Positive PSYCHOLOGY

Positive PSYCHOLOGY

The Scientific and Practical Explorations of Human Strengths

C. R. Snyder & Shane J. Lopez

University of Kansas, Lawrence

SAGE Publications
Thousand Oaks ■ London ■ New Delhi

For information:

Sage Publications, Inc.
2455 Teller Road
Thousand Oaks, California 91320
E-mail: order@sagepub.com

Sage Publications Ltd.
55 City Road
London EC1Y 1SP
United Kingdom

Sage Publications India Pvt. Ltd.
B-42, Panchsheel Enclave
Post Box 4109
New Delhi 110 017 India

Printed in the United States of America

Library of Congress Cataloging-in-Publication Data

Snyder, C. R.
Positive psychology : the scientific and practical explorations of human strengths /
C. R. Snyder, Shane J. Lopez.
    p. cm.
Includes bibliographical references and indexes.
ISBN 0-7619-2633-X (cloth)
   1. Positive psychology. I. Lopez, Shane J. II. Title.
BF204.6.S69 2007
150.19′8   dc22   2006004955

This book is printed on acid-free paper.

06   07   08   09   10   10 9 8 7 6 5 4 3 2

Acquisitions Editor:	Cheri Dellelo
Editorial Assistant:	Karen Ehrmann
Production Editor:	Laureen A. Shea
Copy Editor:	April Wells-Hayes
Typesetter:	C&M Digitals (P) Ltd.
Proofreader:	Dennis Webb
Indexer:	Michael Ferreira

Brief Contents

Detailed Contents

PART IV: POSITIVE COGNITIVE STATES AND PROCESSES

Preface

We once heard it said that 1 out of 10 readers actually reads the prefaces of textbooks. So, if you are one of those rare people who have made it to these infrequently read pages, we are delighted that you have joined us.

This is the third book that we have written together on the general topic of positive psychology. The previous two volumes were positive psychology handbooks—one on theoretical perspectives and the other on assessment issues. We assume that positive psychology will continue to grow and that there will be more courses aimed at teaching about the psychological strengths of people. If these predictions are accurate, then there will be a need for textbooks on positive psychology. This was our thinking in launching this project.

Our agent, Neil Salkind, shared our enthusiasm for writing a textbook on positive psychology. We could not ask for a better friend and agent. Moreover, this project would not have happened without Neil's efforts to find an outstanding publisher who saw a need for this book.

We were graced with a marvelous editor, Jim Brace-Thompson at Sage, who shared our vision of the need for a textbook in positive psychology. Jim hung with us as we encountered various roadblocks along the way, including our own health problems and our aging parents, who were victimized by water (most recently Hurricane Rita). In his own quiet way, Jim practiced the best tenets of positive psychology and nurtured this project to its completion. Any success this book may have is due in large part to his marvelous editorial skills. A full dose of thanks, therefore, is owed to Jim Brace-Thompson and his successor, Cheri Dellelo.

During the evolution of this book project, we also added two new offspring. It is fitting that the newest members of our clan, Trenton Richard Snyder and Parrish Joseph Lopez, have appeared during this time of writing about human strengths. These young gentlemen certainly seem to be graced with a sense of "can do," to judge from their actions so far.

Just as we have added these newest participants in the grand journey of positive psychology, during the time of writing this book we also experienced a huge loss. We were saddened as the grandfather of the positive psychology movement, Donald Clifton, passed away. He was perhaps the gentlest, kindest person we have had the honor to know, and yet he was an absolute powerhouse in advancing the notion that human strengths must be at the top of our agenda in psychology. We are reminded here of a line in the movie *As Good As It Gets,* uttered by the character played by actor Jack Nicholson. This man turned to his would-be lover and said, "You make me a better person." The same was true of Donald Clifton. Farewell, Don, and thank you for the many gifts you left us. At the risk of stating the obvious, you made us better people.

So, too, do our spouses deserve our gratitude for the hours during which this project has taken us away from family matters. Indeed, if we have learned anything in the writing of this text, it is that the family is crucial to a life well lived.

In these pages, we have introduced you to the growing field of positive psychology. We have borrowed from the therapy and research efforts of many outstanding psychologists, and we thank them for their pioneering contributions. So, too, do we thank our clients, our students (especially Matt Gallagher, Lindsey Hammond, Kim Monden, Kristin Rasmussen, and Melinda Roberts), and our colleagues (Lisa Edwards, Jeana Magyar-Moe, Phil McKnight, and Jennifer Teramoto Pedrotti), who assisted on this project; over the years, they have taught us as much about positive psychology as we have taught them. The undergraduate and graduate student members of the Hope Research Group helped in many ways, large and small, to see that various aspects of this project came to fruition.

We have sampled the various areas of positive psychology and have included exercises to help you to experience many of these new concepts.

In Part I, titled "Looking at Psychology from a Positive Perspective," we group four chapters together. We begin with Chapter 1 ("Welcome to Positive Psychology") and introduce you to the field. In Chapters 2 and 3, we explore the Western and Eastern backgrounds of the field. Next, in Chapter 4 ("Classifications and Measures of Human Strengths and Positive Outcomes"), we explain the attempts to categorize various topics in the field.

In Part II, titled "Positive Psychology in Context," we discuss the roles of emotions in a positive life. In Chapter 5 ("Developing Strengths and Living Well in a Cultural Context"), we examine the role of cultural factors in determining what is positive. In Chapter 6 ("Living Well at Every Stage of Life"), we trace the development of human strengths.

Part III, "Positive Emotional States and Processes," comprises two chapters. In Chapter 7, "The Principles of Pleasure: Understanding Positive Affect, Positive Emotions, Happiness, and Well-Being," we show what has been learned about emotions and happiness. And in Chapter 8, "Making the Most of Emotional Experiences: Emotion-Focused Coping, Emotional Intelligence, Socioemotional Selectivity, and Emotional Storytelling," we reveal recent findings on how emotions can contribute positively to effective coping in life.

Part IV, "Positive Cognitive States and Processes," contains three chapters. Chapter 9 ("Seeing Our Futures Through Self-Efficacy, Optimism, and Hope") covers the most powerful positive cognitive and motivational states. Then, in Chapter 10 ("Wisdom and Courage: Two Universal Virtues"), we introduce findings about people at their best under sometimes-difficult circumstances. And in Chapter 11 ("Mindfulness, Flow, and Spirituality: In Search of Optimal Experiences"), we detail the latest findings on the power of mental processes in relation to self and higher forces.

Part V is titled "Prosocial Behavior." In this portion of the book, we examine interpersonal matters. In Chapter 12 ("Empathy and Egotism: Portals to Altruism, Gratitude, and Forgiveness") and Chapter 13 ("Attachment, Love, and Flourishing Relationships"), we show how human ties improve the quality of life.

In Part VI, "Understanding and Changing Human Behavior," we give insights into improving one's life, in Chapter 14 ("Balanced Conceptualizations of Mental Health and Behavior") and Chapter 15 ("Interceding to Prevent the Bad and Enhance the Good").

In Part VII, "Positive Environments," we describe how school (Chapter 16, "Positive Schooling"), work (Chapter 17, "Good Work: The Psychology of Gainful Employment"), and the community (Chapter 18, "The Me/We Balance: Building Better Communities") all contribute to a more productive, happier life.

Finally, in Part VIII, "A Positive Look at the Future of Psychology," we provide an overview of the future direction of the field of positive psychology (Chapter 19, "Going Positive").

For many of you, this is your first educational foray into the new field of positive psychology. We are privileged to introduce you to this work. Furthermore, if your life is in some small way improved by reading the following pages, it will have made our hundreds of hours of labor more than worthwhile.

C. R. S.
S. J. L.
Lawrence, Kansas

C. R. Snyder mailed the final draft of this book to the publisher on December 1, 2005. He was very hopeful that the text would help people find new passions in psychology and in their lives. Indeed, he was committed to bringing this book to life by teaching an undergraduate positive psychology course and by encouraging colleagues across the world to incorporate positive psychology lectures into all their courses. Unfortunately, he will not be able to realize his goal of giving positive psychology away; we will have to do that on his behalf. My mentor and friend, Rick, died of cancer on January 17, 2006. I miss him terribly.

S. J. L.
Lawrence, Kansas

Part I

Looking at Psychology From a Positive Perspective

Welcome to Positive Psychology 1

> *The gross national product does not allow for the health of our children, . . . their education, or the joy of their play. It does not include the beauty of our poetry or the strength of our marriages; the intelligence of our public debate or the integrity of our public officials. It measures neither wit nor courage; neither our wisdom nor our teaching; neither our compassion nor our devotion to our country; it measures everything, in short, except that which makes life worthwhile.*
>
> —Robert F. Kennedy, 1968

The final lines in this 1968 address delivered by Robert F. Kennedy at the University of Kansas point to the contents of this book: *the things in life that make it worthwhile.* In this regard, however, imagine that someone offered to help you understand human beings but in doing so would teach you only about their weaknesses and pathologies. As far-fetched as this sounds, a similar "What is wrong with people?" question guided the thinking of most applied psychologists (clinical, counseling, school, etc.) during the 20th century. Given the many forms of human fallibility, this question produced an avalanche of insights into the human "dark side." As the 21st century unfolds, however, we are beginning to ask another question: "What is right about people?" This question is at the heart of the burgeoning initiative in **positive psychology,** which is the scientific and applied approach to uncovering people's strengths and promoting their positive functioning. (See the article "Building Human Strength," in which positive psychology pioneer Martin Seligman gives his views about the need for this new field.)

Building Human Strength: Psychology's Forgotten Mission

MARTIN E. P. SELIGMAN

President, American Psychological Association

Before World War II, psychology had three missions: curing mental illness, making the lives of all people more fulfilling, and identifying and nurturing high talent. After the war, two events changed the face of psychology. In 1946, the Veterans Administration was created, and practicing psychologists found they could make a living treating mental illness. In 1947, the National Institute of Mental Health was created, and academic psychologists discovered they could get grants for research on mental illness.

As a result, we have made huge strides in the understanding of and therapy for mental illness. At least 10 disorders, previously intractable, have yielded up their secrets and can now be cured or considerably relieved. Even better, millions of people have had their troubles relieved by psychologists.

Our Neglected Missions

But the downside was that the other two fundamental missions of psychology— making the lives of all people better and nurturing "genius"—were all but forgotten.

We became a victimology. Human beings were seen as passive foci: Stimuli came on and elicited "responses," or external "reinforcements" weakened or strengthened "responses," or conflicts from childhood pushed the human being around. Viewing the human being as essentially passive, psychologists treated mental illness within a theoretical framework of repairing damaged habits, damaged drives, damaged childhoods, and damaged brains.

Fifty years later, I want to remind our field that it has been sidetracked. Psychology is not just the study of weakness and damage, it is also the study of strength and virtue. Treatment is not just fixing what is broken, it is nurturing what is best within ourselves.

Bringing this to the foreground is the work of the Presidential Task Force on Prevention, headed by Suzanne Bennett Johnson and Roger Weissberg. This task force will take on a number of jobs: It will attempt to identify the "Best practices in prevention," led by Karol Kumpfer, Lizette Peterson, and Peter Muehrer; it will explore "Creating a new profession: training in prevention and health promotion" by setting up conferences on the training of the next generation of prevention psychologists, led by Irwin Sandler, Shana Millstein, Mark Greenberg, and Norman Anderson; it will work with Henry Tomes of APA's Public Interest Directorate in the ad campaign to prevent violence in children; it will sponsor a special issue on prevention in the 21st century for the *American Psychologist*, edited by Mihaly Csikszentmihalyi; and, led by Camilla Benbow, it will ask what psychology can do to nurture highly talented children.

Building Strength, Resilience, and Health in Young People

But an underlying question remains: How can we prevent problems like depression, substance abuse, schizophrenia, AIDS, or injury in young people who are genetically vulnerable or who live in worlds that nurture these problems? What we have learned is that pathologizing does not move us closer to the prevention of serious disorders. The major strides in prevention have largely come from building a science focused on systematically promoting the competence of individuals.

We have discovered that there is a set of human strengths that are the most likely buffers against mental illness: courage, optimism, interpersonal skill, work ethic, hope, honesty, and perseverance. Much of the task of prevention will be to create a science of human strength whose mission will be to foster these virtues in young people.

Fifty years of working in a medical model on personal weakness and on the damaged brain has left the mental health professions ill equipped to do effective prevention. We need massive research on human strength and virtue. We need practitioners to recognize that much of the best work they do is amplifying the strengths rather than repairing their patients' weaknesses. We need psychologists who work with families, schools, religious communities, and corporations to emphasize their primary role of fostering strength.

The major psychological theories have changed to undergird a new science of strength and resilience. Individuals—even children—are now seen as decision makers, with choices, preferences, and the possibility of becoming masterful, efficacious, or, in malignant circumstances, helpless and hopeless. Such science and practice will prevent many of the major emotional disorders. It will also have two side effects. Given all we are learning about the effects of behavior and of mental well-being on the body, it will make our clients physically healthier. It will also re-orient psychology to its two neglected missions, making normal people stronger and more productive as well as making high human potential actual.

Source: From Seligman, M., Building human strength: Psychology's forgotten mission, in *APA Monitor,* January 1998, p. 2. Copyright © 1998 by the American Psychological Association. Reprinted with permission.

Although other subareas of psychology were not focused on human weaknesses, 20th-century applied psychology and psychiatry typically were. For example, consider the statement attributed to Sigmund Freud that the goal of psychology should be "to replace neurotic misery with ordinary unhappiness" (cited in Simonton & Baumeister, 2005, p. 99). Thus, the applied psychology of yesteryear was mostly about **mental illness** along with understanding and helping the people who were living such tragedies. Positive psychology, on the other hand, offers a balance to this previous weakness approach by suggesting that we also must explore people's strengths along with their weaknesses. In advocating this focus on strengths, however, in no way do we mean to lessen the importance and pain associated with human suffering.

Positive psychological science and practice are situated fortuitously for the identification and understanding of human strengths and virtues as well as for helping people to live happier and more productive lives. As we enter the 21st century, we are poised to study the whole human picture by exploring psychological assets and debits. We present this book as a guide for this journey and to welcome those of you who are new to this approach.

In this chapter, we begin by orienting you to the potential benefits of focusing on the positive in daily life and in psychological research. In this first section, we show how a positive newspaper story can shine a light on what is right in the world and how this type of storytelling can produce very favorable reactions among readers. In the second section, we discuss the importance of a balanced perspective involving the strengths and weaknesses of people. We encourage readers not to become embroiled in the debate between the strengths and weakness camps about which one best reflects the "truth." Third, we explore the attention that psychology to date has given to human strengths. In the fourth section, we allow the reader to get a sense of his or her typical emotional reactions, and we discuss how this can color how the world is seen. Also, we share one of our Saturdays as an example of the thoughts and feelings that characterize positive psychology. In the ensuing fifth section, we walk you through the eight major parts of the book and give brief previews of the chapter contents. Finally, we suggest that positive psychology represents a potential "golden era" in 21st-century America.

We would like to make two final points about our approach in writing this volume. First, we believe that the greatest good can come from a positive psychology that is based on the latest and most stringent experimental methods. In short, an enduring positive psychology must be built on scientific principles. Therefore, in each chapter we present what we see as the best available research bases for the various topics that we explore. In using this approach, however, we describe the theory and findings of the various researchers rather than going into depth or great detail about their methods. Our rationale for this "surface over depth" approach stems from the fact that this is an introductory-level book; however, the underlying methods used to derive the various positive psychology findings represent the finest, most sophisticated designs and statistics in the field of psychology.

Second, although we do not cover in a separate chapter the physiology and neurobiology (and occasionally, the evolutionary) underpinnings of positive psychology, we do view these perspectives as very important. Accordingly, our approach is to discuss the physiology, neurobiology, and evolutionary factors in the context of the particular topics covered in each chapter. For example, in the chapter on self-efficacy, optimism, and hope we discuss the underlying neurobiological forces. Likewise, in the chapter on gratitude we explore the underlying heart and brain wave patterns. Moreover, in discussing forgiveness we touch upon the evolutionary advantages of this response.

Going From the Negative to the Positive

Suppose you were a newspaper reporter and your assignment was to describe the thoughts and actions of people who are stranded one Friday evening at a large airport because of bad weather. The typical content of the newspaper story about such a situation probably would be very negative and filled with actions that portray people in a very unfavorable light. Such stories are of the same ilk as the negative emphases displayed by many 20th-century psychologists toward human beings. But, as we shall see, not all stories are negative about people.

A POSITIVE NEWSPAPER STORY

Juxtapose such negative newspaper stories with the following tale reported by the senior author (Snyder, 2004d, p. D4) in a local newspaper. The scene is the Philadelphia International Airport on a Friday evening as flights arrive late or are canceled.

> . . . people who were trying to make the best of difficult situations. For example, when a young Army soldier just back from Iraq noticed that he had lost his girlfriend's ring, the people working at the airport and all of us in the waiting area immediately began to search for it. In a short period of time, the ring was located, and a cheer went out in the crowd.
>
> Around 7:40 p.m., the announcer told us that there would be yet longer delays on several of the flights. To my amazement and delight, I found that my fellow travelers (and I) just coped. Some broke out supplies of food that they had stashed away in bags, and they offered their treasures to others. Decks of playing cards came out, and various games were started. The airlines people handed out snacks. There were scattered outbreaks of laughter.
>
> As if we were soldiers waiting in the trenches during a lull between battles, someone in the distance began to play a harmonica. Small boys made a baseball diamond, and as their game progressed, no one seemed to mind when one of their home runs would sail by. Although there weren't enough seats for everyone, people creatively made chairs and couches out of their luggage. The people who had computers took them out and played video games with each other. One guy even turned his computer screen into a drive-in-movie-like setup on which several people watched *The Matrix*. I used my computer to write this column.

I once heard it said that grace is doing the average thing when everyone should be going crazy. When hollering and screaming, becoming angry and upset, and generally "losing it" seem to loom just over the horizon, it is wonderful instead to see the warming grace of people—similar to the rays of the sun on a cold day.

REACTIONS TO THIS POSITIVE STORY

After this story appeared, I (CRS) was not prepared for readers' reactions. Never have I written anything that ignited such an outpouring of heartfelt praise and gratitude. In the first week alone after this editorial appeared, I was swamped with favorable e-mails. Some recounted how it reminded them of times they had witnessed people behaving at their very best. Others wrote about how this story made them feel better for the rest of that day and even for several days afterward. Several people said they wished there were more such news stories in the paper. Not a single person among the responses I received had anything negative to say about this column.

Why would people react so uniformly and warmly to this short story about a Friday night at the Philadelphia airport? In part, people probably want to see and hear more about the good in others. Whether it is through newspaper stories such as this one or through the scientific studies and applications we present in this book, there is a hunger to know more about the good in people. It is as if the collective sentiment were, "Enough of all this negativity about people!" In writing this book on positive psychology, we have experienced the uplifting effects of reviewing the many research and clinical applications that are appearing on the study of human strengths and positive emotions. As you read about the assets of your fellow humans and about the many resources that promote the best in people, see whether you, too, feel good. There are many things for which we can praise people, and we will share many examples.

Positive Psychology Seeks a Balanced, More Complete View of Human Functioning

Seeing only the good in one's own actions and the bad in those of others is a common human foible. Validating only the positive or negative aspects of the human experience is not productive. It is very tempting to focus on just the good (or the bad) in the world, *but it is not good science,* and we must not make this mistake in advancing positive psychology. Although we do not agree with the tenets of the previous pathology models, it would be inaccurate to describe their proponents as being poor scholars, poor scientists, poor practitioners, or bad people. Instead, this previous paradigm was advanced by well-meaning, bright people who were responding to the particular circumstances of their times. Likewise, it is not as if these people were wrong in their depictions of people. They developed diagnoses and measurement approaches for schizophrenia, depression, and alcoholism and validated many effective treatments for specific problems such as panic disorder and blood and injury phobia (see Seligman, *What You Can Change and What You Can't*, 1994).

Thus, those operating within the pathology model were quite accurate in their descriptions of some people at some particular times in their lives. Moreover, they were able to help certain people with select problems. Nevertheless, advocates of the pathology approach were incomplete in their portrayals of humankind. Undeniably, the negative is part of humankind, but only a part. Positive psychology offers a look at the other side—that which is good and strong in humankind and in our environs, along with ways to nurture and sustain these assets and resources.

Although we explore the positive, we emphasize that this half is no more the entire story than is the negative side. Future psychologists must develop an inclusive approach that examines both the weaknesses *and* the strengths of people, as well as the stressors *and* the resources in the environment. That approach would be the most comprehensive and valid. We have not reached that point, however, because we have yet to develop and explore fully the science and practice of positive psychology. Only when we have done such detective work on the strengths of people and the many resources of positive environments will we truly be able to understand human beings in a balanced fashion. Our task in these pages, therefore, is to share with you what we do know about positive psychology at this relatively early point in its development.

We look forward to that future time in the field of psychology when the positive is as likely as the negative to be used in assessing people and helping them to lead more satisfying existences. That time will probably come during the lifetimes of the readers of this book; some of you may pursue careers in psychology in which you routinely will consider people's strengths along with their weaknesses. Indeed, we feel strongly that your generation will be the one to implement a psychology that truly balances the tenets of a positive approach with those of the previous pathology orientation. We also hope that today's parents will use positive psychology techniques to shore up families and bring out the best in their children. Likewise, we envision a time when school-age children and youth are valued as much for their major strengths as for their scores on state tests or college entrance examinations.

We have dedicated this volume to you. Because you may be the stewards of the eventual balanced positive–negative psychology, we warn you about the debate that is already in progress as to the superiority of one approach over the other. In the next section, we attempt to inoculate you against such "us-versus-them" thinking.

VIEWS OF REALITY THAT INCLUDE BOTH THE POSITIVE AND THE NEGATIVE

Reality resides in people's perceptions of events and happenings in their world (Gergen, 1985), and scientific perspectives thereby depend on who defines them. Accordingly, the positive psychology and pathology "camps" may clash over how to build meaningful systems for understanding our world. On this process of **reality negotiation** (i.e., moving toward agreed-upon worldviews), Maddux, Snyder, and Lopez (2004, p. 326) have written,

> The meanings of these and other concepts are not *revealed* by the methods of science but are *negotiated* among the people and institutions of society who have an interest in their definitions. What people often call "facts" are not truths but reflect reality negotiations by those people who have an interest in using "the facts."

So, whether one is of a mind to believe the positive psychology or the pathology perspective, we must be clear that this debate involves **social constructions** about those facts. Ultimately, the prevailing views are linked to the social values of society's most powerful individuals, groups, and institutions (Becker, 1963). Likewise, because the prevailing views are social constructions that contribute to ongoing sociocultural goals and values, both the positive psychology and the pathology perspectives provide guidelines about how people should live their lives and what makes such lives worth living.

We believe that both the positive psychology view and the more traditional pathology view are useful. Accordingly, it would be a huge mistake to continue the "us-versus-them" debate between these two groups. Professionals in both camps want to understand and help people. To accomplish these ends, the best scientific and practical solution is to embrace both perspectives. Therefore, although we introduce positive psychology tenets, research, and applications in this textbook, we do so in order to add the strengths approach as a complement to insights derived from the previous weakness model. Accordingly, we encourage the readers of this book—those who eventually will become the leaders in the field—to avoid being drawn into the debate aimed at proving either the positive psychology or pathology model.

Where We Are Now and What We Will Ask

Positive psychology presently is in a period of expansion, not so much in terms of the relative percentage of the entire field that it represents but rather in terms of the influence of these ideas in gaining the attention of the psychology community in particular and society in general. A notable accomplishment of the positive psychology movement in its first decade has been its success in increasing the amount of attention given to its theories and research findings.

University of Pennsylvania psychologist Martin Seligman should be singled out for having ignited the recent explosion of interest in positive psychology, as well as for having provided the label *positive psychology*. (Abraham Maslow actually coined the term *positive psychology* when he used it as a chapter title in his 1954 book, *Motivation and Personality*.) Having grown tired of the fact that psychology was not yielding enough "knowledge of what makes life worth living" (Seligman & Csikszentmihalyi, 2000, p. 5; note the similarity in this sentiment to Robert Kennedy's lament about the gross national product in this chapter's opening quotation), Seligman searched for a provocative theme when he became president of the American Psychological Association in 1998. It was during his presidency that Seligman used his bully pulpit to bring attention to the topic of positive psychology. Since that time, Seligman has worked tirelessly to initiate conferences and grant programs for research and applications of positive psychological research. Throughout his leadership of the developing positive psychology movement, Seligman has reminded psychologists that the backbone of the initiative should be good science. Without question, therefore, we owe a debt of gratitude for Martin Seligman's continued efforts to see that positive psychology prospers.

Martin Seligman

Source: Courtesy of Martin Seligman.

At times, we will make mistakes in our search for human strengths. On balance, however, we firmly believe that our hunt for strengths will result in some marvelous insights about humankind. In judging the success of positive psychology, we hold that it must be subjected to the very highest standards of logic and science. Likewise, positive psychology must undergo the analyses of skeptical yet open minds. We leave this latter important role to you.

What's Your Face? A Positive Psychology Passport Picture

As we begin this journey into positive psychology, we ask you to take your "passport picture." This will serve as your identification picture as you move through the various lands of positive psychology. Close your eyes and relax for a few seconds. Then, think about the face that most people see as you go about your daily activities. Once you have that face in your mind, open your eyes and look at the row of simple faces in Figure 1.1. Go ahead and circle the one face that best fits you among these possibilities. Remember, this is not the face that you *want* others to see but the *face that they really do see*.

At various points in this book, we talk about how people react to others. The human **face** often is what others look at in forming an impression.

Select the face that best fits you most of the time.

Figure 1.1   Selecting Your Face

Jack Nicholson

Source: © Corbis.

Lance Armstrong

Source: © Corbis.

Indeed, the face is related to the root term for the subfield of psychology called *personality*. In early tragedies and comedies, the actors (all of whom were males) held up masks to signify the roles that they were playing. The word for such a mask was *persona*. Thus, our "masks" are what others see. The actor Jack Nicholson is known for his smile, which is his enduring means of displaying his happy-go-lucky, fun-loving approach to his life.

Having decided which face best fits you, we would hasten to add that how you are feeling will be influenced by the things that happened to you this month, this week, today, or perhaps just five minutes ago. Thus, we typically grin when we have succeeded in the pursuit of an important goal. Consider here the sheer glee experienced by cyclist Lance Armstrong as he finally realized that he was going to win his sixth straight Tour de France in the 2004 race. (Of course, a year later, in his final ride before retiring from cycling, Armstrong won his seventh Tour de France).

In the article "You Smile, I Smile" (2002), writer Roger Martin shares a personal incident in which he was profoundly influenced by the smile of a person he encountered. Have you ever suddenly come upon another person who smiled widely at you, and immediately responded with an equally big grin? We are social creatures, and, as we explore in Chapter 7, our emotions are part of our happiness and satisfaction in life. In the Personal Mini-Experiments on page 132, we present different activities you can try in order to improve your emotional state.

A RECENT SATURDAY: AN EXAMPLE OF POSITIVE PSYCHOLOGY

Let me (CRS) use today as an example of where to find positive psychology as well as where not to find it. This being a Saturday, I turn on the radio. My tastes in radio listening have changed recently. I used to listen to country music, in which I heard tales of how someone had lost his lover, his job, his dog, or his pickup truck. The melodies were remarkably similar, as were the lyrics of woe. It may well be that these repeatedly negative lyrics led me to a radio station that plays the classics—not the rock-and-roll classics of the 1960s and 1970s but works by Beethoven, Handel, Chopin, and others. Their melodies seem strong and uplifting.

You Smile, I Smile

ROGER MARTIN

I pass a stranger on the steps of the library. Her smile is bright, her greeting warm. She looks me firmly in the eyes, and her bravery is irresistible. I involuntarily smile back and say hello.

I swing around to watch her walk away.

What was that? I think.

Three days later, same thing happens.

I had this fantasy of people sitting in a living room, one of them saying, "This week, let's smile at strangers and see what happens. Show them that love isn't about receiving—it's about sending. Then we'll get together and talk about what happened."

Just like you, everywhere I go, I see the glazed eyes and the faces behind barricades. In fact, mine's often one of them. As I look around, I sense the rage and sadness and loss of meaning and preoccupation that have sunk so deep into our bones that we hardly know they're there.

But the two strangers made me bold, so I took to having moments with those I don't know. I started making stray remarks in the grocery line to the person next to me, hoping my volley [would] be returned. I rewrote the lines of the quick shop drama of Distracted Customer Meets Bored Clerk. . . . The strangers had given a gift without expecting a return—and in that moment, it no longer seemed strange.

Source: Lawrence Journal-World, May 19, 2002, p. D3. Reprinted with permission of the author.

Personal Mini-Experiments

What You Want to Experience

In this chapter, we provide numerous examples of how a focus on the positive can bring more good feelings and people into your daily life. Reorienting the focus of our thinking can help to determine whether we spend our days in pursuit of meaningful experiences or remain fearful of the bad that might happen. Too often, people act as if their thoughts were out of their control when, in fact, we are the authors of daily scripts that largely determine our daily actions. With the goal of focusing your thoughts on the positive, please go through each of these steps and follow the instructions. It is important to take your time.

- Identify three good things you would like to happen tomorrow.
- Think of one thing that you do not want to happen in the upcoming days.
- Imagine what you want not to happen as a circle that is getting smaller and smaller.

(Continued)

(Continued)

- Of the three good things you want to happen tomorrow, imagine the least important one getting smaller and smaller.
- Imagine the small circle of what you want not to happen getting so small it is hard to see.
- Let go of what you want not to happen. Say goodbye to it.
- Of the two good things you want to happen tomorrow, imagine the least important one getting smaller and smaller.
- Focus your mind on the one good thing that remains as the most important for tomorrow.
- See this good thing happening in your mind's eye.
- Practice having this good thing happen in your mind.
- When you awaken tomorrow, focus on the good thing happening.
- Repeat to yourself during the day, "I make this positive possible."
- Repeat the phrase "I choose how to focus my thoughts."

The point of this exercise is to teach people that they have more control of their mental agendas than they often realize. Furthermore, by attending to what people want to happen, they are more likely to own their daily activities rather than to be reactive. In doing this exercise, feel free to tinker with the exact words that you may say to yourself, but try to retain the empowering message in the words we have selected. In our experiences in working with people, spending mental energies on avoiding certain unwanted outcomes tends to make people reactive to other people and events. On the other hand, thinking of what we want to happen helps to keep the negative away.

For lunch, I splurge and go to Baskin-Robbins for a scoop of chocolate almond on the bottom and a scoop of chocolate chip on the top. Afterward, I mow our lawn and, in a moment of altruism, decide also to mow my neighbor's lawn. Halfway through her lawn, my neighbor bolts out and tells me that "there is no need to do that!" I know this, of course, and this probably is why it is so gratifying. I find helping others to be perhaps the most pleasurable activity in my life. (We will come back to this issue later.)

By now, it is 3:00 p.m., and I am back in the house, working on this chapter. I hear the front doorbell ring. I open it, and there is my 9-month-old grandson, Trenton. His dad asks if I would look after him for the rest of the day (including a sleepover), and I immediately agree. I didn't used to be this gung-ho about being around little children, but a big change has happened to me as I have lived through my fifties. I am fascinated by babies and toddlers and enjoy playing with them, watching them, feeding them, and so on. For much of that afternoon, Trenton and I sit on the front lawn watching birds, squirrels, rabbits, and anything that moves—especially the people who smile as they seem to rush past on the front sidewalk. I wonder where they are going in such a big hurry.

For me, great pleasure comes from watching my grandson take in these sights for the first time—everything seems so fresh to him, and this rubs off on me. I feed him, and I am not bothered by the fact that he gets almost as much on me and the surrounding area as he gets in his mouth. I then put him in the stroller, and we take a long walk. He loves being outside, and I love being with him.

By the time we get back, my wife is home from work, and I am disappointed that she wants to spend time with the baby. So, I put up an old baby swing that we have been given, with my wife hollering at me because I am not using a ladder and instead am standing precariously on a small wooden table. The swing is now affixed to a branch of a redbud tree. After dinner, we decide to put Trenton in the baby seat, and he immediately goes all the way to the ground because he is so heavy. Rebecca and I are now laughing at my not-so-excellent planning.

All too soon, it is time for the bedtime ritual, and for any reader who has (or has had) children this probably is a very familiar process. It involves a tug of wills in which, in this case, the tired and exhausted grandparents and grandson all eventually collapse into sleep. (By the time we are asleep, my wife and I look like the antithesis of the pictures in the romantic and sexy Fredericks of Hollywood catalogues. Instead, our sleep attire typically involves ancient sweatpants, stains from dinner or the "project *du jour*," dried grandchild spit-up, or worse. . . . Our outfits could be labeled "Fredericks of Kansas.")

This brief chronicle of a Saturday illustrates several things about positive psychology. By far the most positive aspect of my day involves doing things for or with other people. Mowing the neighbor's lawn and taking care of my grandson are very gratifying. These activities give you a sense of how and where positive psychology "works" for me. Much of the pleasure that flowed from this summer Saturday stemmed from my ability to keep the focus of my activities on those things that produce pleasure for me. Indeed, the positive is all around most of us. Also notice that not all of these activities result from positive hedonistic actions; instead, by far the most gratifying actions pertain to helping others. Giving is receiving. This is but one of the surprising paradoxes about positive psychology that we will unravel for you in this book.

A Guide to This Book

This book was written with you in mind. Throughout our collaboration, we asked each other, "Will this chapter bring positive psychology to life for the students?" These discussions helped us realize that the book needed to be an excellent summary of positive psychological science and practice *and* that it had to hook you into applying positive psychology principles in your daily lives. With that goal in mind, we have attempted to distill the most rigorous positive psychology studies and the most effective practice strategies, *and* we have constructed dozens of mini-experiments and personal strategies that promote your engagement with the positives in people and the world. Our goal is that, by the time you have finished reading this book, you will be more knowledgeable about psychology *and* will have become more skilled at capitalizing on your human strengths and generating positive emotions.

We have divided this book into eight parts. In Part I, "Looking at Psychology from a Positive Perspective," there are four chapters. Chapter 1, which you are about to complete, is introductory. Our purpose has been to give you a sense of the excitement we feel about positive psychology and to share some of the core issues driving the development of this new field. Chapters 2 and 3 are titled "Western Perspectives on Positive Psychology" and "Eastern Perspectives on Positive Psychology," respectively. In them, you will see that, although there are obvious positive psychology ties to Western cultures, there also are important themes from Eastern cultures. Chapter 4, "Classifications and Measures of Human Strengths and Positive Outcomes," will give you a sense of how psychologists apply labels to the various types of human assets. For readers who are familiar with the more traditional pathology model, this will provide a counterpoint classification that is built on human strengths.

In Part II, "Positive Psychology in Context," we have dedicated two chapters to the factors associated with living well. In Chapter 5, "Developing Strengths and Living Well in a Cultural Context," we examine how the surrounding societal and environmental forces may contribute to a sense of well-being. Moreover, in Chapter 6, "Living Well at Every Stage of Life," we show how childhood activities can help shape a person to become adaptive in his or her later years.

Part III, "Positive Emotional States and Processes," consists of two chapters that cover topics pertaining to emotion-related processes. In Chapter 7, "The Principles of Pleasure: Understanding Positive Affect, Positive Emotions, Happiness, and Well-Being," we address the frequently asked question, "What makes a person happy?" In Chapter 8, "Making the Most of Emotional Experiences: Emotion-Focused Coping, Emotional Intelligence, Socio-emotional Selectivity, and Emotional Storytelling," we introduce new findings regarding emotions as extremely important assets in meeting our goals.

In Part IV, "Positive Cognitive States and Processes," we include three chapters. Chapter 9, "Seeing Our Futures Through Self-Efficacy, Optimism, and Hope," covers the three most-researched motives for facing the future: self-efficacy, optimism, and hope. In Chapter 10, "Wisdom and Courage: Two Universal Virtues," we examine positive psychology topics involving the assets people bring to circumstances that stretch their skills and capacities. Likewise, in Chapter 11, "Mindfulness, Flow, and Spirituality: In Search of Optimal Experiences," we discuss how people become aware of the ongoing process of thinking and feeling, along with humans' needs to believe in forces that are bigger and more powerful than they.

In Part V, "Prosocial Behavior," we describe the general positive linkages that human beings have with other people. In Chapter 12, "Empathy and Egotism: Portals to Altruism, Gratitude, and Forgiveness," we show how kindness-related processes operate to the benefit of people. And in Chapter 13, "Attachment, Love, and Flourishing Relationships," we review the importance of close human bonds for a variety of positive outcomes.

Part VI, "Understanding and Changing Human Behavior," describes how to prevent negative things from happening as well as how to make positive things happen. Chapter 14, "Balanced Conceptualizations of Mental Health and Behavior, " and Chapter 15, "Interceding to Prevent the Bad and Enhance the Good," will help you to see how people can improve their life circumstances.

Part VII, "Positive Environments," looks at specific environments. In Chapter 16, "Positive Schooling," we describe recent findings related to positive learning outcomes for students. In Chapter 17, "Good Work: The Psychology of Gainful Employment," we discuss the components of jobs that are both productive and satisfying. And in Chapter 18, "The Me/We Balance: Building Better Communities," we suggest that the most productive and satisfying environments are those in which the inhabitants can manifest some sense of specialness *and* some sense of similarity relative to other people.

The book closes with Part VIII, "A Positive Look at the Future of Psychology." This section comprises Chapter 19, "Going Positive," in which we speculate about the advances in the field of positive psychology in the next decade. Moreover, we invite experts in the field to give their projections about the crucial issues for the field of positive psychology in the 21st century.

PERSONAL MINI-EXPERIMENTS

In most of the chapters (including this one), we encourage you to put the ideas of leading positive psychologists to the test. In Personal Mini-Experiments, we ask you to bring positive psychology into your life by conducting the kind of experiments that positive psychology researchers might conduct in a lab or the field and that positive psychology practitioners might assign to their clients for homework. Some of these experiments take less than 30 minutes to complete, whereas some will take more than a week.

LIFE ENHANCEMENT STRATEGIES

Finding the positive in daily life does not necessarily require a full-fledged experiment. In fact, we believe that a mindful approach to everyday living will reveal the power of positive emotions and human strengths. Therefore, for the chapters that focus specifically on positive emotions, human strengths, and healthy processes, we devised Life Enhancement Strategies, which can be implemented in a matter of minutes. We decided to develop these strategies to help you attain life's three most important outcomes: connecting with others, pursuing meaning, and experiencing some degree of pleasure or satisfaction. Specifically, love, work, and play have been referred to as the three great realms of life (Seligman, 1998e). Freud defined *normalcy* as the capacity to love, work, and play, and psychological researchers have referred to this capacity as "mental health" (Cederblad, Dahlin, Hagnell, & Hansson, 1995). Developmental researchers have described love, work, and play as normal tasks associated with human growth (Icard, 1996) and as keys to successful aging (Vaillant, 1994). Professionals interested in psychotherapy consider the ability to love, work, and play to be an aspect of the change process (Prigatano, 1992), whereas others view it as one of the primary goals of counseling (Christensen & Rosenberg, 1991). Although full engagement in pursuits of love, work, and play will not guarantee a good life, we believe it is necessary for good living. With this belief in mind, we encourage you to participate in numerous Life Enhancement Strategies that will enhance your ability to love, work, and play.

This concludes our brief rundown of where we plan to go in the ensuing chapters and of our many hopes for you. If you become fully engaged with the material and the exercises in this book, you will gain knowledge and skills that may help you lead a better life.

Rarely does a student have the opportunity to witness the construction of a new field from the ground up. If we have done our jobs properly, you will sense the excitement that comes from being present at the outset.

The Big Picture

Despite the horror and uncertainty of terrorism and natural disasters, the United States of the 21st century is prosperous, stable, and poised for peace. At such a positive point in its evolution, a culture can focus on such issues as virtues, creativity, and hope. Three earlier cultures faced similar positive eras. In the 5th century BC, Athens used its resources to explore human virtues—good character and actions. Democracy was formed during this period. In 15th-century Florence, riches and talents were spent to advance beauty. And Victorian England used its assets to pursue the human virtues of duty, honor, and discipline.

Like the gifts emanating from these three previous eras, perhaps the contribution of 21st-century America lies in adopting and exploring the tenets of positive psychology—the study and application of that which is good in people (Seligman & Csikszentmihalyi, 2000). Certainly, never in our careers have we witnessed such a potentially important new development in the field of psychology. But we are getting ahead of ourselves, because the real test will come when new students are drawn to this area. For now, we welcome you to positive psychology.

Appendix

1. **Wisdom & Knowledge**—Cognitive strengths that entail the acquisition and use of knowledge.

   Creativity: Thinking of novel and productive ways to do things
   Shine (1996)
   Amadeus (1984)

   Curiosity: Taking an interest in all of ongoing experience
   October Sky (1999)
   Amelie (2001, French)

   Open-Mindedness: Thinking things through and examining them from all sides
   No Man's Land (2001, Bosnian)

   Love of Learning: Mastering new skills, topics, and bodies of knowledge
   Billy Elliott (2000)
   A Beautiful Mind (2001)

   Perspective (Wisdom): Being able to provide wise counsel to others
   The Devil's Advocate (1997)
   American Beauty (1999)

2. **Courage**—Emotional strengths that involve the exercise of will to accomplish goals in the face of opposition, external or internal

   Bravery: Not shrinking from threat, challenge, difficulty, or pain
   Schindler's List (1993)
   Life as a House (2001)

   Persistence (Perseverance): Finishing what one starts, persisting in a course of action despite obstacles
   The Piano (1993)
   The Legend of Bagger Vance (2000)

   Integrity (Authenticity, Honesty): Speaking the truth and presenting oneself in a genuine way
   A Few Good Men (1992)
   Erin Brockovich (2000)

Appendix Note: These movies and classification are taken from Rashid (2006), with one alteration: "Vitality" has been moved to the "Transcendence" category. Reprinted with permission of Tayyab Rashid.

3. **Humanity**—Interpersonal strengths that involve tending and befriending others

Love: Valuing close relations with others, in particular those in which sharing and caring are reciprocated; being close to people
   Doctor Zhivago (1965)
   The English Patient (1996)
   Sophie's Choice (1982)
   The Bridges of Madison County (1995)
   Iris (2001)
   My Fair Lady (1964)

Kindness (Generosity, Nurturance, Care, Compassion, Altruistic Love): Doing favors and good deeds for others; helping them; taking care of them
   As Good as It Gets (1997)
   Cider House Rules (1999)
   Promise (1986)

Social Intelligence (Emotional Intelligence, Personal Intelligence): Being aware of the motives and feelings of self and others; knowing what to do to fit into different social situations; knowing what makes other people tick
   Driving Miss Daisy (1989)
   Children of a Lesser God (1986)
   K-Pax (2001)
   The Five Senses (2001, Canadian)

4. **Justice**—Civic strengths that underlie healthy community life

Citizenship (Social Responsibility, Loyalty, Teamwork): Working well as member of a group or team; being loyal to the group; doing one's share.
   L.A. Confidential (1997)
   Finding Forrester (2001)
   Awakenings (1990)

Fairness: Treating all people the same according to notions of fairness and justice; not letting personal feelings bias decisions about others; giving everyone a fair chance
   The Emperor's Club (2002)
   Philadelphia (1993)

Leadership: Encouraging a group of which one is a member to get things done and at the same time maintain good relations within the group; organizing group activities and seeing that they happen
   Lawrence of Arabia (1962)
   Dances With Wolves (1990)

5. **Temperance**—Strengths that protect against excess

Forgiveness and Mercy: Forgiving those who have done wrong; accepting the shortcomings of others; giving people a second chance; not being vengeful
> *Pay It Forward* (2000)
> *Terms of Endearment* (1983)
> *Dead Man Walking* (1995)
> *Ordinary People* (1980)

Humility/Modesty: Letting one's accomplishments speak for themselves; not seeking the spotlight; not regarding oneself as more special than one is
> *Gandhi* (1982)
> *Little Buddha* (1994)

Prudence: Being careful about one's choices; *not* taking undue risks; *not* saying or doing things that might later be regretted
> *Sense and Sensibility* (1995)

Self-Regulation (Self-Control): Regulating what one feels and does; being disciplined; controlling one's appetites and emotions
> *Forrest Gump* (1994)

6. **Transcendence**— Strengths that forge connections to the larger universe and provide meaning

Appreciation of Beauty and Excellence (Awe, Wonder, Elevation): Noticing and appreciating beauty, excellence, and skilled performance in all domains of life, from nature to arts to mathematics to science to everyday experience
> *Out of Africa* (1985)
> *Colors of Paradise* (2000, Iranian)

Gratitude: Being aware of and thankful for the good things that happen; taking time to express thanks
> *Sunshine* (2000)
> *Fried Green Tomatoes* (1991)

Hope (Optimism, Future-Mindedness, Future Orientation): Expecting the best in the future and working to achieve it; believing that a good future is something that can be brought about
> *Gone With the Wind* (1939)
> *Life Is Beautiful* (1998, Italian)
> *Good Will Hunting* (1997)

Humor (Playfulness): Liking to laugh and tease; bringing smiles to other people, seeing the light side; making (not necessarily telling) jokes
> *Patch Adams* (1999)

Spirituality (Religiousness, Faith, Purpose): Knowing where one fits within the larger scheme; having coherent beliefs about the higher purpose and meaning of life that shape conduct and provide comfort

Contact (1997)

Apostle (1997)

Priest (1994, British)

Vitality (Zest, Enthusiasm, Energy): Approaching life with excitement and energy; not doing things halfway or halfheartedly, living life as an adventure, feeling alive and activated

Cinema Paradiso (1988, Italian)

My Left Foot (1993)

One Flew Over the Cuckoo's Nest (1975)

Key Terms

Face: In its most concrete sense, the human features on the front of the head. More generally, and borrowing from sociologist Irving Goffman, the impression that one makes in public display.

Mental illness: Within the pathology psychological approach, refers to a variety of problems that people may have. A catch-all term for someone having severe psychological problems, as in "he is suffering from mental illness."

Positive psychology: The science and applications related to the study of psychological strengths and positive emotions.

Reality negotiation: The ongoing processes by which people arrive at agreed-upon worldviews or definitions.

Social construction: The perspective or definition that is agreed upon by many people to constitute reality (rather than some objectively defined "truth" that resides in objects, situation, and people).

Western Perspectives on Positive Psychology 2

Contributed by Phil McKnight in collaboration with the authors

Hope has been a powerful underlying force in Western civilization. Indeed, looking back through the recorded history of Western civilization, **hope**—the agentic, goal-focused thinking that gets you from *here* to *there*—has been so interwoven into the fabric of our civilization's eras and events that it can be hard to detect, like yeast in bread. In this regard, the belief in a positive future is reflected in many of our everyday ideas and words. For example, words such as *plan* and *trust* carry assumptions about the length of the timeline that stretches ahead of us and the probabilities that our actions will have positive effects on these future events.

This chapter looks backward to foundational ideas and exemplary events that have shaped modern hope and the 21st century. We are purposefully linear in our historical accounting, starting with the Greek myth of Pandora's box and ending with a modern tale of triumph. But first, we explore how and why a robust force such as hope has been absent from parts of the tale of Western civilization.

Hope: Ubiquitous Yet Hidden

Although hope has remarkable and pervasive power, we are often unaware of its presence. Perhaps this is because hope is embedded in many related ideas. On this point, hope often is not identified by name in sources that are essentially all about it (e.g., for a thorough review of how hope is seldom discussed in philosophy, see Ernst Bloch's book *The Principle of Hope* [1959; trans. 1986]). In fact, if we examine the tables of contents or indexes of prominent Western writings, the word *hope* cannot be found. For example, the book *Key Ideas in Human Thought* (McLeish, 1993), contains not one index listing for hope. Imagine the irony of omitting the term *hope* from a supposedly complete archiving of human ideas! According to Bloch, hope has been "as unexplored as the Antarctic" (quoted in Schumacher, 2003, p. 2).

Hope as Part of Greek Mythology

In all of human history, there has been a need to believe that bad could be transformed into good, that ugly could become beautiful, and that problems could be solved. But civilizations have differed in the degree to which they have viewed such changes as possible. For example, consider the classic Greek myth of Pandora's box, a story about the origin of hope. There are two versions of this tale.

In one version, Zeus created Pandora, the first woman, in order to exact revenge against Prometheus (and against humans in general) because he had stolen fire from the gods. Pandora was endowed with amazing beauty and grace but also with the tendency to lie and deceive. Zeus sent Pandora with her dowry chest to Epimetheus, who married her. In using what may be one of the earliest examples of reverse psychology, Zeus instructed Pandora not to open her dowry chest upon arriving on Earth. Of course, she ignored Zeus's order and opened the chest. Out spewed all manner of troubles into the world, except hope, which remained in the chest—not to help humankind but to taunt it with the message that hope does not really exist. In this version, therefore, hope was but a cruel hoax.

A second version of this tale holds that all earthly misfortunes were caused by Pandora's curiosity rather than by any inherent evil nature. The gods tested her with instructions not to open the dowry chest. She was sent to Epimetheus, who accepted her despite the warning of his brother, Prometheus, about gifts from Zeus. When Pandora opened the dowry chest, hope was not a hoax but a blessing and a source of comfort for misfortunes (Hamilton, 1969). And in this positive version of the story, hope was to serve as an antidote to the evils (e.g., gout, rheumatism, and colic for the body, and envy, spite, and revenge for the mind) that escaped when the chest was opened. Whether hope was a hoax or an antidote, these two versions of this story reveal the tremendous ambivalence of the Greeks toward hope.

Pandora's Box

Source: © Corbis.

Religious Hope in Western Civilization

The history of Western civilization parallels the histories of Judaism and Christianity. This is why the phrase *Judeo-Christian heritage* often is linked to Western civilization. It is no accident that the timeline of Western civilization (see Figures 2.1 through 2.4) overlays the Judeo-Christian heritage, including the period before Christ (BC) and the period after the birth of Christ (AD). These timelines highlight significant happenings in the history of religion: the opening of Notre Dame Cathedral, the building of the west façade of Chartres Cathedral, and the publishing of St. Thomas Aquinas's *Summa Theologica*. In this respect, the presence of hope in the early periods of Western civilization is illustrated clearly in such biblical passages as "Thy Kingdom come, thy will be done" (Matthew 6:10) and ". . . there was the hope that creation itself would one day be set free from its slavery to decay and would share the glorious freedom of the children of God" (Romans 8:18, 20, 21). These passages reflect a vision of hope for God's reign on Earth as well as the hope for God's will to be done on Earth as it is in heaven. Or consider Corinthians I, 15:19, in which St. Paul writes about faith in Christ for this life on Earth and beyond: "If our one hope in Christ is for this life only, we are all men most to be pitied." In addition, Christianity's doctrines hold that God's kingdom on Earth is not only awaited—it is anticipated. Thus, it is logical that the belief in hope would influence secular intellectual assumptions and ideas.

As shown by these examples of hope in religion, impressive human endeavors can result from a hopeful disposition. In each case, an active verb is connected to a noun that refers to an outcome—an achievement. Note the words *opening, building,* and *publishing*. It should be noted as well that these verbs were followed by nouns denoting significant achievements in our civilization, such as the cathedrals at Chartres and Notre Dame.

These examples also are important because they are achievements along a road out of a period that is sometimes referred to as the Dark Ages. It is hard for us to appreciate the willpower and efforts of our ancestors, who strove to achieve significant milestones in a period known for the absence of such. Indeed, although these times were not truly dark, the Middle Ages (500–1450), before the Renaissance, certainly were enveloped in the shadows of oppression and ignorance; inertia and intellectual lassitude were the norms. As Davies (1996) writes,

> There is an air of immobility about many descriptions of the medieval world. The impression is created by emphasizing the slow pace of technological change, the closed character of feudal society, and the fixed, theocratic perceptions of human life. The prime symbols of the period are the armoured knight on his lumbering steed; the serfs tied to the land

of their lord's demesne [domain or property]; and cloistered monks and nuns at prayer. They are made to represent physical immobility, social immobility, intellectual immobility. (p. 291)

This intellectual and social immobility reflected a paralysis of curiosity and initiative. From the years of the **Middle Ages** (500–1500), such paralysis precluded the purposeful, sustained planning and action required by a hopeful, advancing society. The fires of advancement were reduced to embers during this dark millennium and kept glowing only by a few institutions such as the monasteries and their schools.

Eventually, as the Dark Ages were ended by of the brightness of the Renaissance and its economic growth and prosperity, hope was seen as more relevant to present life on Earth than to the afterlife (i.e., a better life on Earth became possible, even probable). Therefore, the religious hope that focused on a distant future, after life on Earth, became somewhat less important as the Renaissance emerged. Indeed, the focus during the Renaissance was on the contemporary anticipation of better days in the here and now. Related to this new focus, the philosopher Immanuel Kant decided that the religious nature of hope precluded its inclusion in discussions of how to bring about changes on Earth. With this shift, the religious conception of hope faded as the primary motivation for action. Strengthening and hastening this change was another aspect of religious hope, identified by what Farley (2003) called "wishful passivity," a perspective that still influences religious hope today. Farley notes, "Religious hope . . . gives a false sense that all is really well and 'all shall be well.' Belief in an ultimate future, in this view, short-circuits commitment to a proximate future" (p. 25). In other words, the religious hope that is oriented to the afterlife can become an unconscious barrier to taking action in this life. The problem with this kind of religious hope as described by Farley is that it may give a sense of delayed comfort about future conditions. Unfortunately, in focusing on a desired future state instead of upon what must happen to reach that state, the person's attentions and efforts are drawn away from what is needed in the here and now.

Farley's (2003) comment is similar to an important point made by Eric Fromm in his book, *The Revolution of Hope: Toward a Humanized Technology* (1974). Fromm states that some definitions of hope often are "misunderstood and confused with attitudes that have nothing to do with Hope and in fact are the very opposite" (p. 6). Fromm goes on to point out that hope is not the same as desires and **wishes** (i.e., products of envisioning a possibility for change without having a plan or requisite energy for producing such change). Unlike hope, these latter motives have passive qualities in which there is little or no effort made to realize the desired objective. An extreme level of this passivity yields what Fromm called *nihilism* (p. 8).

Revision of the History of Hope in Western Civilization

THE PRE-RENAISSANCE PERIOD

The positive beliefs and hope of Western civilization solidified after the Renaissance. It should be noted, however, that hope was not totally absent from earlier epochs. Consider, for example, the following brief listing of illustrative hope-related human activities that took place before the Renaissance:

The building of the museum and library at Alexandria (established 307 BC)

The opening of the first English school at Canterbury (598 AD)

Publication of the Exeter Book collection of English poetry (970 AD)

The development of systematic musical notation (990 AD)

Revival of the artistic traditions in Italy (1000)

The attempt to fly or float in the air (1000)

Groundbreaking for York Cathedral in England (1070)

The founding of Bologna University in Italy (1119)

The building of St. Bartholomew's Hospital in London (1123)

Completion of the western façade of Chartres Cathedral in France (1150)

The popularizing of chess in England (1151)

The founding of Oxford University (1167) and Cambridge University (1200) in England

The opening of Notre Dame Cathedral in Paris (1235)

The printing of Thomas Aquinas's *Summa Theologica* (1273)

Development of the Italian city of Florence into the leading commercial and cultural city of Europe (1282)

Consider these events on the timeline in Figure 2.1. They reflect people having the spirit and making the effort needed to reach goals. These historical markers required goal-directed actions instead of mere waiting for better times or good things to happen. With the advent of the Renaissance, these active and hopeful thoughts began to be coupled with goal-directed actions. We turn to the Renaissance and the crucial events in the next section.

St. Thomas Aquinas

Source: © Corbis.

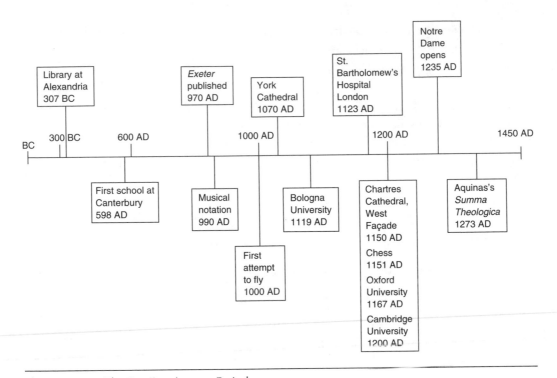

Figure 2.1   The Pre-Renaissance Period

Source: Compiled from Hale (1965).

THE RENAISSANCE

Beginning in Italy around 1450 and extending to approximately 1600, the **Renaissance** produced changes in the customs and institutions that had dominated Europe for the previous millennium. Feudalism, the dominance of the Catholic Church, and rural, isolated living all gave way to an emerging nationalism, trade and commerce, the growth of cities, and the expansion of arts and scholarship. Hope came alive during this period of rebirth. This historical period now is viewed more as an evolution than a revolution, and it was a turning point that facilitated the emergence of active hope.

Given that, in the Renaissance, part of the emphasis was on the past, how could it be seen as the beginning of "modern" hope? The answer to this question is that, although the Renaissance did analyze antiquity, much of the analysis was done to move forward and advance understanding. For example, Roman law emerged as a crucial area for legal studies because Renaissance lawyers wanted to examine the great codes of Roman law, the Digest and the Codex. Thus, the Renaissance perspective was that learning from the past was necessary to meet the demands of the complex, materialistic society that was emerging from the late Middle Ages. Similarly,

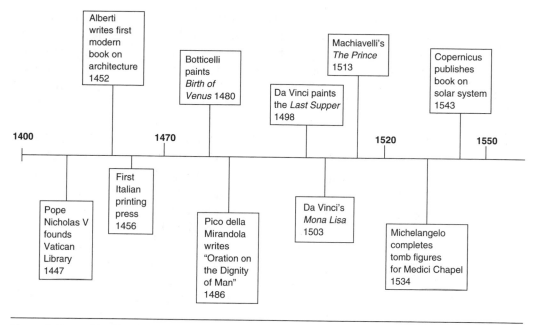

Figure 2.2   The Renaissance

Source: Compiled from Grun (1975) and Hale (1965).

advances in other areas of public life and business were built on accurate understandings of previous literature, philosophy, and art. Although studies of these fields became goals in themselves, they were undertaken primarily to accomplish more worldly objectives, such as facilitation of trade and mercantilist economics. Therefore, Renaissance society began to see worldly fulfillment as more important than preparation for death or fulfillment after death.

During this period, people also began to view themselves as individuals rather than as representatives of a class. Moreover, this emerging interest in the merits of personal achievement led to a focus on doing things related to *this* life. Whereas medieval (500–1500 AD) men and women searched their souls, Renaissance citizens looked outward and forward to achieve the here-and-now goals that were based on their abilities and personal interests. See Figure 2.2 for important events and accomplishments of the Renaissance.

THE ENLIGHTENMENT

The period following the Renaissance, from approximately 1700 to the late 1700s, is known as the **Age of Enlightenment**. This era marked the

Immanuel Kant

Source: © Corbis.

emergence from an immaturity characterized by unwillingness to use one's own knowledge and intelligence. On this point, Immanuel Kant (1784) wrote, "*Sapere aude*! 'Have courage to use your own reason!'—that is the motto of enlightenment" (cited in Gay, 1969, p. 11). In effect, the Enlightenment represented a declaration of independence from the long-established acceptance of authority in religion and politics that dated back to biblical times.

In a cultural atmosphere conducive to exploration and change, the Enlightenment was rooted in the Renaissance revival of interest in Greek and Latin books and ideas, along with an interest in this world rather than the next. As the religious authority of the Church weakened, commercial, political, and scientific influences began to play increasingly strong roles in the spiritual, physical, and intellectual lives of people.

Scientific is a key word in characterizing the Enlightenment. Isaac Newton's 1687 publication of *Mathematical Principles of Natural Philosophy* has been used by some to mark the start of the Enlightenment and the rise of the scientific method. Although the roots of his work extended back to the biblical era, Newton's ideas served other purposes to help in understanding and revering God.

The Scientific Revolution was an integral part of the Enlightenment, and it began when the political atmosphere became more favorable to a climate of discovery as manifested in the works of such scholars as Kepler, Galileo, Newton, and Descartes. Gay (1966) describes this group of thinkers as a kind of "coalition" of scientists and philosophers who viewed research efforts as "steps" in a cumulative process rather than mere accidental and isolated discoveries.

The Enlightenment reflected the nature of hope because of its emphases on rational agencies and rational abilities. These qualities were interwoven in the dominant belief of the age, that reason brought to life with the scientific method led to the achievements in science and philosophy. These latter perspectives are in direct contrast to the prevalence of ignorance, superstition, and the acceptance of authority that characterized the Middle Ages. Described in terms of the use of mathematics as a means of discovery and progress, this process emphasized the rational will. It should come as no surprise, then, that education, free speech, and the acceptance of new ideas burgeoned during the Enlightenment. Indeed, the consequences of such enlightened thinking were long lasting and reflective of the power of hope. On this last point, consider education and how it decreases the probability that actions will be impulsive; that is to say, education should promote thoughtful analyses and plans to reach desired goals. Furthermore, human dignity and worth were recognized during the Enlightenment. Taken together, the idea that knowledge and planning could produce perceived empowerment led Francis Bacon to the goal of improving the human condition. It is no wonder, therefore, that Condorcet noted in his *Sketch for a Historical Picture of the Progress of the Human Mind* (1795) that the Enlightenment assured the present and future progress of human beings.

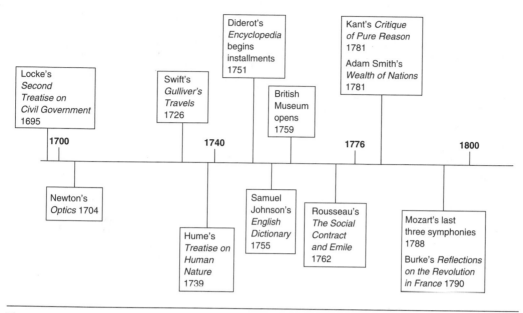

Figure 2.3   The Enlightenment

Source: Compiled from Grun (1975) and Gay (1966).

The results of hopeful beliefs can be seen in the impact of these significant events of the Enlightenment:

The invention of the flying shuttle (1773), which initiated modern weaving

The drafting of the Declaration of Independence (1776)

The ridiculing of fashionable society by poet Alexander Pope in the *Rape of the Lock* (1714)

The opening of the British Museum (1759)

Publication of Kant's *Critique of Pure Reason* (1781)

The writing of Mozart's last three symphonies (1788)

Publication of Edmund Burke's *Reflection on the Revolution in France* (1790)

Other events and milestones are noted in Figure 2.3.

THE INDUSTRIAL REVOLUTION

Beginning approximately in the late 1700s and continuing to the end of the 1800s was the period known as **Industrial Revolution** (or the Age of

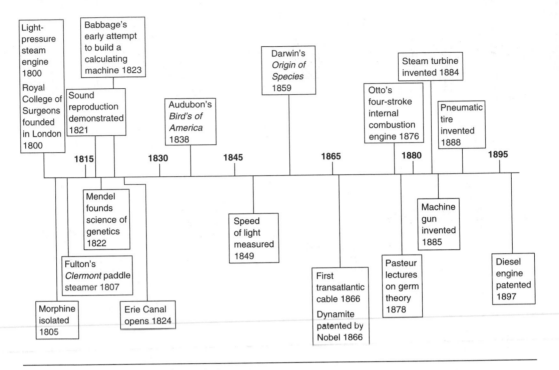

Figure 2.4 The Industrial Revolution

Source: Compiled from Grun (1975) and Burchell (1966).

Industrialization). The movement of production from homes and small workshops to large factories vastly increased material benefits for individual citizens (see Figure 2.4). Although some results of this age were dysfunctional and counterproductive, very real and important contributions took place. Brogan (1960) describes these advances:

> As a result of advances made in the 19th and early 20th centuries, people did live longer, fewer children died as infants, and many were better fed, better housed and better educated. The physical unity of the world was made possible by the steamboat, the locomotive, the automobile, and the airplane. The unity of science was exemplified by the adaptation, within a few years of its discovery, of Louis Pasteur's work with bacteria in Paris to Joseph Lister's practice of antiseptic surgery in Scotland. Areas of the world previously uninhabitable, or habitable only at a very low level of existence, became easier to live in. (in Burchell, 1966, p. 7)

As Bronowski (1973) wrote eloquently in his chapter "The Drive for Power" in *The Ascent of Man,* the Industrial Revolution made the world "ours." Indeed, the Industrial Revolution reflected a turning point in the progress of humankind because it provided so many material and personal benefits. Perhaps even more important, the Industrial Revolution created amenities that most citizens could obtain and enjoy. Goods thus become available for the many rather than only for the few. Such benefits included the steam engine and its many applications, iron and steelmaking, and railroads (efficient transportation and communication for all), to name but a few examples that appeared in the 20th century.

Western civilization has been defined by its critical mass of hopeful events and beliefs. Before the Renaissance, the Enlightenment, and the Industrial Revolution, and even during the Middle Ages, hopeful thinking was a critical part of humankind's belief system. If some historical eras do not reveal major signs, there nonetheless have been implicit markers of hope. Thus, although the Reformation and the Age of Reason (1600–1700) are not highlighted here, these periods nonetheless saw important advances that contributed to society. Following is a sampling of notable achievements in these periods:

Francis Bacon's *The Advancement of Learning* (1604)

Galileo's proportional compass (1606)

The beginning of extensive road building in France (1606)

Galileo's astronomical telescope (1608)

Harvey's discovery of the circulation of blood (1619)

Publication of the *Weekly News* in London (1622)

The opening of the first coffee shop in London (1632)

The abolition of torture in England (1638)

The chartering of Harvard College (1650)

Newton's experiments with gravitation and his invention of differential calculus (1665)

Establishment of the Greenwich observatory (1681)

The opening of the first coffeehouses in Vienna (1683)

Implementation of streetlights in London (1684)

The first modern trade fair, in Leiden, Holland (1689)

Peter the Great's sending of 50 Russian students to study in England, Holland, and Venice (1698)

Looking back at the events of the Renaissance, the Enlightenment, and the Industrial Revolution, perhaps it is reasonable to consider all eras, starting with the Renaissance and continuing until 1900, as part of a new period called the Age of Progress. This Age of Progress characterizes Western civilization and reflects the inherent component of hopeful thinking. As Nisbet (1980) writes in his *History of the Idea of Progress,*

> No single idea has been more important than, perhaps as important as, the Idea of Progress in Western Civilization for 3,000 years. Its flaws and corruptions understood, the idea of progress has been overwhelmingly a noble idea in Western history, noble for what it has celebrated in countless philosophical, religious, scientific, and historical works, and most of all for what it has meant to the motivations and aspirations of those who have made up the human substance of Western Civilization. (p. 4)

This faith in the value and promise of our civilization is essential for the concept of hope, and vice versa. Thus, hope is the essence of faith in the value and promise of our Western civilization.

Conclusions

Hope is the belief that life can be better, along with the motivations and efforts to make it so. More than desires, wishes, or daydreams, hope taps thinking that leads to meaningful actions. A wish envisions change but may not lead to action. One may wish to win the lottery, but this does not necessarily lead to important or sustained activities to fulfill this wish. Furthermore, the conditions surrounding the fulfillment of a wish are not promising, because there may be few reasonable or even realistic means for doing so.

It should be noted that Western European civilization does not have a monopoly on the idea of hope. In every civilization and historical period, there have been hopeful beliefs and activities. But hope often does not appear to be as significant a driving belief in all cultural perspectives. For example, in the Native American culture there is less expectation of progress. Rather, if one respects and takes care of the environment, things should be all right but not necessarily great. The Native American belief is that proper traditions and beliefs may not bring prosperity but will help stave off disasters. Here, then, the difference in the two systems may be more one of degree than of kind. For Native Americans, positive actions are not assumed to lead to positive outcomes as much as they are in Western European civilization's system of beliefs. Accordingly, hope may not be as prominent a motivational force within the Native American tradition as has been the case for other peoples in Western civilization (Pierotti, personal communication, 2005).

The idea of hope has served as an underpinning for thinking in Western civilization. As Bronowski (1973) has noted in regard to the Industrial

Revolution, hope helped to make our world ours. Where hope will take us, in turn, is perhaps the most important question about the unfolding 21st century.

Key Terms

Age of Enlightenment: The period from 1700 to the late 1800s. The Enlightenment brought with it the idea that people could use their own reason, knowledge, and intellect instead of relying on superstition or the authority of the Church and government. The Enlightenment included the Scientific Revolution. Hope was reflected in the belief that people had the ability to use their own rationality to improve themselves and their world.

Hope: As defined by Snyder, goal-directed thinking in which a person has the perceived capacity to find routes to desired goals (pathway thinking) and the requisite motivations to use those routes (agency thinking). Snyder believes that hope is not genetically based but an entirely learned and deliberate way of thinking. (See Chapter 9.)

Industrial Revolution: Part of the Age of Enlightenment; the movement of production from the home and workshop to the factory, which resulted in increased material benefits for the individual and greater mobility due to the invention of the steamboat, locomotive, and airplane. The Industrial Revolution made the hope of the Renaissance (prosperity and happiness in the here and now) possible for most people.

Middle Ages: The period from 500 to 1500 AD; sometimes called the Dark Ages. Social, physical, and intellectual immobility and various forms of oppression mark this period of time. Hope was tied to prosperity and happiness in the afterlife.

Renaissance: The period from 1450 to approximately 1600, which produced many changes in the customs that dominated Europe. During this period, people analyzed the past to move forward and advance the future. Hope was now tied to prosperity and happiness in the here and now. Hopeful thoughts were accompanied by motivation for action in this life instead of preparation for the afterlife.

Wish: The envisioning of the possibility for change without the pathway for action; a passive desire.

Eastern Perspectives on Positive Psychology 3

Contributed by
Jennifer Teramoto Pedrotti
in collaboration with the authors

A Matter of Perspective

"A good fortune may forebode a bad luck, which may in turn disguise a good fortune." This Chinese proverb exemplifies the Eastern perspective that the world and its inhabitants are in a perpetual state of flux. Thus, just as surely as good times occur, so, too, will bad times visit us. In turn, life's challenges may be harbingers of our triumphs. This balance of good and bad is sought throughout life. Indeed, this expectation of and desire for balance distinguishes Easterners' views of optimal functioning from the more linear path taken by Westerners to resolve problems and monitor progress (see Chapter 2). Easterners thereby seek to become one with the march of changes, finding meaning in the natural ups and down of living. Ever adaptive and mindful, Easterners move with the cycle of life until the change process becomes natural and **enlightenment** (i.e., being able to see things clearly for what they are) is achieved. Unlike Westerners, who search for rewards in the physical plane, Easterners seek to transcend the human plane and rise to the spiritual one.

Positive psychology scholars aim to define human strengths and highlight the many paths that lead to better lives (Aspinwall & Staudinger, 2002; Keyes & Haidt, 2003; Lopez & Snyder, 2003; Peterson & Seligman, 2004; Snyder & Lopez, 2002). As Western civilization and European events and values shaped the field of psychology as we know it today in the United States, it is not surprising that the origins of positive psychology have focused more on the values and experiences of Westerners. Increasingly, however, scholars are taking the broader historical and cultural contexts into account to understand strengths and the practices associated with living well (see, e.g., Leong & Wong, 2003; Schimmel, 2000; Sue & Constantine, 2003). The previously neglected wisdoms of the Eastern traditions are being consulted to add different viewpoints about human strengths.

In this chapter, we discuss Eastern perspectives and teachings in terms of their influences on positive psychology research and applications. First, we introduce the main tenets of Confucianism, Taoism, Buddhism, and Hinduism and demonstrate how each tradition characterizes important strengths and life outcomes. Next, we discuss some of the inherent and fundamental differences between Eastern and Western value systems, thought processes, and life outcomes sought. We also articulate the Eastern idea of the "good life" and discuss the associated strengths (embedded more in Eastern cultures than in Western ones) that assist Easterners in attaining positive life outcomes. We then close with a discussion of Eastern views of the concepts of compassion and harmony as the two primary and necessary qualities for achieving the good life.

Confucianism, Taoism, Buddhism, and Hinduism

To summarize thousands of years of Eastern ideology and tradition is obviously beyond the scope of this chapter. Therefore, we highlight the basic tenets of the four influential Eastern disciplines of **Confucianism, Taoism** (traditions generally associated with China), **Buddhism, and Hinduism** (rooted in traditions of Southeast Asia). As is the case in the Western historical context, the concept of the "good life" has existed within the Eastern tradition for many centuries. Contrary to the Western culture's idea of optimal functioning as occurring intrapsychically, Eastern cultures hold that an optimal life experience is a spiritual journey involving transcendence and enlightenment. This latter search for spiritual transcendence parallels the Westerner's hopeful pursuits for a better life on Earth.

CONFUCIANISM

Confucius, or the Sage, as he is sometimes called, held that leadership and education are central to morality. Born during a time when his Chinese homeland was fraught with strife, Confucius emphasized morality as a potential cure for the evils of that time (Soothill, 1968). Confucian ethics, which have been compared to the works of the Western philosopher Immanuel Kant, have clear definitions and relatively inflexibile meanings (Ross, 2003; e.g., "Your job is to govern, not to kill," *Analects,* 12:19, in instructions to rulers who resort to force). The tenets of Confucianism are laden with quotations that encourage looking to the welfare of others. In fact, one of Confucius's most famous sayings is a precursor of the Golden Rule and can be translated, "You would like others to do for you what you would indeed like for yourself" (Ross, 2003; *Analects* 6:28). Such teachings are collected in several books, the most famous of which is the *I Ching* (the *Book of Changes*).

The attainment of virtue is at the core of Confucian teachings. The five virtues deemed central to living a moral existence are *jen* (humanity, the virtue most exalted by Confucius); *yi* (duty); *li* (etiquette); *zhi* (wisdom), and *xin* (truthfulness). The power of *jen* stems from the fact that it was said to encapsulate the other four virtues. The concept of *yi* describes appropriate treatment of others and can be defined as the duty to treat others well. The concept of *li* promotes propriety and good manners along with sensitivity for others' feelings (Ross, 2003). Finally, the ideas of *zhi* and *xin* define the importance of wisdom and truthfulness, respectively. Confucian followers must strive to make wise decisions based on these five virtues and must be true to them as well. Continual striving for these virtues leads the Confucian follower to enlightenment, or the good life.

Confucius

Source: © Corbis.

TAOISM

Ancient Taoist beliefs are difficult to discuss with Western audiences partly because of the untranslatable nature of some key concepts in the tradition of Taoism. Lao-Tzu (the creator of the Taoist tradition) states in his works that his followers must live according to the Tao (pronounced "Dow" and roughly translated as "the Way"). The Chinese character portraying the concept of the Way is a moving head and "refers simultaneously to direction, movement, method, and thought" (Peterson & Seligman, 2004, p. 42; Ross, 2003); moreover, it is meant to embody the ubiquitous nature of this force. Tao is the energy that surrounds everyone and is a power that "envelops, surrounds, and flows through all things" (Western Reform Taoism, 2005, p. 1). In this regard, Lao-Tzu (1994) described the Way in the following lines:

The Way

> The Way can be spoken of,
> But it will not be the constant way;
> The name can be named,
> But it will not be the constant name.
> The nameless was the beginning of the myriad creatures;

The named was the mother of the myriad creatures.

Hence constantly rid yourself of desires in order to observe its subtlety;

But constantly allow yourself to have desires in order to observe what it is after.

These two have the same origin but differ in name.

They are both called dark,

Darkness upon darkness

The gateway to all is subtle. (p. 47)

Lao-Tzu

Source: © Corbis.

Although Lao-Tzu is eloquent in depicting his views on the Way, many readers of these lines are left with some uncertainty about their actual meaning. According to Taoist traditions, the difficulty in understanding the Way stems from the fact that one cannot teach another about it. Instead, understanding flows from experiencing the Way for oneself by fully participating in life. In this process, both good and bad experiences can contribute to a greater understanding of the Way. It also is said to encapsulate the balance and harmony between contrasting concepts (i.e., there would be no light without dark, no male without female, and so on) (Ontario Consultants on Religious Tolerance, 2004). On this latter point, the *yin* and *yang* symbol (described in more detail subsequently) reflects this ever-changing balance of opposing forces and desires.

Achieving naturalness and spontaneity in life is the most important goal in the Taoist philosophy. Thus, the virtues of humanity, justice, temperance, and propriety must be practiced by the virtuous individual without effort (Cheng, 2000). One who has achieved transcendence within this philosophy does not have to think about optimal functioning but behaves virtuously naturally.

BUDDHISM

Buddha

Seeking the good of others is woven throughout the teachings of "the Master" or "the Enlightened One" (i.e., the Buddha). In one passage, the Buddha is quoted as saying, "Wander for the gain of the many, for the happiness of the many, out of compassion for the world" (Sangharakshita, 1991, p. 17). At the same time, the Buddha teaches that suffering is a part of being and that this suffering is brought on by the human emotion of desire. Such desire is reflected in the Four Noble Truths of Buddhism:

1. Life is suffering, essentially painful from birth to death.

2. All suffering is caused by ignorance of the nature of reality and the resultant craving, attachment, and grasping.

3. Suffering can be ended by overcoming ignorance.

4. The way to relief from suffering is the Noble Eightfold Path (right views, right intention, right speech, right action, right livelihood, right effort, right-mindedness, and right contemplation).

As long as craving exists, in Buddhist ideology, true peace cannot be known, and such existence without peace is considered suffering (Sangharakshita, 1991). This suffering can be lessened only upon reaching **nirvana,** which is the final destination in the Buddhist philosophy. Accordingly, nirvana is a state in which the self is freed from desire for anything (Schumann, 1974). It should be noted that both premortal and postmortal nirvana states are proposed as possible for the individual. More specifically, the premortal nirvana may be likened to the idea of the ultimate "good life." Postmortal nirvana may be similar to the Christian idea of heaven.

Like the other Eastern philosophies, Buddhism gives an important place to virtue, which is described in several catalogs of personal qualities. Buddhists speak of the *Brahma Viharas,* those virtues that are above all others in importance (described by Peterson and Seligman, 2004, p. 44, as "universal virtues"). These virtues include love (*maitri*), compassion (*karuna*), joy (*mudita*), and equanimity (*upeksa*) (Sangharakshita, 1991). The paths to achieving these virtues within Buddhism require humans to divorce themselves from the human emotion of desire to put an end to suffering.

HINDUISM

The Hindu tradition differs somewhat from the other three philosophies discussed previously in that it does not appear to have a specific founder, and it is not clear when this tradition began in history (Stevenson & Haberman, 1998). In addition, there is no one text that pervades the tradition, though many refer to the *Upanishads* as the most commonly used set of writings. Instead of following written guidelines, many followers of Hindu "think of their religion as being grounded in a way of action, rather than a written text" (Stevenson & Haberman, p. 45). The main teachings of the Hindu tradition emphasize the interconnectedness of all things. The idea of a harmonious union among all individuals is woven throughout the teachings of Hinduism that refer to a "single, unifying principle underlying all of Earth" (Stevenson & Haberman, p. 46).

The *Upanishads* discuss two possible paths after death: that of reincarnation (or returning to Earth to continue to attempt to achieve necessary enlightenment), or that of no reincarnation (meaning that the highest knowledge possible was achieved in life). The latter path, no reincarnation, is the more glorified path and the one that Hindu followers would attempt to attain. One's goal within this tradition would be to live life so fully and so correctly that one would go directly to the afterlife without having to repeat life's lessons in a reincarnated form (Stevenson & Haberman, 1998). Hindu teachings are very clear about the qualities one must embody to avoid reincarnation: "To return to this world is an indication of one's failure to achieve ultimate knowledge of one's self" (Stevenson & Haberman, p. 53). Thus, the quest of one's life is to attain ultimate self-knowledge and to strive for ultimate self-betterment (notably also a Western concept). This emphasis on personal improvement echoes Buddhist teachings but contrasts sharply with the Confucian belief that citizenship and group good are much more important than self-improvement (Dahlsgaard, Peterson, & Seligman, 2005; Peterson & Seligman, 2004). This is not to say, however, that the focus is solely on the individual within the Hindu tradition. Individuals are encouraged to be good to others as well as to improve themselves; the *Upanishads* state, "A man turns into something good by good action and something bad by bad action" (Stevenson & Haberman, p. 54).

"Good action" is also encouraged in the sense that, if one does not reach ultimate self-knowledge in one's life and thus does have to return to Earth via reincarnation after death, the previous life's good actions correlate directly with better placement in the world in this life (Stevenson & Haberman, 1998). This process is known as *karma*. In this next life, then, the individual must again strive for self-betterment, and so on throughout his lives until the goal of ultimate self-knowledge is attained. The good life in the Hindu tradition, therefore, encompasses individuals who are continually achieving knowledge and continually working toward good actions (Dahlsgaard, Peterson, & Seligman, 2005; Peterson & Seligman, 2004; Stevenson & Haberman).

SUMMARY OF EASTERN PHILOSOPHIES

Each of the Eastern philosophies discussed here incorporates ideas about the importance of virtue, along with human strengths, as people move toward the good life (i.e., transcendence). Similarities also can be drawn among the four, especially in the types of human qualities and experiences that are valued. These are discussed in detail in the subsequent sections, but first it is important to contrast these Eastern beliefs with Western ideology to understand the differences in positive psychology viewed from each perspective.

East Meets West

Eastern and Western ideologies stem from very different historical events and traditions. These differences can be seen explicitly in the value systems of each cultural approach to living, their orientations toward time, and their respective thought processes. These cultural differences give more information about strengths identified in each culture and ways in which positive life outcomes are pursued and achieved.

VALUE SYSTEMS

Cultural value systems have significant effects on the determination of strengths versus weaknesses (Lopez, Edwards, Magyar-Moe, Pedrotti, & Ryder, 2003). Whereas most Western cultures have *individualist* perspectives, most Eastern cultures (Japanese, Chinese, Vietnamese, Indian, and others) are guided by *collectivist* viewpoints (see also Chapter 18). In **individualist** cultures, the main focus is the single person, who is held above the group in terms of importance. Competition and personal achievement are emphasized within these cultures. In **collectivist** cultures, however, the group is valued above the individual, and cooperation is accentuated (Craig & Baucum, 2002). These different emphases on what is valued determine which constructs are considered strengths in each type of culture. For example, Western cultures value highly the ideas of personal freedom and autonomy. Thus, the person who "stands on her own two feet" is seen as possessing strength within this worldview. In an Eastern culture, on the other hand, such assertiveness on behalf of the self would not be viewed as an asset, as society seeks to foster *inter*dependence within the group.

Closely related to the interdependence that is prized within collectivist cultures are the concepts of sharing and duty to the group. In addition, value is placed on staying out of conflict and "going with the flow" within the Eastern ways of thinking. The Japanese story *"Momotaro"* ("Peach Boy," Sakade, 1958) gives an excellent example of the cultural importance of the traits of interdependence, the ability to avoid conflict, and duty to the group. The story begins with an elderly couple who have always wished for a child, although they are not able to conceive. One day, as the woman is washing her clothes in a stream, a giant peach floats to where she is standing and, upon reaching the woman, splits open to reveal a baby! The woman takes Momotaro ("Peach Boy") home, and she and her husband raise him. Momotaro grows into a fine young boy and, at age 15, tells his parents that the ogres in the nearby country have tormented the people of his village long enough. To the great pride of his parents, he decides to go to fight the ogres and bring back their treasure to his village.

Along the way, Momotaro befriends many animals one by one. The animals want to fight each new animal they meet, but at Momotaro's urging, "The spotted dog and the monkey and the pheasant, who usually hated each other, all became good friends and followed Momotaro faithfully" (Sakade, 1958, p. 6). At the end of the story, Momotaro and his animal friends defeat the ogres by working together and bring the treasure back to the village, where all who live there share in the bounty. As the hero, Momotaro portrays the strengths valued in Japanese and other Asian cultures: (a) He sets out for the good of the group, although in doing so risks individual harm (collectivism); (b) along the way, he stops others from petty squabbling (promoting harmony); (c) he works with them to achieve his goal (interdependence and collaboration); and (d) he brings back a treasure to share with the group (interdependence and sharing). In comparison to this tale of Momotaro, the story of a Western hero might differ at several points, especially that of the hero needing help from others, because individual achievement often is valued above group achievement. Thus, the cultural orientation determines which characteristics are transmitted as the valued strengths to its members.

ORIENTATION TO TIME

Differences also exist between East and West in terms of their orientations to time. In Western cultures such as the United States, we often look to the future (see Chapters 2 and 9). Indeed, some of the strengths we seem to value most (e.g., hope, optimism, self-efficacy; see Chapter 9) reflect future-oriented thinking. In Eastern cultures, however, there is a greater focus on, and respect for, the past. This past-oriented focus is revealed in the ancient Chinese proverb, "To know the road ahead, ask those coming back." Thus, certain personality characteristics might be defined as strengths in terms of their compatibility with a particular time orientation. For example, certain types of problem solving might be viewed as more advantageous than others. In a well-known Chinese fable, "Old Horse Knows the Way," a group of soldiers travels far from their home in the mountains and, upon trying to find their way home, they become lost. One of the soldiers comes up with this solution: "We can use the wisdom of an old horse. Release the old horses and follow them, and thereby reach the right road" (Pei, 2005, p. 1). Thus, Eastern cultures value the strength of "looking backward" and recognizing the wisdom of their elders.

THOUGHT PROCESSES

When considering the unique aspects of Western and Eastern thought, we often focus on the nature of specific ideas, but we do not reflect on the process of linking and integrating ideas. Indeed, as researchers (e.g., Nisbett, 2003) have noted, stark differences exist in the very thought processes used by Westerners and Easterners, and this results in markedly divergent worldviews and approaches to meaning making. Richard Nisbett, a professor at the University of Michigan who studies social psychology and cognition, illustrates how he became aware of some of these differences in thinking during a conversation he had with a student from China. Nisbett recalls,

> A few years back, a brilliant student from China began to work with me on questions of social psychology and reasoning. One day early in our acquaintance, he said, "You know, the difference between you and me is that I think the world is a circle, and you think it is a line." . . . The Chinese believe in constant change, but with things always moving back to some prior state. They pay attention to a wide range of events; they search for relationships between things; and they think you can't under-stand the part without understanding the whole. Westerners live in a sim-pler, more deterministic world; they focus on salient objects or people instead of the larger pictures; and they think they can control events because they know the rules that govern the behavior of objects." (p. xiii)

As Nisbett's story shows, the thinking style used by the Chinese student, and not just the ideas themselves, was vastly different from Nisbett's. This more circular thinking style is best exemplified by the Taoist figure of the *yin* and the *yang*. Most people are familiar with the *yin* and *yang* symbol. This figure represents the circular, constantly changing nature of the world as viewed by Eastern thought. The dark part of the symbol represents the feminine and passive, and the light side represents the masculine and active. Each part exists because of the other, and neither could exist alone, according to Taoist beliefs. As one state is experienced, the other is not far to follow; if hard times are occurring, easier times are on the way. This more circular thinking pattern affects the way in which the Eastern thinker maps out his or her life and therefore may influence the decisions a person makes in the search for peace.

Yin Yang

An example of the effects of such different ways of thinking may be found in the life pursuits of the Westerner as compared with those of the Easterner. Whereas in the United States we give high priority to the right to "life, liberty, and the pursuit of happiness," the goals of the Easterner might have a different focus. Take, for instance, the positive psychological construct of happiness (see Chapter 7). Researchers have posited that happiness (whether group or individual) is a state commonly sought by Easterners and Westerners alike (Diener & Diener, 1995). The difference in the philosophical approaches to life, however, may make the searches look very different. For example, a Westerner whose goal is happiness draws a straight line to his goal, looking carefully for obstacles and finding possi-ble ways around them. His goal is to achieve this eternal happiness. For the Easterner who follows the *yin* and the *yang*, however, this goal of happiness may not make sense. If one were to seek happiness and then achieve it, in the Eastern way of thinking, this would only mean that unhappiness was close on its heels. Instead, the Easterner might have the goal of balance, trusting in the fact that, although great unhappiness or suffering may occur in one's life, it would be equally balanced by great happiness. These two different types of thinking obviously create very different ways of forming goals to achieve the good life.

EAST AND WEST: IS ONE BEST?

There are substantial differences in the types of ideas and the way in which they are put together that emerge from Eastern and Western traditions. It is important to remember, however, that neither is "better" than the other. This is especially relevant for discussions regarding strengths. Therefore, we must use culture as a lens for evaluating whether a particular characteristic might be considered a strength or a weakness within a particular group.

Different Ways to Positive Outcomes

So far, we have discussed how thinking styles influence the development of goals in the lives of both Westerners and Easterners. Differences also exist, however, in the routes that each group uses to move toward its goals. Western-oriented thinking focuses on the individual's goal, whereas Eastern philosophers suggest a different focus, one in which the group is highlighted. For example, Confucius said, "If you want to reach your goal, help others reach their goal" (Soothill, 1968, *Analects 6:29*). Accordingly, although hope may be the primary tool of the "rugged individualist" (i.e., Westerner; see Chapter 2) in moving toward the good life, other tools might take precedence in the life of the Easterner. For example, qualities that help to create and sustain interdependent relationships for Easterners may be more valuable in helping them to reach their goals. These virtues may be most important in helping Easterners to develop pathways that ensure that group goals are achieved, thereby assisting Easterners in completing their individual goals.

In the main Eastern philosophical branches of learning (Confucianism, Taoism, Buddhism, and Hinduism), repeated mention is made of the two constructs of compassion for others and the search for harmony or life balance. Thus, each has a clear place in the study of positive psychology from an Eastern perspective.

COMPASSION

The idea of **compassion** has origins in both Western and Eastern philosophies. Within the Western tradition, Aristotle often is noted for early writings on the concept of compassion. Likewise, compassion can be traced in the Eastern traditions of Confucianism, Taoism, Buddhism, and Hinduism. In Confucian teachings, compassion is discussed within the concept of *jen* (humanity) and is said to encapsulate all other virtues. Within the Taoist belief system, humanity also reflects behaviors that must occur naturally, without premeditation. Finally, the Buddha often is described as "perfectly enlightened, and boundlessly compassionate" (Sangharakshita, 1991, p. 3). As such, the idea of compassion, or *karuna*, also is woven throughout Buddhism as a virtue on the path toward transcendence. Finally, within the Hindu tradition, compassion is called for in good actions toward others, which will direct followers upon the path that will not require them to return to Earth after death.

In recent writings in positive psychology, physician Eric Cassell (2002) proposes the three following requirements for compassion: (a) the difficulties of the recipient must be serious; (b) the recipient's difficulties cannot be self-inflicted, and (c) we, as observers, must be able to identify with the recipient's suffering. Compassion is described as a "unilateral emotion" (Cassell, p. 435) that is directed outward from oneself. In Buddhist teachings, the attainment of compassion means being able to "transcend preoccupation with the centrality of self" (Cassell, p. 438)—to focus on others rather than merely on ourselves. The ability to possess feelings for something completely separate from our own suffering allows us to transcend the self and, in this way, to be closer to the achievement of the good life. In fact, transcendental compassion is said to be the most significant of the four universal virtues, and it often is called Great Compassion (*mahakaruna*) to distinguish it from the more applied *karuna* (Sangharakshita, 1991). Similarly, although discussed in somewhat different ways as Confucian, Taoist, and Hindu principles, the capacities to feel and to do for others are central to achieving the good life for each of these traditions as well.

Possessing compassion helps the person to succeed in life and is viewed as a major strength within the Eastern tradition. Feeling for fellow group members may allow identification with others and development of group cohesion. Furthermore, acting compassionately fosters group, rather than personal, happiness.

Compassion also may come more naturally to the person from a collectivist culture than to someone from an individualist culture. On this point, researchers have argued that a collectivist culture may breed a sense of compassion in the form of its members' prosocial behaviors (Batson, 1991; Batson, Ahmad, Lishner, & Tsang, 2002). When a group identity has been formed, therefore, the natural choice may be group benefits over individual ones. More information from qualitative and quantitative studies in this area would be helpful in defining the mechanisms used to foster such compassion.

Peterson and Seligman (2004) indicate that "humanity" may be viewed as a "universal strength" in their book, *Character Strengths and Virtues: A Handbook and Classification*. For both Western and Eastern traditions, they hold that the ability to feel for others is a necessary part of the search for the good life. Compassion, an aspect of humanity, involves looking outside ourselves and thinking about others as we care for and identify with them. This other-than-self focus is needed to transcend one's physical body, according to Eastern traditions. Thus, nirvana can be attained only when one's independent identity and the self-motivated desires that accompany it are eradicated completely.

In moving toward the good life, therefore, compassion is essential for dealing with daily life tasks. As one walks along the path toward this good life, the continual goal is to transcend the human plane and to become enlightened through experiences with others and the world. Compassion asks people to think outside themselves and to connect with others. Additionally, as the person comes to understand others, she or he comes closer to self-understanding. This is yet another key component in attaining transcendence.

HARMONY

In Western history, the Greeks are said to have viewed happiness as the ability "to exercise powers in pursuit of excellence in a life free from constraints" (Nisbett, 2003, pp. 2–3). Thus, the good life was viewed as a life with no ties to duty and the freedom to pursue individual goals. There are clear distinctions in comparing this idea of happiness to Confucian teachings, for example, in which duty (*yi*) is a primary virtue. In Eastern philosophy, happiness is described as having the "satisfactions of a plain country life, shared within a *harmonious* social network" (Nisbett, p. 5–6, emphasis added). In this tradition, **harmony** is viewed as central to achieving happiness.

In Buddhist teachings, when people reach a state of nirvana, they have reached a peacefulness entailing "complete harmony, balance, and equilibrium" (Sangharakshita, 1991, p. 135). Similarly, in Confucian teachings harmony is viewed as crucial for happiness. Confucius had high praise for individuals who were able to harmonize; he compared this capacity to "a good cook blending the flavors and creat[ing] something harmonious and delicious" (Nisbett, 2003, p. 7). Getting along with others allows the person to be freed from individual pursuits and, in so doing, to gain "collective agency" (Nisbett, p. 6) in working out what is good for the group. Thus, the harmonizing principle is a central tenet of the Eastern way of life. The balance and harmony that one achieves as part of an enlightened life often are thought to represent the ultimate end of the good life. In Hindu teachings, one also can see that, as all humans are interconnected by a "single unifying principle" (Stevenson & Haberman, 1998, p. 46), harmony must be pursued. If an individual walks through life without thought of others as connected to him, the effects may be far-reaching for both the individual and the group (Stevenson & Haberman).

The concept of harmony has received minimal attention in the field of positive psychology to date, although some attention has been given to the idea of appreciating balance in one's life in reference to certain other constructs (e.g., wisdom; see Baltes & Staudinger, 2000, and Chapter 10). Moreover, Clifton and colleagues (Buckingham & Clifton, 2001; Lopez, Hodges, & Harter, 2005) include a harmony theme in the Clifton StrengthsFinder (see Chapter 4); they describe this construct as a desire to find consensus among the group, as opposed to putting forth conflicting ideas. Little more scholarly attention has been paid to harmony in American psychological literature. Given the central role of harmony as a strength in Eastern cultures, more research may be warranted on this topic in the future. First, the concept of harmony often is mistakenly equated with the notion of conformity. Studies to ferret out the differences between these two constructs could be beneficial in defining each more clearly. Because the term *conformity* has somewhat negative connotations in our independence-oriented culture, it is possible that some of these same negative characterizations have been extended to the concept of harmony.

Second, qualitative research methods could be used to develop a better definition of harmony. At present, the concept of harmony is reflected in the virtue of justice as discussed by Peterson and Seligman (2004) in their classification of strengths. These authors note that the ability to "work well as a member of a group or team; being loyal to the group; doing one's share" (p. 30) may be a subset of the idea of civic strength. Although this may be one way to classify this strength, it might be argued that the idea of harmony is broader than this particular definition and may be thought of separately from loyalty and "pitching in." Furthermore, the phenomenon of harmony may be both an interpersonal strength (as described in the previous paragraphs) and an intrapersonal strength.

Finally, after more conceptual work is completed, positive psychology scholars interested in harmony would benefit greatly from the development of reliable and valid measuring devices. Such tools would help researchers to uncover the primary contributors and correlates of harmony.

Final Thoughts

It is important to recognize that, in discussing Eastern thoughts in this chapter, a central tenet of Eastern ways of life is broken, in the decidedly Western, didactic teaching method used to bring this information to students of positive psychology. The traditional Easterner would object to the notion that the concepts here could be learned from mere words and would argue that only life experience would suffice. As part of Eastern teachings, self-exploration and actual hands-on experience are essential for true understanding of the concepts that are presented in only an introductory fashion in this chapter. Thus, you are encouraged to seek out more experience of these ideas in everyday life and to attempt to discover the relevance to your own lives of strengths such as compassion and harmony. Although these ideas may stem from Eastern ideology, they are relevant for Westerners who want to discover new ways of thinking about human functioning. As a student of positive psychology, you can to continue to broaden your horizons by considering ideas from the East. Challenge yourself to be open minded about the types of characteristics to which you assign the label *strength*, and remember that different traditions bring with them different values.

Key Terms

Buddhism: A philosophical and religious system based on the teachings of Buddha: Life is dominated by suffering caused by desire; suffering ends when we end desire; and enlightenment obtained through right conduct, wisdom, and meditation releases one from desire, suffering, and rebirth.

Collectivism: A cultural value that prizes the concepts of sharing, cooperation, interdependence, and duty to the group.

Compassion: An aspect of humanity that involves looking outside oneself and thinking about others as we care for and identify with them. In positive psychology, compassion requires (a) that the difficulty of the recipient be serious; (b) that the recipient's difficulties are not self-inflicted; and (c) that we, as observers, are able to identify with the recipient's suffering.

Confucianism: A philosophical and religious system developed from the teachings of Confucius. Confucianism values love for humanity, duty, etiquette, and truthfulness. Devotion to family, including ancestors, is also emphasized.

Enlightenment: A human's capacity to transcend desire and suffering and to see things clearly for what they are.

Harmony: A state of consensus or balance. Eastern traditions view harmony as essential to happiness.

Hinduism: A diverse body of religion, philosophy, and cultural practice native to and predominant in India. Hinduism is characterized by a belief in the interconnectedness of all things and emphasizes personal improvement with the goal of transcending the cycle of reincarnation.

Individualism: A cultural value that emphasizes individual achievement, competition, personal freedom, and autonomy.

Nirvana: A state in which the self is freed from desire. This is the final destination in the Buddhist philosophy.

Taoism: A philosophical and religious system developed by Lao-Tzu which advocates a simple, honest life and noninterference in the course of natural events.

Classifications and Measures of Human Strengths and Positive Outcomes

4

> *Let us imagine that one could set up a kind of scale or yardstick to measure the success of life—the satisfactoriness to the individual and the environment in their mutual attempts to adapt themselves to each other. Toward the end of such a yardstick, positive adjectives like "peaceful," "constructive," "productive," might appear, and at the other end such words as "confused," "destructive," "chaotic." These would describe the situation in general. For the individual himself there might be at one end of the yardstick such terms as "healthy," "happy," "creative," and at the other end "miserable," "criminal," "delirious."*
>
> —Menninger, Mayman, & Pruyser (1963, p. 2)

Karl Menninger, one of the brothers who helped build the world-renowned Menninger Clinic, attempted to change the way that health care professionals viewed the diagnosis, prevention, and treatment of mental illness. As part of his mission, he encouraged clinicians and researchers to dispense with the old, confusing labels of sickness. Then, he called for the development of a simple diagnostic system that described the life *process* rather than *states* or *conditions*. Finally, he reminded us of the power of the "sublime expressions of the life instinct" (Menninger et al., 1963, p. 357), specifically hope, faith, and love. Over

Karl Menninger

Source: Reprinted with permission of The Menninger Clinic.

the last 50 years, psychology and psychiatry have busied themselves with the confused and miserable aspects of human nature, and, as a result of maintaining the pathology focus, health care providers have helped millions of people relieve their suffering. Unfortunately, too few professionals have engaged in the entire exercise in imagination described earlier, and this has resulted in the unmet needs of millions more people. We continue to add complexity to an ever-growing diagnostic system (American Psychiatric Association, 2000); we know little about the process of living; and we spend far too little time and energy making sense of the intangibles of good living—hope, faith, and love. If Menninger were alive, we think he would consider our professional acumen and knowledge lacking in utility and out of balance. Most important, he probably would ask, "What about the productive and healthy aspects of personal functioning?"

Although the missions of many positive psychologists bear similarities to Dr. Menninger's ideas, there is a long way to go in measuring human strengths. (We subscribe to Linley and Harrington's [2006] definition of **strength** as a capacity for feeling, thinking, and behaving in a way that allows optimal functioning in the pursuit of valued outcomes.) In this regard, the argument can be made that work on the classification of illnesses had a 2000-year head start on the more recent efforts to classify strengths and positive outcomes. Therefore, it is easy to understand why we have better understandings of human weaknesses than we do of strengths. In the Menninger et al. (1963) review of the history of classifying disorders, it is noted that the Sumerians and the Egyptians drew distinctions between hysteria and melancholia as early as 2600 BC. The earliest attempt to define a set of virtues is contained in Confucian teachings dating to 500 BC, where Confucius systematically addressed *jen* (humanity or benevolence), *li* (observance of rituals and customs), *xin* (truthfulness), *yi* (duty or justice), and *zhi* (wisdom) (Cleary, 1992; Haberman, 1998; see Chapter 2 for a discussion of Confucian philosophy and other Eastern perspectives on positive psychology).

In the 21st century, two classifications of illness have attained worldwide acceptance. First, the World Health Organization's (1992) *International Classifications of Diseases* (*ICD*) is in its 10th edition and continues to evolve. Second, the American Psychiatric Association's (2000) *Diagnostic and Statistical Manual* (*DSM*) now is in its 6th iteration as the *DSM-IV-TR* (Text Revision). The *ICD* is broader in scope than the *DSM* in that it classifies all diseases, whereas the *DSM* describes only the mental disorders. Currently, no classification of human strengths or positive outcomes has achieved worldwide use or acceptance. Some classifications and measures, however, have been created, refined, and broadly disseminated in the last decade. In this chapter, we discuss the following three classification systems:

1. The Gallup Themes of Talent (Buckingham & Clifton, 2001) as measured by the Clifton StrengthsFinder and the Clifton Youth StrengthsExplorer

2. The Values in Action (VIA) Classification of Strengths (Peterson & Seligman, 2004) as measured by the adult and youth versions of the VIA Inventory of Strengths

3. The Search Institute's 40 Developmental Assets (Benson, Leffert, Scales, & Blyth, 1998) as measured by the Search Institute Profiles of Student Life: Attitudes and Behaviors

Then, we explore the dimensions of well-being commonly used to describe mental health. Next, we call for greater attention to the development of broader descriptions and more sensitive measures of positive outcomes. Finally, we emphasize the need for a comprehensive classification of human behavior.

Classifications and Measures of Human Strengths

Whether for positive traits and behaviors or for negative ones, the development of classification systems and measures is influenced by the values of society and the professionals who create these values. As cultures change over time, it is important that these tools be revised regularly to remain applicable to their targeted groups. We now discuss the present three frameworks, along with measures of strengths and their **psychometric properties** (the measurement characteristics of the tools). Specifically, we comment on the **reliability** (the extent to which a scale is consistent or stable) and the **validity** (the extent to which a scale measures what it purports to measure) of these recently designed tools.

GALLUP'S CLIFTON STRENGTHSFINDER

Over his 50-year career at the University of Nebraska, Selection Research Incorporated, and The Gallup Organization, Donald Clifton[1] studied success across a wide variety of business and education domains (Buckingham & Clifton, 2001; Clifton & Anderson, 2002; Clifton & Nelson, 1992). He based his analysis of success on a simple question: "What would happen if we studied what is right with people?" Furthermore, he focused on straightforward notions that stood the test of time and empirical scrutiny. First, he believed that talents could be operationalized, studied, and accentuated in work and academic settings. Specifically, he defined **talent** as "naturally recurring patterns of thought, feeling, or behavior that can be productively applied" (Hodges & Clifton, 2004, p. 257) and manifested in life experiences

Donald Clifton

Source: Reprinted with permission.

characterized by yearnings, rapid learning, satisfaction, and timelessness. He considered these trait-like "raw materials" to be the products of normal, healthy development and successful childhood and adolescence experiences. Likewise, Clifton viewed strengths as extensions of talent. More precisely, the strength construct combines talent with associated knowledge and skills and is defined as the ability to provide consistent, near-perfect performance in a specific task.

Second, Clifton considered success to be closely allied with personal talents, strengths, and analytical intelligence. Based on these beliefs, he identified hundreds of personal talents that predicted success in work and academics. Moreover, he constructed **empirically based** (grounded in theory and research findings), semistructured interviews for identifying these talents. When developing these interviews, Clifton and his colleagues examined the prescribed roles of a person (e.g., student, salesperson, administrator), visited the job site or academic setting, identified outstanding performers in these roles and settings, and determined the long-standing thoughts, feelings, and behaviors associated with situational success. These interviews also were useful in predicting positive outcomes (Schmidt & Rader, 1999) and subsequently were administered to more than 2 million people for the purposes of personal enrichment and employee selection. When considering the creation of an objective measure of talent in the mid-1990s, Clifton and his colleagues systematically reviewed the data in these interviews and identified about three dozen themes of talent involving enduring, positive human qualities. (See Table 4.1 for a listing and description of the 34 themes in the Gallup classification system.)

The first step in developing the Clifton StrengthsFinder as an online measure (see www.strengthsfinder.com) was to construct a pool of more than 5000 items. Selection of items was based on traditional **construct, content, and criterion validity** evidence suggesting that the tool tapped underlying attributes, the full depth and breadth of content, and the shared relationships and predictive powers, respectively. A smaller pool was derived subsequently on the basis of item functioning. More specifically, the evidence used to evaluate the item pairs was taken from a database of over 100 predictive validity studies (Schmidt & Rader, 1999). Factor and reliability analyses were conducted in multiple samples to produce maximal theme information in an instrument of minimal length. Many sets of items were pilot tested, and those with the strongest psychometric properties were retained.

In 1999, an online version of the Clifton StrengthsFinder was launched. That version had 35 themes. After several months of collecting data, the researchers decided on the 180 item pairs (360 items, 256 of which are scored) and the 34-theme version currently available. Although some theme names have changed since 1999, the theme definitions and 180 item pairs have not been altered. See Figure 4.1 for a summary of the textbook author's (SJL) signature themes.

Table 4.1 The 34 Clifton StrengthsFinder Themes

Achiever: People strong in the Achiever theme have a great deal of stamina and work hard. They take great satisfaction from being busy and productive.

Activator: People strong in the Activator theme can make things happen by turning thoughts into action. They are often impatient.

Adaptability: People strong in the Adaptability theme prefer to "go with the flow." They tend to be "now" people who take things as they come and discover the future one day at a time.

Analytical: People strong in the Analytical theme search for reasons and causes. They have the ability to think about all the factors that might affect a situation.

Arranger: People strong in the Arranger theme can organize, but they also have a flexibility that complements that ability. They like to figure out how all of the pieces and resources can be arranged for maximum productivity.

Belief: People strong in the Belief theme have certain core values that are unchanging. Out of those values emerges a defined purpose for their life.

Command: People strong in the Command theme have presence. They can take control of a situation and make decisions.

Communication: People strong in the Communications theme generally find it easy to put their thoughts into words. They are good conversationalists and presenters.

Competition: People strong in the Competition theme measure their progress against the performance of others. They strive to win first place and revel in contests.

Connectedness: People strong in the Connectedness theme have faith in links between all things. They believe there are few coincidences and that almost every event has a reason.

Consistency: People strong in the Consistency theme are keenly aware of the need to treat people the same. They try to treat everyone in the world with consistency by setting up clear rules and adhering to them.

Context: People strong in the Context theme enjoy thinking about the past. They understand the present by researching its history.

Deliberative: People strong in the Deliberative theme are best characterized by the serious care they take in making decisions or choices. They anticipate the obstacles.

Developer: People strong in the Developer theme recognize and cultivate the potential in others. They spot the signs of each small improvement and derive satisfaction from those improvements.

Discipline: People strong in the Discipline theme enjoy routine and structure. Their world is best described by the order they create.

Empathy: People strong in Empathy theme can sense the feelings of other people by imagining themselves in others' lives and in others' situations.

Focus: People strong in the Focus theme can take a direction, follow through, and make the corrections necessary to stay on track.

Futuristic: People strong in the Futuristic theme are inspired by the future and what could be. They inspire others with their vision of the future.

Harmony: People strong in the Harmony theme look for consensus. They don't enjoy conflict; rather, they seek areas of agreement.

(Continued)

Table 4.1 (Continued)

Ideation: People strong in the Ideation theme are fascinated by ideas. They are able to find connections between seemingly disparate phenomena.

Includer: People strong in the Includer theme are accepting of others. They show awareness of those who feel left out and make efforts to include them.

Individualization: People strong in the Individualization theme are intrigued with the unique qualities of each person. They have a gift for figuring out how people who are different can work together productively.

Input: People strong in the Input theme have a craving to know more. Often they like to collect and archive all kinds of information.

Intellection: People strong in the Intellection theme are characterized by their intellectual activity. They are introspective and appreciate intellectual discussions.

Learner: People strong in the Learner theme have a great desire to learn and want to improve continuously.

Maximizer: People strong in the Maximizer theme focus on strengths as a way to stimulate professional and group excellence. They seek to transform strengths into something superb.

Positivity: People strong in the Positivity theme have an enthusiasm that is contagious. They are upbeat and can get others excited about what they are going to do.

Relator: People who are strong in the Relator theme enjoy close relationships with others. They find deep satisfaction in working hard with friends to achieve a goal.

Responsibility: People strong in the Responsibility theme take psychological ownership of what they say they will do. They are committed to stable values such as honesty and loyalty.

Restorative: People strong in the Restorative theme are adept at dealing with problems. They are good at figuring out what is wrong and resolving it.

Self-Assurance: People strong in the Self-Assurance theme feel confident in their ability to manage their own lives. They possess an inner compass that gives them confidence that their decisions are right.

Significance: People strong in the Significance theme want to be very important in the eyes of others. They are independent and want to be recognized.

Strategic: People strong in the strategic theme create alternative ways to proceed. Faced with any given scenario, they can quickly spot the relevant patterns and issues.

WOO: WOO stands for "winning others over." People strong in the WOO theme love the challenge of meeting new people and winning them over. They derive satisfaction from breaking the ice and making a connection with another person.

Source: Reprinted with permission. Gallup®, StrengthsFinder®, Clifton StrengthsFinder™, and each of the 34 Clifton StrengthsFinder theme names are trademarks of The Gallup Organization, Princeton, NJ.

In the last six years, extensive psychometric research on the Clifton StrengthsFinder was conducted by Gallup researchers (and summarized in a technical report by Lopez, Hodges, & Harter, 2005). Across samples, most scales (i.e., themes) have been found to be internally consistent (despite containing as few as four items) and stable over periods ranging from 3 weeks to 17 months. Specifically, the coefficient alphas have ranged

Your Signature Themes

Many years of research conducted by The Gallup Organization suggest that the most effective people are those who understand their strengths and behaviors. These people are best able to develop strategies to meet and exceed the demands of their daily lives, their careers, and their families.

A review of the knowledge and skills you have acquired can provide a basic sense of your abilities, but an awareness and understanding of your natural talents will provide true insight into the core reasons behind your consistent successes.

Your Signature Themes report presents your five most dominant themes of talent, in the rank order revealed by your responses to StrengthsFinder. Of the 34 themes measured, these are your "top five."

Your Signature Themes are very important in maximizing the talents that lead to your successes. By focusing on your Signature Themes, separately and in combination, you can identify your talents, build them into strengths, and enjoy personal and career success through consistent, near-perfect performance.

Futuristic

"Wouldn't it be great if. . . ." You are the kind of person who loves to peer over the horizon. The future fascinates you. As if it were projected on the wall, you see in detail what the future might hold, and this detailed picture keeps pulling you forward, into tomorrow. While the exact content of the picture will depend on your other strengths and interests—a better product, a better team, a better life, or a better world—it will always be inspirational to you. You are a dreamer who sees visions of what could be and who cherishes those visions. When the present proves too frustrating and the people around you too pragmatic, you conjure up your visions of the future, and they energize you. They can energize others, too. In fact, very often people look to you to describe your visions of the future. They want a picture that can raise their sights and thereby their spirits. You can paint it for them. Practice. Choose your words carefully. Make the picture as vivid as possible. People will want to latch on to the hope you bring.

Maximizer

Excellence, not average, is your measure. Taking something from below average to slightly above average takes a great deal of effort and in your opinion is not very rewarding. Transforming something strong into something superb takes just as much effort but is much more thrilling. Strengths, whether yours or someone else's, fascinate you. Like a diver after pearls, you search them out, watching for the telltale signs of a strength. A glimpse of untutored excellence, rapid learning, a skill mastered without recourse to steps—all these are clues that a strength may be in play. And having found a strength, you feel compelled to nurture it, refine it, and stretch it toward excellence. You polish the pearl until it shines. This natural sorting of strengths means that others see you as discriminating. You choose to spend time with people who appreciate your particular strengths. Likewise, you are attracted to others who seem to have found and cultivated their own strengths. You tend to avoid those who want to fix you and make you well rounded. You don't want to spend your life bemoaning what you lack. Rather, you want to capitalize on the gifts with which you are blessed. It's more fun. It's more productive. And, counterintuitively, it is more demanding.

Arranger

You are a conductor. When faced with a complex situation involving many factors, you enjoy managing all the variables, aligning and realigning them until you are sure you have arranged them in the most productive configuration possible. In your mind, there is nothing special about what you are doing. You are simply trying to figure out the best way to get things done. But others, lacking this theme, will be in awe of your ability. "How can you keep so many things in your head at once?" they will ask. "How can you stay so flexible, so willing to shelve well-laid plans in favor of some brand-new configuration that has just occurred to you?" But you cannot imagine behaving in any other way. You are a shining example of effective flexibility, whether you are changing travel schedules at the last minute because a better fare has popped up or mulling over just the right combination of people and

Figure 4.1   Clifton StrengthsFinder Signature Themes for Shane Lopez   *(Continued)*

Figure 4.1 (Continued)

resources to accomplish a new project. From the mundane to the complex, you are always looking for the perfect configuration. Of course, you are at your best in dynamic situations. Confronted with the unexpected, some complain that plans devised with such care cannot be changed, while others take refuge in the existing rules or procedures. You don't do either. Instead, you jump into the confusion, devising new options, hunting for new paths of least resistance, and figuring out new partnerships—because, after all, there might just be a better way.

Ideation

You are fascinated by ideas. What is an idea? An idea is a concept, the best explanation of the most events. You are delighted when you discover beneath the complex surface an elegantly simple concept to explain why things are the way they are. An idea is a connection. Yours is the kind of mind that is always looking for connections, and so you are intrigued when seemingly disparate phenomena can be linked by an obscure connection. An idea is a new perspective on familiar challenges. You revel in taking the world we all know and turning it around so we can view it from a strange but strangely enlightening angle. You love all these ideas because they are profound, because they are novel, because they are clarifying, because they are contrary, because they are bizarre. For all these reasons, you derive a jolt of energy whenever a new idea occurs to you. Others may label you creative or original or conceptual or even smart. Perhaps you are all of these. Who can be sure? What you are sure of is that ideas are thrilling. And on most days this is enough.

Strategic

The Strategic theme enables you to sort through the clutter and find the best route. It is not a skill that can be taught. It is a distinct way of thinking, a special perspective on the world at large. This perspective allows you to see patterns where others simply see complexity. Mindful of these patterns, you play out alternative scenarios, always asking, "What if this happened? Okay, well what if this happened?" This recurring question helps you see around the next corner. There you can evaluate accurately the potential obstacles. Guided by where you see each path leading, you start to make selections. You discard the paths that lead nowhere. You discard the paths that lead straight into resistance. You discard the paths that lead into a fog of confusion. You cull and make selections until you arrive at the chosen path—your strategy. Armed with your strategy, you strike forward. This is your Strategic theme at work: "What if?" Select. Strike.

Source: Reprinted with permission. Gallup®, StrengthsFinder®, Clifton StrengthsFinder™, and each of the 34 Clifton StrengthsFinder theme names are trademarks of The Gallup Organization, Princeton, NJ.

from .55 to .81 (.70 or above is a desirable psychometric standard) with WOO having the highest internal consistency (.81) and Connection and Restorative having the lowest (both below .60). Regarding the stability of scales, most test-retest correlations were above .70 (considered appropriate for a measure of a personal trait).

Regarding construct validity, the theme score intercorrelations support the relative independence of themes, thereby showing that the 34 themes provide unique information. Finally, a study correlating Clifton StrengthsFinder themes with the Big 5 personality constructs (openness, conscientiousness, extroversion, agreeableness, and neuroticism; McCrae & Costa, 1987) provided initial evidence for the measure's convergent validity (i.e., they were correlated, but not at such a high level suggesting redundancy). To date, there are no published studies examining the intercorrelations between the 34 theme scores and personality measures (other than the Big 5 measure).

Today, the Clifton StrengthsFinder is available in 17 languages, and it is modifiable for individuals with disabilities. It is appropriate for administration to adolescents and adults with reading levels at 10th grade or higher. Although it is used to identify personal talents, the related supporting materials (e.g., Buckingham & Clifton, 2001; Clifton & Anderson, 2002; Clifton & Nelson, 1992) can help individuals discover how to build on their talents to develop strengths within their particular life roles. It should be noted, however, that this instrument is not designed or validated for use in employee selection or mental health screening. Another caveat also is warranted: namely, given that Clifton StrengthsFinder feedback (presented as your "Five Signature Themes") is provided to foster intrapersonal development, using it for comparisons of individuals' profiles is discouraged. (A respondent's top five themes, in order of potency, are included in the feedback. Remaining themes are not rank ordered and shared with respondents. This is also the case with the strengths feedback that results from the Values in Action measure, to be discussed subsequently.) Furthermore, the Clifton StrengthsFinder is not sensitive to change and, as such, it should not be used as a pre-post measure of growth.

The Gallup Organization is in the process of developing a new talent classification system and a measure that is appropriate for children and youth (ages 10 to 14). This is called the Clifton Youth StrengthsExplorer, and it will be released in 2006. StrengthsExplorer developers believe that knowledge about young people's strengths will help in directing their energies to maximize their potentials (personal communication, Pio Juszkiewicz, November 7, 2005). The version of the StrengthsExplorer tested in the summer of 2005 taps 10 themes (Achieving, Caring, Competing, Confidence, Dependability, Discoverer, Future Thinker, Organizing, Presence, and Relating). (The psychometric report for the measure will be available upon its release.) When respondents complete the measure, they will receive a Youth Workbook summarizing their top three themes and including action items and exercises that, if completed, could help youth capitalize on their strengths. Parent and educator guides also will be available so that caregivers can help youth in developing their positive characteristics.

THE VIA CLASSIFICATION OF STRENGTHS

The VIA (Peterson & Seligman, 2004) Classification of Strengths serves as the antithesis of the *DSM*, and it holds promise for fostering our understanding of psychological strengths. Peterson and Seligman make the point that we currently have a shared language for speaking about the negative side of psychology, but we have no such equivalent terminology for describing human strengths. The VIA Classification of Strengths provides such a common language, and it encourages a more strength-based approach to diagnosis and treatment (treatment manuals focused on enhancing strengths may one day accompany the diagnostic manual).

Christopher Peterson

Source: Reprinted with permission.

As these pioneering positive psychologists write, "We . . . rely on the 'new' psychology of traits that recognizes individual differences . . . that are stable and general but also shaped by the individual's setting and thus capable of change" (Peterson & Seligman, 2004, p. 5).

The VIA classification system, originally commissioned by the Mayerson Foundation, was generated in response to two basic questions: "(1) How can one define the concepts of 'strength' and 'highest potential,' and (2) how can one tell that a positive youth development program has succeeded in meeting its goals?" (Peterson & Seligman, 2004, p. v). These questions led to more philosophical and practical questions about human character. Ultimately, Peterson and Seligman and many colleagues decided that components of character included virtues (core characteristics valued by some moral philosophers, religious thinkers, and everyday folk), character strengths (psychological processes and mechanisms that define virtues), and situational themes (specific habits that lead people to manifest strengths in particular situations).

The generation of entries for the classification system first was attempted by a small group of psychologists and psychiatrists after dozens of inventories of virtues and strengths and perspectives of character were reviewed. Upon applying 10 criteria for strength (e.g., a strength is morally valued in its own right; a person's display of a strength does not diminish other people) to a long list of potential constructs, 24 strengths were identified and then organized under 6 overarching virtues (wisdom and knowledge, courage, humanity, justice, temperance, and transcendence) thought to "emerge consensually across cultures and throughout time" (Peterson & Seligman, 2004, p. 29). Table 4.2 lists and describes the 6 virtues and 24 strengths. Peterson and Seligman state that their classification approach is sensitive to the developmental differences in which character strengths are displayed and deployed.

The measure of this system of virtues and strengths, the Values in Action Inventory of Strengths (VIA-IS), was designed to describe the individual differences of character strengths on continua and not as distinct categories. The development of the measure was influenced by a tool once known as the "wellsprings" measure (Lutz, 2000), and it "took inspiration from the Gallup Organization's StrengthsFinder measure . . . by wording items in extreme fashion ("I *always* . . .") and by providing feedback to respondents concerning their top—not bottom—strengths of character" (Peterson & Seligman, 2004, p. 628).

To date, the VIA-IS has been refined several times, and the current version appears reliable and valid for the purposes of identifying strengths in adults (based on summary information presented in Peterson & Seligman [2004] which is referenced heavily in this paragraph). Regarding the reliability of the measure, all scales have satisfactory consistency and stability across a four-month period. Correlations among scales are higher than expected given that the inventory was designed to measure 24 unique

Table 4.2   The VIA Classification of Virtues and Strengths

Wisdom and Knowledge—*Cognitive strengths that entail the acquisition and use of knowledge*

Creativity: Thinking of novel and productive ways to conceptualize and do things

Curiosity: Taking an interest in ongoing experience for its own sake

Open-mindedness: Thinking things through and examining them from all sides

Love of learning: Mastering new skills, topics, and bodies of knowledge

Perspective: Being able to provide wise counsel to others

Courage—*Emotional strengths that involve the exercise of will to accomplish goals in the face of opposition, external and internal*

Bravery: Not shrinking from threat, challenge, difficulty, or pain

Persistence: Finishing what one starts; persisting in a course of action in spite of obstacles

Integrity: Speaking the truth but more broadly presenting oneself in a genuine way

Vitality: Approaching life with excitement and energy; not doing anything halfheartedly

Humanity—*Interpersonal strengths that involve tending and befriending others*

Love: Valuing close relations with others, in particular those in which caring is reciprocated

Kindness: Doing favors and good deeds for others; helping them; taking care of them

Social intelligence: Being aware of the motives and feelings of other people and oneself

Justice—*Civic strengths that underlie healthy community life*

Citizenship: Working well as a member of a group or team; being loyal to a group

Fairness: Treating all people the same according to the notions of fairness and justice

Leadership: Encouraging a group of which one is a member to get things done

Temperance—*Strengths that protect against excess*

Forgiveness and mercy: Forgiving those who have done wrong; accepting others' faults

Humility/Modesty: Letting one's accomplishments speak for themselves

Prudence: Being careful about one's choices; not taking undue risks

Self-regulation: Regulating what one feels and does; being disciplined

Transcendence—*Strengths that forge connections to the larger universe and provide meaning*

Appreciation of beauty and excellence: Noticing and appreciating beauty, excellence, and/or skilled performance in various domains of life

Gratitude: Being aware of and thankful for the good things that happen

Hope: Expecting the best in the future and working to achieve it

Humor: Liking to laugh and tease; bringing smiles to other people

Spirituality: Having coherent beliefs about the higher purpose and meaning of the universe

Source: From Peterson, C., & Seligman, M. E. P., *Character Strengths and Virtues: A Handbook and Classification,* Table 1.1: Classification of Character Strengths, copyright © 2004 by Values in Action Institute. Used by permission of Oxford University Press, Inc.

constructs. Women score higher on humanity strengths than men, and African Americans score higher than members of other ethnic groups on the scale of the spirituality strength. Evidence of the measure's validity includes the following three sets of findings:

1. Nominations of strengths by friends and family correlate at about a .50 level with matching scales' scores for most of the 24 strengths.

2. The majority of the scales correlate positively with scores on measures of life satisfaction.

3. Factor analyses provides some support for the existence of 6 virtues.

The results from the factor analysis conducted on existing data, however, actually suggest 5 factors (strengths of restraint, intellectual strengths, interpersonal strengths, emotional strengths, theological strengths) instead of the 6 proposed virtues. Peterson and Seligman (2004) described studies comparing strengths across groups of people, and they reason that the VIA-IS is an outcome measure that is sensitive to change. The researchers at the VIA Institute plan additional examinations of the psychometric properties of the measure.

The 6th iteration of the VIA-IS currently is available as an online (www.positivepsychology.org) and paper-and-pencil measure in English and several other languages. The 240 items (10 for each strength), answered with a 5-point Likert scale, can be completed in about 30 minutes. The feedback report consists of the top 5 strengths, which are called signature strengths. See Figure 4.2 for the summary of the textbook author's (SJL) findings from the VIA-IS.

An adolescent version of this measure, referred to as the Values in Action Inventory of Strengths for Youth (VIA-Youth), has been developed and is undergoing validation; it may be available in 2006 (Christopher Peterson, personal communication, October 15, 2004). Preliminary information about the VIA-Youth, which contains 198 items (6 to 12 items for each of the 24 strengths with a 5-point Likert scale), suggested that internal consistency of the scales is adequate for most and that the basic structure of the measure may be best described by 4 factors rather than 6 (Peterson & Park, 2003). Child and youth versions of a strengths cardsort (Quinn, 2004; Lopez, Janowski, & Quinn, 2004), based on the 24 VIA strengths, have been developed, initially validated, and widely used by practitioners.

THE SEARCH INSTITUTE'S 40 DEVELOPMENTAL ASSETS

The Search Institute's Developmental Assets (Benson et al., 1998), which originally were conceptualized in the 1980s in response to the question, "What protects children from today's problems?" considers internal and external variables that contribute to a child's thriving. The Search Institute researchers, headed by Peter Benson, conducted numerous research projects

Version 6.8.2004

VIA Strengths Scale

Thank you for taking the time to complete this questionnaire. Its goal is to measure the extent to which people see themselves possessing various human strengths (for details see http://www.psych .upenn.edu/seligman/classification.htm).

Please take these tentative results with a grain of salt, but we would be interested in knowing your reactions to this assessment.
Christopher Peterson
chrispet@umich.edu

Feedback

You completed a preliminary version of this questionnaire. Here is the feedback we promised you. If you would like to save a copy, use File–Save As in your browser's menu and save it as Feedback.html on your computer.

We are just beginning the process of ascertaining the reliability and validity of the questionnaire. However, if we go simply by the face validity of the questions you answered, **your five most notable strengths** are as follows:

1. Gratitude
   You are aware of and thankful for the good things that happen. You take time to express thanks.

2. Perspective [Wisdom]
   You are able to provide wise counsel to others. You have ways of looking at the world that make sense to yourself and to other people.

3. Curiosity [Interest, Novelty-Seeking, Openness to Experience]
   You take an interest in all of ongoing experience for its own sake. You find subjects and topics fascinating. You explore and discover.

4. Hope [Optimism, Future-Mindedness, Future Orientation]
   You expect the best in the future and work to achieve it. You believe that a good future is something that can be brought about.

5. Vitality [Zest, Enthusiasm, Vigor, Energy]
   You approach life with excitement and energy. You don't do things halfway or halfheartedly. You live life as an adventure. You feel alive and activated.

Figure 4.2   VIA-IS Signature Strengths for Shane Lopez

Source: © 2004 Values in Action Institute.

and also held informal discussions and focus groups to ensure that the developmental assets included in their framework were applicable to all people, cultures, and settings in America.

The Search Institute's 40 Developmental Assets are considered commonsense, positive experiences and qualities and are identified as reflecting primary contributors to the thriving of young people. The Developmental Assets framework categorizes assets according to external and internal groups of 20 assets each. The 20 external assets are the positive experiences that children and youth gain through interactions with people and institutions; the 20 internal assets are those personal characteristics and behaviors that stimulate the positive development of young people. (See Table 4.3.)

Table 4.3   The Search Institute's 40 Developmental Assets

EXTERNAL ASSETS	
Support	
Family support	Family life provides high levels of love and support.
Positive family communication	Young person and her or his parent(s) communicate positively, and young person is willing to seek advice and counsel from parent(s).
Other adult relationships	Young person receives support from three or more nonparent adults.
Caring neighborhood	Young person experiences caring neighbors.
Caring school climate	School provides a caring, encouraging environment.
Parent involvement in schooling	Parent(s) are actively involved in helping young person succeed in school.
Empowerment	
Community values youth	Young person perceives that adults in the community value youth.
Youth as resources	Young people are given useful roles in the community.
Service to others	Young person serves in the community one hour or more per week.
Safety	Young person feels safe at home, at school, and in the neighborhood.
Boundaries and Expectations	
Family boundaries	Family has clear rules and consequences and monitors the young person's whereabouts.
School boundaries	School provides clear rules and consequences.
Neighborhood boundaries	Neighbors take responsibility for monitoring young people's behavior.
Adult role models	Parent(s) and other adults model positive, responsible behavior.
Positive peer influence	Young person's best friends model responsible behavior.
High expectations	Both parent(s) and teachers encourage the young person to do well.
Constructive Use of Time	
Creative activities	Young person spends three or more hours per week in lessons or practice in music, theater, or other arts.
Youth programs	Young person spends three or more hours per week in sports, clubs, or organizations at school and/or in community organizations.
Religious community	Young person spends one hour or more per week in activities in a religious institution.
Time at home	Young person is out with friends "with nothing special to do" two or fewer nights per week.

INTERNAL ASSETS	
Commitment to Learning	
Achievement motivation	Young person is motivated to do well in school.
School engagement	Young person is actively engaged in learning.
Homework	Young person reports doing at least one hour of homework every school day.
Bonding to school	Young person cares about her or his school.
Reading for pleasure	Young person reads for pleasure three or more hours per week.
Positive Values	
Caring	Young person places high value on helping other people.
Equality and social justice	Young person places high value on promoting equality and reducing hunger and poverty.
Integrity	Young person acts on convictions and stands up for her or his beliefs.
Honesty	Young person tells the truth even when it is not easy.
Responsibility	Young person accepts and takes personal responsibility.
Restraint	Young person believes it is important not to be sexually active or to use alcohol or other drugs.
Social Competencies	
Planning and decision making	Young person knows how to plan ahead and make choices.
Interpersonal competence	Young person has empathy, sensitivity, and friendship skills.
Cultural competence	Young person has knowledge of and comfort with people of different cultural/racial/ethnic backgrounds.
Resistance skills	Young person can resist negative peer pressure and dangerous situations.
Peaceful conflict resolution	Young person seeks to resolve conflict nonviolently.
Positive Identity	
Personal power	Young person feels he or she has control over "things that happen to me."
Self-esteem	Young person reports having high self-esteem.
Sense of purpose	Young person reports that "my life has a purpose."
Positive view of personal future	Young person is optimistic about her or his personal future.

The 156-item survey, Search Institute Profiles of Student Life: Attitudes and Behaviors, was developed in 1989 and revised in 1996 (see Benson et al., 1998, for a review). The measure (appropriate for children and youth) describes the respondent's 40 Developmental Assets, along with 8 thriving indicators, 5 developmental deficits, and 24 risk-taking behaviors. Unfortunately, there is little information in the public domain about its psychometric properties.

Additional lists of developmental assets (for infants, toddlers, pre-schoolers, etc.) have been created by Dr. Benson and the Search Institute researchers. Parents and other caregivers are directed to observe the assets manifested by children and available in the environment.

DISTINGUISHING AMONG THE MEASURES OF HUMAN STRENGTH

Although the Clifton StrengthsFinder, the VIA-IS, and the Search Institute Profiles of Student Life were created for different reasons, they currently are used for similar purposes. Namely, they identify a person's primary strengths. Table 4.4 illustrates some of the similarities and differences among the measures. This information may help in the selection of the correct instrument for specific purposes, but more data should be solicited from the developers of the measures before making the final choice.

Table 4.4   Characteristics of Measures of Human Strengths

Measure	Cost $	Online	Completed in < 45 Minutes	Multiple Age-Specific Versions	Direct Focus on Environment
Gallup's Clifton StrengthsFinder	Yes	Yes	Yes	Yes	No
Values in Action– Inventory of Strengths	No	Yes	Yes	Yes	No
Search Institute Profiles of Student Life	Yes	No	Yes	Yes	Yes

IDENTIFYING YOUR PERSONAL STRENGTHS

Over the years, we have asked hundreds of clients and students about their weaknesses and strengths. Almost without exception, people are much quicker to respond about weaknesses than strengths. (See the

Personal Mini-Experiments to examine this issue and to explore your strengths by taking the measures discussed in this chapter.) We also have observed that people struggle for words when describing strengths, whereas they have no shortage of words or stories that bring their weaknesses to life.

Personal Mini-Experiments

Discovering and Capitalizing on Your Strengths

In this chapter, we have discussed classifications and measures of human strengths. We encourage you to learn more about your strengths and to share them with friends, family, teachers, and coworkers.

Getting to Know Your Friend's Weaknesses and Strengths: Ask a friend (or several friends), "What are your weaknesses?" and note how quickly they respond to the question, how many weaknesses they identify, and how descriptive they are when telling the story of weaknesses. Then, ask that friend, "What are your strengths?" Make similar mental notes about reaction time, number of strengths, and descriptiveness. If you are asking these questions of more than one friend, alternate between asking the weakness question first and the strength question first. In turn, share your thoughts about your strengths (before or after you complete the measures presented in this chapter), and ask for your friend's feedback on your self-assessment.

Discovering Your Strengths: In just over an hour, you can identify 10 of your personal strengths by completing the Clifton StrengthsFinder (www.strengthsfinder.com) and the Values in Action Inventory of Strengths (www.positivepsychology.org). We encourage you to take both inventories and share the results with people close to you.

Capitalizing on Your Strengths: There are numerous strategies for capitalizing on your strengths (see www.strengthsquest.com, www.reflectivehappiness.com). For now, we would like you to capitalize on one strength. Pick 1 of your 10 strengths and try to use that strength 5 times a day for 5 days. Your 25 attempts to capitalize on that strength have the potential to bolster it and create a habit of using that strength more each day.

We hope that readers take advantage of the opportunity to discover their strengths and that in several decades people will have as much to say about their strengths as they do about their weaknesses. Our observations of people upon the completion of a strengths measure suggest that the new or validated information about your personal strengths will give you a slight, temporary boost in positive emotions and confidence. Also, you will want to share the results with people around you.

THE CASE OF SHANE

As positive psychologists, we have committed ourselves to the development of the positive in others and, of course, we try to practice what we preach. We both have identified our strengths through formal and informal assessment, and we try to capitalize on our strengths every day. Here is a brief account of how one of us (SJL) uses his strengths in daily life.

When I received the results of the Clifton StrengthsFinder (see Figure 4.1) and the VIA-IS (see Figure 4.2), I reflected on the findings and tried to figure out how I could put them to immediate use. Then, I realized that I have been using these strengths every day . . . that is why they are my strengths! Nevertheless, I decided to be more intentional in my efforts to make my strengths come alive. That goal of intentionality addressed *how* I would capitalize on my strengths, but I hadn't addressed *why*. It turns out, however, that it was pretty simple—I wanted to make my good life even better. That was the outcome I desired, and I thought that these "new" strengths would provide pathways to that goal.

Admittedly, my initial efforts to intentionally use my strengths every day were not that successful. Although I thought the findings were accurate, and I was excited to receive the strengths feedback, I was overwhelmed by the idea of refining my use of 5 or 10 strengths at the same time. For that reason, I decided to capitalize on the strengths that I thought would help me the most in making my life better. I chose the top two themes (Futuristic and Maximizer) from the Gallup feedback and the top strength (Gratitude) from the VIA results. Right away, focusing on three strengths seemed doable.

With those "three strengths that matter most" (as I began to refer to them) in hand, I consulted the action items (shared in a printable form as a supplement to the Signature Themes presented in Figure 4.1) associated with my Futuristic and Maximizer themes. For Futuristic, I settled on one daily activity that might spark my tendency to project into the future: Take time to think about the future. Pretty straightforward, but reading this action item made me realize that I would go for a considerable time without thinking about the future, and this led to dissatisfaction with how my life was going. Putting this guidance into action has involved taking daily walks dedicated to thinking about the future. Often, I walk in the evening, and I chat with my wife about the future of our work and our family. At other times, I leave the office around midday and walk through the campus reflecting on some of my aspirations. These walks have turned into a cherished time that yields exciting ideas and considerable satisfaction.

Regarding my Maximizer theme, I believe this talent of making good ideas, projects, and relationships better contributes greatly to my success at work. Through examining my habits at home and work, I realized I was doing a fairly good job of systematically using this strength. This left me feeling unsure about how to proceed in my efforts to capitalize on this strength. Then, one day I encountered a person who prided herself on playing "the devil's advocate" every time an idea was presented during a meeting. I thought about the many devil's advocates whom I have encountered over the years, and I concluded that these people were not necessarily providing constructive feedback that made a good idea better. They also were not offering alternative ideas that would work better. In my opinion, all they were doing was undercutting my creativity and enthusiasm (or that of other people). To maximize, I realized that I had to surround myself with people who knew how to make good ideas better. That criterion has become a critical one when I select friends, colleagues, and students, and I believe it has boosted my creativity and the quality of my work.

I have used Futuristic and Maximizing themes both at work and at home, and I think my efforts have helped me in both domains. I believe that capitalizing on these strengths has led to more creativity and productivity at work and greater sense of purpose for my family and me. Using gratitude (my third "strength that matters most") with more intentionality has not generated more productivity or greater clarity in my personal mission, but it has been rewarding in that it brings joy and a sense of closeness to people. To make the most of my gratitude, I decided to spend part of most Friday afternoons writing thank-you notes (handwritten and mailed the old-fashioned way) to people who have touched my life that week, and at other times I thank people who have done something nice for me that week. Occasionally, I write to a person who did a good deed for me years ago (and whom I had never thanked or whom I wanted to thank again.) Finally, I also write to people who have done good works (I may or may not know them personally) to express my gratitude for their efforts. This practice has enriched my emotional life, and it has strengthened many of my relationships.

By focusing on three of my strengths, I have been successful at making an already good life even better. Over time, I have become more facile at capitalizing on other strengths, particularly ideation, hope, and wisdom. Living my strengths has become a way of life for me, and I look forward to finding out how this will influence the futures of my loved ones and me.

Positive Outcomes for All

DIMENSIONS OF WELL-BEING

The pursuit of happiness has been the topic of discussion in religious writings, philosophical texts, and proclamations of the American forefathers. Most recently, magazine articles and trade books have positioned happiness as the de facto central outcome of positive psychology research and practice. Yet, as described in this text, the pursuit of happiness is only one aspect of positive psychology. As positive psychology researchers and practitioners, we certainly want our participants and clients to be happy, but we also are interested in whether they are realizing their potentials, pursuing their interests, nurturing others, and leading authentic lives. To date, however, happiness (spontaneous reflections of pleasant and unpleasant feelings in one's immediate experience) and **life satisfaction** (a sense of contentment and peace stemming from small gaps between wants and needs) are of major interest in the positive psychology field. In this section of the chapter, we discuss happiness and life satisfaction as components of emotional well-being but not as the single or most important outcome in positive psychology. (This chapter provides a basic description of happiness as a meaningful life outcome. The basic research on happiness is discussed in Chapter 7.)

Theories of *subjective* well-being (also referred to as emotional well-being and happiness), such as the emotional model posited by Diener and others (Diener, 1984; Diener, Suh, Lucas, & Smith, 1999), suggest that individuals' appraisals of their own lives capture the essence of well-being. *Objective* approaches to understanding psychological well-being and social well-being have been proposed by Ryff (1989) and Keyes (1998), respectively. Our view is that psychological and social well-being provide useful frameworks for conceptualizing human functioning. Taken together, subjective descriptions of emotional well-being (i.e., happiness) and objective descriptions of psychological and social well-being constitute a more complete portrayal of mental health (Keyes & Lopez, 2002). Table 4.5 presents the descriptions of the three types of well-being and sample items that tap these components of positive functioning.

Emotional well-being consists of perceptions of avowed happiness and satisfaction with life, along with the balance of positive and negative affects. This threefold structure of emotional well-being consists of life satisfaction, positive affect, and the absence of negative affect, and it has been confirmed in numerous studies (e.g., Bryant & Veroff, 1982; Lucas, Diener, & Suh, 1996; Shmotkin, 1998). Indeed, the coupling of satisfaction and affect serves as a meaningful and measurable conceptualization of emotional well-being.

Ryff (1989) posits that some of the favorable outcomes described by positive psychologists can be integrated into a model of **psychological well-being** (see Table 4.5). Self-acceptance, personal growth, purpose in life, environmental mastery, autonomy, and positive relations with others are the six components of Ryff's conceptualization of positive functioning. This model of well-being has been investigated in numerous studies, and the findings reveal that the six dimensions are independent, though correlated, constructs of well-being. Specifically, Ryff and Keyes (1995) conducted an analysis of the six-part well-being model and found that the multidimensional model was a superior fit over a single-factor model of well-being.

Carol Ryff

Source: Reprinted with permission of Carol Ryff.

Table 4.5   Elements of Psychological, Social, and Emotional Well-Being

Psychological Well-Being	Social Well-Being	Emotional Well-Being
Self-Acceptance: Possess positive attitude toward the self; acknowledge and accept multiple aspects of self; feel positive about past life. • *I like most parts of my personality.* • *When I look at the story of my life, I am pleased with how things have turned out so far.* • *In many ways, I feel disappointed about my achievements in life.* (−)	**Social Acceptance:** Have positive attitudes toward people; acknowledge others and generally accept people, despite others' sometimes complex and perplexing behavior. • *People who do a favor expect nothing in return.* • *People do not care about other people's problems.* (−) • *I believe that people are kind.*	**Positive Affect:** Experience symptoms that suggest enthusiasm, joy, and happiness for life. • *During the last 30 days, how much of the time did you feel cheerful; in good spirits; extremely happy; calm and peaceful; satisfied; and full of life?***
Personal Growth: Have feelings of continued development and potential and are open to new experience; feel increasingly knowledgeable and effective. • *For me, life has been a continuous process of learning, changing, and growth.* • *I think it is important to have new experiences that challenge how I think about myself and the world.* • *I gave up trying to make big improvements/changes in my life a long time ago.* (−)	**Social Actualization:** Care about and believe society is evolving positively; think society has potential to grow positively; think self/society is realizing potential. • *The world is becoming a better place for everyone.* • *Society has stopped making progress.* (−) • *Society hasn't improved for people like me.* (−)	**Negative Affect:** Absence of symptoms that suggest that life is undesirable and unpleasant. • *During the last 30 days, how much of the time did you feel so sad nothing could cheer you up; nervous; restless or fidgety; hopeless; that everything was an effort; worthless?***
Purpose in Life: Have goals and a sense of direction in life; past life is meaningful; hold beliefs that give purpose to life. • *Some people wander aimlessly through life, but I am not one of them.* • *I live life one day at a time and don't really think about the future.* (−) • *I sometimes feel as if I've done all there is to do in life.* (−)	**Social Contribution:** Feel they have something valuable to give to the present and to society; think their daily activities are valued by their community. • *I have something valuable to give to the world.* • *My daily activities do not create anything worthwhile for my community.* (−) • *I have nothing important to contribute to society.* (−)	**Life Satisfaction:** A sense of contentment, peace, and satisfaction from small discrepancies between wants and needs with accomplishments and attainments. • *During the past 30 days, how much of the time did you feel satisfied; full of life?*** • *Overall these days, how satisfied are you with your life? (0–10, where 0 = terrible and 10 = delighted)* • *Satisfaction may be measured in life domains such as work, home, neighborhood, health, intimacy, finances, and parenting or it is measured globally (see the Satisfaction With Life Scale, Diener et al., 1985).*

(Continued)

Table 4.5 (Continued)

Psychological Well-Being	Social Well-Being	Emotional Well-Being
Environmental Mastery: Feel competent and able to manage a complex environment; choose or create personally suitable community. • *The demands of everyday life often get me down. (–)* • *In general, I feel I am in charge of the situation in which I live.* • *I am good at managing the responsibilities of daily life.*	**Social Coherence:** See a social world that is intelligible, logical, and predictable; care about and are interested in society and contexts. • *The world is too complex for me. (–)* • *I cannot make sense of what's going on in the world. (–)* • *I find it easy to predict what will happen next in society.*	**Happiness:** Having a general feeling and experience of pleasure, contentment, and joy. • *Over all these days, how happy are you with your life?**** • *How frequently have you felt (joy, pleasure, happiness) in the past week, month, or year?*
Autonomy: Are self-determining, independent, and regulated internally; resist social pressures to think and act in certain ways; evaluate self by personal standards. • *I tend to be influenced by people with strong opinions. (–)* • *I have confidence in my own opinions, even if they are different from the way most other people think.* • *I judge myself by what I think is important, not by the values of what others think is important.*	**Social Integration:** Feel part of community; think they belong, feel supported, and share commonalities with community. • *I don't feel I belong to anything I'd call a community. (–)* • *I feel close to other people in my community.* • *My community is a source of comfort.*	
Positive Relations With Others: Have warm, satisfying, trusting relationships; are concerned about others' welfare; capable of strong empathy, affection, and intimacy; understand give-and-take of human relationships. • *Maintaining close relationships has been difficult and frustrating for me. (–)* • *People would describe me as a giving person, willing to share my time with others.* • *I have not experienced many warm and trusting relationships with others. (–)*		

Note: A negative sign in parenthesis indicates that the item is reverse scored. Response options range from strongly disagree (1), moderately disagree (2), or slightly disagree (3) to neither agree nor disagree (4), slightly agree (5), moderately agree (6), or strongly agree (7).

** Indicates response range from all the time (1), most of the time (2), some of the time (3), a little of the time (4), none of the time (5).

*** Indicates response range from worst possible situation (0) to best possible situation (10).

72

Keyes (1998) suggests that, just as clinicians categorize the social challenges that are evident in an individual's life, so should they assess the social dimensions of well-being. On this point, he proposes that the dimensions of coherence, integration, actualization, contribution, and acceptance are the critical components of **social well-being.**

Keyes (Keyes & Lopez, 2002) also suggests that complete mental health can be conceptualized via combinations of high levels of emotional well-being, psychological well-being, and social well-being. Individuals with these high levels are described as **flourishing** (see the criteria in Table 4.6). Accordingly, individuals who have no mental illness but who have low levels of well-being are described as **languishing.** (We have found that informal assessment of levels of well-being provides valuable information about the range of functioning between flourishing and languishing.) This conceptualization of mental health describes a syndrome of symptoms that might be amenable to intervention techniques aimed at increasing levels of emotional, social, and psychological well-being. Conceptualization and treatment are well connected in this model.

A new, integrative theoretical perspective on well-being may provide additional assistance in bridging the gap between our research-based understanding of living well and the ability to promote it (Lent, 2004). By describing one model that explains our capacity for positive functioning during normative life conditions and one that provides direction for restoring well-being during difficult life circumstances, Lent highlights numerous treatment alternatives (e.g., setting goals, enhancing efficacy, building social support) that promote this much-prized life outcome.

TOWARD A BETTER UNDERSTANDING OF POSITIVE OUTCOMES

As discussed in this chapter and suggested elsewhere throughout this book, we believe that human strengths are the active ingredients of positive living. This belief can be tested empirically in everyday life and in research studies if, and only if, the definitions and measures of strengths capture the true essence of the best in people. Therefore, we submit information in this chapter about three classifications of strengths and their respective measures for your critical evaluation.

Most of the remaining chapters of this text focus on the science of human strengths (some of these strengths are not listed in the classification systems) that is being developed by clinical, counseling, developmental, health, evolutionary, personality, school, and social psychologists. Numerous chapters address the practice of leading a good life and how you and your friends and family capitalize on strengths and build on positive emotions to attain positive life outcomes. Notice that we do not address the "science of good living." Positive psychology research initiatives have done

Table 4.6   Diagnostic Criteria for Flourishing

FLOURISHING IN LIFE

A. Individual must have had no episodes of major depression in the past year.

B. Individual must possess a high level of well-being as indicated by the individual's meeting all three of the following criteria:
  1. High emotional well-being, defined by 2 of 3 scale scores on appropriate measures falling in the upper tertile.
     a. Positive affect
     b. Negative affect (low)
     c. Life satisfaction

  2. High psychological well-being, defined by 4 of 6 scale scores on appropriate measures falling in the upper tertile.
     a. Self-acceptance
     b. Personal growth
     c. Purpose in life
     d. Environmental mastery
     e. Autonomy
     f. Positive relations with others

  3. High social well-being, defined by 3 of 5 scale scores on appropriate measures falling in the upper tertile.
     a. Social acceptance
     b. Social actualization
     c. Social contribution
     d. Social coherence
     e. Social integration

---

little to describe and measure outcomes other than those associated with happiness and life satisfaction, or "the pleasant life" (Seligman, 2002). Although we encourage a focus on objective aspects of well-being, we contend that a more expanded conceptualization of living well is needed to guide our efforts at change and positive growth. Here, in the remaining portion of this chapter, we dream a little about the future of positive psychology, one where romantic and agapic love, rewarding school and work and civic contributions, and resource-producing play share the spotlight with happiness.

Positive Outcomes Associated With Love

Agape is a spiritual love that reflects selflessness and altruism. This type of love involves concern for another's welfare and being relatively undemanding for oneself. Although this is not the most celebrated form of love, it may be the most beneficial. Our view is that we could use our strengths to be more giving and to build relationships founded on selflessness.

Romantic love, especially passionate romantic love (described further in Chapter 13), is much desired and talked about by people of all ages. There is little celebration, however, of *resilient* romantic love or *sustained* romantic love. What strengths does it take to make a relationship work despite hard times and thereafter flourish for 10 years, 30 years, and 50 years? We could determine this through more systematic study of couples who report high levels of romantic love many years into their relationships.

Positive Outcomes Associated With School, Work, and Civic Contributions

Schools are becoming more accountable for the educational outcomes of their students, and businesses continue to keep a close eye on the bottom line. Although desired outcomes for students and employees are fairly well articulated as learning and productivity, respectively, there must be other positive outcomes associated with these important activities that occupy us for our entire lives.

Certainly the meaningfulness of academic pursuits and work can be described. But could we measure the extent to which positive schooling (see Chapter 16) and gainful employment (see Chapter 17) stimulate psychological growth? And what about distal outcome measures of school and work? Civic contributions of students and employees could be linked to developmental gains attained early during important periods in school or work.

Positive Outcomes Associated With Play

Play introduces us to the social, emotional, and physical skills needed to make the most out of life. Indeed, play is regarded as a "form of practice, or proximal growth, or mastery of skills" (Lutz, 2000, p. 33). The positive outcomes of childhood play are undeniable . . . yet we do not value the role of play in adulthood. The benefits of competitive and noncompetitive adult play have not been delineated, and this topic is ripe for more research.

Identifying Strengths and Moving Toward a Vital Balance

The staid view of mental illness as progressive and refractory was challenged by the noted psychiatrist Karl Menninger (Menninger et al., 1963). He called for psychiatrists to view mental illness as amenable to change. Thus, this new view of mental illness would bring the old view into balance. Positive psychologists now call for a different type of balance— a view of human life that gives attention both to weaknesses and to strengths. Although there is no question that we presently know much more about human fallibilities than about assets, a strong science and robust applications aimed at human strengths will yield not only a more thorough but also a more accurate view of the human condition.

Note

1. In January 2003, Dr. Clifton was awarded an American Psychological Association presidential commendation in recognition of his pioneering role in strengths-based psychology. The commendation states, "Whereas, living out the vision that life and work could be about building what is best and highest, not just about correcting weaknesses, [Clifton] became the father of Strengths-Based Psychology and the grandfather of Positive Psychology."

Key Terms

Agape: A spiritual love that reflects selflessness and altruism.

Construct validity: The extent to which a scale measures the underlying attributes it intends to measure. Construct validity can be achieved by comparing your measure to other measures that assess a similar construct.

Content validity: The extent to which the actual content of the scale represents the domain it is intended to address. In other words, a content-valid measure covers all aspects of the construct it is trying to measure.

Criterion validity: The extent to which scores on a scale can predict actual behavior or performance on another, related measure.

Emotional well-being: A type of well-being consisting of perceptions of affirmed happiness and satisfaction with life, along with a balance of positive and negative affect.

Empirically based: Developed using available research knowledge.

Flourishing: A term pertaining to individuals who have simultaneously high levels of social, emotional, and psychological well-being.

Languishing: A term pertaining to individuals who do not have a mental illness but who are low in social, emotional, and psychological well-being.

Life satisfaction: A sense of contentment and peace stemming from small gaps between wants and needs.

Psychological well-being: A type of well-being that consists of six elements: self-acceptance, personal growth, purpose in life, environmental mastery, autonomy, and positive relations with others.

Psychometric properties: The measurement characteristics of a scale that include its reliability, validity, and statistics on items of the measure.

Reliability: The ability of a scale to produce consistent and reliable results over a number of administrations or after the passage of time.

Social well-being: A type of well-being that consists of coherence, integration, actualization, contribution, and acceptance by others.

Strength: A capacity for feeling, thinking, and behaving in a way that allows optimal functioning in the pursuit of valued outcomes (Linley & Harrington, 2006).

Talent: Naturally recurring patterns of thought, feeling, or behavior that can be productively applied and manifested in life experiences characterized by yearnings, rapid learning, satisfaction, and timelessness.

Validity: The ability of a scale to measure what it is intended to measure.

Part II

Positive Psychology in Context

Developing Strengths and Living Well in a Cultural Context

5

Culture and Psychology

David Satcher, the 16th surgeon general of the United States, who served from 1998 to 2002, sat on a dimly lit stage in the overflowing convention hall. He clutched a copy of a thick document, the report titled *Mental Health: Culture, Race, Ethnicity* (U.S. Department of Health and Human Services [DHHS], 2001), which was being officially released that same day. Psychologists poured into the meeting room to hear Dr. Satcher's summary of this report, which had been years in the making. When it was time to talk, Satcher spoke on the crucial influences of culture on mental health. This excerpt from the report summarizes some of the surgeon general's comments:

> **Culture** [boldface added] is broadly defined as a common heritage or set of beliefs, norms, and values (U.S. DHHS, 1999). It refers to the shared attributes of one group.... [C]ulture bears upon whether people even seek help in the first place, what types of help they seek, what coping styles and social supports they have, and how much stigma they attach to mental illness. All cultures also feature strengths, such as resilience and adaptive ways of coping, which may buffer some people from developing certain disorders. Consumers of mental health services naturally carry this cultural diversity directly into the treatment setting.... The culture of the clinician and the larger health care system govern the societal response to a patient with mental illness. They influence many aspects of the delivery of care, including diagnosis,

treatment, and the organization and reimbursement of services. Clinicians and service systems have been ill equipped to meet the needs of patients from different backgrounds and, in some cases, have displayed bias in the delivery of care (U.S. DHHS, 2001; see the complete executive summary of the report below).

There were two take-home messages from Dr. Satcher's summary. First, "culture counts" in the consideration of the **etiology** (the cause of something, such as an illness), effects, and treatment of educational and psychological problems. Second, psychologists need to incorporate cultural issues into their conceptualizations of psychological problems and treatments.

Main Message: Culture Counts

DAVID SATCHER

Surgeon General of the United States

Culture and society play pivotal roles in mental health, mental illness, and mental health services. Understanding the wide-ranging roles of culture and society enables the mental health field to design and deliver services that are more responsive to the needs of racial and ethnic minorities.

Culture is broadly defined as a common heritage or set of beliefs, norms, and values (DHHS, 1999). It refers to the shared attributes of one group. Anthropologists often describe culture as a system of shared meanings. The term *culture* is as applicable to whites as it is to racial and ethnic minorities. The dominant culture for much of United States history focused on the beliefs, norms, and values of European Americans. But today's America is unmistakably multicultural. And because there are a variety of ways to define a cultural group (e.g., by ethnicity, religion, geographic region, age group, sexual orientation, or profession), many people consider themselves as having multiple cultural identities.

With a seemingly endless range of cultural subgroups and individual variations, culture is important because it bears upon what *all* people bring to the clinical setting. It can account for variations in how consumers communicate their symptoms and which ones they report. Some aspects of culture may also underlie *culture-bound syndromes*—sets of symptoms much more common in some societies than in others. More often, culture bears upon whether people even seek help in the first place, what types of help they seek, what coping styles and social supports they have, and how much stigma they attach to mental illness. All cultures also feature strengths, such as resilience and adaptive ways of coping, which may buffer some people from developing certain disorders. Consumers of mental health services naturally carry this cultural diversity directly into the treatment setting.

Culture is a concept not limited to patients. It also applies to the professionals who treat them. Every group of professionals embodies a "culture" in the sense that they too have a shared set of beliefs, norms, and values. This is as true for health professionals as it is for other professional groups such as engineers and teachers. Any professional group's culture can be gleaned from the jargon they use, the orientation and emphasis in their textbooks, and from their mindset or way of looking at the world.

Health professionals in the United States and the institutions in which they train and practice are rooted in Western medicine, which emphasizes the primacy of the human body in disease and the acquisition of knowledge through scientific and empirical methods. Through objective methods, Western medicine strives to uncover universal truths about disease: its causation, diagnosis, and treatment. Its achievements have become the cornerstone of medicine worldwide.

To say that physicians or mental health professionals have their own culture does not detract from the universal truths discovered by their fields. Rather, it means that most clinicians share a worldview about the interrelationship between body, mind, and environment informed by knowledge acquired through the scientific method. It also means that clinicians view symptoms, diagnoses, and treatments in ways that sometimes diverge from their clients' views, especially when the cultural backgrounds of the consumer and provider are dissimilar. This divergence of viewpoints can create barriers to effective care.

The culture of the clinician and the larger health care system govern the societal response to a patient with mental illness. They influence many aspects of the delivery of care, including diagnosis, treatments, and the organization and reimbursement of services. Clinicians and service systems, naturally immersed in their own cultures, have been ill equipped to meet the needs of patients from different backgrounds and, in some cases, have displayed bias in the delivery of care.

The main message of this Supplement is that "culture counts." The cultures that patients come from shape their mental health and affect the types of mental health services they use. Likewise, the cultures of the clinician and the service system affect diagnosis, treatment, and the organization and financing of services. Cultural and social influences are not the only influences on mental health and service delivery, but they have been historically underestimated—*and they do count.* Cultural differences must be *accounted for* to ensure that minorities, like all Americans, receive mental health care tailored to their needs.

Source: A Summary of the Surgeon General's Report on Mental Health: Culture, Race, Ethnicity, http://www.mentalhealth.samhsa.gov/cre/execsummary-3.asp.

The need to acknowledge broad cultural influences also applies to our efforts to understand educational successes, psychological strengths, and the very nature of the good life. This need, however, has gone unmet, according to the critics of the positive psychology initiative. These critics have observed that most strength-focused scholarship fails to address cultural influences in our research plans, service delivery, and program evaluations (Ahuvia, 2001; Leong & Wong, 2003; Sue & Constantine, 2003). Furthermore, critics call for more discussion about how "culture counts" in positive psychology research and practice activities.

We exhort any future positive psychologists who are reading this chapter to *count culture as a major influence on the development and manifestation of human strengths and good living*. This goal is challenging because psychology as a discipline has been ineffective in including cultural variables in the study of mental health and illness. Likewise, positive psychologists appear to be split on the issue of whether science and practice are culture free (i.e., hold a neutral and objective stance in the examination of "universal" human traits and behaviors) or culturally embedded (i.e., acknowledge the influences of cultural values in the examination of strengths and positive functioning).

In this chapter, we describe (1) psychologists' historical stances regarding the roles of culture on positive and negative behaviors, (2) positive psychologists' approaches to incorporating cultural perspectives into their work, and (3) the role of cultural influences in our future explorations of strengths and positive functioning. We first address the field's historical (and often flawed) attempts to understand the roles of cultural forces in determining our psychological makeups. Second, we examine the assertions that positive psychology is culture free or culturally embedded. Third and finally, we discuss the steps that need to be taken in order to position positive psychology in the cultural context. At the end of this chapter, we may have raised more questions than we have answered. Obviously, we view these questions as central to the future of positive psychology, and many of the readers of this text may be called upon to address these issues in their careers.

Understanding Culture: A Matter of Perspective

Psychology in the 20th century grappled with the topic of individual differences. Many of these discussions of individual differences pertained to culture. Over the last 100 years, for example, psychology moved from identifying differences associated with culture to the identification and appreciation of individual uniqueness.

In the late 1800s and early 1900s, anthropologists and psychologists often referred to race and culture as determinants of positive and negative personal characteristics and behaviors. Research paradigms, influenced by the sociopolitical forces of the times, produced findings that were generally consistent with the belief that the dominant race or culture was superior to all other American ethnic or minority groups. These approaches to highlighting the inferiority of certain racial and cultural groups have been referred to as the *genetically deficient* and *culturally deficient perspectives* on human diversity, whereas the *culturally different perspective* recognizes the potential of each culture to engender unique strengths (Sue & Sue, 2003). Psychologists who subscribed to the **genetically deficient** model hypothesized that biological differences explained perceived gaps in intellectual capabilities between racial groups. Moreover, the proponents of the genetically deficient model argued that people who possessed inferior intelligence could not benefit from growth opportunities and, as such, did not contribute to the advancement of society.

Pseudoscience was used to demonstrate the presumed genetic basis of intelligence and to emphasize the "finding" of intellectual superiority of Europeans and European Americans. For example, craniometry, which is the study of the relationship between skull characteristics and intelligence (sometimes measuring the amount of pepper seeds that filled the brain pan in dried skulls), was a pseudoscientific approach intended to demonstrate the relative superiority of one group over another group.

These notions of genetic inferiority were a prominent focus of **eugenics** (the study of methods of reducing "genetic inferiority" by selective breeding) research led by American psychologists such as G. Stanley Hall and Henry Goddard. Hall "was a firm believer in 'higher' and 'lower' human races" (Hothersall, 1995, p. 360). Goddard held similar views about race and intelligence, and in the early 1900s he established screening procedures (using formal intelligence tests similar to those used today) at Ellis Island to increase the deportation rates of the "feebleminded" (Hothersall, 1995). In this regard, people from around the world were given complex intelligence tests—typically in a language other than their own—the same day that they completed a long, overseas voyage. Not surprisingly, these test results generally were a poor estimate of the immigrants' intellectual functioning.

By the middle of the 20th century, most psychologists had abandoned the belief that race predetermined cognitive capacities and life outcomes. Indeed, the focus shifted from race to culture, or, more specifically, the "cultural deficiencies" evidenced in the daily lives of some people. In the **culturally deficient** approach to understanding differences among people, psychologists (e.g., Kardiner & Ovesey, 1951) identified a host of environmental, nutritional, linguistic, and interpersonal factors that supposedly explained the stunted physical and psychological growth of members of selected groups. It was hypothesized that people were lacking in certain psychological resources because they had limited exposure to the prevailing values and customs of the day, namely, those of European Americans (see the discussion of cultural deprivation in Parham, White, & Ajamu, 1999). Many researchers and practitioners attempted to explain problems and struggles of people by carefully examining the juxtaposition of cultures, specifically those cultures that were viewed as somewhat marginal as compared to those considered mainstream (middle-class, suburban, socially conservative). Deviations from the normative culture were considered "deficient" and cause for concern. Although this model focused greater attention on the effects of external variables than the earlier genetically deficient model, it nevertheless continued to apply a biased, negative, and oversimplified framework for appraising the cognitive capacities of minority group members (Kaplan & Sue, 1997).

After decades in which some psychologists argued that specified races and cultures were better than others (i.e., that European Americans were superior to minorities), many professionals began to subscribe to the **culturally different** perspective, in which the uniqueness and strengths of all cultures were recognized. Recently, researchers and practitioners have begun to consider *culturally pluralistic* (i.e., recognizing distinct cultural entities and adopting some traditional American values) and *culturally relativistic* (i.e., interpreting behaviors within the context of the culture) explanations of the diversities inherent in positive and negative human behaviors. Although pluralistic and relativistic explanations are broadly accepted, there is debate about whether positive psychology research and practice is culture free or culturally embedded. This debate is framed and discussed in the next section.

Positive Psychology: Culture Free or Culturally Embedded?

Positive psychology scientists and practitioners are committed to studying and promoting optimal human functioning. Although we share this common goal, we pursue it along many different routes. Outside observers might conclude that all positive psychology researchers ask similar questions and use similar methods. Such observers also may note that all positive psychology practitioners focus on clients' strengths and help move people toward positive life outcomes. Our educational specialties (e.g., social, health, personality, developmental, counseling, and clinical psychology), however, may determine particular aspects of the questions examined and research tools used. Likewise, our theoretical orientations to counseling (e.g., humanistic, cognitive–behavioral, solution-focused) may influence our efforts to help people to function more optimally. Likewise, the extent to which we view positive psychology research and practice as culture free rather than culturally embedded may shape our foci and methods.

Since 1998, the debate about cultural influences on positive psychology research and practice has been conducted formally at conventions and informally on listservs and in classrooms. Most professionals probably have confidence in the objectivity of their methods. They also are likely to acknowledge the need to make sense of the amazing diversity in human existence. Some professionals adopt more extreme positions (e.g., "Positive psychology IS culture free and IS NOT culturally embedded," or "Positive psychology IS culturally embedded and IS NOT culture free") and defend their views with great vigor. Having witnessed these debates and participated

---

Personal Mini-Experiments

Culture-Free or Culturally Embedded Daily Practice

In this chapter, we have discussed the extent to which you "count culture" in your daily work as a positive psychologist. The polar positions (culture free versus culturally embedded) on culture's role in positive psychology come to life when applied to a real professional situation.

Imagine that you join a professor's lab that is committed to the study of positive functioning of first-generation college students. During your initial discussion with the faculty member, you learn that the project she will be working on involves developing and evaluating a mentoring program for a culturally diverse group of students, some of whom moved to the United States only years ago when their families were providing seasonal labor to regional farmers. At the first meeting of the research group, you, fellow students, and the faculty member brainstorm ideas about the content and process of the mentoring sessions and about the salient outcome measures. As these topics are discussed, the professor interjects the following questions:

- Which of the students' strengths are most likely to aid them in school and in life?
- Should we measure happiness as a desired outcome in addition to academic self-efficacy, performance, and retention?
- What about family-of-origin influence on a student's academic behaviors? Should we account for that?
- How might our own values affect the mentoring process or research?

Please share your response with fellow students, and attempt to determine the extent to which you account for the role of culture in your responses.

---

in a few, the three recurring issues appear to involve (1) the effects of professionals' cultural values on their research and practices, (2) the universality of human strengths, and (3) the universality of the pursuit of happiness. Table 5.1 presents the extremes of each of these three positions. In the following sections, we detail the perspectives of the proponents on each position. Additionally, we present Personal Mini-Experiments to challenge the reader to think about the application of these perspectives.

CULTURE-FREE POSITIVE PSYCHOLOGY RESEARCH AND PRACTICE

Those advocating the culture-free approach hold that positive social science is descriptive and objective and that its results can "transcend particular cultures and politics and approach universality" (Seligman & Csikszentmihalyi, 2000, p. 5). These professionals argue that the cultural values of researchers and practitioners do not influence their professional

Table 5.1   Culture-Free and Culturally Embedded Positions in Positive Psychology

Culture Free	Issue	Culturally Embedded
NO	Cultural values of the researcher and practitioner influence their daily work.	YES
YES	There are numerous human strengths that are valued universally.	NO
YES	The pursuit of happiness is common across cultures.	NO

work. The underlying logic is that rigorous scientists use well-developed methods and validated tools; similarly, conscientious and effective therapists use validated assessments and interventions.

Regarding the universality of numerous human strengths, Peterson and Seligman (2004) detail their comprehensive search for virtues and strengths that are valued by all people across cultures (see Chapter 4 for a discussion of the VIA Classification of Strengths). The 24 personal characteristics identified by Peterson and Seligman are believed to be present in all societies and deemed positive in all cultural groups. Indeed, researchers who have gone to the far ends of the Earth to interview tribal people (e.g., the Inuit of Greenland and the Maasai in Kenya) report anecdotal and quantitative evidence that supports the existence and desirability of these VIA strengths in unique cultures (Biswas-Diener & Diener, in press).

That everyone wants to be happy is the guiding assumption of David Myers's (1993) book, *The Pursuit of Happiness*, and many positive psychologists share this view. On this point, subjective well-being researchers (e.g., Kahneman, Diener, & Schwartz, 1999) surveyed people from around the world and found that happiness defines the emotional experiences (on average) of the people in most nations.

CULTURALLY EMBEDDED POSITIVE PSYCHOLOGY RESEARCH AND PRACTICE

The culturally embedded perspective on positive psychology is closely associated with ongoing efforts to contextualize all research and practice efforts. Specifically, culture-sensitive recommendations for research, practice, and policy making (APA, 2003) encourage professionals to develop specific competencies to help account for cultural influences on psychology. Accordingly, subscribers to the culturally embedded position would agree that research and practice are conducted at the intersections of the professionals' cultures and the research participants' or clients' cultures. Hence, it is argued that cultural values of the researcher and practitioner influence positive psychology.

Although professionals who believe that all strengths are culturally embedded concede that a core group of positive traits and processes might exist across cultures, they nevertheless hold that most positive traits and processes manifest themselves in very different ways for different purposes in different cultures. Sandage, Hill, and Vang (2003) provide a good example of how forgiveness (one of the 24 VIA strengths) is valued cross-culturally and yet operates very differently within cultures. In their examination of the forgiveness process of Hmong Americans, Sandage and colleagues discovered that forgiveness focuses on the restoration of respect and relational repair, emphasizes a spiritual component, and is facilitated by a third party. Although other conceptualizations of forgiveness emphasize relationship repair, the spiritual components and the need for third-party facilitation appear to be rare.

On the notion of happiness as a universally desired human state, psychologists (e.g., Constantine & Sue, 2006; Leong & Wong, 2003; Sue & Constantine, 2003) have noted that suffering and transcendence are the goals for some individuals who adopt an Eastern perspective on positive psychology (see Chapter 3). Thus, happiness may be simply a by-product of the life process. Ahuvia (2001) recounted his experiences with people who did not share the "universal" desire to be happy:

> Some years ago, an Indian doctoral student of mine saw the back cover of Myers's (1993) book, which read, "We all want to be happy. . . ." The student remarked simply, "I don't." I recall another conversation, this with a young Singaporean man, who confided to me that he was going to marry his fiancée because it was socially expected of him, not because he thought he would be happy in the marriage. . . . Similarly, I exchanged lengthy e-mails with a Korean student who was very explicit about choosing a career to be rich, not to be happy, so that he could bring face to his parents by buying them a new Mercedes. (p. 77)

Also, the results of national subjective well-being surveys (Kahneman, Diener, & Schwartz, 1999) suggest that there are differences over the decades in happiness levels across nations.

CULTURE FREE VERSUS CULTURALLY EMBEDDED: AN ONGOING DEBATE?

Debating this issue may not necessarily be the best use of professional resources. John Chambers Christopher (2005) of the University of Montana contends that "positive psychology requires a philosophy of social science that is robust enough to handle ontological, epistemological, and ethical/moral issues and move beyond both objectivism and relativism" (pp. 3–4). The full text of Christopher's article, reprinted here, details his suggestions for undergirding positive psychology with a stronger conceptual framework.

Situating Positive Psychology

JOHN CHAMBERS CHRISTOPHER

To post-modern thinkers of a variety of stripes, ontological and moral commitments are increasingly recognized to be inescapable in the social sciences. This poses problems for positive psychology if it is pursued as if it were a "descriptive" or objective science that can "transcend particular cultures and politics and approach universality" (Seligman & Csikszentmihalyi, 2000, p. 5). Prior initiatives in the field of psychology that claimed to be objective, value free, culture free, ahistorical, and universal were shown by critical psychologists to presuppose individualistic cultural values and assumptions. Preliminary inquiry suggests that theory and research in positive psychology is likewise influenced by Western cultural outlooks (Christopher, 1999, 2003; Guignon, 2002; Woolfolk, 2002). One implication is that positive psychology requires a philosophy of social science that is robust enough to handle ontological, epistemological, and ethical/moral issues and move beyond both objectivism and relativism.

I believe conceptual resources for positive psychology can be found in the philosophical hermeneutics of Charles Taylor and Martin Heidegger and in Mark Bickhard's interactivism. These metatheories provide (a) conceptual tools for critiquing how cultural values and assumptions shape psychological theory, research, and practice, (b) an alternative non-individualistic and non-dualistic metatheory regarding the nature of the self and how the self is related to culture, and (c) ways of thinking interpretively about cultural meanings and discerning their specific manifestations (Campbell, Christopher, & Bickhard, 2002; Christopher, 2001; Christopher, 2004). A useful way of thinking about culture comes from considering how human beings always and necessarily exist within *moral visions*. Moral visions entail a set of ontological presuppositions about the nature of the person or self and a set of moral or ethical assumptions about what the person should be or become. I believe that any positive psychology, whether in the current movement or in the indigenous psychologies of other cultures, is based on moral visions.

From this moral visions framework, positive psychology will need to be able to address how the self varies across culture. To promote subjective well-being, psychological well-being, or character, we need to have a clear understanding of the self that is at stake. Failing to do this can potentially pathologize individuals whose sense of self is not the "bounded, masterful self" of Western psychology (Cushman, 1990). In addition, positive psychology will need to address what role the various configurations of the self have for positive psychology. For example, positive psychology encourages the development and enhancement of the self. Yet for many non-Western indigenous psychologies such as Buddhism and classical yoga, identification with this notion of the self is the source of suffering and the true stumbling block to growth. Or as Alfred Adler suggested, mental health and well-being may in part require a sense of identification with the larger communities of which one is a part. Dialogue and debate regarding these types of underlying assumptions will be essential to help positive psychology not become culture-bound.

The second aspect of moral visions that positive psychology will need to contend with are those assumptions regarding how we should be or become (or what the good person and the good life are). Psychology tends to define its virtues, like autonomy, relatedness, and personal growth, in abstract and decontextualized ways that tend to obscure the local and specific interpretations with which these virtues are actually lived out (Campbell & Christopher, 1996a; Christopher, 1999; Christopher, Nelson, & Nelson, 2004). This is a point that applies to various aspects of positive psychology, including Peterson and Seligman's (2004) VIA project, character education, and well-being (Christopher et al., 2004). I contend that positive psychology will need to more fully consider how interpretation plays a central role in understanding those characteristics and qualities that define the good person and the good life. To the extent that certain virtues can be found to be present across most cultures, there are huge and generally unexplored ways that the meaning of these virtues can be radically different for those who hold them. The virtue of caring, for instance, is generally interpreted within Western cultures to mean caring about other people—yet there are traditions for whom caring about the environment and about the self are also moral imperatives (Campbell & Christopher, 1996a). Moreover, even when there is consensus about the object or domain of caring, there are frequently considerable differences across and within cultures around what it means to care in a particular situation, such as with the elderly. A hasty attempt to declare that certain virtues are universally endorsed can obscure how these common virtues are often prioritized in very different ways. Respect, for example, is an important virtue in most cultures. Yet, while Turkish and Micronesian college students consider respect the most important attribute of the good person, American students ranked it 35th (Smith, Türk-Smith, & Christopher, 1998).

Comprehending how culture shapes peoples' understanding of virtues, values, and well-being will indeed complicate research endeavors. Our commitment to cultural pluralism demands more of us than the inclusion of other countries in standard research relying on self-report measures. One implication of the moral visions perspective is that people already live out positive folk psychologies: The structure of their lives provides an answer to the question of the good person and good life. These implicit and embodied outlooks need to be juxtaposed with notions of the good that are consciously accessible and espoused by lay persons, as well as with indigenous professional theories of well-being. To fully address how positive psychologies exist at a variety of levels of awareness requires the addition of interpretive methods. This will initially result in a kind of messiness, as some moral development theorists now acknowledge is necessary (Campbell & Christopher, 1996b; Walker & Hennig, 2004; Walker & Pitts, 1998), but this is offset by the potential to capture more of the richness and diversity of human experience.

Positive psychology is critical to the well-being of 21st-century psychology. It will require vigilance to ensure that positive psychology does not become yet another form of a disguised individualistic ideology that perpetuates the sociopolitical status quo and fails to do justice to the moral visions of those outside the reigning outlook. I believe that by paying attention to our underlying moral visions, learning about the moral visions of those across cultures and across time, and learning to think culturally, we can avoid prematurely rushing to ethnocentric conclusions that fail to take full measure of the wisdom of non-Western cultural traditions.

Source: Christopher (2005). Reprinted with permission of the author.

Note: Citations for Dr. Christopher's article are presented in the References at the back of the book.

Putting Positive Psychology in a Cultural Context

Psychology's past perspectives on culture, along with the culture-free-versus-culturally-embedded debate, tell of the pitfalls and progress associated with professional attempts to understand the influence of culture on positive psychology research and practice. Here, we provide recommendations to help make sense of culture's role in positive psychology.

EXAMINING THE EQUIVALENCE OF THE "POSITIVES" TO DETERMINE WHAT WORKS

Establishing cross-cultural applicability of positive constructs and processes goes beyond determining whether strengths and coping mechanisms exist and are valued by members of different cultural groups. It requires an understanding of the indigenous psychology of the group (Sandage et al., 2003) that tells the story of how and when the strength or process became valued within the culture and how it currently functions positively. Qualitative study of a people's use of a particular strength in their daily lives could enhance our understanding of how culture counts in the development and manifestation of that strength; and rigorous, quantitative, cross-cultural studies could reveal additional information about how a strength leads to or is associated with a particular outcome in one culture but a different outcome in another.

Another means of uncovering the cultural nuances associated with a positive construct or process is to ask people how a particular strength became potent in their daily lives. For example, the "Head, Heart, Holy Test of Hope" has proven to be an effective means of starting discussions (in and out of counseling sessions) and lectures on hope because it allows people to reflect on their story of how hope came to be meaningful in their lives and to be part of their culture. Here is how we (Lopez, 2005) introduce it:

> Today, we will talk about the power of hope in your lives. Before I get started, I need to know how you understand this thing called hope. Here is what we are going to do, raise both hands (facilitator raises both hands). And on the count of three, I want you to point to where YOUR hope comes from. Given your background and all of your life experiences, where do you think your hope originates . . . in your head (facilitator points to head)—that thinking part of you, in your heart (facilitator points to heart)—from the love you have for others and they have for you, or from the holy (facilitator points up and all around)—your spiritual life? Now, you can use both hands to point to one place if you think all of your hope comes from that place, or you can use one hand to point to one place and the other hand to point to another (facilitator demonstrates.) Any questions? So, on three, point to where your hope comes from . . . 1, 2, 3. (p. 1)

Inevitably, there is a diversity of gestures capturing people's beliefs about their hope. As participants look around the room, they start asking questions of one another and sometimes launch into stories. Some of these stories about hope are shared with the larger group, and the cultural base of each person's hope becomes more evident. Hope, as laypeople understand it, is clearly grounded in beliefs, values, and experiences.

Chang (1996a, 1996b), in a series of quantitative studies on optimism in Asian Americans and Caucasians, highlighted the importance of understanding the equivalence of constructs across cultural groups. In one study, Chang (1996a) examined the utility of optimism and pessimism in predicting problem-solving behaviors, depressive symptoms, general psychological symptoms, and physical symptoms. In general, the results of this study revealed that Asian Americans were significantly more pessimistic than Caucasians (according to the Extended Life Orientation Test; Chang, Maydeu-Olivares, & D'Zurilla, 1997) but not significantly different from Caucasians in their level of optimism. These findings were corroborated when data from an independent sample were examined (Chang, 1996b). Chang points out that his findings might suggest that Asian Americans are generally more negative in their affectivity than Caucasian Americans, *except for the fact that he found no significant differences in reported depressive symptoms between the two groups. In fact, optimism was negatively correlated with both general psychological symptoms and physical symptoms for Asian Americans but not for Caucasians.* Also, problem solving was found to be negatively correlated with depressive symptoms for Asian Americans but unrelated for Caucasians. Finally, it was revealed that, whereas pessimism was negatively correlated with problem-solving behaviors for Caucasians, it was positively correlated for Asian Americans.

Even in cases where common strategies are used in similar ways by people of different backgrounds, the benefits of those strategies often are not shared. Hence, we should be cautious when prescribing particular coping strategies that, on the surface, seem universally beneficial. Consider another example. Shaw et al. (1997) found that the use of four coping strategies seemed to transcend culture (or were equally valued in cultures) for family caregivers (participants were from Shanghai, China, and San Diego, California.) aiding a loved one grappling with Alzheimer's disease. These four strategies involved (1) taking action, (2) utilizing social support, (3) cognitively reappraising life situations, and (4) denying the health problem and demands or avoiding thinking about it. The benefits, however, of these four strategies were not shared across the cultural groups. These results are consistent with other research indicating that common coping strategies have unique effects across cultures (Liu, 1986).

Discussions with clients, along with well-designed quantitative and qualitative studies with research participants, can provide good data on the equivalence of positive constructs and processes across cultures. With these data in hand, we will be better able to assess what strengths benefit whom (in what situations) and what positive interventions might help people create better lives for themselves. As professionals attempt to enhance strengths in culturally diverse groups of people (see Chapter 15 of this text, along with Linley and Joseph [2004] for discussions of positive psychology in practice), we must ask and answer the question, "What works for whom?"

DETERMINING THE FOUNDATIONS OF THE GOOD LIFE

As suggested in the previous section, people's cultural beliefs about forgiveness, hope, optimism, coping, independence, collectivism, spirituality, religion, and many other topics may bear on how particular strengths work in their lives, how they respond to efforts to enhance personal strengths, and which life outcomes they value. Our version of a common story, which we have titled "The Wise Man of the Gulf," brings some of these issues to life.

The Wise Man of the Gulf

An American businessman, Woody, was at the pier of a small Mexican village when a boat with just one fisherman docked. Inside the boat were many pounds of large gulf shrimp.

The American complimented the Mexican on the quality of his catch and asked about the mesh of his cast net, "Why is the mesh so large? Couldn't you catch more with a tighter weave?" Hector, the fisherman, replied, "I catch what I need, *Señor*. And the net, the net is a fine net. I was taught how to weave this net by my father, who was taught by his father. I work on the net every day to keep it strong."

Woody then asked how long it took to seine for his catch. Hector replied, "Only a little while." The American questioned, "So what do you do with the rest of your time?" The Mexican fisherman said, "I sleep late, I pray, go shrimping for a while, play with my children, take *siesta* with my wife, Maria, examine and repair the net, stroll into the village each evening, where I sip wine and play guitar with my *amigos*. On Sundays, I go to mass and spend the rest of the day with *la familia*. I have a full and busy life, *Señor*. I am very happy."

After hearing the fisherman's account of his week, Woody scoffed, "I am a Harvard MBA and could help you be more successful. You should use a net with a smaller weave and spend more time fishing and, with the proceeds, buy a bigger boat with a larger net you could troll for many miles. With the profits from the bigger boat, you could buy several boats; eventually, you would have a fleet of boats. Instead of selling your catch to a middleman, you would sell directly to the processor and then open your own plant. You would control the product, processing, and distribution. You would need to leave the small coastal fishing village and move to Mexico City, then Houston, and then Los Angeles. There, you will run your expanding enterprise."

Hector was somewhat taken aback by the complicated plan and asked, "But, *Señor,* how long will all this take?" Woody replied, "Fifteen to 20 years." "But what then, *Señor?*" The American laughed and said, "That's the best part. When the time is right, you would sell your company stock to the public and become very rich; you would make millions." "Millions, *Señor?* Then what?" Hector questioned. The American said, "Then you would retire, move to a small coastal fishing village, where you would sleep late, pray, fish a little, play with your grandkids, take a siesta with your wife, stroll in the village in the evenings, where you could sip wine and spend time with *la familia.*"

Source: Snyder and Lopez (2002, pp. 700–714).

Views of the good life are personally constructed over our lifetimes. At the beginning of life, we have natural urges that persist, such as eating and sleeping, and, as we become more cognizant of our surroundings, we link our natural urges to cultural ones, such as eating certain foods and adopting sleep rituals. This link of our natural needs to our cultural influences defines the contours of our daily lives (Baumeister & Vohs, 2002). From the experiences of our daily lives, we construe personal views of what life is all about, and we form *worldviews* (Koltko-Rivera, 2004), or "way[s] of describing the universe and life within it, both in terms of what is and what ought to be" (p. 4). Theoretically, our personal view of the world defines what motivations and behaviors are desirable and undesirable and, ultimately, what life goals should be sought (Koltko-Rivera). Given that our cultural experiences may be inextricably linked to what we consider to be the foundations of the good life, is it reasonable to believe that all people (in the world) desire happiness (as American positive psychologists define it; see Chapter 7)? Or are there life outcomes that are just as valued and as valuable as happiness? These are questions that can be explored in a casual debate among friends (we encourage you to do this), but they also must be examined empirically. A world poll conducted in a scientifically rigorous manner, such as that being currently tackled by The Gallup Organization, may shed some light on the big hopes of people. Future positive psychology clinical work and research also must consider the possibility that cultural forces influence what individuals consider to be the basic foundations of the good life.

Final Thoughts on the Complexity of Cultural Influences

Psychology and future positive psychologists will continue to struggle to understand the complexity of cultural influences on the development and manifestation of positive personal characteristics and desirable life outcomes. The increasing cultural diversity in the United States, along with rapid technological advances that facilitate our interaction with people from around the world (Friedman, 2005), will outpace our discoveries of the specific roles that cultures play in psychology. Given that we cannot be certain about issues such as the universality of particular strengths or the extent to which culture modifies how a strength is manifested, we must do our best to determine if and how "culture counts" in each interaction with a client or research participant.

Progress toward the goal of counting culture as a primary influence on the development and manifestation of human strengths and good living in your research and practice may be best facilitated when you become aware of what you believe about the interplay between cultural and psychological phenomena. Through our personal and professional experiences, we have made some progress toward putting the positive in a cultural context. What we now believe or assume is grounded in what is known and what is not known about strengths and culture . . . and it is definitely open to your critical scrutiny and debate. First, psychological strength is universal. Across time, place, and culture, most people have developed and refined extraordinary qualities that promote adaptation and the pursuit of a better life. Second, there are no universal strengths. Although most people manifest strengths, the nature of the manifestation differs subtly and not so subtly across time, place, and culture. Third, life's contexts affect how strengths are developed, defined, manifested, and enhanced, and our understanding of these contexts contributes to diverse presentation of human capacity. History, passage of time, culture, situations and settings, professional perspectives, and human potentialities are reciprocally determined. Fourth, culture is a reflection of and a determinant of the life goals that we value and pursue. The good life is in the mind of the beholder, and the vision of what is meaningful will drive our life pursuits.

Key Terms

Culturally deficient perspective: A view that identifies a host of environmental, nutritional, linguistic, and interpersonal factors (namely, those factors that differ most from European American values) that supposedly explain the physical and psychological growth of members of selected groups.

Culturally different perspective: A view of human diversity that recognizes the potential of each culture to engender unique strengths.

Culture: A common heritage or set of beliefs, norms, and values.

Etiology: The cause, origin, or a reason for something.

Eugenics: The study of methods of reducing "genetic inferiority" by selective breeding, especially as applied to human reproduction.

Genetically deficient perspective: A view of human diversity that suggests that biological difference explains perceived gaps in intellectual capabilities among racial groups. Proponents of this perspective believe that those of inferior intelligence cannot benefit from growth opportunities and do not contribute to the advancement of society.

Living Well at Every Stage of Life

6

"Psychologists have abandoned the missions of identifying and nurturing talent."

"Psychology is half baked! We know very little about optimal human functioning."

With each presenter's statements about psychology's neglect of the positive side of human functioning, Paul Baltes squirmed a little more in his seat. Finally, it was Dr. Baltes's opportunity to share his research on wisdom (see Chapter 10). By now, however, he had something else on his mind. He politely reminded the group of psychologists, most of whom were trained in social, personality, and clinical specialties, that one branch of psychology had never wavered in its commitment to studying adaptability and positive functioning. That branch was developmental psychology. Indeed, developmental psychologists typically had approached their research with questions about what is working instead of what is not working. The efforts of developmental psychologists and other developmentalists (others who maintain life-span perspectives) produced findings that often transcended historical, geographical, ethnic, and class boundaries to focus on people's self-correcting tendencies.

In this chapter, we review developmental researchers' discoveries about "what works" across the life span. For our purposes, the life span is described across childhood (birth to age 11), youth (ages 12 to 25), adulthood (ages 26 to 59), and older adulthood (age 60 to death). We assume that your basic knowledge of prominent development theories (see Table 6.1) will provide a backdrop for the discussions of resilience in childhood, positive youth development, living well as an adult, and successful aging.

Table 6.1   An Overview of Major Theories of Development

	Maturational and Biological	Psychoanalytic	Behavioral	Cognitive–Developmental
What are the basic assumptions of the theory?	The sequence and content of development are determined mostly by biological factors and the evolutionary history of the species	Humans are conflicted beings, and individual differences as well as normal growth result from the resolution of those conflicts	Development is a function of the laws of learning, and the environment has an important influence on growth and development	Development is the result of the individual's active participation in the developmental process in interaction with important environmental influences
What is the philosophical rationale for the theory?	Recapitulation theory, preformationism, and predeterminism	Embryological	*Tabula rasa,* ("blank slate")	Predeterminist
What are the important variables most often studied?	Growth of biological systems	Effects of instincts on needs and the way instincts are satisfied	Frequency of behaviors	Stage-related transformations and qualitative changes from one stage to another
What are the primary methods used to study development?	Cinematic records, anthropological data, normative investigations, and animal studies	Case studies and indirect examination of unconscious processes	Conditioning and modeling paradigms	Social and cognitive problem solving during transitions from stage to stage
In what areas has the theory had its greatest impact?	Child rearing, the importance of biological determinants, aspects of cultural and historical development	Personality development and the relationship between culture and behavior	Systematic analysis and treatment of behavior, and educational applications	Understanding how thinking and cognition develop in light of cultural conditions and demands

Source: Reprinted with permission of Sage Publications, Inc.

Resilience researchers and positive youth development scholars have shared interests in the positive traits and outcomes of young people. As discussed subsequently, professionals who study resilience identify the "naturally occurring" personal and environmental resources that help children and adolescents to overcome life's many challenges. **Positive youth developmentalists** put the findings of resilience researchers and other positive psychologists into action and give growth a nudge by designing and conducting programs that help youth capitalize on their personal assets and environmental resources.

In the first half of this chapter, we highlight what developmental researchers have discovered about healthy growth. Moreover, we address some of the limitations in this line of research. Scholars who study adult development typically are able to provide prospective information about the gradual unfolding of people's lives. Their in-depth knowledge of the past and the present helps them predict the future. Rather than taking snapshots of life, the developmentalists who study adults use a methodology akin to time-lapse photography—thousands of still pictures of life (or interviews of people) are linked together to tell a compelling story of individual development.

In the second half of the chapter, we explore the life tasks associated with adulthood and the characteristics of people who have aged successfully. Additionally, we discuss many of the gaps in our knowledge about adulthood. Throughout this chapter, we encourage the reader to consider the developmental factors associated with adaptation and good living.

Resilience in Childhood

In the 1970s, a core group of developmental scientists began to study children who succeeded in life despite severe challenges. These children who triumphed in the face of adversity were referred to as "resilient," and their stories captivated the interests of clinicians, researchers, and laypeople. In the present section on resilient children, we begin by presenting a brief case history. Then, we define *resilience* and the related issues about which scholars have differed. Next, we describe the work of Emmy Werner and other resilience scholars (e.g., Garmezy and Rutter). Finally, we discuss the internal (personal) and external (environmental) resources that protect children from developmental insults, along with the problems in such resilience research.

THE CASE OF JACKSON

We have met many resilient children in our work as teachers and clinicians. The story of Jackson's struggles and triumphs is one that stands out. Jackson, by all accounts, was charming from birth. His giggles made people laugh. People were naturally drawn to him. And he seemed comfortable with and trusting of all family and friends.

When he entered school, he thrived socially and academically. He seemed to be growing up healthy and strong. Unfortunately, when he was 8 years old, a family member sexually abused Jackson. He quickly learned to protect himself from the perpetrator, and the abuse was limited to one incident. The effects of the abuse, however, were significant. Jackson's trust in people became shaky. Within weeks of the abuse, he became withdrawn, severely anxious, and developed constant stomach pains and headaches. His psychological and physical problems led to school absences and poor academic performance. Once a confident child with an eye toward the future, he now seemed scared, and the look in his eyes suggested that he was lost in the past.

In time, some caring adults in Jackson's life realized that he was struggling. The teachers at his small school realized that he was not the child he used to be. Two of these teachers reached out, one saying, "We don't know what is bothering you, but whatever it is, we are here to help you." Although he would not talk about the abuse incident until 20 years later, Jackson was able to get the support he needed from his teachers. He showed up at school a little early each morning and sat quietly in one teacher's class. Not much talking took place, but the quiet smiles they shared communicated volumes.

The two elementary teachers gave Jackson a safe place to sit and heal. The quiet support helped him to let go of his fears. Over time, he began to interact more comfortably with adults. Within a year, his anxiety had subsided and his grades had improved. He returned to his old, charming ways and built a large circle of friends and mentors throughout his youth. Today, he is happily married and employed in a job he loves. Jackson, as is the case with other resilient children, is a survivor.

WHAT IS RESILIENCE?

Perhaps the most parsimonious definition of resilience is "bouncing back." The following comments on resilience from Masten and Reed (2002) illustrate this positive process. Specifically, **resilience** refers to

> *. . . a class of phenomena characterized by patterns of positive adaptation in the context of significant adversity or risk.* Resilience must be inferred, because two major judgments are required to identify individuals as belonging in this class of phenomena. First, there is a judgment that individuals are "doing OK" or better than OK with respect to a set of expectations for behavior. Second, there is a judgment that there have been extenuating circumstances that posed a threat to good outcomes. Therefore, the study of this class of phenomena requires defining the criteria or method for ascertaining good adaptation and the past or current presence of conditions that pose a threat to good adaptation. (p. 75)

This broad definition is widely accepted; scholars agree that risk or adversity must be present for a person to be considered resilient. Despite this consensus, however, there is considerable debate regarding the universality of protective factors (Harvey & Delfabbro, 2004) and the extent to which children are doing "OK" according to the criteria of good adaptation (Luthar, Cicchetti, & Becker, 2000; Masten, 1999; Wang & Gordon, 1994). Thus, although a long list of protective factors has been identified (see the discussion later in this chapter), there are notable differences in the extent to which these factors "protect" (i.e., how well these factors yield positive outcomes), along with variability in how and when people call upon particular resources when facing risks and disadvantages (Harvey & Delfabbro, 2004). Indeed, given the state of resilience research, scholars can suggest what might work, but they cannot describe a formula for the operation of resilience.

Researchers disagree on the answer to the question, "Bounced back to what?" When determining a resilient child's level of post-threat functioning, observers are looking for a return to normal functioning (i.e., attainment of developmental milestones) and/or for evidence of excellence (functioning that is above and beyond that expected of a child of a similar age). Most investigators, however, "have set the bar at the level of the normal range, no doubt because their goal is to understand how individuals maintain or regain normative levels of functioning and avoid significant problems in spite of adversity—a goal shared by many parents and societies" (Masten & Reed, 2002, p. 76). Certainly, the most celebrated cases of resilience often are depictions of individuals overcoming overwhelming odds to become stronger. (For example, Mattie Lepanak, a child poet, seemingly became more prolific as the neuromuscular disease he battled became more difficult to manage.)

One major consideration that may be ignored in the conceptualization of resilience outcomes is culture (Rigsby, 1994; see Chapter 5 for a related discussion). "Bounced back to what?" must be answered within the context of the values of the culture and the expectations of the community for its youth. Cultural forces dictate whether researchers examine positive educational outcomes, healthy within-family functioning, or psychological well-being—or perhaps all three. Although some consistency is desirable in what scholars measure, the extent to which community members foster particular outcomes is difficult to assess.

Regarding "good adaptation," resilience researchers agree that **external adaptation** (meeting the social, educational, and occupational expectations of society) is necessary in order to determine who is resilient. The network of researchers is split, however, on whether a determination of **internal adaptation** (positive psychological well-being) is necessary as well. This debate creates confusion because some people see bouncing back as inexorably linked to emotional and intrapsychic adaptation.

THE ROOTS OF RESILIENCE RESEARCH

Case studies have long been used to tell the stories of amazing people and their triumphs. Stories about youth who transcended terrible life circumstances have compelled people to find out more about these resilient people and the resilience process. Some researchers (e.g., Garmezy, 1993; Garmezy, Masten, & Tellegen, 1984) approach their work by focusing on the building blocks of resilience and then identifying how these blocks stack up in a large group of people who are at risk due to a stressor. Other researchers (e.g., Werner & Smith, 1982) identify subsamples of larger groups of people who are functioning well or thriving despite having experienced a recent stressor. Then, these latter researchers study the resilient people in depth to determine what similarities they share with each other and with members of less resilient groups and to identify what distinguishes them from the people who fail to bounce back.

Dr. Emmy Werner, sometimes called the "mother of resiliency," is a person-focused resilience researcher. She identified resilient people and then got to know them really well over time. Given her prominence in this area of positive psychology, we discuss her work as an exemplar of informative resilience research. Werner collaborated with her colleague, Ruth Smith (Werner & Smith, 1982, 1992), in a study involving a cohort of 700 children born on the island of Kauai (in Hawaii) from 1955 to 1995. From birth on, psychological data were collected from the children and adult caregivers, many of whom worked in jobs associated with the sugarcane plantations that used to dominate the island. At birth, one-third of these children were considered high risk for academic and social problems because of their deficits in family support and home environments (e.g., poverty, parental alcoholism, and domestic violence).

Of the at-risk students, one-third appeared to be invulnerable to the undermining risk factors. Two primary characteristics accounted for the resiliency of these children: (1) They were born with outgoing dispositions, and (2) they were able to engage several sources of support. (Better care during infancy, intelligence, and perceptions of self-worth also contributed to positive outcomes.) The other two-thirds of the children in the high-risk group did develop significant life problems in childhood or adolescence. By their mid-thirties, however, most research participants in the Kauai study reported (and psychological tests and community reports corroborated) that they had "bounced back" from the challenges faced earlier in their lives. Over time, more than 80% of the original high-risk group had bounced back. In retrospect, many of those who were resilient attributed their buoyancy to the support of one caring adult (e.g., a family member, neighbor, teacher, mentor).

Given these findings, resilience researchers over the last three decades have examined the dispositions of at-risk children along with the physical and social resources of the youngsters who faced these disadvantages.

In this regard, the finding that many children who did not possess protective factors ultimately (by their fourth decade of life) bounced back has not been adequately explained.

RESILIENCE RESOURCES

According to Masten and Reed (2002), findings from case studies, qualitative research, and large-scale quantitative projects "converge with striking regularity on a set of individual and environmental attributes associated with good adjustment and development under a variety of life-course-threatening conditions across cultural contexts" (p. 82). These potent protective factors in development were identified in research and reviews in the 1970s and 1980s (Garmezy, 1985; Masten, 1999; Masten & Garmezy, 1985; Rutter, 1985; Werner & Smith, 1982), and some protective factors continue to be borne out in ongoing studies. Indeed, this broad list has held up reasonably well over time and across groups (see Table 6.2). (These factors are addressed elsewhere in this volume. For example, self-efficacy and a positive outlook on life are discussed in Chapter 9.)

Although we agree that most of these resilience resources are positive for most people in many situations, there are few universal truths in the resilience literature (with the possible exception that one caring adult can help a child or young person adapt). For example, D'Imperio, Dubow, and Ippolito (2000) found that a multitude of previously identified protective factors failed to distinguish between youth who coped well with adversity and those who did not. Culture and other factors (e.g., past experiences with adversity) undoubtedly influence how young people bounce back from adversity.

The resilience resources listed in Table 6.2 have been translated into strategies for fostering resilience. (Note the overlap between some of these recommendations and those discussed in the next section on positive youth development; some of these strategies may simultaneously prevent the "bad" and promote the "good" in people.) By using these strategies, developmentalists have developed thousands of programs that can help young people overcome adversities and build competencies. Some scholars (e.g., Doll & Lyon, 1998) argue that the proliferation of resilience programs has occurred in the absence of rigorous research examining the construct and the effectiveness of the programs that supposedly foster it. Furthermore, Doll and Lyon note that that many resilience programs teach young people life skills that are not reinforced in the cultures in which they live. Given these concerns about programming, policy makers and people who develop promotion efforts should attempt to adopt existing programs that have effectively served similar youth (i.e., promoted resilience-related competencies), or evaluate the effectiveness of programs with small focused samples rather than large community groups. (See Table 6.3.)

Table 6.2   Protective Factors for Psychosocial Resilience in Children and Youth

Within the Child

    Good cognitive abilities, including problem solving and attentional skills

    Easy temperament in infancy; adaptable personality later in development

    Positive self-perceptions; self-efficacy

    Faith and a sense of meaning in life

    A positive outlook on life

    Good self-regulation of emotional arousal and impulses

    Talents valued by self and society

    Good sense of humor

    General appeal or attractiveness to others

Within the Family

    Close relationships with caregiving adults

    Authoritative parenting (high on warmth, structure/monitoring, and expectations)

    Positive family climate with low discord between parents

    Organized home environment

    Post-secondary education of parents

    Parents with qualities listed as protective factors with the child (above)

    Parents involved in child's education

    Socioeconomic advantages

Within the Family or Other Relationships

    Close relationships to competent, prosocial, and supportive adults

    Connections to prosocial and rule-abiding peers

Within the Community

    Effective schools

    Ties to prosocial organizations, including schools, clubs, scouting, etc.

    Neighborhoods with high "collective efficacy"

    High levels of public safety

    Good emergency social services (e.g., 911 or crisis nursery services)

    Good public health and health care availability

Source: Masten and Reed (2002).

Table 6.3   Strategies for Promoting Resilience in Children and Youth

Risk-Focused Strategies: Preventing/Reducing Risk and Stressors

Prevent or reduce the likelihood of low birth weight or prematurity through prenatal care.

Prevent child abuse or neglect through parent education.

Reduce teenage drinking, smoking, or drug use through community programs.

Prevent homelessness through housing policy or emergency assistance.

Reduce neighborhood crime or violence through community policing.

Asset-Focused Strategies:
Improving Number or Quality of Resources or Social Capital

Provide a tutor.

Organize a Girls or Boys Club.

Offer parent education classes.

Build a recreation center.

Process-Focused Strategies:
Mobilizing the Power of Human Adaptational Systems

Build self-efficacy through graduated success model of teaching.

Teach effective coping strategies for specific threatening situations, such as programs to prepare children for surgery.

Foster secure attachment relationships between infants and parents through parental sensitivity training or home visit program for new parents and their infants.

Nurture mentoring relationships for children through a program to match children with potential mentors, such as Big Brothers/Big Sisters of America.

Encourage friendships of children with prosocial peers in healthy activities, such as extracurricular activities.

Support cultural traditions that provide children with adaptive rituals and opportunities for bonds with prosocial adults, such as religious education or classes for children where elders teach ethnic traditions of dance, meditation, etc.

Source: Masten and Reed (2002).

An Excerpt From
Finding Strength: How to Overcome Anything

DEBORAH BLUM

Resilience research is often not bright and shiny at all. If you're going to study people climbing upward, you have to start at the very rocky bottom. "I decided to look at adults who'd had traumatic childhoods because I knew some very neat people who had come from that background," said John DeFrain, PhD, a professor of family studies at the University of Nebraska. "I thought it would be all warm and fuzzy-feeling. But these were people who were sometimes just barely hanging on. They were surviving as children, but just."

He found that it was in adulthood that people really began to transcend the difficulties of childhood and to rebuild. One man, beaten as a child by his father with belts, razor strops, and tree branches, reached a point in his mid-twenties when he decided to die. He wrote a suicide note, put the gun to his head, and then suddenly thought, "I'm not going to die because of what someone else did to me." That day, for the first time, he called a psychologist and went into counseling.

That dramatically emphasizes one of several key aspects of resilience research:

- There is no timeline, no set period, for finding strength, resilient behaviors, and coping skills. People do best if they develop strong coping skills as children, and some researchers suggest the first 10 years are optimum. But the ability to turn around is always there.
- About one-third of poor, neglected, abused children are capably building better lives by the time they are teenagers, according to all resilience studies. They are doing well in school, working toward careers, often helping to support their siblings.
- Faith—be it in the future, the world at the end of the power lines, or in a higher power—is an essential ingredient. Ability to perceive bad times as temporary times gets great emphasis from Seligman [see Chapter 1] as an essential strength.
- Most resilient people don't do it alone—in fact, they don't even try. One of the standout findings of resilience research is that people who cope well with adversity, if they don't have a strong family support system, are able to ask for help or recruit others to help them. This is true for children and adults; resilient adults, for instance, are far more likely to talk to friends and even coworkers about events in their lives.
- Setting goals and planning for the future [are] strong factor[s] in dealing with adversity. In fact, as University of California–Davis psychologist Emmy Werner, PhD, points out, it may minimize the adversity itself. For instance, Werner found that, when Hurricane Iniki battered Hawaii in 1993, islanders who were previously identified as resilient reported less property damage

than others in the study. Why? They'd prepared more, boarded up windows, invested in good insurance.

- Believing in oneself and recognizing one's strengths is important. University of Alabama psychologist Ernestine Brown, PhD, discovered that, when children of depressed, barely functioning mothers took pride in helping take care of the family, they didn't feel as trapped. "You pick yourself up, give yourself value," Brown says. "If you can't change a bad situation, you can at least nurture yourself. Make yourself a place for intelligence and competence, surround yourself with things that help you stabilize, and remember what you're trying to do."

- And it's equally important to actually recognize one's own strengths. Many people don't. Teaching them such self-recognition is a major part of the approach that the Wolins [resilience researchers and developers of Project Resilience] try when helping adults build a newly resilient approach to life. They are among a small group of professionals testing the idea that resilience can be taught, perhaps by training counselors and psychologists to focus on building strengths in their clients.

Source: Reprinted with permission from *Psychology Today,* copyright © 2006, www.psychology today.com.

Positive Youth Development

In this section, we define positive youth development and the socially valued positive outcomes that have been identified by youth advocates and researchers. Additionally, we identify youth development programs that work.

WHAT IS POSITIVE YOUTH DEVELOPMENT?

The teachers, counselors, and psychologists who are committed to positive youth development recognize the good in our youth and focus on each child's strengths and potential (Damon, 2004). Building on Pittman and Fleming's definition (1991, p. ii, first line of our definition), we (Lopez & McKnight, 2002, p. 3) articulate how components of development interact over time to yield healthy adults:

Positive youth development should be seen as an ongoing, inevitable process in which all youth are engaged and all youth are invested. Youth interact with their environment and positive agents (e.g., youth and adults who support healthy development, institutions that create climates conducive to growth, programs that foster change) to meet their basic needs and cultivate assets. Through [their] initiative (sometimes combined with the support of positive agents), momentum builds, and youth who are capable of meeting basic needs challenge themselves to attain other goals; youth use assets to build additional psychological resources that facilitate growth. Ideally, positive youth development generates physical and psychological competencies that serve to facilitate the transition into an adulthood characterized by striving for continued growth.

The positive qualities of our youth combine (in an intentional manner) with the resources of the environment and positive agents (caring youth and adults) in the context of a program (see subsequent descriptions) to promote healthy development. Healthy development is marked by the attainment of some of the following nine positive outcomes (Catalano, Berglund, Ryan, Lonczak, & Hawkins, 1998) targeted by positive programs. (All of these positive outcomes are addressed elsewhere in this book.)

1. Rewarding bonding

2. Promoting social, emotional, cognitive, behavioral, and moral competencies

3. Encouraging self-determination

4. Fostering spirituality

5. Nurturing a clear and positive identity

6. Building beliefs in the future

7. Recognizing positive behavior

8. Providing opportunities for prosocial development

9. Establishing prosocial norms

POSITIVE YOUTH DEVELOPMENT PROGRAMS THAT WORK

The report on Positive Youth Development (Catalano et al., 1998) is a valuable resource for the people who believe that "problem free does not mean fully prepared" (Pittman & Fleming, 1991, p. 3). Indeed, some developmentalists focus their helpful efforts on youth who are not struggling with major life problems but do not possess the personal assets or environmental resources needed to reach many of their goals as they transition into adulthood. As such, the challenge for those who might fall through the cracks is to build the confidences and competencies in young people.

A Positive Youth—Rose Naughtin's Story:
"I Had Two Heart Transplants"

ROSE NAUGHTIN (AS TOLD TO PAM GROUT)

When Rose Naughtin was a child, she was told that, if she didn't have a heart transplant, she could die. Worse, last year Rose's new heart started to fail, and she had to have a second heart replacement. Now the 13-year-old is doing great.

When I was only four, I learned that I had a disease that could kill me within a few years. Doctors diagnosed me with restrictive cardiomyopathy, a potentially fatal illness where your heart muscle can't relax normally and stops working right. My only hope was a heart transplant.

Luckily, I was too young to really understand the seriousness of the situation. I just remember wondering how long it would be until I got a new heart. (I'd ask my mom every night before bed.) Five weeks later, a heart became available, and we flew from my hometown, Lawrence, Kansas, to St. Louis Children's Hospital for the 8-hour operation. I honestly don't remember very much about the surgery or the immediate recovery. But I do know that, amazingly, within 2 weeks I was able to ride a tricycle through the hospital hallways, and within a few months I was back to my old self. Aside from regular checkup[s] with my cardiologist, I led a normal life. I took ballet and piano lessons, and I loved playing with my brother, Hugh. You'd never know what happened to me unless you saw the scar on my chest where the doctors cut me open. I felt really lucky.

Then one day in February 2004, my seventh-grade science class went on a field trip to the Natural History Museum at the University of Kansas. Walking to the campus, I was talking and joking with friends until, suddenly, I got extremely dizzy and passed out. I didn't think a whole lot about it, but my mom was worried, and she decided that I should see my cardiologist. He did a lot of tests and then delivered shocking news: I had severe coronary disease—my arteries were so clogged that my heart couldn't get the blood and oxygen it needed. Untreated, I was looking at a heart attack—and I was 13! My doctor said I could die without another transplant. It was so scary.

This time, I would be old enough to understand the dangers of the surgery. In fact, another transplant would be riskier because patients are more likely to reject a second heart. Yet I think, since I'd already been through a lot, I'd learned to not worry about things I couldn't control. Basically, I wasn't happy about my situation, but I had no choice.

So I signed up to receive a new heart and waited. Meanwhile, I stayed out of school, since my heart was so weak that walking just a little would tire me out. I was anxious about what was going to happen, but all the support I got made me feel much better. Kids at school sent cards; my friends stopped by to see how I was doing. Plus, my friends even raised money for the small portion of my

(Continued)

(Continued)

medical expenses that were not covered by insurance. Some of my neighbors and classmates raised money by making and selling heart-shaped pins. My local food cooperative, the Community Mercantile, set up a benefit for me. It felt so good to know how many people cared about me.

Three weeks after I found out I needed another transplant, we got a call at 2 a.m. I had a heart! I got dressed, threw some CDs into a backpack, and went to the airport with my parents to meet an air ambulance that would take us to the hospital. I prepared myself, so I wasn't really nervous. By 5:30, we'd arrived and the procedure was ready to begin. I kissed my parents, the anesthesia kicked in, and I fell asleep. I didn't wake up for 2 days—but when I did, I learned the transplant was a success.

I was taking high doses of painkillers, so I didn't really feel much where they cut me open. Even though I was grateful to be alive, it was a lot to handle; I was so drained. The painkillers made me sick to my stomach, and whenever I ate, I threw up. But slowly I began to recover. After 8 days in intensive care and 2 more weeks of additional recovery, I was able to go home.

I was so happy. When I arrived, friends were waiting with food, flowers, and cards. My good friend Allison had painted my room blue and put up new posters for me, including a signed Ramones one. I was so overwhelmed!

It has been almost a year now since the transplant, and I feel as good as new. I'm back at school, in the eighth grade, and I love hanging out with my friends. I'll never forget the people who saved my life. I don't really know much about the kids whose hearts I got. But in order to help me live, they had to have their hearts in the right place. I will do my best to keep them that way.

Positive youth development programs come in many forms (Benson & Saito, 2000), including structured or semistructured activities (e.g., Big Brothers and Big Sisters), organizations providing activities and positive relationships (e.g., Boy's Club, YMCA, YWCA), socializing systems promoting growth (e.g., day care centers, school, libraries, museums), and communities facilitating the coexistence of programs, organizations, and communities. The soundness of these programs is determined by the extent to which they promote the "good" and prevent the "bad" in today's youth.

Programs that work help youth move toward competencies that make their lives more productive and meaningful. A brief listing of more than a dozen effective programs was developed after a critical review of published and unpublished program evaluations that included, at a minimum, the following (Catalano et al., 1998; Jamieson, 2005):

- Adequate design and outcome measures
- Adequate description of research methodologies
- Description of the population served
- Description of the intervention and fidelity of implementation
- Effects demonstrated on behavioral outcomes

Regarding effectiveness, Catalano et al. wrote: "Programs were included if they demonstrated behavioral outcomes at any point, even if these results decayed over time. Programs were also included if they demonstrated effects on part of the population studied" (p. 26). These effective programs include some that are well known and others that are less known. For the purpose of illustrating how some of these effective programs engage youth and cultivate personal resources, we describe the basic operations and effects of Big Brothers and Big Sisters and the Penn Resiliency Program. We also describe some of the developmental tasks associated with a positive college experience.

Big Brothers and Big Sisters is a community-based mentoring program (3–5 contact hours per week) initiated in 1905. For no fee, the program matches low-income children and adolescents with adult volunteers who are committed to providing caring and supportive relationships. Typically, mentors are screened carefully and then provided with some training and guidelines for positively influencing youth. Mentoring activities are unstructured or semistructured, and they typically take place in the community. Regarding the effectiveness of the program, Tierney and Grossman (2000) found that this mentoring program did promote the good (academic achievement, parental trust) and prevent the bad (violence, alcohol and drug use, truancy).

The Penn Resiliency Program (Gillham & Reivich, 2004) is a highly structured life-skills development program that is offered to schoolchildren for a fee (or as part of a research study). A highly trained facilitator conducts the scripted sessions in the classroom. The 12 sessions focus on awareness of thought patterns and on modifying the explanatory style of students to change the attributions for events so that they are more flexible and accurate. Extensive evaluation of the program demonstrated its effectiveness at preventing the bad (the onset and severity of depressive symptoms) and promoting optimism and better physical health.

Colleges and universities, as socializing systems, also can promote positive youth development. Chickering's (1969; Chickering & Reisser, 1993) work on education and identity provides a set of developmental tasks that is the joint focus of college students and positive agents (student peers, faculty, and staff). Within the Chickering model, development of competence is identified as a primary developmental direction or goal for college students during their educational experiences. With increased confidence in their resourcefulness, students then begin working on the developmental tasks of managing emotions, moving through autonomy toward interdependence, developing mature interpersonal relationships, establishing identity, developing purpose, and developing integrity. Progress toward each of these goals equips students to succeed in school, work, and life in general. More intentional focus on developing colleges and universities into positive socializing systems could enhance the value of a college education for the students and society at large. Integrating strengths development programming into the college experience also could enhance the positive effects of higher education (Lopez, Janowski, & Wells, 2005).

Now that we know what types of programs promote positive youth development, our attention turns to the question, "Why does that program work?" Although components of each of these programs have not been systematically scrutinized to determine what does and does not work, there are several suggestions about what makes the programs beneficial, including (1) that more is better (more time committed to the youth, the better the results); (2) that earlier is better (the younger the program participant, the more likely he or she is to develop competence); and (3) that structured is better (programs that are purposeful and systematic can replicate what works more easily) (Jamieson, 2005).

The Life Tasks of Adulthood

Some longitudinal studies (e.g., Werner & Smith, 1982) started because of a researcher's interest in childhood experiences yet went on (for decades) to reveal a great deal about adult experiences. In this section, we describe two such prospective studies (Terman's Life Cycle Study of gifted children, and the Harvard study of the "best of the best," known as the Study of Adult Development). It should be noted that many aspects of adult development are addressed in this section and in prominent developmental theories (see Table 6.1), but a great deal is still unknown about how people grow and change between ages 26 and 59.

THE TRAJECTORIES OF PRECOCIOUS CHILDREN

Lewis Terman

Source: Courtesy of
Stanford University Archives.

Lewis Terman (Terman & Oden, 1947) spent most of his life studying intelligence, which he viewed as an adaptive quality that would lead directly to life success and, more specifically, to national leadership. In the 1920s, Terman began an ambitious study of 1500 intellectually gifted children (IQ>140) who were nominated by teachers in California schools; the study participants nicknamed themselves the "Termites."

These participants were physically hardy during childhood and typically were healthier than their peers. Most of the children graduated from college and secured professional jobs. Although many of the Termites were productive in their jobs, few went on to be national leaders as Terman had hypothesized. It should be emphasized, therefore, that elevated childhood IQs did not guarantee adult successes and better mental health.

Although Terman's predictions regarding the adult prowess of bright children were not borne out, his sample has revealed information about adult development. On the negative side of human functioning, Peterson, Seligman, Yurko, Martin, and Friedman (1998) studied the Termites' childhood responses to open-ended questions and found that an explanatory style that was characterized as *catastrophizing* (explaining bad events with global causes) predicted risks of mortality in this sample of healthy children. This link between explanatory style and longevity/mortality is probably meditated by lifestyle choices. Given these findings, it would seem that genius-level IQ and good health in childhood do not protect individuals from making bad choices that lead to poor health and premature death.

WHAT ARE THE PRIMARY TASKS OF ADULTHOOD?

A subset of the Terman sample data was reviewed by George Vaillant, the keeper of decades of data from the Harvard study (described in more detail subsequently). Specifically, 90 women in the Terman sample were interviewed by Vaillant to examine the generalizability of his findings on adult development from his all-male sample. Consideration of the Terman data and review of data from the Study of Adult Development helped Vaillant build on existing developmental theories and identify the life tasks associated with adulthood.

Guided by Erik Erikson's (1950) stage theory of development, Vaillant mapped out (1977) and refined (2002) six tasks of adult development: identity, intimacy, career consolidation, generativity, keeper of meaning, and integrity. **Identity** is typically developed during adolescence or early adulthood, when people's views, values, and interests begin to become their own rather than a reflection of their caregivers' beliefs. (Failure to develop a personal identity can preclude meaningful engagement with people and work.) With the development of identity, a person is more likely to seek an interdependent, committed relationship with another person and thereby achieve **intimacy.** Many of the women in the original Terman sample identified close female friendships as their most intimate relationships, whereas the men in the Harvard study invariably identified their relationships with their wives as the most intimate

George Vaillant

Source: Reprinted with permission of George Vaillant.

connections. A related conclusion reached by Vaillant (2002, p. 13) was, "It is not the bad things that happen to us that doom us; it is the good people who happen to us at any age that facilitate enjoyable old age."

Career consolidation is a life task that requires the development of a social identity. Engagement with a career is characterized by contentment, compensation, competence, and commitment. For many people, career consolidation, like the other tasks, is "worked on" rather than achieved. That is, people may consolidate their career for decades, even as they move toward and into retirement. In today's workforce, consolidation often is compromised by the need to transition into a new job. As a result, career adaptability (Ebberwein, Krieshok, Ulven, & Prosser, 2004; Super & Knasel, 1981) has emerged as a prerequisite of career consolidation.

Regarding tasks associated with **generativity**, people become involved in the building of a broader social circle through a "giving away" of self. As mastery of the first three tasks is achieved, adults may possess the competence and altruism needed to directly mentor the next generation of adults. Indeed, as people age, social goals become more meaningful than achievement-oriented goals (Carstensen & Charles, 1998; Carstensen, Pasupathi, Mayr, & Nesselroade, 2000).

In the context of a larger social circle, some people take on the task of becoming **keepers of meaning**. The keeper of meaning has perspective on the workings of the world and of people, and this person is willing to share that wisdom with others. The keeper protects traditions and rituals that may facilitate the development of younger people. In essence, the keeper links the past to the future.

Finally, achieving the task of developing **integrity** brings peace to a person's life. In this stage, increased spirituality often accompanies a greater sense of contentment with life.

Mastery of these tasks is the object of adulthood. Intentional work on each of these tasks leads sequentially to work on the next task, and the mastery of all tasks is the essence of successful aging.

THE CASE OF SARAH

The ability to anticipate changes at work, plan for future opportunities, develop new skills, and create a social network that would facilitate a transition at work has been displayed by dozens of our clients over the years, but Sarah's story is notable because she had anticipated the need for such flexibility in her sixth decade of life. This is a time when many would say she had achieved career consolidation.

Sarah had been working in the same job for the same company for 33 years. As a graphic designer for a national greeting card company, she knew her position was a cherished one, and she also realized that computer software and high-quality printers were replacing her traditional pencil-and-ink methods. She mastered new computerized design skills, yet she did not experience the same creative satisfaction from this new way of working. How could she continue to feel creative so as to derive pleasure from her work? First, she had to identify exactly what she liked about the creative process. After weeks of pondering, she came to the insight that she enjoyed thinking about the design more than she enjoyed the actual design process, whether it was on a notepad or a computer screen. Could she convince her team leader to pay her to "think about design" rather than to produce designs? At the beginning of a workday, when she was feeling particularly gutsy, she floated the idea to her team leader, who looked intrigued and relieved. It turned out that the team leader was trying to figure out how to let Sarah know that some of the technical aspects of the design work were going to be completed by people from another group (who were much cheaper by the hour) and that the small cadre of current designers was going to be asked to produce concepts for the young computer-based artists. So, for the last 10 years of her career, Sarah envisions that she will be paid for her ideas rather than her artwork. She also has the pleasure of visiting with young graphic artists from around the world. Although fairly confident of her career future, she continues to anticipate changes in the greeting card industry that might shape her work and her life.

Successful Aging

With the baby boomers joining the older adult group of Americans, stories of successful aging are becoming more prominent in today's media. The stories of older adults provide valuable lessons to all of us. This was definitely the case in the life of Morrie Schwartz (the focus of Mitch Albom's 2002 book, *Tuesdays with Morrie*), who lived life to its fullest and found great meaning during his physical decline and death.

The study of the positive aspects of aging (referred to as *positive aging, healthy aging, successful aging,* and *aging well*) is only several decades old. It will become a primary focus of psychological science, however, given the trends in American demography that will demand the attentions of scientists and the general public. Our goal for this section is to describe successful aging based on the MacArthur Study of Successful Aging and the prospective study by Vaillant (2002).

WHAT IS SUCCESSFUL AGING?

The term *successful aging* was popularized by Robert Havighurst (1961) when he wrote about "adding life to years" (p. 8) in the first issue

of *The Gerontologist*. Havighurst also primed scholarly interest in healthy
aspects of getting older. Rowe and Kahn (1998), summarizing the findings
from the MacArthur Study of Successful Aging, proposed three components of **successful aging**: (1) avoiding disease, (2) engagement with life,
and (3) maintaining high cognitive and physical functioning. These three
components are aspects of "maintaining a lifestyle that involves normal,
valued, and beneficial activities" (Williamson, 2002, p. 681). Vaillant
(2002) simplifies the definition further by characterizing successful aging
as joy, love, and learning. These descriptions, though not detailed, provide
an adequate image of successful aging.

THE MacARTHUR FOUNDATION
STUDY OF SUCCESSFUL AGING

The MacArthur Foundation Study of Successful Aging (which ran from
1988 to 1996) was conducted by John Rowe and a multidisciplinary group
of colleagues. They investigated physical, social, and psychological factors
related to abilities, health, and well-being. A sample of 1189 healthy adult
volunteers between the ages of 70 and 79 was selected from a pool of 4030
potential participants, using physical and cognitive criteria. These high-
functioning adults participated in a 90-minute personal interview and
then were followed for an average of 7 years, during which time they
completed periodic interviews.

As mentioned previously, the MacArthur study revealed that the three
components of successful aging were avoiding disease, engaging with life,
and maintaining physical and cognitive functioning (Rowe & Kahn, 1998).
Here, we focus on life engagement because it is the component of successful aging that positive psychologists are most likely to address in their
research and practice. Indeed, the two components of life engagement,
social support and productivity (Rowe & Kahn), parallel the life pursuits
of love, work, and play that we address in many of the chapters in this
book.

Social support is most potent when it is mutual; the support given is
balanced by support received. Two kinds of support are important for successful aging: **socioemotional support** (liking and loving) and **instrumental support** (assistance when someone is in need). Further examination of
the MacArthur data revealed that support increased over time (Gurung,
Taylor, & Seeman, 2003). Moreover, the respondents with more social ties
showed less decline in functioning over time (Unger, McAvay, Bruce,
Berkman, & Seeman, 1999). The positive effects of social ties were shown
to vary according to the individual's gender and baseline physical capabilities (Unger et al.). Gender also influenced how married participants
(a 439-person subset of the total sample) received social support: "Men

received emotional support primarily from their spouses, whereas women drew more heavily on their friends and relatives and children for emotional support" (Gurung et al., p. 487).

Regarding productive activity in later adulthood, Glass et al. (1995) examined patterns of change in the activities of the highly functioning sample of 70-to-79-year-olds and in a group of 162 moderate-to-low-functioning 70-to-79-year-olds over a 3-year period. The highest functioning cohort was found to be significantly more productive than the comparison group. Changes in productivity over time were associated with more hospital admissions and strokes, whereas age, marriage, and increased mastery of certain skills were related to greater protection against declines. These findings are consistent with the work of Williamson (2002), who suggests that sustained physical activity (an aspect of productive activity) helps to maintain healthy functioning. Accordingly, interruptions of physical activity regimens often precipitate declines in overall well-being.

THE ADULT DEVELOPMENT STUDY

Vaillant (2002) acknowledges that subjective evaluation of functioning is not the most rigorous approach to identifying those who age successfully. He has relied on a system of independent evaluations of the functioning (e.g., physical, psychological, occupational) of the participants in the Study of Adult Development. The original 256 Caucasian, socially advantaged participants were identified in the late 1930s by the deans at Harvard (who viewed the students as sound in all regards). For the past 80 years, these participants have been studied via physical examinations, personal interviews, and surveys. More than 80% of the study participants lived past their 80th birthdays, whereas only 30% of their contemporaries lived to that age. His extensive study of these older adults (and members of two other prospective studies) identified the following lifestyle predictors of healthy aging: not smoking, or stopping smoking while young; coping adaptively, with mature defenses; not abusing alcohol; maintaining a healthy weight, a stable marriage, and some exercise; and being educated. These variables distinguished people on the ends of the health spectrum: The happy–well (62 individuals who experienced good health objectively and subjectively, biologically and psychologically) and the sad–sick (40 individuals who were classified as unhappy in at least one of three dimensions: mental health, social support, or life satisfaction.) The most robust predictor of membership in the happy–well group versus the sad–sick group was the extent to which people used mature psychological coping styles (e.g., altruism, humor) in everyday life.

> ### One Man's View of Aging
>
> Contrary to all expectations, I seem to grow happier as I grow older. I think that America has been sold on that theory that youth is marvelous but old age is terror. On the contrary, it's taken me 60 years to learn how to live reasonably well, to do my work and cope with my inadequacies.
>
> For me, youth was a woeful time—sick parents, war, relative poverty, the miseries of learning a profession, a mistake of a marriage, self-doubts, booze, and blundering around. Old age is knowing what I am doing, the respect of others, a relatively sane financial base, a loving wife, and the realization that what I can't beat, I can endure.
>
> *Source:* Vaillant (2002, p. 14).

Nuns

Source: © Corbis.

Perhaps prediction of successful aging is not as complex as the MacArthur studies and Vaillant make it out to be. What if successful aging, or at the very least longevity, boils down to experiencing positive emotions in early life? Danner, Snowdon, and Friesen (2001), in their study of the autobiographies of 180 Catholic nuns written in early 20th century, demonstrated that positive emotional content in the writings was inversely correlated with risk of mortality 60 years later. These nuns, who had seemingly had a lifestyle conducive to successful aging, were more likely to live past their 70th and 80th birthdays if they had told stories of their lives that were laden with positive emotions many decades before.

The body of research on successful aging is growing quickly, and the findings suggest that people have more control over the quality of their lives during the aging process than we once believed. Furthermore, across studies, social support is the one of the psychological factors that promotes successful aging. Despite this communality, as more cross-cultural research is conducted and published, it appears that aging and successful aging may vary depending on the particular nations studied. Therefore, successful aging should not be measured against a universal standard (Baltes & Carstensen, 1996). This suggests that future work should consider the cultural aspects of adaptive aging in pursuing clues to the good life in the later years.

A More Developmental Focus in Positive Psychology

We face daily hassles and adversities. This is true during childhood, adolescence, adulthood, and older adulthood. Hopefully, as we age, we become more resourceful and adaptable. This appears to be the case because there are numerous positive developmental factors that help children and adults to bounce back. The findings discussed in this chapter also suggest that positive psychology is well on its way to identifying and sharing meaningful information about how to live a better life. Try the Personal Mini-Experiments to bring some of these findings to life.

Personal Mini-Experiments

Finding Amazing People of All Ages

In this chapter, we discuss many of the factors that promote healthy development over the life span. Here are a few ideas that might help you discover the positive in people of all ages.

Testing the Effectiveness of Your Mentorship: According to resilience research, a warm relationship with one caring adult can bring out the positive in children and youth. The effectiveness of your own mentorship can be tested out through your ongoing work with Big Brothers and Big Sisters or another community-based mentoring program. A true test would involve giving 3 to 4 hours a week to one child and tracking the child's development over time by considering the enhancement of resources listed in Table 6.2.

Building a Stronger Social Circle: Several of the life tasks of adults are related to developing a stronger social network. Consider the state of your own social network. Draw four concentric circles. In the middle circle, write "Me," and then fill in the remaining circles with the names of the people to whom you give your time and talents on a regular basis; the closer the names are to the center circle, the closer these people are to you. Consider how you can maintain the people in the circles closest to you and bring the other folks closer to you. When you have identified a few strategies, end the exercise by acting on one of your thoughts and giving your time or talent to someone close to you.

Collecting Stories of Aging Well: Every day, you encounter people 60 and older. Some of these folks are exuberant; they could be members of Vaillant's happy–well group. Approach five of these people, and ask them if they would be willing to participate in a brief interview. (Tell them that you have just learned about successful aging and you would like to develop a better understanding of how people live well as they age.) Here are some questions you can ask (derived from Dr. Vaillant's Scale of Objective Mental Health, 2002, p. 342):

- How well are you enjoying your career/retirement?
- How would you describe your last vacation?
- What personal relationships have been important to you since you turned 50? Please describe the most important one.

Log your responses to these questions, and attempt to draw conclusions about successful aging in your community from these five interviews.

Although much is known about how to thrive during each decade of our lives, the next generation of positive psychologists (you and your peers) has many questions to answer regarding topics such as positive adult development and making successful aging possible for more people. Furthermore, more theory and research are needed to help us understand how each human strength is manifested and to describe how culture shapes a given strength and its potency over time. If positive psychology is to grow as a field, we believe that it is crucial to understand the unfolding developmental processes from childhood to older age.

Key Terms

Career consolidation: A life task that requires the development of a social identity and engagement in a career characterized by contentment, compensation, competence, and commitment.

External adaptation: A person's ability to meet the social, education, and occupational expectations of society.

Generativity: A life task that requires one to "give the self away" and expand one's social circle. This may include mentoring the next generation of adults.

Identity: A life task that requires one to develop one's own views, values, and interests instead of simply reflecting the beliefs of one's parents or others.

Instrumental support: Support that involves giving assistance or help when needed.

Integrity: A life task that requires one to cultivate contentment with life and sense of peace. Often accompanied by increased spirituality.

Internal adaptation: A person's ability to achieve emotional and psychological well-being.

Intimacy: A life task that requires one to develop an interdependent, committed, and close relationship with another person.

Keeper of meaning: A life task that engenders perspective on the workings of the world and of people and that is characterized by a willingness to share this wisdom with others. The keeper of meaning is seen as linking the present and the past by protecting traditions and rituals and passing them on to the next generation.

Positive youth development: Positive, healthy youth development is marked by the attainment of nine outcomes: (1) bonding; (2) social, emotional, cognitive, behavioral, and moral competencies; (3) self-determination; (4) spirituality; (5) clear and positive identity; (6) belief in the future; (7) positive behavior; (8) prosocial development; (9) prosocial norms.

Positive youth developmentalists: Professionals who put the findings of resilience researchers and other positive psychologists into action and create opportunities for growth by developing and conducting programs that help youth capitalize on their personal assets and environmental resources.

Resilience: The ability to bounce back or positively adapt in the face of significant adversity or risk.

Resilience researchers: Professionals who study resilience and identify the naturally occurring personal and environmental resources that help children and adolescents overcome life challenges.

Socioemotional support: Support that involves providing friendship, kindness, and love for others.

Successful aging: A lifestyle defined by avoiding disease, engaging in life, and maintaining high cognitive and physical functioning in one's later years.

Part III

Positive Emotional States and Processes

The Principles of Pleasure 7

Understanding Positive Affect, Positive Emotions, Happiness, and Well-Being

Standing at the front of a small lecture hall, Ed Diener, University of Illinois psychologist and world renowned happiness researcher, held up a real brain in a jar with a blue liquid, which he called "joy juice," trickling into it from a small plastic pouch held above. He asked the audience to pretend that their brains could be treated with a hormone (i.e., joy juice) that would make them ecstatically happy, and that they could be happy *all the time*. Then he asked the crucial question, "How many people in this room would want to do this?" Of the 60 audience members, only 2 raised their hands to signify their desires for perpetual happiness.

Given that I (SJL) had had little exposure to philosophy coursework and that my undergraduate and graduate training in psychology had not exposed me to the science of happiness, I hadn't thought much about happiness in its many forms. Dr. Diener's question intrigued me, and since attending his lecture in 1999 I have attempted to develop a better understanding of the positive side of the emotional experience; this has led me to the solid research I summarize here.

Ed Diener

Source: Reprinted with permission of Ed Diener.

In this chapter, we attempt to add to what you know about pleasure by going far beyond Freud's (1936) **pleasure principle** (the demand that an instinctive need be gratified regardless of the consequences) and by fostering an understanding of the many principles of pleasure that have been linked to good living. In this process, we present what we know about that which makes modern life pleasurable. We also summarize research that examines the distinctions between positive and negative affect. Likewise, we highlight positive emotions and their pleasure-expanding benefits, and we explore the many definitions of happiness and well-being, qualities of pleasurable living. To begin, we clarify the numerous terms and concepts used in this chapter.

Defining Emotional Terms

The terms *affect* and *emotion* often are used interchangeably in scholarly and popular literatures. Furthermore, *well-being* and *happiness* appear to be synonymous in psychology articles. Unfortunately, however, the interchangeable use of these terms is very confusing. Although we try to clarify the distinctions among these closely related ideas, we acknowledge the overlap that exists. We begin by suggesting that affect is a component of emotion, and emotion is a more specific version of mood.

AFFECT

Affect is a person's immediate, physiological response to a stimulus, and it is typically based on an underlying sense of arousal. Specifically, Professor Nico Frijda (1999) reasoned that affect involves the appraisal of an event as painful or pleasurable—that is, its *valence*—and the experience of autonomic arousal.

EMOTION

Parsimonious definitions of **emotion** are hard to find, but this one seems to describe the phenomenon succinctly: "Emotions, I shall argue, involve judgments about important things, judgments in which, appraising an external object as salient for our own well-being, we acknowledge our own neediness and incompleteness before parts of the world that we do not fully control" (Nussbaum, 2001, p. 19). These emotional responses occur as we become aware of painful or pleasurable experiences and associated autonomic arousal (i.e., affect; Frijda, 1999), and evaluate the situation. An emotion has a specific and "sharpened" quality, as it always has an object (Fredrickson, 2002), and it is associated with progress in goal pursuit (Snyder et al., 1991; Snyder, 1994). In contrast, a **mood** is objectless, free floating, and long lasting.

HAPPINESS

Happiness is a positive emotional state that is subjectively defined by each person. The term is rarely used in scientific studies because there is little consensus on its meaning. In this chapter, we use this term only when it is clarified by additional information.

SUBJECTIVE WELL-BEING

Subjective well-being involves the subjective evaluation of one's current status in the world. More specifically, Diener (1984, 2000; Diener, Lucas, & Oishi, 2002) defines **subjective well-being** as a combination of positive affect (in the absence of negative affect) and general life satisfaction (i.e., subjective appreciation of life's rewards). The term *subjective well-being* often is used as a synonym for *happiness* in the psychology literature. Almost without exception, the more accessible word *happiness* is used in the popular press in lieu of the term *subjective well-being*.

Distinguishing the Positive and the Negative

Hans Selye (1936) is known for his research on the effects of prolonged exposure to fear and anger. Consistently, he found that physiological stress harmed the body yet had survival value for humans. Indeed, the evolutionary functions of fear and anger have intrigued both researchers and laypeople. Given the historical tradition and scientific findings pertaining to the negative affects, their importance in our lives has not been questioned over the last century.

Historically, positive affects have received scant attention over the last century because few scholars hypothesized that the rewards of joy and contentment went beyond hedonic (pleasure-based) values and had possible evolutionary significance. The potentialities of positive affect have become more obvious over the last 20 years (Fredrickson, 2002) as research has drawn distinctions between the positive and negative affects.

David Watson (1988) of the University of Iowa conducted research on the approach-oriented motivations of pleasurable affects—including rigorous studies of *both* negative and positive affects. To facilitate their research on the two dimensions of emotional experience, Watson and his collaborator Lee Anna Clark (1994) developed and validated the Expanded Form of the Positive and Negative Affect Schedule (PANAS-X), which has become a commonly used measure in this area. This 20-item scale has been used in hundreds of studies to quantify two dimensions of affect: **valence** and **content**. More specifically, the PANAS-X taps both "negative" (unpleasant) and "positive" (pleasant) valence. The content of negative affective states can be described best as general distress, whereas positive affect includes joviality, self-assurance, and attentiveness. (See the PANAS, a predecessor of the PANAS-X, which is brief and valid for most clinical and research purposes.)

David Watson

Source: Reprinted with permission of David Watson.

The Positive and Negative Affect Schedule

This scale consists of a number of words that describe different feelings and emotions. Read each item and then mark the appropriate answer on the line provided. **Indicate to what extent you feel this emotion right now.** Use the following scale as you record your answers.

Feeling or emotion	Very slightly or not at all	A little	Moderately	Quite a bit	Extremely
1. interested	1	2	3	4	5
2. distressed	1	2	3	4	5
3. excited	1	2	3	4	5
4. upset	1	2	3	4	5
5. strong	1	2	3	4	5
6. guilty	1	2	3	4	5
7. scared	1	2	3	4	5
8. hostile	1	2	3	4	5
9. enthusiastic	1	2	3	4	5
10. proud	1	2	3	4	5
11. irritable	1	2	3	4	5
12. alert	1	2	3	4	5
13. ashamed	1	2	3	4	5
14. inspired	1	2	3	4	5
15. nervous	1	2	3	4	5
16. determined	1	2	3	4	5
17. attentive	1	2	3	4	5
18. jittery	1	2	3	4	5
19. active	1	2	3	4	5
20. afraid	1	2	3	4	5

Using the PANAS and other measures of affect, researchers systematically have addressed a basic question; "Can we experience negative affect and positive affect at the same time?" (See Diener & Emmons, 1984; Green, Salovey, & Truax, 1999.) For example, could we go to an engaging movie and come out feeling both pleasure and fear? Although negative and positive affects once were thought to be polar opposites, Bradburn (1969) demonstrated that unpleasant and pleasant affects are independent and have different correlates. Psychologists such as Watson (2002) continue to examine this issue of independence in their research. In a recent study, he found that negative affect correlated with joviality, self-assurance, and attentiveness at only −.21, −.14, and −.17, respectively. The small magnitudes of these negative correlations suggest that, while negative and positive affect are inversely correlated as expected, the relationships are quite weak and indicative of independence of the two types of affect. The size of these relationships, however, may increase when people are taxed by daily stressors (Keyes & Ryff, 2000; Zautra, Potter, & Reich, 1997).

Positive Emotions: Expanding the Repertoire of Pleasure

As some psychologists refine the distinction between the positive and negative sides of the emotional experience through basic research and measurement, other scholars (e.g., Isen, Fredrickson) have begun to explore questions about the potency and potentialities of positive emotions. (Here we use the term *emotion* rather than *affect* because we are addressing the specific response tendencies that flow from affective experience.) Cornell University psychologist Alice Isen is a pioneer in the examination of positive emotions. Dr. Isen found that, when experiencing mild positive emotions, we are more likely (1) to help other people (Isen, 1987), (2) to be flexible in our thinking (Ashby, Isen, & Turken, 1999), and (3) to come up with solutions to our problems (Isen, Daubman, & Nowicki, 1987). In classic research related to these points, Isen (1970; Isen & Levin, 1972) performed an experimental manipulation in which the research participants either did or did not find coins (placed there by the researcher) in the change slot of a public pay phone. Compared to those who did not find a coin, those who did were more likely to help another person carry a load of books or to help pick up another's dropped papers. Therefore, the finding of a coin and the associated positive emotion made people behave more altruistically.

Alice Isen

Source: Reprinted with permission of Alice Isen.

Feeling positive emotion also can help in seeing problem-solving options and finding cues for good decision making (Estrada, Isen, & Young, 1997). In one study related to these latter points, the researchers randomly assigned physicians to an experimental condition in which the doctor either was or was not given a small bag that contained 6 hard candies and 4 miniature chocolates (the doctors were not allowed to eat the candy during the experiment). Those physicians who had, rather than had not, been given the gift of candy displayed superior reasoning and decision making relative to the physicians who did not receive the candy. Specifically, the doctors in the positive emotion condition did not jump to conclusions; they were cautious even though they arrived at the diagnosis sooner than the doctors in the other condition (Alice Isen, personal communication, December 13, 2005). Perhaps, therefore, we should give our doctor some candy next time we see him or her!

Here is a more detailed description of that study that led us to this lighthearted suggestion. (Although Dr. Isen uses the term *affect*, we believe *emotion* would be more appropriate here.)

Forty-four physicians were randomly assigned to 1 of 3 groups: a control group, an affect-induction group (these participants received a small package of candy), or a group that asked participants to read humanistic statements regarding the practice of medicine. Physicians in all three groups were asked to "think aloud" while they solved a case of a patient with liver disease. Transcripts of the physicians' comments were typed, and two raters reviewed the transcripts to determine how soon the diagnosis of liver disease was considered and established, and the extent to which thinking was distorted or inflexible. The affect group initially considered the diagnosis of liver disease significantly earlier in the experiment and showed significantly less inflexible thinking than did controls. The affect and control groups established the diagnosis at similar points in the experiment. So positive affect led to the earlier integration of information (considered liver disease sooner) and resulted in little premature foreclosure on the diagnosis.

Personal Mini-Experiments

In Search of Joy and Lasting Happiness

In this chapter, we discuss positive emotion and happiness. Our review suggests that pleasant emotional experiences can be induced via brief mini-experiments. Here are a few ideas for experiments aimed at boosts in joy and happiness.

The Cartoon/Comedy Pretest/Posttest: Respond to the PANAS (see page 130) based on how you feel at the moment, then watch an episode (5 to 20 minutes without commercials, if possible) of your favorite cartoon or situation comedy that showcases good-natured humor (not sarcastic or sardonic humor). Complete a second PANAS immediately after viewing the show. Then, note the changes that have occurred in your positive and negative affect.

The "Movie, Then What?" Experiment: This experiment requires careful selection of two movies: one that has sad themes and a sanguine ending (a "feel-bad" film), and one that emphasizes joy and triumph (a "feel-good" film). Across two occasions, invite the same group of friends for movie watching at home or in the theater. After the movies, ask your friends, "Hey, if you could do anything at all right now, what would you do? What else?" Make mental notes of how many future activities are mentioned and the exuberance with which your friends discuss these activities. Identify the differences in the thought–action repertoires across the conditions of the "feel-bad" movie and the "feel-good" movie.

Commonsense Definitions of Happiness: Have you ever asked someone about his or her views on happiness? We encourage you to ask friends and acquaintances of various ages and backgrounds, "How do you define happiness in your life? What are some benchmarks or signs of your happiness?" You will be surprised by the diversity of answers and refreshed and entertained by the many stories accompanying people's responses.

Building on Isen's work, Fredrickson (2000) has developed a new theoretical framework, the **broaden-and-build model**, that may provide some explanations for the robust social and cognitive effects of positive emotional experiences. In Fredrickson's review of models of emotions (Smith, 1991), she found that responses to positive emotions have not been extensively studied and that, when researched, they were examined in a vague and underspecified manner. Furthermore, action tendencies generally have been associated with physical reactions to negative emotions (again, imagine "fight or flight"), whereas human reactions to positive emotions often are more cognitive than physical. For these reasons, she proposes discarding the **specific action tendency** concept (which suggests a restricted range of possible behavioral options) in favor of newer, more inclusive term, **momentary thought-action repertoires** (which suggest a broad range of behavioral options; imagine "taking off blinders" and seeing available opportunities).

Barbara Fredrickson

Source: Reprinted with permission of Barbara Fredrickson.

To illustrate the difference in that which follows positive and negative emotions, consider the childhood experience of one of the authors (SJL). Notice how positive emotions (e.g., excitement and glee) lead to cognitive flexibility and creativity, whereas negative emotions (e.g., fear and anxiety) are linked to a fleeing response and termination of activities.

> During a Saturday visit to my grandmother's home, I had the time of my life playing a marathon game of hide-and-seek with my brother and four cousins. The hours of play led to *excitement* and giggling . . . and the creation of new game rules and obstacles. The unbridled *joy* we experienced that afternoon made us feel free; we felt like that day would go on forever. Unfortunately, the fun was interrupted. The abrupt end to the game came when my cousin Bubby spotted me hiding behind the tall grasses on the back of my grandmother's property. I darted out of my hiding place to escape from him. As I ran around the house, I veered off into the vacant lot next door. Laughing with *glee*, I ran as hard as I could. Suddenly, there was an obstacle in my path. I leaped over it as Bub screamed uncontrollably. As I turned around, I realized I had jumped over a four-foot water moccasin, a highly poisonous snake. As my cousin's screaming continued, I grew increasingly *jittery*. Without thinking, we backed away from the snake . . . and then ran for our lives. When we finally stopped running, we could not catch our breaths. No one was hurt, but our *fear* and *anxiety* had taken the fun out of our day.

In testing her model of positive emotions, Fredrickson (2000) demonstrated that the experience of joy expands the realm of what a person feels like doing at the time; this is referred to as the *broadening* of an individual's momentary thought-action repertoire. Following an emotion-eliciting film clip (the clips induced one of five emotions: joy, contentment, anger, fear, or a neutral condition), research participants were asked to list everything

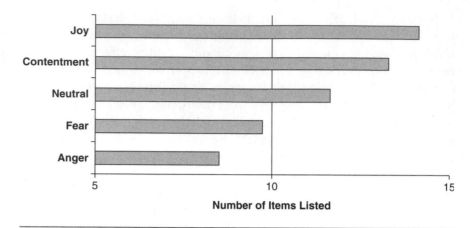

Figure 7.1   The Broadening Effects of Positive Emotions
Source: Fredrickson (2002).

they would like to do at that moment (see the results in Figure 7.1). Those participants who experienced joy or contentment listed significantly more desired possibilities than did the people in the neutral or negative conditions. In turn, those expanded possibilities for future activities should lead the joyful individuals to initiate subsequent actions. Those who expressed more negative emotions, on the other hand, tended to shut down their thinking about subsequent possible activities. Simply put, joy appears to open us up to many new thoughts and behaviors, whereas negative emotions dampen our ideas and actions.

Joy also increases our likelihood of behaving positively toward other people, along with developing more positive relationships. Furthermore, joy induces playfulness (Frijda, 1994), which is quite important because such behaviors are evolutionarily adaptive in acquisition of necessary resources. Juvenile play builds (1) enduring social and intellectual resources by encouraging attachment, (2) higher levels of creativity, and (3) brain development (Fredrickson, 2002).

It appears that, through the effects of broadening processes, positive emotions also can help *build* resources. In 2002, Fredrickson and her colleague, Thomas Joiner, demonstrated this building phenomenon by assessing people's positive and negative emotions and broad-minded coping (solving problems with creative means) on two occasions 5 weeks apart. The researchers found that initial levels of positive emotions predicted overall increases in creative problem solving. These changes in coping also predicted further increases in positive emotions (see Figure 7.2). Similarly, controlling for initial levels of positive emotion, initial levels of coping predicted increases in positive emotions, which in turn predicted increases in coping. These results held true only for positive emotions, *not* for negative emotions. Therefore, positive emotions such as joy may help generate resources, maintain a sense of vital energy (i.e., more positive emotions),

Positive Emotion Styles
Linked to the Common Cold

A. PALMER

Positive emotions may increase resistance to the common cold, according to a recent study in *Psychosomatic Medicine* (Vol. 65, No. 1). The research by Sheldon Cohen, PhD, of Carnegie Mellon University and colleagues adds to a body of literature that suggests that emotional styles influence health. The researchers interviewed 334 healthy volunteers by phone for 7 evenings over 3 weeks to assess their emotional states. Participants described how they felt throughout the day in three positive-emotion areas of vigor, well-being and calm and three negative-emotion areas of depression, anxiety and hostility by rating their emotions on a scale of 0 to 4.

After this initial evaluation, researchers administered a shot of a rhinovirus, the germ that causes colds, into each participant's nose. Afterward, participants were observed for 5 days to see if they became sick and in what ways cold symptoms manifested. The volunteers were considered to have a clinical cold if they were both infected and met illness criteria.

"People who scored low on positive emotional style were three times more likely to get sick than those with high positive emotional styles," Cohen says.

The researchers then measured how emotional style affected all sick participants' reporting of cold symptoms. Each day of the quarantine, researchers asked them to report the severity of such cold symptoms as a runny nose, cough, and headaches on a 4-point scale.

While negative emotional style did not affect whether people developed colds, the study found that people with higher negative emotional styles reported more symptoms than expected from objective health markers, Cohen says. Those with lower positive emotions reported fewer symptoms of illness than expected.

Positive emotional style was also associated with better health practices and lower levels of epinephrine, norepinephrine and cortisol, three stress-related hormones, but the researchers found that this did not account for the link between positive emotional style and illness.

Considering the average adult catches 2 to 5 colds per year and children average 7 to 10 colds per year, developing psychological risk profiles and considering ways to enhance positive emotions might reduce the risk of colds, says Cohen.

Cohen adds that future research should focus on the unique biological role that emotions play in health.

and create even more resources. Fredrickson (2002) referred to this positive sequence as the "upward spiral" of positive emotions (see Figure 7.3).

Extending her model of positive emotions, Fredrickson and colleagues examined the "undoing" potential of positive emotions (Fredrickson, Mancuso, Branigan, & Tugade, 2000) and the ratio of positive to negative emotional experiences that is associated with human flourishing (Fredrickson & Losada, 2005). Fredrickson et al. (2000) hypothesized that, given the broadening and building effects of positive emotions, joy and

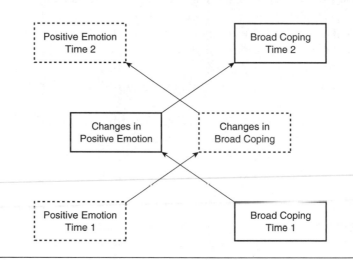

Figure 7.2   The Building Effects of Positive Emotions

Source: From Mayne, T. J., & Bonanno, G. A., *Emotions,* copyright © 2001. Reprinted with permission of Guilford Press.

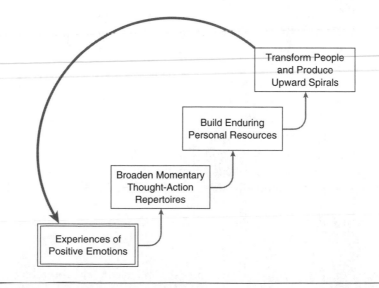

Figure 7.3   The Upward Spiral of Positive Emotions

Source: From Fredrickson, B. L., & Joiner, T., "Positive emotions trigger upward spirals toward emotional well-being," in *Psychological Science, 13*(2), copyright © 2002. Reprinted with permission of Blackwell Publishing.

contentment might function as antidotes to negative emotions. To test this hypothesis, the researchers exposed all participants in their study to a situation that aroused negative emotion and immediately randomly assigned people to emotion conditions (sparked by evocative video clips) ranging from mild joy to sadness. Cardiovascular recovery represented the undoing process and was operationalized as the time that elapsed from the start of the randomly assigned video until the physiological reactions induced by the initial negative emotion returned to baseline. The undoing hypothesis was supported, as participants in the joy and contentment conditions were able to undo the effects of the negative emotions more quickly than the people in the other conditions. These findings suggest that there is an incompatibility between positive and negative emotions and that the potential effects of negative experiences can be offset by positive emotions such as joy and contentment.

Given that positive emotions help people build enduring resources and recover from negative experiences, Fredrickson and Losada (2005) hypothesized that positive emotions might be associated with optimal mental health or flourishing (i.e., positive psychological and social well-being; see the complete mental health model on page 144). By subjecting data on undergraduate participants' mental health (from a flourishing measure) and their emotional experience (students rated the extent to which they experienced 20 emotions each day for 28 days) to mathematical analysis, the researchers found that a mean ratio of 2:9 positive to negative emotions predicts human flourishing. This finding provides diagnostic insight into the effects of daily emotional experiences on our mental health.

Happiness and Subjective Well-Being: Living a Pleasurable Life

AGE-OLD DEFINITIONS OF HAPPINESS

Buddha left home in search of a more meaningful existence and ultimately found enlightenment, a sense of peace, and happiness. Aristotle believed that *eudaimonia* (human flourishing associated with living a life of virtue), or happiness based on a lifelong pursuit of meaningful, developmental goals (i.e., "doing what is worth doing"), was the key to the good life (Waterman, 1993). America's founders reasoned that the pursuit of happiness was just as important as our inalienable rights of life and liberty. These age-old definitions of happiness, along with many other conceptualizations of emotional well-being, have had clear influences on the views of 20th- and 21st-century scholars, but more recent psychological theory and genetic research have helped us to clarify happiness and its correlates.

Theories of happiness have been divided into three types: (1) need/ goal satisfaction theories, (2) process/activity theories, and (3) genetic/ personality predisposition (Diener et al., 2002). (Explore folk definitions of happiness by completing the third exercise in the Personal Mini-Experiments earlier in this chapter.)

In regard to **need/goal satisfaction theories**, the leaders of particular schools of psychotherapy proffered these ideas about happiness. For example, psychoanalytic and humanistic theorists (Sigmund Freud and Abraham Maslow, respectively) suggested that the reduction of tension or the satisfaction of needs lead to happiness. In short, it was theorized that we are happy because we have reached our goals. Such "happiness as satisfaction" makes happiness a target of our psychological pursuits.

In the **process/activity** camp, theorists posit that engaging in particular life activities generates happiness. For example, Mike Csikszentmihalyi (pronounced CHEEK-SENT-ME-HIGH), who was one of the first 20th-century theorists to examine process/activity conceptualizations of happiness, proposed that people who experience **flow** (engagement in interesting activities that match or challenge task-related skills) in daily life tend to be very happy. Indeed, Csikszentmihalyi's (1975/2000, 1990) work suggests that engagement in activity *produces* happiness. Other process/activity theorists (e.g., Emmons, 1986; Snyder, 1994) have emphasized how the *process* of pursuing goals generates energy and happiness. This pursuit-of-happiness perspective mirrors America's founders' promise of "life, liberty, and the pursuit of happiness."

Those who emphasize the **genetic and personality predisposition theories of happiness** (Diener & Larsen, 1984; Watson, 2000) tend to see happiness as stable, whereas theorists in the happiness-as-satisfaction and process/activity camps view it as changing with life conditions. On this latter point, Costa and McCrae (1988) found that happiness changed little over a 6-year period, thereby lending credence to theories of personality-based or biologically determined happiness. Demonstrating this link between happiness and personality, Lucas and Fujita (2000) showed that extroversion and neuroticism, two of the Big 5 factors of personality (openness, conscientiousness, extroversion, agreeableness, neuroticism), were closely related to the characteristics of happiness.

Studies of the biological or genetic determinants of happiness have found that up to 40% of positive emotionality and 55% of negative emotionality are genetically based (Tellegen et al., 1988). Obviously, this leaves about 50% of the variance in happiness that is not explained by biological components. Overall, therefore, a thorough understanding of happiness necessitates an examination of genetic factors *and* the variables suggested by need/goal satisfaction and the activity/process theorists.

SUBJECTIVE WELL-BEING AS A SYNONYM FOR HAPPINESS

Building on a utilitarian tradition and the tenets of hedonic psychology (which emphasizes the study of pleasure and life satisfaction), Diener (1984; 2000; Diener et al., 2002) considers well-being to be the subjective evaluation of one's current status in the world. More specifically, well-being involves our experience of pleasure and our appreciation of life's rewards. Given this view, Diener defines subjective well-being as a combination of positive affect (in the absence of negative affect) and general life satisfaction. Furthermore, he uses the term *subjective well-being* as a synonym for *happiness*. (The satisfaction component often is measured with the Satisfaction With Life Scale; Diener, Emmons, Larsen, & Griffin, 1985).

The Satisfaction With Life Scale

Instructions: Please use one of the following numbers from 1 to 7 to indicate how much you agree or disagree with the following statements.

1	2	3	4	5	6	7
Strongly disagree	Disagree	Slightly disagree	Neither agree nor disagree	Slightly agree	Agree	Strongly agree

1. _____ In most ways, my life is close to my ideal.

2. _____ The conditions of my life are excellent.

3. _____ I am satisfied with my life.

4. _____ So far, I have gotten the important things I want in my life.

5. _____ If I could live my life over, I would change almost nothing.

Note: Scores for all items are summed to calculate a total score.

Subjective well-being emphasizes peoples' reports of their life experiences. Accordingly, the subjective report is taken at face value. This subjective approach to happiness assumes that people from many cultures are comfortable in focusing on individualistic assessments of their affects and satisfaction and that people will be forthright in such personal analyses (Diener et al., 2002). These assumptions guide the researchers' attempts to understand a person's subjective experiences in light of his or her objective circumstances.

DETERMINANTS OF SUBJECTIVE WELL-BEING

When examining college students' (from 31 nations) satisfaction in various life domains, financial status was more highly correlated with satisfaction for students in poor nations than for those in wealthy nations (Diener & Diener, 1995). Moreover, the people in wealthy nations generally were happier than those in impoverished nations. Within-nation examination of this link between income and well-being reveals that, once household income rises above the poverty line, additional bumps in income are not necessarily associated with increases in well-being. When well-being data are divided further by categories of economic status (very poor versus very wealthy), it appears that there is strong relationship between income and well-being among the impoverished but an insignificant relationship between the two variables among the affluent (Diener, Diener, & Diener, 1995).

Data specific to Western samples indicate that married men and women alike report more happiness than those who are not married (never married, divorced, or separated; Lee, Seccombe, & Shehan, 1991). The link between subjective well-being and being married holds for people of all ages, income and educational levels, and racial–ethnic backgrounds (Argyle, 1987). Not surprisingly, marital quality also is positively associated with personal well-being (Sternberg & Hojjat, 1997).

In a study of the happiest 10 percent of American college students, Diener and Seligman (2003) found that the qualities of good mental health and good social relationships consistently emerge in the lives in the sample of happiest young adults. Upon closer inspection of their data, analyses revealed that good social functioning among the happiest subset of students was a necessary but not sufficient cause of happiness.

HAPPINESS + MEANING = WELL-BEING

Psychologists who support the hedonic perspective view subjective well-being and happiness as synonymous. Alternatively, the scholars whose ideas about well-being are more consistent with Aristotle's views on *eudaimonia* believe that happiness and well-being are not synonymous. In this latter perspective, *eudaimonia* is comprised of happiness and meaning. Stated in a simple formula, well-being = happiness + meaning. In order to subscribe to this latter view of well-being, one must understand virtue and the social implications of daily behavior. Furthermore, this view requires that those who seek well-being be authentic and live according to their real needs and desired goals (Waterman, 1993). Thus, living a eudaimonic life goes beyond experiencing "things pleasurable," and it embraces flourishing as the goal in all our actions. Both hedonistic and eudaimonic versions of happiness have influenced the 21st-century definitions.

21st-CENTURY DEFINITIONS OF HAPPINESS

Modern Western psychology has focused primarily on a postmaterialistic view of happiness (Diener et al., 2002) that emphasizes pleasure, satisfaction, *and* life meaning. Indeed, the type of happiness addressed in much of today's popular literature emphasizes hedonics, meaning, and authenticity. For example, Seligman (2002) suggests that a pleasant and meaningful life can be built on the happiness that results from using our psychological strengths.

Excerpts From *Authentic Happiness*

MARTIN E. P. SELIGMAN

When well-being comes from engaging our strengths and virtues, our lives are imbued with authenticity. Feelings are states, momentary occurrences that need not be recurring features of personality. Traits, in contrast to states, are either negative or positive characteristics that bring about good feeling and gratification. Traits are abiding dispositions whose exercise makes momentary feelings more likely. The negative trait of paranoia makes the momentary state of jealousy more likely, just as the positive trait of being humorous makes the state of laughing more likely. (p. 9)

The well-being that using your signature strengths engenders is anchored in authenticity. But just as well-being needs to be anchored in strengths and virtues, these in turn must be anchored in something larger. Just as the good life is something beyond the pleasant life, the meaningful life is beyond the good life. (p. 14)

Source: Seligman (2002).

Beach Man Named Nation's Happiest

JASON SKOG

VIRGINIA BEACH—Who's the happiest man in America?

He's not rich or powerful, so scratch Bill Gates and President Bush. And he's not a famous movie or rock star, so forget Tom Cruise and Bruce Springsteen.

According to the March 7–9 cover story of *USA Weekend* magazine, a Sunday supplement in almost 600 newspapers, the nation's happiest guy is a 45-year-old Virginia Beach stockbroker, J. P. "Gus" Godsey.

Godsey will be introduced early today on ABC's *Good Morning, America*, and he's, well, happy.

"It's real cool," Godsey said. "I didn't realize how big this was going to be."

Since word of the recognition leaked, he's had inquiries for national TV interviews. And there's been talk of appearances with Regis, Oprah, and Letterman.

Godsey's grin is nearly as broad as his shoulders. When he speaks, words tumble out in rambling, overflowing tones that are full, raspy, and fast. He can hardly contain himself.

"I'm not going to believe all the hype," Godsey said, "but I do know, if there are happier people, I haven't met many of them."

(Continued)

(Continued)

Godsey earned the distinction based on studies that suggest that volunteer work and civic involvement contribute to a person's happiness. Virginia Beach's quality of life also helped the magazine pick Godsey.

"It was a combination of science, sleuthing, and surveys," the *USA Weekend* story reads.

The magazine set out to find the happiest man in Virginia Beach, and Godsey's name continued to come up. After some initial interviews, he was subjected to a battery of psychological and emotional tests—five in all—measuring his level of contentment.

Dr. Martin E. P. Seligman, author of *Authentic Happiness* and a University of Pennsylvania professor, spent a day in Virginia Beach administering some of the tests.

Seligman divides happiness into three types: the pleasant life, the good life, and the meaningful life.

"He did great in all three and actually was off the scale in the second one. He's real unusual," Seligman said.

Godsey is a member of the city's Human Rights Commission, founder of local Thanksgiving and holiday food and toy drives, past chairman of the Republican Party of Virginia Beach, and a coordinator of benefit concerts.

He and his wife, Judi, have a son, Jeremy, 23, and a daughter, Jessica, 20. The couple lives on a 1¼-acre lot along the Lynnhaven Inlet in the Wolfsnare Plantation neighborhood.

"Not only is Mr. Godsey a very amiable, pleasant person," said Mayor Meyera E. Oberndorf, "he is a perfect example of the young people we want to return to our city to establish their lives and families and their careers."

Lynda Filipiak-Wilchynski, Godsey's sales assistant at Ferris, Baker, Watts Inc., a regional brokerage house based in Washington, said her boss's good humor is contagious.

"Everything is cool, everything is smooth with J.P.," she said.

Godsey said the key to happiness is simple.

"We wake up every morning full of choices," he said. "And your state of happiness is something you can do every single day. How are you going to make your day this morning? And we only have today. God never promised us tomorrow."

Do the faltering economy, threats of terrorism, and a looming war make this a difficult time to be happy?

"No. Absolutely not," he said. "Because I cannot control those things. . . . Why focus on something I can't control or that will bring me down?"

Reach Jason Skog at jskog@pilotonline.com or 222-5113.

Source: From Skog, J., "Beach Man Named Nation's Happiest," *The Virginian-Pilot*, March 3, 2003, p. A1. Reprinted with permission of *The Virginian-Pilot*.

Describing a new model of happiness, Lyubomirsky, Sheldon, and Schkade (2005) propose that "[a] person's chronic happiness level is governed by three major factors: a genetically determined set point for happiness, happiness-relevant circumstantial factors, and happiness-relevant activities and practices" (p. 111). Lyubomirsky and colleagues' "architecture of sustainable happiness" (p. 114) incorporates what is known about the genetic components of happiness, the circumstantial/demographic determinants of happiness, and the complex process of intentional human change. Based on past research, which they summarize, Lyubomirsky et al. propose that genetics accounts for 50% of population variance for happiness, whereas life circumstances (both good and bad) and intentional activity (attempts at healthy living and positive change) account for 10% and 40% of the population variance for happiness, respectively. This model of happiness acknowledges the components of happiness that can't be changed, but it also leaves room for volition and the self-generated goals that lead to the attainment of pleasure, meaning, and good health.

Undoubtedly, 21st-century scholars will produce many more refined views of happiness. Our prediction is that the pursuit of happiness through positive psychological science and practice ultimately will develop a better sense of the genetic (summarized in Lyubomirsky et al., 2005), neural (Urry et al., 2004), and neurobiological correlates and underpinnings of happiness and will embrace the contentment, peace, and happiness of Eastern philosophy along with the folk wisdom of the Western world. So, imagine a science of happiness that is grounded in what is known about the genetic and biological bases of happiness and that examines the rigor and relevance of Buddha's teachings alongside Benjamin Franklin's recommendations for virtuous living (see Figure 7.4). Through

Figure 7.4   East Meets West in the Discussion of Happiness

Source: Photo credit: Malcolm Tarlofsky. Reprinted with permission.

good biological and psychological science and a universal appreciation of philosophical stances on happiness, we can increase the international relevance of our scholarship in positive psychology.

COMPLETE MENTAL HEALTH: EMOTIONAL, SOCIAL, AND PSYCHOLOGICAL WELL-BEING

Ryff and Keyes (1995; Keyes & Lopez, 2002; Keyes & Magyar-Moe, 2003) combine many principles of pleasure to define complete mental health. Specifically, they view optimal functioning as the combination of **emotional well-being** (as they refer to subjective well-being; defined as the presence of positive affect and satisfaction with life and the absence of negative affect), **social well-being** (incorporating acceptance, actualization, contribution, coherence, and integration), and **psychological well-being** (combining self-acceptance, personal growth, purpose in life, environmental mastery, autonomy, positive relations with others). Taking the symptoms of mental illness into consideration, they define "complete mental health" as the combination of "high levels of symptoms of emotional well being, psychological well-being, and social well-being, as well as the absence of recent mental illness" (Keyes & Lopez, 2002, p. 49). This view of mental health combines all facets of well-being into a model that is both dimensional (because extremes of mental health and illness symptomatology are reflected) and categorical (because assignment to distinct diagnostic categories is possible). This **complete state model** (Keyes & Lopez, p. 49; see Figure 7.5) suggests that combined mental health and mental illness symptoms may be ever-changing, resulting in fluctuations in states of overall well-being ranging from complete mental illness to complete mental health.

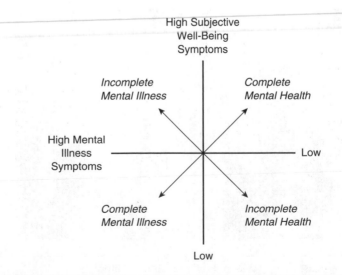

Figure 7.5   A Model of Complete Mental Health

Source: Keyes and Lopez (2002).

INCREASING HAPPINESS IN YOUR LIFE

Although there are numerous theories of happiness and countless definitions of it, researchers (e.g., Sheldon & Lyubomirsky, 2004) have begun to build on past work (Fordyce, 1977, 1983) in their attempts to answer the question many of our clients ask: "Can I learn how to be happier?" David Myers (1993), an expert on the subject and the author of *The Pursuit of Happiness*, provides general strategies for increasing the happiness in your life (see Figure 7.6). We provide Life Enhancement Strategies for boosting happiness in specific domains of your life.

---

1. **Realize that enduring happiness doesn't come from success.** People adapt to changing circumstances—even to wealth or a disability. Thus wealth is like health: its utter absence breeds misery, but having it (or any circumstance we long for) doesn't guarantee happiness.

2. **Take control of your time.** Happy people feel in control of their lives, often aided by mastering their use of time. It helps to set goals and break them into daily aims. Although we often overestimate how much we will accomplish in any given day (leaving us frustrated), we generally underestimate how much we can accomplish in a year, given just a little progress every day.

3. **Act happy.** We can sometimes act ourselves into a frame of mind. Manipulated into a smiling expression, people feel better; when they scowl, the whole world seems to scowl back. So put on a happy face. Talk as if you feel positive self-esteem, are optimistic, and are outgoing. Going through the motions can trigger the emotions.

4. **Seek work and leisure that engages your skills.** Happy people often are in a zone called "flow"—absorbed in a task that challenges them without overwhelming them. The most expensive forms of leisure (sitting on a yacht) often provide less flow experience than gardening, socializing, or craft work.

5. **Join the "movement" movement.** An avalanche of research reveals that aerobic exercise not only promotes health and energy, it also is an antidote for mild depression and anxiety. Sound minds reside in sound bodies. Off your duffs, couch potatoes.

6. **Give your body the sleep it wants.** Happy people live active vigorous lives yet reserve time for renewing sleep and solitude. Many people suffer from a sleep debt, with resulting fatigue, diminished alertness, and gloomy moods.

7. **Give priority to close relationships.** Intimate friendships with those who care deeply about you can help you weather difficult times. Confiding is good for soul and body. Resolve to nurture your closest relationships: to not take those closest to you for granted, to display to them the sort of kindness that you display to others, to affirm them, to play together and share together. To rejuvenate your affections, resolve in such ways to act lovingly.

8. **Focus beyond the self.** Reach out to those in need. Happiness increases helpfulness (those who feel good do good). But doing good also makes one feel good.

9. **Keep a gratitude journal.** Those who pause each day to reflect on some positive aspect of their lives (their health, friends, family, freedom, education, senses, natural surroundings, and so on) experience heightened well-being.

10. **Nurture your spiritual self.** For many people, faith provides a support community, a reason to focus beyond self, and a sense of purpose and hope. Study after study finds that actively religious people are happier and that they cope better with crises.

Figure 7.6   David Myers's Suggestions for a Happier Life

Source: Adapted from Myers, D., *The Pursuit of Happiness,* copyright © 1993. Reprinted with permission of the author.

Life Enhancement Strategies

Following is a list of additional tips for increasing pleasant emotional experiences and happiness and well-being in your life. Although we categorize these suggestions within life's important domains, as we do in most chapters, we do not mean to suggest that all aspects of positive affect and emotions and happiness are domain specific. We do believe, however, that some aspects of both the pleasant life and the meaningful life can be found in each of life's domains.

Love

- Surround yourself with happy people. Their positive affect and emotions will buoy you in your times of distress.
- Tell those close to you that you love them. Your sincere expression of love will bolster your relationship and induce positive affect in others.

Work

- Start a meeting with positive comments about peers' contributions. This may raise positive affect that generates creativity and good decision making.
- Bring homemade treats to work or class. This may generate productive interactions.

Play

- Engage in your favorite play activities from yesteryear—those activities that brought you joy as a child may do so today.
- Participate in brief relaxation activities to break up your day. Relaxation can make your mind and body more sensitive to the pleasurable daily moments.

Moving Toward the Positive

It is very easy to find the unpleasant, negative aspects of emotions and dysfunctions in life (Baumeister, Bratslavsky, Finkenhaur, & Vohs, 2001). All you have to do is read the morning newspaper or watch the nightly news. Our human need to understand the negative is great, given the suffering and loss associated with anger and fear as well as the evolutionary functions of avoidance strategies. Although the positive aspects of emotional experiences rarely capture the attention of media or science, things are beginning to change. It was only three decades ago, for example, that a few brave social scientists (e.g., Bradburn, 1969; Meehl, 1975) shared their thoughts about the lighter side of life. Today, we know that the flow of "joy-juice" (Paul Meehl's flippant term for that which induces pleasant emotional experiences) and biological factors are important, but they do not define our entire emotional experience. In the words of Diener et al.

(2002, p. 68), "It appears that the way people perceive the world is much more important to happiness than objective circumstances."

Key Terms

Affect: A person's instinctive response to a stimulus; characterized by a sense of arousal. Affect is considered the most basic element of feeling and often involves evaluation of a stimulus as good or bad.

Broaden-and-build model of positive emotions: Model developed by Fredrickson (2000), which suggests that positive emotions expand what an individual feels like doing at any given time. Fredrickson calls this expansion *broadening* of an individual's momentary thought-action repertoire. Positive emotions also allow people to *build* resources through the increasing of creative problem solving and recognition of personal resources.

Complete state model: Model developed by Keyes and Lopez (2002), in which mental health is defined as as high levels of emotional, psychological, and social well-being and the absence of mental illness symptoms; the model acknowledges that well-being and mental illness symptomatology changes over time.

Content of affect: A dimension of affect measured by Watson and Clark's (1994) Expanded Form of the Positive and Negative Affect Scale (PANAS-X). Refers to the type of experience within the positive or negative affective state. For example, the content of positive affect may include joviality, self-assurance, or attentiveness, whereas negative affect may include anger, sadness, and fear.

Emotion: A feeling state resulting from the appraisal of an external object as salient to our own well-being. An emotion has a specific, "sharpened" quality, as it always has an object.

Emotional well-being: The presence of positive affect and the absence of negative affect, as well as satisfaction with life.

Eudaimonia: Human flourishing, or happiness associated with living a life of virtue.

Flow: According to Csikszentmihalyi (1990), the pleasurable experience resulting from engagement in an interesting activity that properly matches or challenges a person's skills and abilities.

Genetic/personality predisposition theories of happiness: Theories suggesting that happiness may be a more stable personality trait or a characteristic that is genetically based.

Momentary thought-action repertoire: Suggested by Fredrickson (2000), the broadening of a specific action tendency to include cognitive as well as physical responses to an emotion. Fredrickson suggests that specific action tendencies associated with negative emotions fail to consider responses to positive emotions, which often are more cognitive than physical. See also *specific action tendency.*

Mood: General, free-floating feelings that last longer than an emotion. Mood is thought to be tied to expectations of future positive or negative affect.

Need/goal satisfaction theories of happiness: Theories of happiness suggesting that happiness lies in the reduction of tension through the satisfaction of goals and needs.

Pleasure principle: Freud's idea that humans seek to reduce tension by gratifying instinctive needs. He believed that well-being was the result of satisfied biological and psychological needs and that humans will seek gratification regardless of the consequences.

Process/activity theories of happiness: Theories of happiness suggesting that happiness is produced by engaging in certain activities or working toward a goal.

Psychological well-being: A state of well-being characterized by self-acceptance, personal growth, purpose in life, environmental mastery, autonomy, and positive emotions.

Social well-being: A state of well-being characterized by acceptance, actualization, contribution, coherence, and integration with others.

Specific action tendency: Suggested by most models of emotion, the tendency to act in a specific manner that follows an emotion. The most famous specific action tendency is the "fight or flight" response, the theory of which suggests that, when confronted with a situation that elicits a negative emotion, humans and animals will act either by approaching (fight) or by retreating (flight) from the situation.

Subjective well-being: A person's individual judgment about his or her current status in the world. Often used synonymously with *happiness.*

Valence: The direction of affect: positive (pleasant) or negative (unpleasant).

Making the Most of Emotional Experiences 8

Emotion-Focused Coping,
Emotional Intelligence,
Socioemotional Selectivity,
and Emotional Storytelling

At times during the 20th century, psychology research and practice sullied the reputation of emotions. At worst, helping professionals and the public at large characterize emotions as toxic to our lives or detrimental to rational decision making. At best, emotions have been portrayed as reflections of life satisfaction or signals of specific daily actions that need to be taken. Research popularized in the 21st century (reviewed in Chapter 7 and in this chapter) demonstrates that both positive and negative emotions may determine how adaptive we are in our daily lives (see Chapter 7 to review Nussbaum's [2001] definition of emotion). The purpose of this chapter is to introduce you to how people make the most of their emotional experiences—that is, how they generally handle positive and negative emotions in a manner that leads to a positive outcome—by discussing theory and research associated with emotion-focused coping, emotional intelligence, socioemotional selectivity, and emotional storytelling. We discuss how we *benefit* from engaging our emotions, how we can *learn* to process and use emotion-laden material competently, and how we more efficiently *sort* the good from the bad emotional content of life as we age. Finally, we describe how sharing stories of emotional upheaval helps us *overcome* traumatic stress and pain.

Emotion-Focused Coping:
Discovering the Adaptive Potential of Emotional Approach

Annette Stanton

Source: Reprinted with permission of Annette Stanton.

The power of emotions traditionally is described in such negative terms as "the beast within" (Averill, 1990). Intense emotions were seen as dysfunctional and opposed to rationality. Research in the 20th century often supported this view of emotional experiences by linking them with maladaptive outcomes in life. But when Annette Stanton, a positive psychologist at the University of California at Los Angeles, considered the adaptive potential of emotion-focused coping (i.e., regulating the emotions surrounding a stressful encounter), she found that there was a problem in how emotions were defined and measured in some of the research. Indeed, wide disparity was apparent in the items used to measure the emotion-focused coping phenomenon, and this led to unclear associations between what was referred to as "emotion-focused coping" and psychological adjustment. That is, Stanton, Danoff-Burg, Cameron, and Ellis (1994) found that scales assessing emotion-focused coping contained items in which the respondent had to engage in self-deprecation or admit to having distress or psychopathology whenever he or she acknowledged experiencing intense emotion. Responses to items such as "I blame myself for becoming too emotional" (Scheier, Weintraub, & Carver, 1986) and "I get upset and let my emotions out" (Carver, Scheier, & Weintraub, 1989) most probably would have been positively correlated with responses to items about a negative view of self or about general distress. When questions that framed emotional regulation in such a confounding manner were removed from research protocols, the frequently cited relationship between greater emotion-focused coping and poorer life outcomes was deemed invalid.

Stanton and her colleagues have spent the last decade working to clarify what "emotion-focused coping" means. Specifically, Stanton, Parsa, and Austenfeld (2002, p. 150) stated that "coping through emotional approach might be said to carry adaptive potential, the realization of which may depend on . . . the situational context, the interpersonal milieu, and attributes of the individual." What they call **emotional approach** involves active movement *toward, rather than away from,* a stressful encounter. This distinction between emotional approach and **emotional avoidance** is supported by the existence of two neurobiological systems that govern approach (i.e., appetitive) and avoidance behavior. The *behavioral activation system* regulates our appetitive motivation, which helps us realize emotional or behavioral rewards, whereas the *behavioral inhibition system* functions to help us avoid negative events and punishment (Depue, 1996).

Stanton, Kirk, Cameron, and Danoff-Burg (2000) identified two related but distinct processes involved in approach-oriented emotion-focused coping. One involves **emotional processing**, or attempts to understand

Table 8.1   Measures of Emotion-Focused Coping

Emotional Processing

    I realize that my feelings are valid and important.

    I take time to figure out what I am really feeling.

    I delve into my feelings to get a thorough understanding of them.

    I acknowledge my emotions.

Emotional Expression

    I feel free to express my emotions.

    I take time to express my emotions.

    I allow myself to express my emotions.

    I let my feelings come out freely.

Source: From Stanton, A. L., Kirk, S. B., Cameron, C. L., & Ellis, A. P., Coping through emotional approach: Scale construction and validation, in *Journal of Personality and Social Psychology, 78*(6), pp. 1150–1169. Copyright © 2000 by the American Psychological Association. Reproduced with permission.

emotions, and a second reflects **emotional expression,** or free and intentional displays of feeling. The researchers then created scales to tap these two approaches of emotional processing and emotional expression (see Table 8.1 for a list of components of the two processes).

With emotion-focused coping defined and measured more clearly and objectively, Stanton and colleagues (Stanton et al., 2000; Stanton, Danoff-Burg, & Huggins, 2002) were able to illuminate the functions of emotional approach. Using their revised measures, Stanton et al. (2000) studied the impact of emotion-focused coping on women's adjustment to breast cancer. Over a 3-month period, women who used emotion-focused coping perceived their health status as better, had lower psychological distress, and had fewer medical appointments for cancer-related pain and ailments, as compared to those who did not.

Working with an undergraduate population, Stanton, Kirk, Cameron, and Danoff-Burg (2000) found that students who were dealing with a parent's psychological or physical illness coped better with their stressors if they were assigned to sessions that matched their emotional approach tendencies. That is to say, people who previously had reported a preference for expressing emotions when under duress did better when attending sessions that allowed them to vent emotions rather than receive facts. On the other hand, those participants who did not report a preference for expressing emotions when dealing with stress did better when placed in the information condition rather than the emotion-focused coping condition. These findings suggest that emotional preferences related to coping may interact with environmental contingencies to determine psychological outcomes.

Recent work on emotion-focused coping, summarized in a review by Austenfeld and Stanton (2004), highlights the adaptive potential of emotional expression and processing when coping with infertility, cancer, and chronic pain. Anecdotal evidence collected from the reports of our clients and friends suggests that the adaptive potential of emotional approach also is realized in normal life circumstances. For instance, each day we are challenged by minor stresses (junk mail, mean people, traffic) and real problems (shortages of money, minor illnesses, subtle prejudices) that stir up emotions that we can approach or avoid. Most people seem to benefit, at least in the short run, from expressing their emotions in a meaningful way. Further, emotional processing seems to become more adaptive as people learn more about what they feel and why they feel it.

Given the robust findings linking emotion-focused coping and adaptive outcomes under particular circumstances, it is important to understand how emotional approach works to our benefit. Of course, if we turned our attentions away from unpleasant feelings each time we experienced them, we would learn very little about how these feelings influence us and our friends (Salovey, Mayer, & Caruso, 2002). This approach coping may foster a better understanding of our experiences and direct our attention to central concerns (Frijda, 1994). Furthermore, over time we may develop the tendency to face our stressors directly and repeatedly (instead of avoiding them on occasion) and thereby habituate to certain predictable negative experiences. We learn that emotional pain does subside, and time heals both psychological and physical wounds. As we discuss later in this chapter, understanding one's emotional experience can help one select optimal relationships and environments (Carstensen, 1998). On a neurobiological level, Depue (1996) points to the involvement of the behavioral activation system, and LeDoux (1996) reveals that a particular brain structure, the amygdala, plays a significant role in processing matters of emotional significance. Specifically, LeDoux suggests that, under stress-free life circumstances, our thinking is governed by the hippocampus, but during more stressful times, our thought processes—and hence aspects of our coping—are ruled by the amygdala. Future examination of the neurobiology of emotion-focused coping may further demystify the benefits of approaching emotions and the related workings of brain structures such as the amygdala.

THE CASE OF A HURRICANE SURVIVOR

While standing in a line for hurricane relief with dozens of survivors, I (SJL) witnessed people who were avoiding all emotions, some who were approaching their emotions productively, and some who were frankly overwhelmed by what they were experiencing. My guess is that those who were approaching their emotions are doing better today than those who did not. I was a visitor to the disaster area; my mother's home was damaged, but she was safe and sound. She and I chatted with many of her neighbors who had lost their homes and were trying to pull their lives together.

I struck up a conversation with a fellow about my age; I thought I recognized him from high school. It turned out that Ted was from the New Orleans area, about 150 miles away. He and his family had survived Hurricane Katrina, but his home was uninhabitable. He moved to New Iberia to find a home for his family, and then Hurricane Rita hit that town. Ted told me the whole story. He heard that Katrina had pushed five feet of water into his family's New Orleans home, but he was not allowed to go back and see it because of the unsafe conditions. He found his way to New Iberia and rented an apartment for his wife and two boys. Then, Ted said, "Rita hit and scared the hell out of my family." He told me that he felt frightened because he might never be able to keep his wife and boys safe again. Ted *expressed his emotions* in simple, honest language that communicated the depths of his fear and sadness.

Ted and I chatted some more, and it was clear that he had spent a great deal of time with his wife, *processing their emotions*. I asked him about how his boys were coping. He laughed, "Kids are amazing!" He said that they didn't understand the need for all the changes in their lives, but they had coped well with the ups and downs. At that time, he told me, "Yesterday, we bought the boys bunk beds, and I put them up last night. I placed my son in the top bunk, and then, well, you know what he said? 'Daddy, it is starting to feel like we have a home again.'" Ted teared up and said, "I hope this line starts moving."

Emotional Intelligence:
Learning the Skills That Make a Difference

Daniel Goleman, once a science writer for numerous periodicals and newspapers, popularized the concept of *emotional intelligence* in the 1990s. His 1995 book, *Emotional Intelligence: Why It Can Matter More Than IQ*, introduced the general public to the emotional concepts that had been discussed by psychologists and laypeople for decades. Professionals of all types built on this "next big thing" and shared their views on emotional intelligence in the popular press or in what has been referred to as the "organizational development industry" (which primarily involves training programs designed to help employees reach their professional potential by realizing their personal potential). To date, numerous amalgamations of psychological constructs have been conceptualized as reflective of emotional intelligence (see Bar-On, 1997; Schutte et al., 1998). For example, Bar-On (1997, 2000) defines emotional intelligence as an array of noncognitive capabilities, competencies, and skills that help us deal with the demands of the environment, but the related inventory, the EQ-I (Bar-On, 1997), primarily measures personality and mood variables such as self-regard, empathy, tolerance, and happiness. This atheoretical version of emotional intelligence may be distinct from other forms of intelligence, yet it appears to overlap existing operationalizations of meaningful psychological variables. Therefore, measuring this type of emotional intelligence may not provide a researcher or practitioner with the new information that might help predict positive life outcomes.

We believe that the proliferation of emotional intelligence models and the general appeal and popularity of this positive construct have led to a muddying of the waters. As a result, emotional intelligence now may be one of the most misunderstood and misrepresented constructs in psychology. For that reason, we return to the roots of emotional intelligence research and demonstrate how we learn to manage emotion-laden material for our benefit and the benefit of others.

In 1960, Mowrer addressed the prevailing thoughts about emotions undermining intelligence by suggesting that emotion was, in fact, "a high order of intelligence" (p. 308). Peter Salovey of Yale University and John Mayer of the University of New Hampshire (Mayer, DiPaolo, & Salovey, 1990; Salovey & Mayer, 1990) shared Mowrer's sentiment and theorized that adapting to life circumstances required cognitive abilities and emotional skills that guide our behavior. In their original 1990 papers, Salovey and Mayer constructed a theoretical framework for an emotional intelligence. The framework comprised three core components: appraisal and expression, regulation, and utilization. These fledging ideas about a set of emotional abilities that might provide people with a reservoir of intellectual resources was well received by the general public and psychology scholars.

Peter Salovey

Source: Photo credit: Michael Marsland, Office of Public Affairs, Yale University. Reprinted with permission.

The Salovey and Mayer four-branch ability model of **emotional intelligence** (see Table 8.2; Mayer, DiPaolo, & Salovey, 1990; Mayer & Salovey, 1997; Salovey & Mayer, 1990; Salovey et al., 2002) has been predicated on the belief that skills needed to reason about emotions and to use emotional material to assist reasoning can be learned. Branch 1 of the model involves skills needed to perceive and express feelings. More specifically, perception of emotions requires picking up on subtle emotional cues that might be expressed in a person's face or voice. For example, when chatting with a friend about an emotionally charged political topic, a person skilled in perceiving emotions can determine what aspects of the discussion are safe or unsafe territory based on the friend's nonverbal behavior. These skills in perceiving can be considered a threshold competency that needs to be acquired so that the other three emotional intelligence competencies can be developed.

Branch 2 of this ability model concerns using emotions and emotional understanding to facilitate thinking. Simply stated, people who are

Table 8.2   Salovey and Mayer's Four-Branch Ability Model of Emotional Intelligence

---

Branch 1: Perceiving Emotions

    Ability to identify emotion in a person's physical and psychological states

    Ability to identify emotions in other people

    Ability to express emotions accurately and to express needs related to them

    Ability to discriminate between authentic and inauthentic emotions

Branch 2: Using Emotions to Facilitate Thought

    Ability to redirect and prioritize thinking on the basis of associated feelings

    Ability to generate emotions to facilitate judgment and memory

    Ability to capitalize on mood changes to appreciate multiple points of view

    Ability to use emotional states to facilitate problem solving and creativity

Branch 3: Understanding Emotions

    Ability to understand relationships among various emotions

    Ability to perceive the causes and consequences of emotions

    Ability to understand complex feelings, emotional blends, and contradictory states

    Ability to understand transitions among emotions

Branch 4: Managing Emotions

    Ability to be open to feelings, both pleasant and unpleasant

    Ability to monitor and reflect on emotions

    Ability to engage, prolong, or detach from an emotional state

    Ability to manage emotions in oneself and others

Source: From Salovey, P., & Mayer, J. D., Emotional intelligence, in *Imagination, Cognition, & Personality,* 9(3), pp. 185–211. Copyright © 1990. Reprinted with permission of Baywood Publishing Company.

emotionally intelligent harness emotions and work with them to improve problem solving and to boost creativity. Physiological feedback from emotional experience is used to prioritize the demands on our cognitive systems and to direct attention to what is most important (Easterbrook, 1959; Mandler, 1975). In this regard, imagine that a person has to make an important decision about a relationship. Should she invest more energy in a friendship that has been on the rocks, or should she cut her losses and end the friendship in a civil manner? How she feels physically and emotionally when she thinks about continuing or ending the friendship can provide some clues about how to proceed. This emotional information thus turns attention to alternatives about how to handle the friendship. Also, the more the emotions are used in efforts to make good decisions, the greater the increase in emotional intelligence.

Branch 3 of emotional intelligence highlights the skills needed to foster an understanding of complex emotions, relationships among emotions, and relationships between emotions and behavioral consequences. Someone displaying a heightened level of emotional understanding would know that hope is an antidote to fear (see Chapter 9) and that sadness or apathy are more appropriate responses to lost love than hating is. People with these skills understand that emotions such as jealousy and envy are destructive in their own right (due to their physiological and psychological repercussions) and that they fuel maladaptive interpersonal behavior that probably results in a proliferation of negative emotions. Appreciating the dynamic relationships among emotions and behaviors gives an emotionally intelligent person the sense that they can better "read" a person or a situation and act appropriately, given environmental demands. For example, imagine the emotional struggle of a person who is placed in the awkward situation of being asked by a close friend to betray the confidence of a classmate or work colleague. He might feel disappointment or disgust that the friend asked him to behave in an inappropriate manner. If he were tempted to break the trust, he might experience a wave of shame. Understanding these complex emotions then might help him choose the right course of action at that time.

The more we practice skills that are associated with Branches 1 through 3, the more emotional content there is to manage. Managing emotions, Branch 4, involves numerous mood regulation skills. These skills are difficult to master because regulation is a balancing act. With too much regulation, a person may become emotionally repressed. With too little, one's emotional life becomes overwhelming. People who become very good at regulating their moods also are able to share these skills with others. Often the best parents, teachers, coaches, leaders, bosses, or role models can manage their emotions and at that same time instill confidence in others to be open to feelings and manage them appropriately.

Each of the four dimensions of the ability model is assessed with two sets of tasks in a measure called the Mayer-Salovey-Caruso Emotional Intelligence Test (MSCEIT; Mayer, Salovey, & Caruso, 2001). The tasks concerned with perceiving emotions ask respondents to identify the emotions expressed in photographs of faces as well as the feelings suggested by artistic designs and landscapes. For using emotions to facilitate thought, respondents are asked to describe feelings using nonfeeling words and to indicate the feelings that might facilitate or interfere with the successful performance of various tasks. The understanding emotions dimension is assessed with questions concerning the manner in which emotions evolve and how some feelings are produced by blends of emotions. To tap the ability of managing emotions, the MSCEIT presents a series of scenarios eliciting the most adaptive ways to regulate one's own feelings as well as feelings arising in social situations and in other people.

Practicing some or all of the 16 skills associated with the 4 branches of emotional intelligence is robustly associated with positive interpersonal functioning. For example, Lopes, Brackett, Nezlek, Schutz, Sellin, and Salovey (2004) examined the relationship between self-reported emotional intelligence (using the MSCEIT; Mayer at el., 2001) and social behavior. These researchers found those college students' ($n = 118$) abilities to manage emotions were positively associated with the quality of social interactions. Additional work with a small group ($n = 76$) of college students (Lopes, Salovey, Cote, Beers, & Petty, 2005) revealed that the strengths of emotional regulation skills were associated positively with interpersonal sensitivity (self-reports and peer nominations), with prosocial tendencies, and with the proportion of positive vs. negative peer nominations. These relationships remained meaningful after controlling for the Big Five personality traits as well as verbal and fluid intelligence. Likewise, in a sample of 103 college students, Lopes, Salovey, and Straus (2004) found that individuals with high-level skills in managing emotions were more likely to report positive relationships with other people, as well as perceived parental support, and less likely to report negative interactions with close friends. These associations remained statistically significant even when controlling for significant Big Five personality traits and verbal intelligence. Findings from these latter two studies (Lopes, Salovey, Cote, Beers, & Petty; Lopes, Salovey, & Straus) highlight the added value of emotional intelligence to understanding the nature of person-to-person interactions; that is, emotional intelligence tells us something about social functioning that personality traits and analytical intelligence do not explain.

As revealed in the previous section's review of research on emotion-focused coping, engaging more deeply in your emotional experiences (or perceiving, using, understanding, and managing emotions, to use the parlance of emotional intelligence researchers) has benefits. Additionally, for people who demonstrate emotional intelligence, positive social functioning may be realized. Given that these two lines of research (Stanton's work on emotional approach and Salovey and Mayer's examination of emotional intelligence) establish the potential of working with your emotions, our attention now turns to whether emotional skills can be learned. More than 300 program developers (Salovey et al., 2002) have been intrigued with the teachability of emotional intelligence. On this issue, anecdotal evidence suggests that children, youth, and adults can be taught to use emotional experiences to enrich their daily lives and can be equipped to deal with the good and bad events they encounter. Time and more empirical scrutiny, however, will tell whether intentional skill development actually produces gains in emotional intelligence.

Further research also is needed to determine the neurological substrates of emotional intelligence. There is some evidence that efficient operation of the amygdala and the ventromedial prefrontal cortex may be implicated in emotional intelligence (see Damasio, 1994), but the interplay between brain structures in people with high emotional intelligence has not been elaborated on.

Who Is Emotionally Intelligent—And Does It Matter?

JACK MAYER

A Description of the High EI Individual

Generally speaking, emotional intelligence improves an individual's social effectiveness. The higher the emotional intelligence, the better the social relations. In a recent review, my colleagues and I described the emotionally intelligent person in these terms:

> The high EI individual, most centrally, can better perceive emotions, use them in thought, understand their meanings, and manage emotions, than others. Solving emotional problems likely requires less cognitive effort for this individual. The person also tends to be somewhat higher in verbal, social, and other intelligences, particularly if the individual scored higher in the understanding emotions portion of EI. The individual tends to be more open and agreeable than others. The high EI person is drawn to occupations involving social interactions such as teaching and counseling more so than to occupations involving clerical or administrative tasks.

> The high EI individual, relative to others, is less apt to engage in problem behaviors and avoids self-destructive, negative behaviors such as smoking, excessive drinking, drug abuse, or violent episodes with others. The high EI person is more likely to have possessions of sentimental attachment around the home and to have more positive social interactions, particularly if the individual scored highly on emotional management. Such individuals may also be more adept at describing motivational goals, aims, and missions (Mayer, Salovey, & Caruso, 2004).

Note that the specific kind of boost that emotional intelligence gives the individual will be subtle, and as a consequence, require some effort to identify. It will not be exhibited in all social circumstances.

Nonetheless, EI Is Important

Some of us accomplish certain tasks with great ease and sophistication; others of us simply can't do those tasks. This is the case with most challenges we face in life. Some of us are great chess players, while others of us have trouble just figuring out how the pieces move. Some of us are fabulous conversationalists, while others of us have trouble just saying hello.

Now, the world could do without the game of chess, and the world could do without fabulous conversationalists, but it would be a poorer place for it.

Emotional intelligence is an intelligence having to do with discerning and understanding emotional information. Emotional information is all around us. Emotions communicate basic feeling states from one individual to another—to signal urgent messages such as "let's get together" or "I am hurting" or "I'm going to hurt you."

What ability tests of emotional intelligence tell us is that only some people can pick up and understand and appreciate the more subtle versions of those messages. That is, only the high EI individual understands the full richness and complexities of these communications.

Emotional information is crucial. It is one of the primary forms of information that human beings process. That doesn't mean that everybody has to process it well. But it does mean that it is circulating around us, and certain people who can pick up on it can perform certain tasks very well that others cannot perform.

We all need emotional intelligence to help us through our emotionally demanding days. Even if we are not emotionally intelligent ourselves, we may rely on those higher in emotional intelligence to guide us.

But guide us to what? What is it that people high in emotional intelligence can see that so many others are blind to? The key to this lies in what those high in emotional intelligence are particularly good at doing themselves.

They're particularly good at establishing positive social relationships with others and avoiding conflicts, fights, and other social altercations. They're particularly good at understanding psychologically healthy living and avoiding such problems as drugs and drug abuse. It seems likely that such individuals, by providing coaching advice to others and by directly involving themselves in certain situations, assist other individuals and groups of people to live together with greater harmony and satisfaction.

So, perhaps even more important than scoring high on an emotional intelligence test is knowing one's level at this group of skills. Discovering one's level means that you can know whether and how much to be self-reliant in emotional areas, and when to seek others' help in reading the emotional information that is going on around oneself. Whether one is high or low in emotional intelligence is perhaps not as important as knowing that emotional information exists and that some people can understand it. Knowing just that, one can use emotional information by finding those who are able to understand it and reason with it.

This is the information age. All of us are dependent on information and using it wisely. The advent of the ability model of emotional intelligence enriches our knowledge of the information surrounding us—it tells us emotional information is there and that some people can see it and use it. The model encourages all of us to use emotional information wisely—whether through our own direct understanding, or through the assistance of those who do understand.

Source: Mayer, J. (2005). *Who is emotionally intelligent—And does it matter?* Retrieved September 5, 2005, from http://www.unh.edu/emotional_intelligence/. Reprinted with permission of Jack Mayer.

THE CASE OF MARIA

Maria is a gifted elementary school teacher who loves her job. Several years ago, I (SJL) had the privilege of observing her classroom teaching while I was working on a positive psychology project in her school. The first day I saw her work with students, I developed a hypothesis about effective teaching that has stuck with me: Good educators (at all levels) are emotionally intelligent teachers of knowledge and skills. That is, I believe that, irrespective of the focus of the course (e.g., math, chemistry, Spanish, literature, psychology), good teachers make sense of the emotional content in the room, and they make minor adjustments in their teaching approaches so that they can effectively share their knowledge with the group.

During my first visit to Maria's classroom, I was struck by how she could "read" a room. She seemed to know what each student needed at any given moment, and she seemed to have a sense of the general emotional tenor of the room. For example, before the "daily check-in" (her name for a quiz), Maria responded to the anxiety in the room with soothing comments and a quick relaxation exercise. Her ability to *perceive the emotions* of her students and respond to them in a strategic manner was demonstrated time and time again during my 5 hours of observation.

Based on my interactions with Maria, it seemed as though she also had a keen sense of her own emotional experience. She described herself as intuitive, and that seemed to fit . . . but there was more to it than that. Although she did seem instinctively to know what she and her students were feeling, she also was adept at *using emotions to spark her creativity* in the classroom. She could scrap her lesson plan and create an engaging activity on the spot if the students were getting bored or restless. And she had great timing when she made these major shifts in her plan; the students were not aware that she went off the page to grab more attention.

Perhaps my view of Maria's high emotional intelligence was cemented the day I saw her settle a dispute among five students on the playground. Children were frustrated and tearful, and Maria seemed to *understand their emotions* and their fast-paced exchanges of accusations and explanations. Slowly, she calmed down the situation and helped each student save face . . . and then, all of a sudden, one of the students yelled, "You're not fair! I hate you!" At that moment, she encouraged the other children to return to the game, and she knelt down to talk to the infuriated student eye to eye. With time, his posture and grimace seemed to soften, and then he nodded his head and ran back to his friends. It was clear that her ability to *manage her own emotions* helped this boy manage his.

Maria shared her emotional intelligence with her students every day by modeling adaptive behavior. I believe that some of her students learned how to make the most of their emotions by watching her.

Socioemotional Selectivity: Focusing in Later Life on Positive Emotions and Emotion-Related Goals

The extent to which we are able to make the most of our emotional experiences is determined in part by personal and environmental demands such as our health status, social surroundings, and cultural norms. It now is becoming clear that humans' unique ability to monitor time across their entire span of life also may determine how much energy is dedicated to emotional goals. (See Chapter 9 for a related discussion on the influence of time perspective.) Indeed, in Stanford psychologist Laura Carstensen's (1998; Carstensen & Charles, 1998) **socioemotional selectivity theory,** she posits that youth may be overrated and that our later years (the "golden years") may be valuable as we focus less on negative emotions, engage more deeply with the emotional content of our days, and savor the "good stuff" in life (e.g., establishing and enhancing relationships). Carstensen reasons that we are able to appreciate these benefits in our advanced years because we come to realize that we have a short amount of time left.

Laura Carstensen

Source: Reprinted with permission of Laura Carstensen.

In her laboratory, Carstensen has demonstrated that young people and their older counterparts manage emotion-laden material quite differently. In tests of attention to novel stimuli, for example, the younger participants have attended to negative images more quickly, whereas the older participants oriented faster to images laden with positive emotions (smiling face, happy baby, puppy) (Charles, Mather, & Carstensen, 2003). Regarding recall of emotional events, Charles et al. found that young people (college age and a bit older) remembered the positive and negative material to the same degree, but the older person had a positivity bias in which they recalled the positive material more quickly than the negative material. These studies suggest that process of interacting with emotions is different for young adults and older adults.

Irrespective of our tendencies to attend and remember certain types of events, life provides all of us with blessings and burdens. Related to this point, Carstensen and her colleagues have found that there are age cohort effects for how we handle positive and negative daily life experiences. After monitoring the moods of 184 people (age 18 and up) for a week, Carstensen, Pasupathi, Mayr, and Nesselroade (2000) discovered that their older research participants not only did not "sweat the small stuff" (which is how they viewed negative events), but they also savored the positive events (experienced the good residuals of positive events for longer periods than their younger counterparts did). Given these findings, it appears that positive experiences and positive emotions become our priority as we age and consider our mortality.

Finally, contrary to young people's fascination with future-oriented goals pertaining to acquiring information and expanding horizons, older people seem to orient to here-and-now goals that foster emotional meaning (Kennedy, Fung, & Carstensen, 2001). Recall of positive experience, savoring the good times, and setting and investing in emotion-focused goals systematically influence social preferences, emotion regulation, and cognitive processing. Overall, therefore, the aging process appears to be linked to the striving for a deeper emotional life.

Emotional Storytelling: The Pennebaker Paradigm as a Means of Processing Intense Negative Emotions

Every now and again, we experience life events that shake us to our core. Traumatic events that cause emotional upheaval may outstrip the resources of good emotion-focused copers, the emotionally intelligent, and the young and old alike. It is quite likely (with a 95% probability) that, when we experience an overwhelming emotional event, we will share the experience with a friend or family member within the same day of its occurrence, typically in the first few hours (Rime, 1995). It is almost as if we were compelled to tell the story of our emotional suffering. Is it possible that we have learned that not talking about our intense emotions has dire consequences? This question and many related research hypotheses have served as the impetus for the work of University of Texas psychologist Jamie Pennebaker. In 1989, Dr. Pennebaker broke ground on this research area by making the following request of undergraduate research participants in an experimental group of a study:

> For the next four days, I would like . . . you to write about your deepest thoughts and feelings about your most traumatic experience in your life. In your writing, I'd like you to really let go and explore your very deepest emotions and thoughts. You might tie your topic to your relationships, including parents, lovers, friends, or relatives. You may also want to link your experience to your past, your present, or your future, or to who you have been, who you would like to be, or who you are now. You may write about the same general issues or experiences on all days of writing, or on different traumas each day. All of your writing will be completely confidential. (p. 215)

The control group participants were asked to write for 15 minutes a day for 4 days, but about a nonemotional topic (e.g., the description of the room they were seated in). All participants were asked to write continuously, without regard to spelling, grammar, and sentence structure. The immediate effects of the two interventions were such that the experimental group was more distressed. Then, over time (beginning 2 weeks after the study), the members of the emotional storytelling group experienced numerous health benefits, including fewer physician visits over the next year, than did the members of the control group.

Emotional Storytelling After a Traumatic Event

In January 2000, the author of this account experienced overwhelming fear and guilt while scuba diving. Upon her return from the outing, she was visibly shaken. After hours of one-to-one conversation, she was encouraged to write for 15 minutes about her intense thoughts and feelings associated with the experience in a free-flowing manner with no regard for punctuation, grammar, or sentence structure.

"My 4th dive ever. My 2nd dive in a year. Steve talked me into going on a night dive. I was nervous about it, esp. since my dive 2 days ago had a scary hyperventilating incident. I like Steve and I didn't want to seem a wimp so I said 'sure,' even though compounding my uneasiness was my discomfort over diving without my husband. I don't like to do anything w/o him if it is at all risky. If something happens to me, I want him there to see it, even if he can't stop it. His very presence gives me a lot of my nerve.

"Over the back of the boat holding my regulator and mask. My fat strap slips over my head and the mask fills with water. It's more in my hand than on my head. I swallow sea water. I get the mask back on but was hyperventilating. The dive master seems far away but some guy name Walker came over to help me. He told me to fill my BCD and he held me as I lay on my back. He tried to distract me with small talk to calm me down. The dive master asked if I wanted back in the boat. I said no. So we tried to descend. More hyperventilating. This time I know it wouldn't stop. My body was in alarm mode and I would not be able to descend. The whole group resurfaced and I was back at the surface. Luckily was I was only under about 10 feet.

"The dive master said 'What's wrong with her?' and I said I want back in the boat. They said the boat is over there. The dive master seemed to want me to swim to the boat that seemed far away while the group descended. The group refused to leave me at the surface so far from the boat. After the boat finally got close enough, I swam to it and Walker came to help me again. Once I was in the boat, everyone else started to get in, too. At first I thought someone else had panicked but soon realized the dive master had aborted the dive. I felt guilty and embarrassed that the other 6 people couldn't dive because of me. Guy and Steve tried to reassure me that it was okay and Walker said I had made the right decision and the last person he would blame is me. I was pretty quiet on the way back to La Sirena. Steve drove and chatted with Guy. I tried to participate but all I could think about was getting back to my husband and our room. My limbic system was still going off for a while after that. No more dives this trip."

Understandably, the diver experienced distress for several days, but the inferred long-term effects of the emotional storytelling were quite positive. The diver talks about this event on occasion and experiences little stress when doing so. She enjoys snorkeling to this day but has not had the opportunity to dive again.

Source: Reprinted with permission of Allison Rose Lopez.

This research procedure, involving the mere act of written disclosure of emotional upheaval, what we generally call **emotional storytelling**, is now referred to as the **Pennebaker paradigm** (systematic written disclosure across brief sessions). This technique has been used to address the emotions associated with job loss (discussed in Chapter 17), diagnosis of illness, and relationship breakup (reviewed in Pennebaker, 1997). The positive long-term effects of emotional storytelling are fairly robust, yet it does appear that people with hostility (which typically suggests personal difficulty managing emotions) have greater positive immune response than people with low hostility (Christensen & Smith, 1998), and participants high in the trait of alexithymia (difficulty identifying and making sense of emotions) experienced more salutary effects than those low in the trait (Paez, Velasco, & Gonzales, 1999). We reference these findings in particular because they may suggest that people who typically do not have the tendency (or skills) to work with the emotionally-laden content of life may benefit the most from this means of processing intense negative emotions.

The theoretical explanations for the benefits of emotional storytelling in response to traumatic events continue to be refined. It does appear that disinhibition (letting go of emotion-related stress), cognitive processing, and social dynamics (when disclosure occurs outside the laboratory) are at work (Niederhoffer & Pennebaker, 2002) when someone experiencing emotional upheaval shares his or her story. Plainly stated, "Putting upsetting experiences into words allows people to stop inhibiting their thoughts and feelings, to begin to organize their thoughts and perhaps find meaning in their traumas, and to reintegrate their social networks" (Niederhoffer & Pennebaker, p. 581). We believe these explanations for the potency of emotional storytelling can be summed up as *strategically working with emotions within a social context.*

Working With Emotions to Bring About Positive Change

Practicing psychologists have long discussed the role of emotions in the psychological change process. During our training as psychologists, we were encouraged to identify clients' emotions and reflect the emotional content of clients' stories through empathic statements we shared aloud. Emotions were considered the indicators of quality of functioning; they helped us track how well a client was doing. Now, given the research discussed in this chapter, we train our graduate students to view emotions as determinants of positive change, not just markers of growth. Indeed, how well we and our clients handle emotional events sets, in part, the outer limits of personal well-being.

Now, with what we have learned in our roles as teachers and clinicians in mind, we share ideas that will reveal the potential benefits of strategically working with your emotions. First, we want you to approach the Personal Mini-Experiments as a psychologist gathering data about the phenomena discussed in this chapter. Be as objective as possible when you conduct each experiment, and determine whether your personal results line up with the research findings in this text. Then, make some attempts to hone your personal skills for dealing with the emotional-laden information you encounter every day, by implementing the Life Enhancement Strategies.

Personal Mini-Experiments

Making the Most of Emotions in Everyday Life

In this chapter, we discuss the "how-tos" and benefits of engaging our emotions. Our review suggests that engaging our emotional selves leads to better and deeper living. Here are a few ideas (and don't forget about the Pennebaker writing exercise described on page 162) for experimenting with making the most of emotions in your everyday life.

The Emotions Daily Journal: Based on your physiological reactions or the duration of the emotional experience, carefully identify the intense emotions (see Chapter 7 for listings of positive and negative feelings) that you feel every 4 waking hours for 2 days. Note these feelings in your paper or electronic calendar. At the end of each 4-hour segment, spend 5 minutes reflecting on these experiences to determine if you tend to *approach* or *avoid* provocative emotions. (Use the listing of emotional processing and expression items in Table 8.1 to track reactions. If necessary, create a 5-point Likert-type rating system to gauge your responses.) After 2 day's time, identify the benefits and pitfalls of moving toward and moving away from emotion-laden information.

"Acting As If" You Were Emotionally Intelligent for a Day: Think about the people in your life who manage their emotions very well. Make a list of these people, and informally rank them from good to best in terms of their emotional intelligence. Then, pick a day of the week when you are sure to have a great deal of social inter-action. Spend the day emulating one of your emotionally intelligent role models, and act as if you were highly skilled in working with your emotions. When faced with problems or opportunities to excel, ask yourself, "What would my EI role model do in this situation?" and then do it! At the end of the day, identify the top three emo-tional skills you acted as if you had (see Table 8.2 on page 155 for the list of the 16 skills of emotional intelligence). In the days that follow, use the three skills again and again until you feel like you have mastered them.

The Buoyant Grandparent Visit: Have you ever asked your grandmother or grandfa-ther (or another family elder) how she or he stays optimistic, happy, and loving despite all the life challenges that she or he has endured? Identify your most resilient or most buoyant family elder, and ask this person, "What's important to you these days? What goals have you set for yourself for the next few years? How do your friends figure into your daily life?" Emotional goals and plans for spending time with family and friends are sure to be mentioned.

Life Enhancement Strategies

We encourage you to develop new emotional skills that you can apply in the important domains of your life.

Love

- Practice using more "feeling words" when interacting with friends and family. Adding this to your daily communication will encourage more emotional approach.
- Set new goals for important relationships that might promote your emotional growth and that of the other person. This might enhance the quality of the relationship over time.

Work

- Acknowledge the emotional undercurrents of communication at work. Share these observations in a nonconfrontational way with your coworkers and bosses, and facilitate a dialogue about the roles of emotions in the workplace.
- Seek "emotional intelligence at work" seminars. Many human resources offices or local consulting services offer this type of seminar, and anecdotal evidence suggests that participants feel more efficacious in their use of emotional intelligence skills once they complete such training.

Play

- Become an emotional storyteller. Write down the stories of your good times and bad in a journal or share them with trusted friends. Storytelling may distance you from negative experiences in your life and bring you closer to people who are important to you.
- Learn and practice meditation skills. These skills are believed to "suspend time" and help us engage our emotional experiences more deeply.

An Emotional Balancing Act

Dealing with the emotional aspects of life certainly is a balancing act (Salovey et al., 2002). Sometimes, intense emotional experiences that tax our psychological resources might result in avoidant responses . . . and this is probably adaptive. Dealing with negative emotions in a manner that results in rumination (obsessive thinking), however, may be quite maladaptive. Balancing approach and avoidance tendencies may result in the best functioning.

Some people are well versed in managing negative emotions but can't identify any intense positive emotions. Other people may ignore the important protective messages conveyed by negative emotions while remaining very open to "good" feelings. These unbalanced attempts at processing feelings may result in lots of missing data, which may lead to poor decision making. Making the most of emotional experiences via emotion-focused coping, emotional intelligence, emotional goal setting, and emotional storytelling can help to create a balanced means of dealing with the information gained from all emotional experiences.

Certainly, there are many productive and unproductive ways to deal with the emotion-laden information we process each day. It is important to learn how to work with emotions by diversifying your repertoire of coping skills and then determining what is effective and leads to desired life outcomes.

Key Terms

Emotional approach: Active movement toward, rather than away from, a stressful or emotional encounter.

Emotional avoidance: Active movement away from, rather than toward, a stressful or emotional encounter.

Emotional expression: Free and intentional display of feeling.

Emotional intelligence: According to Salovey and Mayer's four-branch ability model, the skills (1) to perceive and express feelings; (2) to use emotions and emotional understanding to facilitate thinking; (3) to understand complex emotions, relationships among emotions, and relationships between emotions and behavioral consequences; and (4) to manage emotions.

Emotional processing: The attempt to understand one's emotions.

Emotional storytelling: Written disclosure of emotional upheaval.

Pennebaker paradigm: Systematic written disclosure of emotional upheaval often involving several timed sessions.

Socioemotional selectivity theory: Carstensen's theory that, as compared to younger adults, older adults are more able to focus less on negative emotions, to engage more deeply with emotional content, and to savor the positive in life.

Part IV

Positive Cognitive States and Processes

Seeing Our Futures Through Self-Efficacy, Optimism, and Hope　9

Fascination With the Future

In the privacy of their personal thoughts, people can imagine wonderful visions of their tomorrows. Indeed, the future is fascinating precisely because it holds seductive and positive possibilities. Unlike the past and present, therefore, the future offers the chance to change things—to make them different *and better.*

People want to feel as if they can "make things happen" to their satisfaction. This starts from the earliest baby and toddler days. As the weeks and years roll by, however, individuals are left with more and more past events that cannot be changed, and their present lives unfold so quickly that it seems as if they have little chance to make any real changes. On the other hand, the future remains a place where peoples' fantasies and desires can produce the proverbial happy endings.

Their caregivers taught many Americans that the "real action" in life lies ahead. For those who lived in less-than-ideal circumstances, the American dream was that their children would have better lives. So, the children in such environments were taught to look ahead and to focus on what they could accomplish in the "land of opportunity." In the process of looking ahead, therefore, people run the risk of making their lives extremely busy. As a caveat to the general benefits of the future orientations we describe in this chapter, we encourage the reader to consider the thoughts of columnist Ellen Goodman in her essay, "Being Busy Not an End in Itself." Goodman makes a good case for occasionally taking time out from our busy, future-oriented thinking.

Being Busy Not an End in Itself

ELLEN GOODMAN

BOSTON—A friend of mine once worked for a Hollywood executive as chief assistant in charge of the calendar. That wasn't the actual title, of course, but it was the job description.

This executive had a penchant for filling up her Palm Pilot weeks and months in advance. When the day would come, a day invariably brimming over with "unexpected emergencies," she would order another round of cancellations. And begin to fill in the future.

My friend came to think of this as a binge and purge cycle. Out of earshot, she described her boss as a time-bulimic.

I always remember this, because I wonder how many people suffer from timing disorders. How many make commitments *now* with the absolute and inaccurate certainty that we will have more time *then*. Do we look into the mirror and see an image as distorted as the anorexic who looks into the mirror?

This year, a pair of marketing professors from North Carolina published research about time and timing. The students surveyed said repeatedly they would have more free time on the same day of the next week or the next month than they had today. If you asked these students to add a commitment today, they would answer no. But ask them to do it in the future, and they were more likely to say yes.

These students were not just a bunch of cockeyed optimists. The same people had a much more realistic view of their budgets. They were less likely to commit to spending more money in the future than in the present.

But in this sense, time was not money. It was more malleable. When thinking about their spare time, they experienced what the researchers called "irrational exuberance." Even those on overload today would take on a fresh load in the future.

Americans talk a great deal about time-crunch. We ask each other, "How are you?" And we answer: "Busy." We export our "productivity," which has become the international gold standard of workaholism. We think of time as something that's been eaten away, not given away.

In just my own adulthood, Americans have lost Sundays to shopping and lost focus to multitasking. We spend lifetimes on hold.

In this world, the hero of the month must surely be Joseph Williams, the Baltimore lawyer who sued Sears, Roebuck when a no-show repairman left him waiting for four hours. He won a single dollar and a shiny principle: You can't waste my time.

But how many of us are also victims of our own timing disorder, keepers of irrational exuberance? Do we also fill in the future out of an irrational anxiety about "free" time?

"It's difficult to learn that time will not be more abundant in the future," wrote the researchers. Well, it is one thing for students to be fooled repeatedly. But it is quite another for those of us who are older. Time is, to put it quietly, *less* abundant. The refusal to learn a lesson comes with a higher price tag.

I wonder if other cultures suffer from our timing disorder, our "irrational exuberance." Busyness, we believe, is part of our creed. It was that founding father, Thomas Jefferson, who admonished us, "Determine never to be idle. No person will have occasion to complain of the want of time who never loses any. It is wonderful how much can be done if we are always doing."

But these days, I smile more at the words of that cranky radical, Henry David Thoreau, who replied, "It is not enough to be busy, so are the ants. The question is what are we busy about."

Source: Lawrence Journal-World, April 7, 2005. Copyright © 2005, The Washington Post Writers Group. Reprinted with permission.

Note: Ellen Goodman (ellengoodman@globe.com) is a columnist for the Washington Post Writers Group.

In the present chapter, we first examine three major, future-oriented temporal perspectives in positive psychology—self-efficacy, optimism, and hope. We explore the theories that guide these concepts, along with the scales that measure each and the associated research findings. Next, we discuss the potential balance among temporal orientations aimed at past, present, and future. Finally, we provide cautionary comments about how these future-oriented concepts may not apply to samples other than the Caucasian Americans who were the participants in the reported research.

Self-Efficacy

I THINK I CAN, I THINK I CAN . . .

After Stanford University psychologist Albert Bandura published his 1977 *Psychological Review* article titled "Self-Efficacy: Toward a Unifying Theory of Behavior Change," the self-efficacy concept spread in popularity to the point that it now may have produced more empirical research than any other topic in positive psychology (Bandura, 1977, 1982, 1997). What exactly is this concept that has proven so influential? To understand self-efficacy, some people have used the sentiments of the little train engine (from Watty Piper's [1930/1989] children's story, *The Little Engine That Could*) to epitomize self-efficacy. Recall that the tiny engine, thinking about how the little boys and girls on the other side of the mountain would not have their toys unless she helped, uttered the now-famous

Albert Bandura

Source: Reprinted with permission of Albert Bandura.

motivational words, "I think I can. I think I can. I think I can"—and then proceeded to chug successfully up the mountain side to deliver her payload. This belief that you can accomplish what you want is at the core of the self-efficacy idea.

The self-efficacy construct rests upon a long line of historical thinking related to the sense of personal control. Famous thinkers such as John Locke, David Hume, William James, and Gilbert Ryle have focused on willfulness, or volition, in human thinking (Vessey, 1967). More recently, similar ideas have appeared in theories on achievement motivation (McClelland, Atkinson, Clark, & Lowell, 1953), effectance motivation (White, 1959), and social learning (Rotter, 1966). (For a review of personal competence, coping, and satisfaction, see Skinner, 1995). It was this classic line of control-related scholarship upon which Bandura drew in defining the self-efficacy concept.

A DEFINITION

Bandura (1997, p. vii) defined **self-efficacy** as "peoples' beliefs in their capabilities to produce desired effects by their own actions." Similarly, Maddux (2002, p. 278) has described self-efficacy as "what I believe I can do with my skills under certain conditions." Based on an examination of what needs to be done in order to reach a desired goal (these are called *outcome expectancies*), the person supposedly then analyzes his or her capability to complete the necessary actions (these are called *efficacy expectancies*). For Bandura, outcome expectancies are viewed as far less important than efficacy expectancies; consistent with his perspective, studies have shown that outcome expectancies do not add much to efficacy expectancies when predicting various human actions (Maddux, 1991). Thus, situation-specific self-efficacy thoughts are proposed to be the last and most crucial cognitive step before people launch goal-directed actions.

CHILDHOOD ANTECEDENTS: WHERE DOES SELF-EFFICACY COME FROM?

Self-efficacy is a learned human pattern of thinking rather than a genetically endowed one. It begins in infancy and continues throughout the life span. Self-efficacy is based on the premises of **social cognitive theory**, which holds that humans actively shape their lives rather than passively reacting to environmental forces (Bandura, 1986; Barone, Maddux, & Snyder, 1997).

Social cognitive theory, in turn, is built on three ideas. First, humans have powerful symbolizing capacities for cognitively creating models of their experiences. Second, by observing themselves in relation to these cognitive models, people then become skilled at self-regulating their actions as they navigate ongoing environmental events. Thus, cognitive reactions influence the surrounding environmental forces that, in turn, shape subsequent thoughts and actions (i.e., there is a back-and-forth interchange of environmental and thinking forces). Third, people (i.e., their selves) and their personalities are a result of these situation-specific reciprocal interactions of thoughts → environment → thoughts. Given these social cognitive ideas, therefore, a developing child uses symbolic thinking, with specific reference to the understanding of cause-and-effect relationships, and learns self-efficacious, self-referential thinking by observing how she or he can influence the surrounding circumstances (Maddux, 2002).

Bandura (1989a, 1989b, 1977, 1997) proposed that the developmental antecedents of self-efficacy include

1. Previous successes in similar situations (calling on the wellspring of positive thoughts about how well one has done in earlier circumstances)

2. Modeling on others in the same situations (watching other people who have succeeded in a given arena and copying their actions)

3. Imagining oneself behaving effectively (visualizing acting effectively to secure a wanted goal)

4. Undergoing verbal persuasion by powerful, trustworthy, expert, and attractive other people (being influenced by a helper's words to behave in a given manner)

5. Arousal and emotion (when physiologically aroused and experiencing negative emotions, our self-efficacy may be undermined, whereas such arousal paired with positive emotions heightens the sense of self-efficacy)

THE NEUROBIOLOGY OF SELF-EFFICACY

It is likely that the frontal and prefrontal lobes of the human brain evolved to facilitate the prioritization of goals and the planful thinking that are crucial for self-efficacy (as well as hope, discussed later in this chapter) (see Newberg, d'Aquili, Newberg, & deMarici, 2000; Stuss & Benson, 1984). When faced with goal-directed tasks, especially the problem solving that is inherent in much of self-efficacy thinking, the right hemisphere of the brain reacts to the dilemmas as relayed by the linguistic and abstract left hemisphere processes (Newberg et al., 2000).

Experiments, most of which have been conducted on animals, also reveal that self-efficacy or perceived control can be traced to underlying biological variables that facilitate coping (Bandura, 1997). Self-efficacy yields a sense of control that leads to the production of neuroendocrines and catecholamines (neurotransmitters that govern automatic activities related to stress) (Bandura, 1991; Maier, Laudenslager, & Ryan, 1985). These later catecholamines have been found to mirror the level of felt self-efficacy (Bandura, Taylor, Williams, Mefford, & Barchas, 1985). So, too, does a sense of realistic self-efficacy lessen cardiac reactivity and lower blood pressure—thereby facilitating coping.

SCALES: CAN SELF-EFFICACY BE MEASURED?

Bandura (1977, 1982, 1997) has held staunchly to the **situational perspective** that self-efficacy should reflect beliefs about using abilities and skills to reach given goals *in specific circumstances or domains*. In his words, "Efficacy beliefs should be measured in terms of particularized judgments of capacity that may vary across realms of activity, under different levels of task demands within a given domain, and under different situational circumstances" (Bandura, 1997, p. 42). Consistent with Bandura's emphasis upon situations, Betz and colleagues have developed and validated a 25-item measure that taps confidence in making career decisions (Betz, Klein, & Taylor, 1996; Betz & Taylor, 2000). Scores on this scale predict confidence in examining various careers (Blustein, 1989) and actual career indecision (Betz & Klein Voyten, 1997). Likewise, there are other situation-specific self-efficacy indices, including the Occupational Questionnaire (Teresa, 1991) for tapping students' mastery of various vocations, and the Career Counseling Self-Efficacy Scale (O'Brien, Heppner, Flores, & Bikos, 1997) for measuring counselors' confidence in deriving interventions for persons who are having difficulties with their career decisions. (See also Schwarzer and Renner [2000] for situation-specific "coping self-efficacy.")

Although Bandura consistently has argued against the **trait perspective** (in which psychological phenomena are viewed as enduring over time and circumstances), other researchers have developed such dispositional measures of self-efficacy (e.g., Sherer et al., 1982; see also Tipton & Worthington, 1984). Citing evidence that self-efficacy experiences involving personal mastery can generalize to actions that transcend any given target behavior (e.g., Bandura, Adams, & Beyer, 1977), as well as the fact that some people are especially likely to have high self-efficacy expectations across several situations, Sherer et al. (1982) developed and validated a trait-like index called the Self-Efficacy Scale.

The Self-Efficacy Scale consists of 23 items to which respondents rate their agreement on a 14-point Likert scale (1 = Strongly disagree to 14 = Strongly agree). Examples of some items include the following: "When I make plans, I am certain I can make them work," "If I can't do a job the first time, I keep trying till I can," and "When I have something unpleasant to do, I stick to it until I finish it."

Factor analyses have revealed one factor reflecting "general self-efficacy" and a second one tapping "social self-efficacy." The internal consistency of the scale (i.e., the degree to which individual items aggregate together) has ranged from alphas of .71 to .86. Lastly, the concurrent validity of the Self-Efficacy Scale has been supported by its positive correlations with scores on measures of personal control, ego strength, interpersonal competency, and self-esteem (Chen, Gully, & Eden, 2001; Sherer et al., 1982).

More recently, Chen et al. (2001) have developed an 8-item New General Self-Efficacy Scale, and its scores appear to relate positively to those on the Self-Efficacy Scale of Sherer et al. (although there are exceptions). This New General Self-Efficacy Scale may provide yet another valid self-report index for tapping cross-situational self-efficacy.

Contrary to the cross-situational perspective of the Self-Efficacy Scale, Bandura suggests that any measurement of the individual's sense of personal efficacy should be carefully tied to a given performance situation (see Bandura, 1995, 1997 for expositions of how to do this). Although the cross-situational efficacy scales produce significant correlations with other measures, it is when using such situation-specific measures that higher self-efficacy robustly and consistently has predicted (1) lower anxiety, (2) higher pain tolerance, (3) better academic performance, (4) more political participation, (5) effective dental practices, (6) continuation in smoking cessation treatment, and (7) adoption of exercise and diet regimes (Bandura, 1997).

SELF-EFFICACY'S INFLUENCE IN LIFE ARENAS

Self-efficacy has produced huge bodies of research both inside and outside of psychology. In this section, we explore some of this research. For the reader interested in deeper explorations of self-efficacy research findings, we recommend Albert Bandura's volume, *Self-Efficacy: The Exercise of Control* (1997), along with the James Maddux edited volume, *Self-Efficacy, Adaptation, and Adjustment* (1995).

Psychological Adjustment

Self-efficacy has been implicated in successful coping with a variety of psychological problems (Maddux, 1995). Lower self-efficacies have been linked with depression (Bandura, 1977) as well as avoidance and anxiety (Williams, 1995). Likewise, higher self-efficacy is helpful in overcoming eating disorders and abuse (DiClemente, Fairhurst, & Piotrowski, 1995). Bandura was one of the first to take a positive, strengths-based approach when he posed that self-efficacy can play a protective role in dealing with psychological problems and, further, emphasized *enablement factors* that help people, "to select and structure their environments in ways that set a successful course" (Bandura, 1997, p. 177). This latter view regarding enablement factors taps the positive psychology emphasis on enhancing strengths instead of lessening weaknesses.

Physical Health

Maddux (2002) has suggested that self-efficacy can influence positive physical health in two ways. First, elevated self-efficacy increases health-related behaviors and decreases unhealthy ones; moreover, self-efficacy helps to maintain these changes (Maddux, Brawley, & Boykin, 1995). In this regard, theories pertaining to health behaviors all showcase self-efficacy (e.g., the protection motivation theory [Rogers & Prentice-Dunn, 1997], the reasoned action behavior theory [Ajzen, 1988], and the health belief model [Strecher, Champion, & Rosenstock, 1997]).

Second, self-efficacy has an impact on various biological processes that relate to better physical health. Included in such adaptive biological processes are immune functioning (O'Leary & Brown, 1995), susceptibility to infections, the neurotransmitters that are implicated in stress management (i.e., catecholamines), and the endorphins for muting pain (Bandura, 1997).

Psychotherapy

Just as Jerome Frank (see Frank & Frank, 1991) made the case that hope is a common factor in successful psychotherapy, so too has it been reasoned that self-efficacy is a common factor across various psychological interventions (Bandura, 1986; Maddux & Lewis, 1995). As such, self-efficacy enhancement in the context of psychotherapy not only bolsters efficacious thinking for specific circumstances but also shows how to apply such thinking across situations that the client may encounter (Maddux, 2002).

Psychotherapy may use one or more of the following five strategies discussed previously for enhancing self-efficacy:

1. Building successes, often through the use of goal setting and the incremental meeting of those goals (Hollon & Beck, 1994)

2. Using models to teach the person to overcome difficulties (e.g., Bandura, 1986)

3. Allowing the person to imagine himself or herself behaving effectively (Kazdin, 1979)

4. Using verbal persuasion by a trustworthy psychotherapist (Ingram, Kendall, & Chen, 1991)

5. Teaching techniques for lowering arousal (e.g., meditation, mindfulness, biofeedback, hypnosis, relaxation, etc.) to increase the likelihood of more adaptive, self-efficacious thinking

(The reader can refer to the discussion of self-efficacy-based interventions in Chapter 15, which details various positive psychology change techniques.)

THE LATEST FRONTIER: COLLECTIVE SELF-EFFICACY

Although the great majority of work on the self-efficacy concept has centered on individuals reacting to given circumstances, self-efficacy also can operate at the collective level and involve large numbers of people who are pursuing shared objectives (Bandura, 1997). **Collective self-efficacy** has been defined as "the extent to which we believe that we can work together effectively to accomplish our shared goals" (Maddux, 2002, p. 284). Although there is no agreement about how to measure this collective efficacy, the relevant evidence does show that it plays a helpful role in classroom performances (Bandura, 1993) and work teams (Little & Madigan, 1997), to name but two examples. Our prediction is that collective efficacy will become even more influential with the growing focus of positive psychology on cooperative group efforts. For a real-life application of social learning theory and self-efficacy principles as embodied by television heroes, read the article, "Changing Behavior Through TV Heroes."

Changing Behavior Through TV Heroes

MELISSA DITTMANN

Monitor *Staff*

Albert Bandura highlighted how serial dramas grounded in his social learning theory can lead people to make lifestyle changes and alter detrimental social practices.

Long-running TV and radio programs founded on social psychology are helping people around the world make positive changes in their lives, from encouraging literacy to raising the status of women in societies where they are marginalized, said renowned social cognitive psychologist Albert Bandura, PhD, at a presidential invited address at APA's 2004 Annual Convention in Honolulu. Bandura also received APA's Lifetime Achievement Award at the convention. . . .

Bandura's social learning theory—which emphasizes how modeling and enhancing people's sense of efficacy can help them improve their lives—is at the heart of numerous serial dramas now airing in Africa, Asia, and Latin America. And research is finding the dramas' gripping storylines and realistic characters are proving influential by encouraging people to adopt family planning methods, seek literacy programs, improve women's status, and protect against AIDS infection.

(Continued)

(Continued)

"These dramatic productions are not fanciful stories," said Bandura, APA president in 1973 and the David Starr Jordan Professor of Psychology at Stanford University. "They portray people's everyday lives, help them see a better future, and provide them with strategies and incentives that enable them to take the steps to realize it."

These dramas, incorporating Bandura's theory, involve a global effort, partnering television producers, writers, demographers and communication researchers in creating programs that change personal lifestyles and society.

The messages appear to inspire action: In Mexico, for example, nearly one million people enrolled in a study program to learn to read after watching a drama that promoted national literacy by showing people of different ages struggling to read and then becoming literate and managing their lives more effectively.

According to Bandura, the television programs spark such behavioral and social changes using four guiding principles:

- Contrasting role models with positive and negative models exhibiting beneficial or detrimental lifestyles and transitional models changing from detrimental to beneficial styles of behavior.
- Vicarious motivators that serve as incentives to change by showing the benefits of the positive lifestyles and the costs of the detrimental ones.
- Attentional and emotional involvement within the programs to sustain viewers' attention.
- Environmental supports with each program that contain an epilogue providing contact information for relevant community services and support groups.

For example, using these principles, a series of dramas targeted the high fertility rate in Tanzania, which is expected to nearly double its 36 million population in 25 years and has a fertility rate of 5.6 children per woman. After the dramas aired, researchers found that the greater exposure marital partners had to the dramas, the more they discussed the need to control family size and adopted family planning methods.

To help guide such productions, the drama producers study a region's culture and values to identify major social problems and obstacles to overcoming them. Writers and producers use this information to develop realistic characters and plots grounded in respect for human dignity and equity, which are codified in United Nations covenants.

"Global problems produce a sense of paralysis in people that they cannot do anything about them," Bandura said. "Our global applications illustrate how a collective effort combining the expertise of different players can have a worldwide impact on seemingly insurmountable problems."

Source: From Dittmann, M., Changing behavior through TV heroes, in *APA Monitor,* September 2004, p. 70. Copyright © 2004 by the American Psychological Association. Reprinted with permission.

Optimism

In this section, we discuss two theories that have received the overwhelming majority of the attention in regard to the construct of optimism. The first is learned optimism as studied by Martin Seligman and colleagues, and the second is the view of optimism as advanced by Michael Scheier and Charles Carver.

LEARNED OPTIMISM—SELIGMAN AND COLLEAGUES

The Historical Basis of Learned Optimism

Abramson, Seligman, and Teasdale (1978) reformulated their model of helplessness (see also Peterson, Maier, & Seligman, 1993) to incorporate the attributions (explanations) that people make for the bad and good things that happen to them. University of Pennsylvania psychologist Martin Seligman (Seligman, 1991, 1998b; see also Seligman, Reivich, Jaycox, & Gillham, 1995) later used this attributional or explanatory process as the basis for his theory of learned optimism.

A Definition of Learned Optimism

In the Seligman theory of **learned optimism**, the optimist uses adaptive causal attributions to explain negative experiences or events. Thus, the person answers the question, "Why did that bad thing happen to me?" In technical terms, the optimist makes external, variable, and specific attributions for failure-like events rather than the internal, stable, and global attributions of the pessimist. Stated more simply, the optimist explains bad things in such a manner as (1) to account for the role of other people and environments in producing bad outcomes (i.e., an external attribution), (2) to interpret the bad event as not likely to happen again (i.e., a variable attribution), and (3) to constrain the bad outcome to just one performance area and not others (i.e., a specific attribution).

Thus, the optimistic student who has received a poor grade in a high school class would say, (1) "It was a poorly worded exam" (external attribution), (2) "I have done better on previous exams" (variable attribution), and (3) "I am doing better in other areas of my life such as my relationships and sports achievements" (specific attribution). Conversely, the pessimistic student who has received a poor grade would say, (1) "I screwed up" (internal attribution), (2) "I have done lousy on previous exams" (stable attribution), and (3) "I also am not doing well in other areas of my life" (global attribution).

Seligman's theory implicitly places great emphasis upon negative outcomes in determining one's attributional explanations. Therefore, as shown

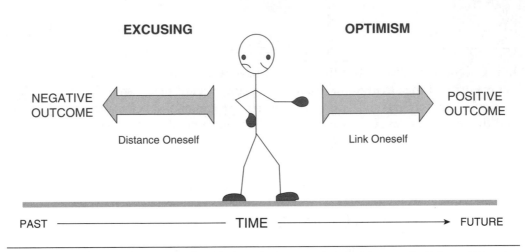

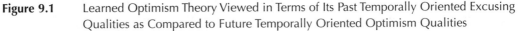

Figure 9.1   Learned Optimism Theory Viewed in Terms of Its Past Temporally Oriented Excusing
Qualities as Compared to Future Temporally Oriented Optimism Qualities

in Figure 9.1, Seligman's theory uses an excuse-like process of "distancing" from bad things that have happened in the past, rather than the more usual notion of optimism involving the connection to positive outcomes desired in the future (as reflected in the typical dictionary definition, as well as Scheier and Carver's definition, which we explore shortly in this chapter). Within the learned optimism perspective, therefore, the optimistic goal-directed cognitions are aimed at distancing the person from negative outcomes of high importance.

Childhood Antecedents of Learned Optimism

Seligman and colleagues (Abramson et al., 2000; Gillham, 2000; Seligman, 1991, 1995, 1998b) carefully described the developmental roots of the optimistic explanatory style. To begin, there appears to be some genetic component of explanatory style, with learned optimism scores more highly correlated for monozygotic than dizygotic twins (correlations = .48 vs. .0; Schulman, Keith, & Seligman, 1993).

Additionally, learned optimism appears to have roots in the environment (or learning). For example, parents who provide safe, coherent environments are likely to promote the learned optimism style in their offspring (Franz, McClelland, Weinberger, & Peterson, 1994). Likewise, the parents of optimists are portrayed as modeling optimism for their children by making explanations for negative events that enable the offspring to continue to feel good about themselves (i.e., external, variable, and specific attributions), along with explanations for positive events that help the offspring feel extra-good about themselves (i.e., internal, stable, and global attributions). Moreover, children who grow up with learned optimism are characterized as having had parents who understood their failures and generally attributed those failures to external rather than internal factors (i.e., they taught their children adaptive excusing; see Snyder, Higgins, & Stucky, 1983/2005). On the other hand, pessimistic people had parents who also were pessimistic. Furthermore, experiencing childhood traumas (e.g., parental death, abuse, incest, etc.) can yield pessimism (Bunce, Larsen, & Peterson, 1995; Cerezo & Frias, 1994), and parental divorce also may undermine learned optimism (Seligman, 1991). (Not all studies have found the aforementioned negative parental contributions to the explanatory styles of their offspring, and thus these conclusions must be viewed with caution. For a balanced overview of parental contributions, see Peterson & Steen, 2002.)

Television watching is yet another potential source of pessimism. American children ages 2 through 17 watch an average of almost 25 hours of television per week (3.5 hours per day; Gentile & Walsh, 2002). As but one recent example of pessimism-related behaviors that stem from children's television watching, Zimmerman, Glew, Christakis, and Katon (2005) found that greater amounts of television watched at age 4 years were related significantly to higher subsequent likelihoods of those children becoming bullies. Likewise, a steady diet of television violence can predispose and reinforce a helpless explanatory style that is associated with low learned optimism in children (Nolen-Hoeksema, 1987).

The Neurobiology of Optimism and Pessimism

Investigators have reported that pessimism and depression are related to abnormal limbic system functioning as well as to dysfunctional operations of the lateral prefrontal cortex and the paralimbic system. Indeed, depression appears to be linked to deficiencies in neurotransmitters (Liddle, 2001). Thus, antidepressant medications aim to increase the effective operation of these neurotransmitters. Likewise, research shows that serotonergic cells located in the dorsal raphe nucleus are reactive to perceived control. Furthermore, there is a predictable, control-induced release of serotonin in the amygdala (Maier & Watkins, 2000). Depression also has been associated with depleted endorphin secretion and defective immune functioning (Peterson, 2000). Finally, Drugan and colleagues (Drugan, Basile, Ha, & Ferland, 1994) have found that, under select conditions of control, there is a molecule released by cells in the brain. Although this research is still in its early phases, it appears that there are neurobiological markers in the brain that are linked to perceived control and pessimism–depression thoughts.

Scales: Can Learned Optimism Be Measured?

The instrument used to measure attributional style in adults is called the Attributional Style Questionnaire (ASQ; Peterson, Semmel, von Baeyer, Abramson, Metalsky, & Seligman, 1982; Seligman, Abramson, Semmel, & von Baeyer, 1979); the instrument for children is the Children's

Attributional Style Questionnaire (CASQ; Kaslow, Tanenbaum, & Seligman, 1978; Seligman, 1995; Seligman et al., 1984). The ASQ poses either a negative or a positive life event, and respondents are asked to indicate what they believe to be the causal explanations of those events on the dimensions of internal/external, stable/transient, and global/specific. Since the development of the ASQ, however, researchers have used expanded versions with more items (E-ASQ; see Metalsky, Halberstadt, & Abramson, 1987; Peterson & Villanova, 1988).

Beyond the explanatory style scales for adults and children, University of Michigan psychologist Chris Peterson and his colleagues (Peterson, Bettes, & Seligman, 1985) have developed the Content Analysis of Verbal Explanation (CAVE) approach for deriving ratings of optimism and pessimism from written or spoken words (Peterson, Schulman, Castellon, & Seligman, 1992). The advantage of the CAVE technique is that it allows an unobtrusive means of rating a person's explanatory style based on language usage. In this latter regard, one can go back and explore the optimism/pessimism of famous historical figures in their speeches, diaries, or newspaper interviews from earlier decades (e.g., Satterfield, 2000). To demonstrate the predictive power of the CAVE, we describe an intriguing application of the technique to predict the performances of major league baseball teams (see "The CAVE and Predicting Baseball Outcomes").

What Learned Optimism Predicts

The various indices of learned optimism have spawned a large amount of research (see Carr, 2004), with the learned optimistic rather than pessimistic explanatory style associated with the following:

1. Better academic performances (Peterson & Barrett, 1987; Seligman, 1998b)

2. Superior athletic performances (Seligman, Nolen-Hoeksema, Thornton, & Thornton, 1990)

3. More productive work records (Seligman & Schulman, 1986)

4. Greater satisfaction in interpersonal relationships (Fincham, 2000)

5. More effective coping with life stressors (Nolen-Hoeksema, 2000)

6. Less vulnerability to depression (Abramson, Alloy et al., 2000)

7. Superior physical health (Peterson, 2000).

In terms of learned optimism-based interventions, the reader is referred to Chapter 15, where details are given about the change techniques for both children and adults (see also Seligman, Steen, Park, & Peterson,

The CAVE and Predicting Baseball Outcomes

Martin Seligman, an avid Philadelphia Phillies baseball fan, decided to see whether his CAVE approach could be used to predict the outcomes of baseball teams. To accomplish this, his research group used the CAVE technique to analyze the optimistic explanatory styles inherent in the comments of National League baseball players reported in the *Sporting News* and the hometown newspaper sports sections from April though October of 1985. This was a huge task in that 12 National League team newspapers had to be read across the season—this involved 15,000 pages of reading! They then used the tabulated learned optimism scores for 1985 to predict various performance outcomes in the next 1986 season.

Of particular focus were the comments of the players on the New York Mets and the St. Louis Cardinals. When they lost, the Mets players' remarks conveyed an optimistic explanatory style. For example, star Mets pitcher Dwight Gooden explained a batter's home run as a simple, "He hit well tonight," and of his wild pitch, Gooden opined, "Some moisture must have gotten on the ball." Mets right field Darryl Strawberry said of a loss, "Sometimes you go through these kind of days." Compare these optimistic comments to the more pessimistic comments of St. Louis Cardinals' manager Whitey Herzog on why his team lost: "We can't hit. What the hell, let's face it," and St. Louis slugger Jack Clark on why he dropped a fly: "It was a real catchable ball."

When the explanatory styles of the Mets and Cardinals were used to predict performance in the next 1986 season, the optimistic comments of the Mets suggested success, and the pessimistic comments of the Cardinals predicted failure. This is precisely what happened. The Mets won the division, the playoffs, and the World Series in 1986, whereas the Cardinals lost more games than they won. The Mets' batting average for 1986 was .263 overall and .277 in pressure situations; the Cardinals, in comparison, had a batting average of .236 overall and .231 in pressure situations. Although we have described the results for only 2 of the 12 National League teams, the CAVE ratings of 1985 optimism were equally robust in predicting the outcomes of the other 10 teams. Because Seligman was skeptical about these findings, he replicated the findings, this time using 1986 comments to predict 1987 performance. He found the same results.

Seligman and his coworkers have performed similar studies on other sports to show the power of players' comments as measured by the CAVE approach to deriving explanatory style scores. More specifically, he has predicted the outcomes of NBA professional basketball teams and 1988 Olympic swimmer Matt Biondi. In yet another form of "sports," American politics (humor intended), Seligman also has found that optimistic explanatory style scores are strong predictors of success.

Note: All these applied studies are described in delightful detail in Seligman's 1991 book, *Learned Optimism.*

2005). Additionally, a good overview of learned optimism interventions can be found in Jane Gillham's edited volume titled *The Science of Optimism and Hope* (2000). Easily understood analyses of learned optimism adult interventions can be found in Seligman's *Learned Optimism: How to Change Your Mind and Your Life* (1998b) and his *Authentic Happiness* (2002). Child interventions are described in Seligman et al.'s *The Optimistic Child* (1995).

OPTIMISM—SCHEIER AND CARVER

Defining Optimism as Expectancies of Reaching a Desired Goal

Michael F. Scheier

Source: Reprinted with permission of Michael F. Scheier.

In their seminal article published in *Health Psychology*, psychologists Michael Scheier and Charles Carver (1985, p. 219) presented their new definition of **optimism**, which they described as the stable tendency "[to]believe that good rather than bad things will happen." Scheier and Carver assumed that, when a goal is of sufficient value, then the individual would produce an expectancy about attaining that goal.

In their definition of optimism, Scheier and Carver (1985) purposefully do not emphasize the role of personal efficacy. They wrote,

> Our own theoretical approach emphasizes a person's expectancies of good or bad outcomes. It is our position that outcome expectancies per se are the best predictors of behavior rather than the bases from which those expectancies were derived. A person may hold favorable expectancies for a number of reasons—personal ability, because the person is lucky, or because others favor him. The result should be an optimistic outlook—expectations that good things will happen (p. 223).

Thus, these generalized outcome expectancies may involve perceptions about being able to move toward desirable goals or to move away from undesirable goals (Carver & Scheier, 1999).

Childhood Antecedents of Optimism

The consensus is that there is a genetic basis to optimism as defined by Scheier and Carver (see also Plomin et al., 1992). Likewise, borrowing from Erikson's (1963, 1982) theory of development, Carver and Scheier (1999) suggest that their form of optimism stems from early childhood experiences that foster trust and secure attachments to parental figures (Bowlby, 1988).

Scales: Can Optimism Be Measured?

Scheier and Carver (1985) introduced their index of optimism, the Life Orientation Test (LOT), as including positive ("I'm always optimistic about my future") and negative ("I rarely count on good things happening to me") expectancies. The LOT has displayed acceptable internal consistency (alpha of .76 in original sample) and a test-retest correlation of .79 over 1 month. In support of its concurrent validity, the LOT correlated positively with expectancy for success and negatively with hopelessness and depression.

After years of extensive research using the LOT, a criticism arose about its overlap with neuroticism (see Smith, Pope, Rhodewalt, & Poulton, 1989). In response to this concern, Scheier, Carver, and Bridges (1994) validated a shorter, revised version of the LOT known as the LOT-Revised (LOT-R). The LOT-R eliminated items that caused the neuroticism overlap concerns. Furthermore, relative to neuroticism, trait anxiety, self-mastery, and self-esteem, optimism as measured by the LOT-R has shown superior capabilities in predicting various outcome markers related to superior coping. For example, higher scores on the LOT-R have related to better recovery in coronary bypass surgery, dealing more effectively with AIDS, enduring cancer biopsies more easily, better adjustment to pregnancy, and continuing in treatment for alcohol abuse (Carver & Scheier, 2002; for a good review of the many beneficial correlates of optimism, see Scheier, Carver, and Bridges, 2001). Additionally, internal consistency of the LOT-R equals or exceeds the original LOT (alpha of .78); its test-retest correlations are .68 to .79 for intervals of 4 to 28 months. Lastly, studies have found varying results on the factor structure of the LOT-R, with Scheier et al. (1994) finding one factor (optimism) and Affleck and Tennen (1996) finding the two independent factors of optimism and pessimism.

What Optimism Predicts

As has the LOT, the LOT-R has generated a large amount of research. When coping with stressors, optimists appear to take a problem-solving approach (Scheier, Weintrab, & Carver, 1986) and are more planful than pessimists (Fontaine, Manstead, & Wagner, 1993). Furthermore, optimists tend to use the approach-oriented coping strategies of positive reframing and seeing the best in situations, whereas pessimists are more avoidant and use denial tactics (Carver & Scheier, 2002). Optimists appraise daily stresses in terms of potential growth and tension reduction more than their pessimistic counterparts do. Also, when faced with truly uncontrollable circumstances, optimists tend to accept their plights, whereas pessimists actively deny their problems and thereby tend to make them worse (Carver & Scheier, 1998; Scheier & Carver, 2001). In other words, an optimist knows when to give up and when to keep plugging, whereas the pessimist still pursues a goal when it is not a smart thing to do.

On the whole, the LOT-R has produced robust predictive relationships with a variety of outcome markers (for reviews, see Carver & Scheier, 1999, 2001, 2002). As but a few specific examples, optimists as compared to pessimists fare better in the following ways:

1. Starting college (Aspinwall & Taylor, 1992)

2. Performing in work situations (Long, 1993)

3. Enduring a missile attack (Zeidner & Hammer, 1992)

4. Caring for Alzheimer's patients (Hooker, Monahan, Shifren, & Hutchinson, 1992) and cancer patients (Given et al., 1993)

5. Undergoing coronary bypass surgeries (Fitzgerald, Tennen, Affleck, & Pransky, 1993) and bone marrow transplants (Curbow, Somerfield, Baker, Wingard, & Legro, 1993)

6. Coping with cancer (Carver et al., 1993) and AIDS (Taylor et al., 1992)

Turning to the interventions to enhance optimism, we again suggest that the reader examine our Chapter 15 discussion of implementing positive psychological change. Presently there appears to be one major therapy approach that expressly seeks to enhance the positive expectancies as conceptualized in the Scheier and Carver model of optimism. John Riskind and his colleagues (Riskind, Sarampote, & Mercier, 1996) have modified standard cognitive therapy to influence optimism and pessimism. Riskind has acknowledged that most cognitive therapy techniques aim to lessen negative thinking (pessimism) but do little to enhance positive thinking (optimism). On this point, it should be noted that the simple decrease in negative thinking does not change positive thinking, owing perhaps to the fact that negative and positive cognitions are not correlated (Ingram & Wisnicki, 1988). In the Riskind approach, cognitive techniques are used to challenge optimism-suppressing schemas as well as to enhance positive and optimistic thinking. Another technique suggested by Riskind et al. is positive visualization, wherein the client rehearses seeing positive outcomes for problematic circumstances (for overview, see Pretzer and Walsh, 2001). Because of the robust findings relating optimism to various health outcomes, we believe that the Scheier and Carver model will continue to expand in influence, especially in the area of interventions to help medical patients who are facing physical health challenges.

Hope

Given the considerable attention that C. R. Snyder's theory of hope (Snyder, 1994; Snyder, Harris, et al., 1991) has received in the last two decades, we explore this approach to explaining hopeful thinking in some detail. (Snyder is professor of psychology at the University of Kansas and the senior author of this book.) An overview of the various theories of hope are set forth in Appendix A. Additionally, the book *Hope and Hopelessness: Critical Clinical Constructs* by Farran, Herth, and Popovich (1995) provides a good overview of various approaches for defining and measuring hope.

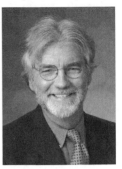

A DEFINITION

C. R. Snyder

Both the Snyder hope theory and the definition of hope emphasize cognitions that are built on goal-directed thought. We define **hope** as goal-directed thinking in which the person utilizes **pathways thinking** (the perceived capacity to find routes to desired goals) and **agency thinking** (the requisite motivations to use those routes).

Only those goals with considerable value to the individual are considered applicable to hope. Also, the goals can vary temporally—from those that will be reached in the next few minutes (short-term) to those that will take months or even years to reach (long-term). Likewise, the goals entailed in hoping may be approach oriented (that is, aimed at reaching a desired goal) or preventative (aimed at stopping an undesired event) (Snyder, Feldman, Taylor, Schroeder, & Adams, 2000). Lastly, goals can vary in relation to the difficulty of attainment, with some quite easy and others extremely difficult. Even with purportedly impossible goals, however, people may join together and succeed through supreme planning and persistent efforts. On this latter issue, coordinated and successful group efforts illustrate why we should refrain from characterizing extremely difficult goals as being based on "false hopes" (Snyder, Rand, King, Feldman, & Taylor, 2002)

Pathways thinking has been shown to relate to the production of alternate routes when original ones are blocked (Snyder, Harris, et al., 1991), as has positive self-talk about finding routes to desired goals (e.g., "I'll find a way to solve this"; Snyder, LaPointe, Crowson, & Early, 1998). Moreover, those who see themselves as having greater capacity for agency thinking also endorse energetic personal self-talk statements, such as "I will keep going" (Snyder, LaPointe, et al., 1998), and they are especially likely to produce and use such motivational talk when encountering impediments.

High hopers have positive emotional sets and a sense of zest that stems from their histories of success in goal pursuits, whereas low hopers have negative emotional sets and a sense of emotional flatness that stems from their histories of having failed in goal pursuits. Lastly, high- or low-hope people bring these overriding emotional sets with them as they undertake specific goal-related activities.

The various components of hope theory can be viewed in Figure 9.2, with the iterative relationship of pathways and agency thoughts on the far left. Moving left to the right from the developmental agency-pathways thoughts, we can see the emotional sets that are taken to specific goal pursuit activities. Next in Figure 9.2 are the values associated with specific goal pursuits. As noted previously, sufficient value must be attached to a goal pursuit before the individual will continue the hoping process. At this point, the pathways and agency thoughts are applied to the desired goal. Here, the feedback loop entails positive emotions that positively reinforce the goal pursuit process, or negative emotions to curtail this process.

Figure 9.2 shows how, along the route to the goal, the person may encounter a stressor that potentially blocks the actual goal pursuit. Hope theory proposes that the successful pursuit of desired goals, especially when circumventing stressful impediments, results in positive emotions and continued goal pursuit efforts (i.e., positive reinforcement). On the other hand, if a person's goal pursuit is not successful (often because that person cannot navigate around blockages), then negative emotions should result (Ruehlman & Wolchik, 1988), and the goal pursuit process should be undermined (i.e., punishment).

Furthermore, such a stressor is interpreted differently depending on the person's overall level of hope. That is to say, high hopers construe such barriers as challenges and will explore alternate routes and apply their motivations to those routes. Typically having experienced successes in working around such blockages, the high hopers are propelled onward by their positive emotions. The low hopers, however, become stuck because they cannot find alternate routes; in turn, their negative emotions and ruminations stymie their goal pursuits.

CHILDHOOD ANTECEDENTS OF HOPE

More details on the developmental antecedents of the hope process can be found in Snyder (1994, pp. 75–114) and Snyder, McDermott, Cook, and Rapoff (2002, pp. 1–32). In brief, however, Snyder (1994) proposes that hope has no hereditary contributions but rather is entirely a learned cognitive set about goal-directed thinking. The teaching of pathways and agency goal-directed thinking is an inherent part of parenting, and the components of hopeful thought are in place by age two. Pathways thinking reflects basic cause-and-effect learning that the child acquires from caregivers and others. Such pathways thought is acquired before agency thinking, with the latter being posited to begin around age one year. Agency thought reflects the baby's increasing insights as to the fact that she is the causal force in many of the cause-and-effect sequences in her surrounding environment.

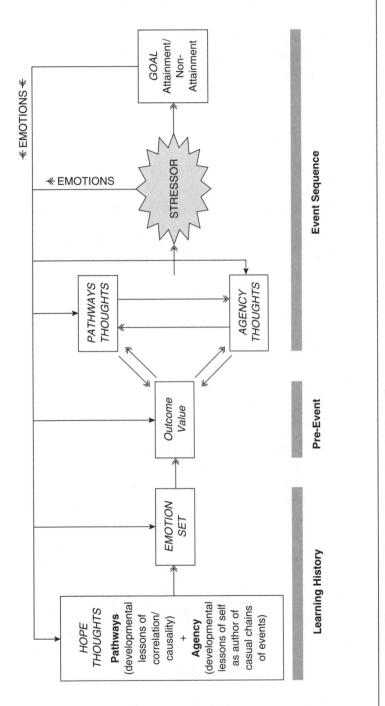

Figure 9.2 The Feedforward and Feedback Functions in Hope Theory

Snyder (1994, 2000a) has proposed that strong attachment to caregivers is crucial for imparting hope, and available research is consistent with this speculation (Shorey, Snyder, Yang, & Lewin, 2003). Traumatic events across the course of childhood also have been linked to the lessening of hope (Rodriguez-Hanley & Snyder, 2000), and there is research support for the negative impacts of some of these traumas (e.g., the loss of parents; Westburg, 2001).

THE NEUROBIOLOGY OF HOPE

Although Snyder and colleagues have held that hope is a learned mental set, this does not preclude the idea that the operations of hopeful thinking have neurobiological underpinnings, especially as related to goal-directed behaviors. Norman Cousins, in his 1991 best-selling book, *Head First: The Biology of Hope and the Healing Power of the Human Spirit*, wrote the following apt description of the brain and hope-related thinking:

> Brain researchers now believe that what happens in the body can affect the brain, and what happens in the brain can affect the body. Hope, purpose, and determination are not merely mental states. They have electrochemical connections that play a large part in the workings of the immune system and, indeed, in the entire economy of the total human organism. In short, I learned that it is not unscientific to talk about a biology of hope. . . . (p. 73)

One exciting new idea here is that goal-directed actions are guided by opposing control processes in the central nervous system. According to Pickering and Gray (1999), these processes are regulated by the *behavioral inhibition system (BIS)* and the *behavioral activation system (BAS)*. The BIS is thought to be responsive to punishment, and it signals the organism to stop, whereas the BAS is governed by rewards, and it sends the message to go forward. A related body of research suggests a *behavioral facilitation system (BFS)* that drives incentive-seeking actions of organisms (see Depue, 1996). The BFS is thought to include the dopamine pathways of the midbrain that connect to the limbic system and the amygdala.

SCALES: CAN HOPE BE MEASURED?

Using hope theory, Snyder and his colleagues have developed several self-report scales. First, Snyder, Harris, et al. (1991) developed a 12-item trait measure for adults ages 16 and older, in which 4 items reflect pathways, 4 items reflect agency, and 4 items are distracters. An example pathways item is "I can think of many ways to get out of a jam," and an example agency item is "I energetically pursue my goals." Respondents respond to each item on an 8-point Likert continuum (1 = Definitely false to 8 = Definitely true).

The internal consistency (alpha level) typically has been in the .80 range, and test-retest reliabilities have been .80 or above over time periods of 8 to 10 weeks (Snyder, Harris, et al., 1991). Furthermore, there are extensive data on the concurrent validity of the Hope Scale in regard to its predicted positive correlations with scales tapping such similar concepts as optimism, expectancy for attaining goals, expected control, and self-esteem, and there have been negative correlations with scales reflecting opposite constructs such as hopelessness, depression, and pathologies. Finally, several factor-analytic studies provide support for the pathways and agency components of the Hope Scale (Babyak, Snyder, & Yoshinobu, 1993).

The Children's Hope Scale (CHS; Snyder, Hoza, et al., 1997) is a six-item self-report trait measure appropriate for children age 8 to 15. Three of the six items reflect agency thinking (e.g., "I think I am doing pretty well"), and three reflect pathways thinking (e.g., "When I have a problem, I can come up with lots of ways to solve it." Children respond to the items on a 6-point Likert continuum (1 = None of the time to 6 = All of the time). The alphas have been close to .80 across several samples, and the test-retest reliabilities for 1-month intervals have been .70 to .80. The CHS has shown convergent validity in terms of its positive relationships with other indices of strengths (e.g., self-worth), and negative relationships with indices of problem (e.g., depression). Lastly, factor analyses have corroborated the two-factor structure of the CHS (Snyder, Hoza, et al., 1997).

Snyder and colleagues (Snyder, Sympson, et al., 1996) also have developed the State Hope Scale (SHS), a six-item self-report scale that taps here-and-now goal-directed thinking. Three items reflect pathways thinking—e.g., "There are lots of ways around any problem that I am facing now"—and three items reflect agency thinking—"At the present time, I am energetically pursuing my goals." The response range is 1 = Definitely false to 8 = Definitely true. Internal reliabilities are quite high (alphas often in the .90 range). Strong concurrent validity results also show that SHS scores correlate positively with state indices of self-esteem and positive affect and negatively with state indices of negative affect. Likewise, manipulation-based studies reveal that SHS scores increase or decrease according to situational successes or failures in goal-directed activities. Finally, factor analysis has supported the two-factor structure of the SHS (Snyder, Sympson, et al., 1996).

WHAT HOPE PREDICTS

For a detailed review of the predictions flowing from Hope Scale scores, see Snyder (2002a). What is noteworthy about the results related to these predictions is that the statistically significant findings typically remain, even after mathematical correction for the influences of a variety of other self-report psychological measures, such as optimism, self-efficacy, and self-esteem. In general, Hope Scale scores have predicted outcomes in academics, sports, physical health, adjustment, and psychotherapy. For example, in the area of academics, higher Hope Scale scores taken at the beginning of college have predicted better cumulative grade point averages and whether students remain in school (Snyder, Shorey, et al., 2002). In the area of sports, higher Hope Scale scores taken at the beginning of college track season have predicted the superior performances of male athletes and have done so beyond the coach's rating of natural athletic abilities (Curry, Snyder, Cook, Ruby, & Rehm, 1977). In the area of adjustment, higher Hope Scale scores have related to various indices of elevated happiness, satisfaction, positive emotions, getting along with others, etc. (Snyder, Harris, et al., 1991). Additionally, hope has been advanced as the common factor underlying the positive changes that happen in psychological treatments (Snyder, Ilardi, Cheavens, et al., 2000).

In regard to interventions to enhance hope, see our discussion of the various approaches in Chapter 15. For the reader with considerable background in psychotherapy, a thorough overview of hope theory interventions can be found in Snyder's edited volume, the *Handbook of Hope* (2000b). For the reader with less experience in psychotherapy, "how-to" descriptions for enhancing adults' hopes can be found in McDermott and Snyder's *Making Hope Happen* (1999) and in Snyder's *The Psychology of Hope: You Can Get There From Here* (1994/2004); "how to" descriptions for raising children's hopes are described in McDermott and Snyder's *The Great Big Book of Hope* (2000) and in Snyder, McDermott, et al.'s *Hope for the Journey: Helping Children Through the Good Times and the Bad* (2002).

THE LATEST FRONTIER—COLLECTIVE HOPE

As with the concept of self-efficacy, hope researchers also have expanded their construct to explore what is called *collective hope* (see Snyder & Feldman, 2000). Simply put, **collective hope** reflects the level of goal-directed thinking of a large group of people. Often, such collective hope is operative when several people join together to tackle a goal that would be impossible for any one person. Snyder and Feldman (2000) have applied the notion of collective hope more generally to the topics of disarmament, preservation of environmental resources, health insurance, and government.

Life Enhancement Strategies

Self-efficacy, optimism, and hope provide the momentum needed to pursue a good life. Therefore, we encourage you to use the self-efficacy, optimism, and hope you already possess to improve functioning in important domains of your life.

Love

- Build new confidence in your relationships by observing someone who is quite skilled in managing friendships and romantic relationships. Emulate his or her behavior as appropriate.
- Approach your next visit with extended family with a flexible explanatory style. When positive events occur, be sure to identify your role in the family success.
- Set goals for important relationships that will help you grow closer to others. Be sure to identify multiple pathways and sources of agency for pursuing these aims.

Work

- Develop new skills for work or school by attending training or study sessions that will help you approach your assignments with increased confidence.
- When a new project is assigned to you, expect that the best will happen. Nurture those optimistic thoughts daily as you work toward successful completion of the project.
- Break down a big task into small goals, and direct your energy toward pursuing small goal after small goal.

Play

- Watch an hour of educational television for children. Attempt to identify the many messages designed to enhance self-efficacy.
- Play a board game or a sport with a friend, and attempt to respond to poor outcome with a flexible explanatory approach.
- Identify a personal goal associated with your favorite leisure activity that you hope to attain in the next month. Identify and procure all the resources you need to make progress toward that goal.

Putting Temporal Futures in Perspective

We now juxtapose the orientations that focus on the future (i.e., the ones we have explored in this chapter) with those that focus on either the past or the present. We do this because comparing these three orientations toward time may foster a better understanding of the possible role of a balanced temporal orientation in producing a productive and satisfying life (see Boniwell & Zimbardo, 2004).

There are advantages and disadvantages to each of the three temporal orientations—the past, the present, and the future. Let us begin, for example, with the **past orientation**, which often is characterized by an emphasis on pleasurable views of previous interpersonal relationships with friends and family. This somewhat sentimental perspective focuses on the happiness to be derived in warm personal interactions. Less positively, however, the past orientation can produce a very conservative, overly cautious approach to one's life, along with a desire to preserve the status quo that makes the person unwilling to experience new things. Likewise, there is no guarantee that the view of the past is positive; those who hold negative views about their pasts are filled with ruminations, anxieties, and depressive thoughts and feelings (often about traumatic childhood events). Of course, this latter content fills many library shelves with books on the pathologies stemming from childhood traumas.

Now, let us explore the person who lives in the here and now. The person who lives for the present can be described in hedonistic terms that have both good and bad consequences. Living in the moment, this individual derives great pleasure in highly intense activities, relishes the thrills and excitements found in the here and now, and remains open to the ongoing adventures of the moment. The person focused on the present also may place a premium on excitement.

One aspect of enjoying the ongoing experience can be savoring (Bryant, 2004; Bryant & Veroff, 2006). Although savoring can be applied to the past or the future, one of the most robust types of savoring pertains to the enjoyment of the moment, perhaps even acting to stretch out an ongoing positive event. As balloonist Bertrand Piccard observed in his 1999 trip around the world, "During the last night, I savor once more the intimate relationship we have established with our planet. I feel so privileged that I want to enjoy every second of this air world. . . . " (Piccard, 1999, p. 44).

When considered from a Western perspective, the concerns that arise from this **present orientation** all reflect the fact that such a person may not think ahead about the potential liabilities of such excitement seeking. Although most of us probably do not remember our toddler years, it is likely that we then lived a here-and-now existence as we pursued our momentary whims and desires to the fullest. When adults are committed solely to this present orientation, however, some may suffer the negative consequences of hedonistic adventures. For example, addictions, injuries from accidents, and various temptations can destroy the career aspirations of the person who lives only with such a hedonistic present orientation. Such people take risks in a variety of arenas, including the driving of automobiles, sexual encounters, and drug use (Keough, Zimbardo, & Boyd, 1999). Much of our current description of the present orientation has a distinctly Western flavor; an Eastern perspective would include a meditative appreciation of the calmness that flows from a here-and-now orientation (see Chapter 11 for discussions of optimal experiences of the present).

If one considers a more Eastern perspective, many of these more negative possibilities are less likely to appear (if they appear at all).

Lastly, there is the future temporal perspective that has formed the core theme of this chapter. The person with a **future orientation** thinks ahead to the possible consequences of his or her actions. As we have learned, future-oriented people form clear goals and conjure the requisite paths to reach those goals. They are likely to engage in preventive behaviors to lessen the likelihood of bad things happening in the future. Furthermore, as we have learned in the literatures of self-efficacy, optimism, and hope reviewed in this chapter, such people are successful in life's endeavors—in academics, jobs, sports, health, and so on. Some future-oriented people may not do very well, however, at experiencing the enormous pleasure that can be derived from just being with others or recalling previous interpersonal activities.

In reading about the past, present, and future orientations, you may be intrigued about which orientation characterizes your own life. Stanford psychologist Philip Zimbardo (Zimbardo & Boyd, 1999) has developed and validated a trait-like measure of temporal orientation, the Zimbardo Time Perspective Inventory (see Appendix B). That is to say, although people have accentuated the past, present, or future at given moments, they also are disposed across situations to one of these temporal orientations. Thus, temporal orientations can have a trait-like quality.

In the Personal Mini-Experiments are two approaches to help you answer the question of how you use your time. First, we encourage you to try the "What's Ahead" exercise. In this exercise, you will monitor your thoughts for one day in order to see to what degree you are focused on the past, present, and future. Students who have tried this exercise report that they find the results surprising and worthwhile.

Philip Zimbardo

Source: Reprinted with permission of Philip Zimbardo.

Personal Mini-Experiments

Balancing Your Perspective on Time

In this chapter, we discuss the benefits of future orientation and balancing time perspectives. Our review suggests that our orientation to time affects positive and negative outcomes alike. Here are a few ideas for experimenting with increasing your awareness of how you view time.

"What's Ahead": Although you may have a rough idea about how much time you spend thinking about the future, we have found it useful for people actually to reflect on their days to produce an estimate of the time spent "in the past," "in the present," and "in the future." Mark a piece of lined paper with columns and rows (see the example following). From the top down in each column, write the hours of your day (1 a.m., 2 a.m., 3 a.m., etc.), and across the top in a row, write the words *Past, Present,*

(Continued)

(Continued)

and *Future*. Now, you have a chart on which you can note how many minutes in each hour were spent in thoughts of the past, present, or future. It helps to print this chart on a small piece of card stock that you can place in your pocket or purse along with a small pencil for the hourly recording of your time spent in each perspective.

Time	Past	Present	Future
7 a.m.			
8 a.m.			
9 a.m.			
10 a.m.			
11 a.m.			
Noon			
1 p.m.			
And so on			
Totals			

If you can, in the last minute of each hour from 7 a.m. to midnight (or whatever your waking hours may be), estimate the number of minutes you spent in that previous hour thinking about past, present, or future. If you found yourself in a flow-like experience, totally engrossed in whatever you were doing, and the time just seemed to fly, count that under Present. Lastly, sum the number of past, present, or future minutes across the hours that you were awake. The next day, figure out how you spent most of your time. For most people, even during busy hours, considerable time was spent thinking ahead about goals and plans to reach those goals. We do this virtually from the moment we awaken and think about what we will be doing that day. Remember, there are no right or wrong ways to spend your time. Instead, the purpose is to sensitize you to the temporal foci of your thinking. Realize also that the results of this experiment may depend on the day of the week, your health, your age, whether you are on vacation, the time of year, where you live, your job, and so on. Most people who complete this exercise, however, are somewhat surprised by how much time they spend thinking about the future.

Toward a Balanced Time Perspective: After completing and scoring the Zimbardo Time Perspective Inventory (see Appendix B), identify the most meaningful event you will experience in the upcoming week (i.e., the event you are most looking forward to or the one you are most dreading). Once you have identified that event, daydream about how you will approach that event with temporal orientation you typically hold across situations (past-negative, past-positive, present-fatalistic, present-hedonistic, future). Jot down notes about how your orientation to time might affect the outcome of that event. Then, consider how you might approach the event if you held one of the other orientations. Are there benefits to this alternative orientation to time? Most people realize that perceptions of time can affect present and future experiences.

As part of the Personal Mini-Experiments, you can take the Zimbardo Time Perspective Inventory (Zimbardo & Boyd, 1999) presented in Appendix B. With this scale, you can ascertain the degree to which each of the following five temporal orientations best characterizes you across situations: (1) past-negative, (2) past-positive, (3) present-fatalistic, (4) present-hedonistic, and (5) future. By completing the "What's Ahead" Personal Mini-Experiment and the "Balance Exercise" associated with the Zimbardo Time Perspective Inventory, you should be able to see the past, present, and future temporal orientations in your life.

The key to having a balance in these three temporal perspectives is your ability to operate in the temporal orientation that best fits the situation in which you find yourself. This balance, according to Boniwell and Zimbardo (2004, p. 176), entails "Working hard when it's time to work. Playing intensively when it's time to play. Enjoying listening to grandma's old stories while she is still alive. Viewing children though the eyes of wonder with which they see the world. Laughing at jokes and life's absurdities. Indulging in desire and passion."

Being flexible and capable of switching to an appropriate temporal orientation yield the most productive approach to how we spend our time. Having said this, however, it is clear that, in Western culture, we typically emphasize the future orientation (see Chapter 2). This is why the positive psychology as practiced in Western societies is built on thinking about the future. Nowhere is this more obvious than in the children's story *The Three Little Pigs,* in which children learn that the present-oriented pigs build flimsy houses from hay or twigs that cannot withstand the onslaught of the big, bad, fearsome wolf. Rather, it is the future-oriented pig who builds his house of bricks and "lives happily ever after." What this children's story does not consider, however, is the Eastern perspective toward time, and we touch on this on the next and final section of this chapter.

Cultural Caveats About Temporal Perspective

What we have offered in this chapter reflects a perspective on temporal orientations that reflects the Caucasian Americans who overwhelmingly have been the research participants in the various reported studies. Be clear, therefore, that some Americans and members of other, non-Western cultures may *not* share the perspectives on self-efficacy, optimism, and hope that we have presented. (See Chapter 5 for a detailed discussion of culture and positive psychology.) Not only may these non-Western perspectives differ in their implementation of self-efficacy, optimism, and hope, they also may not value these to the same degree that we have in writing about them in this chapter.

Additionally, in many cases the instruments we have described may not be sensitive to the nuances of Eastern people. Clearly, the dominant Caucasian cultural groups in the United States and other Western cultures place a priority on the mastery of their futures, along with emphasizing doing- or goal-oriented activities and the individual rather than the collective perspective (Carter, 1991). Moreover, the Caucasian Americans about whom we have reported in this chapter are judged by what they do more so than by what they are. So, too, are these research participants, in a manner similar to Western cultural bias (Stewart, 1972), probably focused on controlling their surrounding environments and, in so doing, view time in a linear manner (and consider planning for the future crucial).

Contrast the former perspective, for example, with the Native American accentuation of the here and now (Trimble, 1976). For Native Americans, time is seen as a kind of flowing and relative resource that is to be focused upon; instead of "going by the clock," things are done as needed (Soldier, 1992). Similarly, Cuban Americans, Mexican Americans, and Puerto Rican Americans all appear to prefer a present orientation to a future one (Chandler, 1979; Inclan, 1985; Szapocnik, Scopetta, & King, 1978). Generally, Native Americans, Latinos/Latinas, African Americans, and Asian Americans perceive time in a *polychromic* manner—many things are conceptualized as happening at once with people. Moreover, time is viewed as a plentiful resource, and human relationships take priority over it (Schauber, 2001). Contrast this with the European American culture, in which time is linear, sequential, and *monochromic* (also consider the value placed on time in the phrase "time is money"; Schauber, 2001).

There is considerable variation, however, even within American culture, and our analysis in this chapter has not addressed this fact. Furthermore, if there are differences within American culture regarding perspectives that relate to self-efficacy, optimism, and hope, it is probably accurate to infer that the differences are even larger when comparisons are made to cultures outside the United States.

In Eastern cultures (as exemplified by Asian countries), the traditional view is to see the self and other people as interrelated (Kim, Triandis, Kagitcibasi, Choi, & Yoon, 1994; Markus & Kitayama, 1991). Thus, contrary to the American values, the Eastern view is to accentuate harmonious interdependence among interacting persons (see Chapter 3; Weisz, Rothbaum, & Blackburn, 1984). Furthermore, in the Eastern perspective the experience of suffering is seen as a necessary part of human existence (Chang, 2001b). This emphasis on people serves to make temporal concerns far less important in Eastern cultures.

Some research has been conducted with the optimism construct in comparing Western and Eastern cultures. Using the learned optimism construct as measured by the ASQ, for example, Lee and Seligman (1997) found that Asian Americans and Caucasian Americans had similar levels of optimism, but the mainland Chinese students were less optimistic.

Using the Scheier and Carver approach to operationalizing optimism (along with a version of the LOT), Ed Chang of the University of Michigan

(1996a) found that Asian American and Caucasian American students were not different on optimism, but the Asian Americans were higher in pessimism than their Caucasian American counterparts. In this same study, Chang found that, for the Caucasian Americans, their higher pessimism was associated with less problem solving—as one would expect. For the Asian Americans, on the other hand, *their higher pessimism was associated with greater problem solving.* In the words of Chang (2001a, p. 226), "Thus, what 'works' for Asian relative to Caucasian Americans simply might be different, *not necessarily more effective*" (emphasis added). (See Chapter 5 for a related discussion of Chang's work.)

Edward C. Chang

Source: © Edward C. Chang 2005.

These studies on optimism show that we cannot assume that this coping approach is manifested in the same degree among Asian Americans and Caucasian Americans, nor can we assume that having more optimism (and less pessimism) even produces the same coping repercussions for these two distinct groups. In closing this chapter by comparing persons from different cultural backgrounds, we seek to point out how the findings discussed in the bulk of this chapter may be culture specific. It is important that future positive psychology thinkers *not* assume that Western-based theories and scales can and will translate in obvious ways to Eastern cultures. We strongly believe that positive psychology should be a worldwide initiative, and thus we must take care to test any theories and measures across cultures before drawing inferences about "universally" applicable findings. As such, we are reminded of the wisdom inherent in the old proverb, "To be uncertain is to be uncomfortable, but to be certain sometimes can be ridiculous."

Appendix A: A Summary of Hope Theories

AVERILL

Averill, Catlin, and Chon (1990) define hope in cognitive terms as appropriate when goals are (1) reasonably attainable (i.e., an intermediate level of difficulty), (2) under control, (3) viewed as important, and (4) acceptable at social and moral levels.

BREZNITZ

Breznitz (1986) proposed five metaphors to capture the operations of hope in response to stressors, with hope as (1) a protected area, (2) a bridge, (3) an intention, (4) performance, and (5) an end in itself. He also cautioned that hope may be an illusion akin to denial.

ERIKSON

Erik Erikson (1964, p. 118) defined hope as "the enduring belief in the attainability of fervent wishes" and posed dialectics between hope and other motives, one of the strongest and most important being trust/hope versus mistrust, which is the infant's first task. Another broad dialectic, according to Erikson (1982), pertains to the generativity of hope versus stagnation.

GOTTSCHALK

For Gottschalk (1974), hope involves positive expectancies about specific favorable outcomes, and it impels a person to move through psychological problems. He developed a Hope Scale to analyze the content of 5-minute segments of spoken words. This hope measurement has concurrent validity in terms of its positive correlations with positive human relations and achievement, and its negative relationships to higher anxiety, hostility, and social alienation.

MARCEL

Basing his definition on the coping of prisoners of war, Marcel (see Godfrey, 1987) concluded that hope gives people the power to cope with helpless circumstances.

MOWRER

Mowrer (1960) proposed that hope was an emotion that occurred when rats observed a stimulus that was linked with something pleasurable. Mowrer also described the antithesis of hope, or fear, which he said entailed a type of dread in which the animal lessened its activity level and that, as such, fear impedes their goal pursuits.

STAATS

Staats (1989, p. 367) defined hope as "the interaction between wishes and expectations." Staats and colleagues developed instruments for tapping the affective and cognitive aspects of hope. To measure affective hope, the Expected Balance Scale (EBS; Staats, 1989) entails 18 items, for which respondents use a 5-point Likert continuum. To measure cognitive hope, the Hope Index (Staats & Stassen, as cited in Staats, 1989) focuses on particular events and their outcomes and contains the subscales of Hope-Self,

Hope-Other, Wish, and Expect. The Hope Index contains 16 items, and respondents use a 6-point Likert continuum (0 = Not at all to 5 = Very much) to rate both the degree to which they "wish this to occur" and "expect this to occur."

STOTLAND

Stotland (1969) explored the role of expectancies and cognitive schemas and described hope as involving important goals for which there is a reasonably high perceived probability of attainment. Using Stotland's (1969) model, Erickson, Post, and Paige (1975) designed the Hope Scale, which consists of 20 general and common (i.e., not situation-specific) goals. This Hope Scale yields scores of average importance and average probability across these goals. There is little reported research, however, using this scale.

Appendix B: Zimbardo Time Perspective Inventory Items

Directions: Read each item carefully. Using the 5-point scale shown below, please select the number to indicate how characteristic each statement is of you in the blank provided.

1	2	3	4	5
Very uncharacteristic	Uncharacteristic	Neutral	Characteristic	Very characteristic

_____ 1. I believe that getting together with one's friends to party is one of life's important pleasures.

_____ 2. Familiar childhood sights, sounds, smells often bring back a flood of wonderful memories.

_____ 3. Fate determines much in my life.

_____ 4. I often think of what I should have done differently in my life.

_____ 5. My decisions are mostly influenced by people and things around me.

_____ 6. I believe that a person's day should be planned ahead each morning.

_____ 7. It gives me pleasure to think about my past.

Appendix B Source: From Zimbardo, P. G., & Boyd, J. N., Putting time in perspective: A valid, reliable individual-differences metric, in *Journal of Personality and Social Psychology, 77,* pp. 1271–1288. Copyright © 1999 by the American Psychological Association. Reprinted with permission.

_____ 8. I do things impulsively.

_____ 9. If things don't get done on time, I don't worry about it.

_____ 10. When I want to achieve something, I set goals and consider specific means for reaching those goals.

_____ 11. On balance, there is much more good to recall than bad in the past.

_____ 12. When listening to my favorite music, I often lose track of time.

_____ 13. Meeting tomorrow's deadlines and doing other necessary work comes before tonight's play.

_____ 14. Since whatever will be will be, it doesn't really matter what I do.

_____ 15. I enjoy stories about how things used to be in the "good old times."

_____ 16. Painful past experiences keep being replayed in my mind.

_____ 17. I try to live my life as fully as possible, one day at a time.

_____ 18. It upsets me to be late for appointments.

_____ 19. Ideally, I would live each day as if it were my last.

_____ 20. Happy memories of good times spring readily to mind.

_____ 21. I meet my obligations to friends and authorities on time.

_____ 22. I've taken my share of abuse and rejection in the past.

_____ 23. I make decisions on the spur of the moment.

_____ 24. I take each day as it is rather than try to plan it out.

_____ 25. The past has too many unpleasant memories that I prefer not to think about.

_____ 26. It is important to put excitement in my life.

_____ 27. I've made mistakes in the past that I wish I could undo.

_____ 28. I feel that it's more important to enjoy what you're doing than to get work done on time.

_____ 29. I get nostalgic about my childhood.

_____ 30. Before making a decision, I weigh the costs against the benefits.

_____ 31. Taking risks keeps my life from becoming boring.

_____ 32. It's more important for me to enjoy life's journey than to focus only on the destination.

_____ 33. Things rarely work out as I expected.

_____ 34. It's hard for me to forget unpleasant images of my youth.

_____ 35. It takes joy out of the process and flow of my activities if I have to think about goals, outcomes, and products.

_____ 36. Even when I am enjoying the present, I am drawn back to comparisons with similar past experiences.

_____ 37. You can't really plan for the future because things change so much.

_____ 38. My life path is controlled by forces I cannot influence.

_____ 39. It doesn't make sense to worry about the future, since there is nothing I can do about it anyway.

_____ 40. I complete projects on time by making steady progress.

_____ 41. I find myself tuning out when family members talk about the way things used to be.

_____ 42. I take risks to put excitement in my life.

_____ 43. I make lists of things to do.

_____ 44. I often follow my heart more than my head.

_____ 45. I am able to resist temptations when I know that there is work to be done.

_____ 46. I find myself getting swept up in the excitement of the moment.

_____ 47. Life today is too complicated; I would prefer the simpler life of the past.

_____ 48. I prefer friends who are spontaneous rather than predictable.

_____ 49. I like family rituals and traditions that are regularly repeated.

_____ 50. I think about the bad things that have happened to me in the past.

_____ 51. I keep working at difficult, uninteresting tasks if they will help me get ahead.

_____ 52. Spending what I earn on pleasures today is better than saving for tomorrow's security.

_____ 53. Often luck pays off better than hard work.

_____ 54. I think about the good things that I have missed out on in my life.

_____ 55. I like my close relationships to be passionate.

_____ 56. There will always be time to catch up on my work.

To obtain the scores for each of the five subfactors, (1) reverse code all the relevant items, (2) add the scores for each item that contributes to the specific subfactor, and (3) divide the subfactor total by the number of questions that constitute the subfactor.

Past-Negative = Items 4, 5, 16, 22, 27, 33, 34, 36, 50, and 54

Past-Positive = Items 2, 7, 11, 15, 20, 25, 29, 41, and 49

Present-Fatalistic = Items 3, 14, 35, 37, 38, 39, 47, 52, and 53

Present-Hedonistic = Items 1, 8, 12, 17, 19, 23, 26, 28, 31, 32, 42, 44, 46, 48, and 55

Future = Items 6, 9, 10, 13, 18, 21, 24, 30, 40, 43, 45, 51, and 56

Key Terms

Agency thinking: The requisite motivations to use routes to desired goals. (Compare with *pathways thinking.*)

Collective hope: Goal-directed thinking in which a group of people have the perceived capacity to find routes to desired goals and the requisite motivations to use those routes.

Collective self-efficacy: The degree to which a group of people believe they can work together to accomplish shared goals.

Future orientation: A perspective in which one emphasizes future events and the consequences of one's actions. Future-oriented people focus on planning for things to come.

Hope: Goal-directed thinking in which a person has the perceived capacity to find routes to desired goals (pathways thinking) and the requisite motivations to use those routes (agency thinking). Hope is not genetically determined but an entirely learned, deliberate way of thinking (Snyder, 1994).

Learned optimism: Characteristic use of a flexible explanatory style in which one has learned to make external (outside oneself), variable (not consistent), and specific (limited to a specific situation) attributions for one's failures. In contrast, pessimists have learned to look at failures as due to internal (characteristics of the self), stable (consistent), and global (not limited to a specific situation) attributions.

Optimism: One's expectancy that good things rather than bad will happen. It is a stable trait in some people and is independent of self-efficacy (Scheier & Carver, 1985).

Pathways thinking: The perceived capacity to find routes to desired goals. (Compare with *agency thinking.*)

Past orientation: A perspective in which one emphasizes past occurrences, pleasurable experiences, or previous relationships when thinking about time.

Present orientation: A perspective in which one emphasizes the here and now, looking to the present to experience pleasure and satisfy needs.

Self-efficacy: Belief that one's skills and capabilities are enough to accomplish one's desired goals in a specific situation.

Situational perspective: A view of psychological concepts (such as self-efficacy) as situationally, or context, specific; that is, that the specific setting influences how a psychological phenomenon is manifested. As the situation varies, the concept varies in turn. (Compare with *trait perspective.*)

Social cognitive theory: A theory suggesting that people's self-efficacy (confidence in their abilities) influences their actions and thoughts in such a way that they shape their environments. For example, a child who thinks she might be good at basketball tries out for the team. Trying out for the basketball team, in turn, gives the child opportunities to develop her skills and gain confidence in her abilities. Then the child thinks more positively about her ability to do a variety of sports. Therefore, the child's beliefs influenced the type of environment in which she pursued goals.

Trait perspective: An approach to understanding a psychological concept (such as self-efficacy) as part of the enduring characteristics of the person, a part of their disposition that is evident across situations. (Compare with *situational perspective.*)

Wisdom and Courage 10

Two Universal Virtues

> *God grant me the serenity to accept the things I can not change,*
> *courage to change the things I can, and the wisdom to know the*
> *difference.*
>
> —Attributed to Reinhold Niebuhr

The serenity prayer has become the credo for many ordinary people who are struggling with life challenges. We open with this reference because it makes two points that we examine throughout this chapter. First, as the prayer reveals, the notions of wisdom and courage have been intermingled, historically, in literature. This link and the reasons for it are examined subsequently. Second, the prayer suggests that the extraordinary qualities of wisdom and courage are available to everyone. This point is discussed in the context of the reviews pertaining to wisdom and courage.

Wisdom and Courage: Two of a Kind

Some philosophers and theologians consider wisdom (prudence) and courage (fortitude) to be two of the four cardinal virtues (along with justice and temperance). These primary virtues, traditionally ranked in the order prudence, justice, fortitude, and temperance, "are cognitive and motivational dispositions that in themselves designate not only adaptive fitness for individual's achievements, but also the idea of convergence of individual goal achievements with becoming and being a good person from a communal and social-ethical point of view" (Baltes,

Glueck, & Kunzmann, 2002, p. 328). The cardinal virtues facilitate personal development; good living through practicing them may foster the development of social resources that spark the growth of other people. Both wisdom and courage can inform human choices and fuel pursuits that lead to enhanced personal functioning and communal good. Courage also can help overcome obstacles that make the practice of other virtues more difficult.

**The Cowardly Lion
(played by Bert Lahr)**

Source: © Corbis.

Wisdom and courage often have been studied together, although their intermingling may cause difficulties in distinguishing them. This construct confusion is captured in a statement from the movie *The Wizard of Oz* (Haley & Fleming, 1939), in which the Wizard says to the Cowardly Lion, "As for you, my fine friend, you are a victim of disorganized thinking. You are under the unfortunate delusion that, simply because you run away from danger, you have no courage. You're confusing courage with wisdom."

Wisdom and strength both exemplify human excellence; they involve a challenge, they require sound decision making, and they typically contribute to the common good. Furthermore, as mentioned in the introduction to this chapter, ordinary people can demonstrate both of these extraordinary qualities. Without question, however, the scholarly discussion aimed at clarifying the relationship between wisdom and courage will be complex. In some cases, wisdom is characterized as the predecessor of courage. Moreover, in the strongest form of the argument, St. Ambrose believed that "[f]ortitude without justice is a level of evil" (cited in Pieper, 1966, p. 125). Some people even reason that wisdom can make courage unnecessary. This view is described in Staudinger and Baltes's (1994) words: "[W]e need courage only in those instances when in fact they [wisdom and faith] do not suffice—either because we simply lack them or because they are irrelevant to or ineffective against our distress. Knowledge, wisdom, and opinion can provide fear with its objects or deprive it of them. They do not impart courage but rather offer an opportunity to exercise it or do without it" (p. 57).

In contrast to this perspective, courage has been portrayed as a precursor of wisdom. The logic here is that the capacity for courageous action is necessary before one can pursue a noble outcome or common good that is defined by wisdom. Courage sometimes is viewed as the virtue that makes all virtuous behaviors possible. Irrespective of their relative power or import, we believe that a discussion of implicit and explicit theories of wisdom and courage will help in understanding their importance in our daily lives.

Theories of Wisdom

Wisdom often is referenced in ancient maxims (e.g., Yang, 2001) and in philosophical reviews. For example, Robinson's (1990) review of early

Western classical dialogues revealed three distinct conceptualizations of wisdom: (1) that found in persons seeking a contemplative life (the Greek term *sophia*); (2) that of a practical nature, as displayed by great statesmen (*phronesis*); and (3) scientific understanding (*episteme*). Aristotle added to the list of types of wisdom by describing *theoretikes*, the theoretical thought and knowledge devoted to truth, and distinguishing it from *phronesis* (practical wisdom). (See the comments of classics professors as shared by Roger Martin.)

During the 15th, 16th, and 17th centuries in the Western world, two issues dominated the scholarly discussion of wisdom. Philosophers, theologians, and cultural anthropologists debated the philosophical versus pragmatic applications of virtue, along with the divine or human nature of the quality (Rice, 1958). Both issues relate to the question of whether wisdom is a form of excellence in living as displayed by ordinary people or is more aptly seen as a fuzzy philosophical quality possessed only by sages. These issues have yet to be resolved, although psychology scholars have suggested recently that ordinary people are capable of living a good life by applying wisdom.

Wisdom Difficult to Define, Attain

ROGER MARTIN

One day, somebody said, "I enjoy reading your column, but I'm not always sure what it does for the university."

It was one of those hot-potato moments.

I thought fast and tossed this back:

"Universities create knowledge through research and distribute it through teaching.

"The column suggests that, in doing that, universities are one of the sources of wisdom. And that's a great thing. Right?"

I wasn't actually that articulate or concise.

But that's what I meant.

Later, I started to wonder if I was jiving.

I think of this piece I do as a knowledge column. I realized I'd defend it because I love to write about the ideas that come to bright people who passionately study one thing.

The possible jive I detected was in my attempt to connect knowledge with wisdom. I wondered whether that was legitimate.

I called two University of Kansas professors of classics, Tony Corbeill and Stan Lombardo, thinking that, because they study the ancient Greeks, they would have thought about the relationship of knowledge and wisdom.

(Continued)

(Continued)

In Greek mythology, knowledge is the domain of the god Hermes, Lombardo said. Hermes is both inventive and tricky, but he's a lightweight compared with Zeus, the Greek god of wisdom.

According to Corbeill, the wisdom of Zeus was given to humans by the god Apollo.

Apollo spoke through prophets who lived in his temple at Delphi. The prophets were always women. They weren't known for their clarity. Their wisdom often came out garbled, or they spoke in riddles.

In *Scientific American* last year, some researchers reported one possible reason. The prophets may have been sitting in a place where a lot of ethane, methane, and ethylene were leaking in.

Imagine sniffing a lot of glue and then channeling Zeus, and you've got the idea.

Whatever the source of the prophets' inspiration, it's significant to me that they weren't easy to understand.

Wisdom sometimes arrives at the door in odd packages, ones that mere mortals have trouble opening.

Another source of the idea that wisdom is difficult is the Greek poet Empedocles.

Empedocles says that, to get wisdom, you have to "sift knowledge through the guts of your being," according to Lombardo.

Now, the university used to love this word *wisdom*.

KU's fifth chancellor, Francis Huntington Snow, thought a KU education was in part about attaining it. He had these words carved on a building that once served as a KU library:

"Whoso Findeth Wisdom Findeth Life."

But the university seldom uses the word *wisdom* anymore, and it's not the exclusive property of scholars, not by a long shot.

Corbeill says, "It's rare for a polymath to be wise. What comes to mind are people who just learn language after language, for example, as if they're collecting them."

Nevertheless, I've been learning things for 25 years in order to write this column, and as the years have passed, I've become increasingly interested in wisdom—if not wise.

Given the difficulty of discovering wisdom, of breaking the puzzling code that contains it, my mule-headed persistence hasn't hurt a bit.

Source: Lawrence Journal-World, May 21, 2004; www.news.ku.edu/archive. Reprinted with permission.

Although our understanding of wisdom has progressed slowly over modern times, this started to change during the late 20th century. Although the first president of the American Psychological Association, G. Stanley Hall, wrote a book in 1922 in which he addressed the wisdom gained during the aging process, this work was considered the bailiwick of religion and moral philosophers until about 1975, when psychologists began to scrutinize the concept of wisdom. These scholarly efforts produced a better commonsense psychological understanding of wisdom. **Implicit theories** (folk theories of a construct that describe its basic elements) of wisdom first were described by Clayton (1975, 1976; Clayton & Birren, 1980) and then further explicated by German psychologist Paul Baltes's (1993) analysis of cultural-historical occurrences. Knowledge gained from these recent studies has informed the development of **explicit theories** (theories detailing the observable manifestations of a construct) of wisdom, the soundest of which presently include the **balance theory of wisdom** (Sternberg, 1998) and the **Berlin wisdom paradigm** (Baltes & Smith, 1990; Baltes & Staudinger, 1993, 2000). In the next section, we explore these implicit and explicit theories of wisdom.

IMPLICIT THEORIES OF WISDOM

Clayton's (1975) dissertation study was one of the first systematic examinations of the wisdom construct. She had people rate similarities between pairs of words believed to be associated with wisdom (e.g., *empathic, experienced, intelligent, introspective, intuitive, knowledgeable, observant*). Through a statistical procedure known as multidimensional scaling, she identified three dimensions of the construct: (1) affective (empathy and compassion), (2) reflective (intuition and introspection), and (3) cognitive (experience and intelligence).

In a later study, Sternberg (1985) asked 40 college students to sort cards (each describing one of 40 wise behaviors) into as many piles as they thought necessary to explain their contents. Again, a multidimensional scaling procedure was used, and the following six qualities of wisdom were identified: (1) reasoning ability, (2) sagacity (profound knowledge and understanding), (3) learning from ideas and environment, (4) judgment, (5) expeditious use of information, and (6) perspicacity (acuteness of discernment and perception). In yet another study, Holliday and Chandler (1986) determined that five factors underlie wisdom: (1) exceptional understanding, (2) judgment and communication skills, (3) general competence, (4) interpersonal skills, and (5) social unobtrusiveness.

The meaning of wisdom also is communicated in our everyday language. In this regard, Baltes (1993) analyzed cultural-historical and philosophical writings and found that wisdom (1) addresses important/difficult matters of life; (2) involves special or superior knowledge, judgment, and advice; (3) reflects knowledge with extraordinary scope, depth, and balance applicable to specific life situations; (4) is well intended and combines mind and virtue; and (5) is very difficult to achieve but easily recognized.

EXPLICIT THEORIES OF WISDOM

Although informed by implicit theories, **explicit theories** of wisdom focus more on behavioral manifestations of the construct. Explicit theories applied to wisdom are intertwined with decades-old theories of personality (Erikson, 1959) and cognitive development (Piaget, 1932), or they emphasize the application of pragmatic knowledge in pursuit of exceptional human functioning (Baltes & Smith, 1990; Baltes & Staudinger, 1993, 2000; Sternberg, 1998).

In his (1932) stage theory of cognitive development, Jean Piaget describes the qualitatively different kinds of thinking that occur during childhood and adulthood. Children typically move from the sensorimotor stage (in which the child's world is experienced through sensing and doing) to the preoperational stage (in which the child's world is framed in symbolic thought) to the concrete operations stage (in which the child's experience begins to be understood through logical thought) during the first 12 years of life. During the formal operations stage, people develop the ability to reason by systematically testing hypotheses. Riegel (1973) built on Piaget's work and considered a form of postformal operational thinking referred to as the dialectical operations stage or, more simply, wisdom. These **dialectical operations** (logical argumentation in pursuit of truth or reality) associated with wisdom involve reflective thinking that attends to a balance of information and to truth that evolves in a cultural and historical context. Such reflective, or dialectical, thinking facilitates an integration of opposing points of view (Kitchener & Brenner, 1990), dual use of logical and subjective processing of information (Labouvie-Vief, 1990), and an integration of motivation and life experiences (Pascual-Leone, 1990).

Life-span theorists (e.g., Erikson, 1959) view wisdom as part of optimal development. For Erikson, wisdom reflects a maturity in which concerns for the collective good transcend personal interests. In Orwoll's (1989) study of people nominated as wise, this Eriksonian integrity was accompanied by elevated concerns for the collective good.

Both Sternberg's (1998) balance theory and Baltes's (Baltes & Smith, 1990; Baltes & Staudinger, 1993, 2000) Berlin wisdom paradigm are similar in that they emphasize the organization and application of pragmatic knowledge. Furthermore, both views of wisdom propose that wise people can discern views of others, develop a rich understanding of the world, craft meaningful solutions to difficult problems, and direct their actions toward achieving a common good.

Yale psychologist Robert Sternberg built on his previous work on intelligence and creativity (Sternberg, 1985, 1990) and proposed the balance theory of wisdom as specifying "the processes (balancing of interests and of responses to environmental contexts) in relation to the goal of wisdom (achievement of a common good)" (Sternberg, 1998, p. 350).

More specifically, Sternberg theorized that the tacit knowledge underlying practical intelligence (i.e., "knowing how" rather than "knowing what") is used in balancing self-and-other interests within the environmental context to achieve a common good (Sternberg, personal communication, October 8, 2003). See Figure 10.1 for a diagram of Sternberg's wisdom model. In this model, the wise person goes through a process that may resemble high levels of moral decision making (Gilligan, 1982; Kohlberg, 1983). First, the person is challenged by a real-life dilemma that activates the reasoning abilities that were first developed in adolescence and then refined in adulthood. Then, the person's life history and personal values bear on his or her use of available tacit knowledge in balancing interests and generating wise responses. The person striving to be wise then examines possible responses to determine the extent to which solutions require adaptation to the environmental context, shaping of the environment to fit the solutions, or selection of a new environment where the solutions

Robert Sternberg

Source: Reprinted with permission of Robert Sternberg.

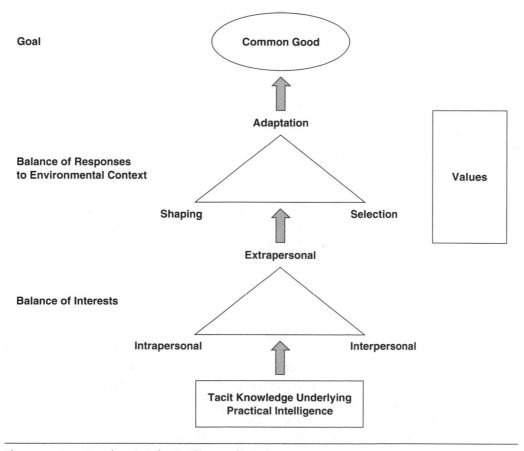

Figure 10.1   Sternberg's Balance Theory of Wisdom

Source: From Sternberg, R., A balance theory of wisdom, in *Review of General Psychology,* 1998, reprinted with permission.

might work. Finally, if balance is achieved, then the common good is addressed with the proposed solution. (For a related discussion of wisdom as a "balance strength," see Bacon, 2005.)

According to Sternberg, wisdom involves forming a judgment when there are competing interests that lack a clear resolution. For example, a wise approach to resolving a conflict over a proposed ban of cigarette smoking on a college campus would consider the interests of all people (smokers, nonsmokers, students, faculty, visitors, etc.), review the options for serving the interests of those people, and act to best serve the common good. As such, balancing personal interests and actions and sharing a wise judgment may entail exceptional problem-solving ability.

In the Berlin wisdom paradigm, Baltes and his colleagues (Baltes & Smith, 1990; Baltes & Staudinger, 1993, 2000), define wisdom as the "ways and means of planning, managing, and understanding a good life" (Baltes & Staudinger, 2000, p. 124). Simply stated, "wisdom is an expertise in conduct and meaning of life" (p. 124). The Baltes group (Baltes & Smith, 1990; Staudinger & Baltes, 1994) has identified five criteria that characterize wisdom (excellence) and wisdom-related (near-excellence) performance.

The two basic criteria, factual and procedural knowledge, indicate that wise performance necessitates expertise. According to Baltes, such expertise requires people to "know what" (i.e., knowledge about topics such as human nature and development, individual differences, social relations and norms, etc.) and to "know how" (i.e., developing strategies for dealing with problems and giving advice, resolving life conflicts, and planning for and overcoming obstacles that could thwart problem resolution). Factual knowledge, or the behavior that is the "product" of that knowledge, could be evaluated with the following question: "To what extent does this product show general (*conditio humana*) and specific (e.g., life events, institutions) knowledge about life matters and the human condition as well as demonstrate scope and depth in the coverage of issues?" (Staudinger & Baltes, 1994, p. 149). "Know how," or procedural knowledge, would be examined in light of the following question: "To what extent does this product consider decision strategies, how to define goals and to identify the appropriate means, whom to consult with and about strategies of advice giving?" (Staudinger & Baltes, 1994, p. 149). The three meta-criteria that are specific to wisdom (i.e., life-span contextualism, relativism of values, and recognition and management of uncertainty) involve flexible thinking and dialectical processing. In particular, **life-span contextualism** requires that wise people consider the contexts of life (e.g., love, work, and play), cultural values, and the passage of time when reviewing problems and their associated solutions. **Relativism of values** and life priorities place the value differences across people and societies in perspective. Lastly, **managing uncertainty** provides the decision-making flexibility that is necessary for processing difficult information and coming up with appropriate solutions. These characteristics of wisdom also may be evaluated with additional probing questions (see Staudinger & Baltes, 1994).

To determine the quality of wisdom, Baltes challenges people with questions about resolving real-life problems. Then, the responses to such questions are transcribed and rated according to the five criteria of wisdom. Reliable wisdom scores can be calculated using this method. Specifically, Baltes asks people to consider how they would advise other people facing dilemmas (referred to as wisdom-related tasks requiring "life planning" or "life management") or to conduct a "life review" by describing their responses to problems experienced in their lives. For example, people are asked to consider the following: "In reflecting over their lives, people sometimes realize that they have not achieved what they had once planned to achieve. What should they do and consider?" (Baltes & Staudinger, 2000, p. 126). One "high-level" (i.e., wise) response to this question demonstrates the value perspective plays in drawing meaning from life:

> First, I would want to say that only very few and most likely uncritical people would say that they are completely satisfied with what they have achieved. . . . It depends very much on the type of goals we are considering, whether they are more of the materialistic or more of the idealistic kind. It also depends on the age of the person and the life circumstances in which he/she is embedded. . . . Next, one would start to analyze possible reasons for why certain goals are not attained. Often, it is the case that multiple goals were pursued at the same time without setting priorities and, therefore, in the end, things get lost. . . . It is important to gradually become realistic about goals. Often, it is helpful to talk to others about it . . . conditions external and internal to the person, or sometimes it is also the match between the two, that can lead to difficulties in life (excerpted from Staudinger & Leipold, 2003, p. 184).

Becoming and Being Wise

DEVELOPING WISDOM

Influential developmental theorists such as Piaget (1932), Jung (1953), and Erikson (1959) provided building blocks for 20th-century wisdom theorists. As mentioned previously, Piaget's work has been extended beyond formal operations to include "dialectical operations" (Riegel, 1973). The work of Erikson and Jung gave modern theorists clues about how resolving conflict leads to enhanced discernment and judgment. In this regard, Erikson emphasized that wisdom is gained through resolving daily crises, specifically those involving integrity and despair. Jung, with his interests in family-of-origin issues, proposed that wisdom develops through the resolution of psychic conflicts pertaining to individuating from the family unit.

Theorists such as Baltes (1993), Labouvie-Vief (1990), and Sternberg (1998) suggest that wisdom builds on knowledge, cognitive skills, and personality characteristics (discussed by Piaget, Jung, Erikson, and others), and that it requires an understanding of culture and the surrounding environment. Moreover, wisdom develops slowly through exposure to wise role models. Sternberg proposed that knowledge, judicial thinking style, personality, motivation, and environmental context precede wisdom, and Baltes and Staudinger (2000) suggested that fluid intelligence, creativity, openness to experience, psychological-mindedness, and general life experiences "orchestrate" to produce wisdom.

Wisdom grows as people learn to think flexibly to solve problems, and such problem solving entails recognizing ideas according to place and culture. In turn, by recognizing that the answers to questions depend both on contextual factors and on the balancing of many interests, people become even more flexible in their thinking. On these points, Baltes and Staudinger (2000) also emphasize the importance of "guidance by mentors or other wisdom-enhancing 'others,'" (p. 127) though such mentoring benefits are indirect sometimes and direct at other times. Indeed, Staudinger and Baltes (1996) agree with the old adage, "Two heads are better than one," when it comes to responding wisely to life challenges. These same researchers also found that people who discussed dilemmas with loved ones (and others) and then were allowed time for reflection showed increases in their wisdom-related performances; moreover, the older participants benefited more from these interactive experiences than did the younger participants.

WISE PEOPLE AND THEIR CHARACTERISTICS

Over centuries and cultures, the *sage* was considered the carrier of wisdom (Assmann, 1994; Baltes, 1993). These mysterious and rare sages were purveyors of life guidance, but they often did little to teach life understanding and the skills needed for wisdom. Modern characterizations of the wise person suggest that the ordinary person can acquire expertise in life matters. In this latter regard, clinical psychologists have been found to possess high levels of wisdom (discussed subsequently; see Smith, Staudinger, & Baltes, 1994; Staudinger, Smith, & Baltes, 1992).

Monika Ardelt, a researcher who has studied aging, measured what she referred to as the "timeless and universal knowledge of wisdom" (2000, p. 71). California residents were the participants in her longitudinal study, the Berkeley Guidance Project. Her analysis of the characteristics that facilitated the development of wisdom revealed that a person's childhood does not have an impact on the development of wisdom, whereas the quality of one's social environment in early adulthood does. Ardelt (1997) also found that wise people achieved greater life satisfaction than unwise people.

Orwoll and Achenbaum (1993) reviewed the role that gender plays in the development of wisdom. In considering the different ways that men and women attain and express wisdom, these researchers concluded that wisdom combines traditional masculine and feminine sensibilities. In their review, they also reported that many of men's wise acts took place in public, whereas women's wise acts took place in private. On this point, Orwoll and Achenbaum wrote, "Differing experiences and social roles of women and men are bound to affect the forms through which wisdom is expressed" (p. 287). Unfortunately, this assumption has yet to be carefully scrutinized via empirical studies.

Life-span researchers also have explored whether wisdom-related performances vary with chronological age (Smith & Baltes, 1990; Staudinger, 1999). In exploring the performances of 533 people, Baltes and Staudinger (2000) found that "for the age range from about 25 to 75 years of age, the age gradient is zero" (p. 128). In this study, therefore, there were no age differences in levels of wisdom. Wisdom does appear to decline, however, in the late seventies and beyond. Furthermore, researchers studying adolescents (e.g., Pasupathi, Staudinger, & Baltes, 1999) have reported that the decade between years 15 to 25 is a major time for acquiring wisdom. Taken alone, these findings suggest that adolescence and young adulthood are fertile times for wisdom development, and the late seventies and beyond bring about declines in wisdom. More research is needed to explain wisdom development during the 50-year period between 25 and 75.

The role of professional background also has been considered in regard to the expression of wisdom (see Smith et al., 1994; Staudinger et al., 1992). This research revealed that clinical psychologists had higher levels of wisdom-related performance than people in other professional jobs who were matched on educational level and age. Although the wisdom displayed by psychologists was elevated, it was not at the expert level. Based on these findings, the researchers concluded that professional specialization does play a role in the manifestation of wisdom. (Of course, it also may suggest that people predisposed to the development of wisdom self-select for certain professions; that is, those who are disposed toward being wise decide to pursue educations and careers in clinical psychology.)

We have met thousands of psychologists during our careers, and we have had the privilege of working with a handful of applied psychologists who could be considered master therapists. In our estimation, these therapists are paragons of wisdom because not only are they prudent in their daily lives, they also are able to impart wisdom to some of the people they counsel and educate. One master therapist whom we have gotten to know through her writings is the popular author Dr. Mary Pipher; we encourage you to get to know her as well. Dr. Pipher's keen ability to provide perspective on complex issues has been demonstrated in books such as the 1995 bestseller, *Reviving Ophelia*, a work that deals with the cultural pressures exerted on adolescent girls in America. Her wisdom as a therapist was shared broadly with psychologists-in-training in her 2003 book, *Letters to a Young Therapist*. Here, she shares pages and pages of "know-how," a basic criterion of wisdom, and she encourages readers to adopt a "back to the basics" approach when helping others. She emphasizes the need to contextualize clients' problems and to recommend treatment strategies that fit with the person at *this* time in their lives. She also addresses the uncertainty that is part and parcel of life, and she describes numerous strategies for managing, or better yet, accepting, this uncertainty. Through her *Letters* book, which is an excellent primer on human change, Piper suggests that young therapists practice wisely and share their perspective-taking skills with their clients.

THE MEASUREMENT OF WISDOM

Several measurement approaches have been used in the models of wisdom described in this chapter. For example, developmental and personality theories of wisdom have yielded self-report questions and sentence completion tasks. The forms of wisdom involving expertise in the conduct and meaning of life have been tapped via problem-solving tasks. Sternberg (1998) has proposed that wisdom problems require a person to resolve conflicts, and he is working toward the development of a formal, standardized test of wisdom. Consistent with his emphasis on pragmatism, Baltes (Baltes & Smith, 1990; Baltes & Staudinger, 1993) has constructed a series of difficult life problems such as the following: "Someone receives a telephone call from a good friend, who says the he or she cannot go on like this and has decided to commit suicide. What might one/the person take into consideration and do in such a situation?" (Baltes & Staudinger, 1993, p. 126). Respondents are encouraged to "think aloud" while considering the resolution of this problem. Their comments and solutions to the problem are evaluated by trained raters, based on the five criteria identified by the Baltes group (factual and procedural knowledge, life-span contextualism, relativism of values, and recognition and management of uncertainty).

A brief self-report measure of wisdom that includes Likert-type items recently was constructed and validated for inclusion in the Values in Action Classification of Strengths (Peterson & Seligman, 2004; see Chapter 4 for a discussion of the classification system). The items are not linked to any of the aforementioned theories, however, and they tap five aspects of wisdom: curiosity, love of learning, open mindfulness, creativity, and perspective. Although all respondents complete the wisdom items, only people who have wisdom as one of their top five strengths (out of 24) receive feedback on their capacity for wise living.

The aforementioned measures of wisdom do not include any items commonly associated with conventional intelligence tests or measures of creativity. The exclusion of markers of intelligence and creativity is deliberate because IQ and creativity are not necessarily associated with wisdom. Hence, the very intelligent or very creative person should not be automatically considered a wise person.

RELATIONSHIPS BETWEEN WISDOM AND INTELLIGENCE

Although implicit theories of wisdom and intelligence are similar (Sternberg, 1985), they can be distinguished by their roles in daily living. Intelligence provides the basic knowledge for accomplishing daily life-supporting tasks for oneself and others, whereas wisdom includes the know-how, judgment, and flexibility to resolve major life problems for the common good (Clayton, 1982; Sternberg, 1985). Clayton (1982) noted that crystallized intelligence is time-bound (knowledge acquired today may be obsolete in 20 years) and wisdom is timeless (knowledge that endures in utility across decades and even centuries). Likewise, Sternberg (1985) characterized wisdom, more than intelligence, as involving inter-personal savvy (listening to and dealing with many different people) and day-to-day life management skills.

Theories of Courage

Like wisdom, courage is a universal virtue. Go to any corner of the earth, and you will find that courage is valued. Read the works of Eastern philosophers and Western thinkers, and you will find that even the wisest people in the history of the world marveled at courage. Socrates is one of many who sought to understand this noble quality, as illustrated in his question to Laches: "[S]uppose we set about determining the nature of courage and in the second place, proceed to inquire how the young men may attain this quality by the help of study and pursuits. Tell me, if you can, what is courage," implored Socrates (Plato, trans. 1953, p. 85). Although this age-old question has long intrigued scholars and laypeople, it is only in the last few decades that researchers from diverse fields (e.g., Finfgeld, 1995; Haase, 1987; Putman, 1997; Rachman, 1984; Shelp, 1984) have established the requisite theoretical and scientific springboards needed for launching more comprehensive examinations of courage. In fact, as can be seen in Table 10.1, there are at least 18 different conceptualizations of courage.

Hemingway's definition (see Table 10.1) appears to be the most parsimonious, whereas Hobbes's view is the most critical of courage. Each of

Table 10.1   Selected Scholarly Definitions of Courage

Aquinas	Defined *fortitudo* as "firmness in mind in enduring or repulsing whatever makes steadfastness outstandingly difficult, that is, particularly serious dangers, primarily sustaining action to overcome fears of bodily harm and death and secondarily in persevering in attacking" (1273/1948, p. 123).
Aristotle	Defined *andreia* (military courage) as the disposition to act appropriately in situations that involve fear and confidence—a rationally determined mean between cowardice and foolhardiness (cited in Rorty, 1988).
Finfgeld	"Being courageous involves being fully aware of and accepting the threat of a long-term health concern, solving problems using discernment, and developing enhanced sensitivities to personal needs and the world in general. Courageous behavior consists of taking responsibility and being productive" (1998, p. 153).
Gergen & Gergen	"To be courageous, then, is to remain steadfast within the bosom of those relationships from which one's sense of personal esteem and identity are derived" (1998, p. 144).
Haitch	"Courage is two-sided: there is an aspect of standing firm or fighting, and an aspect of accepting intractable realities; courage is the psychic strength that enables the self to face danger and death" (1995, p. 86).
Hemingway	Grace under pressure (Parker, 1929).
Hobbes	"The contempt of wounds and violent death. It inclines men to private revenges, and sometimes to endeavor the unsettling of public peace" (cited in Rorty, 1988, p. x).
Kant	Defined *fortudido* as the "capacity and the resolved purpose to resist a strong but unjust opponent; and with regard to the opponent of the moral disposition within us" (Rorty, 1988, p. 65).
Kennedy	(Describing senators with political courage) "Men whose abiding loyalty to their nation triumphed over personal and political considerations" (1956, p. 21).
Kohut	"Oppose the pressures exerted on them and remain faithful to their ideals and themselves" (1979, p. 5).
O'Byrne et al.	"Dispositional psychological courage is the cognitive process of defining risk, identifying and considering alternative actions, and choosing to act in spite of potential negative consequences in an effort to obtain 'good' for self or others, recognizing that this perceived good may not be realized" (2000, p. 6).
Plato	The ability to remember what is worth prizing and what is worth fearing (cited in Rorty, 1988).
Putman	Facing the fears associated with the loss of psychological stability (summarized from Putman, 1997).
Rachman	Persevering in the face of fear (summarized from Rachman, 1984).
Seligman	The capacity to rise to the occasion (Seligman, personal communication, January 7, 2001).

Shelp	"The disposition to voluntarily act, perhaps fearfully, in a dangerous circumstance, where the relevant risks are reasonably appraised, in an effort to obtain or preserve some perceived good for oneself or others, recognizing that the desired perceived good may not be realized" (1984, p. 354).
Snyder	"Responding to extraordinary times with behaviors that seem natural and called for in those circumstances. It is only later, when removed from courage-eliciting events, that the protagonist and others view the behaviors as particularly worthy of the label courageous. This view of courage obviously gives greater weight to situational than to personal factors and suggests that most people are capable of courage if faced with the appropriate circumstances" (Snyder, personal communication, October 17, 2005).
Woodard	"The ability to act for a meaningful (noble, good, or practical) cause, despite experiencing the fear associated with perceived threat exceeding the available resources" (2004, pp. 4–5).

these definitions provides a different historical glimpse of what scholars and society valued in terms of persevering in the face of fear. One other scholarly description, that of the Roman statesman Cicero (as summarized by Houser, 2002), may be the view of courage that best transcends culture and time (as suggested by a comparison to implicit and explicit views on courage detailed later in this chapter). Houser noted that Cicero saw courage as

... (1) magnificence, the planning and execution of great and expansive projects by putting forth ample and splendid effort of mind; (2) confidence, that through which, on great and honorable projects, the mind self-confidently collects itself with sure hope; (3) patience, the voluntary and lengthy endurance of arduous and difficult things, whether the case be honorable or useful, and (4) perseverance, ongoing persistence in a well-considered plan. (p. 305)

IMPLICIT THEORIES OF COURAGE

To examine laypeople's views of courage, O'Byrne, Lopez, and Petersen (2000) surveyed 97 people and found considerable variation. For example, as seen in Table 10.2, some perceive courage as an attitude (e.g., optimism), and others see it as a behavior (e.g., saving someone's life). Some refer to mental strength, others write of physical strength. Some claim that courage involves taking a risk, whereas others accentuate the role of fear. Neither the risk component nor the fear component, however, is found in all descriptions of courage.

Kristin Koetting O'Byrne

Source: Reprinted with permission of Kristin Koetting O'Byrne.

Table 10.2   Laypeople's Responses to the Question, "What Is Courage?"

Taking action (either mental, physical, or spiritual) that is difficult because it makes you uncomfortable (because it is dangerous, threatening, or difficult)

Doing something outside of one's comfort zone—fine line between courage and stupidity

Taking risks in the face of possible failure and uncertainty

Ability to take what life gives and make the best out of one's life (positive attitude involved)

Initiate risk-taking behavior in the face of a threatening situation toward one's emotional/psychological/spiritual/physical health

Standing up for what one believes in even if others don't feel the same

Standing up for oneself in the face of adversity or harm even when the consequences are known

Willingness to take risks, not knowing if one may fail or succeed (being brave)

Sacrificing, working, or helping a cause; faith

Proceeding in a situation even when one is unsure about the outcome; challenging the norm in the best interest of society

Ability to face threats/fears/challenges and overcome obstacles

Ability to contain one's fear enough to progress with a task

Self-confidence, belief in self and situations, making a choice and acting on it, strength

Bravery; act of strength/wisdom in moments of crisis

Defending a viewpoint that is different from the norm; standing up for what one believes in

Having the power and strength to face difficulties or challenges

Taking responsible risks, sacrificing part of oneself

Facing challenges rather than running away or pretending they don't exist

Displaying actions that go along with one's beliefs

Risking failure; determination in the face of failure

Form of assistance during a dangerous or life-threatening event

Selfless behavior; displaying concern for others rather than oneself

Committing acts of perceived bravery that an ordinary person might not do

Being mentally/physically strong

Under strenuous situations/circumstances, engaging in a behavior knowing that negative consequences may occur because of that behavior/action

Note: Major themes: taking risks (possible failure, negative consequences, uncertainty), particular attitude, facing challenges and defending beliefs

Across history and cultures, courage has been regarded as a great virtue because it helps people to face their challenges. Philosophers offered the earliest views on understanding courage. Over the past centuries, efforts to construct socially relevant views of courage have transported it from the hearts of the warriors on the battlefields to the daily experiences and thoughts of every person. Whereas Aristotle analyzed the physical courage of his "brave soldier," Plato marveled at the moral courage of his mentors. The philosophical focus seemed to shift to the deeds and traits of veterans of moral wars with Aquinas's (1273/1948) attention paid to steadfastness in the face of difficulty, and Tillich's (1980) interpretation of courage as the reaffirmation of self and being.) These latter two types of courage (physical and moral) have captured most philosophers' attentions, and the classification of courageous behavior has broadened over the years.

After reviewing work on courage, two groups of researchers developed similar classifications of courage. In their Values In Action classification system, Peterson and Seligman (2004) conceptualized courage as a core human virtue comprised of such strengths as **valor** (taking physical, intellectual, and emotional stances in the face of danger), **authenticity** (representing oneself to others and the self in a sincere fashion), **enthusiasm/zest** (thriving/having a sense of vitality in a challenging situation), and **industry/perseverance** (undertaking tasks and challenges and finishing them).

In a similar model, O'Byrne et al. (2000) identified the three types of courage as physical, moral, and health/change (now referred to as *vital courage*). **Physical courage** involves the attempted maintenance of societal good by the expression of physical behavior grounded in the pursuit of socially valued goals (e.g., a fireperson saving a child from a burning building). **Moral courage** is the behavioral expression of authenticity in the face of the discomfort of dissension, disapproval, or rejection (e.g., a politician invested in a "greater good" places an unpopular vote in a meeting). **Vital courage** refers to the perseverance through a disease or disability even when the outcome is ambiguous (e.g., a child with a heart transplant maintaining her intensive treatment regimen even though her prognosis is uncertain).

Physical courage has evolved slowly from the Greek *andreia*, the military courage of the brave soldier in ancient Greece. Finding the rugged path between cowardice and foolhardiness distinguished a Greek soldier as courageous. From ancient to present times, this disposition to act appropriately in situations involving fear and confidence in the face of physical danger seems to be universally valued (Rorty, 1988). For example, Ernest Hemingway was a major writer on the topic of courage in 20th-century America. His fascination with physical courage in a variety of arenas such as the battlefield, the open sea, and the bullfighting arena seemed to mirror the American fascination with staring danger in the face and persevering. In fact, the "Hemingway code" of living a life characterized by strength, knowledge, and courage provided a code of conduct for many Americans.

Jack Rachman's research on courage stemmed from his realization that courage was the mirror image of fear. He noticed that, when faced with physical jeopardy, some people dealt with the perceived danger better than others. Therefore, Rachman (1984) worked with paratroopers, decorated soldiers, and bomb squad members to gather information on the nature of fear and its counterpart, courage. He found that courageous people persevere when facing fear and thereafter make quick physiological recoveries. He also suggested that courageous acts are not necessarily confined to a special few, nor do they always take place in public. In regard to this latter point, he became intrigued by the inner battles and private courage displayed by his psychotherapy clients. He concluded that clearly there was more to courage than *andreia* and related physical conquest of danger.

Moral courage involves the preservation of justice and service for the common good. Fascinated by moral courage, John F. Kennedy spent years gathering stories of statesmen who followed their hearts and principles when determining what was "best" for the American people—even when constituents did not agree with their decisions or value their representations. Although Kennedy himself was a military hero, in his *Profiles in Courage* (1956) he seemed to give more attention and reverence to moral courage than to physical courage.

Authenticity and integrity are closely associated with the expression of personal views and values in the face of dissension and rejection. Exactly when should one take a stand? In one example, Rosa Parks said that she took a seat at the front of a bus because it was time to do so. Doctors and nurses, when facing difficult situations with patients and families, must be truthful and straightforward even when it would be easier, emotionally, to sugarcoat diagnoses and prognoses (see Finfgeld, 1998; Shelp, 1984). Not only does it take courage to speak the truth (Finfgeld, 1998), it also takes courage to hear the truth. Moral courage can take yet another form when an individual stands up for the rights of the underprivileged and the disadvantaged and confronts someone with power over him or her.

Moral courage might be considered the "equal opportunity" form of this virtue; we all experience situations in which a morally courageous response is provoked, and this behavior requires no special training. Indeed, we may encounter discomfort or dissension and be challenged by the task of maintaining authenticity and integrity in those situations. Physical courage, on the other hand, is sparked only in special circumstances, and often those who engage in physically courageous behavior have received training that helps them overcome fear. (Thankfully, most of us, except for soldiers and first responders, are not called upon to put our lives at risk to protect the common good every day.) Similarly, vital courage is not needed unless we encounter disease or disability, and often professionals teach us how to battle the infirmity. So, how does a common person like you or me respond to situations that challenge our core assumptions about the world and about people? When discomfort or dissension is experienced, and prudence suggests that a stand needs to be taken, we have the opportunity to engage in behavior consistent with moral courage. Unfortunately, we (SJL and CRS) encounter many situations every month in which a person (who is present or not present) is not getting a "fair shake" because of someone's prejudice, be it ageism, racism, or sexism. (We guess that you witness bias of some sort once or more a month as well.) On occasion, we are able to muster up the moral courage to address the perceived injustice; I (SJL) will tell you about one such occasion where I was able to overcome my fear and preserve my integrity and that of others. I hope I can conjure up this kind of courage in similar situations in the future.

My opportunity to practice what I preached occurred on a flight from Lafayette, Louisiana, to Houston, Texas. I was on the first leg of a trip back to Kansas City. I had just spent a week in my hometown of New Iberia helping my mother move into a new house. I was exhausted and more than ready to be reunited with my wife and son. Before boarding the plane, I recognized an acquaintance from my hometown and, I must admit, I avoided him because I remembered him as being somewhat caustic. Much to my chagrin, this man's seat was right behind mine, and, as it turned out, I was surrounded by four of his friends, who were joining him on a hunting trip. I buried my nose in a newspaper and repeatedly thought of being greeted by my family at the Missouri airport. Despite my attempt to ignore the jocular banter of the five men, I overheard first one, then another, then another racist remark about African American hurricane evacuees, politicians, and athletes. There were five racist comments in all, most of which were initiated by my hometown acquaintance. After each comment, my resolve to express my disapproval of these comments grew and grew, as did the fear that made me lightheaded and nauseous. (I reconciled myself to waiting until the plane landed, because the five men had been drinking, and I was concerned that their reaction to my planned remarks would lead to great discomfort among other passengers.) When we landed and the seatbelt sign went off, I took a deep breath, turned to the acquaintance, and said, "I don't approve of the racist comments you shared with your friends during this flight. It is that kind of ignorance that makes people feel unwelcome in our hometown." To my great astonishment, my momentary euphoria was shattered by this man, who proceeded to justify his racist diatribe, and by his friends, who chimed in with a few expletives. As I parted company from the group, I was gratified to realize that the offensive response to my courageous action, which was less than ideal, really was irrelevant to the new confidence it engendered. I had practiced moral courage . . . and I knew I could do it again if I needed to.

Vital courage is at work as the patient battles illness through surgery and treatment regimens. Physicians, nurses, and other allied health professionals use their expertise to save human life or to improve quality of the lives of those whom they serve. Many researchers have examined vital courage (though not calling it such), and their work has captured the phenomenon that captivates us when we hear about someone facing chronic illness. Haase (1987) interviewed nine chronically ill adolescents to answer the question, "What is the essential structure of the lived-experience of courage in chronically ill adolescents?" She found that courage involves developing a deep personal awareness of the potential short-term and long-term effects of the illness.

Amputee Parry Honored as Most Courageous

BERNARD FERNANDEZ

Philadelphia Daily News

1/27/2004—NEIL PARRY has no quit in him. If he did, he never could have exhibited the indomitable will and endless patience required to chase an impossible dream through 3 years and 25 surgical procedures. Somewhere along the way, Parry's excruciating journey of self-discovery transformed the San Jose State football player into a national beacon of hope for the disabled.

You wouldn't think someone like that would suddenly feel a need for instant gratification, but there it was. Parry was back on a football field again, his dream about to become reality, and he wanted the moment to play out as it had so often in his mind.

"It was unbelievable just to be out there for warmups [before a game Sept. 18 against Nevada]," said Parry, 24, last night's recipient of the Most Courageous Athlete Award at the 100th annual Philadelphia Sports Writers Association dinner at the Cherry Hill Hilton. "When you go to a game and you're just going to be on the sideline and not play, it's not the same.

"When I knew I was going to be getting into the game, I was like a kid in a candy store. The crowd is cheering, the band is playing, your family and friends are there.

"For 3 years, I'd run through my head how I wanted it to happen, and it didn't happen like that. I had a little contact, but I didn't really put a big hit on someone, the kind that makes the crowd go, 'Ooooh!' I didn't make the tackle. It wasn't until after the game that I realized what a big deal it was, just being out there."

Big deal? Well, only if you think someone whose right leg had been amputated below the knee in October 2000 had no business even daring to believe he again could compete in Division I-A football. A lot of people thought that. But then, they don't know what Neil Parry is made of. Until the life-altering injury that presented him with an opportunity to go far beyond the universe as he had known it, even Parry couldn't have been sure he had that kind of right stuff.

"People come up to me all the time and say, 'If that happened to me, I wouldn't be able to do what you're doing,'" Parry said. "But nobody knows until you go through it yourself. I could have said the same thing. Before I got hurt, I saw something about that basketball player from Notre Dame [Mike Edwards, the PSWA's 1999 Most Courageous honoree] who played with a [leg] prosthesis. I remember thinking, 'Man, that's awesome.' "

Then, on Oct. 14, 2000, Parry—a walk-on safety at San Jose State—was thrust into the same situation Edwards once found himself in. He made a tackle in the third quarter of an eventual 47–30 loss to Texas-El Paso, but his right leg was mangled in a pile of bodies. He had suffered a compound fracture.

And that wasn't the worst of it. The leg became severely infected, and Parry was given the horrifying news: He would die unless the irreparably damaged limb was amputated. Just 9 days after he was injured, he woke up to see a bandaged stump where his leg had been.

"You never think it's going to happen to you," Parry said. "People say, 'Play every play like it could be your last,' but you never really take it in. When it did happen to me, I thought there had to be a way to save my leg. There wasn't."

San Jose State granted Parry—whose older brother, Josh, also played for the Spartans and was a practice-squad player for the Eagles this season—a full scholarship. But coach Fitz Hill never really thought the young man, who kept talking about playing again, ever would contribute more to the program than a heaping dose of inspiration to his teammates.

But the 25th operation brought Parry's quest into sharper focus, and his doctors informed Hill that Parry, fitted with a new prosthesis, would be able to do virtually everything he had done before the injury. The coach told him to suit up.

Which brings us to the Nevada game and the big hit that Parry had hoped to deliver on his first play back. Miracles do happen, however, and Parry had come too far to be denied the sweet sensation of making a highlight-reel play at some point.

Parry, listed as a 6-1, 175-pound senior safety, would go on to participate in 19 plays last season, all on punt returns. And his presence on the field wasn't the result of a coach taking pity on a nice but physically challenged kid; Division I football doesn't work that way. Parry, whose best time in the 40-yard dash had been 4.6 seconds before the injury, now was being clocked in a tad under 5 seconds. He was still an athlete, maybe not a NFL prospect, but good enough to merit his roster spot.

Perhaps the folks at the East-West Shrine Game in San Francisco invited Parry to play in their Jan. 10 shindig because of his increasingly high profile. He had, after all, met President Bush and been the recipient of awards for courage in Chicago, New Orleans, and Tempe, Ariz. But Parry had one more game to play, and he wanted it to be something more than ceremonial.

In the second quarter, Parry's West team kicked off, and Arkansas' Lawrence Richardson took off on the return. But he didn't get very far, as Parry flew in and flattened him.

"I finally got to lay somebody out," Parry said at the time, his smile indicative of the victory he had achieved, a victory that goes beyond the lines on a football field. He had confronted the worst thing life has presented him to this point, and he had beaten his doubt and fear.

Parry talks of the disabled kids, some amputees, who regard him as a role model, and he takes that responsibility seriously. The walk-on has, in his own way, become a superstar.

Asked whether he would trade all of his awards for the return of his leg, Parry said he had pondered that hypothetical question often.

"It has crossed my mind," he said. "But I don't think I would do it. I've met more people and gone more places than I ever would have.

"I was put in a situation where I can help others. I guess this has brought out my character, shown who I am. I've been able to help more people than I ever would have with two legs."

Source: Fernandez, B. (2004, Jan. 27). Amputee Parry honored as most courageous. *Philadelphia Daily News.* Reprinted with permission of RMS.

In interviews about courage with middle-aged adults with various physical illnesses, Finfgeld (1998) determined that courage involves becoming aware of and accepting the threat of a long-term health condition, solving any related problems through the use of insight, and developing enhanced sensitivities to oneself and others. Finfgeld (1995) also interviewed older adults who were demonstrating courage in the face of chronic illnesses and concluded that being courageous is a lifelong process that entails factors such as significant others, values, and hope. My own (SJL) experience with an elderly client, Carl, led to my fascination with courage and hope and with positive psychology in general. I met Carl on what he referred to as the worst day of his life. He had been diagnosed with kidney failure. The physician realized that this news shook Carl to his core; this observation led to the psychology referral which led Carl to me. Within minutes of meeting Carl, I knew he was suicidal. Within an hour, I knew why he wanted to end his life. In short, the diagnosis of kidney failure was not a surprise; Carl saw it coming. He also realized that kidney failure meant dialysis; dialysis meant a loss of vitality; a loss of vitality meant an inability to work 12-hour days; anything less than full devotion to his work meant that he might lose the family farm. Carl feared his illness because he feared the loss of his purpose and meaning. By hour two, with Carl's permission, I had enlisted his wife in our efforts to develop a plan that would help him cope with this devastating news. By the end of hour three, Carl was stable enough to be allowed to go home rather than being admitted to an inpatient unit. The next morning, he returned for an extended counseling session, and he told me that he was going to battle his illness and learn how to "get the job done" on the farm while undergoing treatment. It was as if he had tapped into a wellspring of hope and courage. Over the next three months, I watched in delight as Carl's health improved . . . without the help of dialysis. His perseverance was unwavering; his vital courage was ever present. It was Carl's courage that helped me realized the power and potential of human strengths.

Regarding the courage of physicians, Shelp (1984) found that this virtue, along with competence and compassion, are very desirable characteristics of health care providers. Moreover, instilling courage through "encouragement" (p. 358) is required of anyone in a profession that exemplifies care and concern. Furthermore, Shelp states that the necessary components of courage are freedom of choice, fear of a situation, and the willingness to take risks in a situation with an uncertain but morally worthy end. We believe that vital courage frequently is exhibited by people who are suffering, by the health care providers who treat them, *and* by the many significant others who care for loved ones during hard times. This vital courage of family and friends who cared for an ailing significant other was one of the many backstories in Jerome Groopman's work, *The Anatomy of Hope: How People Prevail in the Face of Illness.* In this 2004 book, Dr. Groopman told the stories of people who were enduring illness. Often, the sick person was accompanied by a caring doctor and a loving support person. Those caregivers shared, albeit vicariously, in the suffering of the ill person; they faced their own fears, including the fear of the loss of the person who meant so much to them. Hence, vital courage in the face of suffering often is manifested by people other than the identified patient. Groopman's account of a mother with colon cancer and her teenage daughter's coping was particularly poignant. Indeed, the story of Frances and Sharon Walker (pseudonyms for an actual patient and her daughter), discussed in Chapter 2 of the Groopman text, revealed how courage can be seen in the virtuous behavior of those who are ill and the loved ones who suffer alongside them. Furthermore, this case demonstrated that, when one caregiver (the physician in this example) behaves in a cowardly manner, other caregivers might be challenged to rise to the occasion. Frances Walker, during her battle with cancer, was the model patient; she was determined to endure, and she was compliant with treatment. Sharon, her teenage daughter, believed that her mother would be cured; the young woman was a constant source of comfort and support to her mother at every appointment. Unfortunately, Frances's oncologist was not honest with them; her cancer treatment was only palliative, not curative as he boldly asserted. The colon cancer was indeed terminal, a fact the doctor probably knew when first rendering his diagnosis. When Frances was overwhelmed by her true prognosis, and the physician would not keep his appointments with her, young Sharon stood by her mother and stood up to the medical staff. She grappled with her fears about her mother's suffering and her dread of losing her loved one in the near future, and she overcame her hesitancy to challenge authority (the medical staff) when she realized she wasn't getting straight answers. Frances, the patient, and Sharon, the caregiver, embodied the vital courage necessary to fight an illness and maintain dignity.

Psychological courage, as Putman (1997) described it, is strength in facing one's destructive habits. This form of vital courage may be quite common in that we all struggle with psychological challenges in the forms of stress, sadness, and dysfunctional or unhealthy relationships. In light of these threats to our psychological stabilities, we stand up to our dysfunctions by restructuring our beliefs or systematically desensitizing ourselves to the fears. One striking argument that Putman advanced about psychological courage is that there is a paucity of training for psychological courage as compared to physical and moral courage. Putman goes on to say that pop culture presents many physically and morally courageous icons in literary works and movies, but exemplars of psychological courage are rare. Perhaps this is due to the negative stigma surrounding mental health problems and destructive behaviors. It is also possible, however, that the language surrounding vital courage is new relative to that for moral and physical courage (the latter having been acknowledged since the ancient Greeks). The people in Figure 10.2 exemplify moral, physical, and vital courage.

Moral Courage

Rosa Parks stood up to injustice when she sat in a seat in the front of a Birmingham bus during a time of extreme prejudice.

Physical Courage

Firefighters completing a training exercise prepare for their life-threatening work.

Vital Courage

Elie Weisel devoted his life to fighting for human rights after he survived youth in a concentration camp.

Figure 10.2   Exemplars of Three Types of Courage

Consideration of the implicit views of courage and of modern scholars' theoretical examination of courage suggests that our understanding of this virtue has changed little in the 2000 years since Cicero's work. Cicero's definition, summarized previously on page 223, is a timeless one. For example, his comments on courage take into account its multidimensional nature, going beyond the culturally lauded physical courage to honor the patience and perseverance necessary for vital courage and the magnificence inherent in moral courage. Today's implicit views and scholarly operationalizations of courage include references to the qualities of hope, confidence, and honor that appeared in Cicero's definition.

Becoming and Being Courageous

Finfgeld (1995, 1998) says that courageous behaviors follow the identification of a threat, after which there is a shift away from defining the problem as an insurmountable obstacle. Behavioral expectations, role models, and value systems also appear to determine if, when, and how courage unfolds. Courageous behavior may result in a sense of equanimity, or calmness; an absence of regret about one's life; and personal integrity.

Using structured individual interviews, Szagun (1992) asked children ages 5 to 12 to rate the courage associated with 12 different risks (on a 5-point scale ranging from 1 = Not courageous to 5 = Very courageous); moreover, the researcher asked the children to judge courage vignettes. The younger children (ages 5 to 6) likened courage to the difficulty of the task at hand, along with being fearless. The older children (ages 8 to 9) likened courage to subjective risk taking and overcoming fear. Still older children (ages 11 to 12) reported that being fully aware of a risk at the time of acting is a necessary component of courage. Not surprisingly, given their developmental stages, the younger group rated physical risks as entailing more courage than other risks (e.g., psychological risks).

More recently, Szagun and Schauble (1997) investigated courage using an interview technique for younger children and an open-ended questionnaire for adolescents and adults. These researchers asked participants to recall and then describe situations in which they had acted courageously, and to focus on the thoughts and feelings of those situations. Children were asked about courage through the use of a short story about a specific character. Results showed that the young children did not consider fear or overcoming fear in describing the experience of courage, but this propensity to equate courage with the experience of fear increased with age. As in past research (Szagun, 1992), younger research participants conceptualized courage as more physical risk taking, whereas older children focused on psychological risk taking as being necessary for courage. The older children also conceptualized courage as a multifaceted emotional experience that involves fear, self-confidence, and an urge to act.

Several researchers have attempted to determine how people become courageous. This is explored by open-ended questions and interviews in which the individual is asked to describe a situation involving courage (Finfgeld, 1995, 1998; Haase, 1987). Haase (1987) used a phenomenological, descriptive method of assessment. In an unstructured interview format with chronically ill adolescents, participants identified and described their courageous experiences. They were asked the following: "Describe a situation in which you were courageous. Describe your experience as you remember it, include your thoughts, feelings, and perceptions as you remember experiencing them. Continue to describe the experience until you feel it is fully described" (p. 66). This instruction reveals an assumption that all individuals have the capacity for and past experience with courage. Haase's findings regarding courage point to the development of attitudes and coping methods rather than descriptions of so-called "born heroes." In particular, she found that, through daily encounters with "mini-situations" of courage (e.g., treatment, procedures, physical changes, and others that result from the illness), the adolescent comes to an awareness and resolution of the experience as one of courage. Increasingly, over time and experiences, the situation is viewed as difficult but not impossible. Through resolution of the situation of courage, the adolescent develops a sense of mastery, competence, and accomplishment and a feeling of growth.

> ### Late Night's David Letterman's
> ### Take on Courage—September 17, 2001
>
> "And it's very simple . . . there is only one requirement for any of us, and that is to be courageous, because courage, as you might know, defines all other human behavior. And I believe, because I've done a little myself, pretending to be courageous is just as good as the real thing."

> ### United States Senator John McCain's
> ### View on Strengthening Courage—April 2004
>
> "Moral courage we can strengthen. The first time you stand up to a bully, it's hard. The second time, it's not so hard. Physical courage sometimes you run out of. And when I ran out of courage and came back to my cell and tapped on my wall, it was my comrades that picked me up, that lifted me up, that sustained me, that gave me strength to go back and fight again." (transcript of MSNBC's *Hardball With Chris Matthews*)

Courage Research

THE MEASUREMENT OF COURAGE

Over the last 30 years, numerous brief self-report measures of courage have been created for research purposes. Although several of these measures have some strong points, all warrant additional development.

In 1976, Larsen and Giles developed a scale to measure existential (akin to moral) and social (related to physical) courage. The existential courage domain is tapped by 28 items, and 22 examine social courage. Psychometric support for this measure is limited, and little if any work has been done to refine the scale.

Schmidt and Koselka (2000) constructed a seven-item measure of courage. Three items relate to general courage, and four assess what is considered panic-specific courage (possibly a subtype of vital courage). This scale meets basic standards for reliability, but evidence for its validity is limited.

Woodard (2004) used a carefully researched definition of courage as the ability to act for a meaningful (noble, good, or practical) cause, despite experiencing fear (associated with perceived threat exceeding available resources). Based on this definition, Woodard developed a 31-item scale. The total score is computed by multiplying a "willingness to act" score by a "perceived fear" score. Research on this scale suggests that it has promise for measuring courage in future research.

Recent scale development has been completed by positive psychology research teams who were working on what originally was called "wellsprings" measures and now is referred to as the Values in Action Inventory of Strengths (Peterson & Seligman, 2004). The first version of a wellsprings measure included five items (e.g., "I have taken a stand in the face of strong resistance") that tap courage. The current version measures four types of courage, including valor, authenticity, enthusiasm/zest, and industry/perseverance.

The development of measures of courage is in its early stages because a comprehensive theory of courage has not been proposed and carefully examined. It will be difficult to develop a model of courage, but this task should be no more difficult than that accomplished already by several wisdom researchers. An important issue here is whether measurement should assess courage as displayed in a courageous act or as embodied by the courageous actor. To compound matters, it is not clear whether we should focus on the **tonic** (constant) and **phasic** (waxing and waning) elements of courage, or both. This may depend on the type of courage assessed. Moral courage may possess tonic qualities, as a person may demonstrate it steadily across situations, and it also may possess phasic qualities, as it only *appears* when necessary. (Physical and vital courage may be tonic and phasic as well, but the phasic characteristics are more evident.) For example, tapping the tonic elements of moral courage could be achieved with straightforward questions; traditional scales could yield a meaningful representation of this strength. On the other hand, the phasic elements of moral courage, which only emerge in their pure form when needed in a given situation, may require the assessment techniques of observation, narrative reports, experience sampling methods, and critical incident reviews.

RELATIONSHIPS BETWEEN FEAR AND COURAGE

Although the link between fear and courage has been assumed for centuries, the relationship is not well understood. One of the first researchers to examine this link, Rachman (1984) observed that frightened people can perform courageous acts. Though courage and fearlessness often are regarded as synonymous, many (see Table 10.1) have argued that perseverance despite fear is the purest form of courage. Indeed, Rachman proposed that true courage is being willing and able to approach a fearful situation despite the presence of subjective fear. In this case, physiological responses may be measured to assess the presence of fear or stress in a given situation in order to determine how the courageous people respond.

Prior to his research on courage, Rachman's (1978) work focused on describing subjective fear and its associated bodily responses. As he developed a firm understanding of fear and its bodily manifestations and made the shift toward courage research, Rachman and his colleagues (Cox, Hallam, O'Connor, & Rachman, 1983; O'Connor, Hallam, & Rachman, 1985) studied the relationship between fear and courage. These researchers compared bomb operators who had received decorations for gallantry to undecorated operators with comparable training and years of service. (The decoration served as a method of identifying individuals with the experience of courageous acts.) Based on Rachman's (1978) previous research, performances under stressors were determined by various subjective, behavioral, and psychophysiological measures. Comparisons revealed distinctive physiological responses under stress for the decorated as compared to the nondecorated bomb operators, although there were no statistically significant differences found (Cox et al., 1983). In a subsequent experimental replication, O'Connor et al. (1985) demonstrated that, relative to comparison persons, the decorated operators maintained a lower cardiac rate under stress. The findings from these studies suggested that people who had performed courageous acts might respond (behaviorally and physiologically) to fear in a way that is different from people who had not demonstrated courage.

Rachman (1984), trying to understand why some people respond to fear in a manner that might be conducive to courageous behavior, studied beginning paratroopers. His assessment of subjective fear and corresponding physiological markers revealed that paratroopers reported a moderate amount of fear at the beginning of their program, but this fear subsided within their initial five jumps. Furthermore, it was found that the execution of a jump despite the presence of fear (i.e., courage) resulted in a reduction of fear.

This line of research begins to unravel the complex relationship between fear and courage. Given the common assumption that a prerequisite fear must be apparent for there to be courage, the link between fear and physical courage, moral courage, and vital courage needs further examination.

Finding Wisdom and Courage in Daily Life

Wisdom and courage, probably the most valued of the virtues, are in high demand in our world, and fortunately there is not a limited supply. Indeed, we believe that most people, through a mindful approach to life, can develop wisdom and courage. Feel free to test this hypothesis by completing the Personal Mini-Experiments. Then, create some mini-situations of wisdom and courage by implementing the Life Enhancement Strategies.

Can Courage Be Learned?

VIC CONANT

President of Nightingale-Conant Corporation

If you look at the most revered people in history, the people who have done the most for the world, the people who have pushed society forward, you'll invariably find that a major characteristic of those individuals is courage. But what is courage?

S. J. Rachman, a Canadian psychologist specializing in fear and courage, says that many people think of courage as fearlessness. However, Rachman defines courage as perseverance in the face of fear and stress.

Courage is a personal strength, which equates to the ability to act when others of lesser courage will not. It's the ability to act in spite of fear and overwhelming opposition. It's the ability to act in spite of hardship, despair, and sometimes imminent personal physical danger.

Ask yourself, Who's the most courageous individual you've personally known? Next, who's the most courageous person you can identify throughout history? Now, what were the courageous characteristics that caused you to choose these individuals? My personal favorite is Winston Churchill. At the end of World War I, Churchill was in charge of the British navy. After a major naval defeat, he was removed from office and then had to endure more than 20 years of rejection of his political views. He admittedly suffered some very low times. But he never wavered on his beliefs. His views were eventually proven correct when the Germans swept through Europe, and Churchill was the obvious choice to become Britain's wartime prime minister.

Everyone automatically looked to him in this time of need because they knew where he stood, and they witnessed him display courage in battle, putting himself in harm's way over and over again. His personal courage and determination helped inspire an entire nation to continue to resist a force that at the time must have seemed to most . . . insurmountable. And yet Churchill wasn't a likely person to become courageous. According to Stephen Mansfield, in his book *Never Give In: The Extraordinary Character of Winston Churchill,* Churchill didn't have physical strength or towering stature. He was neglected, ridiculed, and misused by friends and family alike. He was brought up in the leisure class, which seldom produces principled men of vision. However, in spite of all that, he developed a staggering moral and physical bravery.

Mansfield goes on to say about courage, "It cannot be taught, though it can be inspired. And it normally springs from something like faith or resolve—a commitment to something larger than oneself. It can burst forth instantly as though awakened by a sudden jolt. But, more often, it waits in silence until aroused by some pressing challenge. What is certain of courage, though," he says, "is that true leadership is impossible without it."

(Continued)

(Continued)

Churchill himself said, "Courage is rightly esteemed the first of human qualities, because it is the quality that guarantees all others."

Mansfield is right to say that it would be difficult to teach someone to operate at, as he says, "the staggering level of courage of a Churchill or a Gandhi or a Martin Luther King." However, it's been proven that courage can be learned, and that is incredibly important for any of us who would like to increase our courage in some area of our lives.

Among S. J. Rachman's research, he observed the military bomb-disposal officers serving in the British army in Northern Ireland. He discovered that these men were able to cultivate a great capacity for courage, even if they initially lacked a high degree of self-confidence or a natural ability to persist under pressure. He found that the ability to persist and function well in the face of great danger was largely the result of intense and specialized training for their job. Not only being prepared, but *knowing you are prepared.*

Denis Waitley describes fear as one of the strongest motivating emotions we can experience. Yet we do have the power to choose an even stronger motivation that can override fear and cause us to act courageously.

Denis used to be a Navy pilot, and he observed the training of our astronauts. After some of the most arduous and intense training ever devised, astronauts have been able to act efficiently and effectively, even in incredibly dangerous situations. As Neil Armstrong said after he walked on the moon, "It was just like a drill. It was just like we planned it."

It's apparent that we can become more courageous with enough preparation. If we venture, we do so by faith, because we cannot know the end of anything at its beginning. Isn't this the ultimate reason that doubt and fear are able to eat away at our courage? We're fearful because we cannot know the end of anything at its beginning, and we start imagining the worst possible scenarios. So, it seems our best chance to overcome fear and become courageous is to prepare and then have faith. Now, in what area of your life would you like to become more courageous?

Source: Reprinted with permission from Vic Conant. www.AdvantEdgeMag.com.

Personal Mini-Experiments

In Search of the Wisdom and Courage of Everyday People . . . Including Yourself

In this chapter, we discuss two of the most celebrated human strengths, wisdom and courage. Our review suggests that both these qualities, although extraordinary, are manifested in one's daily life. Here are a few ideas for finding wisdom and courage in everyday people.

The Wisdom Challenge: Consider your views on the following life event. Think aloud and write them down. "A 15-year-old girl wants to get married right away. What should one/she consider and do?" (Baltes, 1993, p. 587). What questions would you want to ask before offering a comment? Write them down. Then, informally evaluate how well your questions address the five criteria of wisdom (factual and procedural knowledge, life-span contextualism, relativism of values, and recognition and management of uncertainty).

Today's Superheroes: Identify real-life superheroes, people you know, who exemplify each type of courage—physical, moral, and vital. Write a brief biography of each person, and, if you are inclined, write a note to these people telling why you think they possesses courage. You may be surprised by how easy it is to find people who demonstrate courage, as well as how uncomfortable courageous people are with the label.

The Controversial Courage Debate: Debating an emotionally provocative, controversial topic sometimes requires great wisdom. A "controversial courage debate" might require you to apply flexible thinking and consider variations in others' values and life priorities (i.e., value relativism). In a small group, in class or in a social setting, discuss both sides of the following issue: "The terrorists who crashed their planes into the World Trade Center towers were courageous." Focus on personal definitions of courage and on ideas about whose common good needs to be considered when identifying courage.

Life Enhancement Strategies

Pursuits of wisdom and courage have been chronicled in many historical and fictional accounts. For example, Buddha abandoned everything that he knew and loved in order to seek enlightenment, a state of wisdom and love that has defined the Buddhist traditions. And, as we referenced at the beginning of this chapter, the Cowardly Lion trekked through the magical forest in hopes that the Wizard of Oz would grant him the courage that he thought he lacked.

We believe that, over the journey that is your life, you can develop the wisdom and courage to make your life more fulfilling as well as to contribute to a greater good. By no means do we think is easy to develop these qualities, however, but other ordinary people have been able to do so by facing life's challenges . . . and with mindful practice, you also can.

As in most chapters, we categorize the life enhancement strategies across three of life's important domains—love, work, and play. We share two suggestions for each domain, one related to wisdom and one to courage.

(Continued)

(Continued)

Love

- Balancing your love life with your work life will take a tremendous amount of wisdom. Identify one person in your family who is the best role model for using wisdom to balance his or her love life with his or her work life. Interview this person, and determine the four wise acts in which he or she engages to maintain that balance.
- Face the fear often associated with dating and making new friends by introducing yourself to twice as many people today as you did yesterday.

Work

- Share your wisdom about succeeding academically and socially with freshmen at your college or university. Your perspective on how to adapt may prove valuable to other students.
- Stand up for what is just when your rights or the rights of others are violated. Take opportunities to display your moral courage only when you are certain that the act is warranted, but don't decline to act out of concern that the outcome is uncertain.

Play

- Balance your work or school demands with your leisure activities. Reflect on the past week, and determine how well you balanced your daily living.
- Pursue recreational interests with a passion, but do not confuse rashness or fearlessness with courage.

The Value of Wisdom and Courage

"To understand wisdom fully and correctly probably requires more wisdom than any of us have" (Sternberg, 1990, p. 3). Likewise, to understand courage may require a good bit of wisdom. This chapter provides a brief review of what we know about these strengths. Undoubtedly, despite our effort to demonstrate that everyday people embody both of these extraordinary characteristics, the number of times that you are exposed either directly or by the media to images of unwise and rash behavior may outnumber the times that you see virtuous behavior. Given that many people are enamored of the stupid behavior of the unwise and the apparent fearlessness of contestants on television shows such as *Fear Factor*, we feel compelled to make an even stronger case for celebrating virtue: Wisdom and courage have evolutionary value, whereas stupidity and rash fearlessness thin the herd.

A clear argument for the adaptive value of wisdom is made by Csikszentmihalyi and Rathunde (1990). Wisdom guides our action, and through that wisdom we make good choices when challenged by the social and physical world. This practiced wisdom is intrinsically rewarding and beneficial to the common good; it promotes the survival of good ideas, of oneself, and of others. Indeed, wise ideas and wise people may stand the test of time. A similar case can be made for courage. Physical courage and vital courage often extend lives. So, too, does moral courage preserve the ideals of justice and fairness.

Key Terms

Authenticity: A dimension of courage in the Values in Action classification system. Authenticity involves acknowledging and representing one's true self, values, beliefs, and behaviors to oneself and others.

Balance theory of wisdom: A theory developed by Sternberg (1998) that specifies the processes used to balance personal interests with environmental context to achieve a common good. The processes involve using tacit knowledge and personal values to form a judgment of or resolution for competing interests.

Berlin wisdom paradigm: A theory developed by Baltes et al. suggesting that wisdom requires knowledge and insight into the self and others within a cultural context and is "the ways and means of planning, managing, and understanding a good life" (Baltes & Staudinger, 2000, pg. 124). The paradigm addresses life-span contextualism, relativism of values, and managing uncertainty.

Dialectical operations: The use of logical argumentation, discussion, and reasoning as a method of intellectual investigation. Dialectical thinking involves examining and resolving opposing or contradictory ideas and integrating subjective information, motivation, and life experiences.

Enthusiasm/zest: A dimension of courage in the Values in Action classification system. It involves thriving, or having motivation, in challenging situations or tasks.

Explicit theories: Explicit theories examine the externally visible aspects of a construct. For example, in the study of wisdom, explicit theories examine behaviors thought to demonstrate wisdom, such as problem-solving ability. These theories focus on the observable characteristics of a construct.

Implicit theories : Theories that examine the nature or essence of a construct, such as courage, that cannot be directly seen or revealed. Implicit theories or "folk theories" seek to explain through describing characteristics, qualities, and/or dimensions of the desired construct.

Industry/perseverance: A dimension of courage in the Values in Action classification system. It involves undertaking tasks or having initiative and determination to start and complete challenges.

Life-span contextualism: A component of the Berlin wisdom paradigm that requires understanding a problem in terms of its context. These contexts can be aspects of life, such as love, work, and play, as well as cultural and temporal contexts (time and place in society).

Managing uncertainty: A component of the Berlin wisdom paradigm. Using this skill means understanding that any problem-solving strategy or solution involves limitations and requires decision-making flexibility.

Moral courage: Part of O'Byrne, Lopez, and Petersen's (2000) classification of courage; the authentic expression of one's beliefs or values in pursuit of justice or the common good despite power differentials, dissent, disapproval, or rejection.

Phasic: Pertaining to a nonenduring characteristic, a quality that is subject to change depending on the situation, context, or when it is needed.

Physical courage: Part of O'Byrne, Lopez, and Petersen's (2000) classification of courage; an attempted physical behavior or action that seeks to uphold the values of a society or the common good.

Psychological courage: Described by Putman (1997) as a form of vital courage that involves the strength to acknowledge and face personal weaknesses, destructive habits, or threats to one's own psychological stability.

Relativism of values: A component of the Berlin wisdom paradigm; involves understanding that values and priorities are different across people, societies, and time. The value of any idea may vary depending on the context in which it is presented.

Tonic: Pertaining to an enduring characteristic or trait-like quality.

Valor: A dimension of courage in the Values in Action classification system. It involves taking a physical, emotional, or intellectual stance in the face of danger or fear.

Vital courage: Part of O'Byrne, Lopez, and Petersen's (2000) classification of courage, formerly *health/change courage*; a person's persistence and perseverance through a disease, illness, or disability despite an uncertain outcome.

Mindfulness, Flow, and Spirituality

In Search of Optimal Experiences

Perhaps our favorite definition of *insanity* is "doing the same thing over and over again and expecting different results" (attributed to both Albert Einstein and Benjamin Franklin). Why would we engage in the same behavior again and again if we know that the eventual outcome will be negative? Well, passive habits are easy to establish and hard to break (see Bargh & Chartrand, 1999). For example, many of us have done this more than once: turned on the television to "see what's on," watched "nothing" for 3 hours, and then wished we had those 180 minutes back. That kind of habitual, mind-numbing experience may have some short-lived, stress-relieving benefits, but more often it distracts us from what is happening in our worlds. Mindless pursuit of less-than-meaningful goals or unchallenging ones leaves people feeling bored and empty. Conversely, intentional, moment-to-moment searches for optimal experiences give us joy and fulfillment. These positive pursuits may bring about sanity in daily life that is grounded in competence (Langer, 1989, 1997) and happiness (Myers, 2000).

This chapter directs your attention to the moment-to-moment experiences that make up each and every day of our lives. A discussion of mindfulness, flow, and spirituality is framed as searches for optimal experiences. We believe that too many of us walk through everyday life unaware—out of sync with the significance of our experiences and with our emotional selves. Hence, we need to learn more about the psychology of deeper living, a psychology with universal applications that teaches about the depths of enjoyment, contentment, and meaningfulness that can be achieved through engagement with everyday life. In our pursuit of an understanding of optimal experiences, we discuss the searches for novelty, absorption, and the sacred, respectively, and we highlight the possible benefits of a more intentional existence (produced with the aid of sound interventions promoting mindfulness, flow, and spirituality). We begin by considering how the moments of our existence hold the potential for giving our lives pleasure and meaning.

Moment-to-Moment Searches

In a fast-paced, 21st-century world, it is easy to lose sight of the thousands of moments passing in front of our very eyes. Yet, each of these moments is accessible (or can be captured), and each has untapped potential; they all are part of our search for optimal experiences. Daniel Kahneman, a psychologist who won the 2002 Nobel Prize in Economics, values the currency that is time and understands the relationship between individual moments and the broader experience of life, as suggested by this excerpt from one of his recent addresses:

> Now, there are about 20,000 moments of 3 seconds in a 16-hour day, so this is what life consists of; it consists of a sequence of moments. Each of these moments is actually very rich in experience, so if you could stop somebody and ask, "What is happening to you right now?" a great deal is happening to us at any one of these moments. There is a goal, there is a mental content, there is a physical state, there is a mood, there might be some emotional arousal. Many things are happening. And then you can ask, "What happens to these moments?" (Mitchell, 2003, para. 11)

We certainly can agree that moments are plentiful in daily life. And the potential that each moment holds is reflected in the thoughts, feelings, and physiological forces connected to each moment. From a positive psychology perspective, a day presents 20,000 opportunities for engagement, for overcoming the negative, and for pursuing the positive.

To test our contention that each moment of life is novel and potential-packed, try slowing down your day a bit by taking a stroll through a neighborhood . . . with a three-year-old child. A three-year-old (who is well rested and generally content) can turn a two-block walk into a grand adventure that lasts about five times longer than you expected. The child will attend to everything in his or her line of vision and will happily share thoughts about what is being experienced. When the next "moment" arrives (e.g., another child runs across the path), the child can move on to experience it without any "analysis paralysis" (Should I attend to that or to this?). Undoubtedly, sauntering through a neighborhood with a toddler will draw your attention to the slices of life that are there to be experienced. By adding a bit of intentionality to your belief that each moment has potential, we believe you can actively pursue, on a daily basis, a richer life experience that includes more novelty (*mindfulness*), more absorption (*flow*), and attention to the sacred (*spirituality*).

Mindfulness: In Search of Novelty

Some of the best examples of mindfulness are manifested in the everyday behaviors of people. This was indirectly illustrated in the research of Amy Wrzesniewski, a positive psychologist interested in how people function optimally at work (cited in Snyder & Lopez, 2002; Wrzesniewski, McCauley, Rozin, & Schwartz, 1997; also see Chapter 17.). She found that a third of the hospital cleaners in a metropolitan medical center considered their work a "calling" and therefore did everything they could to make the health care experience positive for patients and staff. These members of the cleaning team essentially reconstrued their jobs by mindfully making moment-to-moment choices about what was worthy of attention, thereby also exercising some control over their duties. Their mindfulness resulted in benefits for others. For example, cleaners who had a calling were quite vigilant in their attempts to keep the hospital sanitary. These cleaners would make generous efforts to make the stays of the long-term patients more bearable by changing the placement of pictures in the rooms and repositioning other objects to give patients new views of their surroundings. Each day, the cleaners found novel ways to improve the hospital environment. (See the story about a hospital orderly told by the senior author [CRS] in Chapter 17.)

Ellen Langer, a social psychologist at Harvard University, made sense out of mindfulness behavior by observing the everyday behavior of people from all walks of life (students, businesspeople, retirees). In the context of a research study that examined the effects of perceived control on older adults in a residential care facility, Langer and her colleague Judith Rodin (Langer & Rodin, 1976; Rodin & Langer, 1977) gave a group of residents a "pep talk" about making their own decisions and then allowed these participants each to choose a houseplant to tend over the coming months. Another group of residents received a talk focused on how staff would help them with daily activities and decisions. These participants also received plants, but they were told that the staff would care for them. Over the 3 weeks postintervention, the individuals who were encouraged to make

Ellen Langer

Source: Reprinted with permission of Ellen Langer.

choices and to care for their plants were more alert and happier. They found novelty in every day as their plants and their lives changed little by little.

Langer's follow-up with the facility 18 months later revealed a striking finding: Half as many people in the group encouraged to make choices had died, relative to the group encouraged to take advantage of staff support (7 out of 44 versus 15 out of 43). Langer explained this finding by highlighting the value of "minding" daily choices and the houseplant; this observation launched her into a career dedicated to mindfulness research.

MINDFULNESS AS A STATE OF MIND

Mindfulness, which sometimes is considered a new-age concept, is comparable to the age-old process of cultivating awareness (of everyday happenings and physiological and psychological sensations) in Buddhist traditions and to the modern therapeutic technique of increasing attention in order to identify distorted thinking (an aspect of cognitive and cognitive-behavioral therapies; Miller, 1995). Although a very common psychological phenomenon, mindfulness is not very well understood (Bishop et al., 2004). Therefore, we have done our best in what follows to elaborate on Langer's (2002) definition of **mindfulness** and to describe the benefits of the practice of mindfulness meditation. First, here is Langer's definition of mindfulness, written 25 years after she conducted the study with the elderly residents of the residential care facility:

> [I]t is important to take at least a brief look at what mindfulness is and is not: It is a flexible state of mind—an openness to novelty, a process of actively drawing novel distinctions. When we are mindful, we become sensitive to context and perspective; we are situated in the present. When we are mindless, we are trapped in rigid mind-sets, oblivious to context or perspective. When we are mindless, our behavior is rule and routine governed. In contrast, when mindful, our behavior may be guided rather than governed by rules and routines. Mindfulness is not vigilance or attention when what is meant by those concepts is a stable focus on an object or idea. When mindful, we are actively varying the stimulus field. It is not controlled processing (e.g., 31×267), in that mindfulness requires or generates novelty. (p. 214)

In short, mindfulness is an active search for novelty, whereas mindlessness involves passively zoning out to everyday life. "Automatic pilot" is a form of mindlessness that is attributable to the repetition of behaviors.

Drawing novel distinctions (being mindful) requires us (1) to overcome the desire to reduce uncertainty in daily life, (2) to override a tendency to engage in automatic behavior, and (3) to engage less frequently in evaluations of self, others, and situations. Regarding uncertainty, Langer (2002) argues that "aspects of our culture currently lead us to try to reduce uncertainty" (p. 215). Our desire to control our surroundings by reducing uncertainty often leads to more uncertainty. For example, a child's effort to hold a spirited kitten or puppy demonstrates this point well. The more the child attempts to hold the little pet still, the more it tries to wriggle away. This also happens in daily life when we attempt to hold things (and people's behavior) still in our attempt to reduce uncertainty. Given that life is not static, Langer contends that we should exploit the uncertainty and proposes that mindfulness "makes clear that things change and loosens the grip of our evaluative mind-sets so that these changes need not be feared" (p. 215). Uncertainty keeps us grounded in the present, and awareness of all that is happening in the present creates more uncertainty.

The automaticity of behavior provides quick, well-honed responses to familiar situations. For example, what do most people do when a phone rings? No matter what else is going on around them, many people automatically reach for their phones and answer them. This response is considered the "one best way" to deal with the given situation—but is it? Do we necessarily need to answer the phone when it rings, irrespective of what else we are doing, or has it become an automatic, mindless behavior? Automaticity of behavior relies on the assumption that the quick, well-rehearsed behavior is the easiest behavior in which to engage. In fact, in the case of the ringing phone, the less automatic behavior (e.g., continuing to chat with friends, working on homework, leaving your house so you are not late for class) may be the most efficient way to behave. Perhaps we are distracted from the novelty of the stimuli right before us when a phone rings. What happens if the phone's ringing becomes a signal or a reminder to search for the novelty right in front us? What happens if we don't answer the phone?

Langer, Blank, and Chanowitz (1978) explored the automaticity of behavior by sending an interdepartmental memorandum to university offices that requested that the recipient handle the memo in a particular manner ("Please return this immediately to Room 247") and another memo that demanded particular handling ("This memo is to be returned to Room 247"). To examine the effects of novelty on behavior, half the memos were formatted in the usual form for interoffice memos, whereas the other half of the memos were formatted in a distinctly different manner. In the end, 90% of the memos that looked like the typical interoffice missive were returned to Room 247; 60% of those that looked a bit different from the typical memo were returned. The automaticity of behavior is quite evident given that the majority of the memos were returned. The potency of attention to novelty, however, also was suggested given that a smaller percentage of uniquely formatted memos was returned. Hence, mindfulness will occur when we become less automatic in our daily behavior and search for novelty.

Making evaluations requires us to cast judgment on ourselves, others, and life situations. "Events do not come with evaluations; we impose them on our experiences and, in so doing, create our experience of the event" (Langer, 2002, p. 218). Mindfulness may battle our evaluative nature and lead us to make fewer unnecessary judgments, even positive ones. Here-and-now living does require a refined ability to discriminate between subtleties, and this need not lead to an evaluation. For example, on a walk through a park, a statue may catch your eye and grab a few minutes of your attention. During that short span of time, you may mindfully make numerous observations that discriminate between weathered portions of the statue and less weathered portions, or you may notice that it looks taller from one perspective than another. There is no need or benefit for you to mindlessly activate your criteria for quality artwork and pass judgment on the statue, labeling it as either good art or bad art.

Reducing our tendency to make evaluations of external events is a hallmark of Langer's (2002) conceptualization of mindfulness. On this note, Timothy Miller (1995), author of *How to Want What You Have,* defines *attention* (his term for mindfulness) as "the intention to avoid unnecessary value judgments about your own experience—both internal and external experience" (p. 17).

Miller's focus on avoiding evaluation of internal events as well as external ones is shared with Bishop and colleagues (2004). Bishop et al.'s (2004) operationalization of mindfulness, although similar to Langer's (2002), does discourage continued evaluation of the self, and it draws more attention to the cognitive and emotional components of mindful engagement. In the Bishop et al. two-component system, *self-regulated attention* is honed on current personal experience, and *emotional openness* facilitates the acceptance and appreciation of all internal experiences. Hence, mindfulness from this perspective involves metacognition and emotional awareness.

Turning from Langer's (2002) and Bishop et al.'s (2004) definitions and discussions of mindfulness, we consider a nuts-and-bolts operationalization of mindfulness that often is used by mindfulness meditation practitioners (Kabat-Zinn, 1990; Shapiro, Schwartz, & Santerre, 2002). Mindfulness, in the practice community, is parsimoniously described as attending nonjudgmentally to all stimuli in the internal and external environments. In moments of mindfulness, some "mindfulness qualities" (Shapiro et al., 2002) come into consciousness; see Table 11.1. Many of the these qualities are positive psychological processes discussed elsewhere in this book.

Table 11.1   Mindfulness Qualities

Nonjudging: Impartial witnessing, observing the present moment by moment without evaluation and categorization

Nonstriving: Non-goal-oriented, remaining unattached to outcome or achievement, not forcing things

Acceptance: Open to seeing and acknowledging things as they are in the present moment; acceptance does not mean passivity or resignation, rather a clearer understanding of the present so one can more effectively respond

Patience: Allowing things to unfold in their time, bringing patience to ourselves, to others, and to the present moment

Trust: Trusting oneself, one's body, intuition, emotions, as well as trusting that life is unfolding as it is supposed to

Openness:[1] Seeing things as if for the first time, creating possibility by paying attention to all feedback in the present moment

Letting go: Nonattachment, not holding on to thoughts, feelings, experiences; however, letting go does not mean suppressing

Gentleness: Characterized by a soft, considerate and tender quality; however, not passive, undisciplined, or indulgent

Generosity: Giving in the present moment within a context of love and compassion, without attachment to gain or thought of return

Empathy: The quality of feeling and understanding another person's situation in the present moment—their perspectives, emotions, actions (reactions)—and communicating this to the person

Gratitude: The quality of reverence, appreciating and being thankful for the present moment

Lovingkindness: A quality embodying benevolence, compassion, and cherishing, a quality filled with forgiveness and unconditional love

Source: Shapiro, S. J., Schwartz, G. E. R., & Santerre, C. (2002). Meditation and positive psychology. In C. R. Snyder & S. J. Lopez (Eds.), *The handbook of positive psychology* (pp. 632–645). New York: Oxford University Press. Copyright Oxford University Press, Inc. Used by permission of Oxford University Press, Inc.

Note: These categories are offered heuristically, reflecting the general idea that there are mindfulness qualities that should be part of the intention phase as well as the attention phase of a pathway model. A commitment (intention phase) is made to bring the qualities to the practice, and then the qualities are themselves cultivated throughout the self-regulation practice itself (attention phase). See Kabat-Zinn (1990, pp. 33–40) for detailed definitions of the first seven qualities (cognitive in nature) and Shapiro and Schwartz (2000) for the other five (more affective in nature).

1. Openness: Derived from beginner's mind, defined as "a mind that is willing to see everything as if for the first time" (Kabat-Zinn, 1990, p. 35).

Living With Mindfulness

THE WOMEN'S HEART FOUNDATION

Reactions to stress can have a negative effect on health. [They] can lead to high blood pressure, a rapid resting pulse rate, and . . . heart rhythm disturbances. Reactions to stress can weaken the immune system, which then leads to a variety of illnesses. It is important to learn how to handle stress.

Mindfulness meditation has been shown to help a person manage stressful situations by increasing one's awareness and by making the mind more receptive to one's current situation and internal states. It is a method of fully embracing with minimal resistance one's current life situation and internal states.

One can bring about increased awareness to any activity. Here are some examples:

Being Mindful of Emotions

With mindfulness meditation, one can learn to be less judgmental. Being less judgmental helps to bring about a more relaxed state. One can learn to watch anger and other emotional states with compassion. This enables one to eventually let go of these states or at least keep from intensifying them.

Being Mindful of Eating

Increasing one's awareness of eating may benefit those who are trying to make changes in their eating habits. Here is how to increase your awareness of eating:

- Look at the food you are about to eat. Focus on what it consists of. Ask yourself, "Do I still want to take this food into my body?"
- Pay close attention to every bite. Food eaten mindfully will be easier to digest, and you will be less likely to overeat.
- Just after eating, notice how the food you ate affects your digestive system. Does it agree with you? Notice how you feel when eating a low-fat meal versus a high-fat meal . . . a candy bar snack versus a raw vegetable snack.

Mindful Stretching Exercises

Gentle stretching and strengthening exercises done very slowly with moment-to-moment awareness of breathing and of the sensations that arise is yoga. Yoga seeks to unite the body, mind, and spirit. This can result in improved health and vitality.

Mindful Breathing and Sitting as a Meditation

Mindful breathing and sitting (meditation) help to relax and focus the mind. Just 5 minutes a day can make you feel more refreshed and energetic. Here are some guidelines for practicing mindful breathing and sitting:

1. Make a special time and place for "non–doing."

2. Adopt an alert and relaxed body posture.

3. Look dispassionately at the reactions and habits of your mind.

4. Bring your attention to your breathing by counting silently "1" on inhalation and "2" on exhalation, "3" on inhalation, etc. When you reach number 10, return to number 1. (If you go beyond the number 10, then you know your mind has wandered.)

5. When your mind wanders, name what it wanders to, and come back to the breathing.

6. Once you have practiced focusing on your breathing, you can use sensation, sound, or watching thoughts as your point of concentration.

You cannot prevent stressful situations in life, but you can control your reactions to them. Practicing mindfulness can help.

Source: "Beliefs Surrounding Mindfulness," poem from the Buddhist faith. Mindfulness is used by many Eastern cultures. The positive use of Mindfulness outlined herein was extrapolated from the teachings of Jon Kabat-Zinn. Printed with permission. Grateful acknowledgement to the Women's Heart Foundation, www.womensheart.org.

THE BENEFITS OF MINDFULNESS

The deliberative practice of mindfulness often takes the form of mindfulness meditation. The aim of mindfulness meditation, generally speaking, is the "development of deep insight into the nature of mental processes, consciousness, identity, and reality, and the development of optimal states of psychological well-being and consciousness" (Walsh, 1983, p. 19) through "opening up." The results of several studies examining the effects of mindfulness meditation are discussed here in order to consider the potential benefits of intentionally searching for novelty. It should be noted, however, that this body of research has been criticized because few rigorous, randomized, controlled studies have been published (Bishop, 2002).

Jon Kabat-Zinn (1982) of the University of Massachusetts adapted some of the ancient Eastern meditation practices and created a form of mindfulness meditation that has been used in the successful treatment of chronic pain and anxiety. In one study, Kabat-Zinn and Skillings (1989) examined the effects of an 8-week, mindfulness-based stress reduction program (MBSR) on stress hardiness (commitment, control, challenge; Kobasa, 1990) and sense of coherence (the ability to find the world meaningful and manageable; Antonovsky, 1987) in hospital patients. The researchers found improvement in both hardiness and coherence over the course of the intervention. In turn, patients with the largest improvements in sense of coherence made the biggest gains in psychological and physical symptom reduction. At the 3-year follow-ups (Kabat-Zinn & Skillings 1992), the initial gains were maintained, and even further improvement was made in the extent to which patients considered their worlds manageable.

In a randomized controlled study, Shapiro, Schwartz, and Bonner (1998) tested the effects of mindfulness meditation on 78 premedical and medical students. Their results revealed increased levels of empathy and decreased levels of anxiety and depression in the meditation group as compared to the wait-list control group. Furthermore, these results held during the students' stressful examination period. The findings were replicated when participants in the wait-list control group received the mindfulness intervention.

Brown and Ryan (2003) conducted a clinical intervention study with cancer patients, targeting an increase in positive emotional states and decreased anxiety. The researchers demonstrated that increases in mindfulness over time related to declines in mood disturbances and stresses.

The benefits of mindfulness meditation go beyond stress relief. For example, Weinberger, McCleod, McClelland, Santorelli, and Kabat-Zinn (1990) demonstrated that affiliative trust (trust, openness, and caring) and oneness motivation (a sense of being part of something larger than one's self) increased over the course of the mindfulness intervention. Astin (1997) demonstrated significant increases in spiritual experience after mindfulness meditation interventions in a group of undergraduate students. Similarly, Shapiro and colleagues (1998), in a randomized controlled study, found that higher scores were obtained on a measure of spiritual experience in a meditation group as compared to a control group. Furthermore, these results were replicated when the control group received the same intervention. (To explore the benefits of mindfulness in your relationships, try the Personal Mini-Experiments.)

Flow: In Search of Absorption

Flow experiences have been observed throughout time, across cultures, and in countless creative and competitive endeavors. Such experiences are vividly described in accounts of the responses of the world's great artists, scientists, and religious figures to the challenge of seemingly overwhelming tasks. For example, historical accounts suggest that Michelangelo worked on the ceiling of the Vatican's Sistine Chapel for days at a time. Totally absorbed in his work, he would go without food and sleep and push through discomfort until he ultimately passed out from exhaustion.

Personal Mini-Experiments

In Search of Optimal Experiences

In this chapter, we discuss mindfulness, flow, and spirituality. Our review suggests that intentional pursuits of novelty, absorption, and the sacred can lead you to the good life. Here are a few ideas for experiments aimed at helping you initiate these searches and explore the benefits.

Searching for Novelty: Increasing Mindfulness in Your Relationships: According to Table 11.1, numerous behaviors are associated with mindfulness. For example, *nonjudging* is impartial witnessing, observing the present, moment by moment without evaluation and categorization. *Nonstriving* involves nongoal-oriented behavior, remaining unattached to outcome or achievement, not forcing things. What would happen if you practiced these behaviors for one day in a significant relationship? Try no judgments and no "forcing things." Be an impartial witness, and remain unattached to outcomes for one day. Then, at the end of the day, ask your partner what differences he or she has noticed in your behavior.

Searching for Absorption: Finding Flow in Your School Day: Have you ever wondered how much your screen time (time in front of television, surfing the Internet, instant messaging) affects your ability to immerse yourself in your schoolwork? Take a break from all screen time (except academic use of computers) for 2 days, and determine whether your ability to concentrate increases or decreases. If focused attention increases during this trial period, be sure to decrease screen time during busy times in your academic semester.

Searching for the Sacred: Being More Spiritual in Daily Life: Often, the search for the sacred is cast as a grand journey toward a life-changing goal, but it actually requires small daily steps. Jon Haidt at the University of Virginia (http://wsrv.clas.virginia.edu/~jdh6n/Positivepsych.html) created the following exercises to help folks start the search today. Try these brief exercises and see how they work:

- For 5 minutes a day, relax and think about the purpose of life and where you fit in.
- For 5 minutes a day, think about the things you can do to improve the world or your community.
- Read a religious or spiritual book, or go to a religious service every day.
- Explore different religions. You can do this by going to a library, looking on the Internet, or asking your friends about their religions.
- Spend a few minutes a day in meditation or prayer.
- Invest in a book of affirmations or optimistic quotes. Read a few every day.

He was consumed by work, neglecting self-care and the needs of others. (Legend has it that Michelangelo went weeks without changing his clothes, including his boots. One of his assistants supposedly observed the skin of his foot peel down as a boot was removed.)

Mihaly Csikszentmihalyi

Source: Credit: Christopher
Csikszentmihalyi.

Mihaly "Mike" Csikszentmihalyi was intrigued by the stories about artists who lost themselves in their work. Studying the creative process in the 1960s (Getzels & Csikszentmihalyi, 1976), Csikszentmihalyi was struck by the fact that, when work on a painting was going well, the artist persisted single-mindedly, disregarding hunger, fatigue, and discomfort—yet rapidly lost interest in the artistic creation once it had been completed (Nakamura & Csikszentmihalyi, 2002, p. 89). Csikszentmihalyi (1975/ 2000) also noted that forms of play (chess, rock climbing) and work (performing surgery, landing a plane) often produced similar states of engagement. Over the last 30 years, Csikszentmihalyi has interviewed and observed thousands of people, and his views on the concept of flow guide us in our discussion of this state of "full-capacity" living that is believed to be directly linked to optimal development and functioning.

THE FLOW STATE

Decades of qualitative and quantitative research (summarized in Nakamura and Csikszentmihalyi, 2002) have explored the underpinnings of intrinsic motivation. Indeed, psychology has grappled with the issue of why people pursue particular goals with great fervor in the absence of external rewards (e.g., money and praise). Csikszentmihalyi (e.g., 1978, 1997, 2000) examined this issue in order to understand "the dynamics of momentary experience and the conditions under which it is optimal" (Nakamura & Csikszentmihalyi, 2002, p. 93). Csikszentmihalyi conducted extensive interviews of people from many walks of life; he also developed and used the **experience sampling method**, in which research participants are equipped with programmable watches, phones, or hand-held computers that signal them, at preprogrammed times throughout the day, to complete a measure describing the moment at which they were paged. To date, the conditions of flow appear to be remarkably similar across work settings, play settings, and cultures. These conditions of **flow** include (1) perceived challenges or opportunities for action that stretch (neither underutilizing or overwhelming) existing personal skills, and (2) clear proximal goals and immediate feedback about progress.

Many of Csikszentmihalyi's early research participants described their optimal momentary experiences as being "in flow," hence his use of the term to describe the phenomenon. Based on the early interviews, Csikszentmihalyi (1975/2000) mapped out the landscape of deep flow experiences by graphically representing the relationship between perceived challenges and skills. Three regions of momentary experiences were identified: (1) *flow*, where challenges and skills matched; (2) *boredom*, where challenges and opportunities were too easy relative to skills, and (3) *anxiety*, where demands increasingly exceeded capacities for action (see Figure 11.1).

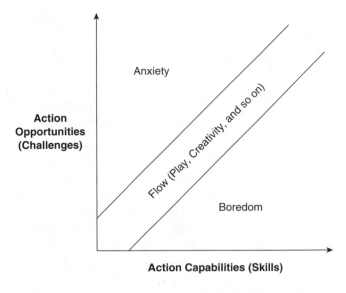

Flow is experienced when perceived opportunities for action
are in balance with the actor's perceived skills.

Figure 11.1   The Original Model of the Flow State

Source: From Csikszentmihalyi, M., *Flow: The Psychology of Optimal Experience.* Copyright
© 1990 by Mihaly Csikszentmihalyi. Reprinted by permission of HarperCollins Publishers.

Under the flow conditions of perceived challenge to skills, clear goals, and feedback on progress, experience unfolds from moment to moment, and the subjective state that emerges has the following characteristics (as listed in Nakamura and Csikszentmihalyi, 2002):

- Intense and focused concentration on what one is doing in the present moment
- Merging of action and awareness
- Loss of reflective self-consciousness (i.e., loss of awareness of oneself as a social actor)
- A sense that one can control one's actions; that is, a sense that one can in principle deal with the situation because one knows how to respond to whatever happens next
- Distortion of temporal experience (typically, a sense that time has passed faster than normal)
- Experience of the activity as intrinsically rewarding, such that often the end goal is just an excuse for the process

The search for absorption in momentary experiences is primarily an intentional attentional process. Intense concentration is dedicated to the present activity, followed by the merging of action and awareness. The loss of self-consciousness occurs as flow emerges. Maintaining the flow state is quite challenging given the many distractions from the outside world and the self-talk that may involve criticism of performance. (Hence, a mindful, nonjudgmental approach to personal performance may be necessary for achieving deep flow.) When considering the quality of flow state, the variable of interest is time spent absorbed, with more engagement in flow being better for the individual.

The conceptualization of flow has not changed much over the last quarter century of research. The model of balancing perceived challenge and skill has been refined, however, by Delle Fave, Massimini, and colleagues (Delle Fave & Massimini, 1988, 1992; Massimini & Carli, 1988; Massimini, Csikszentmihalyi, & Carli, 1987), who, by using the experience sampling method, discovered that the quality of a momentary experience intensifies as challenges and skills move beyond a person's *average* levels. For example, if you play chess with a typical six-year-old, the experience will not present you with an average or above-average challenge that requires higher-level skills. If you play chess with someone with considerably more experience and skill, however, you experience a great challenge, your skills will be stretched, and flow is more likely. See Figure 11.2 for a depiction of a flow model that takes into account these characteristics of flow. Apathy is experienced when perceived challenges and skills are below a person's average levels; when they are above, flow is experienced. Intensity (depicted by the concentric rings) of each experience (e.g., anxiety, arousal, relaxation) increases with distance from a person's average levels of challenge and skill.

THE AUTOTELIC PERSONALITY

The majority of flow research has focused on flow states and the dynamics of momentary optimal experiences. Csikszentmihalyi (1975/2000) did hypothesize, however, that a cluster of personality variables (e.g., curiosity, persistence, low self-centeredness) may be associated with the ability to achieve flow and with the quality of flow that is experienced. He suggested the possible existence of an **autotelic personality** (from the Greek words *autos*, meaning "self," and *telos*, meaning "end"), as exhibited by a person who enjoys life and "generally does things for [his or her] own sake, rather than in order to achieve some later external goal" (Csikszentmihalyi, 1997, p. 117). The amount of time spent in flow has been used as a rough measure of this personality type (Hektner, 1996), but this operationalization does not account for possible environmental influences on flow. A more nuanced operationalization of the autotelic personality focused on the disposition to be intrinsically motivated in high-challenge, high-skill situations. This conceptualization

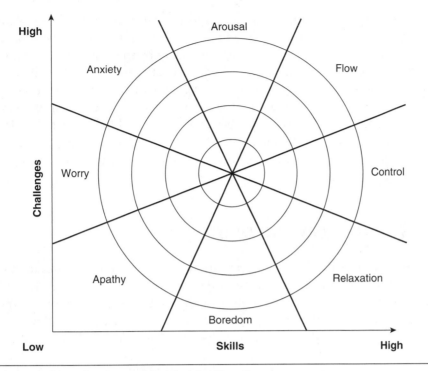

Figure 11.2   The Current Model of the Flow State

Source: From Csikszentmihalyi, M., *Finding Flow*, copyright © 1997 by Mihaly Csikszentmihalyi. Reprinted by permission of Basic Books, a member of Perseus Books, L.L.C.

of the autotelic personality has been measured via quantitative methods (Csikszentmihalyi, Rathunde, & Whalen, 1993).

The autotelic personality in American teenagers appears to be related to positive and affective states and the quality of personal goal statements (Adlai-Gail, 1994). In a sample of American adults, Abuhamdeh (2000) found that, when compared to people who do not have the autotelic personality characteristics, those who do have these characteristics have a preference for high-action-opportunity, high-skills situations that stimulate them and encourage growth. Furthermore, people with the autotelic personality appear to experience little stress when in the flow quadrant (see Figure 11.1), whereas the reverse is true for adults without these characteristics.

LONGITUDINAL FLOW RESEARCH

Longitudinal research on flow reveals how flow experiences are associated with achievement (in academics, work, or sports) over time. For example, Csikszentmihalyi et al. (1993) tracked the development of talented teenagers through high school. These researchers found that commitment to a talent area at age 17 was predicted by the student's identification of this talent area as a source of flow 4 years previously, as well as by the amount of flow and anxiety experienced at the time of the initial data gathering (when the students were 13 years old). Similarly, Heine (1996), who studied students skilled in mathematics, found that those who experienced flow in the first part of a math course performed better in the second half (controlling for initial abilities and grade point average). These findings suggest that commitment, persistence, and achievement exhibited by teenagers are associated with previous experiences of flow.

FOSTERING FLOW AND ITS BENEFITS

According to the flow model, experiencing absorption provides intrinsic rewards that encourage persistence in and return to an activity. Hence, skills related to that activity might be enhanced over time. Therefore, the goal of intervention researchers interested in the applications of flow is to help people identify those activities that give them flow and to encourage people to invest their attentions and energies in these activities.

Flow researchers (e.g., Csikszentmihalyi, 1990, 1996, Csikszentmihalyi & Robinson, 1990; Jackson & Csikszentmihalyi, 1999; Perry, 1999) have assisted people in their search for absorption by describing two paths to becoming more engaged with daily life: (1) finding and shaping activities and environments that are more conducive to flow experiences, and (2) identifying personal characteristics and attentional skills that can be tweaked to make flow more likely.

In his consultation practices, Csikszentmihalyi has modified numerous work environments to increase the chances of producing flow. For example, he worked with the Swedish police to identify obstacles to flow in their daily work routines and then to make their work more conducive to flow on the beat. (Specifically, officers were encouraged to walk the beat alone on occasion, rather with their partners, so that they could become more absorbed in their work.) Flow principles also have been incorporated into the design of workplaces and into the organization of displays at art venues, including the J. Paul Getty Museum in Southern California, to increase the enjoyment of visits to these sites.

Several clinical researchers (e.g., Inghilleri, 1999; Massimini et al., 1987) have used experience sampling method and flow principles to help individuals discover and sustain flow. This use of the experience sampling method data provides feedback on momentary experiences and identifies activities and environments where optimal experience can be increased.

Perhaps the best application of flow principles has occurred at the Key School in Indianapolis, Indiana, where the goal is to foster flow by influencing both the environment and the individual (Whalen, 1999).

In the school's Flow Activities Center, students have regular opportunities to actively choose and engage in activities related to their own interests, and then pursue these activities without demands or distractions (creating what has been described as "serious play" [Csikszentmihalyi et al., 1993]). In support of students' searches for absorption, teachers encourage students to challenge and stretch themselves; teachers also provide new challenges to the children to foster growth. (See the Personal Mini-Experiments for a flow experiment and the Life Enhancement Strategies for tips for enhancing flow within the domains of your life.)

Life Enhancement Strategies

Every day, you make thousands of choices about how to focus your attention and spend your time. We hope that you choose to become more intentional in your searches for novelty, for absorption, and for the sacred (as you define it in your life.) As in most chapters, we categorize the life enhancement strategies across three of life's important domains—love, work, and play. Three suggestions for each domain are shared here, one related to each of the topics of this chapter.

Love

- Orient yourself to the mindfulness relationship skills presented in Chapter 13.
- Identify an activity that helps you and a friend achieve flow at the same time. Then, spend more time jointly engaged in that activity.
- Find out how a significant other defines the sacred, and ask that person how he or she pursues it.

Work

- Practice making nonjudgmental observations when working with classmates or colleagues.
- Volunteer for assignments and projects that challenge or stretch your existing skills. These tasks are more likely to bring about flow than are easy assignments.
- Find a spiritual haven at work or school that allows you to pursue the sacred during your breaks in the day.

Play

- Read a book on mindfulness meditation (e.g., Kabat-Zinn, 1990), and practice some of the basic skills.
- Pursue recreational activities that are known to induce flow: playing chess, riding a mountain bike, rock-wall climbing, learning a second language, etc.
- Make your search for the sacred a communal experience; invite friends to join you in your favorite spiritual pursuit.

Spirituality: In Search of the Sacred

Glancing at someone engaged in everyday behavior can evoke thoughts about spirituality. For example, imagine a picture of an older woman kneeling with a look of utter concentration on her face. Her search for the sacred (that which is set apart from the ordinary and worthy of veneration) may be inferred from her behavior; this is the case if a church interior appears in the background of the woman's image . . . or if a garden serves as the backdrop. This search for the sacred can happen anywhere, any time because, like flow and mindfulness, spirituality is a state of mind, and it is universally accessible.

The term *search for the sacred* is a widely accepted description of spirituality. (Religion and religious behaviors represent the many ways in which the search for the sacred becomes organized and sanctioned in society; for example, through the attendance of religious services and the frequency and duration of prayer.) In 2000, Hill et al. defined **spirituality** as "the feelings, thoughts, and behaviors that arise from a search for the sacred" (p. 66). Pargament and Mahoney (2002) also defined spirituality "as a search for the sacred . . ." and elaborated, "People can take a virtually limitless number of pathways in their attempts to discover and conserve the sacred. . . . Pathways involve systems of belief that include those of traditional organized religions (e.g., Protestant, Roman Catholic, Jewish, Hindu, Buddhist, Muslim), newer spirituality movements (e.g., feminist, goddess, ecological, spiritualities), and more individualized worldviews" (p. 647). These pathways to the sacred also may be described as spiritual strivings, which included personal goals associated with the ultimate concerns of purpose, ethics, and recognition of the transcendent (Emmons, Cheung, & Tehrani, 1998).

Kenneth Pargament

Psychology researchers agree with the foregoing definitions of spirituality, and there is general support for the belief that spirituality is a positive state of mind experienced by most people. Peterson and Seligman (2004) contend that spirituality is a universal strength of transcendence, stating, "Although the specific content of spiritual beliefs varies, all cultures have a concept of an ultimate, transcendent, sacred, and divine force" (p. 601). Similarly, Pargament and Mahoney (2002) argue that spirituality is a vital part of American society and psychology:

First, spirituality is a "cultural fact" (cf. Shafranske & Malony, 1990): The vast majority of Americans believe in God (95%), believe that God can be reached through prayer (86%), and feel that religion is important or very important to them (86%) (Gallup Organization, 1995; Hoge, 1996). Second, in a growing empirical body of literature, the important implications of spirituality for a number of aspects of human functioning are being noted. Included in this list are mental health (Koenig, 1998), drug and alcohol use (Benson, 1992), marital functioning (Mahoney et al., 1999), parenting (Ellison & Sherkat, 1993), the outcomes of stressful life experiences (Pargament, 1997), and morbidity and mortality (Ellison & Levin, 1998; Hummer, Rogers, Nam, & Ellison, 1999). . . . There are, in short, some very good reasons why psychologists should attend more carefully to the spiritual dimension of peoples' lives. (p. 646)

Despite its ubiquitous nature and scholarly agreement on its definition, psychological researchers and the general public continue to muddy the waters when discussing spirituality. For example, Peterson and Seligman's (2004) Values in Action Classifications of Strengths lumped spirituality together with similar, yet different, concepts such as religion and faith. And, in a large group of research participants, nearly 75% identified themselves as being both spiritual and religious (Zinnbauer et al., 1997). The fuzziness of the construct undermines efforts to understand the actual effects of searching for the sacred on a person's functioning.

The True Benefits of Spirituality?

Many positive psychologists (e.g., Peterson & Seligman, 2004; Snyder & Lopez, 2002) have hypothesized that a deep understanding of ourselves and our lives is enhanced by our search for the sacred. Indeed, as noted previously, spirituality is associated with mental health, managing substance abuse, marital functioning, parenting, coping, and mortality (summarized in Pargament & Mahoney, 2002; Thoresen, Harris, & Oman, 2001). One examination of spiritual strivings reveals that these pathways to the sacred may lead to (or at least are associated with) well-being (Emmons et al., 1998). Another examination of spiritual strivings suggests the search for the sacred may lead to what we consider to be the true benefits of spirituality in our lives: purpose and meaning (Mahoney et al., 2005). Despite the findings that demonstrate the benefits of searching for the sacred, the mechanisms by which spirituality leads to positive life outcomes are not clear.

The Search Continues

"Zoning out," experiencing apathy and boredom, and feeling as though we lack direction in our lives are signs that we are not actively engaged with daily experience. What if we use these signs of disengagement as prompts to initiate searches for novelty, absorption, and the sacred? For example, next time you are driving and lose track of a stretch a road, take that as a nudge to search for novelty in the next few miles of highway. When you find yourself thinking, "I'm bored," lose yourself in the activity that brings you the most flow. Finally, when you feel aimless, turn your attention to your search for the sacred.

Practicing mindfulness, flow, and spirituality may have benefits for your psychological and physical health, your academic or work performance, and your social well-being. These practices may have a more profound effect on us. Indeed, these searches may lead us to a deeper existence, one that is filled with meaning.

Key Terms

Autotelic personality: A cluster of traits exhibited by a person who enjoys life and who "generally does things for [his or her] own sake, rather than in order to achieve some later external goal" (Csikszentmihalyi, 1997, p. 117). From the Greek words *autos*, meaning "self," and *telos*, meaning "end."

Experience sampling method (ESM): A research method used to study flow experiences. Participants are signaled via watches, phones, or hand-held computers and asked to answer questions about their experiences at the moment they are paged.

Flow: An optimal state of engagement in which a person perceives challenges to action as neither underutilizing nor overwhelming his or her existing skills and has clear, attainable goals and immediate feedback about progress.

Mindfulness: Openness to novelty and sensitivity to context and perspective. Mindfulness involves cultivating an awareness of everyday happenings and physiological and psychological sensations; overcoming the desire to reduce uncertainty in everyday life; overriding the tendency to engage in automatic behavior; and engaging less frequently in evaluating oneself, others, and situations.

Spirituality: As commonly defined, the thoughts, feelings, and behaviors that fuel and arise from the search for the sacred.

Part V

Prosocial Behavior

Empathy and Egotism 12

Portals to Altruism, Gratitude, and Forgiveness

In this chapter, we explore how empathy and egotism can lead to altruism, gratitude, and forgiveness (see Figure 12.1). As a prelude to describing how empathy and egotism can unleash altruism, gratitude, and forgiveness, we share a story.

Rick went to 12 different schools before graduating from high school. Every year, around the month of October, his family moved because his dad was transferred or promoted, lost his job, or found a new one. Forced to interact with a new group of kids each year, Rick was the outsider—looking yet again toward different peers. Painfully aware of his plight as the "new kid," he became fascinated with the lives of the children around him. He watched, listened, and learned to see the world from the perspectives of the other kids. Not particularly talented in any area, Rick was not much of a threat to the other children of these "little societies" into which he was thrust.

Although he longed to become a real participant in the lives of the other kids, the single year in each location was not enough time for the other children to let him into their lives. Unable to make solid friendship bonds in this short time period, Rick instead became sensitive to the emotional plights and needs of the other kids. This sense of empathy made him want to help the other children, but they did not see him as a legitimate source of help, because he was an outsider. In short, his understanding and empathy produced a compassion and desire to help others, but he could not successfully fulfill this need.

It was only when he grew up and for the first time had the luxury of staying in the same place that he could use his empathy to actually help others. Indeed, Rick's empathy fostered his altruism, gratitude, and forgiveness in the context of these later, enduring, adult relationships.

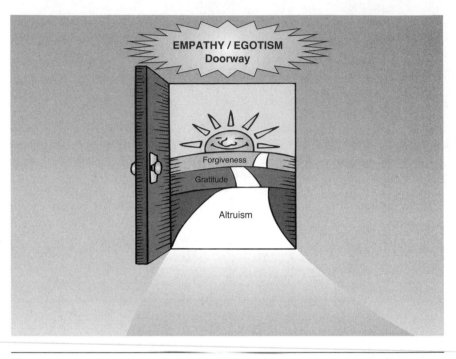

Figure 12.1   Empathy and Egotism as Portals to Altruism, Gratitude, and Forgiveness

In truth, however, he also felt good (enhanced ego and self-esteem) when he expressed altruism, gratitude, and forgiveness in these adult relationships. This story's protagonist is the senior author of this book. Perhaps you have had similar childhood experiences.

Altruism

In this section, we begin by defining *altruism*. Next, we explore the egotism (or esteem) motive and show that it also can drive various types of altruistic actions. We then discuss the empathy altruism hypothesis and follow with a discussion of the genetic and neural underpinnings of empathy. We close with approaches for enhancing and measuring altruism.

DEFINING ALTRUISM

Altruism is behavior that is aimed at benefiting another person. Altruistic behavior can be motivated by personal egotism, or it can be prompted by "pure" empathic desire to benefit another person, irrespective of personal gain (for overviews, see Batson, 1991; Cialdini, Schaller, Houlihan, Arps, Fultz, & Beaman, 1978).

THE EGOTISM MOTIVE

Egotism is the motive to pursue some sort of personal gain or benefit through targeted behavior. Egotism has been heralded as one of the most influential of all human motives. Not surprisingly, therefore, egotism is seen as driving a variety of human actions, including altruism. In this regard, noted Western thinkers such as Aristotle (384–322 BC), St. Thomas Aquinas (1125–1274), Thomas Hobbes (1588–1679), David Hume (1711–1776), Adam Smith (1723–1790), Jeremy Bentham (1748–1832), Friedrich Nietzsche (1844–1900), and Sigmund Freud (1856–1939) have weighed in on the debate as to whether egotism, the sense of empathy, or both, fuel altruistic human actions (see Batson, Ahmad, Lisher, & Tsang, 2002).

Since the Renaissance, a prevailing view has been that altruism is best explained by the motive of egotism. So, too, have several modern scholars reasoned that egotism fuels altruistic behavior (for review, see Wallach & Wallach, 1983). The essence of this position is that we care for other people because it benefits us to do so (Mansbridge, 1990). Furthermore, no matter how noble the altruism may appear, those in the egotism–altruism camp believe that all altruistic actions produce an underlying benefit to the person who is doing the good deeds. Thus, the prevailing motive here is, "I help because it benefits me."

FORMS OF EGOTISM-MOTIVATED ALTRUISM

The forms of such self-beneficial egotism may be straightforward, as when helping another person results in public praise for the individual rendering the aid. In another variant of praise, the helper may receive material rewards or honors for altruistic deeds. In this latter regard, in 2005 the rocker Bob Geldorf of the Irish musical group Boomtown Rats took the initiative to hold Live 8 concerts all over the globe. His efforts raised roughly $100 million for the starving people of Africa. Because of this altruism, a member of the Norwegian parliament nominated Geldorf for the 2006 Nobel Peace Prize (http://edition.cnn.com/2005/WORLD/europe/07/06/ geldpf.npbel.reut/index.html).

There are other examples of self-benefits where the helpers receive no external rewards for their altruistic actions. For example, it is distressing to see another person in some sort of anguishing situation; accordingly, we may help that person to lessen our own sense of personal torment. Or we simply may feel good about ourselves when we act kindly toward another individual. Yet another possibility is that we may escape a sense of guilt for not helping when we step in and lend a hand to a needy person. Moreover, consider the soldier who throws himself upon a live grenade and saves his nearby comrades' lives. Surely this is an act of "pure" altruism, isn't it? Perhaps not, if this soldier imagined the praise and the medals that would be bestowed upon him for his act of courage; or perhaps our hero conjured the image of potential benefits coming to him in the afterlife because of his heroism (Batson et al., 2002).

In posing these various ego-based explanations, we do not mean to be cynical about the helping actions of people. Rather, we are uncovering the many subtle forms that such egotism-based helping can take. Although we have posed several variants, such egotistical or self-benefiting actions involving altruism basically take one of the following three forms:

- The helping person gets public praise or even a monetary reward, along with self-praise for having done that which is good.
- The helping person avoids social or personal punishments for failing to help.
- The helping person may lessen his or her personal distress at seeing another's trauma.

Remember also that, even though the helping person is motivated by personal egotism, the bottom line is that the person renders aid to a fellow human being in need.

THE EMPATHY MOTIVE AND THE EMPATHY–ALTRUISM HYPOTHESIS

C. Daniel Batson

Source: Reprinted with permission of C. Daniel Batson.

Empathy is an emotional response to the perceived plight of another person. One view of empathy is that it involves the ability to match another person's emotions. Instead of this mimic like reproduction of another person's emotions, however, empathy may entail a sense of tenderheartedness toward that other person. University of Kansas social psychologist C. Daniel Batson has described this latter empathy in his 1991 book, *The Altruism Question*. For Batson, altruism involves human behaviors that are aimed at promoting another person's well-being.

Batson and colleagues do not deny that some forms of altruism may occur because of egotism, but their shared view is that, under some circumstances, these egotistical motives cannot account for the helping (see Batson et al., 2002). Indeed, in careful tests of what has come to be called the **empathy–altruism hypothesis** (see Batson, 1991), findings show that there are instances in which egotism does *not* appear to explain such helping behaviors. Moreover, the evidence also supports the view that having empathy for another leads to a greater likelihood of helping that other person (for reviews, see Batson, 1991; Dovidio, Allen, & Schroeder, 1990; Eisenberg & Miller, 1987).

Because of the efforts of Batson and other recent scholars, "pure" altruism arising from human empathy has been viewed as a viable underlying motive for helping, in contrast to the previous emphasis on egotism as the sole motive. In the words of Piliavin and Charng (1990),

> There appears to be a paradigm shift away from the earlier position that behavior that appears to be altruistic must, under closer scrutiny, be revealed as reflecting egoistic motives. Rather, theory and data now being advanced are more compatible with the view that true altruism— acting with the goal of benefiting another—does exist and is a part of human nature. (p. 27)

Void of egotistical gains, therefore, humans at times are sufficiently moved by their empathies to help other people. If we ever need an example of positive psychology in action, this surely is it.

THE GENETIC AND NEURAL FOUNDATIONS OF EMPATHY

The method for measuring genetic heritability is to compare the concordances of empathy scores in monozygotic (identical) twins with the scores of dizygotic (fraternal) twins. For adult males, the empathy correlations for monozygotic and dizygotic twins were found to be .41 and .05, respectively (Matthews, Batson, Horn, & Rosenman, 1981; for similar results, see Rushton, Fulker, Neale, Nias, & Eysenck, 1986). Although both of these studies have been criticized because of concerns that their analytic procedures produced overly elevated heritability scores (e.g., Davis, Luce, & Kraus, 1994), other studies have found monozygotic correlations in the range of .22 to .30 as compared to dizygotic correlations of .05 to .09 (Davis et al., 1994; Zahn-Wexler, Robinson, & Emde, 1992). The latter correlations still suggest a modest level of heritability for empathy.

Recent research has revealed that areas of the prefrontal and parietal cortices are essential for empathy (Damasio, 2002). Empathy requires the capacity to form internal simulations of another's bodily or mental states. Given that people who have damage to their right somatosensory cortices no longer can judge others' emotions, it follows that they have lost a skill that is crucial for empathy (Adolphs, Damasio, Tranel, Cooper, & Damasio, 2000). Likewise, damage to the prefrontal cortex leads to impairments in appraising the emotions of other people (Bechara, Tranel, Damasio, & Damasio, 1996). Furthermore, beginning in the 1990s researchers discovered "mirror neurons" that react identically when an animal performs an action or witnesses another animal performing the same action (Winerman, 2005). In the words of neuroscientist Giacomo Rizzolatti, who was the first to discover these mirror neurons, "the neurons could help to explain how and why we . . . feel empathy" (in Winerman, 2005, p. 49). We must be careful in generalizing these findings to humans, however, because the methodologies to date have involved attaching electrodes directly to brains, and for ethical reasons this only has been done with monkeys.

CULTIVATING ALTRUISM

For clues to how to help someone become more altruistic, we call upon the very processes of egotism and empathy that we have used to explain altruism.

Egotism-Based Approaches to Enhancing Altruistic Actions

In our experiences in working with clients in psychotherapy, we have found that people often may incorrectly assume that feeling good about themselves is not part of rendering help. At least for some portion of Americans, this latter attitude may reflect the Puritan heritage with its emphasis on suffering and total human sacrifice for the good of others. Whatever the historical roots, however, it is inaccurate to conclude that helping another and feeling good about oneself are incompatible. Thus, this is one of the first lessons we use in enabling people to realize that they can help and, because of such actions, have higher esteem. Furthermore, we have found that people seem to take delight in learning that it is legitimate to feel good about helping others.

One way to unleash such positive feelings is to have the person engage in community volunteer work. Local agencies dealing with children, people with disabilities, older people who are alone, and hospitals all need volunteers to render aid. Although this form of helping may begin as voluntary experiences, we have witnessed instances in which our clients have changed their professions to involve activities where they support others *and get paid for it.* Our more general point, however, is that it feels good to help other people, and this simple premise has guided some of our efforts at channeling people into volunteer positions.

Empathy-Based Approaches to Enhancing Altruistic Actions

A way to increase peoples' likelihood of helping is to teach them to have greater empathy for the circumstances of other people. How can such empathy be promoted? One simple approach is to have a person interact more frequently with people who need help. Then, once the individual truly begins to understand the perspectives and motives of the people who are being helped, this insight breaks down the propensity to view interpersonal matters in terms of "us versus them."

Another means of enhancing empathy is to point out similarities with another person that may not have been obvious. These similarities can be as simple as having grown up in the same part of the country, having done work of the same type, having endured comparable hardships, and so on. The shared characteristics of people often are much greater than any of us may realize, and these parallels in life circumstances make people understand that we all are part of the same "grand journey" (see Chapter 18).

One final approach for promoting empathy involves working with those people who especially want to see themselves as different from others (see Snyder & Fromkin, 1980). Uniqueness is something that most people desire to some degree (see Chapter 18) but, taken to an extreme, makes it very difficult for the person to make contact and interact with others. Such people must be taught how they do share characteristics with others and how their illusory specialness needs may be preventing them from deriving pleasure from interacting with other people (Lynn & Snyder, 2002). One personal mini-experiment that you can perform on yourself is to imagine another person and then list all the things (physical, psychological, etc.) that you have in common with this person. This exercise, in our experience, increases the propensity of a person to "walk in the shoes" of another—with greater empathy the result. We explore yet more ways to increase altruism in the following Personal Mini-Experiments.

Personal Mini-Experiments

Exercises in Altruism, Gratitude, and Forgiveness

As suggested in previous exercises, experiment and see what works for you.

Altruism for Thy Neighbor: If you look around your local neighborhood, you will find people who could use a helping hand. The key is to surprise other people and do them favors that they are not expecting. Here are some suggestions:

- Mow the lawn of an elderly person.
- Volunteer to babysit for a single parent who is working hard to make ends meet.
- Go to the local hospital, and see what volunteer work can be done there.
- Offer to read for persons who cannot see.
- Give blood.

(Continued)

(Continued)

You get the idea. Do for others, and make a note of the feelings that altruism engenders in you.

Count Your Blessings (see Emmons & McCullough, 2003): At the beginning and end of each day, list five things for which you are grateful, and then take a few minutes to meditate on the gift inherent in each. One means of elucidating this sense of appreciation is to use the stem phrases, "I appreciate _____ because _____." In the first blank, list the person, event, or thing for which you are grateful, and in the second blank state the reasons for each of the things for which you have expressed gratitude. Discuss the effects of one week of this practice with a classmate, and tweak the exercise as you wish.

Gone but Not Forgiven: If you are contemplating forgiving a person who is no longer alive, or if you cannot locate him or her, use a technique from Gestalt therapy. In this technique, called the "empty chair exercise," one sits facing an empty chair. Then, one imagines the target person sitting in that chair and speaks to the person as though he or she were really there. Occasionally, we may want to forgive ourselves for some transgression that ended up causing us personal harm. The empty chair exercise is a good one for addressing oneself. You can also write yourself a letter and actually mail it to yourself.

MEASURING ALTRUISM

There is a variety of self-report instruments for assessing the altruism of people from childhood through adulthood. Perhaps the best-known self-report instrument is the Self-Report Altruism Scale, a validated 20-item index for adults (Rushton, Chrisjohn, & Fekken, 1981). If one desires an observational index, the Prosocial Behavior Questionnaire (Weir & Duveen, 1981) is a 20-item rating index that can be used by teachers to report prosocial behaviors (using a three-point continuum of applicability ranging from "does not apply" to "applies somewhat" to "definitely applies"). (For a similar index to the Prosocial Behavior Questionnaire, see the Ethical Behavior Rating Scale, a 15-item teacher rating instrument by Hill and Swanson [1985].)

A new and potentially promising self-report instrument for adults is the Helping Attitude Scale, a 20-item measure that taps beliefs, feelings, and behaviors related to helping (Nickell, 1998). The Helping Attitude Scale appears to meet the psychometric criteria for scale reliability and validity, and initial findings show that women have more positive attitudes about helping than do men. The Helping Attitude Scale can be examined in its entirety in Appendix A.

Gratitude

In this section, we discuss the concept of gratitude, which received scant attention prior to the last two decades. We first define gratitude, then discuss how it can be cultivated and measured, review its physiological bases, and close with a real-life example.

DEFINING GRATITUDE

The term *gratitude* is derived from the Latin concept *gratia*, which entails some variant of grace, gratefulness, and graciousness (Emmons, McCullough, & Tsang, 2003). The ideas flowing from this Latin root pertain to "kindness, generousness, gifts, the beauty of giving and receiving" (Pruyser, 1976, p. 69). In the words of noted University of California–Davis researcher Robert Emmons (2005, personal communication), **gratitude** emerges upon recognizing that one has obtained a positive outcome from another individual who behaved in a way that was (1) costly to him or her, (2) valuable to the recipient, and (3) intentionally rendered. As such, gratitude taps into the propensity to appreciate and savor everyday events and experiences (Bryant, 1989; Langston, 1994).

In Emmons's definition, the positive outcome appears to have come from another person; however, the benefit may be derived from a nonhuman action or event. For example, the individual who has undergone a traumatic natural event such as a family member's survival of a hurricane (see Coffman, 1996) feels a profound sense of gratitude. In a related vein, it has been suggested that events of larger magnitude also should produce higher levels of gratitude (Trivers, 1971). Moreover, Ortony, Clore, and Collins (1988) have reasoned that gratitude should be greater when the giving person's actions are judged praiseworthy and when they deviate positively from that which was expected.

In yet another example of gratitude, a person may have come through a major medical crisis or problem and discover benefits in that experience (Affleck & Tennen, 1996). This latter process is called *benefit finding*. As is the case with altruism, it is likely that the ability to empathize is a necessary condition for feeling gratitude toward another person (McCullough, 2005, personal communication).

Gratitude is viewed as a prized human propensity in the Hindu, Buddhist, Muslim, Christian, and Jewish traditions (Emmons et al., 2003). On this point, philosopher David Hume (1888, p. 466) went so far as to say that ingratitude is "the most horrible and unnatural of all crimes that humans are capable of committing." According to medieval scholar Thomas Aquinas (1273/1981), not only was gratitude seen as beneficial to the individual, but it also serves as a motivational force for human altruism.

Of the many famous thinkers who commented on gratitude, only Aristotle (trans. 1962) viewed it unfavorably. In his opinion, magnanimous people are adamant about their self-sufficiencies and, accordingly, view gratitude as demeaning and reflective of needless indebtedness to others.

CULTIVATING GRATITUDE

Michael McCullough

Source: © Elisabeth McCullough. Reprinted with permission.

Robert A. Emmons

Source: Reprinted with permission of Robert A. Emmons.

We begin this section with the words of the writer Charles Dickens (1897, p. 45), "Reflect on your present blessings, of which every man has many, not on your past misfortunes, of which all men have some." In more recent times, psychologists Robert Emmons and Michael McCullough have explored a variety of ways to help people enhance their sense of gratitude (for reviews, see Bono, Emmons, & McCullough, 2004; Emmons & Hill, 2001; Emmons & McCullough, 2004; Emmons & Shelton, 2002; McCullough, Kilpatrick, Emmons, & Larson, 2001). These interventions aimed at enhancing gratitude consistently have resulted in benefits. For example, in comparison to people who recorded either neutral or negative (life stresses) in their diaries, those who kept weekly gratitude journals (i.e., recorded events for which they were thankful) were superior in terms of (1) the amount of exercise undertaken, (2) optimism about the upcoming week, and (3) feeling better about their lives (Emmons & McCullough, 2003). Furthermore, those who kept gratitude journals reported greater enthusiasm, alertness, and determination, and they were significantly more likely to make progress toward important goals pertaining to their health, interpersonal relationships, and academic performances. Indeed, those who were in the "count your blessings" diary condition also were more likely to have helped another person. Finally, in a third study in Emmons and McCullough's (2003) trilogy, people with neuromuscular conditions were randomly assigned to either a gratitude condition or a control condition. Results showed that those in the former condition were (1) more optimistic, (2) more energetic, (3) more connected to other people, and (4) more likely to have restful sleep.

A Japanese form of meditation known as Naikan enhances a person's sense of gratitude (Krech, 2001). Using Naikan, one learns to meditate daily on three gratitude-related questions: First, what did I receive? Second, what did I give? And third, what troubles and difficulties did I cause to others? In Western societies, we may be rather automatic in our expectations of material comforts; gratitude meditation helps to bring this process more into awareness so we can learn how to appreciate such blessings.

One additional comment is noteworthy in regard to gratitude and motivation. In an interview, Dr. Emmons (2004) was asked about the most common *incorrect* assumption that people make about his work on gratitude. In response, he observed that many people assume that gratefulness is synonymous with lack of motivation and greater complacency in life. He then noted that he had never seen a case where gratitude was linked to passivity. On the contrary, gratitude is an active and affirming process, and we share some of the clinical approaches we have used to facilitate it in the Personal Mini-Experiments on pages 271 to 272 (see also Bono et al., 2004). We also present an editorial on the importance of thanking others.

Thanking Your Heroes

RICK SNYDER

It was 1972, and I had just taken a job as an assistant professor at KU. There was one person who had sacrificed her whole life to make it possible for me to reach this point. She worked her regular job, along with part-time jobs, to see that I could go to college. She was a hero in every sense, giving so that I could have a better life than what she had experienced.

This hero was my mother. She told me that my life as an academician was to be her reward. She planned to visit Lawrence later that year, but that visit never happened. Diagnosed with a form of quickly spreading cancer, she spent her last months bedridden in Dallas, Texas.

I visited as much as I could, and we talked about things that were important to both of us. Unfortunately, I never told her that she was my hero. Almost every day over the past 30 years, I have regretted this omission. If you still have a chance to deliver this message to an important hero in your life, do it right now.

Source: From C. R. Snyder. (2004, October 4). Thanking your heroes. *Lawrence Journal-World.*

MEASURING GRATITUDE

Several approaches have been taken to measure gratitude. One tactic was to ask people to list the things about which they felt grateful (*Gallup Poll Monthly,* 1996). This simple method allowed researchers to find those events that produced gratefulness. Another strategy was to take the stories that people wrote about their lives and code these vignettes for gratefulness themes. In this latter approach, Barusch (1999) was surprised to find that gratitude was a common response among older women who were living in poverty. In another study, one in which the findings were more consistent with the researchers' expectations, Bernstein and Simmons (1974) found that kidney recipients frequently cited their gratitude toward their donors. Moreover, the survivors of Hurricane Andrew commonly expressed gratitude for having lived through this natural disaster (Coffman, 1996).

Some attempts also have been made to measure gratitude behaviorally. For example, whether children said thank you during their door-to-door Halloween trick-or-treat rounds was used as an unprompted index of gratitude (Becker & Smenner, 1986). Similarly, the grateful responses of people receiving food in a soup kitchen have been quantified (Stein, 1989).

Working in the context of an overall index called the Multidimensional Prayer Inventory, Laird and his colleagues (Laird, Snyder, Rapoff, & Green, 2004) have developed and validated a 3-item Thanksgiving self-report subscale on which people respond along a 7-point response scale (1 = Never to 7 = All of the time) to each item. The three Thanksgiving items are "I offered thanks for specific things," "I expressed my appreciation for my circumstances," and "I thanked God for things occurring in my life." This Thanksgiving subscale of the Multidimensional Prayer Inventory obviously is worded in terms of religious prayer, and higher scores have correlated with stronger religious practices such as prayer.

Finally, there are two trait-like self-report measures of gratitude that do not inherently link the wording of the items to religious prayer. The first such measure is the Gratitude, Resentment, and Appreciation Test (GRAT), a 44-item index developed and validated by Watkins, Grimm, and Hailu (1998). The GRAT taps the three factors of resentment, simple appreciation, and social appreciation.

The trait self-report index that appears to be most promising is the Gratitude Questionnaire (GQ-6) (McCullough, Emmons, & Tsang, 2002; see also Emmons et al., 2003). The GQ-6 is a 6-item questionnaire (see Appendix B for the entire scale) on which respondents endorse each item on a 7-point Likert scale (1 = Strongly disagree to 7 = Strongly agree). Results show that the 6 items correlate strongly with each other, and one overall factor seems to tap the scale content. Scores of the GQ-6 correlate reliably with peers' rating of target persons' gratitude levels; people scoring high on this scale report feeling more thankful and more grateful (Gray, Emmons, & Morrison, 2001). Additionally, this sense of appreciation as tapped by the GQ-6 endured over a 21-day interval (McCullough, Tsang, & Emmons, 2004).

Scores on the GQ-6 relate in predictable ways to other positive psychology constructs. For example, higher gratitude on the GQ-6 correlated positively with elevated positive emotions, vitality, optimism, hope, and satisfaction with life. Moreover, higher gratitude correlated positively with empathy, sharing, forgiving, and giving one's time for the benefit of others. Those who scored higher in gratitude are less concerned with material goods, and they are more likely to engage in prayer and spiritual matters (McCullough et al., 2002).

THE PSYCHOPHYSIOLOGICAL
UNDERPINNINGS OF GRATITUDE

Although we could not locate research relating directly to psychophysi-ology and gratitude, there is research on appreciation. Whereas gratitude typically refers to another person's actions, appreciation may or may not entail another individual. These two concepts certainly are quite similar, however, and it is for this reason that we briefly explore here the psycho-physiology of appreciation. Although frustration typically elicits dis-ordered and erratic heart rhythms reflecting a lack of synchrony between the parasympathetic and sympathetic branches of the autonomic nervous system, appreciation produces a more coherent pattern of heart rhythms (McCraty & Childre, 2004). This coherent, "calming" pattern of heartbeats per minute can be observed in Figure 12.2 (see Tiller et al., 1996).

Appreciation also has produced another form of physiological coherence, the synchrony between alpha brain wave activity (taken from electroencephalograms [EEGs]) and heartbeats. In research by McCraty and colleagues (McCraty, 2002; McCraty & Atkinson, 2003), for example, under experimental manipulations of appreciation relative to baseline, the synchrony of heartbeat and EEG was higher in the left hemisphere. As shown in Figure 12.3, where the lighter shading signifies the greater degree of synchrony between heartbeat and EEG alpha brain waves, a shift can be seen from the right frontal area at baseline to the left hemisphere in the appreciation manipulation condition. In this regard, McCraty and Childre (2004) have noted that the left hemisphere has been implicated in other

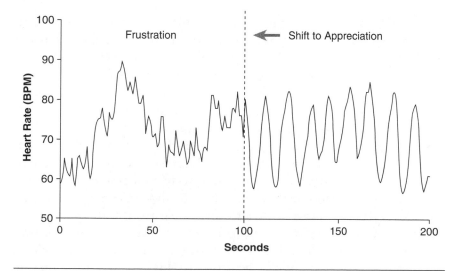

Figure 12.2 Heart Rhythms Under Frustration and Appreciation

Source: From "The grateful heart," by McCraty and Childre, from *The Psychology of Gratitude,* edited by Robert A. Emmons & Michael E. McCullough, copyright © 2004 by Oxford University Press, Inc. Used by permission of Oxford University Press, Inc.

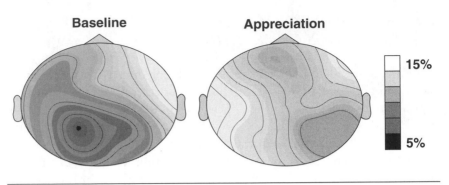

Figure 12.3   Alpha Brain Wave Activity and Heartbeat Synchrony Under Baseline and Appreciation Conditions

Source: From "The grateful heart," by McCraty and Childre, from *The Psychology of Gratitude,* edited by Robert A. Emmons & Michael E. McCullough, copyright © 2004 by Oxford University Press, Inc. Used by permission of Oxford University Press, Inc.

Note: Lighter shading signifies greater synchrony between brain waves and heartbeat.

research with positive emotions (e.g., Lane et al., 1997). Although there obviously is much more research to be done in this area, it is promising that the gratitude-related human response of appreciation appears to have a coherent (McCraty's term) psychophysiological pattern.

GRATITUDE MAKES A HOUSE CALL

As I (CRS) was writing this portion of the chapter, I experienced an incident that evoked a profound sense of gratitude. This event had a mundane beginning—our toilet began to leak water at its base. For years, our plumber, Tommy, has carried out the necessary repairs with the same cheerful demeanor. When we called this time, he promised that he would work our toilet into his busy schedule. In his usual upbeat manner, he arrived early the next morning and spent several hours trying to find the problem, which turned out to be a small crack at the base. When it was almost noon, Tommy said that he would not be able to install the new toilet until the next day because he had to go to a funeral that afternoon. I was relieved, however, that he had taken the time to come over and get the process started. It was only later that I learned a truly eye-opening additional piece of information: The funeral was for his own grown son! He did not mention this to me, though, and in his typical selfless manner, he had helped us on the same day his son was being buried. Using the previously discussed definition of gratitude by Emmons, our plumber intentionally gave us a valuable service when it was costly to him.

Forgiveness

Once a quiet, relatively unexplored concept, there has been an explosion of interest in forgiveness since the 1990s. Part of the reason for this tremendous expansion of theory and research relates to the fact that philanthropist John Templeton initiated calls for grants involving research on forgiveness from the Templeton Foundation. Mr. Templeton believed forgiveness was sufficiently important as a concept to spend his own money to facilitate more research on it!

In this section, we first introduce the various definitions of forgiveness, then describe how it can be cultivated, review its measurement, and end with an overview of its evolutionary and neurobiological bases.

DEFINING FORGIVENESS

Scholars have differed in their definitions of forgiveness (McCullough, Pargament, & Thoresen, 2000a, 2000b; Worthington, 2005). Although views of the exact nature of forgiveness vary, the consensus is that it is beneficial to people (see Worthington, 2005). We discuss the major ways of defining forgiveness in the remainder of this section, starting with the most liberal and inclusive definition and moving to relatively more circumscribed definitions.

Thompson and Colleagues

In the theory espoused by Thompson and her colleagues (Thompson et al., 2005), **forgiveness** is a freeing from a negative attachment to the source that has transgressed against a person. Of all forgiveness theories, Thompson's is the most inclusive in that the source of the transgression, and thus the target of any eventual forgiveness, may be oneself, another person, or a situation that is viewed as out of one's control.

Laura Yamhure Thompson

Source: Reprinted with permission of Laura Yamhure Thompson.

McCullough and Colleagues

According to McCullough (2000; McCullough et al., 1998), forgiveness reflects increases in prosocial motivation toward another such that there is (1) less desire to avoid the transgressing person and to harm or seek revenge toward that individual, and (2) increased desire to act positively toward the transgressing person. Changes in motivation are viewed as being at the core of this theory (McCullough et al., 2000a, 2000b), with the person becoming more benevolent over time; moreover, forgiveness is seen as applicable only when there is another person who has engaged in a transgression.

Enright and Colleagues

The scholar with the longest track record in studying forgiveness is Robert Enright, who defined forgiveness as "a willingness to abandon one's right to resentment, negative judgment, and indifferent behavior toward one who unjustly hurt us, while fostering the undeserved qualities of compassion, generosity, and even love toward him or her" (Enright, Freedman, & Rique, 1998, pp. 46–47). For Enright (2000; Enright et al., 1998), it is crucial that the forgiving person develop a benevolent stance toward the transgressing person. As he put it, "The fruition of forgiveness is entering into loving community with others" (Enright & Zell, 1989, p. 99). Furthermore, Enright was adamant in stating that forgiveness cannot be extended to situations and thus must be directed only at people. On this point, he wrote, "Forgiveness is between people. One does not forgive tornadoes or floods. How could one, for instance, again join in a loving community with a tornado?" (Enright & Zell, 1989, p. 53).

Tangney and Colleagues

In 1999, Tangney and her colleagues (Tangney, Fee, Reinsmith, Boone, & Lee, 1999) suggested that forgiveness reflected

(1) [C]ognitive-affective transformation following a transgression in which (2) the victim makes a realistic assessment of the harm done and acknowledges the perpetrator's responsibility, but (3) freely chooses to "cancel the debt," giving up the need for revenge or deserved punishments and any quest for restitution. This "canceling of the debt" also involves (4) a "cancellation of negative emotions" directly related to the transgression. In particular, in forgiving, the victim overcomes his or her feelings of resentment and anger for the act. In short, by forgiving, the harmed individual (5) essentially removes himself or herself from the victim role. (p. 2)

June Tangney

Source: Reprinted with permission of June Tangney.

The Tangney model suggests that the giving up of the negative emotions is the crux of the forgiving process.

CULTIVATING FORGIVENESS

In this section, we explore how forgiveness can be taught. Accordingly, we show how three sources—another person, oneself, and even a situation or circumstance—can be used as targets in forgiveness instruction.

Forgiving Another Person

In this most typical category of forgiveness, forgiving another individual, one can imagine lyrics of a blues song in which one partner in a relationship has been "done wrong" (e.g., the other partner had an affair). In our therapy experiences with couples dealing with forgiveness in the wake of martial infidelities, we have found that the model of Gordon, Baucom, and Snyder is a useful one (2004, 2005; Gordon & Baucom, 1998). In this model, in which forgiveness is the goal, the first step is to promote a nondistorted, realistic appraisal of the relationship of the two people. The second step is the attempt to facilitate a release from the bond of ruminative, negative affect held toward the violating (transgressing) partner. Finally, the third step is to help the victimized partner lessen his or her desire to punish the transgressing partner. Over time, forgiveness makes it possible for the hurt and the outpouring of negative feelings to diminish—especially for the victimized partner. Likewise, the treatment enhances the empathy for the transgressing partner, and the therapist tries to make both people feel better about themselves.

Forgiveness parallels the stages of recovery from psychological trauma. Over time, the couple progresses from the initial impact stage to a search for meaning or understanding of what happened to them. Finally, the couple moves to a recovery stage, in which they "get on with their lives" (Gordon et al., 2005). In the impact stage, there is typically a rampage of negative emotions—hurt, fear, and anger. At this time, the partners may swing from numbness to very bad feelings. Then, in the meaning stage, the partners search desperately to comprehend why the affair happened. Surely, the couple reasons, there must be some meaning in this relationship-shaking event. Last, the couple slowly begins to recapture a sense of control over their lives; a major goal in this stage is to keep the affair from ruling every waking thought of these two people. To forgive does not necessarily mean that the couple decides to stay together—but at least the forgiving process enables them to make more informed decisions about what to do next.

Everett L. Worthington, Jr.

Another productive approach for helping couples to deal with infidelity is the forgiveness model of Everett Worthington of Virginia Commonwealth University (see Ripley & Worthington, 2002; Worthington, 1998; Worthington & Drinkard, 2000). This model is based on helping the partners through the five steps of the acronym REACH: Recall the hurt and the nature of the injury caused; promote Empathy in both partners; Altruistically give the gift of forgiveness between partners; Commit verbally to forgive the partner, and Hold onto the forgiveness for each other.

Forgiving Oneself

A clinician will be alerted to the potential need for forgiveness of the self when a client is feeling either shame or guilt. In this regard, shame reflects an overall sense that "I am a bad person." As such, shame cuts across particular circumstances, and it reflects an all-encompassing view of the self as powerless and worthless. In contrast, guilt taps a situation-specific negative self-view, for example, "I did a bad thing" (Tangney, Boone, & Dearing, 2005). A person who feels guilt has a sense of remorse and typically regrets something that he or she has done. To correct for such guilt, some sort of reparative action is warranted, such as confessing or apologizing. The process of helping a person to deal with shame is a more difficult one for the helper than is the treatment for guilt. This follows because shame cuts through more situations than the single-situational focus of guilt.

Self-forgiveness has been defined as "a process of releasing resentment toward oneself for a perceived transgression or wrongdoing" (DeShea & Wahkinney, 2003, p. 4). Given that we all must live with ourselves, it can be seen that the consequences of not forgiving oneself can be much more severe than the consequences of not forgiving another person (Hall & Fincham, 2005). Interventions to lessen counterproductive criticism of the self are aimed at helping the individual take responsibility for the bad act or actions and then let go so that she or he can move forward with the tasks in life. In fact, any client who is absorbed in very negative or very positive self-thoughts feels "caught." Accordingly, helpers attempt to help their clients understand how their self-absorbed thoughts and feelings interfere with positive living. Holmgren (2002) has captured this sentiment:

> To dwell on one's own past record of moral performance, either with a sense of self-hatred and self-contempt or with a sense of superiority, is an activity that is overly self-involved and devoid of any real moral value. The client will exercise his moral agency much more responsibly if he removes his focus from the fact that he did wrong and concentrates instead on the contribution he can make to others and on the growth he can experience in the moral and nonmoral realms. (p. 133)

Forgiveness of a Situation

Recall the Enright position (described previously) that forgiveness should be applied only to people, not to inanimate objects such as tornadoes. We disagree with this premise; our views are consistent with the Thompson model of forgiveness, in which the target can be another person, oneself, or a situation.

A psychotherapy case of CRS's some 20 years ago shows how forgiveness can be applied to a situation. We live in Lawrence, Kansas, where tornadoes occasionally descend on our community. In this particular instance, a tornado had damaged houses and their inhabitants. After this tornado, I saw a man in therapy who held severe angry and bitter thoughts toward the tornado for destroying his house and making him feel psychologically victimized. In the course of treatment, the goal was to help this man to stop ruminating about the tornado, as well as to stop blaming it for having ruined his life (Snyder, 2003). Therefore, the man was taught to let go of his resentment toward the tornado. This was part of a larger treatment goal aimed at teaching this person to release the bitterness he felt about a series of "bad breaks" that he had received in life. Moreover, he came to understand that the tornado had struck other houses and families, but those people had picked up the pieces and moved on with their lives. For this client, ruminations about the tornado kept him stuck in the past, and he realized that letting go was part of moving forward so as to have hope in his life (see Lopez, Snyder, et al., 2004; Snyder, 1989).

For professionals who have done considerable psychotherapy, this case will not seem unusual, in that clients often point to their life circumstances as the causes of their problems (i.e., they blame the happenings in their lives). For such clients, therefore, a crucial part of their treatments entails instruction in stopping thoughts about earlier negative life events so that they instead can look ahead toward their futures (Michael & Snyder, in press).

For more insights into raising one's forgiveness, we recommend that you return to the Personal Mini-Experiments.

MEASURING FORGIVENESS

Each of the previously discussed theories of forgiveness is associated with an individual differences self-report measure that has been validated. We cover these measures in the same order as we discussed the theories.

Thompson et al. (2005) developed the Heartland Forgiveness Scale (HFS) as an 18-item trait measure of forgiveness. There are six items to tap each of the three types of forgiveness—self, other, or situation—and respondents use a 7-point scale (1 = Almost always false of me to 7 = Almost always true of me). This scale is reprinted in its entirety in Appendix C. Scores on the HFS have correlated positively with scores on other forgiveness measures; people scoring higher on the HFS also show more flexibility and trust, as well as less hostility, rumination, and depression.

McCullough et al. (1998) developed the Transgression-Related Interpersonal Motivations Inventory (TRIM) as a 12-item self-report measure (respondents use a 5-point continuum from 1 = Strongly disagree to 5 = Strongly agree), with the items tapping either (1) the motive to avoid contact with the transgressing person or (2) the motive to seek revenge against the transgressor. The TRIM can be regarded as a transgression-specific index of forgiveness. This scale is shown in Appendix D.

Enright has developed two forgiveness measures, the first of which is a 60-item version called the Enright Forgiveness Inventory (EVI; Subkoviak et al., 1995). The EVI assesses the respondent's thoughts about a most recent interpersonal transgression. A second Enright-inspired measure is the 16-item Willingness to Forgive Scale (WTF; Hebl & Enright, 1993). The WTF gives a valid estimate of the degree to which a person is willing to use forgiveness as a problem-solving coping strategy.

Tangney and colleagues (1999) have developed a trait self-report index called the Multidimensional Forgiveness Inventory (MFI). The MFI entails 16 different scenarios involving transgressions; 72 items tap these 9 subscales: (1) propensity to forgive self, (2) propensity to forgive others, (3) propensity to ask for forgiveness, (4) propensity to blame self, (5) propensity to blame others, (6) time to forgive self, (7) time to forgive others, (8) sensitivity to hurt feelings, and (9) anger-proneness.

THE EVOLUTIONARY AND NEUROBIOLOGICAL BASES OF FORGIVENESS

In many places throughout this book, we emphasize the communal nature of human beings. We live in groups, and part of such contact unfortunately involves instances in which one person strikes out against another in an injurious manner. In subhuman creatures, animals may at times engage in submissive gestures that stop the aggression cycle (deWaal & Pokorny, 2005; Newberg, d'Aquili, Newberg, & deMarici, 2000). In an analogous fashion, forgiveness may break the violence cycle in humans. Lacking such mechanisms to lessen the potential for aggression and retaliative counteraggression, humans may risk an escalating cycle that threatens the demise of the entire group. In this sense, there is an evolutionary advantage to forgiving actions in that they lower the overall level of hostility (Enright, 1996; Komorita, Hilty, & Parks, 1991), thereby enhancing the survival chances of the larger group. Indeed, people who display forgiveness toward their transgressors produce positive feelings in surrounding people who were in no way involved in the confrontation (Kanekar & Merchant, 1982), thereby stabilizing the social order. In short, forgiveness represents a process that has an adaptive evolutionary advantage in that it helps to preserve the social structure.

Newberg et al. (2000) have described the underlying neurophysiology of the forgiveness process. First, by necessity forgiveness involves a person's sense of self, because it is this source that is damaged during transgression by another. (Incidentally, perception of the self is crucial from an evolutionary standpoint because it is the self that the person strives to preserve over time.) The sense of self is located in the frontal, parietal, and temporal lobes, which receive input from the sensory system and the hippocampus. Second, injury to the self is registered via sensorimotor input, and this input is mediated by the limbic system, the sympathetic nervous system, and the hypothalamus. Third, initiation of the reconciliation process by the person transgressed against involves activation of the temporal, parietal, and frontal lobes, along with limbic system input. Finally, the actual outward direction of the forgiveness occurs through the limbic system and is associated with positive emotions.

The Societal Implications of
Altruism, Gratitude, and Forgiveness

In this portion of the chapter, we turn to the societal repercussions of altruism, gratitude, and forgiveness. As you will learn in this section, these three processes play crucial roles in helping groups of people live together with greater stability and interpersonal accord.

EMPATHY/EGOTISM AND ALTRUISM

Given that the feeling of empathy appears to propel human beings toward "pure" (i.e., nonegotistical) helping or altruistic actions, this motivation generally has positive implications for people living in groups. That is to say, as long as we can feel empathy, we should be more willing to help our fellow citizens.

Unfortunately, however, we often act either consciously or unconsciously so as to mute our sense of empathy toward other people. Consider, for example, the residents of major urban settings who walk down the street and do not even appear to see the street people stretched out on the pavement or sidewalk. Faced daily with such sights, it may be that the inhabitants of cities learn to mute their empathies. City dwellers thus may avoid eye contact or walk to the other side of the street in order to minimize their interactions with such down-and-out people.

To compound matters, social psychologists have shown that, as we live in large, urban settings, we can diffuse any sense of personal responsibility for helping others, a phenomenon known as the "innocent bystander effect" (Darley & Latane, 1968; Latane & Darley, 1970). At times, therefore, urban dwellers may rationalize and deceive themselves that they have behaved morally when, in fact, they have not rendered help to their neighbors (Rue, 1994; Snyder, Higgins, & Stucky, 1983/2005; Wright, 1994).

Realize, however, that even professionals whose training and job descriptions have entailed helping others may undergo similar muting of their sensibilities. For example, both nurses and schoolteachers may experience burnout when they feel blocked and repeatedly sense that they cannot produce the positive changes that they desire in their patients or students (Maslach, 1982; Maslach & Jackson, 1981; Snyder, 1994/2000). In our estimation, positive psychology must find ways to help people to remain empathic so they can continue to help others. Furthermore, we should explore avenues for enhancing empathy so we can address large-scale problems such as AIDS and homelessness (Batson, Polycarpou, et al., 1997; Dovidio, Gaertner, & Johnson, 1999; Snyder, Tennen, Affleck, & Cheavens, 2000).

Turning to the role of egotism-based benefits as they are implicated in the altruism process, our view is that it would be wise to teach people that there is nothing wrong with deriving benefits from or feeling good about helping others. In fact, it is unrealistic to expect that people always will engage in pure, non-ego-based motives as they go about their helping activities. In other words, if people indeed do feel good about themselves in rendering aid to others, then we should convey the societal message that this is perfectly legitimate. Although it certainly is worthwhile to engender the desire to help because it is the right thing to do, we also can impart the legitimacy of rendering help on the grounds that it is a means of deriving some sense of gratification. We should remember both the former and the latter lessons as we educate our children about the process of helping other people.

In fact, child-rearing practices that impart the message that anything other than "pure" altruism is bad may be counterproductive. The senior author once saw a client who was a minister's son; growing up, this young man was taught that any feelings of pleasure when helping another really were not legitimate or acceptable. Accordingly, when this young man found that he did enjoy helping others, he felt extremely guilty. Part of the therapy in this case involved having the young man talk with two other preachers who told him that there was nothing "sinful" about feeling good because of our efforts to help others. When he truly understood this new perspective, we then had an interchange between this young man and his father about this issue. Because the father was deceased, this exercise was conducted using the Gestalt empty chair technique (see the Personal Mini-Experiments), in which the client imagines that the target person is sitting in an empty chair across from him, and a discussion is held in which the client plays the roles of both persons. In doing this exercise, the young man realized that his father had not been mean-spirited in his teaching about helping; instead, his father's major intended lesson was the importance of caring about others. In caring about others, this client also learned that part of the process is to care about oneself and to provide self-love and reinforcement. In turn, his helping of others served both other people and himself, and he was much happier when he reached this insightful resolution. Moreover, the young man taught this lesson about the legitimacy of feeling good about rendering help to his own children so that they would not be caught in the same dilemma that he had experienced.

EMPATHY/EGOTISM AND GRATITUDE

To the degree to which we can understand and take the perspective of another person, it is more likely that we will express our sense of gratitude for the other person's actions. Perhaps another case history will help to clarify this point. One of the very first clients whom I (CRS) saw in psychotherapy, some four decades ago, was a young woman (let's call her Janice) who would never say thank you to others. In growing up, her father had taught her that people only would help another person when they "got something out of it." In other words, as a child she learned that that the help given by other people was not genuine. And, of course, if this help were not genuine, there was no need for Janice to thank other people for it. When she came to therapy, Janice reported that other people saw her as rude because she would not say thank you.

Before even getting into the childhood roots of this maladaptive pattern of behavior, I asked her to simply change her ways and say thanks when someone did something for her. She agreed to try this and immediately found that it made it easier to get along with people. In fact, over time it also made her feel good about herself to express gratitude. Next, we began to explore various ways to help Janice understand the perspectives of other people and that they may at times be quite genuine—that they were not always "out to get something"—in offering their help. Of course, this ran counter to the lessons taught her in childhood by her father, but she gradually did realize that there were not always ulterior motives for the helping behaviors of other people. One important breakthrough in this case came when Janice realized that she herself occasionally would help a friend and, in so doing, was not necessarily "totally out to get something for herself." This case history also shows that both the egotism and empathy perspectives can work to enhance a person's gratitude.

EMPATHY/EGOTISM AND FORGIVENESS

Empathy also is a precursor to forgiving another (McCullough et al., 1998; McCullough, Worthington, & Rachal, 1997; Worthington, 2005). The authors of this book have worked with psychotherapy clients for whom either empathy or egotism served as the routes for unleashing forgiveness. For example, consider the person who is filled with anger at something hurtful that another person has done, and who must first learn to see issues from the perspective of that other person (i.e., empathize) before coming to the point of forgiving him or her.

Occasionally, the person who has engaged in a transgression of some sort has misunderstood the surrounding circumstances. In a case related to this point, a young woman broke off her relationship and began to date other men when she saw her boyfriend sitting in the back of the church with his former girlfriend. It turned out, however, that the reason for this meeting was quite innocent: The former girlfriend's father had died, and the young man was consoling her. When the girl who broke off the relationship realized these circumstances, she was able to emphasize with her boyfriend and forgive him for what was actually an act of kindness. Indeed, she learned that the boyfriend's actions were not even really a transgression!

So too can we forgive—let go of negative ruminations about another person or event—in order to feel better about ourselves. As an example of this egotistical type of forgiveness, consider young people who have gotten into difficulties by breaking the law during their earlier teenage years. To feel better about themselves when they reach young adulthood, these young people may decide to do volunteer work to aid teens with legal problems. Such teenagers often desperately want and need to feel forgiven for their transgressions, and adults in their twenties who have been through similar circumstances make ideal sources of such forgiveness. In this latter regard, these young adults not only can empathize with the teens, but they also can feel good about themselves for providing such forgiveness.

MORAL IMPERATIVES: ALTRUISM, GRATITUDE, AND FORGIVENESS

As we have noted throughout this chapter, empathy and egotism often are precursors of altruism, gratitude, and forgiveness toward another. This notion of the empathy/esteem portal is depicted visually in Figure 12.1. Once a person has expressed altruism, gratitude, and forgiveness toward a recipient, however, the cycle does not stop. Consider, for example, the reactions of the recipient, for example, to gratitude. When the recipient of the gratitude expresses thanks or some other type of appreciation, the giver of such benevolent behavior is rewarded and thereafter may behave prosocially in the future (Gallup, 1998). Likewise, it is possible that some people render prosocial behavior at least in part because they enjoy the reinforcement they receive for it (Eisenberg, Miller, Shell, McNalley, & Shea, 1991).

In this process, depicted in Figure 12.4, the recipient is likely to reciprocate the altruism, gratitude, and forgiveness and, in so doing, may well experience empathy and esteem toward the giver. Moreover, the recipient of the altruism, gratitude, and forgiveness is likely to behave in moral ways toward other people in general (see the right-hand side of Figure 12.4). In other words, when altruism, gratitude, and forgiveness are exchanged, then the recipient should practice the virtues of positive psychology in subsequent interpersonal interactions. In this way, there are ripple effects of altruism, gratitude, and forgiveness. The underlying sentiment here may be, "When I am treated with respect, I will do the same to others."

In Adam Smith's (1790/1976) classic book, *The Theory of Moral Sentiments,* he suggested that gratitude and related constructs such as altruism and forgiveness are absolutely crucial in establishing a moral society. As such, gratitude is a moral imperative in that it promotes stable social interactions that are based on mutual reciprocity and respect (see again Figure 12.4). Using the line of thought developed by Adam Smith, sociologist George Simmel (1950) reasoned that gratitude, in particular, reminds people of their need to reciprocate and their inherent interrelationships to

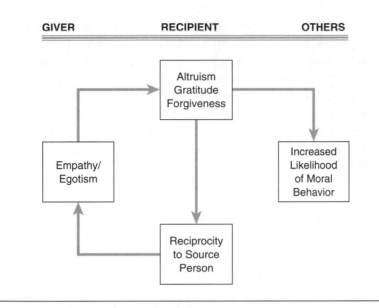

Figure 12.4   Altruism, Gratitude, and Forgiveness From Giver to Recipient to Others

each other. On this point, Simmel penned the beautiful sentiment that gratitude is "the moral memory of mankind. . . . [I]f every grateful action . . . were suddenly eliminated, society (at least as we know it) would break apart" (1950, p. 388). Thus, gratitude and its neighboring concepts of altruism and forgiveness facilitate a society in which there is a sense of cohesion and the ability to continue to function when both good and bad things happen to its citizens (for related discussion, see Rue [1994] and Snyder & Higgins [1997]).

"I Have a Dream": Toward a Kinder, Gentler Humankind

This chapter covers a trilogy of some of the finest behaviors of people—their altruism, gratitude, and forgiveness. It appears that empathy for the target person often is an important precursor to these behaviors. When we have empathy for another, we are more likely to help that person, to feel grateful for his or her actions, and to be forgiving when he or she transgresses. But in feeling such empathy, people also can fulfill their egotism needs. Thus, it need not be an either–or proposition when it comes to the motives of empathy and egotism that unleash altruism, gratitude, and forgiveness.

An implication here is that a kinder and gentler humankind will be one where each of us can understand the actions of others, feel their pains and sorrows, and yet also feel good about our own motives as we help our neighbors. Certainly, empathy is a crucial lesson that should be added to

Martin Luther King Jr.

Source: © Corbis.

the lessons in esteem that are taught to children. Our children may be able to feel good about themselves and get along better with others because of their understanding and compassion. Indeed, much of the future of positive psychology will be built upon people who can attend to their own egotism needs and also get along with and respect each other. Relationships are at the core of positive psychology, and our goal is a more "civilized" humankind in which altruism, gratitude, and forgiveness are the expected, rather than the unexpected, reactions between interacting people.

In what may be one of the most famous oral discourses of modern times, the "I Have a Dream" speech of Martin Luther King Jr., his empathy and altruism/gratitude/forgiveness thoughts and feelings were captured in his call for brotherhood and sisterhood (King, 1968). If positive psychology is to share in such a dream, as it surely aspires to do, then we must continue our quest to understand the science and applications that flow from the concepts of altruism, gratitude, and forgiveness.

Life Enhancement Strategies

Altruism, gratitude, and forgiveness can help you to live a more satisfying life. Here, we offer some tips for being more giving, grateful, and forgiving in all three life arenas.

Love

- Doing things for one's partner fosters a sense of altruism and potentially creates a more giving atmosphere in a relationship.
- A loving relationship is built on praise for one's mate when she or he does positive things; therefore, it is crucial to say thank you and to not take the positive for granted. Thus, your expressed gratitude for your partner keeps the sense of caring alive through an atmosphere of appreciation.
- There may be instances in a loving and intimate relationship where one partner transgresses, and forgiveness is needed for the relationship to endure. Try to become the partner and/or friend who practices forgiveness during difficult times.

Work

- Give your strengths and talents away to others in an effort to help them on their work or school projects.
- Gratitude can be even more important than money as management's way of rewarding workers. If you are given the responsibility of leading a team, give daily thanks for the contributions of others.
- Colleagues are going to be more willing to take chances, to try new things, and to work hard if they know that they will be forgiven should they make an occasional unintended mistake. Spread forgiveness in the workplace or classroom.

Play

- By its very nature, play and leisure activities entail a sense of freedom. Give that sense of freedom to others by inviting them to play your favorite game.
- Sometimes we are given peeks into others' pleasure. When friends and family are having fun around, don't be shy about expressing your gratitude for the "good times."
- Forgive the small rules infractions that are bound to result in competition. Don't let the small stuff get in the way of your fun.

Appendix A: The Helping Attitude Scale

INSTRUCTIONS: This instrument is designed to measure your feelings, beliefs and behaviors concerning your interactions with others. It is not a test, so there are no right or wrong answers. Please answer the questions as honestly as possible. Using the scale below, indicate your level of agreement or disagreement in the space which is next to each statement.

1	2	3	4	5
Strongly disagree	Disagree	Undecided	Agree	Strongly agree

_____ 1. Helping others is usually a waste of time.

_____ 2. When given the opportunity, I enjoy aiding others who are in need.

_____ 3. If possible, I would return lost money to the rightful owner.

_____ 4. Helping friends and family is one of the great joys in life.

_____ 5. I would avoid aiding someone in a medical emergency if I could.

_____ 6. It feels wonderful to assist others in need.

_____ 7. Volunteering to help someone is very rewarding.

_____ 8. I dislike giving directions to strangers who are lost.

_____ 9. Doing volunteer work makes me feel happy.

_____ 10. I donate time or money to charities every month.

Appendix A Source: From Nickell, G. S., "The Helping Attitude Scale," presented at the 106th Annual Convention of the American Psychological Association. Reprinted by permission of Dr. Gary Nickell.

_____ 11. Unless they are part of my family, helping the elderly isn't my responsibility.

_____ 12. Children should be taught about the importance of helping others.

_____ 13. I plan to donate my organs when I die, with the hope that they will help someone else live.

_____ 14. I try to offer my help with any activities my community or school groups are carrying out.

_____ 15. I feel at peace with myself when I have helped others.

_____ 16. If the person in front of me in the checkout line at a store was a few cents short, I would pay the difference.

_____ 17. I feel proud when I know that my generosity has benefited a needy person.

_____ 18. Helping people does more harm than good because they come to rely on others and not themselves.

_____ 19. I rarely contribute money to a worthy cause.

_____ 20. Giving aid to the poor is the right thing to do.

To score the Helping Attitude Scale, reverse the scores for items 1, 5, 8, 11, 18, and 19, then add up all twenty scores to obtain the total score. This score could range from 20 to 100, with a neutral score of 60.

Appendix B: The Gratitude Questionnaire— Six Items From GQ-6

INSTRUCTIONS: Using the scale below as a guide, write a number beside each statement to indicate how much you agree with it.

1	2	3	4	5	6	7
Strongly disagree	Disagree	Slightly disagree	Neutral	Slightly agree	Agree	Strongly agree

_____ 1. I have so much in life to be thankful for.

_____ 2. If I had to list everything that I felt grateful for, it would be a very long list.

Appendix B Source: From McCullough, M. E., Emmons, R. A., & Tsang, J., "The grateful disposition: A conceptual and empirical topography," in _Journal of Personality and Social Psychology, 82,_ copyright © 2002. Reprinted with permission of the American Psychological Association.

_____ 3. When I look at the world, I don't see much to be grateful for.*

_____ 4. I am grateful to a wide variety of people.

_____ 5. As I get older, I find myself more able to appreciate the people, events, and situations that have been part of my life history.

_____ 6. Long amounts of time can go by before I feel grateful to something or someone.*

*Items 3 and 6 are reverse scored.

Appendix C: The Heartland Forgiveness Scale (HFS)

DIRECTIONS: In the course of our lives, negative things may occur because of our own actions, the actions of others, or circumstances beyond our control. For some time after these events, we may have negative thoughts or feelings about ourselves, others, or the situation. Think about how you *typically* respond to such negative events. In the blank lines before each of the following items, please write the number (using the 7-point scale below) that best describes how you *typically* respond to the type of negative situation described. There are no right or wrong answers. Please be as honest as possible.

1	2	3	4	5	6	7
Almost always false		More often false of me		More often true of me		Almost always true of me

_____ 1. Although I feel badly at first when I mess up, over time I can give myself some slack.

_____ 2. I hold grudges against myself for negative things I've done.

_____ 3. Learning from bad things that I've done helps me get over them.

_____ 4. It is really hard for me to accept myself once I've messed up.

_____ 5. With time, I am understanding of myself for mistakes I've made.

_____ 6. I don't stop criticizing myself for negative things I've felt, thought, said, or done.

Appendix C Source: From Thompson, L. Y., Snyder, C. R., Hoffman, L., Michael, S. T., Rasmussen, H. N., Billings, L. S., Heinze, L., Neufeld, J. E., Shorey, H. S., Roberts, J. C., & Roberts, D. E., Dispositional forgiveness of self, others, and situations, in *Journal of Personality, 73,* copyright © 2005. Published with permission of Blackwell Publishing.

_____ 7. I continue to punish a person who has done something that I think is wrong.

_____ 8. With time, I am understanding of others for the mistakes they've made.

_____ 9. I continue to be hard on others who have hurt me.

_____ 10. Although others have hurt me in the past, I have eventually been able to see them as good people.

_____ 11. If others mistreat me, I continue to think badly of them.

_____ 12. When someone disappoints me, I can eventually move past it.

_____ 13. When things go wrong for reasons that can't be controlled, I get stuck in negative thoughts about it.

_____ 14. With time, I can be understanding of bad circumstances in my life.

_____ 15. If I'm disappointed by uncontrollable circumstances in my life, I continue to think negatively about them.

_____ 16. I eventually make peace with bad situations in my life.

_____ 17. It's really hard for me to accept negative situations that aren't anybody's fault.

_____ 18. Eventually, I let go of negative thoughts about bad circumstances that are beyond anyone's control.

REVERSE-SCORED ITEMS

Items 2, 4, 6, 7, 9, 11, 13, 15, and 17 are reverse scored.

OVERALL HFS SCORE

A total forgiveness score is derived by summing the numbers given in response to items 1 through 18 (using the reverse scores for items 2, 4, 6, 7, 9, 11, 13, 15, and 17).

SUBSCALES

Self: Items 1 through 6 compose the forgiveness-of-self subscale.
Other: Items 7 through 12 compose the forgiveness-of-other subscale.
Situations: Items 13 through 18 compose the forgiveness-of-situations subscale.

Appendix D: The Transgression-Related Interpersonal Motivations Scale (TRIM)

Directions: For the following questions, please indicate your current thoughts and feelings about the person who hurt you. Use the following scale to indicate your agreement with each of the questions.

1	2	3	4	5
Strongly disagree	Disagree	Neutral	Agree	Strongly agree

_____ 1. I'll make him/her pay.

_____ 2. I keep as much distance between us as possible.

_____ 3. I wish that something bad would happen to him/her.

_____ 4. I live as if he/she doesn't exist, isn't around.

_____ 5. I don't trust him/her.

_____ 6. I want him/her to get what he/she deserves.

_____ 7. I find it difficult to act warmly toward him/her.

_____ 8. I avoid him/her.

_____ 9. I'm going to get even.

_____ 10. I cut off the relationship with him/her.

_____ 11. I want to see him/her hurt and miserable.

_____ 12. I withdraw from him/her.

AVOIDANCE MOTIVATIONS

Add up the scores for items 2, 4, 5, 7, 8, 10, and 12.

REVENGE MOTIVATIONS

Add up the scores for items 1, 3, 6, 9, and 11.

Appendix D Source: From McCullough, M. E., Rachal, K. C., Sandage, S. J., Worthington, E. L., Jr., Brown, S. W., & Hight, T. L., Interpersonal forgiving in close relationships: II. Theoretical elaboration and measurement, in *Journal of Personality and Social Psychology, 75,* pp. 1586–1603. Copyright © 1998 by the American Psychological Association. Reprinted with permission.

Key Terms

Altruism: Actions or behaviors that are intended to benefit another person.

Egotism: The motive to pursue some sort of personal gain or benefit through targeted behavior.

Empathy: An emotional response to the perceived plight of another person. Empathy may entail the ability to experience emotions similar to the other person's or a sense of tenderheartedness toward that person.

Empathy–altruism hypothesis: The view, borne out by Batson's (1991) findings, that empathy for another person leads to a greater likelihood of helping that person.

Forgiveness (as defined by Thompson and colleagues): A freeing from a negative attachment to the source of the transgression. This definition of forgiveness allows the target of forgiveness to be oneself, another person, or a situation.

Forgiveness (as defined by McCullough and colleagues): An increase in prosocial motivation such that there is less desire to avoid or seek revenge against the transgressor and an increased desire to act positively toward the transgressing person. This theory of forgiveness is applicable only when another person is the target of the transgression.

Forgiveness (as defined by Enright and colleagues): The willingness to give up resentment, negative judgment, and indifference toward the transgressor and to give undeserved compassion, generosity, and benevolence to him or her. Enright and colleagues also limit their definition of forgiveness to people and do not include situations.

Forgiveness (as defined by Tangney and colleagues): A process involving "(1) [C]ognitive-affective transformation following a transgression in which (2) the victim makes a realistic assessment of the harm done and acknowledges the perpetrator's responsibility, but (3) freely chooses to "cancel the debt," giving up the need for revenge or deserved punishments and any quest for restitution. This "canceling of the debt" also involves (4) a "cancellation of negative emotions" directly related to the transgression. In particular, in forgiving, the victim overcomes his or her feelings of resentment and anger for the act. In short, by forgiving, the harmed individual (5) essentially removes himself or herself from the victim role" (Tangney et al., 1999, p. 2).

Gratitude: Being thankful for and appreciating the actions of another. Gratitude emerges upon recognizing that one has received a positive outcome from another person who behaved in a manner that was costly to him or her, valuable to the recipient, and intentionally rendered.

Attachment, Love, and Flourishing Relationships

13

In our clinical work, we see people from all walks of life who talk about feelings of loneliness. For some clients, the conversation focuses on longing for loved ones "back home," along with concerns about finding good friends in a new place. For too many, the loneliness and a sense of alienation stem from relationships that have soured. There are sons who do not feel connected to their fathers, boyfriends who feel invisible to their partners, wives who "don't know" their husbands anymore, and aging parents who haven't seen their children in years. All these people tell painful stories of loss. When our basic needs for love, affection, and belongingness are not met (Maslow, 1970; see Figure 13.1), we feel lonely and worthless. This pain has long-term effects because our growth is stymied when we feel detached and unloved.

We start our discussion of attachment, love, and flourishing relationships with comments on loneliness because much of the positive psychology of social connection was built on scholarship pertaining to traumatic separation (Bowlby, 1969) and failed relationships (Carrere & Gottman, 1999). Only recently have scholars pursued research questions such as, "What are the characteristics of successful relationships?" (e.g., Gable, Reis, & Elliot, 2003; Harvey, Pauwels, & Zicklund, 2001).

Attachment and love are necessary components of flourishing relationships, but they are not sufficient for the maintenance of such relationships. In this regard, attachment and love must be accompanied by what we refer to as *purposeful positive relationship behaviors*.

In this chapter, we discuss the *infant-to-caregiver attachment* that forms the foundation for future relationships, the *adult attachment security* that is closely linked to healthy relationship development, the *love* that is often considered a marker of quality of relationships, and the *purposeful positive*

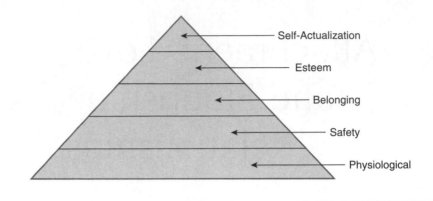

Figure 13.1   The Fulfillment of Needs for Love and Belongingness Is Considered
                    a Prerequisite for Esteem and Self-Actualization

relationship behaviors that sustain interpersonal connections over time and contribute to *flourishing relationships.* Along the way, we describe a hierarchy of social needs that demonstrates how meaningful relationships develop into flourishing relationships. We also describe real-life exemplars of "person-growing" relationships (relationships that promote the optimal functioning of both participants). Moreover, we discuss people who have experienced the best aspects of the interpersonal world. Finally, we summarize the findings on the biology of social support.

Infant Attachment

Attachment is a process that probably starts during the first moment of an infant's life. It is the emotional link that forms between a child and a caregiver, and it physically binds people together over time (Ainsworth, Bell, & Stayton, 1992). John Bowlby (1969), a clinician who worked with delinquent and orphaned children, identified numerous **maladaptive parental behaviors** (chaotic, unplanned attempts to meet a child's needs) and **adaptive parental behaviors** (responsiveness to a child's behavioral cues, e.g., smiling) that were believed to be causally linked to functional behavior and emotional experiences of children. For example, inconsistency in responses to children is associated with children's frustration and later anxiety. On the other hand, consistency in caregivers' responses to children's cues is linked to children's contentment and later development of trust. Adaptive and maladaptive parental behaviors lead to the development of an **attachment system** that regulates the proximity-seeking behaviors connecting infants and caregivers in physical and emotional space. This two-way connection has been described as "a unique, evolutionarily-based motivational system (i.e., independent of the gratification of libidinal needs and drives) whose primary function is the provision of protection and emotional security" (Lopez, 2003, p. 286).

Through the study of children who became disconnected from their caregivers, Bowlby (1969) realized that insecure attachment is a precursor to numerous developmental struggles. A child with insecure attachment to a caregiver may have difficulty in cooperating with others and in regulating moods. These problems make existing relationships fragile and new relationships hard to build. Conversely, children with sound attachment systems become more appealing to their caregivers and other people. Over time, that attachment system becomes more sophisticated, and mutually beneficial patterns of interaction facilitate the psychological development of such children and their caregivers.

A classic behavioral assessment strategy designed by Mary Ainsworth (1979) has allowed psychologists to look into the attachment phenomenon. In the **Strange Situation** assessment, a child is exposed to a novel situation in the company of his or her caregiver, and then the caregiver is removed and reintroduced to the situation twice. During this process, the child participant's reactions are assessed. Here are the basic steps in the assessment paradigm (Steps 2 through 7 last 3 minutes each):

1. Caregiver and child are invited into a novel room.

2. Caregiver and child are left alone. Child is free to explore.

3. Stranger enters, sits down, talks to caregiver, and then tries to engage child in play.

4. Caregiver leaves. Stranger and child are alone.

5. Caregiver returns for the first reunion, and stranger leaves unobtrusively. Caregiver settles child, if necessary, and then withdraws to a chair in the room.

6. Caregiver leaves. Child is alone.

7. Stranger returns and tries to settle child, if necessary, and then withdraws to the chair.

8. Caregiver returns for the second reunion, and stranger leaves unobtrusively. Caregiver settles child and then withdraws to the chair.

Trained observers code behavioral responses in this strange situation and render one of the following assessments of the quality of the attachment: secure, insecure-avoidant, and insecure-resistant/ambivalent. (See Table 13.1 for a description of adult attachment classification systems that have been refined over the years.) The **secure attachment** pattern is characterized by a balance between exploration of the environment and contact with the caregiver. As the strange situation unfolds, the child will engage in more proximity-seeking and contact-maintaining behavior with the caregiver, exploring the environment only to return for comfort when necessary.

Table 13.1　　Three Prominent Classification Systems of Adult Attachment Styles

Main & Goldwyn (1984, 1998)	Description
Secure/Autonomous	Interviewee demonstrates coherent, collaborative discourse. Interviewee values attachment but seems objective regarding any particular event/relationship. Description and evaluation of attachment-related experiences are consistent, whether experiences are favorable or unfavorable.
Dismissing	Interview is not coherent, and interviewee is dismissing of attachment-related experiences and relationships. Interviewee "normalizes" these experiences with generalized representations of history unsupported or actively contradicted by episodes recounted. Transcripts also tend to be excessively brief, violating the maxim of quantity.
Preoccupied	Interview is not coherent, and interviewee is preoccupied with or by past attachment relationships/experiences. Interviewee appears angry, passive, or fearful, and uses sentences that are often long, grammatically entangled, or filled with vague uses. Transcripts are often excessively long, violating the maxim of quantity.
Unresolved/ Disorganized	During discussions of loss or abuse, interviewee shows striking lapse in the monitoring of reasoning or discourse. For example, the person may briefly indicate a belief that a dead person is still alive in the physical sense, or that this person was killed by a childhood thought. Interviewee may lapse into prolonged silence or eulogistic speech.
Hazan & Shaver (1987)	Description
Secure	I find it relatively easy to get close to others and am comfortable depending on them and having them depend on me. I don't often worry about being abandoned or about someone getting too close to me.
Avoidant	I am somewhat uncomfortable being close to others; I find it difficult to trust them completely, difficult to allow myself to depend on them. I am nervous when anyone gets too close, and often love partners want me to be more intimate than I feel comfortable being.
Anxious	I find that others are reluctant to get as close as I would like. I often worry that my partner doesn't really love me or won't want to stay with me. I want to merge completely with another person, and this desire sometimes scares people away.

Bartholomew & Horowitz (1991)	Description
Secure	It is easy for me to become emotionally close to others. I am comfortable depending on others and having others depend on me. I don't worry about being alone or having others not accept me.
Dismissing	I am comfortable without close emotional relationships. It is very important for me to feel independent and self-sufficient, and I prefer not to depend on others or have others depend on me.
Preoccupied	I want to be completely emotionally intimate with others, but I often find that others are reluctant to get as close as I would like. I am uncomfortable being without close relationships, but I sometimes worry that others don't value me as much as I value them.
Fearful	I am uncomfortable getting close to others. I want emotionally close relationships, but I find it difficult to trust others completely, or to depend on them. I worry that I will be hurt if I allow myself to become too close to others.

Source: Adapted from Hesse, E. (1999). The Adult Attachment Interview: Historical and current perspectives. In J. Cassidy & P. R. Shaver (Eds.), *Handbook of attachment: Theory, research, and clinical applications* (pp. 395–433). New York: Guilford Press. Reprinted with permission. Adapted version also published in S. J. Lopez & C. R. Snyder (Eds.), *Positive psychological assessment: A handbook of models and measures* (pp. 285–299). Washington, DC: American Psychological Association.

Insecure patterns involve increasing tension between the child and parent over the course of the strange situation. Children with **insecure-avoidant** patterns avoid the caregiver when he or she is reintroduced into the situation, and those with the **insecure-resistant/ambivalent** pattern passively or actively demonstrate hostility toward the caregiver while simultaneously wanting to be held and comforted. (In the following Personal Mini-Experiments, conduct the jungle gym observation to test your ability to evaluate attachment in relationships.)

Quality of attachment patterns, as measured by the Strange Situation assessment approach, has predicted aspects of children's functioning many years later. For example, a study of preschool children indicated that those who were securely attached were more able to cope with parental absence and to relate to actual strangers more readily. Insecurely attached children seem tongue-tied when communicating with adults, and they had general difficulty relating to their caregivers (Bretherton & Waters, 1985). Other researchers (e.g., Belsky & Nezworski, 1988) have identified long-term consequences of insecure attachment, such as relationship problems, emotional disorders, and conduct problems.

Personal Mini-Experiments

In Search of Love and Flourishing Relationships

In this chapter, we discuss attachment, love, and flourishing relationships. Our review suggests that sound relationships are built on a foundation of secure attachments and that they are maintained with love and purposeful positive relationship behaviors. Here are a few ideas for personal experiments aimed at helping you develop a better understanding of secure, loving relationships—including your own.

The Jungle Gym Observations of Attachment: Conduct your own Strange Situation (Ainsworth, 1979) observations at a jungle gym at the local playground. As a child begins to play and is separated from the caregiver by physical distance, note the frequency of proximity-seeking and contact-maintaining behavior by that child. Hypothesize how the child will react when he or she takes a break from playing . . . or when the caregiver roams a little farther away from the jungle gym (to supervise another child or find a bench). Note whether the child's behavior is consistent with your attachment-related hypotheses.

The Relationship of Two Circles: According to self-expansion theorists (Aron, Aron, & Smollan, 1992), a relationship between two people can be evaluated based on the degree of overlap of two circles representing the two persons in the relationship. To consider the degree of expansion and inclusion in your relationship (the less the two circles overlap, the less inclusion; the more they overlap, the more inclusion), draw a circle that represents your partner, and then draw a circle that represents you and your relationship to your partner. Consider the meaningfulness of the degree of overlap (inclusion and self-expansion) by discussing it with your partner.

Making the Most of Good News: Over the course of your relationship, you may become a master of capitalizing by providing active/constructive responses (see Figure 13.2, page 316) to your partner's attempts to share positive events. To foster this purposeful positive relationship skill, do the following to make the most of the positive daily events in your romantic partner's life:

- Listen actively and empathically to the account of the positive event.
- Mirror your partner's enthusiasm about the positive event (while he/she shares it with you) by engaging in authentic expressions of excitement and delight (e.g., smiling, saying "Great!" or "Wow!," reaching for your partner's hand).
- Ask two constructive questions about the positive event ("How did you feel when it happened?" "How did it happen? Tell me everything!" and other, more specific questions).
- Reintroduce the positive event into conversation later in the day or on the next day to stretch out the benefits of something good having happened in your partner's life.

Attachment is a dynamic force that connects children to their caregivers. Moreover, secure attachment provides the safe environment in which children can take chances, engage in learning activities, initiate new relationships, and grow into healthy, socially adept adults. In the following example, this secure attachment provided the springboard that helped "Crystal" to grow into a happy adult with a thriving family.

Crystal and her brother were always close. He saw her as a little baby who needed more attention, and as she grew up, she saw him as someone she could count on. Crystal warmly greeted her brother when he met her after school to walk her home. Since their early childhood, she has found comfort in her relationship with her older brother. Today, she is fond of telling her children stories about the many good times and occasional bad times she shared with her sibling.

Adult Attachment Security

Personal perspectives on attachment are carried through childhood and adolescence and into stages of adulthood in the form of an internal working model of self and others (Bowlby, 1988; Shaver, Hazan, & Bradshaw, 1988). Early in their social development, children integrate perceptions of their social competence, appeal, and lovability (the self model) with their expectations regarding the accessibility, responsiveness, and consistency of caregivers (the other model). These models are relatively stable over developmental periods because they are self-reinforcing. That is, the internal models consist of a set of cognitive schema through which people see the world, gather information about self and others, and make interpersonal decisions. The model is a "conscious 'mindful state' of generalized expectations and preferences regarding relationship intimacy that guide participants' information processing of relationship experiences as well as their behavioral response patterns" (Lopez, 2003, p. 289). If people carry forward a secure mindful state, they see the world as safe and others as reliable. Unfortunately, negative or insecure schema also may be perpetuated. For example, people who see the social world as unpredictable and other people as unreliable have difficulty overcoming their desires to keep others at a distance.

Numerous theorists (e.g., Bartholomew & Horowitz, 1991; Hazan & Shaver, 1987; Main & Goldwyn, 1984, 1998) have extended attachment theory across the life span in an effort to understand how adults relate to other adults as well as to the children for whom they will serve as caregivers. Developmental psychologists Mary Main and colleagues have conducted interviews of mothers who participated in the Strange Situation assessment, and found that adult attachment could best be described by a four-category system comprising secure/autonomous, dismissing, preoccupied, and unresolved/disorganized. The interview used by Main (George, Kaplan, & Main, 1985; Main & Goldwyn, 1984, 1998), the Adult Attachment Interview, has become the "gold standard" for clinical assessment of adult attachment. (Social psychologists researching attachment tend to use self-report measures such as those reviewed by Brennan, Clark, and Shaver in 1998.)

Phillip Shaver

Source: Reprinted with permission of Phillip Shaver.

Social psychologists Cindy Hazan and Phillip Shaver have studied attachment in the context of adult romantic relationships. They found (Hazan & Shaver, 1987) that the three categories of secure, avoidant, and anxious, akin to Ainsworth's (1979) groups, effectively described the nature of adult attachments to a significant other. In 1991, Bartholomew and Horowitz expanded the three categories of adult attachment to four categories by differentiating two types of avoidant attachment, dismissive and fearful. Most recently, Brennan et al. (1998) considered Bartholomew and Horowitz's system from a different perspective. They conceptualized attachment on the two dimensions of attachment-related avoidance and attachment-related anxiety. The secure style is low on both dimensions, the dismissing style is high on avoidance and low on anxiety, the preoccupied style is low on avoidance and high on anxiety, and the fearful style is high on both avoidance and attachment anxiety. Table 13.1 on pages 300–301 describes the adult attachment classification systems.

Secure adult attachment, as characterized by low attachment-related avoidance and anxiety, involves a comfort with emotional closeness and a general lack of concern about being abandoned by others. Feeling secure in one's attachment to other significant adults has numerous benefits. Most importantly, this approach provides the pathways to survival and healthy development. By successfully recruiting care from significant others, children and adults become stronger and more able to cope with threats (Bowlby, 1988). Moreover, by pursuing growth experiences within the context of safe, secure relationships, we can pursue optimal human functioning or flourishing (Lopez & Brennan, 2000).

Adult attachment security provided "Kelly," in our next example, with a lively confidence that helped her initiate new relationships and sustain existing ones. Kelly introduced herself to her new group of colleagues by sharing a few interesting facts about her life. She had a close family hundreds of miles away and a boyfriend a thousand miles away. Despite her recent goodbyes, she seemed to have a great deal of emotional energy to give to her new friendships. Her first week on the job included three lunch dates with coworkers and numerous quick cell phone calls from Mom and her boyfriend.

Each of you have developed and maintained an attachment system, and based on our history and system, we process new social and emotional stimuli everyday. It determines who is or is not "let in" emotionally. Furthermore, it determines the depths of love.

Love

The capacity for love is a central component of all human societies. Love in all its manifestations, whether for children, parents, friends, or romantic partners, gives depth to human relationships. Specifically, love brings people closer to each other physically and emotionally. When experienced intensely, it makes people think expansively about themselves and the world.

The definitive history of love (Singer, 1984a, 1984b, 1987) highlights the following four traditions, denoted by Greek terms, that define this primary emotional experience: (1) *eros*, the search for the beautiful; (2) *philia*, the affection in friendship; (3) *nomos*, submission and obedience to the divine; and (4) *agape*, or the bestowal of love by the divine. Contrary to the arguments of some researchers (Cho & Cross, 1995; Hatfield & Rapson, 1996) and contrary to the depictions of history in Hollywood movies, it is notable that Singer did not believe that romantic love played a major role in world culture.

Other notable scholars such as Texas Tech University psychologists Susan Hendrick and Clyde Hendrick (1992) hypothesized that only during the last 300 years or so have cultural forces led people to develop a sense of self that was capable of loving and caring for a romantic partner over a lifetime. Despite the uncertainty about the place of romantic love in history, its role in the future of the world is clear. Indeed, love for a companion is considered central to a life well lived, as described in this quotation: "Romantic love may not be essential in life, but it may be essential to joy. Life without love would be for many people like a black-and-white movie–full of events and activities but without the color that gives vibrancy and provides a sense of celebration" (Hendrick & Hendrick, p. 117).

Susan Hendrick

Source: Reprinted with permission of Susan Hendrick.

Given what now can be described as a universal interest in romantic love, we highlight some of the psychological research that explores this type of loving. We describe three conceptualizations of romantic love that may foster an understanding of how it develops between two people.

PASSIONATE AND COMPANIONATE ASPECTS OF ROMANTIC LOVE

Romantic love is a complex emotion that may be best parsed into *passionate* and *companionate* forms (Berscheid & Walster, 1978; Hatfield, 1988), both of which are valued by most people. **Passionate love** (the intense arousal that fuels a romantic union) involves a state of absorption between two people that often is accompanied by moods ranging from ecstasy to anguish. **Companionate love** (the soothing, steady warmth that sustains a relationship) is manifested in a strong bond and an intertwining of lives that brings about feelings of comfort and peace. These two forms can occur simultaneously or intermittently rather than sequentially (from passionate to companionate).

Romantic love is characterized by intense arousal and warm affection. In a study of college students who were probably in the early stages of romantic relationships, nearly half named their romantic partners when asked to identify their closest friend (Hendrick & Hendrick, 1993). This latter finding suggests that passionate and companionate love can coexist in the new relationships of young people. Likewise, in a study of couples married for as long as 40 years, Contreras, Hendrick, and Hendrick (1996) found that companionate love *and* passionate love were alive, and that passionate love was the strongest predictor of marital satisfaction (of all variables measured in the study).

THE TRIANGULAR THEORY OF LOVE

In developing the **triangular theory of love,** psychologist Robert Sternberg (1986) theorized that love is a mix of three components: (1) passion, or physical attractiveness and romantic drives; (2) intimacy, or feelings of closeness and connectedness, and (3) commitment, involving the decision to initiate and sustain a relationship. Various combinations of these three components yield eight forms of love. For example, intimacy and passion combined produce romantic love, whereas intimacy and commitment together constitute companionate love. **Consummate love,** the most durable type, is manifested when all three components (passion, intimacy, commitment) are present at high levels and in balance across both partners.

Some of the research exploring Sternberg's theory of love has focused on the predictive value of these three ingredients of love. In a study of 104 couples (average length of marriage was 13 years, ranging from 2 months to 45 years), both husbands' and wives' intimacy, followed by passion, predicted marital satisfaction (Silberman, 1995). Additionally, research on adults' views about their relationships found that commitment was the best predictor of relationship satisfaction, especially for the long-term partnerships (Acker & Davis, 1992).

THE SELF-EXPANSION THEORY OF ROMANTIC LOVE

Informed by Eastern conceptualizations of love, Arthur Aron and Elaine Aron (1986) developed a theory that humans have a basic motivation to expand the self; moreover, they posited that the emotions, cognitions, and behaviors of love fuel such self-expansion. People seek to expand themselves through love: "The idea is that the self expands toward knowing or becoming that which includes everything and everyone, the Self. The steps along the way are ones of including one person or thing, then another, then still another" (Aron & Aron, 1996, pp. 45–46).

According to the **self-expansion theory** (Aron & Aron, 1996), relationship satisfaction is a natural by-product of self-expansive love. Being in a loving relationship makes people feel good. They then associate those positive feelings with the relationship, thereby reinforcing their commitment to the relationship. The positive consequences of being in love are clear. Aron, Paris, and Aron (1995) studied a group of college students over a 10-week period, and the researchers monitored the reactions of the students to falling in love (if they happened to do so during that particular semester). Those students who fell in love experienced increased self-esteem and self-efficacy. On a more cognitive level, self-expansion means that each partner has made a decision to include another in his or her self. This investment in each other adds to relationship satisfaction. (In the Personal Mini-Experiments, conduct the Relationship of Two Circles experiment to determine the extent to which love has been a self-expanding force in your life.)

COMMENTS ON LOVE RESEARCH

Psychological theories of love—and, more specifically, scholarly ideas about romantic love—provide insights into a mysterious phenomenon. The work of positive psychologists interested in love tells the story of how people first unite and then how positive feelings help to maintain relationships over time. We now turn to another example, the marriage of "Bill" and "Libby," which has taught many people about the potency of love. Each afternoon, Bill and Libby can be seen walking their yellow Labrador retriever in their neighborhood. They chat nonstop about their days at work and about their dreams for the future. They are both near 60, but they have the look of high school friends excitingly planning their lives. Over dinner with friends, they flirt with each other, make occasional overtures, and tell funny stories about themselves and their relationship. When they are at their best, and the relationship is really going well, they make you think that their love will last forever.

The scholarship on love also describes stories of love (Sternberg, 1998) and the meaning of "I love you" (Hecht, Marston, & Larkey, 1994; Marston, Hecht, & Robers, 1987). Our stories of love develop throughout our lives and are carried by us into relationships; theoretically, these stories define the quality of our interactions with our significant others. Sternberg, upon interviewing a large sample of couples, found that there are at least 26 "love stories" (e.g., a fantasy story, a horror story) that are largely unconscious views of romance and relationships that guide our interpersonal choices. By becoming more aware of the stories of love we have told ourselves over the years, we are more able to make mindful choices in approaching and enhancing relationships.

Analysis of the meaning of the statement, "I love you" (Hecht et al., 1994; Marston et al., 1987) reminds us how subjective and personal our views of love can be. Have you ever thought about what you mean when you say, "I love you"? Most people have not examined the many meanings of "I love you," and that spurred Dan Cox, a student in my (SJL's) positive psychology seminar, to ask his colleagues to describe exactly what they meant when they last said, "I love you" to someone. The many meanings of this sentiment included "I understand," "I support you," "Thanks," "I am sorry" and more global statements, such as "This is a good life" and "It is good to be with you." The variability in the meaning of those three little words suggests there is much we don't know about the emotion that connects us to others.

Research on love does not account for all the subjectivity that defines the richness of the experience, nor does it identify the many reasons why some relationships fail and why some flourish. The next section highlights the behaviors, rather than positive emotions, that determine the success of most close relationships.

Flourishing Relationships: A Series of Purposeful Positive Relationship Behaviors

Positive psychologists specializing in close relationships (Harvey et al., 2001; Reis & Gable, 2003) are exploring what makes existing relationships flourish and what skills can be taught directly to partners to enhance their interpersonal connections. (Try to develop some of these behaviors by completing the brief exercises in the Life Enhancement Strategies.) In this section, we discuss theories and research evidence on **flourishing relationships**, which are good relationships that continue to get better due to concerted effort of both partners.

John H. Harvey

Source: Reprinted with permission of John H. Harvey.

BUILDING A MINDFUL RELATIONSHIP CONNECTION

Well-minded relationships are healthy and long lasting. This belief led University of Iowa social psychologist John Harvey and his colleagues (Harvey & Ormarzu, 1997; Harvey et al., 2001) to develop a five-component model of *minding* relationships. This model shows how closeness, or the satisfaction and relationship behaviors that contribute to one another's goals in life, may be enhanced. (See Table 13.2 for a summary of these components and their maladaptive counterparts.)

Life Enhancement Strategies

Additional tips for bringing more security and love into your life are listed here. Although we focus on aspects of romantic love in this chapter, we address many forms of love in this list of strategies.

Love

- Tell the story of your attachment history in a journal entry. Include the language of security/insecurity to describe your childhood and present-day experiences, and identify how your attachment history translates into your current ability to show love to friends, family, and significant others.
- When you are in an ongoing relationship, develop a list of what makes your partner feel appreciated, and attempt to enhance the culture of appreciation in your relationship with five purposeful acts each day.

Work

- Take a mindfulness meditation course (see Chapter 11 for a description) with a partner, and apply your newfound skills when attending to your own behavior and to the relationship. Generalize these skills to behavior with colleagues at work.
- Ignore old advice about making friends at work. Vital friendships (which may involve philial love) at the workplace can enhance your engagement with your work.

Play

- Children benefit socially and emotionally from having one caring adult in their lives. Volunteer some time with a child or youth service and attempt to form a connection with at least one young person. Over time, the benefits of the relationship may become increasingly mutual.
- Identify the couple in your life whom you believe has the best relationship. Arrange to spend some time with them so you can observe relationship behaviors that work for them. If you know the couple well, ask them specific questions about how they maintain their relationship.

Minding is the "reciprocal knowing process involving the nonstop, interrelated thoughts, feelings, and behaviors of persons in a relationship" (Harvey et al., 2001, p. 424). As described in Chapter 11, mindfulness is a conscious process that requires moment-to-moment effort. This need for consciousness in minding relationships is reflected in the first component of the model, *knowing and being known*. According to the model, each partner in the relationship must want to know the other person's hopes, dreams, fears, vulnerabilities, and uncertainties. Furthermore, each

Table 13.2   Minding Relationship Behavior: Adaptive and Nonadaptive Steps

Adaptive	Nonadaptive
Via an in-depth knowing process, both partners in step in seeking to know and be known by the other.	One or both partners out of step in seeking to know and be known by the other.
Both partners use the knowledge gained in enhancing relationship.	Knowledge gained in knowing process is not used or not used well (may be used to hurt other).
Both partners accept what they learn and respect the other for the person they learn about.	Acceptance of what is learned is low, as is respect for the other person.
Both partners motivated to continue this process and do so indefinitely, such that synchrony and synergy of thought, feeling, and action emerge.	One or both partners are not motivated to engage in the overall minding process or do so sporadically; little synchrony and synergy emerge.
Both partners in time develop a sense of being special and appreciated in the relationship.	One or both partners fail to develop a sense of being special and appreciated in the relationship.

Source: From Harvey, J. H., Pauwels, B. G., & Zicklund, S., Relationship connection: The role of minding in the enhancement of closeness, in C. R. Snyder & S. J. Lopez (Eds.), *The Handbook of Positive Psychology*, copyright © 2002 by Oxford University Press, Inc. Used by permission of Oxford University Press, Inc.

partner must monitor the balance between his or her own self-expression and that of the partner, and give preference to learning about the other person rather than focusing on his or her own personal information. People who are successful at knowing and being known in their relationships demonstrate an understanding of how time brings about change, and of how change necessitates renewed opportunities and attempts to learn about the other person.

The second component of relationship minding involves partners *making relationship-enhancing attributions for behaviors.* Attributing positive behaviors to dispositional causes and negative behaviors to external, situational causes may be the most adaptive approach to making sense of another person's behavior. Over time, people in well-minded relationships develop the proper mixture of internal and external attributions and become more willing to reexamine attributions when explanations for a partner's behavior don't jibe with what is known about the loved one. Making charitable attributions (i.e., going beyond the benefit of the doubt; Thomas Krieshok, personal communication, June 21, 2005) occasionally can resolve conflicts before they become divisive.

Accepting and respecting, the third component of the minding model, requires an empathic connection (see Chapter 12), along with refined social skills (such as those described in the next section). As partners become more intimate in their knowledge of one another and share some good and bad experiences, mindful acceptance of personal strengths and weaknesses is necessary for the continued development of the relationship. When this acceptance is linked with respect, it serves as an antidote for contemptuous behavior that can dissolve a relationship (Gottman, 1994).

The final components of the model are *maintaining reciprocity and continuity in minding*. Regarding reciprocity in minding, "each partner's active participation and involvement in relationship-enhancing thoughts and behaviors" (Harvey et al., 2001, p. 428) is necessary for maintaining a mutually beneficial relationship. A lack of conscious engagement displayed by one partner can lead to frustration or contempt on the part of the other partner. Continuity in minding also may require planning and strategizing to become closer as the relationship matures. Partners who frequently check in on the other's goals and needs are likely to identify what is working and what is not working in the minding process (see Snyder, 1994/2000).

Mindfulness is a skill that can be taught and, as such, relationship minding can be enhanced (Harvey & Omarzu, 1997). The mutual practice of mindfulness techniques (discussed in Chapter 11) could benefit partners who are attempting to apply Harvey's relationship-enhancing guidance.

CREATING A CULTURE OF APPRECIATION

John Gottman (1994, 1999) has spent a lifetime "thin-slicing" relationship behavior (Gladwell, 2005). He measures bodily sensations of partners, "reads" the faces of husbands and wives as they interact, and watches people talk about difficult issues while he dissects every aspect of the exchange. He has become so good at his craft that he can use his analyses of brief interactions to predict relationship success (divorce versus continued marriage) with a 94% accuracy.

Gottman achieved this feat of prediction by studying thousands of married couples across many years of their relationships. (Although his original work focused on heterosexual married couples, Gottman's lab's website, www.johngottman.com, indicates that current studies focus on same-sex couples. The applicability of Gottman's findings to people from diverse backgrounds currently is unclear.) The standard research protocol involves a husband and wife entering the "love lab" and engaging in a 15-minute conversation while being closely observed by the researchers and monitored by blood pressure cuffs, EKGs, and other devices. His seminal finding from observations of couples was derived with the assistance of mathematicians (Gottman, Murray, Swanson, Tyson, & Swanson, 2003) who helped him discover what is referred to as the "magic ratio" for marriages. Five positive interactions to one negative interaction (5:1) are needed to maintain a healthy relationship. As the ratio approaches 1:1, however, divorce is likely.

Achieving the 5:1 ratio in a relationship does not require avoiding all arguments. Partners in master marriages can talk about difficult subjects and do so by infusing warmth, affection, and humor into the conversation. On the other hand, a lack of positive interactions during challenging discussions can lead couples to emotional disconnections and to mild forms of contempt.

A Lot of Love in the Lovemaking: Avoiding Chaos, Relationshipwise

MARK D. FEFER

Professor John Gottman is the doctor of love, at least love of the conventional sort—he's an internationally known researcher on what makes marriage last and what makes it fall apart. In his work at the University of Washington, he has managed to apply strict scientific rigor to what seems like the most subjective of areas, and he's popularized his findings in a string of best-selling books (*The Seven Principles for Making Marriage Work* is the most recent).

At his "love lab" near the UW, Dr. Gottman videotapes married couples as they go about a lazy day "at home" and monitors physiological signs like heart rate and blood pressure as they discuss areas of conflict. By toting up the "positive" and "negative" interactions, checking "repair attempts" during fights, watching for incidents of contemptuous behavior, etc., Gottman is able to predict the ultimate fate of the pair with over 90 percent accuracy, he says.

However, as a single guy, I wanted to know how I can keep from getting into a bad marriage in the first place. Wouldn't that save us all a lot of trouble? Warm and affable, the professor met me at the Grateful Bread bakery near his home to discuss the issue.

Seattle Weekly: You study a lot of couples that are on the rocks. And you talk about the four behaviors that foretell divorce—criticism, contempt, defensiveness, stonewalling. But I'm sure that, at one time, most of these couples were in love and gushing about each other. How can I know if my current relationship is going to end up like that? *Dr. Gottman:* People used to think, "Well, you're in love, you're blissed out, you're not going to be doing a lot of real nasty . . . not going to be contemptuous toward your partner, not going to be disrespectful." Not true. If you keep going back and looking at relationships earlier and earlier, to the newlywed phase, the same variability [in behavior] exists for couples there as for later on. Even in the dating relationship—researchers have looked—the same signs are predictive. If you've been going together for 6 months, you can take a look at what's going on and decide if you want to be in that relationship or not.

So how do I make that decision? How can I know if a relationship is right or not? First, what is the quality of the friendship? Are you guys really friends? In other words, is it easy to talk? Like, before you know it, four hours have gone by. It's really a lot like same-sex friendship. It's about being interested in one another, remembering stuff that's important to one another, being affectionate and respectful, and it's about noticing when your friend needs something from you.

Then there's the quality of sex, romance, and passion. Do you feel special to this person? Do you feel attractive? Are you really attracted and turned on by them? Is there a lot of love in the lovemaking? Does it feel passionate?

But everybody feels this stuff at first, don't they? That's the surprising thing: People get married and they don't really like each other, and they're not having good sex together, and they don't feel like their partner's really that interested in them . . . they get married anyway! They're not taking a hard look at their relationship.

OK, but so what if it's really passionate at first—isn't that going to fade? The common belief that passion and good sex start early and then fade is totally wrong— totally wrong. Passion can grow over time in a relationship if people pay attention to it. [In our studies of long-term couples] the thing that came out among those who had a great sex life was friendship—"We've remained really close friends, we're really buddies, we try to understand and help each other."

What about fighting? From what you've written, it seems like fighting in itself isn't bad, right? Right. Conflict does exist in the very beginnings of romantic relationships; it comes out. [But] what's the balance in terms of destructive vs. constructive? Constructive conflict is about accepting influence from your partner, compromising. Destructive conflict is about insulting, being domineering, being defensive, denying any responsibility, withdrawing. Those predict a bad end to the relationship.

How do you get through a time when you're feeling distant, or you're not so sure about the relationship, or you're arguing a lot? Can you repair effectively? It's kind of a sense of confidence. You develop a feeling that you can weather any storm— not that you like the storms. Conflict is inevitable, but coping with it is a way of building the friendship.

Should I feel wildly in love, swept off my feet? You'd be surprised what a small percentage of relationships have had that. Psychologists have called it "limerance," that stage. You're mostly just projecting on your partner what you wish would be there. And when we started interviewing newlyweds about it, couples who had experienced it didn't necessarily have better relationships. It didn't seem necessary or sufficient, except that it is so pleasant to go through. It's very good if you can build from there.

(Continued)

(Continued)

What else should I be on the watch for? There's something called "negative sentiment override." You tend to be walking around with a chip on your shoulder, hypervigilant for put-downs, for ways your partner is saying, "I don't really love you, you're not that special to me." And if you're in that state, it's bad, particularly if you're a male, because that's something that is going to be very difficult to change. And it's really just a question of perception. Two women may be identical in how angry they get, but the one guy is saying, "Boy, she's really stressed right now, but it's OK; I get that way myself sometimes." The other guy's saying, "Nobody talks to me like that; . . . this, who needs this. . . ." What determines the perception, we've discovered, is friendship. If you feel like your partner respects you, is interested in you, turns toward you, then you're in positive sentiment override.

Why are we so bad at this? More than half of all marriages end in divorce. Are we just choosing badly? Are we just bad at being married like we're bad drivers? There are lots of ways to destroy things, and usually only a few ways to really maintain things and keep them working. Things fall apart—this is the entropy idea. Chaos is the more likely event. It really takes a lot of energy to maintain a system that's working well.

Source: From "A lot of love in the lovemaking: Avoiding chaos, relationshipwise," in *Seattle Weekly*, February 13–19, 2002. Reprinted with permission.

Drawing from his decades of research and his "sound marital house" theory, Gottman and colleagues (2002) developed a multidimensional therapeutic approach to couples counseling that moves partners from conflict to comfortable exchanges. The goals of the therapy include the enhancement of basic social skills and the development of an awareness of the interpersonal pitfalls associated with the relationship behaviors of criticism, contempt, defensiveness, and stonewalling. Over time, these four behaviors that undermine relationships are replaced with complaint (i.e., a more civil form of expressing disapproval), a culture of appreciation, acceptance of responsibility for a part of the problem, and self-soothing. These skills also are mentioned in Gottman's (1999) book, *The Seven Principles for Making Marriage Work.*

Based on our reading of Gottman's work, his advice regarding the creation of a culture of appreciation in a relationship may be his most basic, yet most potent, advice to couples of all ages, backgrounds, and marital statuses. The purposeful positive relationship behavior of creating a culture of appreciation is potentially powerful because of (1) the positive reception of the partner and the partner's behavior that it promotes, and (2) the contemptuous feelings that it prevents. Creating a culture of appreciation helps to establish an environment where positive interactions and a sense of security are the norms. Expressing gratitude (see Chapter 13) to a partner is the primary means for creating a positive culture. Saying thanks for the small behaviors that often go unnoticed (picking up around the house, taking the trash out, making the morning coffee, cleaning out the refrigerator) makes a partner feel valued for his or her daily efforts around the home. Sharing appreciation for small favors (taking an extra turn in the car pool, making a coworker feel welcome in the home) and for big sacrifices (remembering a least favorite in-law's birthday, giving up "rainy day" money for a home expense) honors a partner's contributions to the relationship and the family.

CAPITALIZING ON POSITIVE EVENTS

During most of the 20th century, research into relationships focused on negative, or *aversive*, processes such as resolving conflict and dysfunctional communication. Relationship research was grounded in the assumption that these processes are the primary determinants of relationship success. Harvey and Gottman have worked diligently to highlight the role of positive relationship behaviors that often have been overlooked. This focus on the positive, or *appetitive*, processes in relationships may be the primary reason that their theories and research findings are so robust. **Aversive processes** are the eliminating of negative relationship behaviors; **appetitive processes** are the promoting of positive relationship behaviors. Shelly Gable and Howard Reis (Gable & Reis, 2001; Gable et al., 2003; Reis & Gable, 2003) have demonstrated that that these two processes are independent and that they must be conceptualized and researched as independent processes if we are to fully understand human relationships.

Shelly Gable

Source: Reprinted with permission of Shelly Gable.

Gable et al. (2003) noted that differentiating between appetitive and aversive processes provides a new lens for viewing research on the success of close relationships. Now, in a program of research summarized in Gable, Reis, Impett, and Asher (2004), the researchers address the appetitive relationship processes directly by answering the question, "What do you do when things go right?" In a series of studies, Gable and colleagues found that the process of capitalization, or telling others about positive events in one's life, is associated with personal benefits (enhanced positive affect and well-being) as well as interpersonal benefits (relationship satisfaction and intimacy). The personal gains are attributable to the process of reliving the positive experience, and they are enhanced when a partner responds enthusiastically (i.e., active/constructively; see Figure 13.2) to the

How would your friend/relative/partner characterize your habitual responses to their good news?

Active/Constructive

My friend/relative/partner reacts to the positive event enthusiastically.

My friend/relative/partner seems even more happy and excited than I am.

My friend/relative/partner often asks a lot of questions and shows genuine concern about the good event.

Passive/Constructive

My friend/relative/partner tries not to make a big deal out of it but is happy for me.

My friend/relative/partner is usually silently supportive of the good things that occur to me.

My friend/relative/partner says little, but I know he/she is happy for me.

Active/Destructive

My friend/relative/partner often finds a problem with it.

My friend/relative/partner reminds me that most good things have their bad aspects as well.

My friend/relative/partner points out the potential down sides of the good event.

Passive/Destructive

Sometimes I get the impression that my friend/relative/partner doesn't care much.

My friend/relative/partner doesn't pay much attention to me.

My friend/relative/partner often seems uninterested.

Figure 13.2   Capitalizing on Daily Positive Events

Source: Modified portion of the Perceived Responses to Capitalization Attempts Scale. From Gable, S. L., Reis, H. T., Impett, E. A., & Asher, E. R., Capitalizing on Daily Positive Events, *Journal of Personality and Social Psychology, 87,* copyright © 2004. Reprinted with permission.

Note: Shelly Gable of UCLA divides the possible responses into the four categories described above. She has found that the first response style is central to capitalizing, or amplifying the pleasure of the good situation and contributing to an upward spiral of positive emotion.

good news. Improvement in interpersonal relations is contingent upon the quality of the partner's response to the loved one's good news. In Gable et al.'s research, active and constructive responses by partners were found to be the most beneficial.

Praise: Encouraging Signs

WILLOW LAWSON

Summary: Your partner's level of encouragement is a good indicator of how your relationship is going.

Hurdles like jealousy and miscommunication can determine whether a relationship succeeds. But what about how couples "cope" when something positive happens? According to a new set of studies, the way we respond to our mate's good fortune is a strong predictor of marital satisfaction and, at least in the short term, whether a couple will break up.

Shelly Gable, an assistant professor of psychology at the University of California at Los Angeles, examined how couples share everyday positive events because she felt that the lion's share of relationship research focused on how couples handle conflict and trauma. "Thankfully, positive events happen more often than negative ones," she says. "And satisfying and stable relationships are about more than a lack of conflict, insecurity, and jealousy."

In one study, Gable analyzed how men and women respond to a positive event in their partner's life, such as a promotion at work. A partner might respond enthusiastically ("That's wonderful, and it's because you've had so many good ideas in the past few months"). But he or she could instead respond in a less-than-enthusiastic manner ("Hmmm, that's nice"), seem uninterested ("Did you see the score of the Yankees game?") or point out the downsides ("I suppose it's good news, but it wasn't much of a raise").

The only "correct" reaction according to Gable's research—the response that's correlated with intimacy, satisfaction, trust and continued commitment—is the first response, the enthusiastic, active one. Basking in good news or capitalizing on the event seems to increase the effect of happy tidings by reinforcing memory of the occurrence. This is true for both men and women, and holds regardless of whether they are dating or married and whether the positive event is large or small.

Gable says an occasional passive response from a partner probably isn't the end of the world, and she speculates that most of us are able to make excuses for our partners in such situations. "The problem is when that's the chronic response," she says. "If a partner doesn't respond actively and constructively, the person who's trying to disclose something immediately feels less positive and feels less intimacy. Basically they feel less understood, validated, and cared for."

The purposeful positive relationship behavior of capitalizing on positive events for intrapersonal benefits is straightforward. It merely involves telling trusted friends and family about your daily "good stuff." If there are people who attempt to undermine such excitement by pointing out the downside of a positive event ("That promotion will cause you to work harder and longer. Are you sure you are up for that? Really?"), then it is best to avoid telling them the good news. The habit of offering active, constructive responses (mirroring enthusiasm, asking meaningful questions about the event) to the good news of others also is easily developed (see the Personal Mini-Experiments, Making the Most of Good News). And, the more you model this capitalizing behavior, the more likely it is that your partner and other people in your circle of friends and family will reciprocate and practice it themselves.

Few couples master each and every purposeful positive relationship behavior described in this chapter, but some couples seem to dance effortlessly through each day. When you ask them, "How do you make your relationship work?" you get an answer that makes you realize how hard they work at it. In this regard, we turn to the example of "Mitch" and "Linda," who tell the story of the work that goes into their flourishing relationship. "For as long as we have been married, I have sent Linda flowers every Friday," Mitch reported. Linda chimed in that Mitch keeps up with her "new" favorite flowers and honors the tradition even when they are on vacation. "We have been in remote villages living among the locals, and that man will spend an entire Friday seeking out a bouquet of flowers." Mitch expresses his appreciation for Linda through flowers, and Linda shares her gratitude by showering him with thanks and praise, as if it is the first time she had ever received such a gift.

The Neurobiology of Interpersonal Connection

Thus far, we have discussed the emotional and behavioral components of close relationships. Now, we turn to an emerging body of multidisciplinary scholarship that is devoted to explaining the neurobiological underpinnings of attachment and the prosocial emotions and behaviors that are the prerequisites for healthy adult relationships.

Neuropsychoanalyst Allan Schore (1994, 2003) and health psychologist Shelley Taylor (Taylor, Dickerson, & Klein, 2002) have gathered and integrated indirect and direct evidence on the neurobiology of interpersonal connection from their own laboratories, as well as from other researchers. Schore, building on the assumptions of attachment theory, argues that the social environment, mediated by actions of and attachment to the primary caregiver, influences the evolution of structures in a child's brain. More specifically, Schore proposed that the maturation of a region of the right cortex, the orbitofrontal cortex (which may store the internal working models of attachment), is influenced by interactions between the child and the caregiver. As the orbitofrontal cortex matures, self-regulation of emotions is enhanced. The brain–behavior interactions suggest that an upward spiral of growth may explain how infant attachment sometimes produces emotionally healthy adults. That is, when a child and his caregiver have a secure attachment, the part of the brain that helps with the regulation of emotions and behavior is stimulated. As the child's security is maintained, the brain development is promoted, and the abilities to empathize with others and to regulate intrapersonal and interpersonal stress are enhanced. Equipped with well-honed self-regulation skills, the child can develop and sustain healthy friendships and, eventually, healthy adult relationships. (For additional discussion of work related to the link between attachment and neurobiology, we suggest Siegel's [1999] *The Developing Mind.*)

Taylor and colleagues (Taylor et al., 2002), intrigued by the health benefits of social contact and social support (see Seeman, 1996, for a review), reviewed research on social animals and humans to determine the biological mechanisms associated with interpersonal experiences. Like Schore (1994, 2003), Taylor et al. hypothesized that a nurturing relationship between a child and a caregiver promotes the development of regulatory activity, in this case in the hypothalamic-pituitary-adrenocortical (HPA) system (which is activated via hormone secretion). The same biological system may regulate adult social functioning, but little is known about how this system matures over the decades. It is becoming clearer, however, that gender differences in the way the neuroendocrine system works to transform social support into health benefits are associated with the presence of oxytocin in women.

Neuroscientists and psychologists will continue to explore how neurobiology and positive social behavior are intertwined. As the positive psychology of close relationships incorporates neurobiological findings, we will draw closer to knowing how good relationships become great.

More on Flourishing Relationships

As noted in the beginning of this chapter, *infant-to-caregiver attachment* and *adult attachment security* are linked to healthy relationship development. Given the literature revealing the neurobiological underpinnings of attachment (Schore, 1994; Taylor et al., 2002), it appears that interpersonal connection stimulates the brain activity that helps to create the regulatory systems that lead to the development of empathy, enjoyment of positive interactions, and management of the stress associated with negative interactions. The result of this complex brain–behavior interplay is the creation of a foundation of interpersonal experiences and skills on which future relationships are built (see Figure 13.3).

Love, the positive emotion that links us, often is considered a marker of the quality of relationships. We believe that the love we have for another motivates us to engage in *purposeful positive relationship behaviors* that sustain interpersonal connections over time. As relationships grow

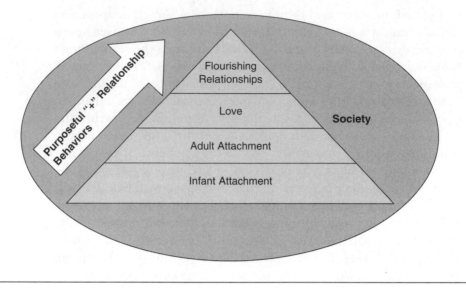

Figure 13.3   The Makings of Flourishing Relationships

stronger, they flourish and facilitate the personal development of both participants. (See Chapter 6 for a discussion of the life tasks of adults.)

Another look at Figure 13.3 reveals the makings of flourishing relationships and summarizes our comments in this section. The hierarchy of social needs presented in this figure suggests that attachment, love, and flourishing relationships are desired by all people but achieved only by some. Indeed, we believe that, of all the individuals who are attached to a caregiver at infancy, only some develop secure adult attachments. And, given that the stability of attachment style across the lifespan has been questioned (Feeney & Noller, 1996), those who experience attachment in early childhood may not necessarily be those who achieve secure attachment in adulthood.

Progressing up the hierarchy, the need for sustained romantic love is met by those who have realized at least a modicum of secure adult attachment. With the benefits generated by applying *purposeful positive relationship behaviors* (see arrow in Figure 13.3), a couple can parlay love into a flourishing relationship.

Building a Positive Psychology of Close Relationships

The study of insecure attachment, lost love, and failed relationships has produced significant findings that are relevant to our lives. Indeed, relationship researchers have been successful in uncovering what does not work and have attempted to teach people how to correct their relationship problems. Nevertheless, most would agree that we all struggle with identifying the right things to do in relationships. The positive psychology of close relationships builds on the work of the past (including the knowledge that secure attachment and love are prerequisites for healthy relationships), incorporates a focus on appetitive processes, and sets an agenda for the future–an agenda that will produce research that will tell the story of flourishing relationships.

Key Terms

Adaptive parental behaviors: Parents' appropriate responsiveness to a child's behavioral cues (i.e., smiling).

Agape: The bestowal of love by the divine.

Appetitive processes: The promotion of positive relationship behaviors.

Attachment system: The sum of emotional and physical proximity-seeking behaviors toward the caregiver, developed by the child as a result of adaptive and maladaptive parent behaviors. Regulates the pattern of attachment characteristic of the child.

Aversive processes: The eliminating of negative relationship behaviors.

Companionate love: A form of romantic love characterized by the soothing and steady warmth that sustains a relationship.

Consummate love: The most durable type of love, manifested when all three components (passion, intimacy, commitment) are present at high levels and in balance across both partners.

Eros: Romantic love, including the search for and possession of the beautiful.

Flourishing relationship: A good relationship that continues to get better due to the concerted effort of both partners.

Insecure-avoidant attachment: In the Strange Situation assessment, an attachment pattern characterized by a tension between the parent and child, resulting in the child's avoidance of the parent when reintroduced.

Insecure-resistant/ambivalent attachment: In the Strange Situation assessment, an attachment pattern characterized by a tension between the parent and child, resulting in the child's passive or active demonstration of hostility toward the caregiver while simultaneously wanting to be held and comforted.

Maladaptive parental behaviors: Parents' chaotic or unplanned attempts to meet a child's needs.

Minding: A form of relationship maintenance that includes knowing and being known, making relationship-enhancing attributions for behaviors, accepting and respecting, and maintaining reciprocity and continuity.

Nomos: A type of love characterized by submission and obedience to the divine.

Passionate love: A form of romantic love characterized by the intense arousal that fuels a romantic union.

Philia: A type of love characterized by affection and friendship.

Secure attachment: In the Strange Situation assessment, a form of attachment that involves a balance between exploration of the environment and contact with the caregiver.

Self-expansion theory of romantic love: A theory developed by Arthur and Elaine Aron suggesting that humans have a basic motivation to expand the self. The Arons hypothesize that the emotions, cognitions, and behaviors of love fuel such self-expansion.

Strange Situation: An assessment strategy first used by Mary Ainsworth to study children's attachment styles. The strange situation exposes a child to a novel situation in the company of his or her caregiver; the caregiver is then removed and reintroduced to the situation twice while the researcher assess the child participant's reactions.

Triangular theory of love: Robert Sternberg's theory that all types of love are made up of different combinations of passion, intimacy, and commitment.

Part VI

Understanding and Changing Human Behavior

Balanced Conceptualizations of Mental Health and Behavior

14

During the 1950s, psychology addressed the full spectrum of human behavior through its scholarship and practice. In 1955, Erich Fromm explored the "sane society," defining mental health as "the ability to love and to create" (Fromm, p. 69). During the same period, social psychologist Marie Jahoda (1958) characterized mental health as the positive condition that is driven by a person's psychological resources and desires for personal growth. She described these six characteristics of the mentally healthy person:

1. A personal attitude toward self that includes self-acceptance, self-esteem, and accuracy of self-perception

2. The pursuit of one's potentials

3. Focused drives that are integrated into one's personality

4. An identity and values that contribute to a sense of autonomy

5. World perceptions that are accurate and not distorted because of subjective needs

6. Mastery of the environment and enjoyment of love, work, and play

Additionally, Fromm and Jahoda wrote volumes on their views of positive mental health and good living. Together, these various efforts to advance ideas regarding positive mental health took place during the same general time period in which psychiatrists drafted a small, pocket-sized book titled *Diagnostic and Statistical Manual* (*DSM*) (American Psychiatric Association, 1952).

At the beginning of the 21st century, it is clear that the focus on the positive has lagged behind the attention paid to the negative. Only recently has the work of Fromm and Jahoda been rediscovered, contextualized, and incorporated into refined conceptualizations of positive mental health. At the same time, the *DSM* has grown tremendously over the last five decades, to the point that that the most recent version is an impressive and influential 943-page document covering the symptoms of mental illness (American Psychiatric Association, 2000).

Why have the efforts to conceptualize positive mental health and optimal human functioning lagged behind the work on mental illness? One explanation is that the attainment of positive mental health is a passive process, whereas the remediation of mental illness is an active process that demands more resources. Another explanation is that the maintenance of mental health does not warrant the same careful attention (from theorists and practitioners) as does the alleviation of suffering. In this regard, it is easy to see why our feelings of compassion are activated in the presence of someone with heightened vulnerabilities (Frankl, 1959; Leitner, 2003). Such attention to profound human suffering has captivated Eastern philosophers (see Chapter 3) for thousands of years, and it defined the meaning of life for some Western thinkers for most of the 20th century. Therefore, the positive mental health of our fellow human beings does not evoke such strong feelings in us. Although these are plausible reasons for our intense focus on mental illness and the associated limited attentions to positive mental health, a more parsimonious explanation is that we are fascinated by abnormal behaviors.

In this chapter, we explore our seeming preoccupation with abnormal behavior and how this has contributed to a limited understanding of positive functioning. We offer recommendations for developing more balanced conceptualizations of behaviors that focus on positive and negative psychological characteristics as influenced by environmental, developmental, and cultural contexts. In short, we believe that conceptualizations of behaviors need to be more balanced. Accordingly, we address the obstacles to such balance and present resources that may help in the development of more comprehensive clinical thinking.

Moving Toward Balanced Conceptualizations

All clinicians, including the two of us, struggle to make sense of the complexity of our clients' behaviors. Beginning clinicians report to us that the sheer volume of information that they collect in a 50-minute session overwhelms them. This challenge is intensified by the fact that such clinical information typically is shared in an emotionally charged interpersonal exchange. Novices and master clinicians alike develop strategies to collect, organize, and interpret the clinical data they collect. We may focus too much or too little on particular aspects and determinants of our clients' behaviors. When conceptualizing a case, rendering a diagnosis, and developing and implementing a treatment plan, we must strike a balance in the type and amount of information we gather and process. Specifically, we emphasize the need to address the following issues that contribute to less-than-optimal mental health care:

- Abnormal behavior seems to more easily gain the attention of the clinician, and aspects of normal behavior and healthy functioning (i.e., what is working in person's life) may not be considered meaningful in the diagnostic and treatment process.
- Attributions for behavior may overemphasize the internal characteristics of a person, whereas the environmental influences on behavior are not adequately addressed.
- Weaknesses and negative emotions often are deemed more salient to the diagnostic and treatment process than are strengths and positive emotions.
- Current behavior may not be considered in light of developmental history and milestones. Specifically, we may not address thoroughly the question, "Is this person's behavior consistent with expectations for his or her developmental history and age?"
- Behaviors often are interpreted without attention to information about the cultural contexts that could influence whether the behaviors are considered adaptive or maladaptive.

By resolving these challenges, we can produce more balanced views of people and how they change. We share here our ideas for improving the conceptualizations of human behavior, but first we attempt to explain the human fascination with abnormal behaviors.

Our Fascination With Abnormal Behavior

Students from all majors vie for seats in the abnormal psychology course that will explain why their roommates are scared to leave the dorm room or why Aunt Nita never takes a bath! Like you, these students also quietly wonder, "Is that normal . . . and how do I know for sure?" Why is this normality question asked so often? And how can it be answered with any degree of confidence?

As practicing psychologists, we would have made some serious money if we had had a dollar for every time we have been asked the question, "Is that normal?" This question has been posed so many times that we have tried to understand the motivation behind the query. Here are our thoughts. A small percentage of people have prurient interests in all behaviors that deviate from the norm. They want to experience, understand, and discuss them. Most people who ask this question, however, seem to have a mixture of curiosities and concerns. This natural desire to know appears whenever we seek to understand a phenomenon, psychological or otherwise. Furthermore, sometimes abnormal behavior makes us uncertain about another's welfare or perhaps even our own. For example, if you walk past someone who is screaming obscenities at the top of her lungs, you may be both curious about why she is doing this and nervous about coming into close contact with her. There is a dance of ambivalence about such interactions, but we believe the underlying fascination with the abnormal is a part of our healthy attempts to make sense out of the world and to ensure the well-being of other people and ourselves.

To answer the question, "Is that normal?" and to further examine abnormal behavior, we must define the criteria for abnormality. Immediately, however, we bump into a problem, because there is no widely accepted definition of *abnormal*. Nevertheless, three criteria commonly serve as markers of **abnormal behavior** in a social context. First, the behavior is *atypical* or *aberrant*, which means that it deviates from what is considered standard or expected. Second, the behavior is considered *maladaptive*—that is, the behavior does not typically lead to socially sanctioned goals. Third, the behavior often is accompanied by *psychological distress*—worry, rumination, and uncomfortable thoughts and feelings.

So, in response to the question, "Is that normal?" the *frequency, function,* and *effects* of the particular behavior must be considered. Furthermore, the context of the behavior must be carefully scrutinized. Consider, for example, a grown man who is kissing the tarmac at an airport. Surely this is atypical behavior. But, if this is a soldier returning to his or her home country after a battle in a foreign land, then this behavior may seem perfectly reasonable and normal. Indeed, such a gesture may be adaptive in that it shows love for one's country as well as relief at coming home. Simply put, the normality conclusion depends on the context of a person's action. Consider another example. College students take off their clothes and run naked across campus. In the 1970s, such "streaking" behaviors were quite the fad, and the campus police typically joined other onlookers in watching these spectacles. Fast-forward three decades—a naked woman races past as you walk to class tomorrow. It is most likely that the campus police would be in hot pursuit, and onlookers would be quick to laugh or shake their heads in disbelief at this behavior. In this example, the temporal context is crucial in determining whether the label "abnormal" should be applied.

Yet another determinant of the abnormality label is whether there is a powerful and influential person in the societal context who is willing to speak out and ostracize a given action by another person. In this regard, Becker (1963) made the important point that a behavior is not necessarily deviant because it merely violates a rule, but rather it often is the reaction of one or more people to that behavior that ultimately determines the label. Furthermore, on occasion there may be no rule or norm violation at all, but the fact that an influential person in the society initiates a "splitting off" process can produce the abnormal label for just about any person. So, we must consider the situational context, the time of the action, and the potential powerful enforcer of the label when considering the application of the label "abnormal" (Snyder & Fromkin, 1980). These examples suggest that consistent identification of abnormal behavior might prove quite difficult. Nevertheless, we do attempt to categorize such behaviors.

Our preoccupation with abnormal behaviors may serve positive functions such as promoting understanding of the world and helping to keep people safe. But this preoccupation seldom leads to a clear answer to the question, "Is that normal?" More times than not, our response to the question is, "It depends." Indeed, as just discussed, it depends on the context of the behavior. Moreover, it depends on additional factors discussed in the next sections of this chapter: severity of the behavior, the developmental factors that defined the person's behavioral repertoire, and the environmental and cultural contexts that frame the behavior. Failure to consider the multiple qualities of a behavior may make the behavior seem more threatening than it needs to be. Equally important for the theme of the present book, our propensity to categorize behavior as abnormal may contribute to the insufficient attention paid to those qualifying factors that may lead to the application of a label on the positive side of the spectrum. We believe the positive side of the human experience also deserves considerable attention because these strengths and positive emotions are the basic ingredients of mental health.

Neglect of the Environment and of the Positive

The desire to understand behavior often leads to a question such as, "Why did he do that?" In search of the answer, however, we unfortunately often forgo asking the actor directly and instead attempt to answer the question from our seat as the observer. When we do this, we expose ourselves to potential errors in thinking that may lead to limited consideration of important environmental influences. Accordingly, the flaws in thinking associated with the *fundamental attribution error* and the *fundamental negative bias* contribute to our tendency to over-pathologize behavior and to view behavior in a manner that is neither comprehensive nor valuing of potential strengths.

When trying to explain the behavior of others in social situations, we are prone to ignore external situational or environmental factors, and instead we attribute the behavior to the other person's internal characteristics (e.g., personality or abilities). This occurs even when the diagnosing clinician knows little about the person and how that person views the environment. This flawed tendency is referred to as the **fundamental attribution error** (Nisbett, Caputo, Legant, & Maracek, 1973). On the other hand, when we explain our own behavior, we are more comprehensive in our conceptualization in that we probably take the environmental variables into account. For example, have you ever received a bad grade on an examination in school? Whereas an outside observer might conclude that you did poorly because you are stupid, you would hasten to make more situation-based explanations, such as the teacher's poor explanation of the material or the instructor's tricky, misleading wording of the test questions.

The **fundamental negative bias** involves the *saliency* (stands out vs. does not stand out), the *value* (negative vs. positive), and the *context* (vague vs. well-defined) of any given behavior (Wright, 1988). Specifically, when a behavior stands out, is considered negative, and occurs in a vague context, the primary factor guiding the perception of the behavior is its negative quality. (Imagine that a friend tells you that her boyfriend was rude to her family during a holiday visit home. With this small amount of information, you know that the behavior is atypical—that it stands out—and negative. With little contextual information, your attention is drawn to the value of the behavior, and you may be left thinking that your friend's boyfriend is a hostile guy. (The same is true for behavior that stands out in a sparse context and is considered positive; the positive quality will define and determine the reactions to the behavior.)

By addressing these biases in our views of behavior, we can create an understanding of the influence of environmental stressors on our functioning. With our increased attention to the environment, we also become more aware of environmental resources that may interact with strengths and result in positive functioning.

ASKING QUESTIONS: THE FOUR-FRONT APPROACH

Recent developments in classifying the full spectrum of human functioning hold much promise. In Beatrice Wright's **four-front approach** (1991; Wright & Lopez, 2002) to developing a comprehensive conceptualization about a person's weaknesses and strengths, as well as in regard to the influence of environmental stressors and resources, she encourages observers to gather information about the following four fronts of behavior:

1. Deficiencies and undermining characteristics of the person

2. Strengths and assets of the person

3. Lacks and destructive factors in the environment

4. Resources and opportunities in the environment

Multiple and complex methods can be used to gather this information, but collaborating with the *actor* (the person being observed) can reveal the answers to these four questions: (1) What deficiencies does the person contribute to his or her problems? (2) What strengths does the person bring to deal effectively with his or her life? (3) What environmental factors serve as impediments to healthy functioning? and (4) What environmental resources accentuate positive human functioning? This balanced approach to conceptualization, refined by the authors of this text (Lopez, Snyder, & Rasmussen, 2003; Snyder & Elliott, 2005; Snyder, Ritschel, Rand, & Berg, 2006), encourages the search for personal strengths as well as environmental resources.

THE CASE OF MICHAEL

Throughout the remainder of this chapter, one of the authors (SJL) tells you about Michael, a 41-year-old, Caucasian male client who was seen in counseling for 4 years. Michael, who was referred by a physician who was treating him for AIDS, reported that he had moderate depression. This depression not only produced sadness, it also caused problems in maintaining relationships and cooperating with his care providers. He started our lengthy relationship with the statement, "I desperately need help with my life." I responded, "What kind of help do you need?" About 100 sessions later, Michael's life story remained intriguing, and I learned something new about him at every meeting. I give a glimpse into Michael's life here and in three other places in this chapter.

Michael told me that he needed help with "everything." I encouraged him to be more specific, and he reached into his jeans pocket and pulled out two pages of handwritten notes about his struggles. He was very descriptive about each and every concern and their effects. It was clear why Michael felt that the world was against him. His car had been totaled, he was having major side effects from medications, the heat was not working in his apartment, and so forth. Although his depression was quite complicated (due to his family history, illness, and side effects of treatment), it was clear that aspects of his situation, and to some extent the quality of his environment, were exacerbating his symptoms.

Near the middle of our first session, I said, "These problems would be overwhelming for anyone. How do you cope?" He looked at me as if he were uncertain about how to respond. Then, I asked him how he handled a particular problem on his list. He was just as descriptive in his storytelling about coping as he was in his accounting of his struggles. At the very end of the session, I said, "Next time, we will talk about your strengths." Part of me knew that he would bring a list of strengths to the next session, and he did. With pages of notes about Michael's strengths and struggles and his environmental stressors and resources, I was able to develop a basic understanding of his depression, his battle with AIDS, and the vitality that kept him moving toward a more positive future.

The Lack of a Developmental Emphasis

Developmental psychologists focus on the origins and functions of behavior (see Chapter 6 for further discussion of human development). Their scientific efforts shed light on normal developmental processes such as cognitive operations (Piaget, 1932), moral judgment (Gilligan, 1982; Kohlberg, 1983), and personality (Allport, 1960; Mischel, 1979). Most of what we know about the origins of everyday behavior we owe to the insights of developmental (and evolutionary) psychologists. Moreover, during the last 25 years developmental psychopathology scholars (e.g., Sameroff, Lewis, & Miller, 2000; Wenar & Kerig, 1999) have begun to unravel the mystery of why some people develop particular disorders and others do not.

Although developmental research has answered many questions about learning and growth over time, some aspects of development remain unexplained and warrant further study. For example, we know very little about how people mature in very specific environments (e.g., a dorm on campus) or how they grow during discrete periods of their lives (e.g., a semester or 4 years of college life). In this regard, a theory about adolescent/adult development during college (developed by Chickering, 1969) contextualizes normal and abnormal behaviors in the unique setting of a college campus.

Although laypeople may be fascinated with such basic questions as, "What happens when bad things happen to good people?" developmental theories often fail to address such basic issues. Such bad things, or "insults," as professionals in the field sometimes describe them, might include traumatic stressors such as abuse or seemingly less painful events such as significant academic failures or relationship breakups. Of particular note here is Allen Ivey and Mary Bradford Ivey's (1998, 1999) developmental counseling and therapy approach, which makes sense out of the life events that potentially could positively or negatively change basic developmental processes.

NORMALIZING NEGATIVE AND POSITIVE BEHAVIOR

In Chickering's (1969; Chickering & Reisser, 1993) theory of the development of college students, the focus is on a circumscribed time period (years in college for traditional and nontraditional learners) and a specific environment (the college academic and social setting). Beyond survival, Chickering proposed that the primary human goal involves the establishment of an identity, the refinement of a unique way of being (called *individuation*). Within the Chickering model, students move toward these goals via seven pathways, or vectors; moreover, Chickering makes the point that movement along multiple pathways at one time is quite likely. **Developing competence** (moving from low-level competence in intellectual, physical, and interpersonal domains to high competence in each area) is identified as a primary developmental driver for young people. (Acquiring competency and developing human strengths are interchangeable and serve as foundations for future growth.) With increased confidence in their resourcefulness, students can pursue Chickering's six other developmental goals. These goals include

1. **Managing emotions,** or growing from little awareness of feelings and limited control over disruptive emotions to increased understanding of feelings and flexible control and constructive expression

2. **Moving through autonomy toward interdependence,** or moving from poor self-direction and emotional dependence to instrumental independence and limited need for reassurance

3. **Developing mature interpersonal relationships,** or growing from intolerance of differences and few relationships to an appreciation of differences and healthy relationships

4. **Establishing identity,** or changing from personal confusion and low self-confidence to a self-concept clarified through lifestyle and self-acceptance

5. **Developing purpose,** or transitioning from unclear vocational goals and distracting self-interests to clear goals and more communal activities

6. **Developing integrity,** or changing from unclear beliefs and values to clear and humanizing values

Chickering's (1969) developmental vectors describe the pathways and goals associated with growth that takes place during a discrete period in a fairly special environment. Understanding optimal functioning during this period can reveal generalizable skills that can be used in other periods and settings. We recommend one basic question to pose to fellow college students to discover what resources they have for the future: What got you ready for college? Consider Chickering and Reisser's (1993) probing questions to determine where you are on your developmental path:

> Briefly describe a change in yourself that had a major impact on how you lived your life. What was the "old" way of thinking or being, vs. the "new" way? What did you move *from,* and what did you move *to*? How did you know that a significant change had occurred? What were the important things (or persons) that *helped* the process? What did the person *do*? What was the experience that catalyzed the shift? Were there any *feelings* that helped or accompanied the process? (p. 45)

When considering the positive and negative circumstances of each person's experiences and environments that may have contributed to his or her current adaptivity and dysfunctionality, the work by Ivey and Ivey (1998, 1999) may be quite useful. In this regard, the Iveys' **developmental counseling and therapy** provides a here-and-now conceptualization in which pathological behaviors are seen as logical responses to life events. (Aspects of the developmental focus and a traditional diagnostic system

Table 14.1   The Contrast Between Traditional and Developmental Meaning-Making Systems

Issue	Traditional Pathological Meaning	Developmental Meaning
Locus of problem	Individual	Individual/family/cultural context
Pathology	Yes	No, logical response to developmental history
Developmental and etiological constructs	Peripheral	Central
Culture	Beginning awareness	Culture-centered
Helper role	Hierarchy, patriarchy	Egalitarian, construction
Cause	Linear, biology vs. environment	Multidimensional considers both biology and environment
Family	Not emphasized	Vital for understanding individual development and treatment
Treatment	Not emphasized	Central issue

are juxtaposed in Table 14.1.) Furthermore, Ivey and Ivey posit that there are many categories for understanding human behavior and experience, and they urge clinicians to reach the most accurate understandings by viewing each person as a whole.

In framing their approach, the Iveys (1999) state that the "contextual self includes relational dimensions of personal and family developmental history, community and multicultural issues, and physiology" (p. 486). Therefore, understanding the individual requires gaining information about him or her along numerous contextual dimensions. Conceptualization of a person's behavior within the Ivey system involves building a framework of background information. For example, when working with someone who has experienced childhood trauma, the Iveys would gather information about environmental or biological insults (Masterson, 1981). The Iveys then recommend examining the connections between such insults and other stress and pain, along with how subjective experiences of stress and pain relate to sadness and depression. Such an examination obviously emphasizes the origins and severity of a person's suffering. Next in this approach, strategies that can be used to combat a negative mood are examined. From the Iveys' point of view, the way in which a personality style helps a person navigate current interpersonal relationships ultimately is linked to a person's psychological well-being.

THE CASE OF MICHAEL

Michael's strengths of "being loving" in relationships and "persevering" in the face of illness and an avalanche of daily obstacles were touchstones throughout treatment. These strengths seemed to be products of the adversity he experienced during his childhood and adolescence, or, at the very least, they were galvanized during that time.

About the quality of "being loving," Michael remarked, "I think I was born with it." He held on to this loving approach as if it were a prized possession even though, from his perspective, this love was not returned by some of the most important people in his life (his stepmother, his brother, and the first person on whom he had a crush). Over the course of counseling, Michael found that he could be loving to the people who did not return his affection and still find some satisfaction in life. It took 41 years for him to realize that his strength was not encumbered by the behaviors of others.

His perseverance took many forms, but I tended to describe it as vital courage. In the face of threats to his psychological well-being and severe illnesses, Michael plugged on. I remember asking him when he had discovered his vital courage. The question clearly brought up a moving memory. Through tears, he told me the story of his stepmother's repeated efforts to "dehumanize me and make me feel like I would never become anything." The many insults that Michael experienced made him more determined to make a good life for himself. When he was diagnosed with AIDS, he was reminded of his commitment to himself. With that in mind and a history of using his strengths, he promised himself and all of his care providers, "I am going to beat this thing."

Difficulties Understanding Behavior in a Cultural Context

The surgeon general's report, *Mental Health: Culture, Race, Ethnicity* (U.S. Department of Health and Human Services, 2001), emphasizes the importance of acknowledging that there are culture-bound syndromes, that culture influences coping strategies and social supports, and that individuals may have multiple cultural identities. Indeed, "culture counts," as it plays a crucial role in determining an individual's thoughts and actions. (See Chapter 5 for an extended discussion of developing strengths and living well in a cultural context.) Clinicians engaging in diagnosis must pay keen attention to the cultural context in forming impressions of any person. This view, which we strongly endorse, runs counter to the **universality assumption**, which holds that what is deemed true for one group may be considered true for other people, irrespective of cultural differences.

Despite the surgeon general's directive to contextualize all behavior, along with the clarion call made by multicultural psychologists to consider

Figure 14.1   *The Jazz Funeral* by Susan Clark depicts how grief and joy intermingle following the death of a New Orleans local. Contrary to the universality assumption, grief looks different across cultures, as do many positive emotions.

Source: Reprinted with permission of Susan Clark.

Madonna Constantine

Source: Reprinted
with permission of
Madonna Constantine.

the cultural factors associated with human functioning, psychologists and laypeople alike may hold the universality assumption. In this regard, Teacher's College, Columbia University psychologists Madonna Constantine and Derald Wing Sue reason that notions of hopefulness and suffering may not be universal. On this issue, Constantine and Sue (2006) wrote,

[Some] Buddhists (many of whom may have an Asian cultural background), for instance, tend to believe that hopelessness is the nature of the world and that life is characterized by suffering. Moreover, present-day suffering is thought to be retribution for transgressions in past lives. Thus, the way to overcome the hopelessness and suffering of the world is through meditation, which will lead to the final state of nirvana, or a higher plane of existence (Obeysekere, 1995). It can be surmised that it is neither optimism nor "realistic optimism" (Schneider, 2001) that results in satisfaction with life for Buddhists. Instead, Western perceptions of depressive affect in Buddhists, in fact, may be the "psychology of the norm" for individuals who adhere to Buddhist philosophy, and an ideal state of well-being would be equivalent to a heightened state of existence. (p. 229)

The empirical data stemming from the research of University of Michigan psychologist Edward Chang (1996a; 1996b; Chang, Maydeu-Olivares, & D'Zurilla, 1997) directly challenge the universality assumption and demonstrates that acting on this false belief could have quite negative consequences. (See Chapters 5 and 9 for more discussion of Dr. Chang's research.) Chang's research demonstrates that optimism, pessimism, problem solving, and possibly psychological and physical symptoms are conceptualized differently and behave differently across cultures. Given these findings, interventions that may benefit one group may be benign or harmful to another.

DETERMINING HOW "CULTURE COUNTS"

Awareness of cultural nuances lends insight into how people of varied backgrounds generate psychological well-being. In addition, examining how adverse experiences could promote adaptive psychological functioning in all people might provide vital clues about how optimal human functioning develops.

Cultural values provide the context in which behaviors, thoughts, and feelings are deemed normal or abnormal (Banerjee & Banerjee, 1995; Constantine, Myers, Kindaichi, & Moore, 2004); these values and their influence on meaning making of experiences contribute to optimal human functioning (Sue & Constantine, 2003). For example, explicit demonstrations of religious faith are considered quite normal in many cultures. In the predominately Catholic parishes of southern Louisiana, home of an ethnic enclave of Cajuns, people put crucifixes above all doorways to ward off evil. In the Cajun culture, this practice is viewed as a common and normal approach to putting one's faith to work to protect personal welfare and ensure well-being.

Focusing specifically on the functioning of people of color in the United States, Constantine and Sue (2006) identified two large classes of variables (see Table 14.2), discussed in previous literature (e.g., Helms & Cook, 1999; Sue & Sue, 2003), that interact in complex environments and contribute to the psychological and social well-being of people of color. Constantine and Sue asserted that these dimensions should be included in psychological conceptualizations pertaining to persons of color.

THE CASE OF MICHAEL

"I am looking for support outside my family and my docs." That is how Michael started one of our sessions during year 3 of our work. We had developed a sort of shorthand in our sessions by then. Michael slid his handwritten notes to me as the session started; he always had them, and I always read them as we kicked off our meetings.

Table 14.2   Optimal Human Functioning of People of Color in the United States: Variables That Interact in Environmental Contexts

Cultural Values, Beliefs, and Practices
- Collectivism
- Racial and ethnic pride
- Spirituality and religion
- Interconnectedness of mind/body/spirit
- Family and community

Strengths Gained Through Adversity
- Heightened perceptual wisdom
- Ability to rely on nonverbal and contextual meanings
- Bicultural flexibility

"What have you tried?" I asked, and Michael listed his many attempts to build his social network. "I think I have tried everything except going to church!" he said with an edge. Michael and I had discussed his religious beliefs and his spirituality at great length over the years. His spirituality was a source of strength, but his religion and, more precisely, his childhood church, were a source of great pain, as he had felt ostracized after coming out as a gay teen. "Why did you bring up church?" I inquired.

I learned that Michael's new case manager had made a big sales pitch about the value of the social support of fellow parishioners. In response, Michael was justifiably angry about the "one size fits all" recommendation. After talking about his frustration with his case manager, we returned to his plans for finding more social connectedness. The discussion soon focused on the gay culture in his small town. Similar to any culture, his town's "gay community," as Michael called it, had norms for behavior, and people held expectations about how single males reached out for support. Our next two sessions were devoted to reviewing Michael's efforts to create a healthier social network in his community.

The Limits of the Categorical Diagnostic System

Once data have been collected in a balanced fashion, clinicians must turn to the task of rendering a diagnosis that describes a client's behavior. In today's mental health practice, clinicians summarize this valuable data in the form of a categorical diagnosis. In this section, we examine the limitations of a categorical diagnostic system and recommend that dimensions be used to more comprehensively describe our fellow men and women.

We have been grouping behaviors into the categories "abnormal" and "normal" for as long as people have possessed language capabilities, but this does not necessarily mean that we are reliably and accurately distinguishing between "abnormal" and "normal." For example, recent factor analyses of data from a sample of individuals who were diagnosed with personality disorders and a sample of individuals with a "normal" personality revealed that personalities reflected in the two groups were more alike than different (see Maddux & Mundell, 1999, for a review). Similarly, Oatley and Jenkins (1992) found that "normal" and "abnormal" emotional experiences were not discretely classified. Specifically, the distress associated with everyday stresses often is hard to distinguish from the criteria of emotional disorders.

Regarding the real-world challenge of making diagnoses by categorizing clients' behaviors, there is evidence of a lack of consistency and accuracy among practicing psychologists. On this point, McDermott (1980) found that, when 72 psychology graduate students and psychologists (24 novices, 24 interns, 24 experts) were presented with the same three case studies, diagnostic agreement was no better than that predicted by chance. A total of 370 diagnostic statements were rendered, and there was no specific pattern of agreement within or between the participant groups.

Barone, Maddux, and Snyder (1997) acknowledged the difficulties in categorizing human functioning. These scholars go on to observe that, despite the fact that all people experience problems, these personal difficulties are best represented as occurring on a continuum from none to slight to moderate to extreme degrees. The inevitable variability of clients' problems cannot be easily explained, however, by using discrete categories. On this latter point, it is impossible to create a true dichotomy between normal and abnormal functioning, because almost every theoretical orientation to psychology acknowledges that it is the *degree* of the dysfunctional behavior that largely drives the distinction between normality and abnormality. Even Freud, who often is criticized for pathologizing behaviors, was clear in stating that conceptualizations depend on the degree to which an unconscious conflict or desire interferes with normal functioning, not on the mere presence or absence of that conflict or desire.

There also may be socially significant problems associated with the categorical system in the American Psychiatric Association's *Diagnostic and Statistical Manual* (*DSM*) (1994, 2000). That is, as mental health professionals, we can become preoccupied with forcing people into negative categories and thereby make little or no attempt to understand the person in a more comprehensive manner. To confound the problem, the labels given to these negative categories then serve as a social wedge between persons who are so labeled and all others who are not. Negative labeling can create stereotypical expectations that can influence how professionals conceptualize and interact with individuals; it can also influence how these labeled individuals may think about themselves.

Once the label of the diagnostic group is applied, the perception of within-group differences tends to be diminished, whereas the perception of between-group differences is enhanced (Wright, 1991). Remember the story about the Sneetches from Dr. Seuss (1961)? In the beginning of that tale, young readers probably view the Sneetches (Star-bellied or Plain-bellied) as a group, as being almost identical to each other, as suggested in Dr. Seuss's singsong verse:

"Now the Star-bellied Sneetches had bellies with stars.

The Plain-bellied Sneetches had none upon thars.

The stars weren't so big; they were really quite small.

You would think such a thing wouldn't matter at all." (p. 3)

The story soon reveals that the small characteristic, the star, did matter quite a bit in the society of Sneetches. The "Star-bellied Sneetches" viewed themselves as quite similar to one another and quite different from and superior to the "Plain-bellied Sneetches." Young readers also quickly become intrigued with the subtle difference between groups, typically making the star a more salient characteristic of the Sneetches and pointing out that one group (whichever has the star at a given time) seems to be happier than the other group. Often, clinicians and laypeople behave like Dr. Seuss's target audience. We overemphasize the meaningfulness of a label, we accentuate the similarities among the group members possessing the label, and we overestimate the differences between the labeled group members and another group of people.

Because diagnostic labels traditionally have been negative, clinicians may ignore the ideographic and potentially positive characteristics of people. Wright (1991; Wright & Lopez, 2002) asserts that information consistent with the diagnostic label will be remembered more easily than inconsistent information. Thus, simply by applying the negative label, professionals attend to and seek information about individual deficits rather than strengths, thereby decreasing accuracy and comprehensiveness in conceptualizing a person's complete psychological make-up.

CONSIDERING NEW PERSONALITY DIMENSIONS

Given the general limitations of a categorical system and the neglect of positive behaviors in the current categorical systems, alternative conceptualizations might advance our understanding of psychological phenomena. In this regard, the dimensional approach puts human behavior on a continuum, thereby allowing the examination of individual differences in negative and positive behavior. It is important to clarify here that viewing psychological behavior does not involve juxtaposing "good" and "evil" on the same continuum. Such a use of dimensional systems may only lead back to the categorizing of behaviors. One view is that it is more informative to consider the degree to which behaviors are adaptive or maladaptive.

Another use of the dimension system involves examining negative and positive behaviors on separate dimensions. Indeed, such an approach is supported by related research. Scores on measures of positive behaviors (e.g., life satisfaction) and scores on measures of negative behaviors (e.g., depression) correlate negatively and modestly, around −.40 or −.50 (see Frisch, Cornell, Villanueva, & Retzlaff, 1992). Accordingly, a report from the United States surgeon general (U.S. Department of Health and Human Services, 1998) indicated that mental illness and mental health are not opposite ends of the same continuum.

In their 1995 book, *New Personality Self-Portrait*, Oldham and Morris (1995) describe a dimensional approach to conceptualizing personality disorders that are often considered the most intractable forms of mental disorders. They contend that each of the 14 personality disorders listed in the *DSM-IV* (APA, 1994) can be viewed as residing on its own continuum of adaptation. At one end of these continua lie less acute, more adaptive presentations of these personality types or styles; on the other end of the continua, we find the actual, less adaptive manifestations of the personality disorders (e.g., borderline, paranoid, histrionic). Oldham and Morris posit that, at any point in time, an individual may move along this continuum, depending on the environmental and endogenous stressors in his or her life. In this conceptualization, an individual may exhibit dysfunctional behaviors that are more indicative of the actual disorder at times of high stress, whereas a clinical presentation may be characterized by a more adaptive symptomatology in times of less stress. Thus, an individual may meet the *DSM-IV* criteria for histrionic personality disorder during extremely stressful periods but might be described merely as "dramatic" at times of low life stress.

As another example, someone with obsessive-compulsive personality disorder in stressful situations may be described as "conscientious" on the lower end of the continuum (see Figure 14.2). In fact, these characteristics may be quite helpful to the individual living at the adaptive end of the continuum. A person who is conscientious as described by Oldham and Morris may find that possessing this quality allows him to be responsible and reliable. A person with features of narcissistic personality disorder may find that certain aspects of this behavior allow him or her to be self-confident and thereby able to function at a superior level. An important point to remember it that it is only when these characteristics become extreme that they cease to be beneficial to a person.

This personality continuum can be used to differentiate between individuals who possess less or more florid symptomatology in their daily lives. With the current *DSM-IV* conceptualization, however, to be diagnosed as "having" the disorder, one must possess a majority of the criteria delineated. An individual possessing one less than the specified number

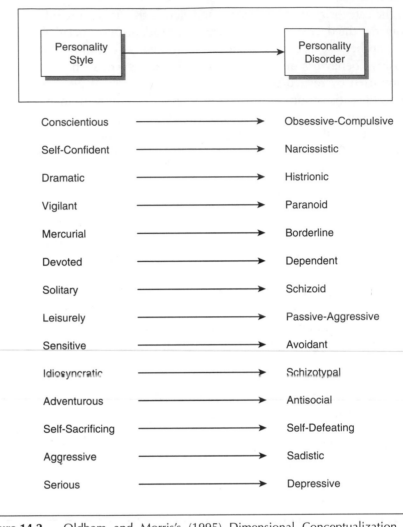

Figure 14.2   Oldham and Morris's (1995) Dimensional Conceptualization of Personality Disorders

Source: From Oldham, J. M., & Morris, L. B., *The New Personality Self-Portrait,* copyright © 1995 by John M. Oldham & Lois B. Morris. Used by permission of Bantam Books, a division of Random House, Inc.

of criteria may be experiencing quite a high level of stress but nevertheless may not receive services because the requisite number of criteria have not been met. The Oldham and Morris (1995) conceptualization leaves room for individuals to be diagnosed according to the degree of dysfunction as well as the degree of positive use of resources. In addition, it may provide more client-friendly terminology for discussion of personality disorder diagnoses during sessions, as well as allowing clinicians to help clients identify strengths and weaknesses in their set of behaviors.

THE CASE OF MICHAEL

Over our 4 years of work, Michael taught me a great deal about the meaningfulness and meaninglessness of labels. It would have been technically accurate to describe him as an "impoverished gay male suffering from AIDS and depression." But this did not tell half the story of Michael's existence. Indeed, his strengths defined him much more than his weaknesses did. Furthermore, as Michael pointed out, these diagnostic terms did not help him make positive changes in his daily life. "I am not poor. Other people can't classify me as poor," Michael told me when his case manager recommended that he claim impoverishment and seek assistance with his utility bills. Michael certainly did not have much of an income—around $9000 a year—but he did believe that he had the right to define his own circumstances. About his identity as a gay male, he often wondered aloud why his sexuality received more attention than that of his heterosexual counterparts. Nevertheless, he did acknowledge that "gay culture" had affected how he saw himself.

Regarding the terms *suffering, AIDS,* and *depression,* at one time or another Michael proclaimed, "the diagnosis doesn't fit." "Suffering is subjective," he reminded me, "and I have felt like I was suffering for a long time." On AIDS, his quarterly medical workups often left us both wondering, "Can AIDS go into remission?" Many of our discussions about diagnoses addressed the classification of depression (records from previous counseling, prior to contracting HIV, indicated that Michael had a history of major depression, recurrent episodes). "But I am coping much better with my depression; doesn't that mean anything in your diagnostic workup?" This was one of Michael's many questions that I could not answer well.

Occasionally, I call Michael to have "booster sessions." Each time, I am impressed with how well he is coping with challenges that might overwhelm other people. Typically, we talk about how he is using his strengths and building a stronger network of friends.

My work with Michael, which was conducted early in my career, taught me about the need to go beyond the client's report of symptoms and to test the limits of the existing diagnostic framework. In time, good mental health care routinely will require us to consider clients' resources and to contextualize their behaviors when we render diagnoses and carry out treatment plans.

Going Beyond the *DSM-IV* Framework

Traditionally, conceptualizations of behavior have focused on symptomatology and dysfunction—those things that are not "working" in a person's life. This focus on negative aspects has occurred at the expense of identifying strengths, and it has not helped people in their pursuit of optimal human functioning. This limited view of psychology undermines the ultimate goal of any psychodiagnostic system: *to understand the person's needs and resources and to facilitate the implementation of helpful therapeutic interventions.* Accordingly, Maddux (2002) points out that the utility of a classification system is closely linked to its ability to lead subscribers to the development and selection of effective treatment. This aspect of the *DSM*'s utility has been repeatedly questioned (see Raskin & Lewandowski, 2000; Rigazio-DiGilio, 2000). Furthermore, the *DSM* system does not explain connections among environment, culture, behavior, thoughts, emotion, external supports, and functioning. Therefore, the *DSM* system can only "suggest somewhat vaguely *what* needs to be changed, but it cannot provide guidelines for *how* to facilitate change" (Maddux, 2002, p. 20).

Going beyond the *DSM* framework requires clinicians to implement the numerous strategies (e.g., using the four-front approach, infusing developmental data into conceptualizations, counting culture's effects on mental health, and dimensioning behavior rather than categorizing it) described in this chapter. Over time, diagnostic practice may evolve into a process that incorporates more meaningful data into a robust system of describing behavior and mental health. Until then, clinicians can make small steps to account for positive and negative aspects of person's functioning. For example, Ivey and Ivey (1998) suggest that one of the first steps toward transcending pathology is to change the language we use to describe client functioning. This includes discovering what is working in a person's life and finding ways to capitalize on personal strengths. Indeed, simply asking about strengths can have a profound effect on the client, the therapeutic relationship, and, ultimately, the clinical conceptualization, as suggested by Snyder et al. (2003):

> By asking about strengths, the diagnostician is fostering several positive reactions in the client. First, the client can see that the helper is trying to understand the whole person. Second, the client is shown that she or he is not being equated with the problem. Third, the client is not reinforced for "having a problem" but rather is encouraged to look at her or his assets. Fourth, the client can recall and reclaim some of the personal worth that may have been depleted prior to coming to the mental health profession. Fifth, a consideration of the client's strengths can facilitate an alliance of trust and mutuality with the mental health professional; in turn, the client is open and giving of information that may yield a maximally productive diagnosis. By asking about strengths, therefore, a positive assessment is at once healing and buoyant in its focus. (p. 38)

Determining "what is not working" and "what is working" for a person honors the client's life experiences and guides clinicians to treatment approaches that make sense (see Chapter 15 for a further discussion of interventions). And, with the ongoing development of positive psychology research and practice, clinicians will be able to link balanced conceptualizations to applications that will help clients achieve optimal mental health.

ATTENDING TO ALL BEHAVIOR

Practicing psychologists get to know people on deep, meaningful levels. We are entrusted with stories that begin, "I wish I had. . . . " and those that start with "I am glad I did. . . . " We learn about hidden regrets and secret dreams. We hear about missed opportunities and planned "next shots." We see and feel deep suffering, and we are carried away by unbridled exuberance. We find out not only that abnormal behavior is fascinating but that *all behavior is intriguing.*

Contextualizing what you see by considering the influences of developmental processes, environmental conditions, and cultural nuances helps create a more balanced, accurate picture of a person and his or her struggles and triumphs. So, next time someone asks you, "Is that normal?" answer, "It depends." Ask a few more questions, and remember to put yourself in the shoes of the person being judged. This is what we try to do in working with people.

Key Terms

Abnormal behavior: A hard-to-define term, most definitions of which include behaviors that are atypical or aberrant, maladaptive, or accompanied by psychological distress. It is also important to consider a person's context and culture when deciding whether their behavior is abnormal.

Developing competence: One of Chickering's developmental goals of college students; involves going from low-level competence in intellectual, physical, and interpersonal domains to high competence in each area.

Developing integrity: One of Chickering's developmental goals of college students; developed when a person changes from unclear beliefs and values to clear and humanizing values.

Developing mature interpersonal relationships: One of Chickering's developmental goals of college students; involves growing from intolerance of differences and few relationships to an appreciation of differences and healthy relationships.

Developing purpose: One of Chickering's developmental goals of college students; involves transitioning from unclear vocational goals and distracting self-interests to clear goals and more communal activities.

Developmental counseling and therapy: Ivey and Ivey's theory of counseling, in which the here and now is examined and information gathered about a variety of contextual dimensions in the process of conceptualizing client's situations. In this theory, pathological behaviors are understood as logical responses to life events.

Establishing identity: One of Chickering's developmental goals of college students; involves changing from personal confusion and low self-confidence to a self-concept clarified through lifestyle and self-acceptance.

Four-front approach: A diagnostic approach that encourages assessment of a person's strengths as well as weaknesses. Observers using this approach gather information on (1) deficiencies and undermining characteristics of the person, (2) strengths and assets of the person, (3) lacks and destructive factors in the environment, and (4) resources and opportunities in the environment.

Fundamental attribution error: The tendency to ignore external situational or environmental factors and instead attribute the behavior of another to that person's internal characteristics (i.e., personality or abilities). In contrast, people are likely to explain their own behavior in terms of situational or environmental influences rather than personal characteristics.

Fundamental negative bias: The tendency to perceive as negative behavior that stands out, is considered negative, and occurs in a vague context. Behavior is remembered according to its saliency (stands out vs. doesn't stand out), its value (negative vs. positive), and its context (vague vs. well-defined).

Managing emotions: One of Chickering's developmental goals of college students; involves going from little awareness of feelings and limited control over disruptive emotions to increased understanding of feelings, flexible control, and constructive expression.

Moving through autonomy toward interdependence: One of Chickering's developmental goals of college students; involves moving from poor self-direction and emotional dependence to instrumental independence and limited need for reassurance.

Universality assumption: The assumption that what is deemed true for one group can be considered true for other people irrespective of cultural differences.

Interceding to Prevent the Bad and Enhance the Good

15

In the Words of a Psychotherapy Client . . .

Eager to get started, a new psychotherapy client passionately announced, "I want to stop the bad things that keep happening, *but that's not all. . . . I want more good!*" Her words tap the two broad categories of intercession that we explore in this chapter.

The first category, stopping the bad, involves efforts to prevent negative things from occurring later, and it can be divided into primary and secondary preventions. *Primary preventions* lessen or eliminate physical or psychological problems *before* they appear. *Secondary preventions* lessen or eliminate problems *after* they have appeared. The latter process often is called psychotherapy.

The second category, making more good, involves enhancing what people want in their lives; it, too, can be divided into primary and secondary types. *Primary enhancements* establish optimal functioning and satisfaction. *Secondary enhancements* go even farther, however, to build upon already-optimal functioning and satisfaction to achieve peak experiences. Primary enhancements make things good (create optimal experiences), whereas secondary enhancements make things the very best that they can be (create peak experiences).

If each of these primary and secondary approaches to prevention and enhancement were to have a slogan, we would suggest the following:

- Primary prevention: "Stop the bad before it happens."
- Secondary prevention (psychotherapy): "Fix the problem."
- Primary enhancement: "Make life good."
- Secondary enhancement: "Make life the best possible."

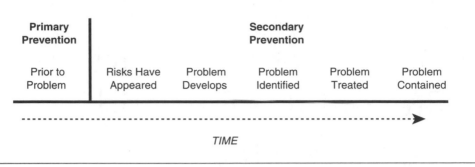

Figure 15.1   Primary and Secondary Preventions

Primary Prevention: "Stop the Bad Before It Happens"

DEFINITION

As shown in the far left of Figure 15.1, **primary preventions** reflect actions that people take to lessen or remove the likelihood of subsequent psychological difficulties (Heller, Wyman, & Allen, 2000) or physical problems (Kaplan, 2000). With primary preventions, people are not yet manifesting any problems, and it is only later that such problems will appear if appropriate protective, or prophylactic, steps are not taken (Snyder, Feldman, Taylor, Schroeder, & Adams, 2000). When primary prevention is aimed at an entire community population, it is called **universal prevention** (e.g., childhood immunizations); when focused on a particular at-risk population, it is called **selective prevention** (e.g., home visitations for low-birth-weight children; Munoz & Mendelson, 2004).

Primary prevention activities are based on hope for the future. As Snyder et al. (2000, p. 256) put it, "*We would suggest that prevention is, at its core, an act of hope—a positive, empowered view of one's ability to act so as to attain better tomorrows.*" As an intriguing example (described in Munoz & Mendelson, 2004) of the fact that a prevention need not entail a full understanding of a given problem or disease, consider the outbreak of cholera in 19th-century London. Although John Snow did not know the actual causal factor at the biochemical level, he did know enough to effectively curtail the epidemic by removing the handle of the water pump at Broad Street! Snow's hunch was that cholera was carried by something in the water supply that was coming from the water at this pump site. Indeed, Snow was able to prevent the spread of cholera by cutting off its source.

Primary prevention sometimes may occur at the governmental level. By setting and enforcing laws that allow people to succeed because of their merits and efforts, for example, a government can lessen subsequent negative consequences for its citizens (Snyder & Feldman, 2000). With legislation against prejudicial hiring practices such as racism and sexism, individual citizens are likely to remain satisfied because they perceive that they have equal opportunities to obtain desirable jobs. Likewise, when citizens perceive that laws allow equitable opportunities to pursue goal-directed activities, they then should (1) become less frustrated and aggressive (an aspect of the frustration-aggression hypothesis [Zillman, 1979]); (2) continue to exert effort in their work settings and personal lives (the negative outcome here has been called *learned helplessness* [Peterson, Maier, & Seligman, 1993]); and (3) be less likely to attempt suicides (Rodriguez-Hanley & Snyder, 2000). On the last point, in a multicountry study Krauss and Krauss (1968) examined the degree to which citizens sensed that their governments blocked them in various goal-pursuit activities. The researchers found that greater perceived blockages correlated significantly with higher suicide rates across countries.

Whatever can be done locally and nationally to raise educational levels also will serve primary prevention purposes by lessening the chances that citizens will be physically unhealthy and psychologically unhappy (Diener, 1984; Veroff, Douvan, & Kulka, 1981). Furthermore, any actions taken to promote employment should prevent people from incurring psychological and physical maladjustments (Mathers & Schofield, 1998; Smith, 1987; see also Chapter 17 on the beneficial aspects of work).

IS PRIMARY PREVENTION EFFECTIVE?

On the whole, primary preventions are quite effective (Albee & Gullotta, 1997; Durlak, 1995; Durlak & Wells, 1997; Mrazek & Haggerty, 1994; Yoshikawa, 1994). To understand the magnitude of the effects of primary prevention efforts, consider the results of a meta-analysis (a statistical technique that allows researchers to combine the results of many studies to discover common trends) conducted by Durlak and Wells (1997). Durlak and Wells examined the effectiveness of prevention programs on children's and adolescents' behavioral and social problems; they found that the preventions yielded effective outcomes similar in magnitude (and in some cases superior) to medical procedures such as cancer chemotherapy and coronary bypass surgery. Moreover, Durlak and Wells observed that, relative to control-group participants, those in the prevention programs were anywhere from 59% to 82% better off in terms of reduced problem behaviors and increased competencies.

COMPONENTS OF EFFECTIVE PRIMARY PREVENTIONS

Heller and his colleagues (Heller et al., 2000, pp. 663–664) have offered five suggestions for implementing successful primary preventions. First, the targeted populations should be given knowledge about the risky behavior to be prevented. Second, the program should be attractive; it should motivate potential participants to increase the desirable behaviors and decrease the undesirable ones. Third, the program should teach problem-solving skills as well as how to resist regressing into previous counterproductive patterns. Fourth, the program should change any norms or social structures that reinforce counterproductive behaviors. On this latter point, social support and approval often are needed in order to overcome the rewarding qualities of problematic behaviors. Fifth, data should be gathered to enable evaluation of the program's accomplishments. These evaluation data then can be used to make a case for implementing primary prevention programs in other settings.

HEAD START: AN EXAMPLE OF PRIMARY PREVENTION

Perhaps the most noteworthy example of primary prevention is the Head Start program, which began in the 1960s as a part of President Lyndon Johnson's War on Poverty. Head Start was implemented in response to widespread concerns that poor American children were not receiving sufficient cognitive and intellectual stimulation to benefit adequately from their schooling. Unfortunately, some children often were failing from the moment they began school.

The goal of Head Start was to provide poor children with a level of preparation that mirrored that of their economically more advantaged counterparts. In addition to its education components, Head Start added nutritious meals, medical screenings, and parental education. The parental training proved to be especially efficacious. Results showed that, when children attended Head Start for at least 3 days per week for 2 years or more, and when parents were involved, social and academic benefits were reliable and lasting over time (Ramey & Ramey, 1998). Head Start also showed children and parents that they need not slip into previous counterproductive behaviors; moreover, this program showed that a better life was possible for the children. Finally, compared to the various other prevention programs, Head Start has received repeated and extensive testing to show that it works. Perhaps the most crucial result has been that children in the program have been better off in their academic performances than their counterparts who did not participate in Head Start (Ramey & Ramey, 1998).

PRIMARY PREVENTIONS FOR ETHNIC MINORITIES

In a modification of Bierman's (1997) risk reduction programs for rural children, Alvy (1988) developed an effective parent training program for African American parents. This program emphasized pride, study skills, discipline, and obedience to authorities. Likewise, the parents were taught the importance of family support for their children. Alvy was careful to use a multiracial staff and to consult both locally and nationally with African American experts. A similarly effective program has been implemented for the parent training of Mexican American mothers (D. L. Johnson, 1988).

The fact that the community and family members were approached in culturally sensitive ways appears to have been a major factor in the success of these programs. Also, the programs all emphasize that the support of the surrounding community is crucial to the adoption of new attitudes (pride, studying, discipline, etc.). Lastly, although there has been some empirical testing of the effectiveness of these programs, examination must be continued to consider their utilities both inside and outside the given minority cultures.

PRIMARY PREVENTIONS FOR CHILDREN

Several primary prevention programs target at-risk children and youth. The work of Shure and Spivak (Shure, 1974; Shure & Spivak, 1988; Spivak & Shure, 1974) is exemplary in teaching problem-solving skills to children who were likely to use inappropriate, impulsive responses when encountering interpersonal problems. Such children were projected to have unhappy lives in which they would resort to crime and aggressive behaviors. As an antidote to these predicted problems, the children were taught to come up with ways other than aggressive outbursts to reach their goals. These successful problem-solving primary prevention programs have been expanded to middle schools (Elias, Gara, Ubriaco, Rothbaum, Clabby, & Schuyler, 1986) and to teenage children identified as likely to abuse drugs (Botvin & Toru, 1988), become pregnant (Weissberg, Barton, & Shriver, 1997), or contract HIV (Jemmot, Jemmot, & Fong, 1992).

We now discuss a program that has been quite successful in helping children at risk for depression. Using Seligman's learned optimism model (see Chapter 9), Gillham, Reivich, Jaycox, and Seligman (1995) implemented a 12-week primary prevention program to fifth- and sixth-grade children. The prevention program helped children to identify negative, self-referential beliefs and to change their attributions to more optimistic and realistic ones. Relative to a control group of children who did not receive this prevention package, those in the experimental group were significantly lower in depression; these findings were directly linked to their learning to make more optimistic attributions. (For analogous findings with high school students, see Clarke, Hawkins, Murphy, Sheeber, Lewinsohn, and Seeley [1995].) The Seligman program is especially laudatory because it continually has assessed its effectiveness in terms of the positive outcomes of the participant children who otherwise would be at risk for serious depression.

PRIMARY PREVENTIONS FOR THE ELDERLY

Prevention programs for the elderly can focus on many different objectives, including screening to lessen the probability of later physical health problems and diseases (Ory & Cox, 1994), checking living arrangements to remove physical hazards that can lead to falls and other accidents (Stevens et al., 1992), and attempts to maximize the elders' work, social, and interpersonal engagements (Payne, 1977). One such intriguing prevention program, called Grandma Please, involves grandchildren who telephone their grandparents after school (Szendre & Jose, 1996). Although the results of this program have been mixed, they are based on the compelling premise that keeping the elderly involved and actively participating in their families prevents them from spiraling into lives of isolation and depression. Unfortunately, these programs for the elderly have not necessarily produced uniformly beneficial results. For example, Baumgarten, Thomas, Poulin de Courval, and Infante-Rivard (1988) assumed that having older adults volunteer to help their debilitated neighbors would be beneficial to these helpers, but in fact the researchers found no such positive results. Related to this latter failure to find the expected benefits, it may be that spending time with family is more important in such prevention activities for elders than spending time meeting new friends (Thompson & Heller, 1990). Obviously, more research is needed to understand what types of preventions actually work with the elderly, and this will become especially important as the large cohort of baby boomers (people born after the end of World War II in 1945) moves into the senior years.

CAVEATS ABOUT PRIMARY PREVENTIONS

Several factors make it difficult to implement primary prevention programs. First, people tend to believe that the future will result in the good things happening to them, whereas the bad things will happen to other people. This phenomenon has been called the **illusion of uniqueness** (Snyder & Fromkin, 1980) or **unique invulnerability** (Snyder, 1997). One approach to lessening these inaccurate views is to give people actuarial information about how typical it is to encounter some problems. This makes it seem more "normal" to have the problem, and the recipients of such information then may be more willing to seek help before the problem grows to such a large size that is difficult to treat.

In an empirical test of this approach, Snyder and Ingram (1983) told college students, half of whom were high in test anxiety, about the high prevalence of anxiety among college students. Results showed that only the highly test-anxious students then perceived their anxiety as normal and that they then were more likely to seek treatment. A similar approach is to show short television spots in which famous athletes or movie stars disclose that they sought treatment and now are better (Snyder & Ingram, 2000b). In short, by normalizing the problem, people with the problem may become more willing to seek help for it.

Another force undermining prevention activities is the difficulty in convincing people that these programs are effective and worth the effort. People tend to remain passive and to believe that "things will work out." Furthermore, funding agencies may not see the payoff—that doing something now will result in benefits years later. One way to correct this misperception is to conduct research to show the direct payoffs in terms of increased productivity and money saved by the agencies where the preventions may be applied (businesses, government organizations, etc.) (Snyder & Ingram, 2000b). If research shows a company that primary prevention efforts actually would save money in the long run, the company is likely to invest money in primary prevention activities.

Lastly, even though advances have been made in the area of prevention, there is a sizable lag time until such findings are published and become part of the knowledge base in psychology (Clark, 2004). Although we have considerable knowledge about how to intervene against psychopathologies (because of the previous widespread application of the pathology model), we have far less understanding of prevention to promote health and lessen the probability of future problems among identified populations (Holden & Black, 1999). Nevertheless, primary prevention can be applied effectively to target behaviors involving both psychological and physical health. Primary prevention can help keep physical illnesses at bay and enhance the psychological quality of life in subsequent years (Kaplan, 2000; Kaplan, Alcaraz, Anderson, & Weisman, 1996; Kaplan & Anderson, 1996).

Secondary Prevention (Psychotherapy): "Fix the Problem"

DEFINITION

Secondary prevention addresses a problem as it begins to unfold. Compared with primary prevention, therefore, secondary prevention occurs later in the temporal sequence of the unfolding problem (see Figure 15.1). Snyder et al. (2000, p. 256) have described **secondary prevention** as occurring when "the individual produces thoughts or actions to eliminate, reduce, or contain the problem once it has appeared." Therefore, time in relation to the problem is a key differentiating factor in these two types of prevention, with primary prevention involving actions *initiated before a problem has developed,* and secondary prevention involving actions *taken after the problem has appeared.*

Secondary prevention is synonymous with psychotherapy interventions. Although most people probably realize that there are numerous forms of psychotherapies, it surprise many to learn that helpers presently are practicing over 400 different types of interventions (Roth, Fonagy, & Parry, 1996).

We view psychotherapy as a prime example of secondary prevention because people who come for such treatments know that they have specific problems that are beyond their capabilities to handle, and this is what leads them to obtain help (Snyder & Ingram, 2000a). Indeed, the related literature reveals that specific problems and life stressors trigger the seeking of psychological assistance (Norcross & Prochaska, 1986; Wills & DePaulo, 1991). Of course, when psychotherapy is successful, it also may produce the primary prevention characteristic of lessening or preventing recurrence of similar problems in the future.

IS SECONDARY PREVENTION EFFECTIVE?

From the earliest summaries of the effectiveness of psychotherapies (e.g., Smith, Glass, & Miller, 1980) to more contemporary ones (see Ingram, Hayes, & Scott, 2000), there is consistent evidence that psychotherapy improves the lives of adults and children. When we say that psychotherapy "works," we mean that there is a lessening of the severity and/or frequency of the client's problem and symptoms. On average, for example, a person who has undergone psychotherapy has improved by a magnitude of 1 standard deviation (that is, she or he is about 34% better off) on various outcome markers, relative to the person who has not undergone psychotherapy (Landman & Dawes, 1982; Shapiro & Shapiro, 1982). Thus, there is strong scientific support for the effectiveness of what are called *evidence-based treatments* for adults (Chambless et al., 1998; Chambless & Hollon, 1998; Chambless et al., 1996), children (Casey & Berman, 1985; Kasdin, Siegel, & Bass, 1990; Roberts, Vernberg, & Jackson, 2000; Weisz, Weiss, Alicke, & Klotz, 1987), the elderly (Gallagher-Thompson et al., 2000; Woods & Roth, 1996), and ethnic minorities (Malgady, Rogler, & Costantino, 1990). Furthermore, clients who have undergone psychotherapy treatments report being very satisfied with their experiences (Seligman, 1995).

For the reader interested in overviews of effective treatments for depressions, bipolar disorders, phobias, generalized anxiety disorders, panics, agoraphobias, obsessive-compulsive disorders, eating disorders, schizophrenia, personality disorders, alcohol dependency and abuse, and sexual dysfunctions, we recommend the 1996 book, *What Works for Whom? A Critical Review of Psychotherapy Research*, edited by Anthony Roth and Peter Fonagy. Effective interventions for specific problems are summarized in Appendix A on pages 373–374.

COMMON COMPONENTS
OF SECONDARY PREVENTIONS

On the effectiveness of psychotherapy, noted psychiatrist and psychotherapy researcher Jerome Frank (1968, 1973, 1975) suggested that hope was the underlying process common to all successful psychotherapy approaches. Building on Frank's pioneering ideas, Snyder and his colleagues (Snyder, Ilardi, Cheavens, et al., 2000; Snyder, Ilardi, Michael, & Cheavens, 2000; Snyder, Parenteau, Shorey, Kahle, & Berg, 2002) have used hope theory

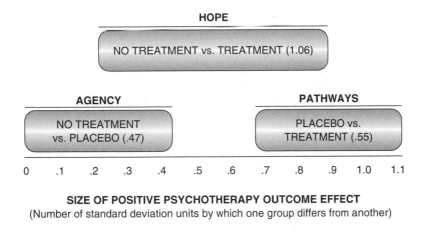

HOPE

NO TREATMENT vs. TREATMENT (1.06)

AGENCY

NO TREATMENT
vs. PLACEBO (.47)

PATHWAYS

PLACEBO vs.
TREATMENT (.55)

0   .1   .2   .3   .4   .5   .6   .7   .8   .9   1.0   1.1

SIZE OF POSITIVE PSYCHOTHERAPY OUTCOME EFFECT
(Number of standard deviation units by which one group differs from another)

Figure 15.2   Primary and Secondary Enhancements

(see Chapter 9) to show how pathways and agency goal-directed thinking facilitate successful outcomes in psychotherapy. We elaborate on the application of these agency and pathways processes to psychotherapy next.

Placebo effects in psychotherapy research represent how much clients will improve if they are motivated to believe that change will happen. Therefore, if the size of the placebo therapeutic outcome effect is compared to the size of therapeutic effect for clients who get no such motivational expectancies, we can produce what amounts to an agency (or motivation) effect. Likewise, if we take the full treatment outcome effect (comprising agency plus the pathways of treatment) and subtract the placebo effect (agency), a pathways-like effect remains. The typical agency effect size has been shown to be .47 standard deviation in magnitude (i.e., clients are 16% better off than had they received no treatment), and the pathways effect has been .55 standard deviation in magnitude (i.e., clients are 19% better off than had they received no treatment; data taken from Barker, Funk, & Houston, 1988). Summing these agency and pathways effects produces an overall hope effect size of 1.02 standard deviation (i.e., clients are about 35% better off than had they received no treatment). As shown in Figure 15.2, we can see that about half of the robust psychotherapy outcome effect relates to agency motivation, and the other half of the psychotherapy effect relates to the pathways learned in the specific interventions.

SECONDARY PREVENTION PROGRAMS FOR ADULTS

Most psychotherapy approaches have used what Berg and de Shazer (1992) call "problem talk" rather than "solution talk." That is to say, the traditional focus has been on decreasing negative thoughts and behaviors rather than focusing on the building of positive thoughts and behaviors (Lopez, Floyd, Ulven, & Snyder, 2000). Even though the pathology approach to thinking about human behavior still is the prevailing model, in recent years many therapists have begun to attend to clients' strengths. Likewise, a client sometimes must unlearn negative thoughts and behaviors before learning positive ones.

Before turning to examples of the newer therapeutic approaches of positive psychology, it would be useful to describe previous approaches that have proven effective in lessening client problems. In this regard, some psychotherapy interventions involve self-management (Rokke & Rehm, 2001). One such is Bandura's self-efficacy model, discussed previously in Chapter 9. According to this model, a client can learn efficacy beliefs through (1) actual performance accomplishments in the problematic area, (2) modeling another person who is coping effectively, (3) verbal persuasion by the helper, and (4) controlling negative cognitive processes by learning to implement positive moods (Forgas, Bower, & Moylan, 1990). It is important to note that there are specific target problems in such self-efficacy approaches.

A second type of self-management involves Meichenbaum's (1977) self-instructional training, which typically is aimed at the problem of anxiety. The initial stage of this approach is gathering information about the problem, including maladaptive cognitions. This is accomplished when the helper asks the client to imagine the problem and then describe the ongoing internal dialogue. In the second stage of Meichenbaum's treatment approach, the client is taught more adaptive internal dialogues. Lastly, the client practices these new coping dialogues in order to strengthen the likelihood of actually using them.

A third self-management approach is Kanfer's (1970) three-stage self-control model, which often is used with anxiety problems. In the first stage, self-monitoring, the client observes the problematic behavior in the context of its antecedents and consequences. In the second stage, self-evaluation, the client learns to compare the ongoing problematic behavior with the desired, improved standard of performance, and realizes that she or he is falling below this standard. In the third stage, self-reinforcement, the client learns to reinforce him- or herself (with rewards and punishments) for controlling the undesired behavior. Additionally, the client must be committed to change and must perceive that the given behaviors are under his or her control.

We cannot describe all the major psychotherapeutic approaches in detail here. For reviews of the various psychotherapy approaches, see the 2000 *Handbook of Psychological Change: Psychotherapy Processes & Practices for the 21st Century*, edited by C. R. Snyder and R. E. Ingram, and the 2004 *Handbook of Psychotherapy and Behavior Change*, edited by M. J. Lambert. The major psychotherapy models have included psychodynamic approaches, behavioral techniques, cognitive-behavioral strategies, humanistic models, and family system approaches, along with the possible use of psychotropic medications (Plante, 2005).

We now turn to approaches to secondary prevention that are described within the new field of positive psychology. For a review of these approaches to psychotherapy, we recommend the 2004 *Positive Psychology in Practice*, edited by P. A. Linley and S. Joseph.

Seligman has used his learned optimism theory as an attributional retraining framework for developing a therapeutic approach for depression. For overviews of his adult therapy, we suggest Seligman's 1991 book, *Learned Optimism,* and his 2002 book, *Authentic Happiness.*

Seligman's attributional retraining for adults starts with teaching people the "ABCs" related to negative events in their lives. Specifically, A is for the adversity, B is for the belief about the underlying reason for the bad event, and C is the consequence in terms of feelings (usually negative or depressed). Seligman then teaches the adult to add a D to the ABC sequence; this D represents the client's learning to dispute the previous counterproductive, depression-producing belief with compelling, accurate evidence. For example, in the following sequence, consider a hypothetical client named Jack:

Adversity = Jack's perception that his friend Bob has been ignoring him.

Belief (of Jack) = Bob does not like him because Jack is "no fun."

Consequence = Jack feels lousy.

With disputation training to learn other explanations for Bob's behavior, Jack will be able to feel better about himself. For example, consider this next sequence, in which disputation is added:

Adversity = Bob does not talk with Jack all afternoon at work.

Belief (of Jack) = Bob doesn't like Jack.

Consequence = Jack feels bad.

Disputation = Jack invokes the more optimistic attribution that Bob had been quiet with other people at work. Additionally, Jack notes that, in fact, Bob had spoken with him at the coffee break that morning. Thus, having made these more optimistic attributions, Jack is able to feel much better about the situation.

In addition to learned optimism therapy, some attention has been given to implementing what has been called "hope therapy" in one-on-one settings (Lopez et al., 2000; Lopez et al., 2004; McDermott & Snyder, 1999), with couples (Worthington et al., 1997), and in groups (Klausner et al., 1998). For example, Klausner and her colleagues (Klausner et al., 1998; Klausner, Snyder, & Cheavens, 2000) have developed a valid group intervention for depressed older adults. Specifically, in a series of 10 group sessions, learning the goal-directed activities that are inherent in hope theory have diminished depression and raised physical activity levels for depressed older persons. Moreover, these improvements based on hope treatment were superior to those attained by a comparison group who underwent Butler's (1974) reminiscence group therapy (this later approach entails elders recalling earlier, pleasurable times in their lives). Also using hope theory as a base, Cheavens and her colleagues (Cheavens, Feldman, Gum, Michael, & Snyder, in press; Cheavens et al., 2001) have developed an effective eight-session intervention for depressed adults.

In yet other therapeutic hope applications, outpatients visiting a community mental health center were given a pretreatment therapy preparation based on hope theory (i.e., they were taught the basic principles of this theory), and these clients then received the normal psychotherapy interventions implemented at this facility. Results showed that the people who were given the pretreatment instructions in hope theory improved in subsequent treatments more than those who did not receive such pretreatment preparations (Irving et al., 2004). It should be emphasized that all clients in this study received comparable actual treatments, but the one group that was given pretreatment education in hope theory profited more from their interventions. In yet another hope intervention, Trump (1997) devised a videotaped treatment using hopeful narratives of women who had survived childhood incest. Results showed that viewing this tape increased the hope levels of these women relative to those who viewed a control tape.

As shown in Appendix B (pages 374–375), which is a worksheet for use in implementing hope therapy for adults, the client undergoing hope therapy initially is probed for his or her goals in differing life arenas. Next, the client is asked to select a particular life domain on which to work. Over the ensuing sessions, the therapist then helps the client to clarify the goals by making lucid marker points for assessing progress in attaining these goals. Various pathways for reaching the goals are then taught, along with ways to motivate the person to actually use those routes. Impediments to the desired goals are anticipated, and the clients are given instructions in how to institute backup routes to the goals. As different goals are practiced over time, the clients learn how to apply hope therapy naturally in their everyday goal pursuits. The overall purpose is to teach clients how to use hope therapy principles to attain ongoing life goals, especially when encountering blockages (Cheavens, Feldman, Woodward, & Snyder, in press).

SECONDARY PREVENTIONS FOR ETHNIC MINORITIES

The following comments about psychotherapy for ethnic minority clients should be considered in light of the fact that people of color tend not to seek treatment. For example, whereas members of minority groups represent roughly 30% of the U.S. population, they make up only 10% of those who seek psychotherapy (Vessey & Howard, 1993). This problem is magnified by the fact that the members of minority groups who do enter psychotherapy are more likely than Caucasian clients to terminate treatment early (Gray-Little & Kaplan, 2000).

We mention these facts to highlight that the system is not effective in reaching and helping people of color. Furthermore, so little research has been done with psychotherapy clients who are African, Hispanic, or Asian Americans that we presently cannot make statements about the best approaches for such treatments. In commenting on the lack of sufficient samples of minority clients, Gray-Little and Kaplan (2000, p. 608) have written, "Our review has left us feeling like the dinner guest who remarked that the food was disappointing and 'such small portions.'" Obviously, one of the missions of positive psychology should be to understand the reasons for the underutilization of mental health professionals by members of minority groups, as well as to increase their propensities to seek such services and remain in treatment.

SECONDARY PREVENTIONS FOR CHILDREN

For overviews of secondary preventions for children, check the two Internet locations http://www.state.hi.us/doh/camhd/index.html and http://www.clinicalchildpsychology.org. We now turn to specific positive psychology interventions for children. Previously in this chapter, we discussed the Seligman approach to optimism as it was used in a primary prevention program for depression in fifth graders (see also Jaycox, Reivich, Gillham. & Seligman, 1994). In his 1995 book, *The Optimistic Child*, Martin Seligman shows teachers and parents how to instruct children in attaining the necessary life skills so as to diminish depression. This program also improves self-reliance, school performance, and physical health.

Using hope theory as developed by Snyder and colleagues, there also have been exploratory intervention programs to raise the hope of children. In these hope training programs, children are taught to set clear goals and to find several workable routes to those goals. The children then are taught to motivate themselves to use the routes to their desired goals. In their book *Hope for the Journey,* Snyder, McDermott, Cook, and Rapoff (2004) use stories to implant hopeful thoughts and behaviors in children. Furthermore, initial programs in grade schools (McDermott et al., 1996) and junior high schools (Lopez, 2000) have used stories to promote modest increases in hope. Likewise, McNeal (1998) reported that children's hope increased after 6 months of psychotherapy, and Brown and Roberts (2000) found that a 6-week summer camp resulted in significant improvements in children's hope scores (these changes remained after 4 months). (For another overview of hope interventions for children, read *The Great Big Book of Hope* by McDermott and Snyder [2000].)

SECONDARY PREVENTIONS FOR THE ELDERLY

Depression is the most frequent problem among older persons who come for psychotherapy. As Blazer (1994) puts it, depression is analogous to the common cold in the psychological life of the elderly. The most prevalent therapeutic approach with the elderly is the cognitive-behavioral one (Thompson, 1996), although the psychodynamic (Newton, Brauer, Gutmann, & Grunes, 1986), interpersonal (emphasizing communication skills; Klerman, Weissman, Rounsaville, & Chevron, 1984), and reminiscence (Butler, 1974) approaches also have been used effectively. Because the elderly typically confront negative events that are almost inevitable (the lessening of income and health, loss of friends and spouse, etc.), the development of more adaptive views about one's circumstances and self is especially applicable (Gallagher-Thompson et al., 2000). In this approach, it is important to make sure that the elderly client (1) has appropriate expectancies of what will transpire in treatment, (2) can hear and see clearly in the sessions, and (3) has sessions structured to move slowly enough for the needed lessons to be absorbed. Although the usual approach is to conduct such treatment in a one-on-one setting, group formats also can work. In this regard, the psychoeducational approach with older adults will be increasingly important in the future. (For a manual in conducting such a class, see Thompson, Gallagher, and Lovett, 1992).

A CAVEAT ABOUT SECONDARY PREVENTIONS

Unfortunately, there is a stigma linked to seeing a mental health professional for psychotherapy. Although most people probably do not refrain from seeing other health professionals, such as ophthalmologists or surgeons, they are reticent about seeing a psychiatrist or professional psychologist. A noteworthy example of this stigma occurred during the 1972 presidential elections when Democratic candidate George McGovern selected Senator Thomas Eagleton as his vice-presidential running mate. When the American public discovered that Senator Eagleton had been treated for clinical depression with electroconvulsive shock therapy, there was a concern that a depressed person would be "a heartbeat away from the presidency" should something happen to McGovern (if he were to be elected president). The stigma associated with the depression eventually led McGovern to remove Eagleton from the ticket.

Another example comes from former first lady Rosalynn Carter (Carter, 1977), who wrote,

When I was growing up in Plains, GA, I did not hear the words "mental health" or "mental illness." Over the years, I picked up that a neighbor of ours had had a "nervous breakdown," and that another friend was "not quite right" and that a distant cousin was locked up in a state institution where, I assumed, everyone was crazy. I remember vividly when my cousin came home once to visit his family. I suppose I remember the occasion with such clarity because he chased me down the road—and I have never been more terrified. I do not know why I had to get away. . . . As a nation, we are still running away from persons who have had or still have mental and emotional disorders. And the stigma attached to their plight is an undeserved disgrace. . . . In sum, mental illness is still not acceptable in our society." (p. D4)

The media touches these issues through occasional television shows such as *The Bob Newhart Show* and *Frasier*, at which we laugh at the humor inherent in the behaviors of quirky psychotherapists. Such television does nothing to reduce the stigma, however, and it may well feed into the negative stereotypes. Indeed, there is little doubt that this stigma remains in American society, because most people still refrain from speaking of their mental health care. The tragedy here is that this stigma prevents many people from seeking needed treatment. Moreover, if people were able to seek treatment in the early phases of their psychological problems, then the likelihood of their having effective treatment outcomes would be improved. As it is, however, people may wait until the psychological problem becomes so severe that it is extremely difficult to intervene effectively. Perhaps positive psychology can work to lessen such prejudicial thinking by making people think of psychotherapy not only as solving problems but also as building on one's strengths and talents to become more productive and happier. In other words, with the growth of positive psychology, the stigma associated with psychotherapy may lessen because people come to view treatment as involving processes to accentuate their assets.

Primary Enhancement: "Make Life Good"

Primary enhancement involves the effort to establish optimal functioning and satisfaction. As shown in the left side of Figure 15.3, primary enhancement involves attempts either to increase hedonic well-being by maximizing the pleasurable, or to increase eudaemonic well-being by setting and reaching goals (Ryan & Deci, 2001; Waterman, 1993). Whereas **hedonic primary enhancements** tap indulgence in pleasure and the satisfaction of appetites and needs, **eudaemonic primary enhancements** emphasize effective functioning and happiness as a desirable result of the goal pursuit process (Seligman, 2002; Shmotkin, 2005). In this regard, it should be noted that factor-analytic research has supported the distinction between hedonic and eudemonic human motives (Compton, Smith, Cornish, & Qualls, 1996; Keyes, Shmotkin, & Ryff, 2000).

Before describing the various routes to primary enhancement, some comments are necessary about the role of evolution. In an evolutionary sense, particular activities are biologically predisposed to produce satisfaction (Buss, 2000; Pinker, 1997). An evolutionary premise is that people

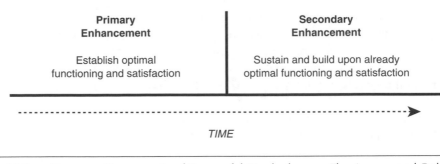

TIME

Figure 15.3   Common Components of Successful Psychotherapy: The Agency and Pathways of Hope

experience pleasure under the circumstances favorable to the propagation of the human species (Carr, 2004). Accordingly, happiness results from close interpersonal ties, especially those that lead to mating and the protection of offspring. Indeed, research shows that happiness stems from (1) a safe and supportive living unit with people who work together, (2) an environment that is fertile and productive of food, (3) "stretching" of our bodies through exercise, and (4) the pursuit of meaningful goals in one's work (Diener, 2000; Kahneman, Diener, & Schwartz, 1999; Lykken, 1999).

One more caveat is warranted. Many of the experiences placed in the category of primary enhancement also could fit into the category of secondary enhancement, involving peak experiences. The line between an optimal experience and a peak experience may be very subtle.

PRIMARY ENHANCEMENT: PSYCHOLOGICAL HEALTH

Many people on their deathbeds may think, "I wish I had spent more time with my family." This suggests that *our relationships are crucial for life satisfaction* (as noted in Chapters 1 and 13). Indeed, for most people, interpersonal relationships with lovers, family, and good friends provide the most powerful sources of well-being and life satisfaction (Berscheid & Reis, 1998; Reis & Gable, 2003).

Engaging in shared activities that are enjoyable enhances psychological well-being (Watson, Clark, & Tellegen, 1988), especially if such joint participation entails arousing and novel activities (Aron, Norman, Aron, McKenna, & Heyman, 2000). Likewise, it is beneficial for couples to tackle intrinsically motivated activities in which they can share aspects of their lives and become absorbed in the ongoing flow of their behaviors (Csikszentmihalyi, 1990).

Beyond the relationship with one's mate, primary enhancement satisfactions also can come from other relationships, such as family and friends. Arranging living circumstances to be within close physical proximity to kin also can produce the social supports that are so crucial for happiness. So, too, can the close network of a few friends produce contentment. Finally, there are compelling evolutionary arguments (Argyle, 2001) and supportive empirical research (Diener & Seligman, 2002) as to why such kin and friend relationships are crucial for happiness.

Another relationship that produces happiness is involvement in religion and spiritual matters (Myers, 2000; Piedmont, 2004). In part, this may reflect the fact that religiosity and prayer are related to higher hope (Laird, Snyder, Rapoff, & Green, 2004; Snyder, 2004c). Likewise, some of the satisfaction from religion probably stems from the social contacts it provides (Carr, 2004). Happiness also may result from the spirituality stemming from the individual's relationship with a higher power. On this point, there is accruing scientific evidence of a possible genetic link to human spirituality needs (see Hamer, 2004).

Gainful employment also is an important source of happiness (Argyle, 2001; see also Chapter 17). To the degree to which people are satisfied with their work, they also are happier (an overall correlation of .40 between being employed and level of happiness; Diener & Lucas, 1999). The reason for this finding is that, for many people, work provides a social network, and it also allows for the testing of talents and skills. To attain such satisfactions from work, however, it is crucial that the jobs have considerable variety in the activities undertaken. Moreover, the job duties should match the worker's skills and talents. Furthermore, it helps if there is a supportive boss who fosters autonomy (Warr, 1999) and at the same time enables the individual worker to understand and embrace larger company goals (Hogan & Kaiser, 2005).

Leisure activities also can bring pleasure (Argyle, 2001). Relaxing, resting, and eating a good meal all have the short-term effect of making people feel better. Recreational activities such as sports, dancing, and listening to music allow people to make enjoyable contacts with others. Although it may seem inconsistent with the term *leisure*, people often are quite active as they participate in recreational activities. Thus, sometimes happiness comes from stimulation and a sense of positive arousal, whereas at other times happiness reflects a quiet, recharging process.

Whatever the particular primary enhancement activities may be, those actions that are totally absorbing are the most enjoyable. Csikszentmihalyi and his colleagues (Csikszentmihalyi, 1990; Nakamura & Csikszentmihalyi, 2002) have studied the circumstances that lead to a sense of total engagement. Such activities typically are intrinsically fascinating, and they stretch talents to satisfying levels in which persons lose track of themselves and the passage of time. This type of primary enhancement has been called a **flow** experience, and artists, surgeons, and other professionals report such flow in their work (see Chapter 11 for further discussion of flow).

Yet another route to attaining a sense of contentment is through here-and-now contemplation of one's external or internal environment. Indeed, a common thread in Eastern thought is that immense pleasure is to be attained through "being" or experiencing. Even in Western societies, however, meditation upon internal experiences or thoughts has gained many followers (Shapiro, Schwartz, & Santerre, 2002). **Meditation** has been defined as "a family of techniques which have in common a conscious attempt to focus attention in a nonanalytic way, and an attempt not to dwell on discursive, ruminating thought" (Shapiro, 1980, p. 14). For example, mindfulness meditation (Langer, 2002) involves a nonjudgmental attention that allows a sense of peacefulness, serenity, and pleasure. Kabat-Zinn (1990) has posed the following seven qualities of mindfulness meditation: nonjudging, acceptance, openness, nonstriving, patience, trust, and letting go (see Chapter 11). Likewise, in what is called *concentrative meditation*, awareness is restricted by focusing on a single thought or object such as a personal mantra, breath, word (Benson & Proctor, 1984), or even a sound (Carrington, 1998).

Another process that is meditation-like in its operation is savoring. **Savoring** involves thoughts or actions that are aimed at appreciating and perhaps amplifying a positive experience of some sort (see Bryant, 2004; Bryant & Veroff, 2006). According to Fred Bryant (2005), who is the psychologist who coined this term and who has produced the major theory and research on it, savoring can take three temporal forms:

Fred B. Bryant

Source: Reprinted with permission of Fred B. Bryant.

1. Anticipation, or the enjoyment of a forthcoming positive event

2. Being in the moment, or thinking and doing things to intensify and perhaps prolong a positive event as it occurs

3. Reminiscing, or looking back at a positive event to rekindle the favorable feelings or thoughts

Furthermore, savoring can take the form of

Sharing with others

Taking "mental photographs" to build one's memory

Congratulating oneself

Comparing with what one has felt in other circumstances

Sharpening senses through concentration

Becoming absorbed in the moment

Expressing oneself through behavior (laughing, shouting, pumping one's fist in the air)

Realizing how fleeting and precious the experience is

Counting one's blessings

As an example of savoring, consider the comments (taken from his diary) of Bertrand Piccard (1999) as he contemplated the last night of his record-breaking 1999 balloon trip around the world:

> During the last night, I savor once more the intimate relationship we have established with our planet. Shivering in the pilot's seat, I have the feeling I have left the capsule to fly under the stars that have swallowed our balloon. I feel so privileged that I want to enjoy every second of this air world. . . . Very shortly after daybreak, [the balloon] will land in the Egyptian sand . . . [and I will] immediately need to find words to satisfy the public's curiosity. But right now, muffled in my down jacket, I let the cold bite of the night remind me that I have not yet landed, that I am still living one of the most beautiful moments of my life. . . . The only way that I can make this instant last will be to share it with others. (p. 44)

There is yet more that people can do beyond savoring. In this regard, University of North Carolina psychologist Barbara Fredrickson (2002) developed her pioneering broaden-and-build model (see Chapter 7 for a more detailed discussion of the model) after observing that negative emotions such as anger and anxiety tend to constrict a person's thought and action repertoires. That is to say, when feeling negative emotions, people become concerned with protection, and their thoughts and actions become limited to a few narrow options aimed at remaining "safe." On the other hand, Fredrickson proposed that, when experiencing positive emotions, people open up and become flexible in their thinking and behaviors. Thus, positive emotions help to produce a "broaden-and-build" mentality, in which there is a positive carousel of subsequent emotions, thoughts, and actions. Therefore, anything a person can do to experience joy, perhaps through play or other activities, can yield psychological benefits.

In her research, Fredrickson (1999, 2001, 2002) has induced positive emotions by having research participants remember a joyful event, listen to a favorite piece of music, watch a good movie, and receive positive self-referential feedback, to name but few examples. These positive emotional inducements, in turn, make people happier, more perceptive, better at problem solving, more facile in social interactions, more creative, and so on. The broaden-and-build cycle is depicted in Chapter 7, in Figure 7.3 (page 136). The positive emotions open the person to surrounding circumstances as well as to the important, task-relevant cues in those circumstances. Furthermore, the positive emotions remind the person of other related, successful episodes in his or her life, thereby enhancing the perceived probability of doing well in the present circumstances. Therefore, Fredrickson's broaden-and-build process sets a positive carousel in motion.

Psychologist Steve Ilardi and his colleagues at the University of Kansas have initiated a new treatment for the prevention of depression and the enhancement of personal happiness, called the Therapeutic Lifestyle

Stephen Ilardi

Source: Reprinted with permission of Stephen Ilardi.

Change (TLC) (Ilardi & Karwoski, 2005; for more about this program, visit the website www.psych.ku.edu/TLC). The basic tenet of TLC is that engaging in certain approaches to one's lifestyle, especially those activities that were natural parts of the lives of our ancestors who lived ages ago, brings about a lessening of depression and the enhancement of happiness.

The components of TLC are exercise, omega-3 fatty acid supplements, exposure to light, decreased rumination and worrying, social support, and good sleep. First, 35 minutes of aerobic exercise at least three times a week is recommended. The idea here is to get one's heart rate to 120 to 160 beats per minute. Second, over-the-counter omega-3 fatty acid supplements (fish oils) can be purchased at a drugstore. It appears that our ancestors consumed higher quantities of fish than we do today. Third, try to obtain at least 30 minutes of bright sunlight per day. This can be done naturally by being outside in the sunlight, or by sitting next to a special light box that emits very bright light (10,000 lux). Fourth, stop ruminating. Things that work to lessen such worrying include calling a friend, exercising, putting one's negative thoughts in a journal, or engaging in other pleasant activities. Fifth, be sure to stay around other people. This also helps to distract you from rumination. Sixth, get at least 8 hours of sleep per night. Do this by getting a bedtime ritual, and be sure to avoid caffeine and alcohol for several hours before retiring. In summary, TLC appears to be a promising new approach (based upon age-old human actions) that may enhance our happiness. Also, it should be noted that TLC inherently seems to involve many of the processes already discussed in this section on the primary enhancement of psychological health.

Martin Seligman and his colleagues have undertaken a program of research aimed at finding interventions that are effective as primary enhancements (see Seligman, Steen, Park, & Peterson, 2005). In particular, Seligman recruited 577 adults who visited the website of his book, *Authentic Happiness* (Seligman, 2002). Most of these people were Caucasian, with some college education, 35 to 54 years old, and 58% were women. Before and after undergoing the primary enhancement intervention, each participant took self-report measures of happiness. (Although participants were randomly assigned to several conditions, we focus on one control and three primary enhancement intervention conditions.)

The control comparison condition was a placebo exercise in which the participants wrote for a week about their early memories. Participants assigned to the gratitude intervention were given a week to "deliver a letter of gratitude in person to someone who had been especially kind to them but had never been properly thanked" (Seligman et al., 2005, p. 416). Participants assigned to the condition involving three good things in life were to write for a week about three things that went well each day, along with the underlying causes of each positive thing. Lastly, a group of participants was asked to examine their character strengths in a new way for a week.

Results showed that each of these three primary enhancement interventions had robust positive effects in terms of raising the participants' happiness levels relative to the levels of the participants in the placebo control condition. The gratitude visit produced the largest increases in happiness, but these lasted for only a month. Furthermore, the writing about three good things that had happened, along with the use of the signature strengths in a new way, made people happier, and these positive changes endured for as long as 6 months.

Taken together, these findings suggest that psychologists can help in the development and implementation of primary enhancement interventions that raise the happiness of people. In their closing comments about these pioneering findings, Seligman et al. (2005, p. 421) concluded, "Psychotherapy has long been where you go to talk about your troubles. . . . We suggest that psychotherapy of the future may also be where you go to talk about your strengths."

Before we close this section on primary enhancement in psychological health, the following observation may surprise you; One goal that does not appear to qualify for primary enhancement is the pursuit of personal financial wealth. Beyond providing for life's basic necessities, money does little to raise well-being (Diener & Biswas-Diener, 2002; Myers, 2000). Think about the people you know. Chances are that the ones who are consumed with acquiring wealth probably are not all that happy. Indeed, as we noted in our earlier chapter on the antecedents of happiness (Chapter 7), acquiring great monetary riches is not the royal road to satisfaction in life.

PRIMARY ENHANCEMENT: PHYSICAL HEALTH

Exercise is a common route for attaining a sense of physical conditioning, fitness, and stamina. An important part of physical exercise and fitness is that it gives people greater confidence in their capacities to carry out the activities that form their daily routines. Beyond the physiological improvements that result from exercising, the resulting confidence also enhances happiness and well-being (Biddle, Fox, & Boutcher, 2000). Although short-term exercise raises positive moods, it is long-term exercise that produces greater happiness (Argyle, 2001; Sarafino, 2002). In this sense, exercise could be added to the previous section on primary enhancement and psychological health.

Part of the motivation to exercise may be to look good and to attain an improved physical image (Leary, Tchividijian, & Kraxberger, 1994). Moreover, another underlying motive to exercise may be the desire for good physical health. On this point, some people find pleasure in taking vitamins and eating nourishing foods.

Regular physical activities produce both psychological and physical benefits. For example, physical activity relates to the following benefits (taken from Mutrie & Faulkner, 2004, p. 148): (1) lessened chance of dying prematurely, (2) diminished probability of dying prematurely from heart disease, (3) reduced risk of protracting diabetes, (4) less likelihood of developing high blood pressure, (5) smaller chance of developing colon cancer, (6) weight loss and control, and (7) healthy bones, muscles, and joints.

A CAVEAT ABOUT PRIMARY ENHANCEMENT

People should take care, in primary enhancements, not to overdo such activities. When seduced by the pleasures derived from building strengths, a person may lose a sense of balance in his or her life activities. As with any activity, moderation may be needed.

Secondary Enhancement: "Make Life the Best Possible"

Compared to primary enhancement, in which the person seeks optimal performance and satisfaction via the pursuit of desired goals, in **secondary enhancement** the goal is to augment already-positive levels to reach the ultimate in performance and satisfaction (see the right side of Figure 15.3). In a temporal sense, secondary enhancement activities take place after basic levels of performance and satisfaction have been reached in primary enhancement.

SECONDARY ENHANCEMENT: PSYCHOLOGICAL HEALTH

Secondary enhancement of psychological health enables people to maximize their pleasures by building on their preexisting positive mental health. Peak psychological moments often involve important human connections, such as the birth of child, a wedding, the graduation of a loved one, or perhaps the passionate and companionate love of one's mate.

There are psychological group experiences the purpose of which is to help people to achieve the extreme pleasures of in-depth relating with others. As early as the 1950s, for example, the training groups, or T-groups, as they were called (Benne, 1964), emphasized how people could gather together to fully experience their positive emotions (Forsyth & Corazinni, 2000). (Sometimes, such groups were called "sensitivity training" [F. Johnson, 1988].)

The existentialist contemplation of the meaning in life is yet another approach to achieving a transcendently gratifying experience. Viktor Frankl (1966, 1992), in considering the question, "What is the nature of meaning?" concluded that the ultimate in experienced life meaning comes from thinking about our goals and purposes. Furthermore, he speculated that the ultimate satisfaction comes from contemplating our purpose during times in which we are suffering. Positive psychology researchers have reported that such meaning in life is linked to very high hope (Feldman & Snyder, 2005). For the reader interested in self-report instruments related to meaning in life, we recommend the Purpose in Life Test (Crumbaugh & Maholick, 1964; Crumbaugh & Maholick, 1981), the Life Regard Index (Battista & Almond, 1973), and the Sense of Coherence Scale (Antonovsky & Sagy, 1986).

Sometimes, secondary psychological enhancements occur in contexts where people can compete against each other. These "normal competitions" (see Snyder & Fromkin, 1980) involve engagements in competitive contests. There are rules for these contests and, over time, one or more people emerge as winners. The high level of pleasure that such winners experience often is described as "pure joy."

Occasionally, the very highest levels of pleasure are derived from involvements that are larger than any one person alone can attain (Snyder & Feldman, 2000). Working together, people can strive for achievements that would be unthinkable for any one individual (see Lerner, 1996). Then, as part of this collective unit, people can experience a sense of meaning and emotions that are of the grandest scale. History is filled with such instances of collective triumph in the face of adversity. Likewise, literature often details the sheer ecstasy experienced by the people who have worked together to overcome difficult and challenging blockages to reach their collective goals. Some psychologists already have begun wilderness coping experiences, in which a small group of people learn the supreme joys of cooperating as a group to successfully complete various challenges in raw, natural settings (diving, kayaking, rafting, mountain climbing, etc.).

So, too, does helping other people make people feel very good about themselves. In the Personal Mini-Experiments following are tips for facilitating volunteering among people. In our experience, volunteering is one of the most gratifying human activities, and we encourage you to explore the suggestions presented.

Yet another transcending experience involves seeing another person doing something that is so special that it is awe-inspiring or elevating. In such instances, it is as if we have been treated to witnessing the very best that is possible in people, and watching this produces a state of profound wonder and awe (see Haidt, 2000, 2002). Consider an actual example of such awe that I (CRS) had the privilege of witnessing. Here is what happened. I had been having a very bad day. Not only had things gone badly in my

Personal Mini-Experiments

Enhancing Your Daily Life

Throughout this chapter, we make the case that people can make changes that will make their lives better. You can put this thesis to the test by engaging in these two mini-experiments.

Finding Pleasure in Helping Another? Popular responses to the question, "What brings you pleasure?" typically cite engaging in some sort of hedonic activity—watching a good movie, eating a favorite meal, playing a favorite sport or game, or having sex with one's partner. What about helping activities that bring pleasure? Examples of such altruistic actions have included volunteering as an aid at a local hospital, serving as a Big Brother or Big Sister to a grade school student or junior high student, helping an older person with yard work, tutoring a student who is having difficulty in a given subject matter, running an errand for a disabled person, reading to a person who is blind, taking a child to a sporting event. Certainly both hedonic and helping activities bring personal pleasure. For you, which type of activity brings more pleasure? Engage in one of each kind of activity (hedonic and helping), and then write a paragraph explaining why you think one brought you more pleasure than the other. Think about what it may mean for the way you spend your time. Although most of us may think we know what brings us pleasure, this exercise shows that we may have some lessons to learn from positive psychology. We are curious to know how this exercise turns out for you, so please feel free to e-mail Shane Lopez at sjlopez@ku.edu with your personal experiences. Some of the examples people send us will appear in the second edition of this book.

Renewing the "Wonder Years": After the teenage years have passed, most adults cease to find new skills. What a shame that is! Recall the wonder and excitement that you had as a child when you learned to walk, tie your shoes, count to 10, ride a bike, fly a kite, drive a car, and so on? Perhaps our youth is called "the wonder years" in large part because of the excitement and sense of marvel that attended all the new skills we mastered. But why did this stop around age 20? We do not think it needs to. Indeed, the point of this positive psychology experiment is to help you regain the joys that come with aquiring new skills. Our instructions here are quite simple: *Learn a new skill that you always have wanted.* Chances are you have talents of which you are not fully aware or which you have not used. Cultivating them is one of the most satisfying and rewarding changes you can make in your adult life. So, go ahead and recapture the spirit of trying new things that used to be a normal part of your daily experience as a child or adolescent. Take some chances.

work (I had received word that my grant application had been rejected), but I also was feeling lousy physically. I went to lunch with my colleagues in the student union, only to find that they, too, were in foul moods. Suddenly, a young man in a Kansas University athletic letter jacket ran over to a table across the aisle and administered the Heimlich maneuver to an older man who was choking. The cafeteria immediately grew quiet as people witnessed this heroic act that may have saved the man's life. Once the food was dislodged from the man's throat, the silence was broken as people applauded the young man's act. Looking a bit embarrassed, he smiled and scurried off. I felt a tremendous psychological lift that lasted throughout the rest of that day (and over the next several days). It was one of the most moving events in which I ever have been involved, and my only role was to witness this amazing, selfless action. Without a doubt, to observe such a truly exceptional act can produce a type of secondary enhancement.

Finally, through the arts—such as music, dancing, theatre, and painting—great pleasures are afforded to the masses. The viewing of stellar artistic performances can lift audiences to the highest levels of satisfaction and enjoyment (Snyder & Feldman, 2000). We also encourage older adults to recapture some of the joys and pleasures that came with the explorations and attainments of new skills when they were younger. (See the Personal Mini-Experiment, "Renewing the 'Wonder Years,'" for suggestions for recapturing the amazement of acquiring new skills.)

SECONDARY ENHANCEMENT: PHYSICAL HEALTH

Secondary enhancement of physical health pertains to the peak levels of physical health—levels that are beyond those of well-conditioned people. People who seek secondary enhancement strive for levels of physical conditioning that far surpass those typically obtained by people who simply engage in exercise. Be clear, however, that such persons need not be Olympic-level athletes who compete against other elite athletes with the goal of achieving the very best performance in a sport. Instead, those athletes who pursue the highest levels of competition may see physical fitness as a means of enhancing the probability of winning. On the other hand, people who typify the secondary enhancement of physical health are motivated to reach very high levels of physical prowess per se. This latter superior level of physical fitness mirrors what Dienstbier (1989) has defined as *toughness*.

CAVEATS ABOUT SECONDARY ENHANCEMENT

As strange as it may sound, people may become almost addicted to the peak experiences that reflect secondary enhancement. There is natural balancing force, however, in that the mundane activities of life necessitate that people attend to them. This leaves people with only limited amounts of time to pursue primary and secondary enhancements.

We also have a serious concern about the potential development of personal coaches to help people attain the peak experiences of secondary enhancement. Our concern is that only the wealthy will be able to afford such coaches, which would be antithetical to the spirit of equity that we believe should guide the field of positive psychology. The proliferation of personal positive psychology coaches should occur in such a way that people from all ethnic and socioeconomic groups can have access to them. As we have said elsewhere, positive psychology should be for the many rather than the few (Snyder & Feldman, 2000).

The Balance of Prevention and Enhancement Systems

In this chapter, we describe the prevention and enhancement intercessions separately. Primary and secondary preventions entail efforts to see that negative outcomes do not happen, whereas primary and secondary enhancements reflect efforts to ensure that positive outcomes will happen. Unchained from their problems via primary and secondary preventions, people then can turn their attentions to primary and secondary enhancements related to reaching optimal, even peak, experiences and life satisfactions (Snyder, Thompson, & Heinze, 2003). Together, preventions and enhancements form a powerful dyad for coping and excelling.

It is noteworthy that prevention and enhancement parallel the two major motives in all of psychology. Namely, prevention mirrors those processes aimed at avoiding harmful outcomes, and enhancement mirrors the processed that focus upon attaining beneficial outcomes. The juxtaposing of the avoidance and approach systems has a long heritage in psychology; it includes the early ideas about defenses in Freud's (1915/1957) psychoanalytic theory, behavioral research (Miller, 1944) and phenomenological research (Lewin, 1951) on the topic of human conflict, and, more recently, health psychology (Carver & Scheier, 1993, 1994).

Although the avoidance system has been portrayed as counterproductive (for review, see Snyder & Pulvers, 2001), these earlier views have ignored the possibility that, via avoidant thinking, people are proactively thinking and behaving to avoid a later bad outcome. Indeed, this latter definition is at the core of the primary and secondary prevention approaches, in which obvious benefits do result. Instead of suggesting that avoidance is always "bad," we close this chapter by suggesting that the avoidant and approach processes (or, as they sometimes are called, the aversive and appetitive processes) both act to help people cope. Thus, prevention and enhancement intercessions provide challenges that people must balance in their daily lives.

Appendix A: Effective Secondary Preventions (Psychotherapies) for Adult Problems

Problem	Effective Psychotherapy Treatments
Depression	Social skills training to change depression-eliciting environments; cognitive therapy to alter counterproductive thinking; hope training to change goal-directed thinking; interpersonal/marital training to alter depression-maintaining styles of interacting
Bipolar Depression	Medication (lithium carbonate) plus cognitive behavioral therapy aimed at refuting elated or depressive thinking; family intervention to lower stress and to enhance problem solving and communication
Social Phobias	Cognitive behavioral therapy that challenges threat orientations, plus practice in pairing social avoidance behaviors with coping skills and relaxation
Simple Phobias	Step-by-step, intensive exposure to fear-inducing stimuli, paired with coping skills and relaxation in the context of behavior therapy
Panic/Agoraphobia	Cognitive behavioral therapy with slowly increasing exposure to anxiety-eliciting stimuli, along with family support, coping skills/relaxation training, and disputation of threat-inducing thought patterns
Generalized Anxiety Disorders	Cognitive behavioral therapy with therapeutic support to challenge threat-inducing thought patterns, along with pairing anxiety-eliciting stimuli with skills/relaxation training
Obsessive-Compulsive Disorders	Behavior therapy with graded exposure to obsession-eliciting cues, pairing of compulsion with coping skills/relaxation, all in the context of family support
Anorexia	Teaching less destructive approaches to assert autonomy; psychodynamic therapy to understand early relationships with caregivers, and insight into present relationship problems (including with helper)
Bulimia	Cognitive behavioral therapy aimed at teaching self-monitoring and problem solving, understanding the precursors of the binge-purge cycle, and disputing the thinking that guides binging-purging
Post-Traumatic Stress Disorders	Pairing of coping skills/relaxation with graded exposure to stimuli that evoke traumatic memories in the context of behavior therapy
Relationship Difficulties	Marital behavioral therapy in which exchange contracts are used, along with skills training in problem solving and communication; couple therapy focused on emotional needs, with special focus on discussing unfulfilled attachment needs and the associated feelings of sadness

(Continued)

(Continued)

Problem	Effective Psychotherapy Treatments
Alcohol Addiction	Multimodal interventions, with family involvement being important; teaching of self control in drinking contexts; attendance at Alcoholics Anonymous (AA); stress-management training, perhaps along with social skills training
Insomnia	Sleep restriction, along with graded withdrawal of any medications, plus relaxation training and disputing of thought patterns that perpetuate insomnia
Smoking Cessation	Cognitive behavioral therapy in which client is given psychoeducation, in addition to teaching of scheduled smoking, gradual withdrawal, and relapse prevention
Heart Disease	Cognitive behavioral therapy, psychoeducation, and family support; dietary counseling, along with physical exercise program and coping/relaxation training
Chronic Pain	Cognitive behavioral therapy, relaxation, and guided imagery training; family work to avoid reinforcing invalid thoughts and behaviors, positive reinforcement for more active lifestyle, and gradual reduction of pain medication

Source: From Carr (2000a, 2000b), Linley & Joseph (2004), Nathan & Gorman (2002), Roth & Fonagy (1996), Snyder (1999a), and Snyder & Ingram (2000a and 2000b).

Appendix B: Hope Therapy Worksheet

Domain	Importance Rating	Satisfaction Rating
Academic		
Family		
Leisure		
Personal Growth		
Health/Fitness		
Romantic		
Social Relationships		
Spiritual		
Work		

My selected domain is:

What would I have to do to increase my satisfaction in this domain?

What is my goal?

What is my pathway to the goal?

How much do I believe that I can make it? (circle one)
A little   Medium   Very much

How much energy do I have to accomplish my goal? (circle one)
A little   Medium   Very much

What makes me think I can attain my goal?

What will slow me down or stop me from reaching my goal?

What is my backup plan?

What are the first three steps to my goal?

1.

2.

3.

Key Terms

Eudaemonic primary enhancements: Enhancements that increase well-being through the setting and reaching of goals. These enhancements are the desirable result of the goal pursuit process, which results in effective functioning and happiness.

Flow: A state of mind that occurs when intrinsically fascinating and engaging activities stretch talents to satisfying levels, in which one loses track of oneself and the passage of time.

Hedonic primary enhancements: Enhancements that increase well-being by maximizing pleasure. This often involves the satisfaction of appetites.

Illusion of uniqueness: The common belief that, in the future, good things will happen to oneself but bad things will happen to other people. This belief is also called *unique invulnerability.*

Meditation: A collection of techniques aimed at focusing the attention in a nonanalytic way that avoids ruminative, rambling, or digressive thought.

Primary enhancements: Enhancements made to establish optimal functioning and satisfaction.

Primary preventions: Actions intended to stop, or lessen the likelihood of, physical or psychological problems before they appear.

Savoring: Thoughts and actions aimed at appreciating and perhaps amplifying a positive experience.

Secondary enhancements: Enhancements that build upon already-optimal functioning and satisfaction to achieve peak experiences.

Secondary preventions: Actions that lessen, eliminate, or contain problems after they appear.

Selective prevention: Primary prevention focused on a particular at-risk population.

Unique invulnerability: See *illusion of uniqueness.*

Universal prevention: Primary prevention aimed at an entire community.

Part VII

Positive Environments

Positive Schooling 16

If you can read this, thank a teacher.

—Car bumper sticker

Because schools play a major role in promoting the tenets of positive psychology, we have included an entire chapter on schooling. *Schooling,* an older word for "education," conveys the importance of the entire community in teaching children. This is why we use the word *schooling* in the title of this chapter. We begin by addressing the unfortunate negative views held by some people about teachers and their work, and explore the characteristics of those few truly bad teachers. Next, we describe the support (or lack thereof) for education in America. Thereafter, we devote most of the chapter to an examination of the six components of effective schools. We then summarize the educational application developed by positive psychology pioneer Donald Clifton, and give a glimpse of some amazing teachers who exemplify positive teaching. Last, we share ideas about thanking teachers who have made positive differences in the lives of their students.

"Teachers Can't Get Jobs in the Real World!"

The very existence of this sentiment suggests that teachers are not recognized for their efforts (Buskist, Benson, & Sikorski, 2005). Not only do teachers receive relatively low salaries for professional work, they also are the targets of derisive comments. On this latter point, I (CRS) was waiting in line to purchase some stamps at the post office when a gentleman ahead of me complained loudly to his friend about "those lazy professors on the hill." Being one of "those lazy professors," I kept quiet, just wanting to get the stamps. Then, this same fellow announced for all in the lobby to hear, "Those professors wouldn't be teaching if they were good enough to get real jobs!" He followed that with a doozy: "As we all know, those who can't make it in the real world are the ones who end up teaching!" No longer could I bite my tongue, and a lively exchange ensued.

Although there is no merit to "those who can't, teach" statements (such as "Those who can, do; those who can't, teach; those who can't teach, teach teachers"), it is likely that all of us unfortunately have endured some bad teachers. So too, however, have we had some truly wonderful teachers. In this regard, many of the ideas in this chapter come from award-winning teachers who have used positive psychology principles in their classroom efforts (see Snyder, 2005b). These instructors *are* talented . . . they could succeed in many life arenas beyond the classroom. As such, we dedicate this chapter to "Those who can, teach!"

Negative Psychology: "Those Who Can't, Shouldn't Be Teaching"

We agree that some instructors are so bad that they should not go near classrooms. Such teachers are the ones "who, when given the honor and the privilege to teach, bore rather than inspire, settle for the lowest common denominator rather than aspire to the highest possible numerator, take the job for granted rather than being continually amazed at the blessing—sins against all the minds they have closed, misinformed and alienated from education" (Zimbardo, 2005, p. 12).

That these bad teachers can do harm is more than sheer speculation; the related research consistently shows that poor teachers have adverse effects on their students (for an overview, see Jennifer King Rice's 2003 book, *Teacher Quality*). In fact, the low quality of teachers has been found to be the most influential of all school-related factors in terms of undermining students' learning and their attitudes about education in general (Rice, 2003). Furthermore, the effects of poor teachers are both additive and cumulative over time (Sanders & Rivers, 1996), with teacher quality accounting for 7.5% of the variance in students' achievements (Hanushek, Kain, & Rivkin, as reported in Goldhaber, 2002).

What factors determine teacher quality? Of the various ways of tapping quality, a teacher's relevant educational background and degrees are two of the most influential sources when it comes to enhancing students' learning (Monk & King, 1994; Rowan, Chiang, & Miller, 1997). Likewise, Darling-Hammond and Youngs (2002) reported that indices of teacher achievements and adequate preparation were robust predictors of students' achievements in the areas of mathematics and reading. To concretize the impact of teacher quality, consider the finding that the difference between having had a bad teacher and a good teacher reflects an entire grade level in student achievement (Hanushek, 1994). Overall, therefore, poor teachers leave behind trails of intellectual boredom and disrespect.

Of course, there are legitimate reasons that some teachers "turn bad." The most obvious is burnout, where the instructor loses enthusiasm after repeatedly encountering blockages and lack of support for his or her efforts (see Maslach, 1999). There is no excuse, however, for a teacher who does nothing to address such burnout. It is hard to have sympathy for the teachers who continue to just "send it in" when it comes to enthusiasm and preparation for their students. Not only have they failed to teach formative young minds when they are most open to the excitement of learning, but they also may have turned off these minds for life (see Zimbardo, 1999).

Although negative teachers are relatively rare, even one is too many. It would be bad enough if these poor teachers only impaired the learning of their students, but they also may inflict psychological pain and damage. Students tragically may become the unwilling participants in self-fulfilling prophecies in which they fail in both the academic and interpersonal spheres. Thus, as impassioned as we are about seeing to it that positive psychology fills the minds and classrooms of our teachers and their students, so, too, are we adamant about wanting poor teachers identified very early in their careers and either taught to change or shown the door out of the classroom.

Should your own education have included one or more poor teachers, we have prepared an exercise for you. We encourage you to follow the steps outlined in the Personal Mini-Experiments, which may help you to "bury" the bad influences of your previous poor teachers. These teachers did enough damage when you were in their classes; we developed this exercise to lessen the likelihood of any lingering negative effect on your life.

"No Child Left Behind" and Beyond

In a letter to John Adams (anthologized in Barber & Battistoni, 1993, p. 41), Thomas Jefferson shared his vision of changing the American aristocracy of "privilege by inheritance" to a more natural type of aristocracy based on talent. Since those early times, the American ideal has been that public education should make one's life outcomes less dependent upon family status and more dependent on the use of public education. Thus, schools were idealized as making huge differences in the lives of our children.

Personal Mini-Experiments

The Power of Positive (and Negative) Teachers

Throughout this chapter, we are reminded of the powerful effects of teachers on our lives. Here, we ask that you consider the effects of a bad teacher and a good teacher on your life.

Letting Go of a Bad Teacher: Think back over your days in grade school, junior high school, high school, college, and perhaps even graduate school. Think about one teacher in particular who made you deplore going to school, not to mention learning. Take a blank piece of paper, and see how much you can remember about this teacher. Write down what she or he looked like, along with the grade and place where you met. Describe how this teacher ran the class. What were the most negative things you can remember this teacher doing? Did this teacher make fun of you in front of the other students? Would this teacher not trust or believe you? Did this teacher make you feel dumb? Did this teacher make fun of your speech or clothes? Did this teacher give you the impression that he or she couldn't care less about you and your success in life?

Once you have written a fairly good summary of this negative teacher, then turn the page over and write what you took away from that class and that instructor for the rest of your life. Do messages that started in that class still play in your mind today? Do you think certain things about yourself even now because of something that happened with that teacher? When you have answered these questions, then say to yourself, "I am going to bury any influence this teacher had on the way I think." Then, repeat several times, "I am going to stop the bad lessons that [teacher's name] taught me!" Feel free to make any other statements that you want—just as if this old teacher were sitting in a chair across from you.

When you have finished making your statements to this bad teacher, grab a shovel and go outside and dig a hole. That's right, dig a hole! Now, put the shovel down, and say goodbye to the bad things you learned from this teacher. Next, take the sheet of paper on which you wrote about this teacher, and tear it into many pieces. Then, throw the pieces of paper into the hole, and cover it over with dirt. Walk away (don't forget the shovel), and vow to yourself that this lousy teacher never again will influence your life. Finally, buy yourself a treat to celebrate this ritual.

Saying Thank You to a Good Teacher: We again ask that you look back over your school days. But, this time, recall those teachers who were superb. They were so good that you actually looked forward to going to their classes. You enjoyed learning from these teachers. Now, take a blank piece of paper, and write the teacher's name at the top of the page. Then, write everything you can remember about this teacher. Write down what this teacher looked like, the grade and place where you met, and how this teacher ran the class. What were some of the most positive things that you can remember this teacher doing?

Once you have a good summary of this positive teacher, turn the page over, and write what you took away from this teacher for the rest of your life. Are there any messages that you still play in your mind that were cultivated in that teacher's class?

Because of things that happened with that teacher, do you now hold certain positive views of yourself? Perhaps this teacher made you feel smart or clever. Did this teacher make a point to give you credit when you did well? Did this teacher truly care that you succeeded in life? Do you still practice certain positive behaviors that you owe to your interactions with this teacher?

Once you have completed this assignment for one or more teachers, then try to find out where they can be reached today. Some still may be teaching. Others probably will be retired. With the advent of e-mail, it has become easier to contact people whom we met earlier in our lives. Now, go ahead and write a thank-you note to each of these positive teachers. You will feel great for having done this, and we can assure you that the teacher will get a tremendous lift from your message. There is nothing more gratifying to a teacher than to be told that she or he played a positive role in the life of a former student. We often do not take the time to thank the truly important people in our lives for the things they have done on our behalf. Your former teachers will treasure your note all the more if you describe specific instances where they helped you. So, too, will they cherish hearing about the successes and accomplishments in your life.

Unfortunately, this romanticized view of schools in America often has been more a dream than a reality. It is ironic that President Lyndon Johnson believed strongly in the power of schools as the "great equalizer" (a phrase popularized by 19th-century educational philosopher and leader Horace Mann) of people. Accordingly, he commissioned a huge study, the results of which he (and others) believed would show once and for all that the quality of school resources (e.g., facilities, curricula, books) was responsible for the superior educational outcomes of Caucasian Americans, compared to those of people of color. Contrary to these expectations, however, the publication of the Coleman Report (technically called the Equality of Educational Opportunity Report) in 1966 (Coleman et al., 1966) led to the conclusion that "schools do not make much of a difference" in the outcomes of students (see Fritzberg, 2001, 2002). This was an extremely disturbing bottom line for educators as well as President Johnson.

Do the findings of the Coleman et al. (1966) report mean that there is nothing that can be done in the way of schooling to improve the learning of students? Fortunately, the answer is no, and we already have touched upon the factor that does seem to yield better student learning: teacher quality. Before we address what can be done to improve the quality of our teachers, however, we describe the present environment of education in the United States.

With the passage of the No Child Left Behind Act in 2001, the emphasis increasingly has been upon accountability of teachers and school systems for producing targeted learning and performance objectives. For an excellent overview of this approach, we suggest the edited volume *No Child Left Behind? The Politics and Practice of Accountability* by Peterson and West (2003). (Appendix A at the end of this chapter illustrates the efforts of psychology departments to monitor the effectiveness of their educational efforts.)

As we have noted, research shows that the quality of teachers is crucial to better learning-related outcomes (Monk & King, 1994; Rice, 2003; Rowan et al., 1997). How, then, can we increase the number of qualified teachers in our schools? As with many questions, money appears to play an important role here. That is to say, the relevant research shows that school districts with higher salaries and better physical facilities are likely to attract and keep the higher-quality teachers (Hanushek, Kain, O'Brien, & Rivkin, 2004). Furthermore, competition between schools does raise the quality of teachers as well as improve the overall quality of education generally (Hanushek & Rivkin, 2003). (It should be noted, however, that teachers are not totally driven by salary, and the race or ethnicity and achievement of the students in given schools also play roles [Hanushek & Rivkin, 2004].)

It appears that legislation to increase taxes to pay for schools and teachers is not receiving strong support among American voters. We see two harmful implications of this trend. First, only the most affluent school districts will be able to pay the high salaries necessary to attract the best teachers. Obviously, this perpetuates the problem of the lack of outstanding teachers in poor school districts. Second, wealthier families are sending their children to private schools. Accordingly, the public schools are left to get by with lower-quality teachers.

Because of these trends, we foresee major challenges to the contributions of positive psychology to 21st-century American schooling. These challenges are magnified by the fact that approximately 3,000,000 teachers, from kindergarten through high-school, will need to be replaced in the next decade because of retirements (Goldhaber, 2002).

The Components of Positive Schooling

Before reviewing the components of **positive schooling** (which is an approach to education that consists of a foundation of care, trust, and respect for diversity, where teachers develop tailored goals for each student to engender learning and then work with him or her to develop the plans and motivation to reach their goals), we acknowledge briefly some of the major educators who have paved the way for this approach. Noted philosophers such as Benjamin Franklin, John Stuart Mill, Herbert Spencer, and John Dewey focused on the assets of students (Lopez, Janowski, & Wells, 2005). Alfred Binet (Binet & Simon, 1916) often is considered the father of the concept of mental age, but he also emphasized the enhancement of student skills rather than paying attention only to the remediation of weaknesses. Likewise, Elizabeth Hurlock (1925) accentuated praise as more influential than criticism as a determinant of students' efforts. Similarly, Lewis Terman (Terman & Oden, 1947) spent his whole career exploring the thinking of truly brilliant learners, and Arthur Chickering (1969) sought to understand the evolution of students' talents. (See Chapter 14 for a discussion of Chickering's views of college student development.) More recently, Donald Clifton identified, and then expanded on, the particular talents of students, rather than focusing on their weaknesses (see Buckingham & Clifton, 2001; Clifton & Anderson, 2002; Clifton & Nelson, 1992; Rath & Clifton, 2004).

We next explore the major components of positive schooling (see Buskist et al., 2005; Lopez et al., 2005; Ritchel, 2005). For the reader interested in an actual one-week curriculum to instill positive psychology ideas in a high-school course, we recommend Amy Fineburg's (2002) unit; moreover, details of various college curricula for positive teaching can be attained at http://www.positivepsychology.org/teachingpp.htm.

Figure 16.1 is a visual representation of the lessons that are common in positive schooling. This figure shows the positive psychology schoolhouse as being built of six parts, from the ground up. We begin with the foundation, where we describe the importance of care, trust, and diversity. Then, the first and second floors of our positive schoolhouse represent teaching goals, planning, and the motivation of students. The third floor holds hope, and the roof represents the societal contributions and paybacks produced by our positive psychology school graduates.

CARE, TRUST, AND RESPECT FOR DIVERSITY

We begin with a foundation that involves caring, trust, and respect for diversity. It is absolutely crucial to have a supportive atmosphere of care and trust because students flourish in such an environment. In attending award ceremonies for outstanding teachers, we have noticed that both the teachers and their students typically comment on the importance of a sense of caring. Students need as role models teachers who consistently are responsive and available. Such teacher care and positive emotions provide the secure base that allows young people to explore and find ways to achieve their own important academic and life goals (Shorey, Snyder, Yang, & Lewin, 2003).

Perhaps a personal story will help to show the importance of teachers caring for students. I (CRS) always thought that I wanted to be a teacher, and I knew this even when I started my college education. In the fall of 1963, I was a first-semester freshman at Southern Methodist University, and the beginning of my college career was going well. Then, on November 22, 1963, not 10 miles from my college, President

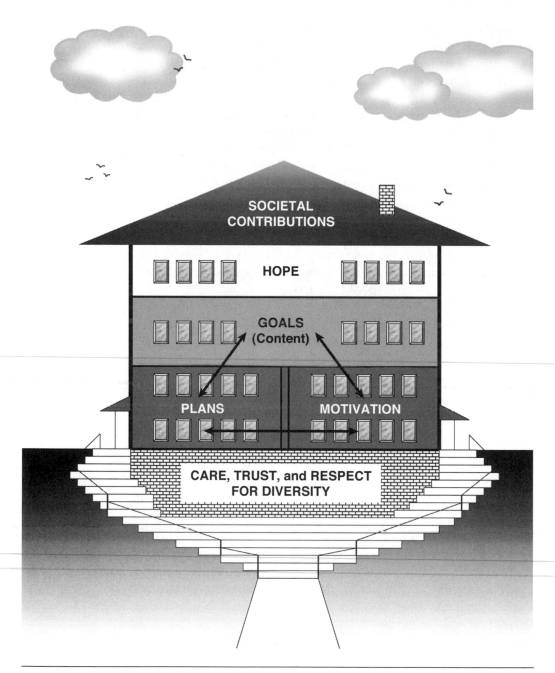

Figure 16.1   The Components of Positive Schooling

John F. Kennedy was assassinated in downtown Dallas, Texas. Having campaigned for Kennedy, I found his death so devastating that I told my instructors I was going to drop out of college. I had not been able to go to my classes, and, when I did attend, I was so upset that I couldn't take notes.

In response to my announcement, my instructors spent considerable time talking with me, and they told me that I needed to grieve. Their caring reactions kept me from leaving college, and I probably would not have been able to become a college professor years later had these instructors not helped me at that crucial time. Good teachers know when to reach out and help students who are facing crises.

Trust in the classroom has received considerable attention among educators, and the consensus is that it yields both psychological and performance benefits for students (Bryk & Schneider, 2002; Collins, 2001). Trust is crucial from the earliest grades on up. For example, in their influential 2003 book, *Learning to Trust: Transforming Difficult Elementary Classrooms Through Developmental Discipline*, Marilyn Watson (an educational psychologist) and Laura Ecken (an elementary school teacher) tackle the thorny problem of classroom management and discipline in the elementary schools. Their approach is to establish trusting relationships with the most difficult students, with the logic that this then will have ripple effects that spread to the rest of the class.

Watson and Ecken (2003) advocate what they call **developmental discipline**. This notion is derived from the principles of attachment theory (see Chapter 13), which advocates helping those students who have insecure attachments to caregivers. Watson and Ecken write, "The building of caring and trusting relationships becomes the most important goal in the socialization of these children. Of course, while we are building these relationships, we must find nonpunitive ways to prevent the children who are aggressive and controlling from harming others and to encourage self-reliance and confidence in those who are withdrawn and dependent" (p. 12). For the reader interested in how to establish trust in secondary school classrooms with at-risk students, we also suggest the 1998 volume, *Empowering Discipline* by Vicki Phillips.

Instructors must make sure that there is a sense of trust in their classrooms. They must avoid becoming cynical about students, because this undermines the trust that is so crucial for learning. Often, students would rather misbehave (and suffer any punishment) than look dumb in front of their peers. In their interactions with students, therefore, positive teachers try to find ways to make students look good. Unless students sense the teacher's respect, they will not take the risks that are so important for learning. At times, the very best teaching results when the instructor is quiet and listens to the views of the students in a class. Award-winning teacher Jeanne Stahl of Morris Brown College has commented, "Silence is the best approach when you are not sure where a student is coming from or heading" (Stahl, 2005, p. 91).

A major part of caring for students involves spending large amounts of time with them. When undergraduates were asked what they thought were the most important aspects of being a college professor (e.g., research, preparing lectures and exams, committee meetings), they consistently reported that teachers' willingness to spend time with them was the most important characteristic (Bjornesen, 2000).

Another aspect of the positive psychology foundation for schooling involves the importance of diversity of student backgrounds and opinions in the classroom. This starts by encouraging students to become sensitive to the ideas of people other than those from their own ethnic or age cohort. This can be accomplished by revealing to students that they have much in common with those who are different from them. Likewise, it is crucial to make certain that the views of all the different constituencies in a class are given voices in the classroom. The positive psychology premise is to foster a "WE/ME" viewpoint—an environment for US. (The "WE/ME" perspective is discussed extensively in Chapter 18.) A useful visual means of helping students to think beyond their own viewpoints (ME) is to have them consider the mirror-like views of others (WE).

Elliot Aronson

Source: Reprinted with permission of Elliot Aronson.

A superb approach for developing a "WE/ME" atmosphere is to implement the "jigsaw classroom" designed by University of California–Santa Cruz professor emeritus Elliot Aronson (Aronson & Patnoe, 1997). In this approach, the students and teachers use group-based goals, and the students from different backgrounds are placed in work units where they must share information in order for the group—and therefore each member—to succeed. In the jigsaw classroom, each student has part of the information that is vital to the success of the group as a whole, and thus there is strong motivation to include each student's input. The jigsaw classroom teaches cooperation rather than competition; the related research shows that students learn the content along with respect for their fellow students. The jigsaw classroom also helps keep students from becoming "grade predators," who want to succeed through invidious competitions and social comparisons with each other (Aronson, 2000; Aronson, Blaney, Stephin, Sikes, & Snapp, 1978).

Before leaving this section on diversity, we emphasize how crucial it is to have compensatory programs aimed at students who may have difficulty in learning. We discuss such programs in detail in Chapter 15 on interceding to help people. One point that was not emphasized in that chapter, and that must be a part of positive psychology schooling, is that we must have programs to stimulate our truly gifted students. Very often, the unfortunate attitude prevails that gifted students already have such tremendous advantages that we should "just leave them alone." We applaud the words of Martin Seligman (1998d):

> Before World War II, high talent was a focal mission of psychology. As our field became increasingly focused on clinical populations, genius was all but forgotten. But central to the presidential theme of positive psychology—psychology dedicated to building the best things in life as well as healing the worst—is the search for and building of the full expression of high talent.

It is not just psychology that has neglected gifted and talented children. [Neglect is] found throughout society—even up to the top policy makers in the government. I had a striking encounter with a high official of the U.S. Department of Education at a meeting of the Council of Science Society Presidents recently. He had given a speech on the Clinton administration's uphill, but laudable, policy of attempting to raise the average science and math scores of all American children.

"The future of American science and math depends not only on a scientifically literate citizenry but more crucially on the very talented young people who will become our future scientists and mathematicians," I commented. "What are you doing to help these children?"

"Gifted children take care of themselves," he replied.

This widespread belief is both mistaken and dangerous. It consigns a very large number of gifted children to fall by the wayside in despair and frustration. Intellectual giftedness comes in many guises, and parents, peers, and schools all too often fail to recognize or support high talents—and worse, reject them into mediocrity. This neglect is not benign; it squanders a precious, irreplaceable national resource under the banner of "anti-elitism."

Psychology must take up their cause again. (p. 3)

Having made this point about stimulating our brightest students, we would close this section by noting that the foundation of positive psychology schooling rests upon an atmosphere in which teachers and students have respect and care for various points of view and backgrounds. Such respect flows from teachers to students and from students to teachers.

GOALS (CONTENT)

The component of goals is represented by the second floor of the strengths schoolhouse (see Figure 16.1). Exploring the responses of students from kindergarten to college, Stanford University Professor Carol Dweck has put together an impressive program of research showing that goals provide a means of targeting students' learning efforts. Moreover, such goals are especially helpful if agreed upon by the teacher and students (Dweck, 1999; Locke, & Latham, 2002). Perhaps the most conducive targets are the stretch goals, in which the student seeks a slightly more difficult learning goal than attained previously. Reasonably challenging goals engender productive learning, especially if the goals can be tailored to particular students (or groups of students).

It is important for students to feel some sense of input in regard to their teachers' conduct of classes. Of course, the instructors set the classroom goals, but in doing so they are wise to consider the reactions of their

Carol Dweck

Source: Photo by Steve Goldband. Reprinted with permission.

previous students. The success of class goals involves making the materials relevant to students' real-life experiences whenever possible (Snyder & Shorey, 2002). In turn, tailoring to students' experiences makes it more likely that students will become involved in and learn the material (see Dweck, 1999).

We advise against emphasizing grades too strictly once learning goals are set. Adherence to grading curves, for example, can turn students into grade predators who are more fascinated with their performances and with doing better than their peers than they are with learning. Indeed, this set has been linked to lower levels of hope (Shorey et al., 2004) and more test-taking anxieties (Dweck, 1999).

It also helps to make the goals understandable and concrete, as well as to take a larger learning goal and divide it into smaller subgoals that can be tackled in stages. Likewise, as we noted with respect to diversity issues in the previous section, goal setting is facilitated when teachers allow part of students' grades to be determined by group activities in which cooperation with other students is essential. Again, Aronson's "jigsaw classroom" (www.jigsaw.org) paradigm is very useful in setting such goals.

PLANS

In Figure 16.1, the first floor of the strengths schoolhouse is divided into plans and motivation, both of which interact with the educational goals on the second floor (and with content). Like building science on accumulating ideas, teaching necessitates a careful planning process on the part of instructors.

Robert Cialdini

Source: Reprinted with permission of Robert Cialdini.

Yet another planning approach is championed by the noted social psychologist Robert Cialdini of Arizona State University (see Cialdini, 2005). Once Professor Cialdini has established a teaching goal regarding given psychological content, he then poses mystery stories for students. By solving the mystery, the student has learned the particular content. (The inherent need for closure [see Kruglanksi & Webster, 1996] regarding the mysteries also motivates the students; motivation is the companion to planning, which we discuss in the next section. Likewise, because the mystery stories have beginnings, middles, and ends, there is the inherent desire on the part of students to get to the conclusion [see Green, Strange, & Brock, 2002, on the drive to traverse a narrative].)

Another consideration in raising students' motivations is to make the material relevant to them (Buskist et al., 2005). At the most basic level, when the course information is relevant, students are more likely to attend class, to pay attention, and to make comments during the lectures (Lowman, 1995; Lutsky, 1999). To increase the relevance of material, instructors can develop classroom demonstrations and at-home exploration (such as the Personal Mini-Experiments and Life Enhancement Strategies in this book) of various phenomena applicable to situations that the students encounter outside the classroom. Some instructors conduct surveys at the beginning of a semester, in which they ask students to describe positive and negative events that have happened in their lives. Then, the instructor can use the more frequently cited events to construct classroom demonstrations (Snyder, 2004). Or, once the instructor has described a phenomenon, students can be asked to give examples from their own experience.

Before leaving the topic of relevance, we caution aging instructors against trying to co-opt the lifestyle manifestations of much younger students. This is a sure-fire way to turn off student motivation. In the words of Snyder (2004),

> Have you ever seen a 50- or 60-something professor who is trying everything possible to be as "hip" as his or her 21-year-old students? I do not know what is most pitiful about this specter. Is it the aging professor's youthful clothes that look so wrong? Is it the out-of-place punked hairstyle fashioned on the head with far too few hairs? Or it is the graying professor's awkward attempts to borrow college students' language? It is folly, in my view, for an older instructor to try to remain "hip" and be part of the young crowd. Indeed, I think that such professors come across as ludicrous and pandering. Give it up, I say, for it is only when we are young—for it is who we really are then—that such hipness is appropriate. Additionally, the truth is that our students do not want a hip-hop "pal" as their instructor. (pp. 17–18)

MOTIVATION (PLUS ENLIVENING THE COURSE CONTENTS FOR STUDENTS)

Teachers must be enthused about their materials so as to carry out the plans that they have made for their classes (see the interactive arrow between plans and motivation on the first floor of Figure 16.1). Instructors are models of enthusiasm for their students. Therefore, when instructors make lesson goals and plans interesting to themselves, their students easily can pick up on this energy.

Motivated teachers are sensitive to the needs and reactions of their students. Strengths-based instructors also take students' questions very seriously and make every effort to give their best answers. If the teacher does not know the answer to a student question, it is enlivening to the class to inform them that, although the instructor doesn't know the answer at that time, he or she will make every effort to find it. Then, the teacher follows through to locate the answer to the question and presents it at the next class period; students typically are very appreciative of such responsiveness.

Teachers also raise the motivational level when they take risks and try new approaches in class (Halperin & Desrochers, 2005). When such risk-taking results in a classroom exercise that does not work, the instructor can have a good laugh at him- or herself. Humor raises the energy for the next classroom exercise, along with the effort level of the teacher. A strengths-based teaching motto is, "If you don't laugh at yourself, you have missed the biggest joke of all" (Snyder, 2005a).

Anything an instructor can do to increase students' accountability also can raise their motivation (Halperin & Desrochers, 2005). Relatedly, students who expect to be called upon by their instructors typically are prepared for each class—they read the material and follow the lecture (McDougall & Granby, 1996).

Recall that the previously discussed jigsaw classroom approach fosters the learning and planning of group goals and that in doing so it also imparts motivation to students as they work together. Indeed, a sense of energy can come from being part of a team effort.

Lastly, praise is very motivating. It is best to deliver this privately, however, because an individual student may feel uncomfortable when singled out in front of peers. Public praise also may raise the propensities of students to compete with each other. An office visit or a meeting with the student outside the classroom is a good time to note the student's good work or progress (or even to offer praise for asking good questions). Furthermore, e-mail is a ready-made vehicle for privately delivering positive feedback that may be motivating. The opportunities for appropriately interacting with and motivating students are many, and positive psychology teachers often try to convey such energizing feedback.

HOPE

If the previously mentioned lessons regarding goals, planning, and motivation have been applied in a classroom, then there will be a spirit of inquiry that students will pick up (Ritschel, 2005). As Auburn University award-winning teacher William Buskist and his colleagues (2005) put it,

> [A]n essential aspect of our teaching is to pass the torch—to share our academic values, curiosities, and discipline-focused enthusiasm and to encourage students to embrace these values and qualities and to own them. Teaching is not about being dispassionate dispensers of facts and figures. Teaching is about influence. It is about caring deeply about ideas and how those ideas are derived, understood, and expressed. It is about caring deeply for the subject matter and for those students with whom we are sharing it. And it is through such passionate caring that we inspire students. (p. 116)

William Buskist

Source: Reprinted with permission of William Buskist.

When students acquire this spirit, their learning expands to increase their sense of empowerment. Thus, students are empowered to become lifelong problem solvers. This "learning how to learn" pulls from goals-directed pathways thinking as well as from the "I can" motivation. Therefore, positive psychology schooling not only imparts the course contents, it also produces a sense of hope in the student learners. (See Chapter 9 for a detailed discussion of hope.) Hope is depicted in the attic of the positive schoolhouse in Figure 16.1. A hopeful student believes that she or he will continue to learn long after stepping out of the classroom. Or perhaps it is more apt to say that hopeful thinking knows no walls or boundaries in the life of a student who never stops learning.

SOCIETAL CONTRIBUTIONS

A final positive psychology lesson is that students understand that they are part of a larger societal scheme in which they share what they have learned with other people. As shown in the potentially nourishing cloud above the metaphorical schoolhouse in Figure 16.1, these societal contributions represent the lasting "paybacks" that an educated person gives to those around him or her—whether this means teaching children to think positively or sharing insights and excitement with the multitude of others with whom they come into contact over the course of their lifetimes. Positive education thus turns students into teachers who continue to share what they have learned with others. In this way, the benefits of the learning process are passed on to a wide range of other people. In positive schooling, therefore, students become teachers of others.

One Example of Positive Schooling: The StrengthsQuest Program

StrengthsQuest is a program to develop and engage high school and college students so that they can succeed in their academic pursuits in particular and in their lives in general. This program owes its existence to positive psychologist Donald Clifton, who began his work on this approach as a professor of education psychology at the University of Nebraska–Lincoln in the 1950s. Before elaborating on his theory and related educational program, we salute this remarkable man. Don Clifton has been commended by the American Psychological Association as a "father" of the strengths-based approach in psychology as well as the "grandfather" of positive psychology (McKay & Greengrass, 2003). Contrary to the intellectual and applied currents of the 1950s through 1990s, which swam in the murky water of weakness-oriented psychology, Professor Clifton always seemed to have a crucial and different question: "What would result if we studied what is right rather than wrong with people?"

This question is at the core of the StrengthsQuest Program (see Clifton & Anderson, 2002). Of course, this positive approach contrasts with the traditional approach to education, wherein students are explicitly and implicitly taught that they must "fix" their deficiencies, and if they do not, they are flunked (Anderson, 2005). In terms of the hope and related motivations discussed in the previous section, the StrengthsQuest Program energizes students. This follows from students' realizations that they are perceived as having the necessary natural cognitive talents to succeed in school.

The StrengthsQuest Program begins by having students complete the Clifton StrengthsFinder, an online, computerized assessment of the five areas of their greatest natural talents. The assessment involves 180 items; for each item, the respondent selects the most applicable descriptor of a pair (e.g., "I read instructions carefully" vs. "I like to jump right into things"). The student also rates the degree to which the selected statement is better than the one with which it is paired. There are 34 possible themes (as shown in Table 4.1, pages 55–56), and the student learns which five themes are the most applicable to him or her.

To date, more than 100 studies have used the StrengthsFinder assessment approach in accurately predicting a variety of outcome markers (Schmidt & Rader, 1999). Moreover, this technique has undergone considerable empirical construct validation (Lopez, Hodges, & Harter, 2005).

Next, the students complete (either online or in a printed format) the workbook *StrengthsQuest: Discover and Develop Your Strengths in Academics, Career, and Beyond* (Clifton & Anderson, 2002). This workbook helps students (as well as teachers, counselors, residence hall coordinators, and others who work with students) to understand and build their signature strengths in ongoing school efforts. Lastly, the students undertake more in-depth training by signing onto the StrengthsQuest website (www.strengthsquest.com).

In the second and third stages of this educational approach, students work on their signature strengths as revealed in the five most robust StrengthsFinder themes. Clifton and his colleagues, including the researchers at the Gallup Organization (which the Clifton family owns and operates), based this second phase on their research findings that the very best achievers and students (1) clearly recognize their talents and develop them; (2) apply strengths in those areas where there are good matches to natural talents and interests, and (3) come up with ways to apply their assets in the pursuit of desired goals. This part of the program is similar to the goals and pathways components discussed in the previous section on positive schooling (Anderson, 2005).

Parallel with these three steps in the Clifton approach, students appear to go though three distinct stages (as reflected in papers written by students undergoing this program; Clifton & Harter, 2003). In the first stage, it appears that students identify their talents; in the second and third stages, respectively, they have revelations about integrating these areas of strengths into their self-conceptualizations, and they thereafter make behavioral changes (Buckingham & Clifton, 2001). As the program advances, participating students notice examples of things they are doing that reflect their natural predilections and talents (e.g., taking a leadership role in difficult situations, giving instructions to others, learning particular new skills in given areas very easily). Not only do students recognize their talents, they also increasingly begin to "own" them.

The Baylor University StrengthsQuest Program

Baylor University is located in Waco, Texas. It is the largest Baptist university in the world, with more than 14,000 students presently enrolled. The faculty and staff of Baylor University support the mission statement "to educate men and women for worldwide leadership and service by integrating academic excellence and Christian commitment within a caring community." Accordingly, they have developed a strengths-based development program that incorporates Chapel Friday StrengthsQuest Presentation.

This program included over 2,000 freshman students in the fall 2004 semester. It begins during the summer, when students attend a university orientation. Students initially complete the Clifton StrengthsFinder (parents also may choose to take the measure). Later, when they arrive in the fall, they participate in the 6-week Chapel Friday curriculum. Faculty and staff who have been trained to disseminate a strengths development curriculum lead small groups of students in Friday sessions. The program goal is to help students identify "callings" based on students' understanding of their personal talents and strengths.

To assist in building a campus-wide effort to use strengths in everyday life, junior and senior students are trained as resident assistants (RAs) whose job it is to encourage the development of individual students' strengths. Each RA is informed of particular student's strengths; the RA then uses the student's strengths during planning sessions. Career counselors also use information about strengths to assist in career and major decision making. Certain student populations are targeted for the strengths program, including those in the study skills courses, student athletes, and leadership programs.

Along with the students, Baylor University faculty and staff complete the measure. Additionally, new staff members take part in an orientation seminar that encourages a strengths approach to education.

Baylor University educators believe that the Chapel Friday StrengthsQuest Presentation helps students to both understand and use their personal strengths, specifically those pertaining to vocational developments. This is especially true of students who work with juniors and seniors individually to create strong mentoring relationships. Anecdotal evidence suggests that the Chapel Friday StrengthsQuest Presentation appears to benefit students. In the words of one of the Baylor students, "This useful information undoubtedly has given many students on the Baylor campus a better understanding of their place in life and perhaps some prospective areas to which they may shape their academic studies."

The StrengthsQuest Program is gaining more attention in high schools and colleges across the United States. Furthermore, the available outcome studies suggest that the StrengthsQuest Program has positive effects for students (see Hodges & Harter, 2005). A study conducted with 212 UCLA students who underwent the StrengthsQuest Program, for example, found that they reported significant increases in altruism, confidence, efficacy, and hope (Crabtree, 2002; Rath, 2002). Likewise, a study conducted at another large state university found that student's state hope (i.e., goal-focused motivation linked to a particular time and situation, see Snyder et al. [1996] and Chapter 9) increased because of their involvement in the StrengthsQuest Program (Hodges & Clifton, 2004). What is especially noteworthy about these findings, taken as a whole, is the degree to which the activities involved in the StrengthsQuest Program map onto the hope-related components (agency, pathways, and goals) described earlier in this chapter and shown in Figure 16.1.

Teaching as a Calling

Just as negative teachers have damaged this process, so, too, have positive teachers unleashed the enthusiasm and joys of learning. These teachers in positive schooling see their efforts as a calling rather than work (Wrzesniewski, McCauley, Rozin, & Schwartz, 1997). A **calling** is defined as a strong motivation in which a person repeatedly takes a course of action that is intrinsically satisfying (see Buskist, Benson, & Sikorski, 2005). When positive psychology tenets are applied to teaching, we believe that the instructors behave as if they had callings in that they demonstrate a profound and strong love for teaching.

Some examples from master teachers may give the reader a better sense of their dedication. Wilbert McKeachie of the University of Michigan, who is widely heralded as having "written the book" on positive teaching at the college level, is approaching his 60th year of teaching. About his teaching, McKeachie (2002, p. 487) states that he looks forward to "preparing for the next week's classes, leading discussions, lecturing, presenting demonstrations, working with teaching assistants, interacting with students from diverse backgrounds, reading student journals—even commenting on and grading tests." To give the reader an appreciation of the common factors shared by effective teachers, Appendix B at the end of this chapter contains an essay written by Professor McKeachie in which he traces the teaching process from the times of William James to the present.

Another patriarch among college teaching is Charles Brewer of Furman University. Professor Brewer depicts his teaching as "delightful, invigorating, mysterious, frustrating, passionate, precious, and sacred." Professor Brewer (2002, p. 507) even admits that "teaching is more fun than most

Charles Brewer

Source: Reprinted with permission of Charles Brewer.

people should have." To give the reader a sense of the brilliance and dedication that Dr. Brewer brings to his teaching, we include the following article written about him by the president of Furman University.

Dr. Brewer Has Passion for Art of Teaching

DAVID SHI

President, Furman University

Furman has always been blessed with exceptional professors. One of our finest is Dr. Charles Brewer. A native of Arkansas, he has taught psychology at Furman for over 35 years, and he has received every major award the university can bestow, including the Meritorious Teaching Award and the William Kenan Jr. Chair of Psychology. Alumni and friends have endowed a fund in the Psychology Department to honor him. He has also received the South Carolina Governor's Distinguished Professor Award as well as the Career Achievement Award and Distinguished Teaching Award from the American Psychological Association.

Over the years, Dr. Brewer has become a legendary campus figure. When students say they are taking "Brewer," it carries special meaning. Teaching to him is a noble calling rather than simply a career. He displays an almost holy reverence for learning, and he shares such passion with his students and colleagues.

People quickly realize that Dr. Brewer views learning as an exalted activity, a rare human privilege that should not be shirked or sullied. He assaults lazy thinking, and he lets students know when they fall short of his expectations and their own abilities. Whatever the specific title or topic of his course, whatever the actual material to be covered, he remains focused on a broader goal: to teach students how to think and speak and write for themselves.

"Much of what teachers do," he once told the Furman faculty, "is inappropriate and a waste of time." Dispensing information, he explained, should not be the primary purpose of higher education. Instead of such "fact-limited teaching," he seeks to help students see the principles behind the details and to become independent thinkers themselves. He wants them to ask why as often as they ask what.

Blessed with a rapier wit, keen mind, extraordinary intelligence, and an unflagging elegance and brilliance of language, Dr. Brewer demonstrates an important truth: Great teaching cannot be reduced to a formula. It is an art, not a science, a messy, complicated human endeavor that springs from the sincerity and energy of the teacher.

In his case, he sees teaching as a dramatic art; he transforms his classroom into a stage. He is as entertaining as he is learned. His teaching is theatrical, his methods eccentric, his ideals transparent. His style is urgent, intense, and embodied.

(Continued)

(Continued)

He himself is a perpetual student, and he is willing to go to great lengths to excite his students about learning. During his classes, he is known to climb on the desk or circulate through the room, all the while displaying his many different moods and manners with an actor's sense of timing.

Whatever his methods, he demands excellence. Like an ultimatum, he implores students not to fall short of their potential. "Write with clarity, conciseness and felicity of expression," he tells students as they begin their own research projects. And, he reminds them, such investigative projects "always take longer than they do."

Charles Brewer is passionate about professoring—and it shows. His eagerness to help students borders on a compulsion. When asked about his office hours, he replied: "Seven a.m. to 7 p.m., 7 days a week." He means it. Students are welcome to contact him anytime about a question or concern.

To be sure, learning with Dr. Brewer is not easy; he has a falcon's eye for error and a passion for precision that forces students to think before they speak. Impatient with mediocrity, he prods and cajoles students to do their best. Yet his demanding courses have made students better scholars and stronger persons. Over 50 of his former students have gone on to earn doctoral degrees in psychology, another 50 have earned master's degrees, and another 30 are currently in graduate school.

Dr. Brewer loves to quote the late–19th-century historian Henry Adams, who said, "A teacher affects eternity; he can never tell where his influence stops." Likewise, Professor Brewer's luminous teaching continues to brighten generations of Furman students and alumni. He is an audacious, exhilarating force. His credo is reminiscent of what Kenneth Tynan, the provocative British drama critic, adopted as his motto: "Rouse tempers, goad and lacerate, raise a whirlwind."

Those who have been fortunate enough to know Professor Brewer as a student or colleague will never forget his cyclonic power—or his infectious love for learning.

Source: Posted Sunday, May 9, 2004, 12:12 a.m. Reprinted with permission of David Shi.

Note: David Shi is a historian, a writer, and president of Furman University. His campus address is 3300 Poinsett Highway, Greenville, SC 29613, or send e-mail to david.shi@furman.edu.

David Worley (2001, p. 279) portrays his teaching as " a dream come true" that he is allowed "to live every day." Moreover, Worley tells his students, "I went back to graduate school and did the difficult and challenging work required for one reason: I wanted to be here with you today."

For all these master teachers, their calling represents a perceived privilege: the chance to make a positive difference in the lives of students

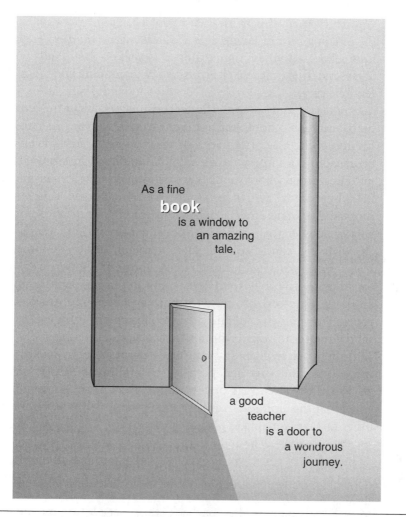

Figure 16.2   The Parallels of Books and Teachers

(Buskist et al., 2005). The student and teacher together undertake an amazing journey. This journey is illustrated in Figure 16.2.

Giving Back to Teachers

Our final observations about positive schooling pertain to the role that you can play in making teachers better. You can do several things to help teachers in particular and the school system in general. First, you can work with teachers to help in whatever ways possible to improve your own children's learning. Learning obviously happens outside of school, and we encourage you to try various activities with your children to reinforce and practice the ongoing lessons taught at school. Likewise, volunteer to help with various school activities. Your children as well as the other children will be impressed by the fact that learning is not something about which only their teachers care.

You also can visit with the teachers in your local elementary, junior high, and high schools and ask them what they need to make their teaching more effective. The needs of teachers may vary with the particular course, but computers are useful gifts for most classrooms. If new computers or other school supplies are needed, perhaps a bake sale or car wash held by parents and community members could raise the necessary money. See what other supplies the teachers may need for their classrooms. Maybe your old books could be donated to the school library. Do what you can to see that these items or services are obtained. If you have special skills, volunteer to come into class and give demonstrations to students. You may want to become politically active to increase local school taxes in order to raise teacher pay and benefits or build new classrooms. You are part of the positive psychology solution to making the schools better in your community.

If there are teachers in your local school system who did a wonderful job of teaching you, and perhaps even of teaching your children, find out when these teachers plan to retire. They have dedicated their lives to educating the children in your community, so why not get together with other former students to plan a reunion? Or help plan a going-away party for the beloved teacher.

In a similar spirit, we ask that you close this chapter with an exercise aimed at saying thank you to those special teachers in your local community. Please try "Saying Thank You to a Good Teacher" (in the Personal Mini-Experiments). This "payback" takes very little time, but it would be tremendously meaningful to the teacher whom you remember. Don't forget that these teachers were there for you at many crucial points in your life, so take some time now and reach out to them. It does not matter whether they have retired yet, because a thank-you at any time is greatly appreciated by your former teachers.

Appendix A: Assessing Educational Success

BRIDGET MURRAY

Monitor *Staff*

More than 200 people gathered in Atlanta Sept. 27–29 for a conference APA's Div. 2 (Society for the Teaching of Psychology) organized to help psychology instructors handle the growing pressure to demonstrate what students have learned.

In workshop sessions and speaker presentations, conference participants learned strategies for preparing for departmental reviews, improving students' writing, compiling evaluative portfolios for students and administrators, and assessing student learning online. Speakers offered tips for building faculty consensus on student learning objectives and for crafting and using comprehensive and standardized tests. They also shared ways to develop exit and alumni surveys and to evaluate student research projects.

"At a time of increased accountability in higher education, this conference provided an invaluable opportunity for participants to analyze issues associated with outcomes assessment in the psychology curriculum and to learn about a variety of assessment methods," says Cynthia Belar, PhD, APA's executive director for education.

The . . . conference organizers recruited keynote speakers from across educational contexts:

Diane Halpern of Claremont McKenna College opened the conference by describing how to cover your assessment needs and maintain the "godliness" required to advocate for ethically appropriate assessment.

Randy Ernst, a high school teacher from Lincoln High School in Nebraska, offered insights into "high-stakes hysteria" that attends assessment decisions and policies.

Donna Duffy, a service-learning scholar from Middlesex Community College, explored how service-learning courses can achieve objectives consistent with the Undergraduate Psychology Learning Goals and Outcomes . . . available at www.apa.org/ed/pcue/taskforcereport.pdf.

Robert Sternberg of Yale University offered teaching and assessment insights from a triarchic approach to the classroom that fosters analytic, practical, and creative gains in students.

In addition, six psychology departments described their distinctive approaches . . . :

- Frostburg State University. The department assesses students' ability to "think and behave like a psychologist" through measures of

Appendix A Note: Jane S. Halonen, PhD, professor and director of the James Madison University School of Psychology, contributed to this report. *APA Monitor,* December 2002, p. 33. Reprinted with permission.

content knowledge (e.g., the ETS Major Field Achievement Test in Psychology), skills (e.g., differentiation between research methods and critical reading of literature reviews), and willingness to use those skills (e.g., research consumption attitudes and counselor self-efficacy).

- Mansfield University. Psychology faculty there favors papers and group projects that students gather into evaluative portfolios. The portfolios and various tests assess students' ability to understand psychology's conceptual bases, gather and assess library and computerized information, think critically about key disciplinary issues, use the discipline's language, understand research methods and statistics, communicate clearly with others, understand psychologists' various roles and work settings, appreciate diversity, and understand ethics in psychology.

- Spelman College. Student learning is gauged through institutional assessment (e.g., the Myers-Briggs Type Indicator, student course evaluations and senior exit surveys), departmental assessment (e.g., the ETS field exam and a comprehensive exam given to sophomore and seniors and alumnae surveys) and honors and experiential outcomes (e.g., participation in honors societies, engagement in research and practica, and acceptance into jobs and graduate schools).

- James Madison University. The department approaches assessment in steps according to *why* it's done: to focus faculty on shared curriculum objectives, gather information on student competencies, guide program administration, demonstrate program strengths, identify program weaknesses, inform instructional delivery, and evaluate program change.

- Fordham University. Faculty emphasizes building faculty buy-in to an overall assessment plan.

- Kennesaw State University. The department assesses its students on 11 learning outcomes using alumni and senior exit surveys, student research proposals, senior capstone course assignments, and a research test. Recently, it has added the ETS field exam and an advisement survey as part of its efforts to offer strong academic and career advising.

In closing the meeting, conference program chair Jane Halonen, PhD, discussed how psychology departments can tap 10 BEA-endorsed achievement goals for undergraduate students. Halonen, who chaired the APA task force that developed the goals, explained that the group has produced an Assessment Cyber Guide, which will soon be available at www.apa.org/ed, to guide departments' reading and use of the goals.

Appendix B: Teaching Tips
From Two "Wills"—James and McKeachie

WILBERT McKEACHIE

Today in higher education, the "in" words are *learner-centered* and *active learning*. We need learner-centered education. Yet I question the premise that learner-centered is a revolutionary new idea. Hear the words of William James (1899) in the Preface to *Talks to Teachers on Psychology: And to Students on Some of Life's Ideals:* "My main desire has been to make (teachers) conceive, and, if possible, reproduce sympathetically in their imagination, the mental life of their pupils as the sort of active unity which the pupil feels it to be" (p. iv).

Also, in the first edition of *Teaching Tips* (McKeachie & Kimble, 1950), we wrote, "If we grant that a rigid authoritarian method of teaching is one way of handling student anxiety, we still may not grant that this is the most desirable method to be used in an educational system which has as its aim preparation for life in a democracy" (p. 83).

In my early research, it was apparent that teaching that works for some students may not work for others. I wrote *Teaching Tips* to provide teachers with a larger repertoire of strategies to enable them to reach different learners. In short, learner-centered has a long history.

WHAT HAS CHANGED?

What We Know About Learning and Memory. I thought, when I began preparing this article, that I would find that much had changed since James's *Talks to Teachers* in 1899 and even since the first edition of *Teaching Tips* (McKeachie & Kimble, 1950). There is no doubt that we know a lot more about cognition than James did or than Greg Kimble and I did when we first wrote *Teaching Tips*. Nonetheless, I'm impressed that most changes are presaged in James and our early editions. Probably the best-known chapter in James's *Principles of Psychology* (1890) was the chapter on habit, and that chapter is largely repeated in the *Talks to Teachers* (James, 1899).

Researchers' current conceptions of learning have moved a long way from simple repetition and reinforcement. We now see students as actively constructing knowledge, each getting it a little differently because they store it in terms of their prior knowledge and experience. We emphasize

Appendix B Note: This appendix represents parts of an article by Professor McKeachie in *Teaching of Psychology,* 1999.

reflection and deep processing. Yet, here again, James had it right. Regarding memory, he said, "To remember, one must think and connect" (James, 1899, p. x).

Researchers now know that most of human behavior is not consciously determined but is automatic. Here, James's chapter on habit seems right on target. In 1899, James said, "Ninety-nine hundredths or, possibly, nine hundred and ninety-nine thousandths of our activity is purely automatic and habitual.... The great thing in all education is to make our nervous system our ally instead of our enemy...." (p. 65–67)

Changes in Cognitive Goals. Today, most colleges and universities emphasize teaching thinking as one of their goals.... When I began teaching, a common assumption was that some students were simply not suited for higher education. Many public universities used the first year to weed out those who did not belong. That attitude persisted in math and science up until the last few years. Now even the science faculty (at least at the University of Michigan) realizes that everyone can learn and think, and we have chemistry, physics, math, and engineering classes that use cooperative learning and open-ended problems.

Changes in Affective and Behavioral Goals. When I began teaching in 1946, educators believed that psychology should be completely objective and value free. Yet, when I became a full-time faculty member, one of my assignments was to teach a course on psychology and religion, and I soon realized that it was impossible to avoid values issues. In his chapter "The Will," James (1899) wrote, "Your task is to build up character" (p. 184), and in "Habit," "Perhaps you can help our rising generation of Americans toward the beginning of a better set of personal ideals" (p. 75).

James wrote during the time of the robber barons, a period of great disparities between the rich and the poor, a period not very different from the greed and extravagant wealth displayed today. Perhaps we need today another Teddy Roosevelt and a Congress less indebted to the wealthy. Certainly our task as teachers cannot neglect the basic values of our culture.

WHAT HAS NOT CHANGED OVER THE 10 EDITIONS

In *Talks to Teachers*, James (1899) laid out much of what we now have research to support. I had expected to find a lot that had changed over the 10 editions of *Teaching Tips*, but four themes were stable.

1. The importance of students' feeling that the teacher cares about their learning and about them as individuals.

2. The value of getting students to participate in discussion.

3. The role of testing and grading in student motivation and learning.

4. The value of getting feedback to improve a course.

WHAT OF THE FUTURE?

We ended the first edition of *Teaching Tips* (McKeachie & Kimble, 1950) with a theory of teaching. In rereading it, I was struck with the fact that I see it as still valid for the 21st century. I stressed three points:

1. The college is part of a culture. Today, context is emphasized in all of psychology and education.

2. The instructor's power to give grades can be a major motivational factor for good or ill. Heavy emphasis on grades increases student anxiety, which may be detrimental to performance.

3. Student-centered, group-centered teaching with clarity about tasks and goals leads to what teachers called "gut learning." Cooperative learning (now commonly used) results in greater elaboration of concepts, more clearing up of confusion, higher motivation, and better decision making.

These three themes seem to me to fit nicely with researchers' current theories of teaching and learning. I wish I could be around for another 55 years to see what happens, but I'm confident that teaching will still be fun!

REFERENCES

James, W. (1890). *The principles of psychology*. New York: Holt

James, W. (1899). *Talks to teachers on psychology: And to students on some of life's ideals*. New York: Holt.

McKeachie, W. J. (1999). *Teaching tips: Strategies, research, and theory for college and university teachers* (10th ed.). Boston: Houghton Mifflin.

McKeachie, W. J., & Kimble, G. (1950). *Teaching tips: A guidebook for the teacher of general psychology*. Ann Arbor, MI: Unpublished manuscript. (Psychology Dept., University of Michigan, Ann Arbor).

Key Terms

Calling: A strong motivation in which a person repeatedly takes a course of action that is intrinsically satisfying. For example, a person who experiences a calling to teach teaches because the job is personally fulfilling, not just because of the paycheck.

Developmental discipline: An attempt, based on attachment theory, at socialization that involves building caring and trusting relationships with students who have insecure attachments with their primary caregivers.

Positive schooling: An approach to education that consists of a foundation of care, trust, and respect for diversity, where teachers develop tailored goals for each student to engender learning and then work with him or her to develop the plans and motivation to reach their goals. Positive schooling includes the agendas of instilling hope in students and contributing to the larger society.

Good Work 17

The Psychology of Gainful Employment

No punch clocks
Means
I produce of
My own accord

You bestow credence
On my talent
So I give my best
Willingly

Not asking what
I cannot produce
But rather that
Which I can

Offering a chance
To be and do
Here it feels as if
My efforts count

And mostly
I can build a fortune
Not from money
But respect

Gainful Employment

These opening lines were penned by the senior author of this book (CRS) during my first month on the job as an assistant professor. Then, as now, some 33 years later, I felt remarkably privileged and happy to have such a livelihood (this term always has seemed so apt). This positive sentiment captures the essence of gainful employment, which we explore in this chapter.

It was Sigmund Freud who first made the bold statement that a healthy life is one in which a person has the ability to love and to work (O'Brien, 2003). In the many decades since Freud presented these ideas, the psychological literature has reinforced the importance of positive interpersonal relationships and employment. After reviewing the growing body of literature on the role of one's job in producing a healthy life, we searched for a phrase that captured the essence of the many benefits that can flow from work. In the end, we decided to use the phrase *gainful employment.*

Although many people awaken only to dread getting up and going to work, gainfully employed people actually look forward to it. **Gainful employment** is work that is characterized by the following eight benefits:

1. Variety in duties performed

2. A safe working environment

3. Income for the family and oneself

4. A purpose derived from providing a product or service

5. Happiness and satisfaction

6. Positive engagement and involvement

7. A sense of performing well and meeting goals

8. The companionship of and loyalty to coworkers, bosses, and companies

In this chapter, we explore the growing body of positive psychology findings and look at gainful employment from the perspectives of the employee, the boss, and the company. We begin with an employee's perspective in the case history of Jenny.

"We Have an Opening": Jenny Loses a Job and Finds a Career

The first time I (CRS) saw Jenny, she had come into psychological treatment because she was depressed. A 32-year-old single woman, Jenny had finished a year and a half of junior college before dropping out. Normally an outgoing person, Jenny reported that her mood had changed for the worse when she lost her job as the executive assistant for the chairperson of the English Department at the local state university. University cutbacks had resulted in the loss of her job. She spent most of her days and nights in bed contemplating the "unfairness of it all."

Jenny's friends either worked in the English Department or were graduate students there. It was only when she lost this job that she realized how much of her world was wrapped up in this work setting. Shortly after being laid off, she would show up at the English Department and try to strike up conversations with her pals. She reported that this was very awkward and that it just wasn't the same as when she worked there. After a few visits, Jenny stopped returning. Jenny's initial coping strategy was to find another job as soon as possible. Although she was relentless in applying for jobs like her old position, such high-paying assistant positions were virtually nonexistent because the entire university was suffering financial woes. In our sessions together, we discussed how all Jenny's friends came from her former work setting. This deepened her sense of despair as she realized how friendless she now was. Moreover, her ruminative thoughts didn't help matters. She was concerned that her former friends only liked her because she was the chairperson's executive assistant. Were they trying to "suck up" to the boss through her? Jenny had one obvious talent, however, about which everyone agreed: People appreciated her ability to remember a person's name after being introduced.

At the beginning of one session, Jenny recounted a dream that she had had for three consecutive nights during the previous week. In this dream, the professors who chaired the various units at the university called her and begged her to apply for positions in their departments. At the beginning of each call, the chair would excitedly announce, "We have an opening in our department that is just right for you!" Puzzled as to why she suddenly was getting all this attention, Jenny (still in her dream) asked the chairs why they were calling. They replied, "You don't know?" To this, Jenny said that she didn't have a clue. Each chairperson then told her how much people loved the fact that she remembered their names. At this point in her dream, Jenny awoke.

This dream provided a breakthrough for Jenny. Her interpretation was that this capacity to remember names was an important asset that she should put to her advantage in seeking new employment. When asked in the session how she might do this, a productive discussion ensued about jobs other than secretarial ones. Another part of her insight was that she began to look at jobs with lower starting salaries than her former executive assistant position had paid.

As you may have guessed by now, there is a happy ending to this case history. Following her hunch about using her skills at remembering the names of people, Jenny decided to take a fairly low-paying job working at the counter of a local dry-cleaning business. A customer needed to visit the dry cleaners only once for Jenny to remember that person's name.

Whenever the customer revisited the shop, Jenny would greet the customer by calling out his or her name. "Good morning, Mr. Parker," "Hello. Ms. Davis," "Alice Marshall . . . How are you doing?" The owner of the dry-cleaning business loved the fact that Jenny could remember the names of each and every customer. Indeed, customers told Jenny that the reason they wanted to do business there was that she remembered their names. In turn, the amount of business at this dry-cleaners' flourished. As a reward for this huge increase in new customers, the owner raised Jenny's salary. So, too, did she thrive in this job, and her depression lifted. In short, she was extremely happy with her work and her life in general.

Take-Home Messages From Jenny's Story

Jenny's case has several implications for this chapter on the role of work in people's lives. Perhaps most important, it gives us a glimpse of the sheer power of work in a person's life. More specifically, it shows the importance of work in determining how a person feels about himself or herself. It reveals the need for an engagement of the worker's talents in the employment setting. It tells us how a person's friends often come from the workplace. Although Jenny's new job provided an income, her tale also illustrates how "chasing the buck" and wanting a high starting salary may backfire. Her new work also gave Jenny a setting in which to stretch her talents and capacities in working with people—this being one of her signature strengths. Along with her growth in areas of talent, her work gave her daily reminders that she was helping people by providing a service. Finally, as had been the case with her English Department job, Jenny's new profession gave her a sense of attachment, companionship, and loyalty to her customers, coworkers, and boss. The bottom line was that Jenny felt very productive and satisfied in her new career. These and other gainful employment messages emerge from the story of Jenny. We pick up on these various themes throughout the chapter.

Gainful Employment: Happiness, Satisfaction, and Beyond

As shown in Figure 17.1, eight benefits are derived from gainful employment. We place happiness and satisfaction at the center because of their key role (see Amick et al., 2002; Kelloway & Barling, 1991). As Henry (2004) describes it,

> The centrality of work to well-being is not surprising when you think of the number of benefits it offers, notably: an identity, opportunities for social interaction and support, purpose, time filling, engaging challenges, and possibilities for status apart from the provision of income. (p. 270)

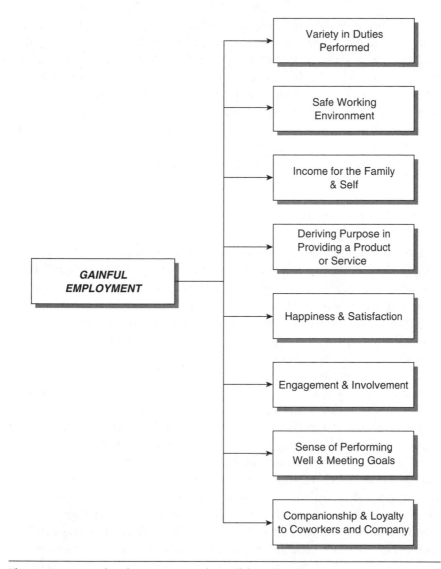

Figure 17.1   Eight Characteristics of Gainful Employment

Not surprisingly, the literature on job satisfaction is huge. Consider, for example, Locke's estimate, made in 1976, that more than 3,300 articles had been published on job satisfaction. Further, a PsycINFO search of the years 1976 though 2000 yielded 7,855 articles on job satisfaction (Harter, Schmidt, & Hayes, 2002).

If a person is happy at work, chances are that his or her overall satisfaction with life will be higher (Hart, 1999; Judge & Watanabe, 1993). The correlation of job satisfaction with overall happiness is about .40 (Diener & Lucas, 1999). Employed people consistently report being happier than their counterparts without jobs (Argyle, 2001; Warr, 1987, 1999).

Why should work, happiness, and satisfaction go hand in hand? In the next sections, we explore the various work factors that appear to be linked to greater happiness. Although we acknowledge the strong role that happiness and satisfaction play in overall gainful employment, we hasten to add that there often is a reciprocal relationship in that one or more factors may influence each other to produce a sense of gainful employment. For example, as we explain in next section, performing well at work heightens the sense of satisfaction. But so, too, does the sense of satisfaction contribute to an employee's better performance in the work arena.

PERFORMING WELL AND MEETING GOALS

How often has your friend or partner commented, "You are really grumpy. Did you have a bad day at work?" Or it can go the other way: "Wow, you are in a great mood. Did things go well at the office?" Without question, what happens at work spills over into various other aspects of our lives.

Related to the previous hypothetical interchanges, one school of thought about the happy worker is that such an employee has a sense of effectiveness and efficiency in performing his or her work activities (Hertzog, 1966). To test the notion that performance on the job relates to satisfaction, Judge, Thoresen, Bono, and Patton (2001) performed a meta-analysis (a statistical procedure for testing the robustness of results across many studies) of 300 samples (about 55,000 workers). They found a reliable relationship of approximately .30 between performance and general satisfaction.

By far the most research related to the sense of performing well has emerged from Bandura's influential self-efficacy construct (see Chapter 9; for a review of the role of self-efficacy in promoting work happiness, see O'Brien [2003]; also see Bandura, Barbaranelli, Vittorio Caprara, and Pastorelli [2001]). **Career self-efficacy**, which is defined as the personal confidence in one's capacity to handle career development and work-related goal activities, has been significantly related to both success and satisfaction with one's occupational efforts and decisions (Betz & Luzzo, 1996; Donnay & Borgen, 1999).

Performing well at work is more likely to occur when workers have clear goals. As shown in relevant literature (e.g., Emmons, 1992; Snyder, 1994/2000), lucid goals offer satisfaction when they are met. Accordingly, when work goals are clearly delineated and employees can meet established standards, heightened personal pleasure and a sense of accomplishment result. In this regard, the high-hope leader's clear goal setting and facile communication provide lucid short- and long-term objectives for the work group. A high-hope boss also can provide greater satisfaction at work. This sequence unfolds this way: The high-hope boss clearly identifies achievable work subgoals, which in turn increases workers' motivation and the chances of reaching larger, organizational goals (Snyder & Shorey,

2004). In this process, the hopeful leader also facilitates workers' willingness to embrace the company's overall objectives (Hogan & Kaiser, 2005).

DERIVING PURPOSE BY PROVIDING A PRODUCT OR SERVICE

One's work also is an important potential source of purpose in life. A major underlying force that drives such purpose is the sense of providing needed products or services to customers. Workers want, sometimes in very small ways, to feel that they are making a contribution to other people and to their society.

Although we talk about her important research later in this chapter, we note here that Amy Wrzesniewski and her colleagues (e.g., Wrzesniewski, McCauley, Rozin, & Schwartz, 1997) have described how workers, from the very highest organizational status to the lowest, can perceive their work as a calling (a vocation to which the employee brings a passion—a commitment to the work for its own sake).

ENGAGEMENT AND INVOLVEMENT

Engagement is the employee's involvement with his or her work, whereas **satisfaction** is what we might call employee enthusiasm at work (Harter et al., 2002). Engagement is said to occur when employees find that their needs are being met. Specifically, engagement reflects those circumstances in which employees "know what is expected of them, have what they need to do their work, have opportunities to feel something significant with coworkers whom they trust, and have chances to improve and develop" (Harter et al., 2002, p. 269). Similarly, Warr (1999) has reported that the most engaging jobs are those with special duties and in which there is a good match between the required activities and the skills and personality of the employees. For example, in a meta-analysis of roughly 300,000 employees in more than 50 companies, responding positively to the engagement item, "I have the opportunity to do what I do best" was related reliably to work productivity and success (Harter & Schmidt, 2002). Furthermore, in their overall analyses, Harter and his colleagues (2002) found a reliable correlation of .37 between employee performance and several items measuring engagement at work.

Engaged involvement at work bears a resemblance to the concept of flow, which entails any circumstances in which a person's skills facilitate success at challenging tasks (Csikszentmihalyi, 1990; Csikszentmihalyi & Csikszentmihalyi, 1988; see Chapter 11). In the flow state, the worker can become so engrossed and involved with the work tasks that she or he loses track of time. What is especially important for our present discussion is that these flow experiences are more likely to happen at work than during leisure activities or relaxation at home (Haworth, 1997). (This does not imply, however, that flow cannot happen in arenas outside of work, because research shows that it can [Delle Fave, 2001].)

VARIETY IN JOB DUTIES

If the tasks performed at work are sufficiently varied, satisfactions come more easily. Indeed, boredom at work can cast a pall. People should maintain as much variety and stimulation as possible in their work activities (Hackman & Oldham, 1980). One fairly common practice for maintaining variety in workers' duties in industrial and technological job settings is *cell manufacturing*. In cell manufacturing, groups of multiskilled workers take responsibility for an entire sequence in the production process (Henry, 2004). These work teams then put their identifying insignia on the product or portion of the product. Cell manufacturing has been used with some success in the construction of automobiles by work teams. (There have been concerns about this approach costing more, however, which has lessened its popularity among some companies).

Lacking variability in work, the employee may lapse into what recently has been called *presenteeism* (in contrast to *absenteeism*). In presenteeism, the employee may physically be at work, but because of the mental health problems that often result from aversive and repetitive work experiences, he or she is unproductive and unhappy (as reported by Dittmann [2005] in citing the views of Daniel Conti, the employee assistance director of J. P. Morgan Chase). Faced with repetitious and tedious tasks and inflexible schedules, employees can become demoralized and lose their motivation.

When seeking a new job, it may be advisable to take a position that offers great variety but lower pay instead of a higher-paying position that involves unchangeable, repetitive activities. Thus, the old maxim, "Variety is the spice of life," is nowhere more applicable than in work settings.

INCOME FOR FAMILY AND SELF

Without question, a minimum income is necessary to provide for the needs of one's family and oneself. As discussed in Chapter 7, however, money is overrated as a source of happiness. Indeed, two survey studies show that people seem to understand that happiness and meaning in life are not related in any major degree to the amount of money they make (King & Napa, 1998).

Whether this "rational" approach to monetary rewards and work is actually practiced, however, remains questionable (King, Eells, & Burton, 2004). For example, making money has been rated as more important than having a cohesive philosophy of life (Myers, 1992, 2000). Additionally, though interpersonal relationships have been valued above work (Twenge & King, 2003), Americans still may think quality of life in terms of how much money they make. The present generation of American workers is spending more time on the job than their parents did (Schor, 1991). In many two-partner relationships, for example, both people have jobs (perhaps this also differs from their parents' generation). Furthermore, when making important life decisions, people are most likely to cite financial reasons (Miller, 1999). It seems as if we are of two minds about acquiring monetary wealth, and this ambivalence is played out in our work.

One promising trend in this area is the development of the Positive Parenting Program (Triple P). This program consists of small group sessions in which parents learn how to balance family life with the pursuit of money through work (Dittmann, 2005). Australian psychologist Matthew Sanders (Sanders, Markie-Dadds, & Turner, 2003; Sanders, Mazzucchelli, & Studman, 2004; Sanders & Turner, in press) originated Triple P, and his intention was to lessen the negative effects of parents' long work hours on their children. Workers must make sure that the pursuit of money does not undermine important family pleasures and obligations. Indeed, if both parents work furiously to make money and do not attend to their offspring, the unfortunate result may be that their children end up behaving in the very same way when they grow up and have children. The irony here is that the same work that is meant to provide the financial resources to raise a family may grow like a cancer and cause problems in the family it is intended to support.

COMPANIONSHIP AND LOYALTY TO COWORKERS AND BOSSES: FRIENDS AT WORK

Another reason that work may be associated with happiness is seen in the case of Jenny, where her friendship network was located entirely within the employment setting. Work offers people a chance to get out of the house and interact with other people. Because workers may share experiences, including obstacles and triumphs in the work setting, there are reasons for people to form bonds with each other.

For the last 30 years or so, corporate America has discouraged the development of friendships at work. This practice was based on the assumption that socializing among coworkers, especially fraternizing between a worker and a manager, would lead to poor productivity. This assumption was not examined by systematic research until Tom Rath and colleagues at The Gallup Organization developed the Vital Friends Assessment and surveyed 1,009 people about the effects of friendships on their happiness, satisfaction, and productivity (Rath, 2006). The work of the Gallup researchers, presented in the book *Vital Friends*, confirmed that the sense of community at a given workplace is a contributing factor to happiness and satisfaction on the job (Mahan, Garrard, Lewis, & Newbrough, 2002; Royal & Rossi, 1996). Furthermore, Rath found that, if you have a "best friend" at work, you are likely to have fewer accidents, increased safety, more engaged customers, and increased achievement and productivity. These findings are attributable to the fact that people with a best friend at work are seven times more likely to be psychologically and physically engaged on the job (Rath, 2006).

SAFE WORK ENVIRONMENTS

Part of happiness at work is a safe and healthy physical environment where it is obvious that management cares about the welfare of workers. In the previously discussed meta-analytic report by Harter et al. (2002), perceived safety of the workplace was one of the most robust predictors of employee satisfaction.

Are there reasons to be concerned about work and actual physical health? The answer to this question is a resounding yes. Many physical injuries occur at work; moreover, there are high-risk professions where serious accidents are quite prevalent. Keeping workers physically safe and injury free leads to better physical health elsewhere (Hofmann & Tetrick, 2003). We do not leave the pain and suffering of a workplace-induced physical impediment at the door of the factory at quitting time.

In summary, the good news is that several factors in the work setting can contribute to a greater sense of happiness and satisfaction in particular and to gainful employment in general. Equally important is the fact that unhappiness with one's work is not inevitable; we expand on this theme in the remainder of this chapter.

Measuring Gainful Employment

In this section, we introduce an instrument that we have developed to help people to concretize their views about work. This approach allows one to attach importance ratings to the eight categories of gainful employment, to rate how well one is doing in each category, and to produce an overall grade for one's job. We now describe this instrument and how it works, then give examples of two clients with whom this exercise was used.

YOUR JOB

In working with people on issues related to their jobs, we suggest the grading system shown in Figure 17.2. This approach vividly shows a person where things are going very well at work and where things are

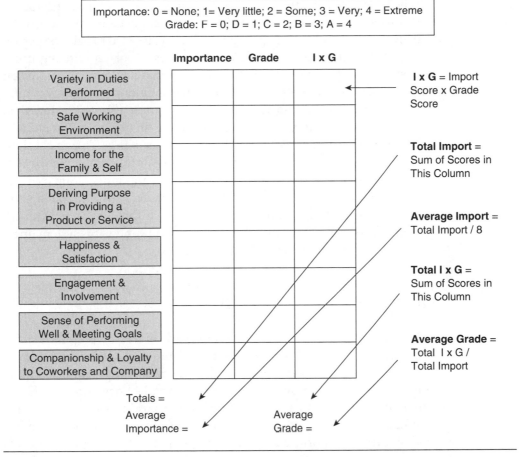

Figure 17.2   Scoring Gainful Employment

going badly. It also helps a worker understand what is important to him or her in the work setting. We developed this technique to help a person rate the importance of the eight categories of gainful employment and to provide a good means for judging success in each category. Let's go though the gainful employment grading system to get an idea of how it works.

First, the client is asked to rate the importance to him or her of each of the eight categories of gainful employment, according to a 5-point scale (0 = None; 1 = Very little; 2 = Some; 3 = Very; 4 = Extreme), and to write the rating in the appropriate blank space in the left-hand blank column headed "Importance." The client is then asked to think about his or her job in terms of each category of gainful employment and to assign a grade that reflects how well things are going (F = 0; D = 1; C = 2; B = 3; A = 4); this grade is written in the middle blank column headed "Grade," Next, the numbers in the first two columns are multiplied for each gainful employment category; the result is placed in the blank third column headed "I x G." Then, the client sums the eight numbers in the "Importance" column; this total is then divided by eight to derive the average importance of the gainful employment categories. This average number can be used to help the person see to what degree she or he perceives the present job as fulfilling needs related to importance; moreover, the scores in each box provide the person with insights about those aspects of work that are more or less important.

By summing the numbers in the third column ("I × G") and then dividing by the total Importance score from the first column, the individual determines the average grade for his or her work. This is the best overall index of how well a job is fulfilling the gainful employment needs of the worker. It is interpreted in the same manner as grade point average, with 0 equaling a grade of F; 1.0 a D; 2.0 an average grade, C; 3.0 a good grade, B; and anything closer to 4.0 meaning that the job has an excellent gainful employment grade of A. Now that you know how this system operates, you can try it on your own job (if you have one).

BACK TO THE CASE OF JENNY

Returning to the case history presented early in this chapter, the gainful employment grade of Jenny is shown in Figure 17.3. This figure depicts Jenny's ratings for her new job at the dry-cleaners. Jenny's average importance rating is 3.38, meaning that she perceived her new job as fulfilling her needs in regard to perceived importance. Additionally, her average gainful employment grade was 3.74. This meant that Jenny perceived her work in extremely positive terms across the eight gainful employment categories. In brief, in those categories of gainful employment to which Jenny gave the very highest importance ratings, she also generally saw herself as performing extremely well.

THE ASSISTANT PROFESSOR WHO DIDN'T GET TENURE

Another client of the senior author (CRS) came to treatment when he realized that he was not going to be promoted in his position of assistant professor. Because he had not published any of his research, this client was to be sacked after 7 years on the job. His self-ratings for work can be seen in Figure 17.4. What is noteworthy is that the average importance rating was 3.50, reflecting his perception that the duties of the assistant professorship were very important. Note, however, that, in contrast to these high importance ratings, he gave low grades for all categories of the job except companionship and loyalty. Finally, notice that his gainful employment average grade was a low 2.13. If the companionship and loyalty category had been omitted, his gainful employment grade would have been even lower.

Importance: 0 = None; 1= Very little; 2 = Some; 3 = Very; 4 = Extreme Grade: F = 0; D = 1; C = 2; B = 3; A = 4

	Importance	Grade	I x G
Variety in Duties Performed	4	3	12
Safe Working Environment	2	4	8
Income for the Family & Self	2	4	8
Deriving Purpose in Providing a Product or Service	4	4	16
Happiness & Satisfaction	4	4	16
Engagement & Involvement	4	4	16
Sense of Performing Well & Meeting Goals	4	4	16
Companionship & Loyalty to Coworkers and Company	3	3	9

Totals = 27   101

Average   Average
Importance − 3.38   Grade − 3.74

Figure 17.3   The Gainful Employment Scores of Jenny

This exercise revealed this young professor's perceptions of his job and his abilities. In the engagement and involvement category and the sense of performing well and meeting goals category, there seemed to be a disconnect in his responses. Although he had rated both of these latter categories very high (i.e., 4s) in terms of importance, the related performance grades (i.e., 0s) were failing. Unfortunately for him, these two categories of engagement and involvement and the sense of performing well and meeting goals were weighed heavily by his department chairperson and dean when judging his promotion to associate professor.

After exploring his gainful employment grade through the aforementioned exercise, our out-of-work assistant professor then was guided through an expressive writing experience in which he wrote for 30 minutes about his thoughts and feelings regarding the loss of his job. He did this on five separate occasions. Previous research by social psychologist Jamie Pennebaker has tested the positive effects of expressive

Jamie Pennebaker

Source: Reprinted with permission of Jamie Pennebaker.

writing (i.e., emotional storytelling, Chapter 8). The results of several experiments have shown that it yields beneficial results in terms of lessening number of physician visits, increasing academic performance, raising immune system functioning, and making people feel better, to name but a few examples of positive outcomes (Pennebaker, 1990; Smyth & Pennebaker, 1999).

What prompted my (CRS) actual use of this technique, however, were results showing that the expressive writing experience decreased employee absenteeism and increased the likelihood that unemployed people would gain other jobs (Spera, Buhrfeind, & Pennebaker, 1994). As had been the case with previous research on this approach, when this former assistant professor tried the expressive writing technique, it seemed to unleash his enthusiasm for seeking another academic position. And, yes, there is a happy ending to this case history! This same man later was able to obtain another assistant professorship at a smaller school. In this new setting, he

	Importance: 0 = None; 1= Very little; 2 = Some; 3 = Very; 4 = Extreme Grade: F = 0; D = 1; C = 2; B = 3; A = 4		
	Importance	**Grade**	**I x G**
Variety in Duties Performed	4	3	12
Safe Working Environment	2	3	6
Income for the Family & Self	2	3	6
Deriving Purpose in Providing a Product or Service	4	2	8
Happiness & Satisfaction	4	2	8
Engagement & Involvement	4	0	0
Sense of Performing Well & Meeting Goals	4	0	0
Companionship & Loyalty to Coworkers and Company	4	4	16

Totals = 28   56

Average Importance = 3.50   Average Grade = 2.13

Figure 17.4   The Gainful Employment Scores of the Assistant Professor Who Didn't Get Tenure

used what he had learned from his problems at his first academic job. Indeed, he succeeded at his new school and was promoted to associate professor. Because he no longer was in treatment, however, there was no gainful employment grade available for his second, more favorable job. Presumably, his average gainful employment grade was higher the second time around.

Having or Being a Good Boss

The boss is a crucial resource in helping employees to have productive and satisfying job experiences. Notice that we include being a good boss in our section heading; we do so because many readers will find themselves in the role of boss at some point in their careers—if they are not already there. Supervisors who provide clear job definitions and duties as well as support to employees foster job satisfaction and production (Warr, 1999). Managers and leaders who are focused on employees' strengths (Buckingham & Clifton, 2001), good at communicating the company goals, and facile at giving feedback contribute to employees' positive experiences. High-hope bosses also enjoy their social interactions with employees; moreover, they often take an active interest in how employees are doing, both at work and outside it (Snyder & Shorey, 2004).

It also is helpful for a boss to be genuine and authentic in interactions with employees (Avolio, Luthans, & Walumbwa, 2004; Gardner & Schermerhorn, 2004; George, 2003; Luthans & Avolio, 2003). But what, exactly, is authenticity? In the words of Avolio et al. (2004), **authentic bosses** are

> [T]hose individuals who are deeply aware of how they think and behave and are perceived by others as being aware of their own and others' values/moral perspective, knowledge, and strengths; aware of the context in which they operate; and who are confident, hopeful, optimistic, resilient, and high on moral character. (p. 4)

Bruce J. Avolio

Source: Reprinted with permission of Bruce Avolio.

Authentic bosses foster trust and positive emotions among their employees along with high engagement and motivation to reach shared goals. Authentic leaders hold deep personal values and convictions that guide their behaviors. In turn, their employees respect and trust them, and these positive views are reinforced as the authentic boss encourages differing views and interacts collaboratively with workers. Thus, authentic bosses value diversity in their employees and want to identify and build on employee talents and strengths (Luthans & Avolio, 2003). The authentic boss sets high standards for his or her own behavior and models integrity and honesty to employees. Through such modeling, the authentic work leader is able to establish a sense of employee teamwork. So, too, does the authentic boss set clear goals and foster employee hope (Snyder & Shorey, 2004). As noted previously, a good boss also encourages the workers to be team players (Hogan & Kaiser, 2005). In summary, authenticity in bosses appears to be associated with gainful employment and a variety of positive outcomes in the workplace.

In our consultation work with various organizations over the years, we have observed these "top ten" characteristics common to the very best bosses:

- They provide clear goals and job duties to employees.
- They are not just friends to employees but can deliver corrective feedback so that it is heard.
- They are genuine and authentic in their interactions with everyone.
- They are ethical and demonstrate moral values in their interactions with people.
- They are honest and model integrity.
- They find employee talents and strengths and build on them.
- They trust workers and facilitate their employees' trust in them.
- They encourage diverse views from employees and can take feedback about themselves.
- They set high but reasonable standards for employees and for themselves.

What is intriguing about these qualities is the degree to which the employees seem to agree that they are important to employees, too. Employees attribute this consistency of views to the fact that they talk among themselves about what they like and do not like in their superiors. Furthermore, when a boss has these characteristics, this appears to play a huge role in employees' productivity and happiness at work.

The sense of engagement, productivity, and satisfaction all seem to go together in a positive workplace. Without a doubt, the boss plays a crucial role in making such positive outcomes happen. Think about these characteristics of a good boss, and then apply them to your work setting. Do these qualities apply to your supervisors? Do you think that you yourself have many of these qualities? Although you may not be a boss right now, whether you possess these "top ten" characteristics may determine whether you become one, as well as whether you succeed in this role.

The Strengths-Based Approach to Work

In this section, we describe a bold new approach for matching employee duties to their strengths and talents that has been spearheaded at The

Gallup Organization. We explore the various aspects of this trend-setting, strengths-based approach next. A longtime champion of the strengths-based approach has been The Gallup Organization, where the leaders practice a "strengths finder" approach to hiring and cultivating employees. Instead of spending millions of dollars to repair or "fix" deficiencies in their employees' skills, the leaders of The Gallup Organization suggest that such money and energy is better spent in discovering employees' strengths and talents and then finding job duties that provide a good match for those talents (Hodges & Clifton, 2004). The focus is not on changing worker weaknesses and deficiencies but on building on their assets. As Buckingham and Coffman (1999, p. 57) put it, "Don't waste time trying to put in what was left out. Try to draw out what was left in. That is hard enough."

MATCH PEOPLE, DON'T FIX THEM

The underlying premise of the strengths-based approach to work is a simple one: Instead of "fixing" all employees so that each has the same basic level of skills, find out what a worker's talents are, and then assign the worker to jobs where those talents can be used, or shape the job activities around the workers' talents and skills. As obvious as this approach may seem, when Gallup performed a survey in different countries, the response was surprising when respondents were asked, "Which would help you be more successful in your life—knowing what your weaknesses are and attempting to improve your weaknesses, or knowing what your strengths are and attempting to build on your strengths?" (Hodges & Clifton, 2004, p. 256). Timothy Hodges and Donald Clifton of Gallup summarized the responses to these questions and found that the majority of respondents across different countries answered in favor of "improving your weaknesses." In terms of the percentages of respondents who favored the building on strengths approach, these researchers found the following: United States = 41%; Great Britain = 38%; Canada = 38%; France = 29%; Japan = 24%; and China = 24%. Obviously, most people still favor the traditional "fix it" model.

Timothy L. Hodges

Source: Reprinted with permission of Timothy Hodges.

THE STAGES OF THIS APPROACH

According to Clifton and Harter (2003), there are three stages in the **strengths-based approach to gainful employment.** The first stage is the identification of talents, which involves increasing the employee's awareness of his or her own natural or learned talents. If you are interested in finding these talents in yourself, we suggest The Gallup Organization's online assessment (http://www.strengthsfinder.com), which is described in Chapter 4. (The authors of this text have completed the measure on this website and found the results to be very useful. Note that there may be a charge for this if you have not purchased a book containing a Clifton StrengthsFinder code.)

The second stage is the integration of the talents into the employee's self-image; the person learns to define him- or herself according to these talents. Gallup has developed books aimed at helping particular groups of people to integrate their talents. There are an enjoyable volume for workers across potential employment areas (see Buckingham & Clifton, 2001), a workbook for students (see Clifton & Anderson, 2002), a book for people in sales (Smith & Rutigliano, 2003), and one for members and leaders of faith-based organizations (see Winseman, Clifton, & Liesveld, 2003).

The third stage is the actual behavioral change, in which the individual learns to attribute any successes to his or her special talents. In this stage, people report being more satisfied and productive precisely because they have begun to own and accentuate their strengths.

DOES IT WORK?

Does the strengths-based approach work for the betterment of employees? The answer appears to be a firm yes. In a survey of 459 people who had taken the Clifton StrengthsFinder assessment through the aforementioned website (Hodges, 2003), 59% agreed or strongly agreed with the item, "Learning about my strengths has helped me to make better choices in my life"; 60% agreed or strongly agreed with the item, "Focusing on my strengths has helped me to be more productive," and 63% agreed or strongly agreed with the item, "Learning about my strengths has increased my self-confidence."

Beyond these self-reported benefits, the strengths-based approach also has produced positive workplace results for "hard" markers. For example, in a study of the Toyota North American Parts Center California (Connelly, 2002), the warehouse workers completed the Clifton StrengthsFinder and then attended lunchtime sessions aimed at answering any related questions. Also, the managers of this company took a 4-day course in this approach. Relative to the previous 3 years, in which per-person productivity increased or decreased by less than 1%, the year following this strengths-based intervention saw a 6% increase in productivity.

Other examples of actual work improvements stemming from the strengths-based approach can be reviewed in Hodges and Clifton (2004). For example, the strengths-based approach, when implemented in work settings, resulted in greater employee engagement (Black, 2001; Clifton & Harter, 2003) and engagement among members of a church congregation (Winseman, 2003). Furthermore, education in the strengths-based approach has produced increases in students' confidence in themselves and their future outcomes (Clifton, 1997; Rath, 2002). In summary, the strengths-based approach has yielded considerable empirical support within the last decade.

THE ASSETS EXERCISE

An exercise that we have used in working with people as they consider new professions or jobs bears similarities to the strengths-based approach used by Gallup. Our technique is much simpler. We start by asking our client to make two columns on a blank piece of paper, heading the first column "Assets" and the second column "Debits." Here, we cite the real case of the senior author (CRS) to illustrate how the helper proceeds from here. I was seeing a man who was about 30 years old. He was a disk jockey but no longer felt any sense of satisfaction in this line of work. What he wanted to do was to go back to school and become a social worker. In order to help him clarify how good a match this new schooling and line of work would be for him, I asked him to take a few minutes to think about his strengths and weaknesses in relation to making this change. Once he had thought about this briefly, I asked him to list all of his assets related to becoming a social worker in the first column, and his debits related to this same move in the second column. His efforts are shown in Figure 17.5.

Note here that our would-be social worker's assets list is much longer than his debits list. This is a good prognostic sign. Additionally, you can see that he had several strengths that would aid him in this transition. First, he had the basic interests and talents required for social work—he had people skills, he was a natural helper, and people opened up to him. His motivation was high, he was certain about what he wanted, and he was poised and ready for change. He also had a solid base of social support,

Assets	Debits
1. People skills	1. Lacked planning
2. Many friends	2. Some low and high grades
3. High motivation	3.
4. Family support	4.
5. Nearby school	5.
6. Saved some $	6.
7. Knew what he wanted	7.
8. Knew faculty member	8.
9. Ready for change	9.
10. A natural helper	10.
11. People opened up to him	11.

Figure 17.5   The Assets of a Would-Be Social Worker

which augurs well for a person undergoing a major, potentially stressful change. On the other side of the ledger, his two debits were not fatal—he could learn how to plan to go back to school, and his grades, although varying from Ds to As, were still above the required minimum. Overall, this assets exercise showed that our would-be social worker had the requisite assets as well as strengths that were good matches to his new profession.

Capital at Work

Fred Luthans

University of Nebraska positive psychologist Fred Luthans has proposed a new way of thinking about resources or capital, one that can be applied to the work force. This view of capital places the greatest emphasis on the individual worker. As Carly Fiorian of Hewlett-Packard has put it (in Luthans & Youssef, 2004, p. 143), "The most important ingredient in the transformed landscape is people." In the spirit of positive psychology research and applications, Luthans begins with the traditional view of economic capital and then expands into new frontiers of positive psychological thinking. We share the evolution of his thinking in the next sections.

TRADITIONAL ECONOMIC CAPITAL

As shown in Figure 17.6, **traditional economic capital** involves an organization's answer to the question, "What do you have?" The answer usually has been a list of the concrete facilities that make a given company unique. Included here would be the buildings or plants, the equipment, data, patents, technology, and so forth. Obviously, this type of capital is very expensive in terms of monetary outlay. Often, a marker of the success of an organization is that other companies attempt to copy these sources of capital (euphemistically called *benchmarking*). Because modern technology now enables the products of an industry leader to be copied by reverse engineering, however, the traditional advantages enjoyed by an organization that develops a new product have been greatly curtailed. Historically, these physical resources of economic capital have received most of the attention in analyses of work settings (Luthans, Luthans, & Luthans, 2004), but this is changing in the 21st century.

HUMAN CAPITAL

The term *human capital* refers to the employees at all levels of an organization. In this regard, business phenom Bill Gates has commented that

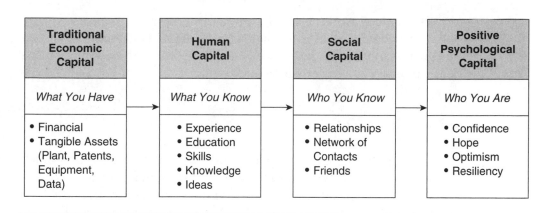

Figure 17.6 Types of Capital

the most important assets of his company "walk out of the door every night." In making such a comment, he is emphasizing how the skills, knowledge, and abilities of his employees reflect the ultimate assets that set Microsoft above its competitors. Thus, in the older, economic capital model, the guiding question for an organization was, "What do you have?" whereas the core question in the human capital perspective is, "What do you know?" The answer to the latter query entails human capital—employee assets such as experience, education, skills, talents, knowledge, and new ideas (Luthans et al., 2004). The knowledge inherent in human capital is made up of the explicit skills of workers. Such skills and tacit knowledge are organization specific; for example, Nike has been characterized as superb at brand management, General Electric at global cooperation; and Microsoft has been lauded for having employees who excel at trying new ideas (Luthans & Youssef, 2004).

In the American workforce, human capital increasingly involves workers of diverse ethnic backgrounds. In the words of John Bruhn (1996),

A healthy organization is one in which an obvious effort is made to get people with different backgrounds, skills, and abilities to work together toward the goals or purpose of the organization. While we have not accomplished this at the societal level, it is achievable at the organizational level. (p. 11)

The need for cultural diversity is being understood both at the managerial and worker levels. University of Michigan professor Taylor Cox (1994) has suggested four good reasons for such diversity of social capital. First, diverse backgrounds within an organization enhance the overall level of energy and talent, thereby raising the problem-solving potential of the organization. Second, a core value of American society is equal opportunity; it is therefore ethically and morally right to enhance diversity among workers. Third, cultural diversity raises the performance of all workers. Fourth, the legislation pertaining to equal pay, civil rights, pregnancy and age discrimination, and Americans with disabilities mandates diversity as a legal requirement.

SOCIAL CAPITAL

Closely related to human capital is **social capital**, with respect to which the key question is, "Who do you know?" Throughout all levels of an organization, an important set of assets taps into the relationships, network of contacts, and friends (see Figure 17.6). Such social capital makes an organization facile in setting goals and solving any challenges that may arise. Because employees know with whom they should talk both within and outside the company, they can reach their goals even under difficult circumstances. Thus, advice is a precious commodity in social capital.

POSITIVE PSYCHOLOGICAL CAPITAL

The last and newest form of capital discussed by social scientists is **positive psychological capital**, which, for Luthans and his colleagues (Luthans et al., 2004; Luthans & Youssef, 2004), comprises four positive psychology variables (see Figure 17.7). These four variables involve Bandura's (1997) efficacy (confidence in one's ability to reach a desired goal; see Chapter 9), Snyder's (2002a) hope (the capacity to find pathways to desired goals, along with the motivation or agency to use those pathways; see Chapter 9), Seligman's (2002) optimism (the ability to attribute good outcomes to internal, stable, and pervasive causes; see Chapter 9), and Masten's (2001) resiliency (the capacity to endure and succeed in adversity; see Chapter 6).

Luthans argues that, as we move into the 21st century, it is time for businesses to lessen their dependency on the traditional sources of capital (e.g., economic) (Luthans et al., 2004; Luthans & Youssef, 2004). Instead, he suggests that there already are compelling theoretical reasons, along with beginning reports from research programs (see Luthans, Avolio, Walumbwa, & Li, in press), to move to these psychological forms of capital. We explore one form of psychological capital, hope, in greater detail in the next section.

Hope: A Prime Psychological Capital

As we discuss in detail in Chapter 9, hopeful thinking can produce benefits in several life arenas, one of the more important of which is work

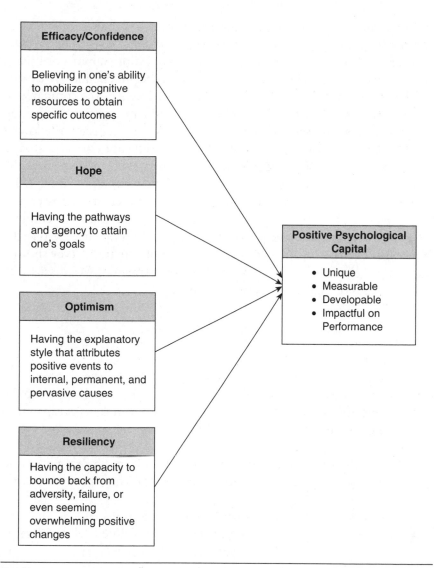

Figure 17.7   Positive Psychological Capital

(Peterson & Luthans, 2003). Indeed, hope can characterize the productive work setting or company as well as the successful worker. Recall that hope as defined by Snyder and his colleagues (see Chapter 9) involves having clearly defined goals, along with the perceived capacities to produce the routes to those goals (called *pathways thinking*), and the requisite energies to use those routes (called *agency thinking*). Generally, using the principles of hope theory, it is adaptive in work settings to clarify the important goals, to break larger goals into subgoals that are easier to reach, and to learn to come up with alternate routes to desired goals—especially in stressful circumstances (Luthans & Jensen, 2002).

To explore the role of hope in American businesses, the senior author of this textbook (CRS) conducted a survey in *Success* magazine in 2001 (Snyder, 2004b). This survey asked a variety of questions about a company, and it required that it be completed and returned independently by one employee each from the top, middle, and lower levels of the company. In other words, the chief executive officer or president represented the top level, managers represented the middle, and laborers reflected the lowest echelon. The responses were returned to the investigator and tabulated so as to rank the top 100 companies on hope; moreover, the top 10 of the entire group of companies were identified. These companies varied from mom-and-pop operations that had only a few workers and grossed less than $150,000 per year to huge organizations with thousands of employees and yearly financial receipts in excess of a billion dollars. Despite the differences of these organizations in size and makeup, this survey showed very similar characteristics for the high-hope companies. We discuss the characteristics of high-hope companies next.

THE HIGH-HOPE COMPANIES

Generally, the higher-hope companies appeared to be very successful in terms of their profits. Thus, hope plays a positive role when it comes to the bottom line. We also found that high-hope work settings (as compared to low-hope ones) shared the following characteristics:

- No one, including management, was greatly feared by employees.
- There was a level playing field where everyone had an equal chance to succeed.
- Advancement and benefits were linked to effort expended.
- The lowest person in the organization was treated with the same respect as every other employee, including management.
- The first priority of management was to help the employees to do the best job possible.
- There was open, two-way communication between employees and management.
- Employee feedback was solicited and viewed as a means of making the company better.
- As many decisions as possible were given to the employees who were doing the particular work.
- Employees were included in the setting of company goals.
- Employees were given responsibility for finding solutions to problems.
- Whether it was solving a problem or trying a new idea, employees were given the responsibility for implementing the changes.
- The objective was to establish enduring relationships with customers instead of to accomplish a given sales objective.

HIGH-HOPE EMPLOYEES

Using the same survey data (i.e., Snyder, 2004), the highest-hope employees also were identified. It also should be noted that these high-hope employees tended to work at the high-hope companies. Results showed that the high-hope employees (as compared to the low-hope ones) shared the following characteristics:

- They were conscientious about their jobs.
- They showed helping attitudes toward other workers and the local communities.
- They were courteous to fellow workers and customers, especially during difficult discussions or interactions.
- They were good sports when it came to fellow workers getting rewards (raises, advancement, recognition, etc.).
- They did not blame fellow workers, the management, or customers when difficulties arose.
- They set clear work goals.
- They found good and multiple routes to desired goals.
- They were able to motivate themselves under normal circumstances and were especially energized during difficult circumstances.

PUTTING HOPE TOGETHER AT WORK

Taken together, these findings regarding the characteristics of high-hope companies and high-hope employees enable several inferences to be drawn. To begin, there are at least four major consequences of being employed in a low-hope setting (Snyder & Feldman, 2000). First, it appears that workers at such settings have low motivation. This follows because they do not have much input in defining their activities. Second, workers may not feel very conscientious and thus would be likely to produce low-quality output. Third, these employees generally are low in self-esteem, and their job morale is low. Fourth, they seem to be disrespectful of other workers and management when they do work, but their work often is spotty in that they have high absenteeism rates.

These survey results paint a different picture, however, for the high-hope work setting and high-hope employee. Such employees are allowed a say in establishing their own work goals. Because they are conscientious and motivated about various aspects of their jobs, they do not have to punch a time clock and instead are trusted to report their hours accurately. They enjoy their work, and this shows in their courtesy to fellow workers and customers; they are likewise helpful in their interactions with coworkers (i.e., they are likely to aid another employee in reaching his or her work-related goals and thus are not overly competitive). Finally, when it comes to the bottom line, the high-hopers are productive. In short, workers who have hopeful outlooks are likely to fare better in work settings (Snyder, 1994), and this is especially true if the work environments involve considerable stress (Kirk & Koesk, 1995). (For similar findings about self-efficacy and work-related performance, see Stajkovic and Luthans [1998].)

CAN HOPE BE INCREASED AT WORK?

One question you may asking at this point is whether an employee can learn to increase his or her hope in the work setting. In two tests of this question, Hodges and Clifton (2004) examined whether completing the Clifton StrengthsFinder and undergoing strengths-enhancing exercises resulted in any increases in situation hope as measured by the State Hope Scale (Snyder et al., 1996). In a first study, students were given the assessment as part of a course they were taking, in addition to which each student was given a 30-minute session with a professional about the test results. Two months later, they retook the State Hope Scale, and scores increased about 12% (in statistical terms, .36 standard deviation units). In a second study, conducted at a rehabilitation hospital, employees initially completed the State Hope Scale and then received the StrengthsFinder assessment. Hospital employees also could meet with a coach to discuss their strengths if they so desired. After one year, 488 hospital employees once again completed the State Hope Scale. For the employees who had sought coaching, as compared to those who did not, there was a significant ($p < .001$) increase in state hope scores. Together, these studies suggest that hope can be raised in the work context.

The Dark Side: Workaholics, Burnouts, and Jobs Lost

In this section, we review those workers who may be most in need of the benefits of positive psychology: people who work all the time, those who have burned out at their jobs, and those who have lost their jobs.

WORKAHOLICS

Some people, referred to as **workaholics,** become obsessed by their work—so much so that they cannot attend to the responsibilities of their friends and family. Workaholism also entails staying late on the job long after others have departed, and working much harder than others, almost to the point of seeking perfectionism (McMillan, O'Driscoll, Marsh, & Brady, 2001). For a workaholic, there is no balance in life activities, and this person even may begin to exhibit the Type A behavior pattern of hypervigilance with regard to time constraints and angry outbursts at coworkers (Houston & Snyder, 1988).

BURNOUT

Do you ever feel as though you work harder and harder at your job, yet the things that you need to get done just seem to grow despite your best efforts? Do you feel tired at work? Does your job lack any sense of reward? Perhaps you have watched you own parents working long and hard and have adopted their workaholic approach for yourself. If these sentiments seem to apply, you may be suffering from *burnout* (Pines, Aronson, & Kafry, 1981; Rodriguez-Hanley & Snyder, 2000).

Burnout is cyclical. Initially, the employee has a high level of energy, but this begins to wane over time. The employee encounters severe time constraints in getting the work done, there are barriers to the work goals, the bosses tend not to give rewards and yet ask more and more of the employee because she or he is getting things done. Paradoxically, the effective, hard-working person is asked to do more. As this cycle continues, the employee becomes totally exhausted in both mind and body, and the burnout truly undermines the employee's ability to carry out the necessary duties of the job. When his or her energy is totally depleted, the employee needs time to recover and recharge (see Baumeister, Faber, and Wallace's [1999] theory of ego depletion).

The authors of this book have worked with schoolteachers who have burned out, and the surprising aspect of these cases is that the new teachers who entered their classrooms with the most enthusiasm appear to be the most vulnerable to burnout. Unfortunately, people in the helping professions may be the most prone to burnout (Carpenter & Steffen, 2004). For example, in a study of social workers, many of those who felt burned out also had burdensome, excessive workloads and bosses who rarely gave praise (Ngai, 1993). Similarly, nurses may burn out when they undergo job pressures and lack of reinforcement like the social workers. Not surprisingly, then, nurses who score high on the Maslach Burnout Inventory (Maslach & Jackson, 1981, 1986) also are low in hope and feel blocked and unable to meet the many demands of their jobs (see Sherwin et al., 1992). For the reader interested in this topic, we recommend the articles of University of California at Berkeley psychologist Christina Maslach. She has produced excellent theoretical and measurement approaches to burnout.

Christina Maslach

Source: Reprinted with permission of Christina Maslach.

What Can Be Done to Improve Your Work?

To help you think somewhat more deeply about your job, we encourage you to study Figure 17.8. We use the boxes in this figure as an aid in going through the steps to improve one's work.

MAKING THE JOB BETTER

In our clinical interactions with people who were exploring issues related to their work, we have found it useful to ask about the first thoughts that a person has, early in the morning, about going to work. If you feel good about your job and look forward to work, we congratulate you on this fortuitous state of affairs. Even if you do like your job, however, we suggest that it helps to look constantly for ways to make it better. In Figure 17.8, this is represented by the left-hand route, labeled "Make Job Better."

Some additional discussion of the various decision points on the "Make Job Better" side is warranted. We believe that employees often have much more power and latitude than they typically realize in making positive changes in their jobs. This is especially true if you have performed well in your job. Your value to your boss may be far greater than you think. One change, however, may be tricky: You may think that having a raise would greatly increase your job satisfaction; as we have discussed, however, money is not as important as is commonly believed.

If a raise is not a panacea, are there other changes in your job that would make your life more enjoyable? Perhaps you could ask for a better office, longer or more frequent vacations, time to spend with family, a larger expense account, an assistant, a company car, or increased and varied retirement benefits. Flexible work schedules are very important for workers' mental health and well-being (Dittmann, 2005). Another possibility here is working at home. See the Personal Mini-Experiments to explore the possibility of working at home. On flexibility and working at home, Dittmann (2005) has written,

> IBM introduced flexible work schedules—such as giving many employees the option to work part-time or at home—based on another of its survey findings that such scheduling contributes to improved worker satisfaction. Now, one-third of IBM employees do not work at a traditional office. Indeed, IBM researchers have found that employees who work at home have the least difficulty with motivation and retention and are more willing to put in extra effort in their job. Plus, 55 percent of the employees surveyed agreed that working at home at least one day per week is acceptable, and 64 percent said that they are likely to work from home in the next five years. (p. 37)

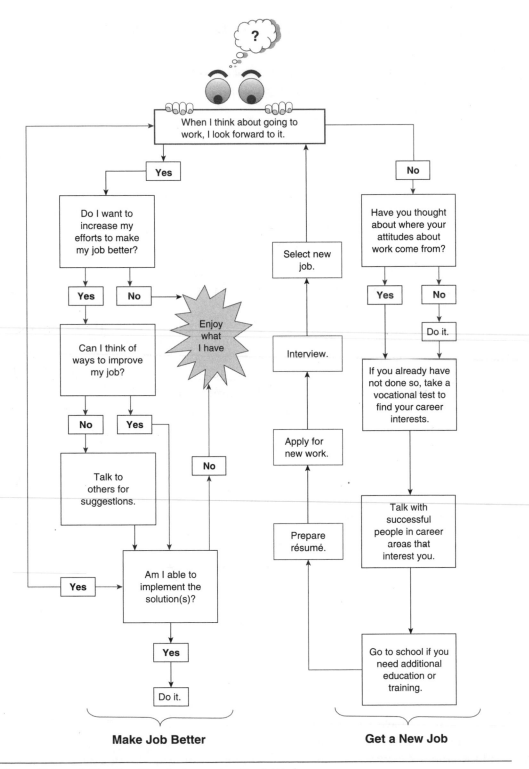

Figure 17.8   A Decision Tree for Improving One's Work

Personal Mini-Experiments

Becoming Gainfully Employed

We hope you have realized how crucial work is to our personal well-being and satisfaction. The following activities encourage you to consider the roots of some of your vocational interests and to experiment with the ideas for making your work situation better.

Can You Work at Home? Whether you are working (or will work) part- or full-time, perhaps you should consider what more and more professionals are doing—working at home. If your reaction to this suggestion is that the activities of your job necessitate your physical presence, then this may not be a good idea. But if your concern is something along the lines of "My boss wouldn't even consider that!" or "I wouldn't be able to work at home because I would just goof off!," there are ways to address this. Keep in mind that bosses are most concerned about productivity; how or where you get the job done is often less important. Eliminating the commute from your daily routine and increasing the flexibility of your schedule may lead to greater productivity. We encourage you to experiment with this idea of working at home by taking an online (or distance education) college course or continuing education workshop. (Many popular undergraduate and graduate courses are offered in online formats, and they typically require viewing of video lectures or completion of web-based assignments and some e-mail participation.) During the course or workshop, keep a journal in which you compare your engagement, satisfaction, and productivity to that typically achieved in a traditional course. This experience will provide valuable information about your work habits and productivity that can inform your future decisions (and negotiations with your boss).

Are You a "Chip Off the Old Block" When It Comes to Work Attitudes? As you think about your own work and your attitudes toward it, have you ever thought about where and how you got your work beliefs? The answer, as with many things, may come from your developmental experiences. Here is an exercise that we have used with our clients to help them to uncover the roots of their work attitudes. Begin by writing down your answers to the following questions:

1. How important is work in your life? (Give details.)
2. What has been your attitude about work throughout your life? (Give details.)
3. Do you enjoy working? If so, why? If not, why not?
4. If you have children, what are you trying (or what did you try) to teach them about the role of work in their lives?
5. Based on what you have seen of them so far, do you think your children have followed your ideas about work?

(Continued)

(Continued)

Once you have answered these questions, think about the people who raised you. These may be your biological parents, stepparents, or a multitude of others who take on the role of caregiver for children. Think about the caregiver who was the biggest influence on you when you were growing up. Once you have a good image in your mind of this person, then do a mental role-play in which you ask that person the same questions you just answered. Write down the answers that you expect your primary caregiver to give to these questions. Now, assuming that this primary caregiver is still alive and otherwise accessible, visit the person or give him or her a call. Ask these same five questions, and write down his or her answers.

At this point, you can see whether or not you are a "chip off the old block." Write each of the five questions in a column on the left side of a piece of paper, and then make three columns to the right. Head the first column "My Attitudes About Work"; the second column, "My Imagined Attitudes for My Caregiver," and the third column, "My Caregiver's Actual Attitudes About Work." In our experience, most people are amazed at the similarity of the attitudes across the three columns. This means that we truly do adopt the attitudes and beliefs of our primary caregivers when it comes to work. A workaholic caregiver will impart her values about work to her offspring. Likewise, the caregiver who has found great meaning in a calling often transmits the quest for a purpose-driven life to his offspring. Remember, if you do not particularly like the attitudes that you have about work, this exercise also provides an excellent starting point for making some changes.

Where Did You Get Your Vocational Interests? Do you know how your interests relate to those of successful people in various lines of work? Are your career choices really ones that you have made, or have other people, such as your parents (or friends, teachers, etc.) made these decisions for you (Saccuzzo & Ingram, 1993)? As a beginning point, please think about each of the following people and rate the percentage of influence that each has had on your career choice to date:

Person	Influence Percentage
Mother	_____
Father	_____
Sister	_____
Brother	_____
Spouse/Mate	_____
Teachers	_____
Friends	_____
Other	_____
YOU	_____
Total	_____ (This should be 100%)

Are you surprised to see who is wielding the most influence in your career selection? Our point is not that you should ignore the input of other people, but rather that you should become more aware of these influences and then decide whether you need or want to take more control of this process.

A good guide for improving your work situation is to consider the various factors that we have discussed previously as contributing to gainful employment (see Figure 17.1, page 411). Look for ways of attaining the following in your job: (1) variety in duties performed; (2) a safe working environment; (3) sufficient income; (4) a sense of purpose; (5) personal happiness and satisfaction; (6) positive engagement; (7) a sense that you are performing well and meeting the goals, and (8) companionship and friendship. Some of these eight characteristics of gainful employment may be more important to you than others. Accordingly, you should try to maximize the fulfillment of your needs in the most important areas.

Another step that we have found helpful is for workers to talk with their fellow employees about ways the work setting can be improved. Your coworkers may have good ideas for changes in the physical aspects of your job. Moreover, they may have tips about how to deal more effectively with other workers and bosses.

A last strategy that comes from the "Make Job Better" side of Figure 17.8 is to learn to enjoy what you have. Appreciation and savoring (Bryant, 2005; Bryant & Veroff, 2006) are important positive psychology attributes, and you may want to take more time to simply realize and enjoy what you have.

APPLYING FOR A NEW JOB

As you can see in Figure 17.8, if your answer is no to the question of awakening and looking forward to work, then you go to the right side of the guide, labeled "Get a New Job," and follow the steps outlined there.

It may take courage to launch a search for a new position. A key to this process is to remain flexible as you consider various options. In this regard, have you ever thought about where you got your attitudes about work, as well as your interests in specific types of work? We have found that parents, family members, and peers are strong influences. This topic is sufficiently important that we have prepared two exercises presented in the Personal Mini-Experiments. In "Chip Off the Old Block," you can see to what degree you learned your attitudes from your parents or caregivers.

You can think about an even wider sample of potentially influential people in regard to your attitudes about work. We believe it is important to think about these influences because, in our experience, considering these sources helps people change their attitudes. Previous readers have found "Where Did You Get Your Vocational Interests?" to be useful in ascertaining the factors that influenced their work attitudes.

The next step in Figure 17.8 is to take a vocational/interest test (if you have not already done so) to see how your interests align with various career trajectories. In our experience, the problem for some people is that they have been pursuing jobs that were not matched to their interest patterns. Our suggestion, especially if you are a college student who is reading this book as part of a course, is to walk over to the student services center and ask to talk to someone about getting career counseling. The key notion here is that you should be pursuing a career in which the activities truly tap your interests (and strengths, as noted previously). Most colleges have one or more professionals who are trained to administer vocational tests and then counsel students about the results. Be clear here that vocational tests do not tell you what job is right for you, but they do provide excellent tips about professions where you should be most satisfied given your interests. These tests may cost a nominal amount, or they may be part of the services offered to all students. We encourage you to do this, not only because it is very useful in making decisions about your career, but it also will be a bargain relative to the several hundred dollars that you would have to pay in the private sector for such services.

These vocational tests have been carefully validated to give you a sense of what your career interests may be as well as an idea of how your particular interests may relate to those of people who are happy and successful in various careers (for general overviews, see Harmon, Hansen, Borgen, & Hammer [1994], and Swanson & Gore [2000]; for specific discussions of cross-cultural and ethnic issues, see Day & Rounds [1998] and Fouad [2002]). The counselor will talk with you about your pattern of interests and, although you may think that you know what these are, you may be in for a surprise. You also will receive helpful feedback about how your interests fit with various professions. The decision about what direction to take will remain yours, but it will be an informed one, unlike that of the typical college student who selects a major, and therefore delimits subsequent jobs, by a hit-and-miss process of accumulating hours in that major. Is that the best way to plan for one of the most important aspect of your entire life? We think not.

Assuming that you do know what jobs are appropriate for you based on your interests and talents, then it may help to conduct informational interviews with people who are doing well in such careers. Find out what their jobs really entail, and then get their advice about finding jobs in the same area. At this stage, you may realize that you need to go back to school to get a new or different degree that will open doors to the jobs that you covet.

If you do have the appropriate education, the next step is to prepare a résumé and have other people read it to make sure that it is in its best form. You may want to go to an employment agency for help in your job search, but whether or not you do, the next step is to get your application and résumé to as many employers as possible.

The next stage involves interviews. Prepare carefully for these. Before an interview, practice with people whom you can trust to give you candid feedback. Learn everything you can about a company and its personnel before the interview. Dress appropriately for the setting. During the interview, show enthusiasm for the job. Listen to what your interviewers are saying, and pay attention. If you do not have the answer to a question, don't try to fake it—admit that you do not know but will learn! And, know your strengths; most interviewers will ask about them.

Congratulations! You now are being offered a job. It is at this stage that you have the most power to influence the content of your job offer. Think about things other than money. Pay attention to the gainful employment factors shown in Figure 17.1 as you negotiate with your potential new employer (for an overview of the application, interview, and negotiation process, see Snyder, 2002b). Finally, select the job you want to take—the one that best fulfills your gainful employment needs.

THE POWER TO CHANGE

In helping people who were less than happy with their work circumstances, we have found that, almost without exception, they eventually realized that they had more options and alternatives than they initially imagined. Therefore, as you work your way through this guide, realize that you can do things to make your job better. An important principle of positive psychology is that we can effectively change our lives—of which work is a crucial aspect—for the better.

When Work Becomes a Calling:
The Tale of a Hospital Orderly

One point that comes across loud and clear is that a person need not be gainfully employed in a high-paying, high-status position to gain enormous satisfaction from the work itself. An example may help to bring this point to life. In 1999, the senior author (CRS) of this textbook underwent a complex operation at the University of Kansas Medical Center. I was in the medical center for 2 weeks, and during that time I had the pleasure of interacting with many people who were wonderful in how they conducted themselves in their jobs. There was a high-status surgeon with his team of "baby docs" who followed him everywhere, as well as my world-class gastroenterologist. Small armies of other physicians and nurses also made my life more bearable. But as marvelous and accomplished as these professionals were, they did not leave the same impression on me as did a person who arguably was the very lowest in the status hierarchy. I am ashamed to say that I do not remember this person's name, but I can vividly remember what she brought to her job.

This amazing woman was an orderly who worked the graveyard shift from midnight until 8 a.m. These were the times when my pain medication often was not working well, when the bed seemed especially hard and uncomfortable, and when I longed to escape the suffering. It was during these dark hours that this orderly, a physically small woman, would fluff my pillow and talk with me about how things would be better. I asked her about her job, which seemed mostly to involve emptying bedpans, cleaning up messes, and replacing dirty gowns and blankets.

An immigrant from Iran, she was very proud of her work, and she told me so! She said that her job was to make sure that the postoperative patients were comfortable during the wee hours of the morning. When I wanted to scream because of the pain, she would tell me about my family, who would be showing up at sunrise.

Doing things that others might deem to be demeaning, this orderly expressed pleasure in the tasks that were part of her job. Many times I remember thanking her for the kindnesses she had delivered, and the next time I awakened, her prophecy had come true—there stood my wife, family members, and friends, and I *was* feeling better.

This orderly also was proud of what she did. Very proud. She saw herself as an important part of the health care team, *and she was.* Each night, she brought a fresh selection of cut flowers in a small vase and placed it on the table beside my bed. I asked her about these flowers, and she said that she went to a nearby grocery store when she came to work in the evening. The store was going to throw away these cut flowers that they would not use, so instead she brought them to work to make small floral arrangements for "her" patients. I would look at these flowers in the early morning hours, and their beauty was magnified when I learned the story that went with them.

My point in telling the story of this orderly is to show how any job, even one seemingly low status, can be a source of dignity and self-respect. Any task, when done well, can bring pleasure to the worker and those whom that person serves. I never will forget this orderly.

As positive psychology pioneer Martin Seligman (2002) notes in describing workers such as this one, they do not see themselves as just having jobs; instead, they have callings. Credit should be given to Amy Wrzesniewski of New York University for her groundbreaking research on the notion of calling (see Wrzesniewski, McCauley, Rozin, & Schwartz, 1997; Wrzesniewski, Rozin, & Bennett, 2001). Again, in the words of Seligman (2002),

> Individuals with a calling see their work as contributing to the greater good, to something larger than they are, and hence the religious connotation is entirely appropriate. The work is fulfilling in its own right, without regard for money or for advancement. When the money stops and the promotions end, the work goes on. Traditionally, callings were reserved to very prestigious and rarified work—priests, supreme court justices, physicians, and scientists. But there has been an important discovery in the field: Any job can become a calling, and any calling can become a job. (p. 168)

Amy Wrzesniewski

Source: Reprinted with permission of Amy Wrzesniewski.

A New Accounting:
An Eye Toward People Rather Than Money

Money talks, but evidently not as loudly as the common stereotype would suggest. This is what we have found in reviewing the literature in preparation for writing this chapter on work. If money is not so important, then, what about our source—our work—for making money? In this regard, we have been impressed with the potential power of work. Next to our interpersonal relationships, work probably is the most important source for making our lives better. Think about this when it comes to your own life.

The positive psychology message that emerges from this chapter is a strong and consistent one: Make your work the best that it can be. Or search for a new job that has the markers of gainful employment discussed in this chapter. If positive psychology succeeds in the 21st century, it will have helped employers and employees alike to create and find work that supports people not only financially but psychologically as well. Therefore, along with the present accounting system that emphasizes low percentages of unemployed people, we focus on having high percentages of gainfully employed people. The latter approach would productively engage the talents of more workers and, at the same time, raise their sense of satisfaction. These are worthy work-related goals for positive psychology.

Key Terms

Authentic boss: A supervisor who is one of "those individuals who are deeply aware of how they think and behave and are perceived by others as being aware of their own and others' values/morals perspective, knowledge, and strengths; aware of the context in which they operate; and who are confident, hopeful, optimistic, resilient, and high on moral character" (Avolio et al. 2004, p. 4).

Burnout: An employee's feeling that, despite working hard, he or she is unable to do everything that needs to be done. The employee is tired and perceives a lack of reward from his or her job.

Career self-efficacy: Personal confidence in one's capacity to handle career development and work-related activities.

Engagement: An employee's involvement with his or her work. Engagement often depends on employees knowing what is expected of them, having what they need to do their work, having a chance to improve and develop, and having opportunities to develop relationships with coworkers.

Gainful employment: Work that contributes to a healthy life by providing variety, a safe working environment, sufficient income, a sense of purpose in work done, happiness and satisfaction, engagement and involvement, a sense of performing well and meeting goals, and companionship and loyalty to coworkers, bosses, and companies.

Human capital: The skills, knowledge, education, experience, ideas, and abilities of employees that are assets to a company.

Positive psychological capital: Assets to a company that result from employee's efficacy (confidence in one's ability to reach desired goals), hope (the capacity to find pathways to desired goals along with the motivation to use those pathways), optimism (the attribution of good outcomes to internal, stable, and pervasive causes) and resiliency (the capacity to endure and succeed in adversity).

Presenteeism: A state in which employees may be physically at work but, because of mental health problems resulting from aversive and repetitive work experiences, are unproductive and unhappy.

Satisfaction: An employee's enthusiasm for his or her work.

Social capital: Assets of a company or person that result from their social relationships, network of contacts, and friends; i.e., assets based on "who you know."

Strengths-based approach to gainful employment: The strengths-based approach to employment involves increasing an employee's awareness of his or her natural and learned talents, integration of these talents into the employee's self-image, and behavioral change in which the employee learns to attribute successes to his or her talents.

Traditional economic capital: The physical facilities and assets of a company, such as plants and buildings, equipment, data, patents, and technology.

Workaholic: A person so engaged in and obsessed by work that he or she is unable to disengage from it and attend to responsibilities of families and friends.

The Me/We Balance

Building Better Communities

Where We Are Going: From ME to WE to US

In this chapter, we use two important human motives as a framework. The first motive is the individualistic focus, in which one pursues a sense of specialness relative to others. A second motive is the collectivistic focus, in which one tries to maximize the link to others (Bellah, Madsen, Sullivan, Swidler, & Tipton, 1985, 1988; Snyder & Fromkin, 1980). We first explore the individualistic focus on the one—the ME—followed by the collectivistic focus on the many—the WE. Last, we propose a blend of the one and the many—the WE/ME, or, more simply, US. This approach represents an intermingling in which both the individual and the group are considered essential for satisfying and productive lives. As we see it, the US perspective reflects a viable positive psychology resolution for the future of humankind.

Individualism: The Psychology of ME

In this section, we touch on the American history of rugged individualism (also discussed in Chapter 2), along with the core and secondary emphases that define a person as individualistic. We then discuss one aspect of individualism, the need for uniqueness, and show how this need can be measured and manifested in a variety of activities.

A BRIEF HISTORY OF AMERICAN INDIVIDUALISM

Alexis de Tocqueville

Source: © Corbis.

Since the publication of Alexis de Tocqueville's (1835/2003) *Democracy in America,* the United States has been known as the land of the "rugged individualist." The essence of this view is that any person with a good idea, through hard work, can succeed in the pursuit of personal goals. In the words of de Tocqueville, Americans "form the habit of thinking of themselves in isolation and imagine that their whole destiny is in their own hands" (p. 508). Such individualism was linked to the American emphases on equal rights and freedom (Lukes, 1973), as well as to its capitalistic economy and open frontiers (Curry & Valois, 1991). Since the establishment of American independence in 1776, this rugged individualism has metamorphosed into the "Me generation" that held sway from the 1960s through the early 1990s (Myers, 2004).

EMPHASES IN INDIVIDUALISM

When concern for the individual is greater than concern for the group, then the culture is said to be **individualistic**; however, when each person is very concerned about the group, then the society is **collectivistic**. As shown in Figure 18.1, when the average person in a society is disposed toward individual independence, that society is deemed individualistic (see the bell-shaped curve drawn with the dotted line).

Core Emphases

We have used the terms *core emphases* and *secondary emphases* to capture the more and less central aspects of individualistic and collectivistic societies. We have also prepared Table 18.1 to help the reader understand the core and secondary emphases within the individualistic and collectivistic perspectives.

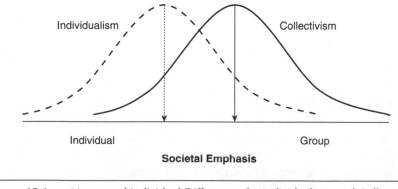

Figure 18.1   Norms and Individual Differences for Individualistic and Collectivistic Societies

Table 18.1   Core and Secondary Emphases of Individualism and Collectivism

Individualism	Collectivism
Core Emphases	
Independence ———————	Dependence
Uniqueness or desire to stand out ———————	Conformity or desire to fit in
Unit of analysis is self/individual ———————	Unit of analysis is others/group
Secondary Emphases	
Goals for self ———————	Goals for others/group
Success for self ———————	Success for group
Satisfaction from self ———————	Satisfaction depends on harmony
Personal payoff ———————	Mutual generosity and equity
Does cost/benefit analysis ———————	Unconditional relatedness
Spontaneity ———————	Duties
Short-term thinking ———————	Long-term thinking
Informal interactions ———————	Formal interactions

As shown in the top portion of Table 18.1, the three core emphases within individualism involve a sense of independence, a desire to stand out relative to others (a need for uniqueness), and the use of the self or the individual as the unit of analysis in thinking about life. We discuss each of these core emphases next.

Underlying each culture is a set of expectations and memories about what is thought to be appropriate for the members of that society. In individualistic societies such as America, social patterns resemble a loosely interwoven fabric, and it is the norm for each person to see him- or herself as independent of the surrounding group of people (Triandis, 1995). On this point, research involving many studies supports the conclusion that American individualism reflects a sense of independence rather than dependence (see Oyserman, Coon, & Kemmelmeier, 2002).

A second core emphasis within individualism is that the person wants to stand out relative to the population as a whole. Within individualistic societies, therefore, people follow their own motives and preferences instead of adjusting their desires to accommodate those of the group (this sometimes is called *conforming*). The individualistic person thus sets personal goals that may not match those of the groups to which he or she belongs (Schwartz, 1994; Triandis, 1988, 1990). Because of the individualistic propensity to manifest one's specialness, coupled with societal support for actions that show such individuality, it follows that the citizens of individualistic societies such as the United States will have a high need for uniqueness. Research related to this point supports the robustness of uniqueness-seeking thoughts and actions among Americans (e.g., Snyder & Fromkin, 1977, 1980). We explore this fascinating motive in greater detail later in this section.

A third core emphasis of individualism is that the self or person is the unit of analysis in understanding how people think and act in a society. That is, explanations of events are likely to involve the person rather than the group. Therefore, the various definitions of individualism draw upon worldviews in which personal factors are emphasized over social forces (Bellah et al., 1985; Kagitcibasi, 1994; Triandis, 1995).

Secondary Emphases

Several secondary emphases flow from the individualistic focus upon the self rather than the group. These are listed in Table 18.1. Goals set by citizens of an individualistic society typically are for the self; moreover, success and related satisfactions also operate at the level of the self. Simply put, the payoffs are at the personal level rather than the group level. The individualistic person pursues what is enjoyable to him or her, in contrast to collectivistic people, who derive their pleasures from things that promote the welfare of the group. Of course, the individualist at times may follow group norms, but this usually happens when she or he has deduced that it is personally advantageous to do so.

As may be obvious by now, individualists are focused upon pleasure and their own self-esteem in interpersonal relationships and beyond. Individualists also weigh the disadvantages and advantages of relationships before deciding whether to pursue them (Kim, Sharkey, & Singelis, 1994). Thus, individualistic persons engage in benefit analyses to determine what may profit them, whereas collectivists are more likely to give their unconditional support to their group and think first and foremost in terms of their duties to the group. Unlike individualists, collectivists are not likely to behave spontaneously, because of their concerns about their peer group. Individualists tend to be rather short-term in their thinking, whereas collectivists are more long-term in their thought patterns. Last, as shown in Table 18.1, people in individualistic societies often are somewhat informal in their interactions with others, whereas people in collectivistic societies are more formal in their interactions, as they attend to the expected and important norms that determine such behaviors. (For a thorough discussion of all these secondary emphases, we recommend the review article by Oyserman et al., 2002.)

PERSONAL EXAMPLES OF INDIVIDUALISM

Somewhere in my journey into adulthood, I (CRS) bought into rugged individualism and got the impression that asking for help was not a good option. During my childhood, I must have received the advice, "Don't ask for help." For some reason, I was thinking about this guiding maxim as I was writing this chapter today—Sunday, December 26th, 2004—my 60th birthday.

We all get many messages from the surrounding community as we grow up. Some make sense, but many do not. Although this "Don't ask for help" lesson fits into the latter category, I understand its seductiveness. Perhaps it can be traced to our rootedness in rugged individualism, whereby we learned the rewards of accomplishing something entirely on our own. But what nonsense this can be, because even when we think that we are doing something totally "on our own," in fact we are using the ideas and inventions of our ancestors to reach our goals. At other times, it is sheer folly *not* to reach out and ask the simple question, "Could you please give me a hand here?"

There are many examples of my foolish adherence to this "Don't ask for help" rule, but one will suffice. When I was in graduate school, I prided myself in carrying as many grocery bags as I could possibly lift. With two paper bags on each arm, I would walk precariously toward the door of my apartment building. At that point, I faced a dilemma—unlocking and then opening the large entry door while holding the four grocery bags. Although several neighbors often passed by, and some even offered help, I would have none of it. Putting down the sacks somehow represented another contorted violation of "Don't ask for help." Instead, I went through a balancing act in which I tried to extract my keys from my jeans pocket, find the correct key, insert it in the door, and open the door—all the while balancing the bags of groceries.

Of course, you can predict what sometimes happened: I dropped the bags. At other times, the paper sacks ripped open, and the contents tumbled out. Once, this happened during a rare Nashville snowstorm. Having fallen on my back with my groceries strewn around me, I remained in the snow, laughing. It was then that I changed my policy of not asking for help, and I have not regretted it since. Not once.

Since those graduate school days, I have found that people are more than willing to help when I ask. Likewise, as we noted in the exercise in Chapter 12, it makes people feel good to help another person. If you would like to explore your own willingness to ask for help, as well as your thoughts and feelings about giving help, please try "Asking for Help" and "Volunteering for Help," the first two exercises in this chapter's Personal Mini-Experiments.

Personal Mini-Experiments

Getting and Giving Help

In this chapter, we explore how the sense of community can promote optimal human functioning. The following exercises encourage you to think about how your relationships to others and the broader community can make a positive difference in your life.

Asking for Help: If you are a person who finds it difficult to ask for the help of another, this exercise offers you a chance to break that habit. Select some activity for which you are especially unlikely to ask for help, and the next time you are in this situation, instead of trying to struggle through it by yourself, go ahead and ask another person for a hand. Here are some questions to ask yourself about a recent situation in which you could have asked for help:

1. Describe the circumstance, included all your thoughts and feelings. What did you imagine people would say if you asked for help? What would you have thought about yourself if you had asked for help?

2. Did you ask for help? If not, why not? If so, how did you overcome your rule, "Don't ask for help"?

3. How did the situation turn out when you did ask for help? What were the reactions of the person you asked for help? Did you get the needed help? If you did, how did you feel? Do you think you could ask for help in a future, similar situation?

Part of being in a community is being able to call upon the people in that community for assistance. Contrary to what you have been taught about not asking for help, it is not a weakness to ask for help. Indeed, it is a strength. You are human. . . . You do need other people to get things accomplished. This is not a bad thing, but a wonderful reality that is part of being a member of a community. As we have suggested in this exercise, give it a try. Once people do, they rarely turn back.

Volunteering Your Help: Remember the last time you offered your assistance to someone else? It probably took very little of your time, and you made a small improvement in your community. The other beautiful aspect of offering help is that it feels absolutely wonderful. (See the Personal Mini-Experiments in Chapter 12, pages 271–272.) Helping thus provides two benefits: one to the recipient and one to the giver. To implement this exercise, just look around your local community and watch your neighbors. Part of this may be a simple wave or greeting. At other times, it may be obvious that someone really could use a helping hand. There are many flat tires needing to be fixed, people who need assistance carrying packages, guidance warranted in getting across the street, directions needed, and so on. To see how you have fared in this exercise, try the following questions:

1. Describe the last circumstance in which you noticed that a person needed help, and include all your thoughts and feelings. What did you imagine people would say if you offered help? What did you think about yourself after offering help?

2. Did you offer help? If not, why not? If you did, how were you able to overcome any rule to the contrary (such as "Don't bother others")?

3. How did the situation turn out when you offered help? How did the person to whom you offered help react? Did you give the needed help? If you did, how did you feel? Do you think you could do this again in a future, similar situation?

Being Alone or With Others: To complete this exercise, merely think about the goal-related activity listed in the left column, and place a check mark in the column to the right that reflects your preferences about doing this alone or with others. Under each general life category, briefly write your desired goal. If you have more than one goal under each category, write each of these goals. Likewise, if you do not have a goal in a given category, then ignore it. Go through each of the goal categories and write a goal (or goals) on the blank line below each one. Then, go back to each goal category and, if you would prefer to seek the goal totally alone, place a check mark under the "Alone" column. If you would prefer to seek the goal with another person, place a check mark under the "Another" column. Finally, if you would prefer to seek the goal with two or more other people, place a check mark under the "Others" column.

Goal Category	Alone	Another	Others
Religious/Spiritual Goal(s)			
_____	____	____	____
Sport Goal(s)			
_____	____	____	____
Academic Goal(s)			
_____	____	____	____
Physical Health Goal(s)			
_____	____	____	____
Psychological Health Goal(s)			
_____	____	____	____
Work Goal(s)			
_____	____	____	____

(Continued)

┌───┐

(Continued)

   Now that you have completed this inventory, simply count the life goals you want
to pursue alone, those you want to do with another person, and those you want to
do with two or more other people. Are you a person who wants to go it alone? If so,
you truly may be prone to the individualistic perspective. Did you find that most of
your goals involved one or more other people? If so, you probably have a more collectivistic perspective. This should give you a rough idea of the importance of other
people to you as you seek the major goals in your life.

   For some of your goals, you may prefer going it alone, whereas for other goals,
you may want to be with one or more others. This is useful information, and it is part
of our general belief that a balanced life entails some things done alone and others
done in concert. Stated another way, you can determine the areas of your life in
which you are an individualist and those in which you are a collectivist.

└───┘

A SUMMARY OF INDIVIDUALISM

The individualistic perspective appears to center on the three core elements shown in Table 18.1—independence, uniqueness, and the self as the
unit of analysis. As to whether Americans are high on such individualism,
the conclusion based on the aggregated body of research appears to be a
qualified yes. In the most sophisticated analysis of this general question,
Oyserman et al. (2002) found that European Americans were more individualistic than members of other countries in that they valued personal
independence. Oyserman et al. also found, however, that European
Americans were not more individualistic than African Americans or
Latinos/Latinas.

THE NEED FOR UNIQUENESS

Now, let's take another look at Figure 18.1. Although it is true that the
norms in individualistic societies emphasize the person (see the dotted
line with an arrow at the bottom), you will notice that some people belong
toward the group end of the continuum and others toward the individual
end. In this latter regard, we now explore the desire to manifest specialness
relative to other people.

The pursuit of individualistic goals to produce a sense of specialness has
been termed the **need for uniqueness** (see Lynn & Snyder, 2002; Snyder &
Fromkin, 1977, 1980). This need is posited to have some universal appeal,
as people seek to maintain some degree of difference from others (as well
as to maintain a bond to other people). In the 1970s, researchers Howard
Fromkin and C. R. Snyder (see Snyder & Fromkin, 1977, 1980) embarked
on a program of research based on the premise that most people have

some desire to be special relative to others. They called this human motive the *need for uniqueness*. Beyond establishing that some specialness was desirable for most of the people in their American samples, these researchers also reasoned that some people have a very high need for uniqueness, whereas others have a very low need for uniqueness. In short, there are individual differences in need for uniqueness.

Encoding of Similarity Information

People define themselves along a variety of identity dimensions. An identity dimension is defined as "a set of person attributes which have a common core of meaning" (Miller, 1963, p. 676). In their theory of uniqueness, Snyder and Fromkin (1980) proposed that people think about their perceived similarity to others and use a dimension (in their minds) on which they evaluate how correct any given feedback seems about their degree of similarity to other people (technically, this is encoded on a uniqueness identity schema). In brief, people evaluate the acceptability of their having varying degrees of similarity to other people. These hypothetical encodings on the uniqueness identity dimension are shown in Figure 18.2.

As can be seen in Figure 18.2, the similarity information is encoded as increasingly higher in acceptability, from very slight, to slight, to moderate, to high levels of perceived similarity to others, with a drop to low acceptability for very high similarity. Thus, the moderate-to-high sense of

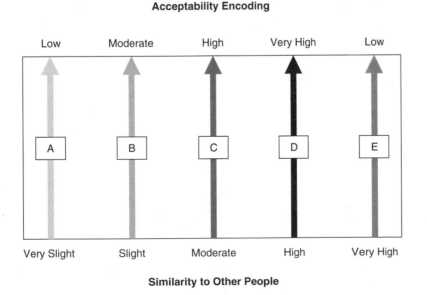

Acceptability Encoding

Low	Moderate	High	Very High	Low
A	B	C	D	E
Very Slight	Slight	Moderate	High	Very High

Similarity to Other People

Figure 18.2   Acceptability Encoding as a Function of Perceived Similarity to Other People

similarity is rated as the most comfortable, most accurate one for people—the reasons being that people realize that most others are somewhat similar to them (see Brown, 1991) and that people desire some specialness. In other words, in terms of *reality as people actually have perceived it* and *how they want it to be,* people prefer the moderate-to-high range of similarity (points C and D in Figure 18.2). Finally, people are not comfortable with either of the extremes of low similarity (point A in Figure 18.2) or high similarity (point E in Figure 18.2).

Emotional and Behavioral Reactions to Similarity Information

When confronted with the varying degrees of perceived similarity that produce the acceptability encodings of Figure 18.2, people then should have the most positive emotional reactions when they perceive that they are highly similar to others (point D in Figure 18.2). Consistent with this hypothesis, the research of Bryne (1969, 1971; Bryne & Clore, 1970) and the efforts of Snyder and Fromkin (1980; see also Lynn & Snyder, 2002) have yielded support for the emotional reactions shown in Figure 18.3. More specifically, people's emotional reactions become more and more positive as levels of similarity increase from the very slight to slight to moderate to high, becoming negative as the level of similarity enters the very high range. (For similar predictions and findings, see the research of Ohio State University psychologist Marilyn Brewer [1991] and Brewer & Weber [1994].) Note that the very highest positive emotional reactions occur when people perceive that they have a relatively moderate to high degree of similarity, thereby showing the maximal pleasure derived from human bonds.

It may help here to give an example of how moderate similarity to another person is emotionally satisfying. The senior author (CRS) once worked with a young woman named Molly who was having difficulties in her college dating relationships. She initially thought that it would be very fun and exciting to date guys who were extremely different from her in terms of their interests. She was the offspring of parents who were college professors, and in rebellion against her parents' backgrounds, her first attempts at college dating involved what she later derisively called her "truck phase" (meaning that she dated guys who drove very big trucks). These were guys who were not serious about school and who spent a good deal of time drinking beer and working on their truck engines. After her first year in college, she settled into a pattern of dating men who shared some of her interests and values about doing well in school but who were majoring in different subjects. These males gave Molly a sense of moderate-to-high similarity, and she reported that she was much happier than she had been with the "truck guys" who were not very similar to her.

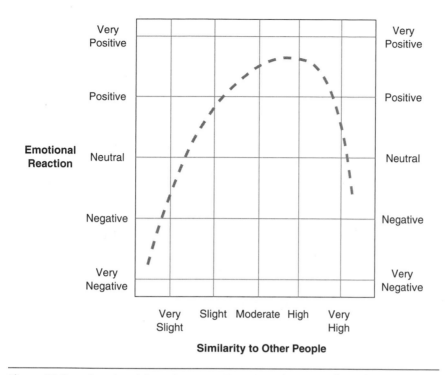

Figure 18.3   Emotional Reactions as a Function of Perceived Similarity to Other People

The acceptability reactions that result from degree of perceived similarity to others (see Figure 18.2) also can cause people to change their actual behaviors to become more or less similar to another person. More specifically, the most positive acceptability (i.e., high similarity) not only produces the highest positive emotional reactions, but it also should result in no need to make any behavioral changes relative to other people. On the other hand, the very slight level of similarity to others yields low acceptability; therefore, people should change to become more similar to others. Moreover, the very high level of similarity to other people is low in acceptability, and therefore people should change to become less similar to others. In this latter sense, because peoples' need for uniqueness is not being satisfied, they should strive to reestablish their differences. Consistent with these predicted behavioral reactions, the results of several studies (see Figure 18.4) have supported this proposed pattern (Snyder & Fromkin, 1980).

To illustrate how people actually may change because of feedback that they are extremely similar to others, consider the reactions of a young woman named Shandra. After joining a sorority at the beginning of college, she was required to wear the same outfits as her sorority sisters whenever they went on group trips. From the beginning, Shandra reacted negatively to what she saw as "uniform requirements" that were being

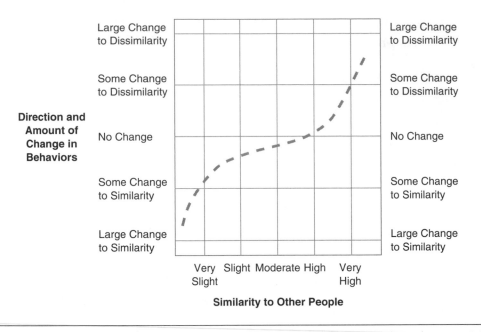

Figure 18.4   Direction and Amount of Change as a Function of Perceived Similarity to Other
People

placed on her. In a bold attempt to break away and assert her uniqueness,
Shandra started wearing outfits that differed from those of her sorority sisters. Her "sisters" tried to get her to conform, but Shandra stood fast in
her desire to dress differently. In fact, she later resigned from this sorority
because of their reaction to her desire to dress differently.

Taken together, these findings suggest that people are drawn to moderate to high levels of perceived similarity to their fellow humans but that
there are upper limits to this desire for the human bond. Furthermore,
there appears to be a desire to balance one's perceived similarity so that it
is kept at the high level; research shows that people are motivated by a need
for uniqueness when they feel too much similarity and that they will strive
for similarity when they feel too different. Most of us have a balance of
"we" and "me" motives; thus, just as an extreme desire for uniqueness can
lead to dysfunction in relating to others and potential social exclusion, so,
too, can an extreme desire for similarity lead to such immersion in "getting
along" that one loses one's power in interpersonal relationships.

Development of the Need for Uniqueness Scale

Based on the previously discussed theoretical predictions and findings
on uniqueness-related behaviors, Snyder and Fromkin (1977) proposed
that there should be individual differences in self-reported need for

uniqueness. Accordingly, they developed and validated the Need for Uniqueness Scale (Snyder & Fromkin, 1977). This self-report scale appears in the Appendix. If you would like to get a sense of your own desire for specialness by completing the scale, refer to this Appendix.

The Need for Uniqueness Scale has been translated into several languages and administered to thousands of people over the years. An average score is around 100; scores higher than this reflect increasingly elevated levels of need for uniqueness, and scores lower than this reflect increasingly diminished levels (Snyder & Fromkin, 1977, 1980). People who score higher on the Need for Uniqueness Scale also have higher self esteem and less anxiety, especially relative to interpersonal matters.

In thinking about the Need for Uniqueness Scale, however, it is important to remember that these scores tap the need to be special, but in many instances this need translates into actual behaviors or actions that represent such specialness. For example, in subsequent discussions of uniqueness attributes, you will learn that people with a higher need for uniqueness, as measured by their scores on the Need for Uniqueness Scale, actually do manifest behaviors that signify their specialness.

Uniqueness Attributes

Having explored the personal need for uniqueness, at this point we describe the acceptable societal processes by which our uniqueness needs are met. People are punished when they deviate from normal or expected behaviors in a society (Goffman, 1963; Schachter, 1951). Thus, unusual behaviors quickly may elicit societal disapprovals and rejections (see Becker, 1963; Freedman & Doob, 1968; Goffman, 1963; Palmer, 1970; Schur, 1969). On the other hand, the following of rules (normal behaviors) typically do not elicit much reaction from other people.

How, then, are people to show their specialness? Fortunately, each society has some acceptable attributes whereby its citizens can show their differences, and these are called *uniqueness attributes*. On this point, Snyder and Fromkin (1980, p. 107) have written, "There are a number of attributes (physical, material, informational, experiential, etc.) that are valued because they define the person as different from members of his or her reference group and that, at the same time, will not call down the forces of rejection and isolation for deviancy. We give examples of these uniqueness attributes in the ensuing sections.

Commodities as Uniqueness Attributes

One of the earliest and most famous psychologists, William James (1890), reasoned that people often define themselves by their possessions. It should come as no surprise, then, to learn that we are attracted by scarce

William James

commodities. This is why we find the sales pitch "Hurry on down while the supply lasts," so seductive. Of special importance, however, is the fact that people who are very high (as opposed to low) in need for uniqueness as measured by the Need for Uniqueness Scale are the most attracted to scarce commodities (see Lynn & Snyder, 2002).

A variety of commodities can be used to define a person as unique— clothes, cars, houses, jewelry, vacations, even special mates (see Walster, Walster, Piliavin, & Schmidt, 1973). Certainly, advertisers are aware of the appeal of special commodities because they promote it in their efforts to sell products. For example, a travel agency uses the message "Birds of a feather need not flock together" to entice potential customers to take unique vacations; a shoe company runs advertisements noting that their "boots will not be available to all customers"; and a perfume is touted as "a fragrance as individual as you are."

In what has been called a "catch-22 carousel" (Snyder, 1992), advertisers use uniqueness appeals to persuade people to buy products, and then, by making yearly changes in their products (styles of clothes, cars, etc.), motivate customers to purchase the latest version. The irony is that, after the latest uniqueness-based advertisement has persuaded people to buy, they notice that what they have bought is now quite common— many other people also have it. Of course, the yearly change of styles keeps people on the consumer "catch-22 carousel."

The role of products as uniqueness attributes has received sufficient attention and support that researchers have developed and validated specific self-report measures aimed at tapping the need for uniqueness in people as they purchase products. For example, Lynn and Harris (1997a, 1997b) developed the Desire for Unique Products Scale; and Tian, Bearden, and Hunter (2001; see Tian & McKenzie, 2001) have validated the Consumer's Need for Uniqueness Scale.

Names as Uniqueness Attributes

Noted personality psychologist Gordon Allport (1961, p. 117) wrote that one's name might be "the most important anchorage of our self-identity." Our name singles out our individuality in a sea of other people. In this regard, have you ever noticed that a person typically becomes annoyed if someone does not remember his or her name after being introduced? So, too, are people bothered to find out that another person has his or her name.

In large urban settings, where people feel deindividuated because so many people live in proximity, it makes sense that name graffiti prolifer- ates on the sides of buildings and trains. It is as if people are striking out to state their specialness by writing their nicknames in huge letters. Consistent with this, Snyder, Omens, and Bloom (1977) reasoned that people with a higher need for uniqueness should have a greater desire to "show their names." Therefore, these researchers had people take the Need for Uniqueness Scale and then sign their names. As hypothesized, those with higher scores in need for uniqueness wrote their names larger (i.e., area of signature as measured by length by height, controlling for the number of letters in the names). In a similar study, Zweigenhaft (reported in Snyder & Fromkin, 1980) gave the Need for Uniqueness Scale to a large number of female college students and then found that those with higher scores also had names that were statistically unusual.

Attitudes and Beliefs as Uniqueness Attributes

Attitudes and beliefs also provide a means for defining a person's special self. In fact, college students often perceive their attitudes and beliefs as their most special characteristics and their behaviors as far less special (Fromkin & Demming, 1967, as reported in Snyder & Fromkin, 1980). Furthermore, research shows that the more we want our attitudes to be different, the more we actually think these attitudes *are* different (Weir, 1971). Ironically, however, when a check is made of whether such special attitudes actually do differ from those of peers, research shows that people's supposedly special attitudes are not different (Brandt & Fromkin, 1974, as reported in Snyder & Fromkin, 1980). This finding is analogous to an earlier phenomenon called **pluralistic ignorance**—the mistaken notion that one's beliefs are nonconforming (Katz & Schanck, 1938). Obviously, there is something satisfying about thinking one's attitudes and beliefs are special, even if it is an illusion (for a demonstration of this illusion, see Snyder, 1997, 1999b).

Performances as Uniqueness Attributes

Our performances in society also can serve as uniqueness attributes. In this regard, the individualistic pursuit of uniqueness through performance usually takes one of three forms, which we discuss next (see Chapter 9 of Snyder and Fromkin [1980] for a full exposition of these three types of performance).

A first type of performance is what we call *individualistic normal competition,* or "Playing the Game." As can be seen in Figure 18.5, the person initially starts out in a group in which there are rules for the competition. Playing by the rules, a winner then emerges by selling more cars, getting better grades, throwing the javelin farthest, or some such. Typically, this winner then must go to yet another group, in which the competition is even stiffer. This "normal competition" is widespread in western societies, especially individualistic and capitalistic ones. If you are a college student, for example, how often have your exam grades been based on a curve (i.e., some As, Bs, Cs, Ds, and Fs)?

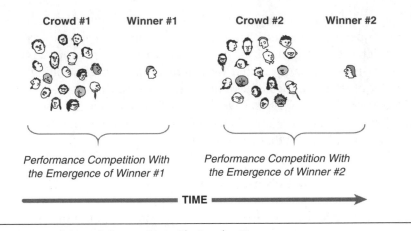

Figure 18.5   Normal Competition: Playing the Game

A second type of performance is *individualistic successful differentiation,* or "Changing the Game." Sometimes, the person finds him- or herself in a group where there are clearly defined rules or statements about the nature of reality. As shown in Figure 18.6, the person comes up with a new idea or way of playing the game and decides to break off from the group to espouse a new perspective or idea. If the person is successful, over time she or he may attract followers, along with countergroups who oppose this new perspective. It is likely that every idea we presently take for granted reflects the efforts of someone who, at an earlier point in time, broke off from an older model or perspective. Thus, whether it is the invention of the light bulb, the discovery of DNA, or the view that the world is round, civilization owes a debt of gratitude to these successful differentiators because they have given us new, improved ideas.

A third type of performance is *individualistic deviance,* or "You Cannot Play the Game." As can be seen in Figure 18.7, this results when a powerful person in the group decides to ostracize a particular group member and kicks that person out of the group. Having been pushed from the group, this person indeed is different, but not in a positive manner as is the case for the successful differentiators who get their views accepted. Instead, the deviant loses face, and even though he or she may get a few followers, history proves that such people are outcasts who have no impact on the thinking of the majority of people. We cannot give a historical example of people who exemplify "You Cannot Play the Game," because they made no impact with their views and thus have not been remembered. This lack of success in being recognized suggests that such people's views did not attract strong followings.

We have reviewed the theory and measurement of the need for uniqueness, which is perhaps a quintessential American motive. We now turn to a different motive: collectivism.

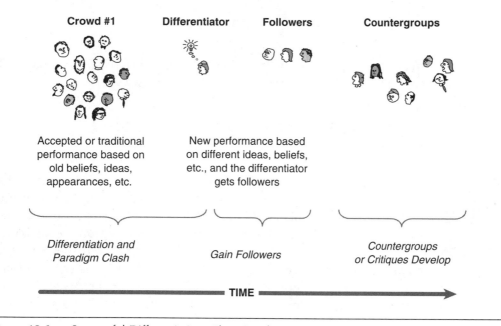

Figure 18.6   Successful Differentiation: Changing the Game

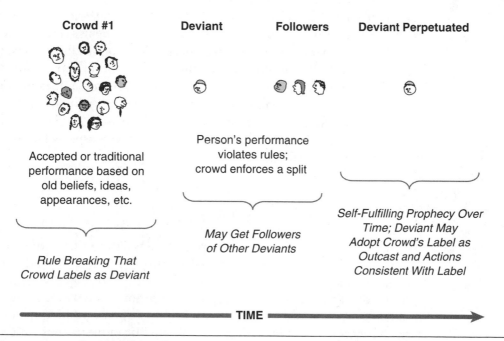

Figure 18.7   Unsuccessful Differentiation or Deviance: "You Cannot Play the Game"

Collectivism: The Psychology of WE

In this section, we comment on the history of collectivism (see Chapter 3) and then describe its core and secondary emphases.

Roy F. Baumeister

Source: Reprinted with permission of Roy F. Baumeister.

A HISTORICAL COMMENT ON COLLECTIVISM: WE CAME TOGETHER OUT OF NECESSITY

Thousands of years ago, our hunter-gatherer ancestors realized that there were survival advantages to be derived from banding together into groups with shared goals and interests (Chency, Seyforth, & Smuts, 1986; Panter-Brick, Rowley-Conwy, & Layton, 2001). These groups contributed to a sense of belonging, fostered personal identities and roles for their members (McMillan & Chavis, 1986), and offered shared emotional bonds (Bess, Fisher, Sonn, & Bishop, 2002). Moreover, the resources of the people in groups helped them fend off threats from other humans and animals.

Simply stated, groups offered power to their members (Heller, 1989). The people in such groups protected and cared for each other, and they formed social units that were effective contexts for the propagation and raising of offspring. Gathered into groups, humans reaped the benefits of community (Sarason, 1974).

Mark Leary

Source: Reprinted with permission of Mark Leary.

By today's standards, our hunter-gatherer relatives were more primitive in their needs and aspirations. But were they really that much different from people today in the satisfactions and benefits they derived from their group memberships? We think not, because human beings always have had the shared characteristics of what social psychologist Elliot Aronson (2003) has called "social animals." In this regard, one of our strongest human motives is to belong—to feel as if we are connected in meaningful ways with other people (Baumeister & Leary, 1995). Social psychologists Roy Baumeister and Mark Leary (1995) and Donelson Forsyth (1999; Forsyth & Corazzini, 2000) have argued that people prosper when they join together into social units to pursue shared goals.

EMPHASES IN COLLECTIVISM

Donelson Forsyth

Source: Reprinted with permission of Donelson Forsyth.

Now, let's return to Figure 18.1 on page 446. As shown there, when the average person in a society is disposed toward group interdependence, then that society is labeled "collectivist" (see the bell-shaped curve drawn with the solid line). At this point, you may be curious as to which country most markedly adheres to collectivistic values. In response to this question, research suggests that China is the most collectivistic of the various nations around the globe (see Oyserman et al., 2002).

Core Emphases

As shown in Table 18.1 on page 447, the three core emphases of collectivism are dependence; conformity, or the desire to fit in; and perception of the group as the fundamental unit of analysis. First, the dependency within collectivism reflects a genuine tendency to draw one's very meaning and existence from being part of an important group of people. In collectivism, the person goes along with the expectations of the group, is highly concerned about the welfare of the group, and is very dependent upon the other members of the group to which he or she belongs (Markus & Kitayama, 1991; Reykowski, 1994).

Regarding the desire to fit in, Oyserman et al. (2002, p. 5) wrote, "The core element of collectivism is the assumption that groups bind and mutually obligate individuals." As such, collectivism is an inherently social approach in which the movement is toward in-groups and away from out-groups (Oyserman, 1993).

Turning to the third core emphasis, the group as the perceived unit of analysis, the social patterns in collectivist societies reflect close linkages in which people see themselves as part of a larger, more important whole. In brief, the collectivist concern is for the group as a whole rather than its constituents (Hofstede, 1980).

Secondary Emphases

The collectivist is defined in terms of the characteristics of the groups to which she or he belongs. Thus, collectivist-oriented people pay close attention to the rules and goals of the group and often may subjugate their personal needs to those of the group. Moreover, success and satisfaction stem from the group's reaching its desired goals and from feeling that one has fulfilled the socially prescribed duties as a member of that effective, goal-directed, group effort (Kim, 1994).

Collectivist people obviously become very involved in the ongoing activities and goals of their group, and they think carefully about the obligations and duties of the groups to which they belong (Davidson, Jaccard, Triandis, Morales, & Diaz-Guerrero, 1976; Miller, 1994). Furthermore, the interchanges between people within the collectivist perspective are characterized by mutual generosity and equity (Sayle, 1998). For such people, interpersonal relationships may be pursued even when there are no obvious benefits to be attained (see Triandis, 1995). In fact, given the great emphasis that collectivists place on relationships, they may pursue such relationships even when such interactions are counterproductive.

Because of their attentions to the guidelines as defined by the group, the individual members with a collectivist perspective may be rather formal in their interactions. That is, there are carefully followed, role-defined ways of behaving. Additionally, the person within the collectivistic perspective monitors the social context carefully to form impressions of others and to make decisions (Morris & Peng, 1994).

Recall our earlier discussion of the need for uniqueness as reflecting individualism. In this regard, Kim and Markus (1999) have reasoned that advertisements in Korea should accentuate collectivist themes related to conformity, whereas ads in the United States should be based more on themes of uniqueness. Consistent with this proposal, Kim and Markus's research shows that the need for uniqueness is lower in collectivistic societies than in individualistic ones (Yamaguchi, Kuhlman, & Sugimori, 1995).

Collectivist societies appear to have core elements of dependency, conformity (low need for uniqueness), and definition of existence in terms of the important group to which one belongs. The research also corroborates the fact that collectivism rests on a core sense of dependency as well as an obligation or duty to the in-group and a desire to maintain harmony between people (Oyserman et al., 2002). Before leaving this section, we salute Daphne Oyserman and her colleagues at the University of Michigan Institute for Social Research for their seminal scholarly review of the characteristics of individualism and collectivism.

DEMOGRAPHICS RELATED TO COLLECTIVISM

Positive psychologists must consider what the future will bring in regard to collectivism. For example, related research suggests that the gulf between the wealthy and the poor in societies throughout the world is widening as we move farther into the 21st century (see Ceci & Papierno, 2005). Research reveals that people in the lower social classes, as compared to the upper ones, are more likely to be collectivist in their perspectives (Daab, 1991; Kohn, 1969; Marjoribanks, 1991). Turning to the role of aging as yet another demographic issue pertaining to collectivism, it appears that people become more collectivist as they grow older (Gudykunst, 1993; Noricks et al., 1987).

ME/WE Balance: The Positive Psychology of US

BOTH THE INDIVIDUALISTIC AND THE COLLECTIVISTIC PERSPECTIVES ARE VIABLE

Social scientists often have conceptualized individualism and collectivism as opposites (Hui, 1988; Oyserman et al., 2002), and this polarity typically has been applied when contrasting the individualism of European Americans with the collectivism of East Asians (Chan, 1994; Kitayama, Markus, Matsumoto, & Norasakkunkit, 1997). This polarity approach strikes us as being neither good science nor necessarily a productive strategy for fostering healthy interactions among people from varying ethnicities within and across societies. In the watershed review on this topic, Oyserman and colleagues (2002) found that Americans indeed were high in individualism, but they were *not necessarily lower* than others in collectivism. Thus, there was support for only half the stereotype.

Viewing individualism and collectivism as opposites also has the potential to provoke disputes, in which the members of each camp attempt to demonstrate the superiority of their approach. Such acrimony between these two perspectives seems especially problematic given that the distinctions between individualism and collectivism have not been found to be clear cut. For example, Vandello and Cohen (1999) found that, even within individualistic societies such as the United States, the form of the individualism differs in the Northeast, the Midwest, the Deep South, and the West. Moreover, cultures are extremely diverse; each has dynamic and changing social systems that are far from the monolithic simplicities suggested by the labels "individualist" and "collectivist" (Bandura, 2000). Likewise, there may be generational differences in the degree to which individualism and collectivism are manifested (e.g., Matsumoto, Kudoh, & Takeuchi, 1996). And when different reference groups become more salient, propensities toward individualism and collectivism vary (Freeman & Bordia, 2001). Furthermore, a seemingly individualistic propensity in actuality may contribute to collectivism; for example, consider the fact that a robust personal sense of efficacy may contribute to the collective efficacy of a society (Fernandez-Ballesteros, Diez-Nicolas, Caprara, Barbaranelli, & Bandura, 2002).

Based on findings such as these, Oyserman and her colleagues (2002) suggested that we should move beyond the rather static view of individualism and collectivism as separate categories, and instead take more dynamic approaches to culture to find when, where, and why these mental sets operate. They argued for an understanding of how individualism and collectivism can operate together to benefit people. We, too, believe that both the individualist and collectivistic perspectives have advantages for people and that the best resolution is to learn to embrace aspects of each.

One characteristic of a happy and productive life is a sense of balance in one's views and actions. We believe that a positive psychology approach to this issue would equate the ME and the WE emphases. As shown in Figure 18.8, the ME/WE perspective allows a person to attend to both the person and the group. Indeed, this is what has been found to characterize the perspectives of high-hope people about their lives and their interactions with others (Snyder, 1994/2000, 2000b). That is to say, in their upbringings, the high-hope children learned about the importance of other people and their perspectives and the role that consideration for others plays in the effective pursuit of personal goals. Just as the high-hopers think of ME goals, then, they simultaneously can envision the WE goals of other people. Thus, ME

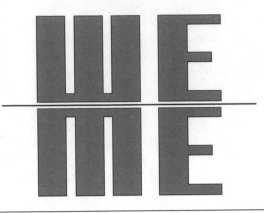

Figure 18.8   The Balanced Perspective: ME/WE

and WE become reflections of each other (see Figure 18.8). The high-hope people thereby think automatically of both the ME goals and the WE goals. Remember, too, that it is the high-hopers who seem to reap the greatest rewards in terms of successful performances and life satisfactions.

THINKING ABOUT YOUR OWN LIFE

Now that you have explored various issues related to the individualist and collectivist perspectives, it also may be informative to take a closer look at your own life. Have you ever thought about all the activities you undertake with an eye toward whether you would prefer to do them alone or with other people? We sometimes go about our lives on "automatic pilot" and do not give much thought to how we want to spend our time. Our point here is to help you getter a better sense of your preferences for doing things alone or with others. Accordingly, we have developed a short exercise to help you to gain insights about your own desires to pursue goals alone or with others. If you have not done so already, complete the exercise "Being Alone or With Others" in the Personal Mini-Experiments (pages 450–452).

Most people who have undertaken this "Being Alone or With Others" exercise have been somewhat surprised at how important other people are to them as they try to reach desired goals. In fact, other people may be quite helpful when it comes to the goals we deem most important. Many of us, especially if we are individualists, see ourselves as being fairly independent as we go about our lives. But is this really so? As we pursue our goals, we also may be explicitly and implicitly intertwined with other people who help us reach them. Thus, our collectivist tendencies may be far stronger than we may have thought. A typical insight reached by people after completing the Personal Mini-Experiment is that they are *both* individualists and collectivists. Likewise, such individualistic and collectivistic thoughts and actions may vary according to the surrounding circumstances and people.

SUGGESTIONS FOR WE PEOPLE (COLLECTIVISTS)

You now should have better ideas about your individualist and collectivist tendencies. In this and the next sections, therefore, we offer some suggestions to help you navigate more effectively in environments in which people hold perspectives that differ from the individualistic or collectivistic ones that you typically hold. In this section, we offer advice for collectivists who will at times interact with individualists. (For an in-depth analysis of how individualists and collectivists can interact more effectively, we recommend the 1988 article by Triandis, Brislin, and Hui, "Cross-Cultural Training Across the Individualism-Collectivism Divide.")

Collectivists often see individualists as too competitive. One useful lesson here is to understand that individualists see their status as based on their personal accomplishments rather than on their memberships in groups. Moreover, the more recent the accomplishments, the more power they wield in terms of status. Thus, collectivists should not be shocked when individualists do not seem impressed with group successes that are based in large part on lineage, family name, age, or sex (males have more status in some collectivistic societies). It may help the collectivist to use recent accomplishments to attain status in the eyes of individualists with whom they interact.

Collectivists also take for granted their relationships with the other members of their groups and thus are not likely to thank or compliment other people for their relevant contributions. Therefore, to provide a "social lubricant" for interactions between people (Triandis, 1995), collectivists should remember that individualists have considerable need for such praise.

Collectivists' dependence on cooperative solutions to dilemmas may not work when they are dealing with individualists. Instead, the collectivist must be able to take into account the "what's in it for me" perspective of the individualist in order to understand the latter's reactions during negotiations. Likewise, the normal arguing of individualists should not be interpreted by collectivists as intentionally hurtful behavior; this is just how the individualist conducts business. Thus, whereas a collectivist interacting with another collectivist may interpret "Let's have lunch" as a genuine invitation, it is often merely social talk when uttered by the individualist.

People from collectivist cultures who move to more individualistic societies may have difficulties with contracts or agreements between people. The problem here is that collectivists may take a much more casual approach to contracts. For example, a student from another country tells a landlord in an American college town that he or she is considering renting an apartment. The student from outside the United States views this statement to the landlord as allowing the necessary time for the student to contact homeland relatives to discuss it. Unfortunately for the American landlord, however, the student may have told several different landlords the very same thing. Of course, the American landlord thinks that a deal has been struck, whereas the student from the other country does not.

SUGGESTIONS FOR ME PEOPLE (INDIVIDUALISTS)

In this section, we offer advice for individualists to interact more effectively with collectivists. To begin, individualists often perceive collectivists as being far too "laid back" and lacking in competitiveness. In this regard, it helps to realize that collectivists derive their sense of status from their group memberships and not from their personal accomplishments.

Individualists must understand that collectivists tend to take for granted their relationships with the other members in their groups and, accordingly, they see no need to compliment others. Individualists who routinely expect thank-yous when interacting with other individualists, therefore, must learn to not interpret collectivists' lack of such social courtesies as signs of disrespect. Despite collectivists *not* practicing social thank-yous, individualists must take into account the collectivist norms in conducting business. That is to say, whereas the individualist may want to immediately get down to business when negotiating, the collectivists often expect some initial warm-up banter to set the stage. In this regard, collectivists want respect and patience between people (Cohen, 1991). When problem solving is needed, collectivists prefer that it be done at the group level, whereas individualists desire more one-on-one negotiating. Obviously, there are subtle differences, including important nonverbal gestures and cues, that must be honored when individualists and collectivists interact.

Individualists should understand that collectivists want interpersonal harmony and therefore try very hard to avoid situations involving conflict (Ting-Toomey, 1994). In such circumstances, the individualists may view conflicts as a useful means of clearing the air so that people can move on to other matters, but they should realize that collectivists are quite concerned with saving face after such conflicts. Thus, individualists can help by solving problems before they escalate into huge confrontations. Similarly, the individualist should not push the collectivist into a corner by repeatedly asking confrontational "Why?" questions in response to which the collectivist must defend his or her position. Moreover, if conflict is necessary, the individualist should try, whenever possible, to help the collectivist maintain his or her pride (what sociologists call *face*).

CLOSING THOUGHTS

Stepping back and taking a "big-picture" view of how the people from various parts of our planet get along with each other, it is obvious that we do not have a very good record. Think of the irony in the fact that historians tend to view peace as anomalous periods between major conflicts of cultures. We wonder to what degree the previous warring of nations has reflected the difficulties of individualists and collectivists in understanding and getting along with each other (see Huntington, 1993).

There is an exceedingly important lesson here for citizens of the United States. Namely, Americans with individualist perspectives must realize that their views are not widely shared around the world. It has been estimated that 70% of the present six and a half billion or so people on Earth take a collectivist view of people and their interactions (Triandis, 1995). Let's do the math here: *That is about four and a half billion collectivists and two billion individualists.* As cherished as the individualist perspective held by many United States citizens may be, *individualistic Americans are the minority in a world populated by collectivists.*

The realization that all people are part of a larger whole may grow in the 21st century. We are becoming increasingly interdependent, and nowhere is this more obvious than in the operation of global markets that influence many countries (Keohane, 1993). The rapid change in our telecommunication technologies also has led to a globalization that has raised our consciousness about other peoples around the globe (Friedman, 2005; Holton, 2000; Robey, Khoo, & Powers, 2000).

In thinking about our relationships with each other, our futures will rest upon a willingness to cooperate and come together. Although the pursuit of specialness certainly can and has produced benefits for humankind, if too many people act in pursuit of their own individuality, we will miss our chance to work together to build shared cultures. As Baumeister (2005) argued cogently in his book, *The Cultural Animal,* there is a fundamental need for shared moral guidelines so that our societies can function effectively. Such shared moralities in the future will limit the degree to which people are counterproductive in following their personal whims. Thus, morality may serve as the very means by which culture is able to assert its precedence over extreme individualism (Baumeister).

We are poised on the cusp of a major change in the balancing of individualism and collectivism—the needs of the "one" and the "many" (Newbrough, 1995; Snyder & Feldman, 2000). As such, the positive psychology of US may be just around the corner.

Appendix: The Need for Uniqueness Scale

Directions: The following statements concern your perceptions about yourself in several situations. Rate your agreement with each statement by using a scale in which 1 denotes strong disagreement, 5 denotes strong agreement, and 2, 3, and 4 represent intermediate judgments. In the blanks before each statement, place a number from 1 to 5 from the following scale:

1	2	3	4	5
Strongest				Strongest
disagreement				agreement

There are no right or wrong answers, so select the number that most closely reflects you on each statement. Take your time, and consider each statement carefully.

_____ 1. When I am in a group of strangers, I am not reluctant to express my opinion publicly.

_____ 2. I find that criticism affects my self-esteem.

_____ 3. I sometimes hesitate to use my own ideas for fear that they might be impractical.

_____ 4. I think society should let reason lead it to new customs and throw aside old habits or mere traditions.

_____ 5. People frequently succeed in changing my mind.

_____ 6. I find it sometimes amusing to upset the dignity of teachers, judges, and "cultured" people.

_____ 7. I like wearing a uniform because it makes me proud to be a member of the organization it represents.

_____ 8. People have sometimes called me "stuck-up."

_____ 9. Others' disagreements make me uncomfortable.

_____ 10. I do not always need to live by the rules and standards of society.

_____ 11. I am unable to express my feelings if they result in undesirable consequences.

_____ 12. Being a success in one's career means making a contribution that no one else has made.

_____ 13. It bothers me if people think I am being too unconventional.

_____ 14. I always try to follow rules.

_____ 15. If I disagree with a superior on his or her views, I usually do not keep it to myself.

_____ 16. I speak up in meetings in order to oppose those whom I feel are wrong.

_____ 17. Feeling "different" in a crowd of people makes me feel uncomfortable.

_____ 18. If I must die, let it be an unusual death rather than an ordinary death in bed.

_____ 19. I would rather be just like everyone else than be called a "freak."

_____ 20. I must admit I find it hard to work under strict rules and regulations.

_____ 21. I would rather be known for always trying new ideas than for employing well-trusted methods.

_____ 22. It is better to agree with the opinions of others than to be considered a disagreeable person.

_____ 23. I do not like to say unusual things to people.

_____ 24. I tend to express my opinions publicly, regardless of what others say.

_____ 25. As a rule, I strongly defend my own opinions.

_____ 26. I do not like to go my own way.

_____ 27. When I am with a group of people, I agree with their ideas so that no arguments will arise.

_____ 28. I tend to keep quiet in the presence of persons of higher ranks, experience, etc.

_____ 29. I have been quite independent and free from family rule.

_____ 30. Whenever I take part in group activities, I am somewhat of a nonconformist.

_____ 31. In most things in life, I believe in playing it safe rather than taking a gamble.

_____ 32. It is better to break rules than always to conform with an impersonal society.

To calculate the total Need for Uniqueness Scale score, first reverse each of the scores on items 2, 3, 5, 7, 9, 11, 13, 14, 17, 19, 22, 23, 26, 27, 28, and 31. That is, on these items only, perform the following reversals: 1—> 5; 2—> 4; 3—> 3; 4—> 2; 5—> 1. Then, add the scores on all 32 items, using the reversed scores for the aforementioned items. Higher scores reflect a higher need for uniqueness.

Key Terms

Collectivism: A perspective in which the needs of the group are placed above the needs of the individual. The core emphases of collectivism are dependence, conformity, the desire to fit in, and the group as the fundamental unit of analysis.

Individualism: A perspective in which the needs of the individual are placed above the needs of the group. The core emphases of individualism are independence, uniqueness, and the individual as the fundamental unit of analysis.

Need for uniqueness: The pursuit of individualistic goals to produce a sense of specialness.

Pluralistic ignorance: The mistaken notion that one's beliefs are nonconforming.

Part VIII

A Positive Look
at the Future of
Psychology

Going Positive 19

To be broken is no reason to see all things as broken.

—Mark Leno, *The Book of Awakening,* p. 100

We start this final chapter by describing a psychotherapy client who had an agenda that reflects a key tenet of positive psychology—the desire to accentuate the good in life. We then discuss a puzzle for positive psychologists: Why does negative information seem to be more powerful for people than positive information (i.e., "bad is stronger than good")? Next, we assess the attentions given to positive psychology in the media and the field, and follow this with a call for positive psychology to be a worldwide phenomenon. We argue that positive psychology should be for all people rather than just a few. We also examine the degree to which young people have been recruited to study positive psychology. We explore the implications of the fact that many more females than males are obtaining doctorates in clinical and counseling psychology. In a subsequent major section, various leaders in this new field will share the ideas about the future of positive psychology. Finally, we close with two stories that vividly illustrate the power of focusing on the positive.

Trading the Bad for Some Good: The Case of Molly

The changes that we have described as a result of the positive psychology initiative are similar to the processes that people undergo in successful psychotherapy—they are able to exchange some negative thoughts and actions for more positive ones. Consider, for example, the case of Molly, a sharp-tongued, 75-year-old woman who came to one of the authors (CRS) for psychotherapy. Molly's initial statement was, "I want to trade in some of my crappy habits for some better ones!" It turned out that this case wasn't quite as simple as her words suggested—but such cases rarely are.

First, Molly said she wanted to stop being so crabby. When asked what she might get out of being cranky and difficult, Molly looked puzzled. "You mean, I do it for a reason?" she asked. Thinking about her possible motivations for being cranky, Molly paused and then asserted, "I want to be more in control." She also said that she did not like how her family seemed to pay more attention when she complained about her aches and pains.

I suggested that she begin volunteer work at the local hospital. This idea had several advantages, the most important being that her family and friends, rather than attending to her complaints, would praise her for helping others. Molly liked this plan because it gave her a positive way to achieve a sense of control. When she began the volunteer work, it also made Molly realize that her aches and pains were quite minor relative to those of the hospital patients. Therefore, Molly's first "trade-in" was to find a more positive means of gaining a sense of control in her life.

Molly's second "trade-in" involved her desire to maintain her body weight. As she got older, she wanted to avoid what she called "the march of fat." Although Molly loved to eat, she was so concerned with getting fat that she actually ate very little. Patterning herself after the rail-thin, 20-year-old female models in magazines, Molly was not enjoying her semi-starvation approach to weight management. After discussing this weight issue, she decided that a healthy, physically fit body was a more enjoyable goal that she wanted for her senior years. This meant that she began to exercise and allowed herself to gain weight that was muscle. Her positive "trade-in" was a more realistic body weight that allowed her to enjoy eating, plus a new physical exercise program that helped her to feel stronger and more physically able.

Our point in describing the case of Molly is to show how peoples' goals sometimes may be sidetracked, thereby producing more harm than benefit. For such people, there typically are other, positive ways to reach goals. Thus, positive psychology is not radical in the strengths-based solutions that it offers people. In the many case histories we have shared throughout this book is a similar pattern, in which people learn to trade their less healthy lifestyles for more positive ones.

If Molly and others like her are to be helped in putting more "positive" in their lives, then we must address the question of how people often attend to the bad things rather than the good things in their lives. That "bad is stronger than good" is a core dilemma for positive psychologists; we address this puzzle next.

Tackling a Fundamental Dilemma:
Bad Is Stronger Than Good

In the 2001 article, "Bad Is Stronger Than Good," social psychologist Roy Baumeister and his colleagues pose one of the thorniest of all problems for positive psychology. As the provocative title of his review suggests, those things in life that can be characterized as "bad" appear to hold greater power in human lives than the things that are "good." More specifically, Baumeister and his colleagues suggest that the greater power of bad over good events can be witnessed in a multitude of life arenas and activities, including interpersonal interactions, outcomes in close relationships, traumas, and various learning processes. They review literature showing that the bad—whether in parents, emotions, or feedback—wields more impact than the good counterparts. To compound matters, information that is bad appears to be processed more completely than good information. So, too, are we more likely to form bad impressions than good ones; and stereotypes that are bad rather than good form more quickly and are more resistant to being disconfirmed. Likewise, we may be more motivated to keep away from bad self-referential feedback than to pursue good feedback. Baumeister and his colleagues conclude by noting that exceptions to "bad is stronger than good" are very rare.

We approach this important issue by using hope as an example of the good and fear as an example of the bad. As oppositional systems, hope and fear are analogous to other dialectical processes such as acquisition vs. protection, approach vs. withdrawal, and action vs. conservation. In making such pairs of opposed processes, it is useful to think of hope as a rather deliberate cognitive activity that is accompanied by positive emotions, whereas fear is a more automatic emotion that crops up in very stressful circumstances.

Hope and fear operate at different levels of the brain. On this point, LeDoux (1986) reported that limbic excitations (between the thalamus and the amygdala) occur without cortical interference, thereby suggesting that the cognitions of hope actually are independent of the fear that emanates from affective systems. LeDoux (1995) also found that the affective encoding of fear in the brain often does not reach awareness. Therefore, because fear is not necessarily reflected in conscious perceptions, it does not have to undergo any "updating" processes. Accordingly, LeDoux (1996) has suggested that there are two roads over which impulses travel to elicit emotions. The low road involves relatively short connections between receptors and the central nervous system (the thalamus to the amygdala). This low road yields fearful reactions to threatening stimuli, and this process occurs below awareness. Second, the high road involves hopeful thinking links (the thalamus and amygdala with the cortex) that occur within awareness.

Fear is aimed at protecting life and preserving things the way they are (homeostasis). Furthermore, given that fear has numerous connections from the limbic (affective) system to the cortical structures, it is potentially more powerful than future-directed thinking. To magnify the power of fear, it can be elicited by diverse human memories; prolonged experiences of fear expand the associative mental networks, thereby resulting in overestimation of its prevalence and importance. As such, fear limits cognitive processing and generally amplifies our human tendencies to avoid risk. Thus, fear is protective and defensive, and makes us less open to new perspectives.

Unlike fear, future-directed thinking comes into play when we conjure a concrete goal. Future-directed thinking entails visualizations and expectations, and the emotions that flow from such thinking typically make us feel good. Unlike fear, in which the emotions are the centerpiece, in future-directed thinking the emotions that are experienced are secondary in that they reflect cognitive appraisals of how well we are doing in our goal pursuit activities. Obviously, therefore, positive emotions play a larger role in future-directed thinking than they do in fear, where negative emotions rule.

Both future-directed thinking and fear have implications for natural selection in an evolutionary sense. Our early survival as a species may have depended more on passing on fear-based thought processes to offspring than future-directed thinking. Over the eons, however, fear may have become less essential, perhaps even irrational and maladaptive in environments where it was not warranted. Furthermore, as human evolution continues, future-directed thinking may well be the most rational coping approach and may have advantages over fear. It is here that we pose our answer to Baumeister and colleagues' persuasive "bad is stronger than good," which, for earlier evolutionary reasons, made sense. *As we have evolved as a species, therefore, our progress today may necessitate a different emphasis, one in which we carefully nurture hope instead of allowing fear to rule our lives.* By analogy, then, we must promote the good rather than let the bad control our lives.

This is precisely where positive psychology offers a solution for untying the knot of "bad is stronger than good." If we so choose, we can think and feel such that the good gains ascendancy over the bad in our lives. This will be no easy task, but the proponents of positive psychology never have held that such change will be effortless. On the contrary, it will be very difficult, but positive psychology offers blueprints to see that the good triumphs over the bad. Part of the success of positive processes like hope will rest on the increased attention of society to issues involving human strengths. Our assessment of issue of the recognition of human strengths follows.

Positive Psychology Is Gaining Attention

How much attention is the media giving to the ideas of positive psychology? Likewise, how seriously are journalists taking the psychological findings related to positive psychology? In a relatively short time, positive psychology has gotten off to a good start in gaining attention both inside and outside of psychology (see Seligman, Steen, Park, & Peterson, 2005). It is important, however, to repeat our findings from the first chapter: Positive psychology researchers are *not* swamping the field with their work, as some have lamented (e.g., Lazarus, 2003). It does appear, however, that work that has been done in positive psychology has captured the attention of people inside and outside the field. Another encouraging sign is that, in January 2006, *The Journal of Positive Psychology,* edited by Robert Emmons, began publishing articles that focus solely on the study of human strengths and positive emotions.

Media attention to the positive runs counter to the old maxim, "Bad news sells newspapers." For this reason, the willingness of print and visual media to discuss the findings of positive psychology is even more noteworthy. When the authors of this text asked newspaper, magazine, and television newspeople about this phenomenon, they expressed the opinion that the public is sick of constant bad news. As such, positive psychology offers a "feel-good" antidote to the trails of tragedy left by acts of nature and human hands. Additionally, these same newspeople have observed that the solid scientific underpinning of positive psychology makes related findings all the more important. This latter point is an important one; positive psychology researchers should be careful about the claims they make about their research findings. As Snyder (2000c) has written,

> As we craft a new psychology of how the mind can work for the good of people, we must adhere to appropriate sampling, causal designs whenever possible, and strict applications of statistical inference. We must be judicious in our claims, mindful that overzealous statements undermine the positive psychology case. And we must have patience for the fact that the science of psychology is built on accumulating evidence. Throughout, those who seek to test various positive psychology tenets would be well advised to remain skeptical. (p. 24)

Not only does the news media hunger for the positive slant on people, but the average person also may be drawn to the strengths approach. For years, when the authors of this book traveled, they frequently encountered the question, "So, what do you do for a living?" Our previous answer, that we were clinical or counseling psychologists, tended to stop conversations, so we changed our answer to, "We are college professors." Now, however, we announce that we are positive psychologists, and this unleashes lively and enjoyable conversations. People want to learn about this, and we want to talk about it with others. Such reactions may reflect the fact that people truly have grown weary of the previous pathology or weakness approach, or perhaps there are intrinsic favorable reactions to the overall strengths approach. In either case, it portends an openness on the part of laypeople to the tenets of positive psychology.

Positive Psychology as a Worldwide Phenomenon

As we noted in the first chapter, the modern impetus for the emergence of positive psychology came through the leadership of Martin Seligman during his term as president of the American Psychological Association (see the Seligman editorial in the Appendix at the end of this chapter). Dr. Seligman urged psychology to focus on the positive in people. Since that time, he has worked tirelessly to see that positive psychology takes root.

Given that Seligman is an acclaimed American psychologist, it is not surprising that his efforts initially were focused in the United States. To his great credit, however, he has reached out to the many positive psychology scholars around the globe. For example, at the Third Annual International Positive Psychology Summit in Washington, DC (sponsored by The Gallup Organization and Toyota University), psychologists from 23 countries attended; students and adults from around the world were both presenters and attendees. Furthermore, the venues for presenting positive psychology research and applications increasingly are located in various countries. In July 2004 in Italy, for example, the European Network of Positive Psychology sponsored its second conference (Seligman et al., 2005).

Positive psychology must continue its worldwide approach because the ideas and findings are crucial for all people. It is important that scholarly leaders include voices from around the globe in books about positive psychology. In our survey of recent, major, edited volumes on positive psychology, the percentage of scholars outside the United States has varied from a low of 7% to a high of 37%, with a mode of 21%. If positive psychology truly is to become a worldwide phenomenon, we must do even better at including researchers and practitioners from around the world in our key books. The same is true of articles published in our professional journals. It cannot be a club with members from just a few countries (see Snyder & Feldman, 2000). Instead, it should welcome the many people from diverse cultures and countries around the world. We discuss this issue in the next section, in which we suggest that the benefits of positive psychology should be available to people around the world.

For the Many, Not Just the Few

As has been the case overall in psychology, positive psychology's emphasis to date has been on the individual rather than the community. Indeed, the late 20th century has been characterized as the time of the Me Generation. Thus, given that there usually are cycles to such matters, it was time for the pendulum to swing back toward the group and what is good for the many rather than just the one.

Certain potential developments may limit the effects of positive psychology to a select few, however, and these concern us as scientists and practitioners. In particular, some people believe that applied psychology should metamorphose into a profession of personal coaches. The problem with this change, in our estimation, is that those who are wealthy will be able to afford the high costs of such personal coaches. We already are witnessing a worldwide widening of the gulf between the financially affluent and the poor (Ceci & Papierno, 2005), and it seems antithetical to the tenets of positive psychology that it should contribute to this disturbing distancing between the haves and the have-nots. In the words of John F. Kennedy in his inaugural address of January 20, 1961, "If a society cannot help the many who are poor, it cannot save the few who are rich."

One way to ensure that the benefits of positive psychology are made available to more people is to value and honor the diverse goals that presently exist in societies throughout the world. Likewise, we should increase the number of goals that are valued within each of these societies. Traditionally, valued goals have included making money, achievements (intellectual and athletic), and physical appearance. As we have reasoned elsewhere (Snyder & Feldman, 2000, p. 391), greater emphasis should be given to "(1) caring for others; (2) producing durable and dependable products; (3) inventing new products; (4) conducting basic and applied research; and (5) promoting safety in the workplace and elsewhere." By encouraging more goal opportunities for people, we are making it possible for more people to experience the benefits related to reaching those coveted goals.

Another means of increasing the opportunities of the many is to place greater emphases on long-range goals. Unfortunately, short-term goals often are self-centered (e.g., "What can I get out of this?" see Lerner [1996]). Positive psychology for the many also may entail deferring gratification instead of "getting mine now." Furthermore, long-range and huge goals may necessitate several people getting together as a collective.

Yet another goal of positive psychology for the many is to change our attitudes and behavior toward older people and aging. Instead of the all-too-common view of older people as being "put out to pasture," we must provide more opportunities for their continued input and rigorous mental activities. Think of the enormous loss of talent when we do not use the many skills acquired by older people! Anything that can be done to ensure that older people contribute, from the societal level to the family level, will help us. Programs are needed in school and perhaps even in the mass media to change the negative stereotypes about aging. After all, people should remember that this is the only minority group that all of us will join with the passing of the years. Most of all, positive psychology for the many should counteract the self-fulfilling prophecies related to the perceived loss of capacities with aging. This would prevent what has called *psychological recession*, the unnecessary deterioration of mental faculties with advanced age (see Snyder in foreword of Williamson, Shaffer, & Parmalee, 2000).

One last goal of positive psychology for the many is to preserving the commons. This notion of the commons came from earlier times, in which villages contained central grazing areas shared by several livestock owners. Over time, the term *commons* has come to signify any environmental resource, such as water, timber, ground, minerals, and oil, that can benefit many people. The problem, of course, is that natural resources are limited, and if we do not do something to curb individualistic desires to use them, they will be depleted (see Edney & Harper, 1978). Positive psychology would teach people how to cooperate and act collectively to preserve our natural resources. Working together in smaller units, people are more likely to cooperate and take responsibility for their individual actions (see Dawes, 1980), thereby assuring that these precious natural resources will be there for our children.

Young People and Education in Positive Psychology

It is too soon to judge whether positive psychology is attracting new cohorts of students who will use this approach as the framework for their scholarly or applied careers. Education will be crucial in such future migration of students to positive psychology's approach to research and practice. Already, introductory psychology textbooks and the instructors of these courses are including coverage of positive psychology. Likewise, nearly 100 universities and colleges have instituted undergraduate and graduate courses that introduce students to the principles of positive psychology. The existence of this and other textbooks on positive psychology signals the growth of such courses.

As these undergraduates obtain their degrees, they also will read various books with positive psychology content as part of the optional requirements of courses such as personality, individual differences, health, abnormal psychology, and clinical psychology, to name but a few. Indeed, in the last decade or so, there has been an explosion of books dedicated to various topics in positive psychology. As shown in Table 19.1, a wide range of issues is addressed in these positive psychology volumes.

Table 19.1   Recent Books on Positive Psychology

Aspinwall, L. G., & Staudinger, U. M. (Eds.). (2002). *A psychology of human strengths: Fundamental questions and future directions for a positive psychology.* Washington, DC: American Psychological Association.

Averill, J. R., Catlin, G., & Chon, K. K. (1990). *Rules of hope.* New York: Springer-Verlag.

Averill, J. R., & Nunley, E. P. (1992). *Voyages of the heart: Living an emotionally creative life.* New York: Free Press.

Baltes, P. B. (2005). *Wisdom: The orchestration of mind and character.* Boston: Basil Blackwell.

Bandura, A. (1997). *Self-efficacy: The exercise of control.* New York: Freeman.

Bass, E., & Davis, L. (1994). *The courage to heal.* New York: HarperPerennial.

Batson, C. D. (1991). *The altruism question: Toward a social-psychological answer.* Hillsdale, NJ: Lawrence Erlbaum.

Branden, N. (1994). *The six pillars of self-esteem.* New York: Bantam Books.

Buckingham, M., & Clifton, D. O. (2001). *Now, discover your strengths.* New York: Free Press.

Buckingham, M., & Coffman, C. (1999). *First, break all the rules: What the world's greatest managers do differently.* New York: Simon & Schuster.

Clifton, D. O., & Nelson, P. (1992). *Soar with your strengths.* New York: Delacorte Press.

Colby, A., & Damon, W. (1992). *Some do care: Contemporary lives of moral commitment.* New York: Free Press.

Csikszentmihalyi, M. (1990). *Flow: The psychology of optimum experience.* New York: Harper & Row.

Csikszentmihalyi, M. (1996). *Creativity: Flow and the psychology of discovery and invention.* New York: HarperCollins.

Etzioni, A. (1993). *The spirit of community: Rights, responsibilities, and the communitarian agenda.* New York: Crown.

Goleman, D. (1995). *Emotional intelligence: Why it can matter more than IQ.* New York: Bantam.

Goleman, D. (1998). *Working with emotional intelligence.* New York: Bantam.

Hendrick, S. S., & Hendrick, C. (1992). *Romantic love.* Newbury Park, CA: Sage.

Hewitt, J. P. (1998). *The myth of self esteem: Finding happiness and solving problems in America.* New York: St. Martin's Press.

Karen, R. (1994). *Becoming attached.* New York: Warner.

Kerr, B. A. (1997). *Smart girls: A new psychology of girls, women, and giftedness.* Scottsdale, AZ: Great Potential Press.

Lefcourt, H. M. (2001). *Humor: The psychology of living buoyantly.* New York: Kluwer.

Linley, P. A., & Joseph, S. (Eds.) (2004). *Positive psychology in practice.* Hoboken, NJ: Wiley.

Lopez, S., & Snyder, C. R. (Eds.). (2003). *Positive psychological assessment: A handbook of models and measures.* Washington, DC: American Psychological Association.

(Continued)

Table 19.1 (Continued)

McAdams, D., & de St. Aubin, E. (Eds.). (1998). *Generativity and adult development: Perspectives on caring for and contributing to the next generation.* Washington, DC: American Psychological Association.

McCullough, M. E., Pargament, K. I., & Thoresen, C. E. (Eds.). (2000). *Forgiveness: Theory, research, and practice.* New York: Guilford Press.

McDermott, D., & Snyder, C. R. (1999). *Making hope happen: A workbook for turning possibilities into realities.* Oakland, CA: New Harbinger Publications.

McDermott, D., & Snyder, C. R. (2000). *The great big book of hope.* Oakland, CA: New Harbinger Publications.

Pargament, K. I. (1997). *The psychology of religion and coping: Theory, research, and practice.* New York: Guilford Press.

Saarni, C. (1999). *Developing emotional intelligence.* New York: Guilford.

Saleebey, D. (1996). *A strengths perspective in social work practice* (2nd ed.). White Plains, NY: Longman.

Schwarzer, R. (Ed.). (1992). *Self-efficacy: Thought control of action.* Washington, DC: Hemisphere.

Seligman, M. E. P. (1991). *Learned optimism.* New York: Knopf.

Seligman, M. E. P. (2002). *Authentic happiness: Using the new positive psychology to realize your potential for lasting fulfillment.* New York: Free Press.

Seligman, M. E. P., Reivich, K., Jaycox, L., & Gillham, J. (1995). *The optimistic child.* New York: Houghton Mifflin.

Snyder, C. R. (1994/2000). *The psychology of hope: You can get there from here.* New York: Free Press.

Snyder, C. R. (Ed.). (1999). *Coping: The psychology of what works.* New York: Oxford University Press.

Snyder, C. R. (Ed.). (2000). *Handbook of hope: Theory, measures, and applications.* San Diego, CA: Academic Press.

Snyder, C. R. (Ed.). (2001). *Coping with stress: Effective people and processes.* New York: Oxford University Press.

Snyder, C. R., & Lopez, S. J. (Eds.). (2002). *The handbook of positive psychology.* New York: Oxford University Press.

Snyder, C. R., McDermott, D., Cook, W., & Rapoff, M. (2002). *Hope for the journey: Helping children through the good times and the bad* (Rev. ed). Clinton Corners, NY: Percheron.

Sternberg, R. J. (Ed.). (1990). *Wisdom: Its nature, origins, and development.* New York: Cambridge University Press.

Wong, P. T., & Fry, P. (Eds.). (1998). *The human quest for meaning.* Mahwah, NJ: Lawrence Erlbaum.

Instructors also will have films to help them teaching positive psychology. For example, two half-hour films on the science of human strengths are available, in which noted positive psychology scholars share their insights in conversations with laypeople who range from teenagers to ninety-year-olds. The films focus on such important topics as finding one's signature strengths, selecting work that matches one's talents, preserving health, and aging well. The titles of the films are *Introducing Positive Psychology: Personal Well-Being, Social Support, Health, and Aging Well* and *Introducing Positive Psychology: Signature Strengths, Flow, and Aging Well.* (For more information about these films, e-mail Jackie Harrison [jackie_harrison@montanapbs.org] or Chris Seifert [chris_seifert@ montanapbs.org].) Also, oral histories of positive psychology researchers are available at www.gallupippi.com.

At the graduate level, positive psychology principles undergird all of the offerings at Gallup University and are appearing in doctoral programs in counseling, clinical psychology, health, social psychology, child psychology, personality psychology, educational leadership, and special education. Furthermore, the first graduate program focused entirely on positive psychology is the Master of Applied Positive Psychology, which has been initiated at the University of Pennsylvania. This applied program is aimed at helping people who are working full-time to learn to use the strengths approach to benefit various clienteles. If you are interested in learning more about this pioneering program, check out the website at www .sas.upenn.edu/CGS/graduate/mapp.

To learn more about positive psychology, you may wish to visit additional websites. The major sites include the following:

www.positivepsychology.org/

www.apa.org/science/positivepsy.html

www.authentichappiness.org

www.bus.umich.edu/Positive/

www.div17.org/positivepsychology

Furthermore, a listserv on positive psychology can be joined at

http://www.ppc.sas.upenn.edu/listservsignup.htm

For young researchers who wish to learn more about the experimental approach from senior leaders in the field, the annual Positive Psychology Institute is held each summer. Additionally, the Positive Psychology Network funds more than 150 scholars from around the world. Last, centers for positive psychology are springing up, with present locations in Philadelphia, Pennsylvania; Urbana-Champaign, Illinois; Claremont, California; and Ann Arbor, Michigan.

Although the information discussed in this section certainly suggests that new opportunities are becoming available for students who are interested in positive psychology, we do not know yet whether increasing numbers of students are being attracted to this approach. It may be a decade before we can judge whether there are reliable increases in the number of students pursuing positive psychology in one form or another.

Women in Positive Psychology

Given the huge recent increase in the number of women, relative to the number of men, in clinical and counseling psychology, the field will change from its traditional male-dominated perspective. What will this portend for positive psychology? Generally, we believe that women will impart the characteristics they value. Research (for review, see Snyder, McDermott, Leibowitz, & Cheavens, 2000) shows these priorities as valued by women: (1) ready emotional access; (2) nonconfrontational behavior; (3) communal and other awareness; (4) harmony and relationships; (5) egalitarianism; (6) understanding of struggle and social inequality; (7) nonthreatening behavior, and; (8) contextual and holistic thinking.

Although we cannot trace all eight characteristics here, we do explore some. For example, we believe that women, more than was the case when men controlled the agenda in psychology, will want to attend to matters pertaining to the family in general and children in particular. Given the huge role that the family plays in the development of children, we foresee that women will make certain that the research and applied activities of positive psychology attend to these pivotal issues. As more attention is paid to the family and children, therefore, we envision greater status accorded matters pertaining to children and families. This follows because what is valued should be esteemed.

Women also are likely to oppose the individualistic view that child care is the sole responsibility of the female partners in relationships (see Crosby, 1991). Therefore, the future view in positive psychology probably will be that the care of children is a community- and family-wide responsibility. As Snyder and Feldman (2000, p. 395) have written,

> Males need to change. The "tough-guy" male stereotype of the movies has merely changed clothes and mode of transportation over the years—he used to wear a cowboy outfit and ride a horse, and now he is found in various garbs driving an assortment of powerful vehicles. The salient messages, however, are the same: "Real men don't need other people. . . . " If these messages were altered so as to extol adult males remaining in relationships, then it is more likely that the families throughout our country would have more visible male role models for children.

Another characteristic that women value and promulgate in others is helping. Accordingly, women should imbue future positive psychology activities with the importance of assisting other people. We see the women leaders of positive psychology promoting the importance of teaching empathy to children, especially toward people who have been harmed by their actions (see Koestner, Franz, & Weinberger, 1990). Women also will be likely to impart praise for such prosocial actions (Cialdini, Baumann, & Kenrick, 1981). Moreover, these future female leaders should encourage parents to model helping to their offspring (Midlarsky & Bryan, 1972), as well as promoting more public service announcements about prosocial actions (Liebert & Sprafkin, 1988).

This point leads to another unfortunate fact about American society— one that future female leaders may change: The amount of violence that our children view is alarming. Women leaders are likely to promote standards to lessen the carnage depicted in television shows, movies, and video games viewed by children. Consider the frightening reality that some of our children are worried about dodging gunfire as they walk to and from school. In this regard, we have found that, in the Kansas City area, inner-city children who have personally witnessed physical violence are likely to have low hope (Hinton-Nelson, Roberts, & Snyder, 1996). Such fear needs to be curbed, and future female leaders in positive psychology may well lead the way.

Likewise, women probably will accentuate matters related to the physical health of others in 21st-century positive psychology. It is a matter of time before there is reliable national health care insurance for all Americans, and women leaders in positive psychology may be in the forefront of such an important change. As with attention to family and children, interest in helping and attending to the physical health of others should make the future positive psychology more of a WE- than a ME-oriented approach (see Chapter 18; Triandis, 1995). As part of this communal perspective, female leaders in positive psychology will be more likely than their earlier male counterparts to study underrepresented populations.

Experts' Views on 21st-Century Positive Psychology

Whether positive psychology truly prospers in the 21st century depends, in our estimation, on how it addresses several potential challenges, explored earlier in this chapter. To provide other views of the challenges ahead, we contacted several experts and asked them to share their visions of key issues. In this section, we share the views of these scholars.

Imagine Our World
If Positive Psychology Succeeds

ED DIENER

University of Illinois, Urbana-Champaign, Illinois

I pose five major questions for positive psychology in the coming decades. First, are there cross-cultural universal virtues, and do their forms differ according to culture? Second, are there tradeoffs between these virtues, and can a person have too much of a particular virtue? Third, can we determine when, why, and what forms of subjective well-being are beneficial to the individual and society more generally? Fourth, what effective interventions will arise for optimizing happiness and virtues? And the fifth and biggest question is to ask how our 21st- and 22nd-century world would look if positive psychology were able to succeed in making people happier, healthier, wiser, and more virtuous, and if we also could create strength-inducing institutional structures. Imagine how these potentially creative and virtuous people of the future will spend their time—aided by computers and robots, long lives, and plentiful resources.

Embracing Positive Psychology Tenets
as Crucial Advice for Clinical Psychology

JAMES MADDUX

George Mason University, Fairfax, Virginia

In the 21st century, clinical psychology must embrace the principles of positive psychology. Of all of the subfields of psychology, the unfortunate reality is that clinical always has been the most "negative." For example, the training of most clinical psychologists instills overly pathological, pessimistic views about both human behavior and the potential for healthy change. Furthermore, the faults and flaws of people have been amplified into "disorders," with the strengths and assets typically being ignored, dismissed, or construed as "defense mechanisms." The condescension lurking behind such weakness-focused thinking is not healthy for the profession or the people it serves. In facing a changing "mental health" marketplace in which millions will want to enhance the quality of their lives rather than just seeking "cures" for "disorders," clinical psychology needs the more uplifting views of positive psychology. Indeed, if clinical psychology does not fill this need, other professions will.

Spirituality and Positive Psychology

KENNETH I. PARGAMENT

Bowling Green State University, Bowling Green, Ohio

Although it is one of the least understood of human dimensions, spirituality is what makes us uniquely human. For much of the 20th century, however, psychologists either disregarded religion and spirituality or treated [them] as a form of pathology. Fortunately, it is becoming clearer that we are more than physical, psychological, and social beings. We also are spiritual beings in search of relationships with the sacred, however we may define it. Accordingly, people draw on many spiritual resources—from prayer and meditation to passage and involvement rites in religious institutions. Furthermore, empirical studies are showing that spirituality often is the source of life meaning, hope, and direction. Likewise, spirituality can sustain people in traumatic situations. It can facilitate deep and long-lasting transformations when people have reached their personal limits. The 21st century should witness a tremendous growth in our positive psychological understanding of spirituality.

Joining Other Scientists in Search of the Spiritual

ROBERT EMMONS

University of California, Davis, California

Similar to negative emotions, positive emotions are interwoven into the human fabric—inextricably connected with our nervous and physiological systems, our evolutionary histories, our behavior and actions, our consciousness, and our philosophies and religions. Although research programs already are yielding insights into specific positive emotions, we know very little about the category of emotions labeled as *spiritual* or *sacred:* joy, sorrow, fear, gratitude, awe, reverence, compassion, contrition, hatred, and zeal. These sacred emotions explicitly reference God and the transcendent, and they move beyond the objects in the empirically accessible world. Significant future progress in understanding sacred emotions and their place in human life will require collaboration between psychologists who specialize in the study of emotion and the experts in evolutionary biology, neuroscience, philosophy, anthropology, and cognitive science. As such, I see positive psychology building upon the advances in these related scientific disciplines.

Building on the "Third Pillar": Positive Communities

DAVID MYERS

Hope College, Holland, Michigan

When first articulating positive psychology, Marty Seligman envisioned three pillars beneath it: the study and advancement of

- positive subjective well-being (happiness, life satisfaction, optimism),
- positive character (creativity, courage, compassion, integrity, self-control, leadership, wisdom, spirituality), and
- positive groups, communities, and cultures.

Having substantially erected the first two pillars, one 21st-century task lies in building the third, with a social ecology that fosters thriving families, communal neighborhoods, effective schools, socially responsible media, and civil dialogue.

In response to the last half-century's rising individualism and declining civic health—we are more often *Bowling Alone*, notes Robert Putnam, and also voting, visiting, entertaining, carpooling, trusting, joining, and meeting less—a positive social renewal movement is underway. The Communitarian Network urges balancing individualism with concern for communal well-being. The National Marriage Project aims to strengthen the state of our unions. And a kindred-spirit positive psychology initiative will join in nurturing a society that respects human rights while supporting human attachments.

The Role of Positive Psychology in Maintaining Hope and Balance

MICHAEL MAHONEY

Salve Regina University, Newport, Rhode Island

A central challenge for positive psychology in the 21st century will be the maintenance of hope and balance in contexts of extreme adversity. Technological innovations and global connections are likely to present unprecedented challenges for psychological life. Changes in world order and threats of chaos may evoke polarizing extremes (e.g., in distinguishing "us" from "them," freedom from tyranny, and good from evil). The propagation of dangerous disintegrative processes will be a challenge. Positive psychology will need to embrace the developmental dynamics of order-stabilizing ("conservative") and change-generating ("liberating") processes at individual, family, community, and larger collective levels. An engaged (activist) faith in human potential and the connectedness of all planetary life will be crucial. So, too, will be compassion and perseverance.

Learning From the 2005 Hurricanes

NANCY G. WESTBURG

Rider University, Lawrenceville, New Jersey

During and after the devastating 2005 hurricanes in the Gulf Coast areas, I witnessed the despair and hopelessness of survivors who had lost everything. Yet, out of these catastrophes, stories of hope, resiliency, spirituality, optimism, and heroism surfaced. As we face the 21st century, we can learn a great deal from those who are rebuilding their lives. More studies are needed to investigate the positive factors that helped people "to keep on going" during and after these disasters. Although the answers may be complex, the results will be useful in helping other traumatized individuals to cope effectively with adversities that are outside of their control. These findings also can be incorporated into large-scale positive psychology prevention programs. Thus, we need to be more proactive in advocating for increased resources to conduct positive psychology research and to develop positive psychology strategies that will teach children and adults to build futures of hope, meaning, and purpose. Nowhere is positive psychology more viable than under adverse circumstances.

Toward a Positive Psychology of the Whole Person

CHRISTINE ROBITSCHEK

Texas Tech University, Lubbock, Texas

Thus far, positive psychologists' examination of human beings has focused on dissecting positive human functioning and examining the many "parts" or "positive characteristics." As we move into the 21st century, one important focus will be to reassemble the human being who is functioning well so that we can understand how the whole person may be different [from] simply the sum of the positive parts. Will the "positively functioning person" have high levels of ALL positive psychology characteristics? I think that is unlikely. Perhaps there will be multiple profiles of positively functioning people. Perhaps the profiles will differ by culture. Perhaps the blending of positive characteristics results in higher-order metacharacteristics.

The reassembly of human beings also needs to include movement from the artificial separation of "positive" and "negative" psychology to an integrated whole. The reality is that no person is entirely positive or negative in terms of functioning. By acknowledging this reality in our theory, research, and practice in psychology, we can work toward reassembling human beings, more accurately characterizing the human condition, and understanding people in more realistic and holistic ways. Psychologists, positive or otherwise, in the 21st century need to embrace this complexity.

A Positive Psychology of Reaching Out and Bridging

P. ALEX LINLEY

University of Leicester, United Kingdom

What does the future hold for positive psychology? Does positive psychology have a future? These are instructive questions, and the answer depends primarily on how we understand "positive psychology." If positive psychology is understood as an effort to redress the imbalance in psychological research and practice, it only has a future if it fails. If successful, positive psychology does not have a future: It will have succeeded in its aim of re-orienting psychology to study the positive as well as the negative, leading to a more unified, integrated psychology which absolves the need for a specific "positive psychology."

If positive psychology does not succeed in this aim, it is likely that its future will be one of increasing specialization. In my opinion, this would be an opportunity lost. The great advantage that positive psychology offers is its ability to build bridges across all areas of psychology, demonstrating to researchers and practitioners how an understanding of the positive, as well as the negative, is integral to understanding the human condition.

Understood in this way, the future of positive psychology is in our hands. As positive psychologists, we need to reach out to all areas of psychology and make the case as to what the positive psychological perspective offers that is novel but, above all, valuable.

Proactive Coping

RALF SCHWARZER

Freie Universität Berlin, Germany

Positive psychology will become the mainstream of psychology. Professionals and academics will think more often in terms of positive than negative constructs. The focus on health will replace the focus on illness. The study of mental and physical fitness, wellness, and health will require a better definition and measurement of positive psychological constructs such as hope, optimism, self-efficacy, engagement, or goal orientation. To understand how people live their lives, we will put less emphasis on the examination of reactive coping with adverse life events and more emphasis on proactive coping. The latter refers to goal setting, goal pursuit, personal growth and corresponding self-regulatory processes. Proactive coping is not preceded by negative appraisals, such as harm, loss, or threat. Proactive coping can be considered as an effort to build up general resources that facilitate promotion toward challenging goals and personal growth. In proactive coping, people have a vision. They see risks, demands, and opportunities in the far future, but they do not appraise them as a threat, harm, or loss. Rather, they perceive demanding situations as personal challenges. Coping becomes goal management instead of risk management. The proactive individual strives for life improvement and builds up resources that assure progress and quality of functioning. Proactively creating better living conditions and higher performance levels is experienced as an opportunity to render life meaningful or to find purpose in life.

The Role of Positive Psychology in Urban Migration and Increased Life Spans

EVERETT L. WORTHINGTON, JR.

Virginia Commonwealth University, Richmond, Virginia

The largest mass migration the world has ever known—from rural to urban areas—has been occurring and will continue. Genetic advances will result in people living much longer. In 1900, the life expectancy was 47. By 2000, it was 78. Some experts say it will be 150 by 2100. Thus, because people likely will live longer, population will increase and will increase proportionately more in urban areas. By 2100, the world's biggest problem will be . . . how people live together in a stressful urban environment. Urban stresses not only will increase stress-related disorders, they also will also increase violence, general discord, anxiety, and depression. Psychologists who deal with stress in an urban environment will be at the center of preventing and solving the world's problems. By promoting positive coping, forgiveness, and reconciliation, positive psychologists will enrich lives, prevent problems, and promote human flourishing.

Health and Care for All: The Challenges for the 21st Century

COREY L. M. KEYES

Emory University, Atlanta, Georgia

Americans are living longer, but not necessarily healthier, lives. Although spending more per capita on health, the U.S. trails many countries in health care. As a threat to our economic stability, health care soon will consume one-quarter of the U.S. gross

(Continued)

(Continued)

domestic product. Positive psychology can be part of the solution by focusing on health and disparities rather than, for example, the happiness of the wealthy (e.g., private happiness coaches). There presently are disturbing social inequalities such as African Americans' dramatically lower life expectancies relative to other racial groups; moreover, disadvantaged Americans face the greatest risks for diseases. Reducing such inequalities is crucial. As such, we must emphasize "promotion" and "health" for all citizens in our future medicine and public health efforts. Thus, in pursuing happiness, the goals of positive psychology not only should be to add sheer number of years to life spans, but also to add healthy and meaningful quality years.

The Need for Greater Commitment to a Broader Sense of Community

CHARLES CARVER

University of Miami, Miami, Florida

The crucial issue for civilization, as well as positive psychology, is the struggle between personal desires and the needs of the community. We live in a time when entitlement is rampant. Many people care about their own wealth and well-being and perhaps the well-being of a very small circle around them: family, close associates, others like themselves. Few care about the well-being of Americans on the poor side of town. Even fewer care about the well-being of people on the other side of the world. We want lower taxes and bigger toys more than we want adequate roads, education, or mental health services for people in need. We are a collection of tribes, not a community: tribes defined by our culture, religion, and skin color. It is harder to care about the broad community of humanity than about one's tribe. But if we do not learn to do so, we will destroy not just the competing tribes but also all of civilization.

Happiness Is the Best Medicine

ELLEN LANGER

Harvard University, Cambridge, Massachusetts

Positive psychology did not exist in the 1970s when I was studying how to increase the health and well-being of people. Although mind/body issues often were rejected previously in the medical community, psychological factors now are seen as having potent health effects. I predict that the impact of such positive psychology research should increase exponentially, and that we will adopt new views about healthcare. "Patients" previously have tended to give total control for their care to health care professionals. This subordinate relationship, in my view, needs to change so that people can adopt more mindful roles in every aspect of their health care. Given that no one knows us better than we do, the information arising from our personal expertise should result in health improvements. Finally, although happiness heretofore has taken a back seat to health, my prediction is that the future may promulgate the view that "happiness is the best medicine."

Acknowledging the Good With the Bad

JAMIE PENNEBAKER

University of Texas, Austin, Texas

The appeal of positive psychology is its optimism about the human condition. As a reaction against traditional psychology, much of positive psychology seems to reject the realities of heartbreak, trauma, fear, and other states that often define us. People line up to see sad movies and go on terrifying amusement rides. We eagerly watch horrific manmade or natural disasters on television. Some of the most haunting songs and poems ever written deal with loss and failure. Whereas traditional psychology failed to see the joy of life, I worry that positive psychology will not see the darker side. We need a psychology that embraces the entire human. Often, we can't realize our potential without acknowledging and understanding our weaknesses. Even country singers such as the Oak Ridge Boys know that "it never hurts to hurt sometime."

Mainstreaming Positive Psychology Ideas

SHELLEY TAYLOR

University of California, Los Angeles, California

A chief task of positive psychology in the coming decades will be to integrate our research and insights with the mainstream of science more generally. Uncovering the biological underpinnings of positive states and identifying the underlying biopsychosocial mechanisms whereby positive psychological states and good relationships affect health beneficially will be among the most important roots to this

(Continued)

(Continued)

integration. Exploring underlying brain mechanisms regarding the impact of positive psychological states on behavior, using techniques such as MRI, will be an increasingly important integrative thrust for positive psychology as well. The psychological and biological sciences are coming together as never before, and the most creative discoveries of the next decades will integrate the biological, psychological, and social levels of analysis. Positive psychology is poised to be in the vanguard of this exciting integrative science.

On Partnering and Getting Our Message Out

SUSAN HENDRICK

Texas Tech University, Lubbock, Texas

The positive psychology movement/force is poised to contribute in unique ways to the crisis and opportunity that face our wider world. For example, technology offers opportunities for connection, yet the elusiveness of "real" connection plagues many people. Rising interest in spirituality co-occurs with rising tides of religious fundamentalism. Life-saving medicines are developed, while illicit drugs seem ever more available. These phenomena can be viewed as cups that are either half empty or half full. Positive psychology can employ increasing knowledge and dissemination of such knowledge about love, hope, resilience, and the like that can be used to help people better understand how to maximize what is positive and minimize what is negative. It is important to maintain a cohesive force within positive psychology, composed of contributors from many areas of psychology. It is also important to look outward—beyond narrow disciplinary boundaries. To really have social impact, I believe we must partner with colleagues in other disciplines such as political science and economics so that dissemination of our knowledge can be broad. We have a good message—now we need to be even better at delivering it.

Maintain Scientific Integrity in the Quest for Relevance and Application

TIMOTHY R. ELLIOTT

University of Alabama, Birmingham, Alabama

It was an awkward situation: A junior colleague from an "allied health profession" was giving a presentation on spiritual beliefs and health to the senior scientists of our research center. She discussed how her profession could conduct research in this area that would enhance practice and attract grant funds. She cited "big names" and current books in positive psychology. Unfortunately, she could not answer basic questions about the mechanisms through which specific behaviors develop, nor could she explain mechanisms of change. She could articulate no testable, theoretical model. As the psychologist on the panel with some familiarity with the topic, colleagues posed a few questions—and some disapproving eyebrows—in my direction.

Positive psychology should be in included in large-scale research projects to further understand these constructs and their relevance to health and well-being. But we must maintain high expectations for scientific rigor and integrity. Acceptance and inclusion bring risks to forgo the essential qualities we expect of theories, constructs, and measures (and multidisciplinary teams are notoriously intolerant of theory in pursuit of applicability and relevance). If scientific integrity is compromised, positive psychology may ascend the flagpole of popularity to heights of cargo cult mentalisms and Barnum statements.

Building a Universal Positive Psychology

SAMUEL HO

University of Hong Kong

Ever since Wundt established the first psychology laboratory in 1879, the knowledge of psychology is, to a very large extent, a one-way traffic from the West to the East. When I was learning psychotherapy at college, I had to accept what was taught to us according to the western models. Some of them may not be totally synchronize with the Asian cultures, and yet there were few channels for giving feedback regarding our experience to colleagues in the West.

Positive psychology is developed in the era of globalization. Many empirical studies of positive psychology are multinational collaborative projects, and the existing accumulative knowledge of positive psychology already reflects the collective wisdom of scholars from different cultures. The future development of positive psychology should further cultivate the mutual exchange of knowledge between scholars in different parts of the world. The establishment of a feedback loop for scholars in Asia to contribute to the development of positive psychology, to me, is especially important. The result would be the building of a universal positive psychology that even may shape the future of psychology in general.

Positive Psychology in a Cultural Context

JENNIFER TERAMOTO PEDROTTI

California Polytechnic State University, San Luis Obispo, California

For positive psychology to remain a viable area of research and practice, we must continue to move our focus from identifying "universal strengths" to viewing all types of strength-based behavior from within a cultural context. By including cultural context in our discussions of the positive, both in the person and in the environment, we can make positive psychology accessible to people from all walks of life.

Giving Positive Psychology Away

TAL BEN-SHACHAR

Harvard University, Cambridge, Massachusetts

Teaching positive psychology is about rigorous fun. At present, the realm of self-help—of enhancing the quality of our lives—is dominated by pop-psychology. In the multitude of self-help seminars and books that are currently being offered, there's a lot of fun and charisma and relatively little substance. These seminars and books promise five quick steps to happiness, the three secrets of success, and four ways to find your perfect lover. On the other side we have academia, with writing and research that is substantive, but that does not find its way into most households. The realm of life flourishing is too important to be left at the hands of charismatic self-help gurus or in the obscurity of academic libraries. As I see it, the role of positive psychology is to bridge between the ivory tower and the main street—between the rigor of academe and the fun of the self-help movement.

The Power of Attitude: The Tales of Johnsy and Jerry

In this book, we show you numerous examples of the sheer power of the human mind in making the lives of people better. Perhaps one of the most beautiful short stories in all of English literature, *The Last Leaf* by O. Henry (1945), tells of this power just as well as the many pages of research we have cited. In this story, a young woman named Johnsy contracts pneumonia, and soon it has worsened to the point that it threatens her life. It is winter, and Johnsy gets sicker with each passing day. Outside of her bedroom, she can view an ivy vine through a window. She becomes convinced that this vine will foretell her impending death. Johnsy concludes that, when this vine drops its last leaf, she, too, will perish. Therefore, she spends her waking hours looking out the window, watching the leaves fall one by one.

To her amazement, one leaf clings to the vine even as winter deepens. Surely, this is an omen—the sign of a miracle as this one stubborn leaf clings to life. Seeing this, Johnsy day by day becomes more convinced that she, too, has been chosen to live. And live she does, having traded a bad prognosis for a favorable one. When she is fully recovered, Johnsy discovers that her artist friend had painted this last leaf on the wall where the vine grew! It matters not to Johnsy then, however, for she realizes that it was the power of her own mind that fueled her triumph over the pneumonia.

O. Henry understood the power of the expectations that can grow in human minds; so, too, does modern positive psychology teach us that what we believe will happen often does happen. Think and feel good things, and so these things become more likely to occur. Of course, this does not mean that you merely can sit idly by to await the good; rather, you may have to work hard—very hard. But, in thinking that you can survive, like Johnsy and her leaf, you are more likely to live and live well. It mattered not that the leaf was not "real," because in the most important place, Johnsy's mind, it was real. And the love and care of her artist friend also was very real.

Similar to Johnsy's good attitude, consider the attitude of Jerry (Baltazar-Schwartz, http://pr.erau.edu/~madler/atttitude.html). Always in a good mood, Jerry could manage to say something positive in almost any situation. His favorite reply, when asked about how he was doing, was, "If I were any better, I would be twins."

For Jerry, life was all about choices. His view was that you could choose to feel lousy or good. For Jerry, who managed a restaurant, this attitude was put to the test one day when armed robbers came into his restaurant and shot him. Rushed to the emergency room, he saw the grim faces of the doctors and nurses. Their expressions said, "This guy is dead." At that point, the head nurse asked him if he was allergic to anything. Jerry said that he was, and the room grew quiet as everyone awaited his response. At that point, Jerry hollered out, "I am allergic to BULLETS!" The people in the emergency room exploded in laughter, and Jerry told them that he was choosing to live. And after hours of skilled surgery, he did live.

The tales of Johnsy and Jerry show the power of positive attitudes. Not only can we live, we can live well if we believe. Indeed, the tale of positive psychology and the science upon which it is built both leave us with an empowering attitude: "We can!"

Appendix: Positive Social Science

MARTIN E. P. SELIGMAN, PhD

President, American Psychological Association

In her biography of Franklin and Eleanor Roosevelt, a distinguished political scientist analyzes Eleanor's tireless pursuit of justice for poor people and black people as an attempt to compensate for her father's alcoholism and her mother's narcissism. The possibility that Eleanor was simply pursuing virtue is not considered. Research psychology has spent half a century documenting the many negative mental effects of isolation, trauma, abuse, physical illness, war, poverty, discrimination, early parental death, and divorce. But this relentless focus on the negative has left psychology blind to the many instances of growth, mastery, drive, and insight that develop out of undesirable, painful life events.

How has it happened that the social sciences view the human strengths and virtues—altruism, courage, honesty, duty, joy, health, responsibility, and good cheer—as derivative, defensive, or downright illusions, while weakness and negative motivations—anxiety, lust, selfishness, paranoia, anger, disorder, and sadness—are viewed as authentic?

When a culture faces military threat, or poverty, or social upheaval, or shortage of goods, it is most naturally concerned with questions about the negative side of life. The sciences it underwrites will be about defense and damage. Modern psychology accordingly has been preoccupied with healing. It has, by and large, understood functioning within a disease model, and its main mode of intervention has been the repair of damage. Theoretically, it has been a victimology in which human beings are viewed as passive, "responding" to external stimuli, or as consumed with unresolved conflicts dictated by childhood trauma, or as acting from tissue needs, drives, and instincts, or as the helpless victims of oppressive cultural and economic forces.

At those few times in history when cultures have been prosperous, at peace, and stable, some have turned their attention from concerns with defense and damage to the promotion of the highest qualities of life. In so doing, these cultures have made monumental contributions to human progress. Athens in the 5th century BC, Victorian England, and Florence of the 15th century are examples.

Athenian prosperity encouraged philosophy, which bred a new form of politics—democracy. Victorian England, sustained by the bounty of empire, enshrined honor, valor, discipline, and duty. Florence's wool and banking trades made it the richest and most stable city-state in Europe.

Whereupon Florence decided to devote much of its surplus not to making it the mightiest power in Europe, but to the creation of beauty.

I believe that America today is entering such a world-historical moment. I do not propose that we build an aesthetic monument, but rather a humane scientific monument: that social science, working at the individual level, will take as its mission the delineation, measurement, and promotion of human fulfillment and will, working at the group level, take civic virtue as its proper subject. My vision is that social science will finally see beyond the remedial and escape from the muckraking that has claimed it, that social science will become a positive force for understanding and promoting the highest qualities of civic and personal life.

Remedial psychology has had its victories: most prominently, a science of mental illness. As a result, the causes of at least 10 of the major mental disorders have been illuminated, and these disorders can now be markedly relieved by psychological and pharmacological interventions. But sadly, while plumbing the depths of what is worst in life, psychology lost its connection to the positive side of life—the knowledge about what makes human life most worth living, most fulfilling, most enjoyable, and most productive.

Such science is possible. The major psychological theories have changed to undergird the investigation of strength and responsibility. No longer do the dominant theories all view the individual as passive; rather, individuals are now seen as decision makers, with choices, preferences, and the possibility of becoming masterful, efficacious or, in malignant circumstances, helpless and hopeless. We have a field of measurement in which the negative states of depression, fear, anomie, aggression, and hopelessness can be reliably and validly assessed. We have a field able to investigate the relevant brain states and neuropharmacology. Our field developed ingenious experimental methods and sophisticated causal modeling for looking at how experience shapes such states and how these states develop over a life span. And we pioneered the interventions that proved effective for undoing such undesirable states. Now we can call upon these same methods to measure and understand how to build personal human strengths and civic virtues.

This kind of scientific activity is not a chimera: There are viable empirical bodies of knowledge about flow and about optimism, for example. But these represent only a minute fraction of the corpus in social science. The thorough investigation of personal strength and civic virtue will not come easily or cheaply. It can be the "Manhattan Project" of the social sciences, but it will require substantial resources.

The positive social science of the 21st century will have as a useful side effect the possibility of prevention of the serious mental illnesses; for there are a set of human strengths that most likely buffer against mental illness: courage, optimism, interpersonal skill, work ethic, hope, responsibility, future-mindedness, honesty, and perseverance, to name several. But it will have as its direct effect a scientific understanding of the practice of civic virtue and of the pursuit of the best things in life.

References

Abramson, L. Y., Alloy, L., Hankin, B., Clements, C., Zhu, L., Hogan, M., et al. (2000). Optimistic cognitive style and invulnerability to depression. In J. Gillham (Ed.), *The science of optimism and hope* (pp. 75–98). Philadelphia, PA: Templeton Foundation Press.

Abramson, L. Y., Seligman, M. E. P., & Teasdale, J. D. (1978). Learned helplessness in humans: Critique and reformulation. *Journal of Abnormal Psychology, 87,* 49–74.

Abuhamdeh, S. (2000). *The autotelic personality: An exploratory investigation.* Unpublished manuscript, University of Chicago.

Acker, M., & Davis, M. H. (1992). Intimacy, passion and commitment in adult romantic relationships: A test of the triangular theory of love. *Journal of Social and Personal Relationships, 9,* 21–50.

Adlai-Gail, W. (1994). *Exploring the autotelic personality.* Unpublished doctoral dissertation, University of Chicago.

Adolphs, R., Damasio, H., Tranel, D., Cooper, G., & Damasio, A. R. (2000). A role for somatosensory cortices in the visual recognition of emotion as revealed by three-dimensional lesion mapping. *Journal of Neuroscience, 20,* 2683–2690.

Affleck, G., & Tennen, H. (1996). Construing benefit from adversity: Adaptational significance and dispositional underpinnings. *Journal of Personality, 64,* 899–922.

Ahuvia, A. (2001). Well-being in cultures of choice: A cross-cultural perspective. *American Psychologist, 56,* 77–78.

Ainsworth, M. D. S. (1979). Infant-mother attachment. *American Psychologist, 34,* 932–937.

Ainsworth, M. D. S., Bell, S. M., & Stayton, D. J. (1992). Infant-mother attachment and social development: "Socialization" as a product of reciprocal responsiveness to signals. In M. Woodhead, R. Carr, & P. Light (Eds.), *Becoming a person* (pp. 30–55). London: Routledge.

Ajzen, I. (1988). *Attitudes, personality, and behavior.* Chicago: Dorsey.

Albee, G. W., & Gullotta, T. P. (Eds.). (1997). *Primary prevention works.* Thousand Oaks, CA: Sage.

Albom, M. (2002). *Tuesdays with Morrie: An old man, a young man, and life's greatest lesson.* New York: Broadway.

Allport, G. W. (1960). *Personality and social encounter.* Boston: Beacon Press.

Allport, G. W. (1961). *Pattern and growth in personality.* New York: Holt, Rinehart & Winston.

Alvy, K. T. (1988). Parenting programs for black parents. In L. A. Bond & B. M. Wagner (Eds.), *Families in transition: Primary prevention programs that work* (pp. 135–169). Newbury Park, CA: Sage.

American Psychiatric Association. (1952). *Diagnostic and statistical manual of mental disorders.* Washington, DC: Author.

American Psychiatric Association. (1994). *Diagnostic and statistical manual of mental disorders* (4th ed.). Washington, DC: Author.

American Psychiatric Association. (2000). *Diagnostic and statistical manual of mental disorders* (Text revision). Washington, DC: Author.

American Psychological Association. (2003). Guidelines on multicultural education, training, research, practice, and organizational change for psychologists. *American Psychologist, 58,* 377–402.

Amick, B. C., III, McDonough, P., Chang, H., Rogers, W. H., Duncan, G., & Pieper, C. (2002). The relationship between all-cause mortality and cumulative working life course psychological and physical exposures in the United States labor market from 1968–1992. *Psychosomatic Medicine, 64,* 370–381.

Anderson, E. (2005). Strengths-based educating. *Educational Horizons, 83,* 80–89.

Antonovsky, A. (1987). *Unraveling the mystery of health: How people manage stress and stay well.* San Francisco: Jossey-Bass.

Antonovsky, A., & Sagy, S. (1986). The development of a sense of coherence and its impact on responses to stress situations. *Journal of Social Psychology, 126,* 213–225.

Aquinas, T. (1948). *Introduction to St. Thomas Aquinas: The Summa Theologica, The Summa Contra Gentiles* (A. Pegis, Ed.). New York: Random House. (Original work published 1273)

Aquinas, T. (1981). *Summa theologica.* Westminster, MD: Christian Classics. (Original work published 1273)

Ardelt, M. (1997). Wisdom and life satisfaction in old age. *Journals of Gerontology: Psychological Sciences and Social Sciences, 52,* 15–27.

Ardelt, M. (2000). Antecedents and effects of wisdom in old age: A longitudinal perspective on aging well. *Research on Aging, 22,* 350–394.

Argyle, M. (1987). *The psychology of happiness.* London: Methuen.

Argyle, M. (2001). *The psychology of happiness* (2nd ed.). London: Routledge.

Aristotle. (1962). *Nichomachean ethics* (M. Ostwald, Trans.). Indianapolis, IN: Bobbs-Merrill.

Aron, A., & Aron, E. N. (1986). *Love and the expansion of self: Understanding attraction and satisfaction.* New York: Hemisphere.

Aron, A., Aron, E. N., & Smollan, D. (1992). Inclusion of other in the self scale and the structure of interpersonal closeness. *Journal of Personality and Social Psychology, 63,* 596–612.

Aron, A., Norman, C. C., Aron, E. N., McKenna, C., & Heyman, R. E. (2000). Couples' shared participation in novel and arousing activities and experienced relationship quality. *Journal of Personality and Social Psychology, 78,* 273–284.

Aron, A., Paris, M., & Aron, E. N. (1995). Falling in love: Prospective studies of self-concept change. *Journal of Personality and Social Psychology, 69,* 1102–1112.

Aron, E. N., & Aron, A. (1996). Love and expansion of the self: The state of the model. *Personal Relationships, 3,* 45–58.

Aronson, E. (2000). *Nobody left to hate: Teaching compassion after Columbine*. New York: Freeman.

Aronson, E. (2003). *The social animal* (9th edition). New York: Worth.

Aronson, E., Blaney, N., Stephin, C., Sikes, J., & Snapp, M. (1978). *The jigsaw classroom*. Beverly Hills, CA: Sage.

Aronson, E., & Patnoe, S. (1997). *The jigsaw classroom: Building cooperation in the classroom* (2nd ed.). New York: Addison Wesley Longman.

Ashby, F. G., Isen, A. M., & Turken, A. U. (1999). A neuropsychological theory of positive affect and its influence on cognition. *Psychological Review, 106*, 529–550.

Aspinwall, L. G., & Staudinger, U. M. (Eds.). (2002). *A psychology of human strengths: Fundamental questions and future directions for a positive psychology*. Washington, DC: American Psychological Association.

Aspinwall, L. G., & Taylor, S. E. (1992). Modeling cognitive adaptation: A longitudinal investigation of the impact of individual differences and coping on college adjustment and performance. *Journal of Personality and Social Psychology, 61*, 755–765.

Assmann, A. (Ed.). (1994). *Wisdom: Archeology of communication*. Munich, Germany: Fink Verlag.

Astin, J. A. (1997). Stress reduction through mindfulness meditation: Effects on psychological symptomatology, sense of control, and spiritual experiences. *Psychotherapy & Psychosomatics, 66*, 97–106.

Austenfeld, J. L., & Stanton, A. L. (2004). Coping through emotional approach: A new look at emotion, coping, and health-related outcomes. *Journal of Personality, 72*, 1335–1363.

Averill, J. (1990). Inner feelings, works of the flesh, the beast within, diseases of the mind, driving force, and putting on a show: Six metaphors of emotion and their theoretical extensions. In D. E. Leary (Ed.), *Metaphors in the history of psychology* (pp. 104–132). New York: Cambridge University Press.

Averill, J. R., Catlin, G., & Chon, K. K. (1990). *Rules of hope*. New York: Springer-Verlag.

Avolio, B., Luthans, F., & Walumbwa, F. O. (2004). Authentic leadership: Theory-building for veritable sustained performance (Working paper). Gallup Leadership Institute, University of Nebraska, Lincoln.

Babyak, M., Snyder, C. R., & Yoshinobu, L. (1993). Psychometric properties of the Hope Scale: A confirmatory factor analysis. *Journal of Research in Personality, 27*, 154–169.

Bacon, F. (2005). *The advancement of learning*. Boston: Elibron Class. (Original work published 1604)

Bacon, S. F. (2005). Positive psychology's two cultures. *Review of General Psychology, 9*, 181–192.

Baltazar-Schwartz, F. *Attitude is everything*. Retrieved January 16, 2005, from http://pr.erau.edu/~madler/atttitude.html

Baltes, M. M., & Carstensen, L. L. (1996). The process of successful aging. *Aging in Society, 16*, 397–422.

Baltes, P. B. (1993). The aging mind: Potential and limits. *The Gerontologist, 33*, 580–594.

Baltes, P. B., Glueck, J., & Kunzmann, U. (2002). Wisdom: Its structure and function in regulating successful life-span development. In C. R. Snyder &

S. J. Lopez (Eds.), *The handbook of positive psychology* (pp. 327–347). New York: Oxford University Press.

Baltes, P. B., & Smith, J. (1990). The psychology of wisdom and its ontogenesis. In R. J. Sternberg (Ed.), *Wisdom: Its nature, origins, and development* (pp. 87–120). New York: Cambridge University Press.

Baltes, P. B., & Staudinger, U. (1993). The search for a psychology of wisdom. *Current Directions in Psychological Science, 2,* 75–80.

Baltes, P. B., & Staudinger, U. (2000). Wisdom: A metaheuristic (pragmatic) to orchestrate mind and virtue toward excellence. *American Psychologist, 55,* 122–136.

Bandura, A. (1977). Self-efficacy: Toward a unifying theory of behavior change. *Psychological Review, 84,* 191–215.

Bandura, A. (1982). Self-efficacy mechanism in human agency. *American Psychologist, 37,* 122–147.

Bandura, A. (1986). *Social foundations of thought and action.* New York: Prentice Hall.

Bandura, A. (1989a). Human agency in social cognitive theory. *American Psychologist, 44,* 1175–1184.

Bandura, A. (1989b). Regulation of cognitive processes through perceived self-efficacy. *Developmental Psychology, 25,* 729–735.

Bandura, A. (1991). Self-efficacy mechanism in physiological activation and health-promoting behavior. In J. Madden IV (Ed.), *Neurobiology of learning, emotion and affect* (pp. 229–270). New York: Raven.

Bandura, A. (1993). Perceived self-efficacy in cognitive development and functioning. *Educational Psychologist, 28,* 117–148.

Bandura, A. (1995). *Manual for the construction of self-efficacy scales.* Available from Albert Bandura, Department of Psychology, Stanford University, Stanford, CA 94305–2130.

Bandura, A. (1997). *Self-efficacy: The exercise of control.* New York: Freeman.

Bandura, A. (2000). Social cognitive theory in context. *Journal of Applied Psychology: An International Review, 51,* 269–290.

Bandura, A., Adams, N. E., & Beyer, J. (1977). Cognitive processes mediating behavioral change. *Journal of Personality and Social Psychology, 35,* 125–139.

Bandura, A., Barbaranelli, C., Vittorio Caprara, G., & Pastorelli, C. (2001). Self-efficacy beliefs as shapers of children's aspirations and career trajectories. *Child Development, 72,* 187–206.

Bandura, A., Taylor, C. B., Williams, S. L., Mefford, I. N., & Barchas, J. D. (1985). Catecholamine secretion as a function of perceived coping self-efficacy. *Journal of Consulting and Clinical Psychology, 53,* 406–414.

Banerjee, T. & Banerjee, G. (1995). Determinants of help-seeking behavior in cases of epilepsy attending a teaching hospital in India: An indigenous explanatory model. *International Journal of Social Psychiatry, 41,* 217–230.

Barber, B. R., & Battistoni, R. M. (1993). *Education for democracy: A sourcebook for students and teachers.* Dubuque, IA: Kendall/Hunt.

Bargh, J., & Chartrand, T. (1999). The unbearable automaticity of being. *American Psychologist, 54,* 462–479.

Barker, S. L., Funk, S. C., & Houston, B. K. (1988). Psychological treatment versus nonspecific factors: A meta-analysis of conditions that engender comparable expectations of improvement. *Clinical Psychology Review, 8,* 579–594.

Bar-On, R. (1997). *Bar-On Emotional Quotient Inventory: A measure of emotional intelligence.* Toronto, Ontario: Multi-Health Systems.

Bar-On, R. (2000). Emotional and social intelligence: Insights from the Emotional Quotient Inventory. In R. Bar-On & J. D. A. Parker (Eds.), *The handbook of emotional intelligence* (pp. 363–388). San Francisco: Jossey-Bass.

Barone, D., Maddux, J., & Snyder, C. R. (1997). The social cognitive construction of difference and disorder. In D. Barone, J. Maddux, & C. R. Snyder (Eds.), *Social cognitive psychology: History and current domains* (pp. 397–428). New York: Plenum.

Barone, D., Maddux, J. E., & Snyder, C. R. (1997). *Social cognitive psychology: History and current domains.* New York: Plenum.

Bartholomew, K., & Horowitz, L. M. (1991). Attachment styles among young adults: A test of a four-category model. *Journal of Personality and Social Psychology, 61,* 226–244.

Barusch, A. S. (1999). Religion, adversity, and age: Religious experiences of low-income elderly women. *Journal of Sociology and Social Welfare, 26,* 125–142.

Batson, C. D. (1991). *The altruism question: Toward a social-psychological answer.* Hillsdale, NJ: Lawrence Erlbaum.

Batson, C. D., Ahmad, N., Lishner, D. A., & Tsang, J. (2002). Empathy and altruism. In C. R. Snyder & S. J. Lopez (Eds.). *The handbook of positive psychology* (pp. 485–498). New York: Oxford University Press.

Batson, C. D., Polycarpou, M. P., Harmon-Jones, E., Imhoff, H. J., Mitchener, E. C., Bednar, L. L., et al. (1997). Empathy and attitudes: Can feeling for a member of a stigmatized group improve feelings toward the group? *Journal of Personality and Social Psychology, 72,* 105–118.

Battista, J., & Almond, R. (1973). The development of meaning in life. *Psychiatry, 36,* 409–427.

Baumeister, R. F. (2005). *The cultural animal: Human nature, meaning, and social life.* New York: Oxford University Press.

Baumeister, R. F., Bratslavsky, E., Finkenhaur, C., & Vohs, K. D. (2001). Bad is stronger than good. *Review of General Psychology, 5,* 323–370.

Baumeister, R. F., Faber, J. E., & Wallace, H. M. (1999). Coping and ego depletion. In C. R. Snyder (Ed.), *Coping: The psychology of what works* (pp. 50–69). New York: Oxford University Press.

Baumeister, R. F., & Leary, M. R. (1995). The need to belong: Desire for interpersonal attachment as a fundamental human motivation. *Psychological Bulletin, 117,* 497–529.

Baumeister, R. F., & Vohs, K. D. (2002). The pursuit of meaningfulness in life. In C. R. Snyder & S. J. Lopez (Eds.), *The handbook of positive psychology* (pp. 608–618). New York: Oxford University Press.

Baumgarten, M., Thomas, D., Poulin de Courval, L., & Infante-Rivard, C. (1988). Evaluation of a mutual help network for the elderly residents of planned housing. *Psychology and Aging, 3,* 393–398.

Bechara, A., Tranel, D., Damasio, H., & Damasio, A. R. (1996). Failure to respond autonomically to anticipated future outcomes following damage to prefrontal cortex. *Cerebral Cortex, 6,* 215–225.

Becker, H. S. (1963). *Outsiders.* New York: Free Press.

Becker, J. A., & Smenner, P. C. (1986). The spontaneous use of *thank you* by preschoolers as a function of sex, socioeconomic status, and listener status. *Language in Society, 15,* 537–546.

Bellah, R. N., Madsen, R., Sullivan, W. M., Swidler, A., & Tipton, S. M. (1985). *Habits of the heart: Individualism and commitment in American life.* Berkeley: University of California Press.

Bellah, R. N., Madsen, R., Sullivan, W. M., Swidler, A., & Tipton, S. M. (1988). *Individualism and commitment in American life: Readings on the themes of habits of the heart.* New York: Harper & Row.

Belsky, J., & Nezworski, T. (Eds.). (1988). *Clinical implications of attachment.* Hillsdale, NJ: Lawrence Erlbaum.

Benne, K. D. (1964). History of T-group in the laboratory setting. In L. P. Bradford, J. R. Gibb, & K. D. Benne (Eds.), *T-group and laboratory method: Innovation in re-education* (pp. 80–135). New York: Wiley.

Benson, H., & Proctor, W. (1984). *Beyond the relaxation response.* New York: Putnam/Berkley.

Benson, P. L. (1992). Religion and substance use. In J. F. Schumaker (Ed.), *Religion and mental health* (pp. 211–220). New York: Oxford University Press.

Benson, P. L., Leffert, N., Scales, P. C., & Blyth, D. A. (1998). Creating healthy communities for children and adolescents. *Applied Developmental Science, 2,* 138–159.

Benson, P. L., & Saito, R. N. (2000). The scientific foundations of youth development. In N. Jaffe (Ed.), *Youth development: Issues, challenges, and directions* (pp. 125–147). Philadelphia: Public/Private Ventures.

Berg, I. K., & de Shazer, S. (1992). Making numbers talk: Language in therapy. In S. Friedman (Ed.), *The new language of change: Constructive collaboration in psychotherapy* (pp. 5–24). New York: Guilford Press.

Bernstein, D. M., & Simmons, R. G. (1974). The adolescent kidney donor: The right to give. *American Journal of Psychiatry, 131,* 1338–1343.

Berscheid, E., & Reis, H. T. (1998). Attraction and close relationships. In D. T. Gilbert, S. T. Fiske, & G. Lindsey (Eds.), *The handbook of social psychology* (4th ed., Vol. 2, pp. 193–281). New York: McGraw-Hill.

Berscheid, E., & Walster, E. (1978). *Interpersonal attraction* (2nd ed.). Reading, MA: Addison Wesley.

Bess, K. D., Fisher, A. T., Sonn, C. C., & Bishop, B. J. (2002). Psychological sense of community. In A. T Fisher, C. C. Sonn, & B. J. Bishop (Eds.), *Psychological sense of community: Research, applications, and implications* (pp. 3–22). New York: Kluwer Academic/Plenum Publishers.

Betz, N. E., Klein, K., & Taylor, K. M. (1996). Evaluation of a short form of the Career Decision-Making Self-Efficacy Scale. *Journal of Career Assessment, 4,* 47–57.

Betz, N. E., & Klein Voyten, K. (1997). Efficacy and outcome expectations influence career exploration and decidedness. *Career Development Quarterly, 46,* 179–189.

Betz, N. E., & Luzzo, D. A. (1996). Career assessment and the Career Decision-Making Self-Efficacy scale. *Journal of Career Assessment, 4,* 413–428.

Betz, N. E., & Taylor, K. M. (2000). *Manual for the Career Decision-Making Self-Efficacy Scale and CDMSE-Short Form.* Unpublished document, Ohio State University, Columbus.

Biddle, S. J. H., Fox, K. R., & Boutcher, S. H. (Eds.). (2000). *Physical activity and psychological well-being.* London: Routledge.

Bierman, K. L. (1997). Implementing a comprehensive program for the prevention of conduct problems in rural communities: The Fast Track experience. *American Journal of Community Psychology, 25,* 493–514.

Binet, A., & Simon, T. (1916). *The development of intelligence in children* (E. S. Kit, Trans.). Baltimore: Williams & Williams.

Bishop, S. R. (2002). What do we really know about mindfulness-based stress reduction? *Psychomatic Medicine, 64,* 71–84.

Bishop, S. R., Lau, M., Shapiro, S., Carlson, L., Anderson, N. D., Carmody, J., et al. (2004). Mindfulness: A proposed operational definition. *Clinical Psychology: Science and Practice, 11,* 230–241.

Biswas-Diener, R., & Diener, E. (in press). Cross-cultural study of strengths. *Journal of Happiness Studies.*

Bjornesen, C. A. (2000). Undergraduate student perceptions of the impact of faculty activities in education. *Teaching of Psychology, 27,* 205–208.

Black, B. (2001). The road to recovery. *Gallup Management Journal, 1,* 10–12.

Blazer, D. (1994). Epidemiology of late-life depression. In L. Schneider, C. F. Reynolds, B. Lebowitz, & A. Friedhoff (Eds.), *Diagnosis and treatment of depression in late life* (pp. 9–19). Washington, DC: American Psychiatric Association.

Bloch, E. (1986). *The principle of hope.* (N. Plaice, S. Plaice, & P. Knight, Trans.). Cambridge: MIT Press (Vol. 1). (Original work published 1959)

Blum, D. (n.d.). Finding strength: How to overcome anything. *Psychology Today,* Retrieved August 30, 2004, from http://www.psychologytoday.com/articles/pto-19980501-000024.html

Blustein, D. L. (1989). The role of goal instability and career self-efficacy in the career exploration process. *Journal of Vocational Behavior, 35,* 194–203.

Boniwell, I., & Zimbardo, P. G. (2004). Balancing one's time perspective in pursuit of optimal functioning. In P. A. Linley & S. Joseph (Eds.), *Positive psychology in practice* (pp. 165–180). Hoboken, NJ: Wiley.

Bono, G., Emmons, R. A., & McCullough, M. E. (2004). Gratitude in practice and the practice of gratitude. In P. A. Linley & S. Joseph (Eds.), *Positive psychology in practice* (pp. 464–481). Hoboken, NJ: Wiley.

Botvin, G. J., & Toru, S. (1988). Preventing adolescent substance abuse through life skills training. In R. H. Price, E. L. Cowen, R. P. Lorion, & J. Ramos-McKay (Eds.), *Fourteen ounces of prevention: A casebook for practitioners* (pp. 98–110). Washington, DC: American Psychological Association.

Bowlby, J. (1969). *Attachment and loss. Vol. I: Attachment.* London: Tavistock.

Bowlby, J. (1982). Attachment and loss: Retrospect and prospect. *American Journal of Orthopsychiatry, 52,* 664–678.

Bowlby, J. (1988). *A secure base: Parent-child attachment and healthy human development.* New York: Basic Books.

Bradburn, N. M. (1969). *The structure of psychological well-being.* Chicago: Aldine.

Brennan, K. A., Clark, C. L, & Shaver, P. R. (1998). Self-report measures of adult attachment: An integrative overview. In J. A. Simpson & W. S. Rholes (Eds.) *Attachment theory and close relationships* (pp. 46–76). New York: Guilford Press.

Bretherton, I., & Waters, E. (Eds.). (1985). Growing points of attachment theory and research. *Monograph of the Society for Research in Child Development, 50*(209).

Brewer, C. L. (2002). Reflections on an academic career: From which side of the looking glass? In S. F. Davis & W. Buskist (Eds.), *The teaching of psychology: Essays in honor of Wilbert J. McKeachie and Charles L. Brewer* (pp. 499–507). Mahwah, NJ: Lawrence Erlbaum.

Brewer, M. B. (1991). The social self: On being the same and different at the same time. *Personality and Social Psychology Bulletin, 17*, 475–482.

Brewer, M. B., & Weber, J. G. (1994). Self-evaluation effects of interpersonal versus intergroup social comparison. *Journal of Personality and Social Psychology, 36*, 917–927.

Breznitz, S. (1986). The effect of hope on coping with stress. In M. H. Appley & P. Trumbull (Eds.), *Dynamics of stress: Physiological, psychological, and social perspectives* (pp. 295–307). New York: Plenum.

Brogan, D. W. (1960). *France (Life world library).* New York: Time Life Books.

Bronowski, J. (1973). *The ascent of man.* Boston: Little, Brown.

Brown, D. E. (1991). *Human universals.* Philadelphia: Temple University Press.

Brown, K. J., & Roberts, M. C. (2000). *An evaluation of the Alvin Ailey Dance Camp, Kansas City Missouri.* Unpublished manuscript, University of Kansas, Lawrence.

Brown, K. W., & Ryan, R. M. (2003). The benefits of being present: Mindfulness and its role in psychological well-being. *Journal of Personality and Social Psychology, 84*, 822–848.

Bruhn, J. G. (1996). Creating an organizational climate for multiculturalism. *Health Care Supervisor, 14*, 11–18.

Bryant, F. B. (1989). A four-factor model of perceived control: Avoiding, coping, obtaining, and savoring. *Journal of Personality, 57*, 773–797.

Bryant, F. B. (2004 May). *Capturing the joy of the moment: Savoring as a process in positive psychology.* Invited address at the meeting of the Midwestern Psychological Association, Chicago.

Bryant, F. B. (2005 February). *Pleasure—Happiness in the present.* Invited international Internet lecture, Authentic Happiness Coaching (www.authentic-happinesscoaching.com), Bethesda, MD.

Bryant, F. B., & Veroff, J. (1982). The structure of psychological well-being: A sociohistorical analysis. *Journal of Personality and Social Psychology, 43*, 653–673.

Bryant, F. B., & Veroff, J. (2006). *The process of savoring: A new model of positive experience.* Mahwah, NJ: Lawrence Erlbaum.

Bryk, A. S., & Schneider, B. (2002). *Trust in schools: A core resource for improvement.* New York: Russell Sage.

Bryne, D. (1969). Attitudes and attraction. In L. Berkowitz (Ed.), *Advances in experimental social psychology* (Vol. 4, pp. 36–86). New York: Academic Press.

Bryne, D. (1971). *The attraction paradigm.* New York: Academic Press.

Bryne, D., & Clore, G. (1970). A reinforcement model of evaluative responses. *Journal of Personality, 1*, 103–108.

Buckingham, M., & Clifton, D. O. (2001). *Now, discover your strengths.* New York: Free Press.

Buckingham, M., & Coffman, C. (1999). *First, break all the rules: What the world's greatest managers do differently.* New York: Simon & Schuster.

Bunce, S. C., Larsen, R. J., & Peterson, C. (1995). Life after trauma: Personality and daily life experiences of traumatized people. *Journal of Personality, 63*, 165–188.

Burchell, S. (1966). *Age of progress.* New York: Time Life Books.

Burger, J. M., & Cooper, H. M. (1979). The desirability of control. *Motivation and Emotion, 3,* 381–393.

Buskist, W., Benson, T., & Sikorski, J. F. (2005). The call to teach. *Journal of Social and Clinical Psychology, 24,* 110–121.

Buss, D. (2000). The evolution of happiness. *American Psychologist, 55,* 15–23.

Butler, R. (1974). Successful aging and the role of life review. *Journal of the American Geriatric Society, 22,* 529–535.

Campbell, R. L., & Christopher, J. C. (1996a). Moral development theory: A critique of its Kantian presuppositions. *Developmental Review, 16,* 1–47.

Campbell, R. L., & Christopher, J. C. (1996b). Beyond formalism and altruism: The prospects for moral personality. *Developmental Review, 16,* 108–123.

Campbell, R. L., Christopher, J. C., & Bickhard, M. H. (2002). Self and values: An interactivist foundation for moral development. *Theory & Psychology, 12,* 795–822.

Carpenter, B. N., & Steffen, P. R. (2004). Stress. In L. Haas (Ed.), *Handbook of primary care psychology* (pp. 563–578). New York: Oxford University Press.

Carr, A. (2000a). *Family therapy: Concepts, process, and practice.* Chichester, England: Wiley.

Carr, A. (2000b). Evidence based practice in counseling and psychotherapy. In A. Carr (Ed.), *Clinical psychology in Ireland: Volume 2. Empirical studies of problems and treatment processes in adults* (pp. 1–52). Ceredigion, UK: Edwin Mellen Press.

Carr, A. (2004). *Positive psychology: The science of happiness and human strengths.* New York: Brunner-Routledge.

Carrere, S., & Gottman, J. (1999). Predicting divorce among newlyweds from the first three minutes of a marital conflict discussion. *Family Process, 38,* 293–301.

Carrington, P. (1998). *The book of meditation.* Boston: Element Books.

Carstensen, L. (1998). A life-span approach to social motivation. In J. Heckhausen & C. S. Dweck (Eds.), *Motivation and self-regulation across the lifespan* (pp. 341–364). Cambridge, England: Cambridge University Press.

Carstensen, L. L., & Charles, S. T. (1998). Emotion in the second half of life. *Current Directions in Psychological Science, 7,* 144–149.

Carstensen, L. L, Pasupathi, M., Mayr, U., & Nesselroade, J. R. (2000). Emotional experience in everyday life across the adult life span. *Journal of Personality and Social Psychology, 79,* 644–655.

Carter, R. (1977, November 29). Mentally ill still carry stigma. [*New York Times* feature]. *Lawrence Journal-World,* p. D4.

Carter, R. T. (1991). Cultural values: A review of empirical research and implications for counseling. *Journal of Counseling & Development, 70,* 164–173.

Carver, C. S., Pozo, C., Harris, S. D., Noriega, V., Scheier, M. F., Robinson, D. S., et al. (1993). How coping mediates the effect of optimism on distress: A study of women with early stage breast cancer. *Journal of Personality and Social Psychology, 65,* 375–390.

Carver, C. S., & Scheier, M. F. (1993). Vigilant and avoidant coping in two patient samples. In H. W. Krohne (Ed.), *Attention and avoidance: Strategies in coping with aversiveness* (pp. 295–320). Seattle, WA: Hogrefe & Huber.

Carver, C. S., & Scheier, M. F. (1994). Situational coping and coping dispositions in a stressful transaction. *Journal of Personality and Social Psychology, 66,* 184–195.

Carver, C. S., & Scheier, M. F. (1998). *On the self-regulation of behavior.* New York: Cambridge University Press.

Carver, C. S., & Scheier, M. F. (1999). Optimism. In C. R. Snyder (Ed.), *Coping: The psychology of what works* (pp. 182–204). New York: Oxford University Press.

Carver, C. S., & Scheier, M. F. (2002). Optimism. In C. R. Snyder & S. J. Lopez (Eds.), *The handbook of positive psychology* (pp. 231–243). New York: Oxford University Press.

Carver, C. S., Scheier, M. F., & Weintraub, J. K. (1989). Assessing coping strategies: A theoretically based approach. *Journal of Personality and Social Psychology, 56,* 267–283.

Casey, R. J., & Berman, J. S. (1985). The outcome of psychotherapy with children. *Psychological Bulletin, 98,* 388–400.

Cassell, E. J. (2002). Compassion. In C. R. Snyder & S. J. Lopez (Eds.). *The handbook of positive psychology* (pp. 434–445). New York: Oxford University Press.

Catalano, R. F., Berglund, M. L., Ryan, J. A. M., Lonczak, H. S., & Hawkins, J. D. (1998). *Positive youth development in the United States: Research findings on evaluations of positive youth development programs.* Retrieved July 5, 1999, from http://aspe.hhs.gov/hsp/PositiveYouthDev99/

Ceci, S. J., & Papierno, P. B. (2005). The rhetoric and reality of gap closing: When the "have-nots" gain but the "haves" gain even more. *American Psychologist, 60,* 149–160.

Cederblad, M., Dahlin, L., Hagnell, O., & Hansson, K. (1995). Intelligence and temperament as protective factors for mental health: A cross-sectional and prospective epidemiological study. *European Archives of Psychiatry and Clinical Neuroscience, 245,* 11–19.

Cerezo, M. A., & Frias, D. (1994). Emotional and cognitive adjustment in abused children. *Child Abuse and Neglect, 18,* 923–932.

Chambless, D. L., Baker, M., Baucom, D. H., Beutler, L. E., Calhoun, K. S., Crits-Christoph, P., et al. (1998). Update: On empirically validated therapies, II. *Clinical Psychology, 51,* 3–16.

Chambless, D. L., & Hollon, S. D. (1998). Defining empirically supported therapies. *Journal of Consulting and Clinical Psychology, 66,* 7–18.

Chambless, D. L., Sanderson, W. C., Shoham, V., Bennett Johnson, S., Pope, K. S., Crits-Christoph, P., et al. (1996). An update on empirically validated therapies. *Clinical Psychology, 49,* 5–18.

Chan, D. K. (1994). COLINDEX: A refinement of three collectivism measures. In U. Kim, H. C. Triandis, C. Kagitcibasi, S. Choi, & G. Yoon (Eds.), *Individualism and collectivism: Theory, method, and applications* (pp. 200–210). Thousand Oaks, CA: Sage.

Chandler, C. R. (1979). Traditionalism in a modern setting: A comparison of Anglo and Mexican-American value orientations. *Human Organization, 38,* 153–159.

Chang, E. C. (1996a). Cultural differences in optimism, pessimism, and coping. Predictors of subsequent adjustment in Asian American and Caucasian American college students. *Journal of Counseling Psychology, 43,* 113–123.

Chang, E. C. (1996b). Evidence for the cultural specificity of pessimism in Asians vs. Caucasians: A test of the negativity hypothesis. *Personality and Individual Differences, 21,* 819–822.

Chang, E. C. (2001a). A look at the coping strategies and styles of Asian Americans: Similar and different? In C. R. Snyder (Ed.), *Coping with stress: Effective people and processes* (pp. 222–239). New York: Oxford University Press.

Chang, E. C. (2001b). Cultural influences on optimism and pessimism: Differences in Western and Eastern construals of the self. In E. C. Chang (Ed.), *Optimism & pessimism: Implications for theory, research, and practice* (pp. 257–280). Washington, DC: American Psychological Association.

Chang, E. C., Maydeu-Olivares, A., & D'Zurilla, T. J. (1997). Optimism and pessimism as partially independent constructs: Relationship to positive and negative affectivity and psychological well-being. *Personality and Individual Differences, 23*(3), 433–440.

Charles, S. T., Mather, M., & Carstensen, L. L. (2003). Aging and emotional memory: The forgettable nature of negative images for older adults. *Journal of Experimental Psychology: General, 132,* 310–324.

Cheavens, J., Feldman, D., Woodward, J. T., & Snyder, C. R. (In press). Hope in cognitive therapies: Working with client strengths. *Journal of Cognitive Psychotherapy: An International Quarterly.*

Cheavens, J. S., Feldman, D. B., Gum, A., Michael, S. T., & Snyder, C. R. (In press). Hope therapy in a community sample: A pilot investigation. *Social Indicators Research.*

Cheavens, J., Michael, S. T., Gum, A., Feldman, D., Woodward, J. T., & Snyder, C. R. (2001). *A group-based intervention for depressed adults.* Unpublished manuscript, University of Kansas, Lawrence.

Chen, G., Gully, S. M., & Eden, D. (2001). Validation of a new general self-efficacy scale. *Organizational Research Methods, 4,* 62–83.

Chency, D., Seyforth, R., & Smuts, B. (1986). Social relationships and social cognition in non-human primates. *Science, 234,* 1361–1366.

Cheng, D. H. (2000). *On Lao Tzu.* Belmont, CA: Wadsworth.

Chickering, A. W. (1969). *Education and identity.* San Francisco: Jossey-Bass.

Chickering, A. W., & Reisser, L. (1993). *Education and identity.* San Francisco: Jossey-Bass.

Cho, W., & Cross, S. E. (1995). Taiwanese love styles and their association with self-esteem and relationship quality. *Genetic, Social, & General Psychology Monographs, 121,* 283–309.

Christensen, A. J., & Smith, T. W. (1998). Cynical hostility and cardiovascular reactivity during self-disclosure. *Psychosomatic Medicine, 55,* 193–202.

Christensen, A. L., & Rosenberg, N. K. (1991). A critique of the role of psychotherapy in brain injury rehabilitation. *Journal of Head Trauma Rehabilitation, 6,* 56–61.

Christopher, J. C. (1999). Situating psychological well-being: Exploring the cultural roots of its theory and research. *Journal of Counseling & Development, 77,* 141–152.

Christopher, J. C. (2001). Culture and psychotherapy: Toward a hermeneutic approach. *Psychotherapy: Theory, Research, Practice, and Training, 38,* 115–128.

Christopher, J. C. (2003, October). *The good in positive psychology.* Paper presented at the International Positive Psychology Summit, Washington, DC.

Christopher, J. C. (2004). Moral visions of developmental psychology. In B. Slife, F. C. Richardson, & J. Reber (Eds.), *Critical thinking about psychology: Hidden assumptions and plausible alternatives.* Washington, DC: American Psychological Association.

Christopher, J. C. (2005). Situating positive psychology. *Naming and nurturing: The e-newsletter of the Positive Psychology Section of the American Psychological Association's Counseling Psychology Division 17, 2,* 3–4.

Christopher, J. C., Nelson, T., & Nelson, M. D. (2004). Culture and character education: Problems of interpretation in a multicultural society. *Journal of Theoretical and Philosophical Psychology, 23,* 81–101.

Cialdini, R. B. (2005). What's the best secret device for engaging student interest? The answer is in the title. *Journal of Social and Clinical Psychology, 24,* 22–29.

Cialdini, R. B., Baumann, D. J., & Kenrick, D. T. (1981). Insights from sadness: A three-step model of the development of altruism as hedonism. *Developmental Review, 1,* 207–223.

Cialdini, R. B., Schaller, M., Houlihan, D., Arps, K., Fultz, J., & Beaman, A. L. (1978). Empathy-based helping: Is it selflessly or selfishly motivated? *Journal of Personality and Social Psychology, 52,* 749–758.

Clark, D. A. (2004). Design considerations in prevention research. In D. J. A. Dozois & K. S. Dobson (Eds.), *The prevention of anxiety and depression* (pp. 73–98). Washington, DC: American Psychological Association.

Clarke, G. N., Hawkins, W., Murphy, M., Sheeber, L. B., Lewinsohn, P. M., & Seeley, M. S. (1995). Targeted prevention of unipolar depressive disorder in an at-risk sample of high school adolescents: A randomized trial of a group cognitive intervention. *Journal of the American Academy of Child and Adolescent Psychiatry, 34,* 312–321.

Clayton, V. (1975). Erikson's theory of human development as it applies to the aged: Wisdom as contradictory cognition. *Human Development, 18,* 119–128.

Clayton, V. (1976). *A multidimensional scaling analysis of the concept of wisdom.* Unpublished doctoral dissertation, University of Southern California, Los Angeles.

Clayton, V. (1982). Wisdom and intelligence: The nature and function of knowledge in later years. *International Journal of Aging and Human Development, 15,* 315–321.

Clayton, V., & Birren, J. E. (1980). The development of wisdom across the life span: A reexamination of an ancient topic. In P. B. Baltes & O. G. Brim (Eds.), *Life-span development and behavior* (Vol. 3, pp. 103–135). New York: Academic Press.

Cleary, T. (1992). Introduction. In T. Cleary (Trans.), *The essential Confucius* (pp. 1–11). New York: HarperCollins.

Clifton, D. O. (1997). *The self-reflection scale.* Princeton, NJ: Gallup Organization.

Clifton, D. O., & Anderson, E. (2002). *StrengthsQuest: Discover and develop your strengths in academics, career, and beyond.* Washington, DC: Gallup Organization.

Clifton, D. O., & Harter, J. K. (2003). Strengths investment. In K. S. Cameron, J. E. Dutton, & R. E. Quinn (Eds.), *Positive organizational scholarship* (pp. 111–121). San Francisco: Berrett-Koehler.

Clifton, D. O., & Nelson, P. (1992). *Soar with your strengths.* New York: Delacorte Press.

Coffman, S. (1996). Parents' struggles to rebuild family life after Hurricane Andrew. *Issues in Mental Health Nursing, 17,* 353–367.

Cohen, R. (1991). *Negotiating across cultures.* Washington, DC: United States Institute of Peace Press.

Coleman, J. S., Campbell, E. Q., Hobson, C. J., McPartland, J., Mood., A. M., Wienfeld, F. D., et al. (1966). *Equality of Educational Opportunity.* Washington, DC: U.S. Government Printing Office.

Collins, J. (2001). *Good to great.* New York: HarperCollins.

Compton, W., Smith, M., Cornish, K., & Qualls, D. (1996). Factor structure of mental health measures. *Journal of Personality and Social Psychology, 76,* 406–413.

Condorcet, Marquis de (1979). *Sketch for a historical picture of the progress of the human mind.* Westport, CT: Greenwood. (Original work published 1795)

Connelly, J. (2002). All together now. *Gallup Management Journal, 2,* 13–18.

Constantine, M., & Sue, D. W. (2006). Factors contributing to optimal human functioning of people of color in the United States. *The Counseling Psychologist, 34,* 228–244.

Constantine, M. G., Myers, L. J., Kindaichi, M., & Moore, J. L. (2004). Exploring indigenous methods of mental health treatment: The roles of healers and helpers in promoting psychological, physical, and spiritual well-being in people of color. *Counseling & Values, 28,* 110–125.

Contreras, R., Hendrick, S. S., & Hendrick, C. (1996). Perspectives on marital love and satisfaction in Mexican American and Anglo couples. *Journal of Counseling and Development, 74,* 408–415.

Costa, P. T., & McCrae, R. R. (1988). Personality in adulthood: A six-year longitudinal study of self-reports and spouse ratings on the NEO Personality Inventory. *Journal of Personality and Social Psychology, 54,* 853–863.

Cousins, N. (1991). *Head first: The biology of hope and the healing power of the human spirit.* New York: Penguin.

Cox, D., Hallam, R., O'Connor, K., & Rachman, S. (1983). An experimental analysis of fearlessness and courage. *British Journal of Psychology, 74,* 107–117.

Cox, T. (1994). *Cultural diversity in organizations: Theory, research, and practice.* San Francisco: Berrett-Koehler.

Crabtree, S. (2002). Talent 101: Self-discovery helps students adjust. *Gallup Management Journal, 2.*

Craig, G. C., & Baucum, D. (2002). *Human Development.* Upper Saddle River, NJ: Prentice Hall.

Crosby, F. J. (1991). *The unexpected advantages of balancing career and home for women and their families.* New York: Free Press.

Crumbaugh, J. C., & Maholick, L. T. (1964). An experimental study in existentialism: The psychometric approach to Frankl's concept of noogenic neurosis. *Journal of Clinical Psychology, 20,* 200–207.

Crumbaugh, J. C., & Maholick, L. T. (1981). *Manual of instructions for the Purpose in Life Test.* Murfreesboro, TN: Psychometric Affiliates.

Csikszentmihalyi, M. (1978). Attention and the holistic approach to behavior. In K. S. Pope & J. L. Singer (Eds.), *The stream of consciousness* (pp. 335–358). New York: Plenum.

Csikszentmihalyi, M. (1990). *Flow: The psychology of optimal experience.* New York: Harper & Row.

Csikszentmihalyi, M. (1996). *Creativity: Flow and the psychology of discovery and invention.* New York: HarperCollins.

Csikszentmihalyi, M. (1997). *Finding flow.* New York: Basic Books.

Csikszentmihalyi, M. (1975/2000). *Beyond boredom and anxiety.* San Francisco: Jossey-Bass.

Csikszentmihalyi, M., & Csikszentmihalyi, I. S. (Eds.). (1988). *Optimal experience: Psychological studies of flow in consciousness.* New York: Cambridge University Press.

Csikszentmihalyi, M., & Rathunde, K. (1990). The psychology of wisdom: An evolutionary interpretation. In R. J. Sternberg (Ed.), *Wisdom: Its nature, origins, and development* (pp. 25–51). New York: Cambridge University Press.

Csikszentmihalyi, M., Rathunde, K., & Whalen, S. (1993). *Talented teenagers.* Cambridge, England: Cambridge University Press.

Csikszentmihalyi, M., & Robinson, R. (1990). *The art of seeing.* Malibu, CA: J. Paul Getty Museum and the Getty Center for Education in the Arts.

Curbow, B., Somerfield, M. R., Baker, F., Wingard, J. R., & Legro, M. W. (1993). Personal changes, dispositional optimism, and psychological adjustment to bone marrow transplantation. *Journal of Behavioral Medicine, 16,* 423–443.

Curry, L. A., Snyder, C. R., Cook, D. L., Ruby, B. C., & Rehm, M. (1997). The role of hope in student-athlete academic and sport achievement. *Journal of Personality and Social Psychology, 73,* 1257–1267.

Curry, R. O., & Valois, K. E. (1991). The emergence of an individualist ethos in American society. In R. O. Curry & L. B. Goodheart (Eds.), *American chameleon: Individualism in trans-national context* (pp. 20–43). Kent, OH: Kent State University Press.

Cushman, P. (1990). Why the self is empty: Toward a historically situated psychology. *American Psychologist, 45,* 599–611.

Daab, W. Z. (1991, July). *Changing perspectives on individualism.* Paper presented at the International Society for Political Psychology. Finland: University of Helsinki.

Dahlsgaard, K., Peterson, C., & Seligman, M. E. P. (2005). Shared virtue: The convergences of valued human strengths. *Review of General Psychology, 9,* 203–213.

Damasio, A. (1994). *Descartes' error.* New York: Grosset/Putnam.

Damasio, A. R. (2002). A note on the neurobiology of emotions. In S. G. Post, L. G. Underwood, J. P. Schloss, & W. B. Hurlbut (Eds.), *Altruism and altruistic love: Science, philosophy, and religion in dialogue* (pp. 264–271). New York: Oxford University Press.

Damon, W. (2004). What is positive youth development? *The Annals of the American Academy of Political and Social Science, 591,* 13–24.

Danner, D. D., Snowdon, D. A., & Friesen, W. V. (2001). Positive emotions in early life and longevity: Findings from the nun study. *Journal of Personality and Social Psychology, 80,* 804–813.

Darley, J. M., & Latane, B. (1968). Bystander intervention in emergencies: Diffusion of responsibilities. *Journal of Personality and Social Psychology, 8,* 377–383.

Darling-Hammond, L., & Youngs, P. (2002). Highly qualified teachers: What does scientifically based research tell us? *Educational Researcher, 31*, 13–25.

Davidson, A. R., Jaccard, J. J., Triandis, H. C., Morales, M. L., & Diaz-Guerrero, R. (1976). Cross-cultural model testing: Toward a solution of the etic–emic dilemma. *International Journal of Psychology, 11*, 1–13.

Davies, N. (1996). *Europe: A history.* New York: Oxford University Press.

Davis, M. H., Luce, C., & Kraus, S. J. (1994). The heritability of characteristics associated with dispositional empathy. *Journal of Personality, 62*, 369–391.

Dawes, R. M. (1980). Social dilemmas. *Annual Review of Psychology, 31*, 169–193.

Day, S. X., & Rounds, J. (1998). Universality of vocational interest structure among racial and ethnic minorities. *American Psychologist, 53*, 728–736.

Delle Fave, A. (2001, December). *Flow and optimal experience.* Paper presented to Economic and Social Research Council Individual and Situational Determinants of Well-Being, Seminar 2: Work, employment, and well-being. Manchester, England: Manchester Metropolitan University.

Delle Fave, A., & Massimini, F. (1988). Modernization and the changing contexts of flow in work and leisure. In M. Csikszentmihalyi & I. Csikszentmihalyi (Eds.), *Optimal experience* (pp. 193–213). Cambridge, England: Cambridge University Press.

Delle Fave, A., & Massimini, F. (1992). The experience sampling method and the measurement of clinical change: A case of anxiety disorder. In M. deVries (Ed.), *The experience of psychopathology* (pp. 280–289). Cambridge, England: Cambridge University Press.

Depue, R. (1996). A neurobiological framework for the structure of personality and emotions: Implications for personality disorder. In J. Clarkin & M. Lenzenweger (Eds.), *Major theories of personality* (pp. 347–390). New York: Guilford Press.

DeShea, L., & Wahkinney, R. L. (2003, November). *Looking within: Self-forgiveness as a new research direction.* Paper presented at the International Campaign for Forgiveness Conference, Atlanta, GA.

de Tocqueville, A. (2003). *Democracy in America.* London: Penguin. (Original work published 1835)

DeWaal, F. B. M., & Pokorny, J. J. (2005). Primate conflict and its relations to human forgiveness. In E. L. Worthington (Ed.), *Handbook of forgiveness* (pp. 17–32). New York: Taylor & Francis.

Dickens, M. (1897). *My father as I recall him.* Westminster, England: Roxburghe Press.

DiClemente, C. C., Fairhurst, S. K., & Piotrowski, N. A. (1995). Self-efficacy and addictive behaviors. In J. E. Maddux (Ed.), *Self-efficacy, adaptation, and adjustment: Theory, research, and application* (pp. 109–142). New York: Plenum.

Diener, E. (1984). Subjective well-being. *Psychological Bulletin, 95*, 542–575.

Diener, E. (1995). The personality structure of affect. *Journal of Personality and Social Psychology, 69*, 130–141.

Diener, E. (2000). Subjective well-being: The science of happiness and a proposal for a national index. *American Psychologist, 55*, 34–43.

Diener, E., & Biswas-Diener, R. (2002). Will money increase subjective well-being? *Social Indicators Research, 57*, 119–169.

Diener, E., & Diener, M. (1995). Cross-cultural correlates of life satisfaction and self-esteem. *Journal of Personality and Social Psychology, 68,* 653–663.

Diener, E., Diener, M., & Diener, C. (1995). Factors predicting the well-being of nations. *Journal of Personality and Social Psychology, 69,* 653–663.

Diener, E., & Emmons, R. A. (1984). The independence of positive and negative affect. *Journal of Personality and Social Psychology, 47,* 1105–1117.

Diener, E., Emmons, R. A., Larsen, R. J., & Griffin, S. (1985). The Satisfaction With Life Scale. *Journal of Personality Assessment, 49,* 71–75.

Diener, E., & Larsen, R. J. (1984). Temporal stability and cross-situational consistency of affective, behavioral, and cognitive responses. *Journal of Personality and Social Psychology, 47,* 871–883.

Diener, E., & Lucas, R. (1999). Personality and subjective well-being. In D. Kahneman, E. Diener, & N. Schwartz, N. (Eds.). *Well-being: The foundations of hedonic psychology* (pp. 213–229). New York: Russell Sage.

Diener, E., Lucas, R. E., & Oishi, S. (2002). Subjective well-being: The science of happiness and life satisfaction. In C. R. Snyder & S. J. Lopez (Eds.), *The handbook of positive psychology* (pp. 63–74). New York: Oxford University Press.

Diener, E., & Seligman, M. E. P. (2003). Very happy people. *Psychological Science, 13,* 81–84.

Diener, E., Suh, E. M., Lucas, R. E., & Smith, H. (1999). Subjective well-being: Three decades of progress. *Psychological Bulletin, 125,* 276–302.

Dienstbier, R. A. (1989). Arousal and physiological toughness: Implication for mental and physical health. *Psychological Review, 96,* 84–100.

D'Imperio, R. L., Dubow, E. F., & Ippolito, M. F. (2000). Resilient and stress-affected adolescents in an urban setting. *Journal of Clinical Child Psychology, 29,* 129–142.

Dittmann, M. (2005). Building a mentally healthy work force. *Monitor, 36,* 36–37.

Doll, B., & Lyon, M. A. (1998). Risk and resilience: Implications for the delivery of educational and mental health services in schools. *School Psychology Review, 27,* 348–363.

Donnay, D. A. C., & Borgen, F. H. (1999). The incremental validity of vocational self-efficacy: An examination of interest, self-efficacy, and occupation. *Journal of Counseling Psychology, 46,* 432–447.

Dovidio, J. F., Allen, J. L., & Schroeder, D. A. (1990). The specificity of empathy-induced helping: Evidence for altruism motivation. *Journal of Personality and Social Psychology, 59,* 249–260.

Dovidio, J. F., Gaertner, S. L., & Johnson, J. D. (1999, October). *New directions in prejudice and prejudice reduction: The role of cognitive representations and affect.* Paper presented at the annual meeting of the Society of Experimental Social Psychology, St. Louis, MO.

Drugan, R. C., Basile, A. S., Ha, J. H., & Ferland, R. J. (1994). The protective effects of stress control may be mediated by increased brain levels of benzodiazepine receptor agonists. *Brain Research, 661,* 127–136.

Durlak, J. A. (1995). *School-based prevention programs for children and adolescents.* Newbury Park, CA: Sage.

Durlak, J. A., & Wells, A. M. (1997). Primary prevention mental health programs for children and adolescents: A meta-analytic review. *American Journal of Community Psychology, 25,* 115–152.

Dweck, C. S. (1999). *Self theories: Their role in motivation, personality, and development.* Philadelphia: Psychology Press.

Easterbrook, J. A. (1959). The effects of emotion on cue utilization and the organization of behavior. *Psychological Review, 66,* 183–200.

Ebberwein, C. A., Krieshok, T. S., Ulven, J. S., & Prosser, E. C. (2004). Voices in transition: Lessons on career adaptability. *Career Development Quarterly, 52,* 292–308.

Edney, J. J., & Harper, C. S. (1978). The commons dilemma: A review of contributions from psychology. *Environmental Management, 2,* 491–507.

Eisenberg, N., & Miller, P. (1987). Empathy and prosocial behavior. *Psychological Bulletin, 101,* 91–119.

Eisenberg, N., Miller, P. A., Shell, R., McNalley, S., & Shea, C. (1991). Prosocial development in adolescence: A longitudinal study. *Developmental Psychology, 27,* 849–857.

Elias, M. J., Gara, M., Ubriaco, M., Rothbaum, P. A., Clabby, J. F., & Schuyler, T. (1986). Impact of a preventive social problem-solving intervention on children's coping with middle school stressors. *American Journal of Community Psychology, 14,* 259–275.

Ellison, C. G., & Levin, J. S. (1998). The religion–health connection: Evidence, theory, and future directions. *Health Education and Behavior, 25,* 700–726.

Ellison, C. G., & Sherkat, D. E. (1993). Obedience and autonomy: Religion and parenting values reconsidered. *Journal for the Scientific Study of Religion, 32,* 313–329.

Emmons, R. A. (1986). Personal strivings: An approach to personality and subjective well-being. *Journal of Personality and Social Psychology, 51,* 1058–1068.

Emmons, R. A. (1992). Abstract versus concrete goals: Personal striving level, physical illness, and psychological well-being. *Journal of Personality and Social Psychology, 62,* 292–300.

Emmons, R. A. (2004). *Cultivating gratitude: An interview with Robert Emmons.* Retrieved June 6, 2005, from http:www.todoinstitute.com/library/public/cultivating_gratitude_an_interview_with_robert_emmons_phd.php)

Emmons, R. A., Cheung, C., & Tehrani, K. (1998). Assessing spirituality through personal goals: Implications for research on religion and subjective well-being. *Social Indicators Research, 45,* 391–422.

Emmons, R. A., & Hill, J. (2001). *Words of gratitude for body, mind, and soul.* Radnor, PA: Templeton Foundation Press.

Emmons, R. A., & McCullough, M. E. (2003). Counting blessings versus burdens: Experimental studies of gratitude and subjective well-being. *Journal of Personality and Social Psychology, 84,* 377–389.

Emmons, R. A., & McCullough, M. E. (Eds.). (2004). *The psychology of gratitude.* New York: Oxford University Press.

Emmons, R. A., McCullough, M. E., & Tsang, J. (2003). The assessment of gratitude. In S. J. Lopez & C. R. Snyder (Eds.), *Positive psychological assessment: A handbook of models and measures* (pp. 327–342). Washington, DC: American Psychological Association.

Emmons, R. A., & Shelton, C. S. (2002). Gratitude and the science of positive psychology. In C. R. Snyder & S. J. Lopez (Eds.), *The handbook of positive psychology* (pp. 459–471). New York: Oxford University Press.

Enright, R. D. (1996). Counseling within the forgiveness triad: On forgiving, receiving forgiveness, and self-forgiveness. *Counseling and Values, 40,* 107–126.

Enright, R. D. (2000). *Helping clients forgive: An empirical guide for resolving anger and restoring hope.* Washington, DC: American Psychological Association.

Enright, R. D., Freedman, S., & Rique, J. (1998). The psychology of interpersonal forgiveness. In R. D. Enright & J. North (Eds.), *Exploring forgiveness* (pp. 46–62). Madison: University of Wisconsin Press.

Enright, R. D., & Zell, R. L. (1989). Problems encountered when we forgive another. *Journal of Psychology and Christianity, 8,* 52–60.

Erickson, R. C., Post, R. D., & Paige, A. B. (1975). Hope as a psychiatric variable. *Journal of Clinical Psychology, 31,* 324–330.

Erikson, E. (1950). *Childhood and society.* New York: Norton.

Erikson, E. H. (1959). *Identity and the life cycle.* Madison, CT: International Universities Press.

Erikson, E. H. (1963). *Childhood and society* (2nd ed.). New York: Norton.

Erikson, E. H. (1964). *Insight and responsibility.* New York: Norton.

Erikson, E. H. (1982). *The life cycle completed: A review.* New York: Norton.

Estrada, C. A., Isen, A. M., & Young, M. J. (1997). Positive affect facilitates integration of information and decreases anchoring in reasoning among physicians. *Organizational Behavior and Human Decision Processes, 72,* 117–135.

Farley, M. (2003). Feminism and hope. In M. Thompson (Ed.), *Full of hope: Critical social perspectives on theology* (pp. 20–40). New York: Paulist Press.

Farmer, H. S. (1983). Career and homemaking plans for high school youth. *Journal of Counseling Psychology, 30,* 40–45.

Farran, C. J., Herth, A. K., & Popovich, J. M. (1995). *Hope and hopelessness: Critical clinical constructs.* Thousand Oaks, CA: Sage.

Feeney, J., & Noller, P. (1996). *Adult attachment.* Thousand Oaks, CA: Sage.

Fefer, M. D. (2002, February 13). A lot of love in the lovemaking: Avoiding chaos, relationshipwise. *Seattle Weekly,* n.p.

Feldman, D., & Snyder, C. R. (2005). Hope and meaning in life. *Journal of Social and Clinical Psychology, 24,* 401–421.

Fernandez-Ballesteros, R., Diez-Nicolas, J., Caprara, G. V., Barbaranelli, C., & Bandura, A. (2002). Determinants and structural relation of perceived personal efficacy to perceived collective efficacy. *Journal of Applied Psychology: An International Review, 51,* 107–125.

Fincham, F. (2000). Optimism and the family. In J. Gillham (Ed.), *The science of optimism and hope* (pp. 271–298). Philadelphia: Templeton Foundation Press.

Fineburg, A. C. (2002). *A 7-day unit plan for high-school positive psychology.* Retrieved January 25, 2005, from http://www.positivepsychology.org/teachinghighschool.htm

Finfgeld, D. L. (1995). Becoming and being courageous in the chronically ill elderly. *Issues in Mental Health Nursing, 16,* 1–11.

Finfgeld, D. L. (1998). Courage in middle-aged adults with long-term health concerns. *Canadian Journal of Nursing Research, 30*(1), 153–169.

Fitzgerald, T. E., Tennen, H., Affleck, G., & Pransky, G. S. (1993). The relative importance of dispositional optimism and control appraisals in the quality of life after coronary artery bypass surgery. *Journal of Behavioral Medicine, 16,* 25–43.

Fontaine, K. R., Manstead, A. S. R., & Wagner, H. (1993). Optimism, perceived control over stress, and coping. *European Journal of Psychology, 7,* 267–281.

Fordyce, M. W. (1977). Development of a program to increase personal happiness. *Journal of Counseling Psychology, 24,* 511–520.

Fordyce, M. W. (1983). A program to increase happiness: Further studies. *Journal of Counseling Psychology, 30,* 483–498.

Forgas, J. P., Bower, G. H., & Moylan, S. J. (1990). Praise or blame? Affective influences on attributions for achievement. *Journal of Personality and Social Psychology, 59,* 809–819.

Forsyth, D. R. (1999). *Group dynamics* (3rd ed.). Pacific Grove, CA: Brooks/Cole.

Forsyth, D. R., & Corazzini, J. G. (2000). Groups as change agents. In C. R. Snyder & R. E. Ingram (Eds.), *Handbook of psychological change: Psychotherapy processes and practices for the 21st century* (pp. 309–336). New York: Wiley.

Fouad, N. A. (2002). Cross-cultural differences in vocational interests: Between-group differences on the Strong Interest Inventory. *Journal of Counseling Psychology, 49,* 282–289.

Frank, J. D. (1968). The role of hope in psychotherapy. *International Journal of Psychiatry, 5,* 383–395.

Frank, J. D. (1973). *Persuasion and healing* (Rev. ed.). Baltimore: Johns Hopkins University Press.

Frank, J. D. (1975). The faith that heals. *The Johns Hopkins Medical Journal, 137,* 127–131.

Frank, J. D., & Frank, J. B. (1991). *Persuasion and healing: A comparative study of psychotherapy* (3rd ed.). Baltimore: Johns Hopkins University Press.

Frankl, V. (1959). *Man's search for meaning.* New York: Beacon Press.

Frankl, V. (1966). What is meant by meaning? *Journal of Existentialism, 7,* 21–28.

Frankl, V. (1992). *Man's search for meaning: An introduction to logotherapy* (I. Lasch, Trans.). Boston: Beacon Press.

Franz, C. E., McClelland, D. C., Weinberger, J., & Peterson, C. (1994). Parenting antecedents of adult adjustment: A longitudinal study. In C. Perris, W. A. Arrindell, & M. Eisemann (Eds.), *Parenting and psychopathology* (pp. 127–144). San Diego, CA: Academic Press.

Fredrickson, B. L. (1999). What good are positive emotions? *Review of General Psychology, 2,* 300–319.

Fredrickson, B. L. (2000). Cultivating positive emotions to optimize health and well-being. *Prevention and Treatment, 3.* Retrieved January 20, 2003, from http://journals.apa.org/prevention

Fredrickson, B. L. (2001). The role of positive emotions in positive psychology: The broaden-and-build theory of positive emotions. *American Psychologist, 56,* 218–226.

Fredrickson, B. L. (2002). Positive emotions. In C. R. Snyder & S. J. Lopez (Eds.), *The handbook of positive psychology* (pp. 120–134). New York: Oxford University Press.

Fredrickson, B. L., & Joiner, T. (2002). Positive emotions trigger upward spirals toward emotional well-being. *Psychological Science, 13,* 172–175.

Fredrickson, B. L., & Losada, M. F. (2005). Positive affect and the complex dynamics of human flourishing. *American Psychologist, 60,* 678–686.

Fredrickson, B. L., Mancuso, R. A., Branigan, C., & Tugade, M. M. (2000). The undoing effects of positive emotions. *Motivation and Emotion, 24,* 237–258.

Freedman, J. L., & Doob, A. N. (1968). *Deviancy: The psychology of being different.* New York: Academic Press.

Freeman, M. A., & Bordia, P. (2001). Assessing alternative models of individualism and collectivism: A confirmatory factor analysis. *European Journal of Personality, 15,* 105–121.

Freud, S. (1936). *The problem of anxiety.* (H. A. Bunker, Trans.). New York: Norton. (Original work published 1926)

Freud, S. (1957). Instincts and their vicissitudes. In J. Strachey (Ed.), *Standard edition of the complete psychological works of Sigmund Freud* (pp. 111–142). London: Hogarth. (Original work published 1915)

Friedman, T. L. (2005). *The world is flat: A brief history of the 21st century.* New York: Farrar, Straus & Giroux.

Frijda, N. H. (1994). Emotions are functional, most of the time. In P. Ekman & R. Davidson (Eds.), *The nature of emotion: Fundamental questions* (pp. 112–122). New York: Oxford University Press.

Frijda, N. H. (1999). Emotions and hedonic experience. In D. Kahneman, E. Diener, & N. Schwartz (Eds.), *Well-being: The foundations of hedonic psychology* (pp. 190–210). New York: Russell Sage.

Frisch, M. B., Cornell, J., Villanueva, M., & Retzlaff, P. J. (1992). Clinical validation of the Quality of Life Inventory: A measure of life satisfaction for use in treatment planning and outcome assessment. *Psychological Assessment, 4,* 92–101.

Fritzberg, G. J. (2001). Opportunities of substance: Reconceptualizing equality of educational opportunity. [First article in a two-part series]. *Journal of Thought, 36*(1).

Fritzberg, G. J. (2002). Freedom that counts: The historic underpinnings of positive liberty and equality of educational opportunity. [Second article in a two-part series]. *Journal of Thought, 37*(2).

Fromm, E. (1955). *The sane society.* New York: Holt, Rinehart & Winston.

Fromm, E. (1974). *The revolution of hope: Toward a humanized technology.* New York: Perennial Library, Harper & Row.

Gable, S. L., & Reis, H. T. (2001). Appetitive and aversive social interaction. In J. Harvey & A. Wenzel (Eds.), *Close romantic relationships: Maintenance and enhancement* (pp. 169–194). Mahwah, NJ: Lawrence Erlbaum.

Gable, S. L., Reis, H. T., & Elliot, A. J. (2003). Evidence for bivariate systems: An empirical test of appetition and aversion across domains. *Journal of Research in Personality, 37*(5), 349–372.

Gable, S. L., & Reis, H. T., Impett, E. A., & Asher, E. R. (2004). What do you do when things go right? The intrapersonal and interpersonal benefits of sharing positive events. *Journal of Personality and Social Psychology, 87,* 228–245.

Gallagher-Thompson, D., McKibbon, C., Koonce-Volwiler, D., Menendez, A., Stewart, D., & Thompson, L. W. (2000). Psychotherapy with older adults. In C. R. Snyder & R. E. Ingram (Eds.), *Handbook of psychological change: Psychotherapy processes and practices for the 21st century* (pp. 614–628). New York: Wiley.

Gallup, G. G. (1998). Self-awareness and the evolution of social intelligence. *Behavioral Processes, 42,* 238–247.

Gallup Organization. (1995). *Disciplining children in America: Survey of attitude and behavior of parents.* Project registration #104438. Princeton, NJ: Author.

Gallup Poll Monthly. (1996, November). Princeton, NJ: Gallup Organization.

Gardner, W. L., & Schermerhorn, J. R. (2004). Unleashing individual potential: Performance gains through positive organizational behavior and authentic leadership. *Organizational Dynamics, 33,* 270–281.

Garmezy, N. (1985). Stress-resistant children: The search for protective factors. In J. E. Stevenson (Ed.), *Recent research in developmental psychopathology:*

Journal of Child Psychology and Psychiatry Book Supplement 4 (pp. 213–233). Oxford, England: Pergamon Press.

Garmezy, N. (1993). Children in poverty: Resilience despite risk. *Psychiatry: Interpersonal and Biological Processes, 56,* 127–136.

Garmezy, N., Masten, A. S., & Tellegen, A. (1984). The study of stress and competence in children: A building block for developmental psychopathology. *Child Development, 55,* 97–111.

Gay, P. (1966). *Age of enlightenment.* New York: Time Life Books.

Gay, P. (1969). *The Enlightenment: An interpretation: Vol 2. The science of freedom.* New York: Norton.

Gentile, D. A., & Walsh, D. A. (2002). A normative study of family media habits. *Applied Developmental Psychology, 23,* 157–178.

George, B. (2003). *Authentic leadership: Rediscovering the secrets to creating lasting value.* San Francisco: Jossey-Bass.

George, C., Kaplan, N., & Main, M. (1985). *The Adult Attachment Interview.* Unpublished protocol, Department of Psychology, University of California at Berkeley.

Gergen, K. J. (1985). The social constructionist movement in modern psychology. *American Psychologist, 40,* 266–275.

Gergen, M. M., & Gergen, K. J. (1998). The relational rebirthing of wisdom and courage. In S. Srivastva & D. L. Cooperrider (Eds.), *Organizational wisdom and executive courage* (134–153). San Francisco: New Lexington Press.

Getzels, J. W., & Csikszentmihalyi, M. (1976). *The creative vision.* New York: Wiley.

Gillham, J. E. (Ed.) (2000). *The science of optimism and hope.* Philadephia: Templeton Foundation Press.

Gillham, J. E., & Reivich, K. J. (2004). Cultivating optimism in childhood and adolescence. *The Annals of the American Academy of Political and Social Science, 591,* 146–153.

Gillham, J. E., Reivich, K. J., Jaycox, L. H., & Seligman, M. E. P. (1995). Prevention of depressive symptoms in school children: Two year follow-up. *Psychological Science, 6,* 343–351.

Gilligan, C. (1982). *In a different voice: Psychological theory and women's development.* Cambridge, MA: Harvard University Press.

Given, C. W., Stommel, M., Given, B., Osuch, J., Kurtz, M. E., & Kurtz, J. C. (1993). The influence of cancer patients' symptoms and functional states on patients' depression and family caregivers' reaction and depression. *Health Psychology, 12,* 277–285.

Gladwell, M. (2005). *Blink: The power of thinking without thinking.* New York: Little, Brown.

Glass, T. A., Seeman, T. E., Herzog, A. R., Kahn, R., et al. (1995). Change in productive activity in late adulthood: MacArthur studies of successful aging. *Journal of Gerontology, 50,* 65–76.

Godfrey, J. J. (1987). *A philosophy of human hope.* Dordrecht, Germany: Martinus Nijhoff.

Godfrey, K. F., Bonds, A. S., Kraus, M. E., Wiener, M. R., & Toch, C. S. (1990). Freedom from stress: A meta-analytic view of treatment and intervention programs. *Applied H. R. M. Research, 1,* 67–80.

Goffman, I. (1963). *Stigma: Notes on the management of spoiled identity.* Englewood Cliffs, NJ: Prentice Hall.

Goldhaber, D. (2002). *The mystery of good teaching.* Retrieved January 14, 2005, from http://www.educationnext.org/20021/50.html

Goleman, D. (1995). *Emotional intelligence: Why it can matter more than IQ.* New York: Bantam Books.

Gordon, K. C., & Baucom, D. H. (1998). Understanding betrayals in marriage: A synthesized model of forgiveness. *Family Process, 37,* 425–450.

Gordon, K. C., Baucom, D. H., & Snyder, D. K. (2004). An integrative intervention for promoting recovery from extramarital affairs. *Journal of Marital and Family Therapy, 30,* 213–231.

Gordon, K. C., Baucom, D. H., & Snyder, D. K. (2005). Forgiveness in couples: Divorce, infidelity, and couples therapy. In E. Worthington (Ed.), *Handbook of forgiveness* (pp. 407–422). New York: Routledge.

Gottman, J. M. (1994). *Why marriages succeed or fail and how you can make yours last.* New York: Simon & Schuster.

Gottman, J. M. (1999). *The seven principles for making marriage work.* New York: Crown.

Gottman, J. M., Driver, J., & Tabares, A. (2002). Building the sound marital house: An empirically derived couple therapy. In N. S. Jacobsen & A. S. Gurman (Eds.), *Clinical handbook of couple therapy* (3rd ed., pp. 373–399). New York: Guilford Press.

Gottman, J. M., Murray, J. D., Swanson, C., Tyson, R., & Swanson, K. R. (2003). *The mathematics of marriage: Dynamic nonlinear models.* Cambridge: MIT Press.

Gottschalk, L. (1974). A hope scale applicable to verbal samples. *Archives of General Psychiatry, 30,* 779–785.

Gray, S. A., Emmons, R. A., & Morrison, A. (2001, August). *Distinguishing gratitude from indebtedness in affect and action tendencies.* Poster session presented at the annual meeting of the American Psychological Association, San Francisco.

Gray-Little, B., & Kaplan, D. (2000). Race and ethnicity in psychotherapy research. In C. R. Snyder & R. E. Ingram (Eds.), *Handbook of psychological change: Psychotherapy processes and practices for the 21st century* (pp. 591–613). New York: Wiley.

Green, D. P., Salovey, P., & Truax, K. M. (1999). Static, dynamic, and causative bipolarity of affect. *Journal of Personal and Social Psychology, 76,* 856–867.

Green, M. C., Strange, J. J., & Brock, T. C. (2002). *Narrative impact: Social and cognitive foundations.* Mahwah, NJ: Lawrence Erlbaum.

Groopman, J. (2004). *The anatomy of hope: How people prevail in the face of illness.* New York: Random House.

Grun, B. (1975). *The timetables of history.* New York: Simon & Schuster.

Gudykunst, W. B. (Ed.). (1993). *Communication in Japan and the United States.* Albany: State University of New York Press.

Guignon, C. (2002). Hermeneutics, authenticity and the aims of psychology. *Journal of Theoretical & Philosophical Psychology, 22,* 83–102.

Gurung, R. A. R., Taylor, S. E., & Seeman, T. E. (2003). Accounting for changes in social support among married older adults: Insights from the MacArthur Studies of Successful Aging. *Psychology and Aging, 18,* 487–496.

Haase, J. E. (1987). Components of courage in chronically ill adolescents: A phenomenological study. *Advances in Nursing Science, 9*(2), 64–80.

Haberman, D. L. (1998). Confucianism: The way of the sages. In L. Stevenson & D. L. Haberman, *Ten theories of human nature* (3rd ed., pp. 25–44). New York: Oxford University Press.

Hackman, J. R., & Oldham, G. R. (1980). *Work design.* Reading, MA: Addison-Wesley.

Haidt, J. (2000, January). *Awe and elevation.* Paper presented at the Akumal II: A Positive Psychology Summit, Akumal, Mexico.

Haidt, J. (2002). The positive emotion of elevation. In C. R. Snyder & S. J. Lopez (Eds.), *The handbook of positive psychology* (p. 753). New York: Oxford University Press.

Haidt, J. (2003). Elevation and the positive psychology of morality. In C. L. M. Keyes & J. Haidt (Eds.), *Flourishing: Positive psychology and the life well-lived* (pp. 275–289). Washington, DC: American Psychological Association.

Haidt, J. (2004). Untitled document. Retrieved September 20, 2005, from http://wsrv.clas.virginia.edu/~jdh6n/Positivepsych.html

Haitch, R. (1995). How Tillich and Kohut find courage in faith. *Pastoral Psychology, 44,* 83–97.

Hale, J. (1965). *Renaissance.* New York: Time Life Books.

Haley, J. (Producer), & Fleming, V. (Director). (1939). *The wizard of Oz* [Motion picture]. United States: MGM.

Hall, G. S. (1922). *Senescence: The last half of life.* New York: D. Appleton.

Hall, J. H., & Fincham, F. D. (2005). Self-forgiveness: The stepchild of forgiveness research. *Journal of Social and Clinical Psychology, 24,* 621–637.

Halperin, D., & Desrochers, S. (2005). Social psychology in the classroom: Applying what we teach as we teach it. *Journal of Social and Clinical Psychology, 24,* 51–61.

Halsall, P. (1997). *Immanuel Kant: What Is Enlightenment?1784.* Internet Modern History Sourcebook. Retrieved August 12, 2004, from halsall@murray.fordham.edu

Hamer, D. (2004). *The God gene: How faith is hardwired into our genes.* New York: Doubleday.

Hamilton, E. (1969). *Mythology: Timeless tales of gods and heroes.* New York: Mentor.

Hanushek, E. A. (1994). *Making schools work: Improving performance and controlling costs.* Washington, DC: Brookings Institution.

Hanushek, E. A., Kain, J. F., O'Brien, D. M., & Rivkin, S. G. (2004). *The market for teacher quality* (Working paper # 11154). Washington, DC: National Bureau of Economic Research.

Hanushek, E. A., & Rivkin, S. G. (2003). Does public school competition affect teacher quality? In C. M. Hoxby (Ed.), *The economics of school choice* (pp. 23–47). Chicago: University of Chicago Press.

Hanushek, E. A., & Rivkin, S. G. (2004). Why public schools lose teachers. *Journal of Human Resources, 39,* 326–354.

Harmon, L. W., Hansen, J. C., Borgen, F. H., & Hammer, A. L. (Eds.). (1994). *Strong Interest Inventory: Applications and technical guide.* Palo Alto, CA: Consulting Psychologists Press.

Hart, P. M. (1999). Predicting employee satisfaction: A coherent model of personality, work and nonwork experiences, and domain satisfaction. *Journal of Applied Psychology, 84,* 564–584.

Harter, J. K., & Schmidt, F. L. (2002). Employee engagement and business-unit performance. *Psychologist-Manager Journal, 4,* 215–224.

Harter, J. K., Schmidt, F. L., & Hayes, T. L. (2002). Business-unit-level relationship between employee satisfaction, employee engagement, and business outcomes: A meta-analysis. *Journal of Applied Psychology, 87,* 268–279.

Harvey, J., & Delfabbro, P. H. (2004). Resilience in disadvantaged youth: A critical overview. *Australian Psychologist, 39,* 3–13.

Harvey, J. H., & Ormarzu, J. (1997). Minding the close relationship. *Personality and Social Psychology Review, 1,* 223–239.

Harvey, J. H., Pauwels, B. G., & Zicklund, S. (2001). Relationship connection: The role of minding in the enhancement of closeness. In C. R. Snyder & S. J. Lopez (Eds.), *The handbook of positive psychology* (pp. 423–433). New York: Oxford University Press.

Hatfield, E. (1988). Passionate and companionate love. In R. J. Sternberg & M. L. Barnes (Eds.), *The psychology of love* (pp. 191–217). New Haven, CT: Yale University Press.

Hatfield, E., & Rapson, R. L. (1996). *Love and sex: Cross-cultural perspectives.* Boston: Allyn & Bacon.

Havighurst, R. J. (1961). Successful aging. *The Gerontologist, 1*(1), 8–13.

Haworth, J. T. (1997). *Work, leisure and well-being.* London: Routledge.

Hazan, C., & Shaver, P. (1987). Romantic love conceptualized as an attachment process. *Journal of Personality and Social Psychology, 52,* 511–524.

Hebl, J. H., & Enright, R. D. (1993). Forgiveness as a psychotherapeutic goal with elderly females. *Psychotherapy, 30,* 658–667.

Hecht, T. L., Marston, P. J., & Larkey, L. K. (1994). Love ways and relationship quality. *Journal of Social and Personal Relationships, 11,* 25–43.

Heine, C. (1996). *Flow and achievement in mathematics.* Unpublished doctoral dissertation, University of Chicago.

Hektner, J. (1996). *Exploring optimal personality development: A longitudinal study of adolescents.* Unpublished doctoral dissertation. University of Chicago.

Heller, K., Wyman, M. F., & Allen, S. M. (2000). Future directions for prevention science: From research to adoption. In C. R. Snyder & R. E. Ingram (Eds.), *Handbook of psychological change: Psychotherapy processes and practices for the 21st century* (pp. 660–680). New York: Wiley.

Heller, K. J. (1989). The return to community. *American Journal of Community Psychology, 17,* 1–16.

Helms, J. E., & Cook, D. A. (1999). *Using race and culture in counseling and psychotherapy: Theory and process.* Needham Heights, MA: Allyn & Bacon.

Hendrick, S. S., & Hendrick, C. (1992). *Romantic love.* Newbury Park, CA: Sage.

Hendrick, S. S., & Hendrick, C. (1993). Lovers as friends. *Journal of Social and Personal Relationships, 10,* 459–466.

Henry, J. (2004). Positive and creative organization. In P. A. Linley & S. Joseph (Eds.), *Positive psychology in practice* (pp. 269–285). Hoboken, NJ: Wiley.

Henry, O. (1945). *The best short stories of O. Henry.* New York: The Modern Library.

Hertzberg, F. (1966). *Work and the nature of man.* Chicago: World Publishing.

Hesse, E. (1999). The Adult Attachment Interview: Historical and current perspectives. In J. Cassidy & P. R. Shaver (Eds.), *Handbook of attachment: Theory, research, and clinical applications* (pp. 395–433). New York: Guilford Press.

Hill, G., & Swanson, H. L. (1985). Construct validity and reliability of the Ethical Behavior Rating Scale. *Educational and Psychological Measurement, 45,* 285–292.

Hill, P. C., Pargament, K. I., Hood, R. W., Jr., McCullough, M. E., Swyers, J. P., Larson, D. B., et al. (2000). Conceptualizing religion and spirituality: Points of communality, points of departure. *Journal for the Theory of Social Behavior, 30,* 51–77.

Hinton-Nelson, M. D., Roberts, M. C., & Snyder, C. R. (1996). Early adolescents exposed to violence: Hope and vulnerability to victimization. *American Journal of Orthopsychiatry, 66,* 346–353.

Hodges, T. D. (2003). *Results of the 2002 StrengthsFinder follow-up survey.* Princeton, NJ: Gallup Organization.

Hodges, T. D., & Clifton, D. O. (2004). Strengths-based development in practice. In P. A. Linley & S. Joseph (Eds.), *Positive psychology in practice* (pp. 256–268). Hoboken, NJ: Wiley.

Hodges, T. D., & Harter, J. K. (2005). A review of the theory and research underlying the StrengthsQuest Program for students. *Educational Horizons, 83,* 190–201.

Hofmann, D. A., & Tetrick, L. E. (Eds.). (2003). *Health and safety in organization: A multilevel perspective.* San Francisco: Jossey-Bass.

Hofstede, G. (1980). *Culture's consequences.* Beverly Hills, CA: Sage.

Hogan, R., & Kaiser, R. B. (2005). What we know about leadership. *Review of General Psychology, 9,* 169–180.

Hoge, D. R. (1996). Religion in America: The demographics of belief and affiliation. *Religion and the clinical practice of psychology* (pp. 21–42). Washington, DC: American Psychological Association.

Holden, E. W., & Black, M. M. (1999). Theory and concepts of prevention sciences as applied to clinical psychology. *Clinical Psychology Review, 19,* 391–401.

Holland, J. L. (1997). *Making vocational choices: A theory of vocational personalities and work environments* (3rd ed.). Odessa, FL: Psychological Assessment Resources.

Holliday, S. G., & Chandler, M. J. (1986). *Wisdom: Explorations in adult competence.* Basel, Switzerland: Karger.

Hollon, S. D., & Beck, A. T. (1994). Cognitive and cognitive-behavioral therapies. In A. E. Bergin & S. L. Garfield (Eds.), *Handbook of psychotherapy and behavior change* (4th cd., pp. 428–466). New York: Wiley.

Holmgren, M. R. (2002). Forgiveness and self-forgiveness in psychotherapy. In S. Lamb & J. G. Murphy (Eds.), *Before giving: Cautionary views of forgiveness in psychotherapy* (pp. 112–135). New York: Oxford University Press.

Holton, R. (2000). Globalization's cultural consequences. *Annals, American Academy of Political and Social Science, 570,* 140–152.

Hooker, K., Monahan, D., Shifren, K., & Hutchinson, C. (1992). Mental and physical health of spouse caregivers: The role of personality. *Psychology and Aging, 7,* 367–375.

Hothersall, D. (1995). *History of psychology.* New York: McGraw-Hill.

Houser, R. E. (2002). The virtue of courage. In S. J. Pope (Ed.), *The ethics of Aquinas* (pp. 304–320). Washington, DC: Georgetown University Press.

Houston, B. K., & Snyder, C. R. (Eds.). (1988). *Type A behavior pattern: Current trends and future directions.* New York: Wiley-Interscience.

Hudson, J. L., Flannery-Schroeder, E., & Kendall, P. C. (2004). Primary prevention of anxiety disorders. In D. J. A. Dozois & K. S. Dobson (Eds.), *The prevention of anxiety and depression* (pp. 101–130). Washington, DC: American Psychological Association.

Hui, C. H. (1988). Measurement of individualism–collectivism. *Journal of Research in Personality, 22,* 17–36.

Hume, D. (1888). *A treatise of human nature.* Oxford, England: Clarendon Press.

Hummer, R. A., Rogers, R. G., Nam, C. B., & Ellison, C. G. (1999). Religious involvement and U.S. adult mortality. *Demography, 36,* 273–285.

Huntington, S. P. (1993). The clash of civilizations. *Foreign Affairs, 72,* 22–49.

Hurlock, E. B. (1925). An evaluation of certain incentives in school work. *Journal of Educational Psychology, 16,* 145–159.

Icard, L. (1996). Assessing the psychosocial well-being of African American gays: A multidimensional perspective. In J. F. Longres (Ed.), *Men of color: A context for service to homosexually active men* (pp. 25–49). New York: Haworth Press.

Ilardi, S., & Karwoski, L. (2005). *The depression cure.* Unpublished book-length manuscript, University of Kansas, Lawrence.

Inclan, J. (1985). Variations in value orientations in mental health work with Puerto Ricans. *Psychotherapy: Theory, Research, and Practice, 22,* 324–334.

Inghilleri, P. (1999). *From subjective experience to cultural change.* Cambridge, England: Cambridge University Press.

Ingram, R. E., Hayes, A., & Scott, W. (2000). Empirically supported treatments: A critical analysis. In C. R. Snyder & R. E. Ingram (Eds.), *Handbook of psychological change: Psychotherapy processes and practices for the 21st century* (pp. 40–60). New York: Wiley.

Ingram, R. E., Kendall, P. C., & Chen, A. H. (1991). Cognitive-behavioral interventions. In C. R. Snyder & D. R. Forsyth (Eds.), *Handbook of social and clinical psychology: The health perspective* (pp. 509–522). New York: Pergamon.

Ingram, R. E., & Wisnicki, K. S. (1988). Assessment of positive automatic cognition. *Journal of Consulting and Clinical Psychology, 56,* 898–902.

Irving, L. M., Cheavens, J., Snyder, C. R., Gravel, L., Hanke, J., Hilberg, P., & Nelson, N. (2004). The relationships between hope and outcome at pre-treatment, beginning, and later phases of psychotherapy. *Journal of Psychotherapy Integration, 14,* 419–443.

Isen, A. M. (1970). Success, failure, attention, and reaction to others: The warm glow of success. *Journal of Personality and Social Psychology, 17,* 107–112.

Isen, A. M. (1987). Positive affect, cognitive processes, and social behavior. *Advances in Experimental Social Psychology, 20,* 203–253.

Isen, A. M., Daubman, K. A., & Nowicki, G. P. (1987). Positive affect facilitates creative problem solving. *Journal of Personality and Social Psychology, 21,* 384–388.

Isen, A. M., & Levin, P. F. (1972). The effect of feeling good on helping: Cookies and kindness. *Journal of Personality and Social Psychology, 17,* 107–112.

Ivey, A. E., & Ivey, M. B. (1998). Reframing *DSM-IV:* Positive strategies from developmental counseling and theory. *Journal of Counseling and Development, 76,* 334–350.

Ivey, A. E., & Ivey, M. B. (1999). Toward a developmental diagnostic and statistical manual: The vitality of a contextual framework. *Journal of Counseling and Development, 77,* 484–490.

Jackson, S., & Csikszentmihalyi, M. (1999). *Flow in sports.* Champaign, IL: Human Kinetics.

Jahoda, M. (1958). *Current concepts of positive mental health.* New York: Basic Books.

James, W. (1890). *Principles of psychology* (Vol. 1). New York: Holt.

Jamieson, K. H. (Ed.). (2005). *Treating and preventing adolescent mental health disorders: What we know and what we don't know.* New York: Oxford University Press.

Jaycox, L. H., Reivich, K. J., Gillham, J., & Seligman, M. E. P. (1994). Prevention of depressive symptoms in school children. *Behavior Research and Therapy, 32,* 801–816.

Jemmott, J. B., Jemmott, L. S., & Fong, G. T. (1992). Reductions in HIV risk-associated sexual behaviors among black male adolescents: Effect of an AIDS prevention intervention. *American Journal of Public Health, 82,* 372–377.

Johnson, D. L. (1988). Primary prevention of behavior problems in young children: The Houston Parent-Child Development Center. In R. H. Price, E. Cowen, R. Lorion, & J. Ramos-McKay (Eds.), *Fourteen ounces of prevention: A casebook for practitioners* (pp. 44–52). Washington, DC: American Psychological Association.

Johnson, F. (1988). Encounter group therapy. In S. Long (Ed.), *Six group therapies* (pp. 115–158). New York: Plenum.

Judge, T. A., & Watanabe, S. (1993). Another look at the job satisfaction–life satisfaction relationship. *Journal of Applied Psychology, 78,* 939–948.

Judge, T. A., Thoresen, C. J., Bono, J. E., & Patton, G. K. (2001). The job-satisfaction performance relationship: A qualitative and quantitative review. *Psychological Bulletin, 127,* 376–407.

Jung, C. (1953). *Two essays on analytical psychology.* New York: Pantheon Books.

Kabat-Zinn, J. (1982). An outpatient program in behavioral medicine for chronic pain patients based on the practice of mindfulness meditation: Theoretical considerations and preliminary results. *General Hospital Psychiatry, 4,* 33–47.

Kabat-Zinn, J. (1990). *Full catastrophe living.* New York: Delacorte Press.

Kabat-Zinn, J., & Skillings, A. (1989, March). *Sense of coherence and stress hardiness as predictors and measure of outcome of a stress reduction program.* Poster presented at the Society of Behavioral Medicine Conference, San Francisco.

Kabat-Zinn, J., & Skillings, A. (1992). *Sense of coherence and stress hardiness as outcome measures of a mindfulness-based stress reduction program: Three-year follow-up.* Unpublished raw data. University of Massachusetts Medical Center, Boston.

Kagitcibasi, C. (1994). A critical appraisal of individualism and collectivism: Toward a new formulation. In U. Kim, H. C. Triandis, C. Kagitcibasi, S.-C. Choi, & G. Yoon (Eds.), *Individualism and collectivism: Theory, method, and applications* (pp. 52–65). Thousand Oaks, CA: Sage.

Kahneman, D., Diener, E., & Schwartz, N. (1999). *Well-being: The foundations of hedonic psychology.* New York: Russell Sage.

Kaluza, G. (1997). Evaluation of stress management interventions in primary prevention—A meta-analysis of (quasi) experimental studies. *Zeitschrift für Gesundheitspsychologie, 5,* 149–169.

Kanekar, S., & Merchant, S. M. (1982). Aggression, retaliation, and religious affiliation. *Journal of Social Psychology, 117,* 295–296.

Kanfer, F. H. (1970). Self-regulation: Research, issues, and speculations. In C. Neuringer & J. L. Michael (Eds.), *Behavior modification in clinical psychology* (pp. 178–220). New York: Appleton-Century-Crofts.

Kaplan, J. S., & Sue, S. (1997). Ethnic psychology in the United States. In D. F. Halpern & A. E. Voiskounsky (Eds.), *States of mind: American and post-Soviet perspectives on contemporary issues in psychotherapy* (pp. 349–369). New York: Oxford University Press.

Kaplan, R. M. (2000). Two pathways to prevention. *American Psychologist, 55,* 382–396.

Kaplan, R. M., Alcaraz, J. E., Anderson, J. P., & Weisman, M. (1996). Quality-adjusted life years lost to arthritis: Effects of gender, race, and social class. *Arthritis Care and Research, 9,* 473–482.

Kaplan, R. M., & Anderson, J. P. (1996). The general health policy model: An integrated approach. In B. Spilker (Ed.), *Quality of life and pharmacoeconomics in clinical trials* (pp. 309–322). New York: Raven.

Kardiner, A., & Ovesey, L. (1951). *The mark of oppression: A psychological study of the American Negro.* New York: Norton.

Kasdin, A. E., Siegel, T. C., & Bass, D. (1990). Drawing on clinical practice to inform research on child and adolescent psychotherapy: Survey of practitioners. *Professional Psychology: Research and Practice, 21,* 189–198.

Kaslow, N. J., Tanenbaum, R. L., & Seligman, M. E. P. (1978). *The KASTAN-R: A children's attributional style questionnaire (KASTAN-R-CASQ).* Unpublished manuscript, University of Pennsylvania.

Katz, D., & Schanck, R. L. (1938). *Social psychology.* New York: Wiley.

Kazdin, A. E. (1979). Imagery elaboration and self-efficacy in the covert modeling treatment of unassertive behavior. *Journal of Consulting and Clinical Psychology, 47,* 725–733.

Kelloway, E. K., & Barling, J. (1991). Job characteristics, role stress, and mental health. *Journal of Occupational Psychology, 64,* 291–304.

Kennedy, J. F. (1956). *Profiles in courage.* New York: Harper.

Kennedy, Q., Fung, H. H., & Carstensen, L. L. (2001). Aging, time estimation, and emotion. In R. C. Atchley & S. H. McFadden (Eds.), *Aging and the meaning of time: A multidisciplinary exploration* (pp. 51–73). New York: Springer.

Kennedy, R. F. (1968, March 18). Address. University of Kansas, Lawrence.

Keohane, R. O. (1993). Sovereignty, interdependence and international institutions. In L. Miller & M. Smith (Eds.), *Ideas and ideals: Essays on politics in honor of Stanley Hoffman* (pp. 91–107). Boulder, CO: Westview.

Keough, K. A., Zimbardo, P. G., & Boyd, J. N. (1999). Who's smoking, drinking, and using drugs? Time perspective as a predictor of substance abuse. *Basic and Applied Social Psychology, 21,* 149–164.

Keyes, C., Shmotkin, D., & Ryff, C. (2000). Optimizing well-being: The empirical encounter of two traditions. *Journal of Personality and Social Psychology, 82,* 1007–1022.

Keyes, C. L. M. (1998). Social well-being. *Social Psychology Quarterly, 61,* 121–140.

Keyes, C. L. M., & Haidt, J. (Eds.). (2003). *Flourishing: Positive psychology and a life well lived.* Washington, DC: American Psychological Association.

Keyes, C. L. M., & Lopez, S. J. (2002). Toward a science of mental health: Positive directions in diagnosis and treatment. In C. R. Snyder & S. J. Lopez (Eds.), *The handbook of positive psychology* (pp. 45–59). New York: Oxford University Press.

Keyes, C. L. M., & Magyar-Moe, J. L. (2003). The measurement and utility of adult subjective well-being. *Positive psychological assessment: A handbook of models and measures* (pp. 411–426). Washington, DC: American Psychological Association.

Keyes, C. L. M., & Ryff, C. D. (2000). Subjective change and mental health: A self-concept theory. *Social Psychology Quarterly, 63,* 264–279.

Kim, M., & Markus, H. R. (1999). Deviance or uniqueness, harmony or conformity? A cultural analysis. *Journal of Personality and Social Psychology, 77,* 785–800.

Kim, M., Sharkey, W. F., & Singelis, T. M. (1994). Relationship between individuals' self-construals and perceived importance of interactive constraints. *International Journal of Intercultural Relations, 18,* 117–140.

Kim, U. (1994). Individualism and collectivism: Conceptual clarification and elaboration. In U. Kim, H. C. Triandis, C. Kagitcibasi, S.-C. Choi, & G. Yoon (Eds.), *Individualism and collectivism: Theory, method, and applications* (pp. 19–40). Thousand Oaks, CA: Sage.

Kim, U., Triandis, H. C., Kagitcibasi, C., Choi, S.-C., & Yoon, G. (1994). *Individualism and collectivism: Theory, method, and applications.* Newbury Park, CA: Sage.

King, L. A., Eells, J. E., & Burton, C. M. (2004). The good life, broadly and narrowly considered. In P. A. Linley & S. Joseph (Eds.), *Positive psychology in practice* (pp. 25–52). Hoboken, NJ: Wiley.

King, L. A., & Napa, C. K. (1998). What makes a good life? *Journal of Personality and Social Psychology, 75,* 156–165.

King, M. L., Jr. (1968). *The peaceful warrior.* New York: Pocket Books.

Kirk, S., & Koesk, G. (1995). The fate of optimism: A longitudinal study of managers' hopefulness and subsequent morale. *Research in Social Work Practice, 86,* 80–92.

Kitayama, S., Markus, H. R., Matsumoto, H., & Norasakkunkit, V. (1997). Individual and collective process in the construction of the self: Self-enhancement in the United States and self-criticism in Japan. *Journal of Personality and Social Psychology, 72,* 1245–1267.

Kitchener, K. S., & Brenner, H. G. (1990). Wisdom and reflective judgment: Knowing the face of uncertainty. In R. J. Sternberg (Ed.), *Wisdom: Its nature, origins, and development* (pp. 212–229). New York: Cambridge University Press.

Klausner, E., Snyder, C. R., & Cheavens, J. (2000). A hope-based group treatment for depressed older adult outpatients. In G. M. Williamson, D. R. Shaffer, & P. A. Parmelee (Eds.), *Physical illness and depression in older adults: A handbook of theory, research, and practice* (pp. 295–310). New York: Plenum.

Klausner, E. J., Clarkin, J. F., Spielman, L., Pupo, C., Abrams, R., & Alexopoulos, G. S. (1998). Late-life depression and functional disability: The role of goal-focused group psychotherapy. *International Journal of Geriatric Psychiatry, 13,* 707–716.

Klerman, G., Weissman, M. M., Rounsaville, B. J., & Chevron, E. S. (1984). *Interpersonal psychotherapy of depression.* Northvale, NJ: Jason Aronson.

Kobasa, S. C. O. (1990). Stress-resistant personality. In R. Ornstein & C. Swencionis (Eds.), *The healing brain: A scientific reader* (pp. 219–230). New York: Guilford Press.

Koenig, H. G. (Ed.). (1998). *Handbook of religion and mental health.* San Diego, CA: Academic Press.

Koestner, R., Franz, C., & Weinberger, J. (1990). The family origins of empathic concern: A 26-year longitudinal study. *Journal of Personality and Social Psychology, 58,* 709–717.

Kohlberg, L. (1983). *The psychology of moral development.* New York: Harper & Row.

Kohn, M. L. (1969). *Class and conformity.* Homewood, IL: Dorsey Press.

Kohut, H. (1979). *Self-psychology and the humanities: Reflections on a new psychoanalytic approach.* New York: Norton.

Koltko-Rivera, M. E. (2004). The psychology of worldviews. *Review of General Psychology, 8,* 3–58.

Komorita, S. S., Hilty, J. A., & Parks, C. D. (1991). Reciprocity and cooperation in social dilemmas. *Journal of Conflict Resolution, 35,* 494–518.

Krauss, H. H., & Krauss, B. J. (1968). Cross-cultural study of the thwarting-disorientation theory of suicide. *Journal of Abnormal Psychology, 73,* 352–357.

Krech, G. (2001). *Naikan: Gratitude, grace, and the Japanese art of self-reflection.* Berkeley, CA: Stone Bridge Press.

Kruglanski, A. W., & Webster, D. M. (1996). Motivated closing of the mind: "Seizing" and "freezing." *Psychological Review, 103,* 263–283.

Labouvie-Vief, G. (1990). Wisdom as integrated thought: Historical and developmental perspectives. In R. J. Sternberg (Ed.), *Wisdom: Its nature, origins, and development* (pp. 52–83). New York: Cambridge University Press.

Laird, S. P., Snyder, C. R., Rapoff, M. A., & Green, S. (2004). Measuring private prayer: The development and validation of the Multidimensional Prayer Inventory. *The International Journal for the Psychology of Religion, 14,* 251–272.

Lambert, M. J. (Ed.). (2004). *Handbook of psychotherapy and behavior change* (5th ed.). New York: Wiley.

Landman, J. T., & Dawes, R. M. (1982). Psychotherapy outcome: Smith and Glass' conclusions stand up under scrutiny. *American Psychologist, 37,* 504–516.

Lane, R. D., Reiman, E. M., Bradley, M. M., Lang, P. J., Ahern, G. L., Davidson, R. J., et al. (1997). Neuroanatomical correlates of pleasant and unpleasant emotion. *Neuropsychologia, 35,* 1437–1444.

Langer, E. (1989). *Mindfulness.* Reading, MA: Addison-Wesley.

Langer, E. (1997). *The power of mindful learning.* Reading, MA: Addison-Wesley.

Langer, E. (2002). Well-being: Mindfulness versus positive evaluation. In C. R Snyder and S. J. Lopez (Eds.), *The handbook of positive psychology* (pp. 214–230). New York: Oxford University Press.

Langer, E., Blank, A., & Chanowitz, B. (1978). The mindlessness of ostensibly thoughtful action: The role of placebic information on interpersonal interaction. *Journal of Personality and Social Psychology, 36,* 635–642.

Langer, E. J., & Rodin, J. (1976). The effects of enhanced personal responsibility for the aged: A field experiment in an institutional setting. *Journal of Personality and Social Psychology, 34,* 191–198.

Langston, C. A. (1994). Capitalizing on and coping with daily-life events: Expressive responses to positive events. *Journal of Personality and Social Psychology, 67,* 1112–1125.

Lao-Tzu. (1994). *Tao Te Ching* (D. C. Lau, Trans.). New York: Knopf.

Larsen, K. S., & Giles, H. (1976). Survival or courage as human motivation: Development of an attitude scale. *Psychological Reports, 39,* 299–302.

Latane, B., & Darley, J. M. (1970). *The unresponsive bystander: Why doesn't he help?* New York: Appleton-Century-Crofts.

Lawson, W. (2004, January/February). Praise: Encouraging signs. *Psychology Today*. Retrieved November 20, 2005, from http://www.psychologytoday.com/articles/pto-20040209-000003.html

Lazarus, R. S. (2003). The Lazarus Manifesto for positive psychology and psychology in general. *Psychological Inquiry, 14,* 173–189.

Leary, M. R., Tchividijian, L. R., & Kraxberger, B. E. (1994). Self-presentation can be hazardous to your health: Impression management and health risk. *Health Psychology, 13,* 461–470.

LeDoux, J. E. (1986). Sensory systems and emotion: A model of affective processing. *Integrative Psychiatry, 4,* 237–248.

LeDoux, J. E. (1995). Emotion: Clues from the brain. *Annual Review of Psychology, 46,* 209–235.

LeDoux, J. E. (1996). *The emotional brain: The mysterious underpinnings of emotional life.* New York: Simon & Schuster.

Lee, G. R., Seccombe, K., & Shehan, C. L. (1991). Marital status and personal happiness: An analysis of trend data. *Journal of Marriage and the Family, 53,* 839–844.

Lee, Y.-T., & Seligman, M. E. P. (1997). Are Americans more optimistic than the Chinese? *Personality and Social Psychology Bulletin, 23,* 32–40.

Leitner, L. M. (2003). *Honoring suffering, tragedy, and reverence: The fully human is more than positive.* Paper presented at the American Psychological Association Annual Convention, Toronto, Canada.

Lent, R. (2004). Toward a unifying theoretical and practical perspective on well-being and psychosocial adjustment. *Journal of Counseling Psychology, 51,* 482–509.

Leong, F. T. L., & Wong, P. T. P. (2003). Optimal human functioning from cross-cultural perspectives: Cultural competence as an organizing framework. In W. B. Walsh (Ed.), *Counseling psychology and optimal human functioning* (pp. 123–150). Mahwah, NJ: Lawrence Erlbaum.

Lerner, M. (1996). *The politics of meaning.* Reading, MA: Addison-Wesley.

Lewin, K. (1951). *Field theory in social science.* New York: Harper & Row.

Liddle, P. (2001). *Disordered mind and brain.* London: Gaskell.

Liebert, R. M., & Sprafkin, J. (1988). *The early window: Effects of television on children and youth* (3rd ed.). Elmsford, NY: Pergamon.

Linley, P. A., & Harrington, S. (2006). Playing to your strengths. *The Psychologist, 19,* 85–89.

Linley, P. A., & Joseph, S. (Eds.). (2004). *Positive psychology in practice.* Hoboken, NJ: Wiley.

Little, B. L., & Madigan, R. M. (1997). The relationship between collective self-efficacy and performance in manufacturing work teams. *Small Group Research, 28,* 517–534.

Liu, W. T. (1986). Culture and social support. *Research on Aging, 8,* 57–83.

Locke, E. A. (1976). The nature and causes of job satisfaction. In M. D. Dunnette (Ed.), *Handbook of industrial and organizational psychology* (pp. 1297–1347). Chicago: Rand McNally.

Locke, E., & Latham, G. P. (2002). Building a practically useful theory of goal setting and task motivation: A 35-year odyssey. *American Psychologist, 57,* 705–717.

Long, B. C. (1993). Coping strategies of male managers: A prospective analysis of predictors of psychosomatic symptoms and job satisfaction. *Journal of Vocational Behavior, 42,* 184–199.

Lopes, P. N., Brackett, M. A., Nezlek, J. B, Schutz, A., Sellin, I., & Salovey, P. (2004). Emotional intelligence and social interaction. *Personality and Social Psychology Bulletin, 30,* 1018–1034.

Lopes, P. N., Salovey, P., Cote, S., Beers, M., & Petty, R. E. (2005). Emotion regulation abilities and the quality of social interaction. *Emotion, 5,* 113–118.

Lopes, P. N., Salovey, P., & Straus, R. (2004). Emotional intelligence, personality, and the perceived quality of social relationships. *Personality and Individual Differences, 35,* 641–658.

Lopez, F. G. (2003). The assessment of adult attachment security. In S. J. Lopez & C. R. Snyder (Eds.), *Positive psychological assessment: A handbook of models and measures* (pp. 285–299). Washington, DC: American Psychological Association.

Lopez, F. G., & Brennan, K. A. (2000). Dynamic processes underlying adult attachment organization: Toward an attachment-theoretical perspective on the healthy and effective self. *Journal of Counseling Psychology, 47,* 283–300.

Lopez, S. J. (2000). *Positive psychology in the schools: Identifying and strengthening our hidden resources.* Unpublished manuscript, University of Kansas, Lawrence.

Lopez, S. J. (2005). *Head, heart, holy test of hope.* Unpublished document. University of Kansas, Lawrence.

Lopez, S. J., Edwards, L. M., Magyar-Moe, J. L., Pedrotti, J. T., & Ryder, J. A. (2003). Fulfilling its promise: Counseling psychology's efforts to understand and promote optimal human functioning. In B. Walsh (Ed.), *Optimal human functioning* (pp. 297–308). Mahwah, NJ: Lawrence Erlbaum.

Lopez, S. J., Floyd, R. K., Ulven, J. C., & Snyder, C. R. (2000). Hope therapy: Helping clients build a house of hope. In C. R. Snyder (Ed.), *Handbook of hope: Theory, measures, and applications* (pp. 123–150). San Diego, CA: Academic Press.

Lopez, S. J., Hodges, T. D., & Harter, J. K. (2005). *Clifton StrengthsFinder technical report: Development and validation.* Omaha, NE: Gallup Organization.

Lopez, S. J., Janowski, K. M., & Quinn, R. (2004). *KU Strengths Cardsort for Children.* Unpublished manuscript. University of Kansas, Lawrence.

Lopez, S. J., Janowski, K. M., & Wells, K. J. (2005). *Developing strengths in college students: Exploring programs, contents, theories, and research.* Unpublished manuscript, University of Kansas, Lawrence.

Lopez, S. J., & McKnight, C. (2002). Moving in a positive direction: Toward increasing the utility of positive youth development efforts. *Prevention and Treatment, 5,* http://journals.apa.org/prevention/volume5/pre0050019c.html

Lopez, S. J., & Snyder, C. R. (2003). *Positive psychological assessment: A handbook of models and measures.* Washington, DC: American Psychological Association.

Lopez, S. J., Snyder, C. R., Magyar-Moe, J. L., Edwards, L. M., Pedrotti, J. T., Janowski, K., et al. (2004). Strategies for accentuating hope. In P. A. Linley & S. Joseph (Eds.), *Positive psychology in practice* (pp. 388–404). Hoboken, NJ: Wiley.

Lopez, S. J., Snyder, C. R., & Rasmussen, H. N. (2003). Striking a vital balance: Developing a complementary focus on human weakness and strength through Positive Psychological Assessment. *Positive psychological assessment: A handbook of models and measures* (pp. 3–20). Washington, DC: American Psychological Association.

Lowman, J. (1995). *Mastering the techniques of teaching* (2nd ed.). San Francisco: Jossey-Bass.

Lucas, R. E., Diener, E., & Suh, E. (1996). Discriminant validity of well-being measures. *Journal of Personality and Social Psychology, 71,* 616–628.

Lucas, R. E., & Fujita, F. (2000). Factors influencing the relations between extraversion and pleasant affect. *Journal of Personality and Social Psychology, 79,* 1039–1056.

Lukes, S. (1973). *Individualism.* Oxford, England: Basil Blackwell.

Luthans, F., & Avolio, B. (2003). Authentic leadership: A positive development approach. In K. S. Cameron, J. E. Dutton, & R. E. Quinn (Eds.), *Positive organizational scholarship* (pp. 241–258). San Francisco: Berrett-Koehler.

Luthans, F., Avolio, B. J., Walumbwa, F. O, & Li, W. (In press). The psychological capital of Chinese workers: Exploring the relationship with performance. *Management and Organizational Review.*

Luthans, F., & Jensen, S. M. (2002). Hope: A new positive strength for human resource development. *Human Resource Development Review, 3,* 304–322.

Luthans, F., Luthans, K. W., & Luthans, B. C. (2004). Positive psychological capital: Beyond human and social capital. *Business Horizons, 47,* 45–50.

Luthans, F., & Youssef, C. M. (2004). Investing in people for competitive advantage. *Organizational Dynamics, 33,* 143–160.

Luthar, S. S., Cicchetti, D., & Becker, B. (2000). The construct of resilience: A critical evaluation and guidelines for future work. *Child Development, 71,* 543–562.

Lutsky, N. (1999, August). *Not on the exam: Teaching, psychology and the examined life.* Paper presented at the annual convention of the American Psychological Association, Boston, MA.

Lutz, S. (2000). Mapping the wellsprings of a positive life: The importance of measure to the movement. *Gallup Review, 3,* 8–11.

Lykken, D. (1999). *Happiness: The nature and nurture of joy and contentment.* New York: St. Martin's Press.

Lynn, M., & Harris, J. (1997a). The desire for unique consumer products: A new individual difference scale. *Psychology and Marketing, 14,* 601–616.

Lynn, M., & Harris, J. (1997b). Individual differences in the pursuit of self-uniqueness through consumption. *Journal of Applied Social Psychology, 27,* 1861–1883.

Lynn, M., & Snyder, C. R. (2002). Uniqueness. In C. R. Snyder & S. Lopez (Ed.), *The handbook of positive psychology* (pp. 395–410). New York: Oxford University Press.

Lyubomirsky, S., Sheldon, K. M., & Schkade, D. (2005). Pursuing happiness: The architecture of sustainable change. *Review of General Psychology, 9,* 111–131.

Maddux, J. E. (1991). Self-efficacy. In C. R. Snyder & D. R. Forsyth (Eds.), *Handbook of social and clinical psychology: The health perspective* (pp. 57–58). New York: Pergamon.

Maddux, J. E. (Ed.). (1995). *Self-efficacy, adaptation, and adjustment: Theory, research, and application.* New York: Plenum.

Maddux, J. E. (2002). Self-Efficacy: The power of believing you can. In C. R. Snyder & S. J. Lopez (Eds.), *The handbook of positive psychology* (pp. 277–287). New York: Oxford University Press.

Maddux, J. E. (2002). Stopping the "madness": Positive psychology and the deconstruction of the illness ideology and the *DSM*. In C. R. Snyder & S. J. Lopez (Eds.), *The handbook of positive psychology* (pp. 13–25). New York: Oxford Press.

Maddux, J. E., Brawley, L., & Boykin, A. (1995). Self-efficacy and healthy decision making: Protection, promotion, and detection. In J. E. Maddux (Ed.), *Self-efficacy, adaptation, and adjustment: Theory, research, and application* (pp. 173–202). New York: Plenum.

Maddux, J. E., & Lewis, J. (1995). Self-efficacy and adjustment: Basic principles and issues. In J. E. Maddux (Ed.), *Self-efficacy, adaptation, and adjustment: Theory, research, and application* (pp. 37–68). New York: Plenum.

Maddux, J. E., & Mundell, C. E. (1999). Disorders of personality: Diseases or individual differences? In V. J. Derlega, B. A. Winstead, & W. H. Jones (Eds.), *Personality: Contemporary theory and research* (pp. 541–571). Chicago: Nelson-Hall.

Maddux, J., Snyder, C. R., & Lopez, S. (2004). Toward a positive clinical psychology: Deconstructing the illness ideology and constructing an ideology of happiness and human strengths. In P. A. Linley & S. Joseph (Eds.), *Positive psychology in practice* (pp. 320–334). Hoboken, NJ: Wiley.

Mahan, B. B., Garrard, W. M., Lewis, S. E., & Newbrough, J. R. (2002). Sense of community in a university setting. In A. T. Fisher, C. C. Sonn, & B. J. Bishop (Eds.), *Psychological sense of community: Research, applications, and implications* (pp. 123–140). New York: Kluwer/Plenum.

Mahoney, A., Pargament, K. I., Cole, B., Jewell, T., Magyar, G. M., Tarakeshwar, N., et al. (2005). A higher purpose: The sanctification of strivings in a community sample. *International Journal for the Psychology of Religion, 15*, 239–262.

Mahoney, A., Pargament, K. I., Jewell, T., Swank, A. B., Scott, E., Emery, E., et al. (1999). Marriage and the spiritual realm: The role of proximal and distal religious constructs in marital functioning. *Journal of Family Psychology, 13*, 321–338.

Maier, S. F., Laudenslager, M. L., & Ryan, S. M. (1985). Stressor controllability, immune function, and endogenous opiates. In F. R. Brush & J. B. Overmier (Eds.), *Affect, conditioning, and cognition: Essays on the determinants of behavior* (pp. 183 201). Hillsdale, NJ: Lawrence Erlbaum.

Maier, S. F., & Watkins, P. R. (2000). The immune system as a sensory system: Implications for psychology. *Current Directions in Psychological Science, 9*, 98–102.

Main, M., & Goldwyn, R. (1984). *Adult attachment scoring and classification system.* Unpublished manuscript, University of California at Berkeley.

Main, M., & Goldwyn, R. (1998). *Adult attachment interview scoring and classification system.* Unpublished manuscript, University of California at Berkeley.

Malgady, R. G., Rogler, L. H., & Costantino, G. (1990). Culturally sensitive psychotherapy for Puerto Rican children and adolescents: A program of treatment outcome research. *Journal of Consulting and Clinical Psychology, 58*, 704–712.

Mandler, G. (1975). *Mind and emotion.* New York: Wiley.

Mansbridge, J. J. (Ed.). (1990). *Beyond self-interest.* Chicago: University of Chicago Press.

Marjoribanks, K. (1991). Sex composition of family sibships and family learning environments. *Psychological Reports, 69*, 97–98.

Markus, H. R., & Kitayama, S. (1991). Culture and self: Implications for cognition, emotion and motivation. *Psychological Review, 98,* 224–253.

Marston, P. J., Hecht, M. L., & Robers, T. (1987). "True love ways": The subjective experience and communication of romantic love. *Journal of Social and Personal Relationships, 4,* 387–407.

Martin, R. (2002, May 19). Columnist finds himself in awe. *Lawrence Journal-World,* p. D3.

Maslach, C. (1982). *Burnout—The cost of caring.* Englewood Cliffs, NJ: Prentice Hall.

Maslach, C. (1999). Progress in understanding teacher burnout. In R. Vandenberghe & A. M. Huberman (Eds.), *Understanding and preventing teacher burnout* (pp. 211–222). Cambridge, England: Cambridge University Press.

Maslach, C., & Jackson, S. E. (1981). The measurement of experienced burnout. *Journal of Occupational Behavior, 2,* 99–113.

Maslach, C., & Jackson, S. E. (1986). *Maslach burnout inventory manual* (2nd ed.). Palo Alto, CA: Consulting Psychologists Press.

Maslow, A. (1954). *Motivation and personality.* New York: Harper.

Maslow, A. (1970). *Motivation and personality.* New York: Harper & Row.

Massimini, F., & Carli, M. (1988). The systematic assessment of flow in daily experience. In M. Csikszentmihalyi & I. Csikszentmihalyi (Eds.), *Optimal experience* (pp. 266–287). Cambridge, England: Cambridge University Press.

Massimini, F., Csikszentmihalyi, M., & Carli, M. (1987). The monitoring of optimal experience: A tool for psychiatric rehabilitation. *Journal of Nervous and Mental Disease, 175*(9), 545–549.

Masten, A. S. (1999). Resilience comes of age: Reflections on the past and outlook for the next generation of research. In M. D. Glantz, J. Johnson, & L. Huffman (Eds.), *Resilience and development: Positive life adaptations* (pp. 282–296). New York: Plenum.

Masten, A. S. (2001). Ordinary magic: Resilience process in development. *American Psychologist, 56,* 227–239.

Masten, A. S., & Garmezy, N. (1985). Risk, vulnerability, and protective factors in the developmental psychopathology. In B. B. Lahey & A. E. Kazdin (Eds.), *Advances in clinical child psychology.* (Vol. 8, pp. 1–51). New York: Plenum.

Masten, A. S., & Reed, M. G. J. (2002). Resilience in development. In C. R. Snyder & S. J. Lopez (Eds.), *The handbook of positive psychology* (pp. 74–88). New York: Oxford University Press.

Masterson, J. (1981). *The narcissistic and borderline disorders.* New York: Brunner/Mazel.

Mathers, C. D., & Schofield, D. J. (1998). The health consequences of unemployment: The evidence. *Medical Journal of Australia, 168,* 178–182.

Matsumoto, D., Kudoh, T., & Takeuchi, S. (1996). Changing patterns of individualism and collectivism in the United States and Japan. *Culture and Psychology, 2,* 77–107.

Matthews, K. A., Batson, C. D., Horn, J., & Rosenman, R. H. (1981). "Principles in his nature which interest him in the fortune of others . . . ": The heritability of empathic concern for others. *Journal of Personality, 49,* 237–247.

Mayer, J. (2005). *Who is emotionally intelligent—And does it matter?* Retrieved September 5, 2005, from http://www.unh.edu/emotional_intelligence/

Mayer, J. D., DiPaolo, M. T., & Salovey, P. (1990). Perceiving affective content of ambiguous visual stimuli: A component of emotional intelligence. *Journal of Personality Assessment, 54,* 772–781.

Mayer, J. D., & Salovey, P. (1997). What is emotional intelligence? In P. Salovey & D. Sluyter (Eds.), *Emotional development and emotional intelligence: Implications for educators* (pp. 3–31). New York: Basic Books.

Mayer, J. D., Salovey, P., & Caruso, D. (2001). *The Mayer-Salovey-Caruso Emotional Intelligence Test (MSCEIT).* Toronto: Multi-Health Systems, Inc.

Mayer, J. D., Salovey, P., & Caruso, D. (2004). Emotional intelligence: Theory, findings, and implications. *Psychological Inquiry, 15,* 197–215.

Mayne, T. J., & Bonanno, G. A. (Eds.). (2001). *Emotions: Current issues and future directions.* New York: Guilford Press.

McClelland, D. C., Atkinson, J. W., Clark, R. W., & Lowell, E. L. (1953). *The achievement motive.* New York: Appleton-Century-Crofts.

McCrae, R. R., & Costa, P. T. (1987). Validation of the five-factor model of personality across instruments and observers. *Journal of Personality and Social Psychology, 52,* 81–90.

McCraty, R. (2002). Influence of cardiac afferent input on heart-brain synchronization and cognitive performance. *International Journal of Psychophysiology, 45,* 72–73.

McCraty, R., & Atkinson, M. (2003). *Psychophysiological coherence.* Boulder Creek, CA: HeartMath Research Center, Institute of HeartMath, Publication No. 03-016.

McCraty, R., & Childre, D. (2004). The grateful heart: The psychophysiology of appreciation. In R. A. Emmons & M. E. McCullough (Eds.), *The psychology of gratitude* (pp. 230–255). New York: Oxford University Press.

McCullough, M. E. (2000). Forgiveness as a human strength: Theory, measurement, and links to well-being. *Journal of Social and Clinical Psychology, 19,* 43–55.

McCullough, M. E., Emmons, R. A., & Tsang, J. (2002). The grateful disposition: A conceptual and empirical topography. *Journal of Personality and Social Psychology, 82,* 112–127.

McCullough, M. E., Kilpatrick, S., Emmons, R. A., & Larson, D. (2001). Is gratitude a moral affect? *Psychological Bulletin, 127,* 249–266.

McCullough, M. E., Pargament, K. I., & Thoresen, C. E. (2000b). The psychology of forgiveness: History, conceptual issues, and overview. In M. E. McCullough, K. I. Pargament, & C. E. Thoresen (Eds.), *Forgiveness: Theory, research, and practice* (pp. 1–14). New York: Guilford Press.

McCullough, M. E., Pargament, K. I., & Thoresen, C. E. (Eds.). (2000a). *Forgiveness: Theory, research, and practice.* New York: Guilford Press.

McCullough, M. E., Rachal, K. C., Sandage, S. J., Worthington, E. L., Jr., Brown, S. W., & Hight, T. L. (1998). Interpersonal forgiving in close relationships: II. Theoretical elaboration and measurement. *Journal of Personality and Social Psychology, 75,* 1586–1603.

McCullough, M. E., Tsang, J., & Emmons, R. A. (2004). Gratitude in intermediate affective terrain: Links of grateful moods to individual differences and daily emotional experience. *Journal of Personality and Social Psychology, 86,* 295–309.

McCullough, M. E., Worthington, E. L., Jr., & Rachal, K. C. (1997). Interpersonal forgiving in close relationships. *Journal of Personality and Social Psychology, 73,* 321–336.

McDermott, D., Hastings, S., Gariglietti, K. P., Gingerich, K., Callahan, B., & Diamond, K. (1996, April). *Fostering hope in the classroom.* Paper presented at the meeting of the Kansas Counseling Association, Salina, KS.

McDermott, D., & Snyder, C. R. (1999). *Making hope happen: A workbook for turning possibilities into realities.* Oakland, CA: New Harbinger.

McDermott, D., & Snyder, C. R. (2000). *The great big book of hope.* Oakland, CA: New Harbinger.

McDermott, P. A. (1980). Congruence and typology of diagnoses in school psychology: An empirical study. *Psychology in the Schools, 17,* 12–24.

McDougall, D., & Granby, C. (1996). How expectation of questioning method affects undergraduates' preparation for class. *Journal of Experimental Education, 65,* 43–54.

McKay, J., & Greengrass, M. (2003). People. *Monitor, 34,* 87.

McKeachie, W. J. (2002). Ebbs, flows, and progress in the teaching of psychology. In S. F. Davis & W. Buskist (Eds.), *The teaching of psychology: Essays in honor of Wilbert J. McKeachie and Charles L. Brewer* (pp. 487–498). Mahwah, NJ: Lawrence Erlbaum.

McLeish, K. (Ed). (1993). *Key ideas in human thought.* New York: Facts on File.

McMillan, D. W., & Chavis, D. M. (1986). Sense of community: A definition and theory. *Journal of Community Psychology, 14,* 6–23.

McMillan, L. H. W., O'Driscoll, M. P., Marsh, N. V., & Brady, E. C. (2001). Understanding workaholism: Data synthesis, theoretical critique, and future design strategies. *International Journal of Stress Management, 8,* 69–91.

McNeal, R. E. (1998). Pre and post-treatment hope in children and adolescents in residential treatment: A further analysis of the effects of the teaching family model. *Dissertation Abstracts International, 59 (5-B),* 2425.

Meehl, P. (1975). Hedonic capacity: Some conjectures. *Bulletin of the Menninger Clinic, 39,* 295–307.

Meichenbaum, D. H. (1977). *Cognitive-behavior modification: An integrative approach.* New York: Plenum.

Meier, S. F., & Watkins, L. R. (1999). The neurobiology of stressor controllability. In J. E. Gillham (Ed.), *The science of optimism and hope* (pp. 41–56). Philadelphia: Templeton Press.

Menninger, K., Mayman, M., & Pruyser, P. W. (1963). *The vital balance.* New York: Viking Press.

Metalsky, G. I., Halberstadt, J., & Abramson, L. Y. (1987). Vulnerability to depressive mood reactions: Toward a more powerful test of the diathesis-stress and causal mediation components of the reformulated theory of depression. *Journal of Personality and Social Psychology, 52,* 386–393.

Michael, S. T., & Snyder, C. R. (In press). Hope, anxiety, and rumination. *Journal of Death Studies.*

Midlarsky, E., & Bryan, J. H. (1972). Affect expression and children's imitative altruism. *Journal of Experimental Research in Personality, 6,* 195–203.

Miller, D. R. (1963). The study of social relationships: Situation, identity, and social interaction. In S. Koch (Ed.), *Psychology: A study of science* (Vol. 5, pp. 639–737). New York: McGraw-Hill.

Miller, D. T. (1999). The norm of self-interest. *American Psychologist, 54,* 1053–1060.

Miller, J. G. (1994). Cultural diversity in the morality of caring: Individually-oriented versus duty-oriented interpersonal scales. *Cross-Cultural Research, 28,* 3–39.

Miller, N. E. (1944). Experimental studies of conflict. In J. M. Hunt (Ed.), *Personality and behavior disorders* (Vol. 1, pp. 431–465). New York: Ronald Press.

Miller, T. (1995). *How to want what you have: Discovering the magic and grandeur of ordinary existence.* New York: Avon Books.

Mischel, W. (1979). On the interface of cognition and personality: Beyond the person situation debate. *American Psychologist, 34,* 740–754.

Mitchell, N. (2003). Interview with Nobel Laureate Daniel Kahneman: Toward a science of well-being Retrieved September 13, 2005, from http://www.abc.net.au/rn/science/mind/s923773.htm

Monk, D. H., & King, J. A. (1994). Subject area preparation of secondary mathematics and science teachers and student achievement. *Economics of Education Review, 13,* 125–145.

Morris, M. W., & Peng, K. (1994). Culture and cause: American and Chinese attributions for social and physical events. *Journal of Personality and Social Psychology, 67,* 949–971.

Mowrer, O. H. (1960). *Learning theory and behavior.* New York: Wiley.

Mrazek, P. J., & Haggerty, R. J. (1994). *Reducing risks for mental disorders: Frontiers for preventive intervention research.* Washington, DC: National Academy Press.

Munoz, R. F., & Mendelson, T. (2004). Prevention of mental disorders. In W. E. Craighead & C. B. Neroff (Eds.), *The Corsini concise encyclopedia of psychology and behavioral science* (pp. 724–725). New York: Wiley.

Murray, B. (2002, December). Assessing educational success. *APA Monitor, 33.*

Mutrie, N., & Faulkner, G. (2004). Physical activity: Positive psychology in motion. In P. A. Linley & S. Joseph (Eds.), *Positive psychology in practice* (pp. 146–164). Hoboken, NJ: Wiley.

Myers, D. (1993). *The pursuit of happiness.* New York: Avon Books.

Myers, D. G. (1992). *The pursuit of happiness.* New York: Morrow.

Myers, D. G. (1993). *The pursuit of happiness.* New York: HarperCollins.

Myers, D. G. (2000). The funds, friends, and faith of happy people. *American Psychologist, 55,* 56–67.

Myers, D. G. (2004). Human connections and the good life: Balancing individuality and community in public policy. In P. A. Linley & S. Joseph (Eds.), *Positive psychology in practice* (pp. 641–657). Hoboken, NJ: Wiley.

Nakamura, J., & Csikszentmihalyi, M. (2002). The concept of flow. In C. R. Snyder & S. J. Lopez (Eds), *The handbook of positive psychology* (pp. 89–105). New York: Oxford University Press.

Nathan, P., & Gorman, J. (2002). *A guide to treatments that work* (2nd ed.). New York: Oxford University Press.

Naughtin, R., as told to Pam Grout. (2005, May). I had two heart transplants. *Teen People,* p. 115.

Newberg, A. B., d'Aquili, E. G., Newberg, S. K., & deMarici, V. (2000). The neuropsychological correlates of forgiveness. In M. E. McCullough,

K. I. Pargament, & C. E. Thoresen (Eds.), *Forgiveness: Theory, research, and practice* (pp. 91–110). New York: Guilford Press.

Newbrough, J. R. (1995). Toward community: A third position. *American Journal of Community Psychology, 23,* 9–31.

Newton, I. (2003). *Mathematical Principles of Natural Philosophy.* Kila, MT: Kessinger Publishing. (Original work published 1687)

Newton, N. A., Brauer, D., Gutmann, D. L., & Grunes, J. (1986). Psychodynamic therapy with the aged: A review. *Clinical Gerontologist, 5,* 205–229.

Ngai, S. S. (1993). Occupational stress and burnout among outreaching social workers in Hong Kong. *International Social Work, 36,* 101–117.

Nickell, G. S. (1998, August). *The Helping Attitude Scale.* Paper presented at the American Psychological Association Convention, San Francisco.

Niederhoffer, K. G., & Pennebaker, J. W. (2002). Sharing one's story: On the benefits of writing or talking about emotional experience. In C. R. Snyder & S. J. Lopez (Eds.), *The handbook of positive psychology* (pp. 573–583). New York: Oxford University Press.

Nisbet, R. (1980). *History of the idea of progress.* New York: Basic Books.

Nisbett, R. E. (2003). *The geography of thought: How Asians and Westerners think differently . . . and why.* New York: Free Press.

Nisbett, R. E., Caputo, C., Legant, P., & Maracek, J. (1973). Behavior as seen by the actor and as seen by the observer. *Journal of Personality and Social Psychology, 27,* 154–164.

Nolen-Hoeksema, S. (1987). Sex differences in depression: Theory and evidence. *Psychological Bulletin, 101,* 259–282.

Nolen-Hoeksema, S. (2000). Growth and resilience among bereaved people. In J. Gillham (Ed.), *The science of optimism and hope* (pp. 107–127). Philadelphia: Templeton Foundation Press.

Norcross, J. C., & Prochaska, J. O. (1986). The psychological distress and self-change of psychologists, counselors, and laypersons. *Psychotherapy, 23,* 102–114.

Noricks, J. S., Atgler, L. H., Bartholomew, M., Howard-Smith, S., Martin, D., Pyles, S., et al. (1987). Age, abstract thinking, and the American concept of person. *American Anthropologist, 89,* 667–675.

Nussbaum, M. (2001). *Upheavals of thought: The intelligence of emotions.* London: Cambridge University Press.

Oatley, K., & Jenkins, J. M. (1992). Human emotion: Function and dysfunction. *Annual Review of Psychology, 43,* 55–86.

Oatley, K., & Jenkins, J. M. (1996). *Understanding emotions.* Cambridge, MA: Basil Blackwell.

Obeysekere, G. (1995). Depression, Buddhism, and the work of culture in Sri Lanka. In A. Kleinman & B. Good (Eds.), *Culture and depression: Studies in the anthropology and cross-cultural psychiatry of affect and behavior* (pp. 134–152). Berkeley: University of California Press.

O'Brien, K. M. (2003). Measuring career self-efficacy: Promoting confidence and happiness at work. In S. J. Lopez & C. R. Snyder (Eds.), *Positive psychological assessment: A handbook of models and measures* (pp. 109–126). Washington, DC: American Psychological Association.

O'Brien, K. M., Heppner, M. J., Flores, L. Y., & Bikos, L. H. (1997). The Career Counseling Self-Efficacy Scale: Instrument development and training applications. *Journal of Counseling Psychology, 44,* 20–31.

O'Byrne, K. K., Lopez, S. J., & Petersen, S. (2000, August). *Building a theory of courage: A precursor to change?* Paper presented at the 108th Annual Convention of the American Psychological Association, Washington, DC.

O'Connor, R., Hallam, R., & Rachman, S. (1985). Fearlessness and courage: A replication experiment. *British Journal of Psychology, 76,* 187–197.

Oldham, J. M., & Morris, L. B. (1995). *New personality self-portrait: Why you think, work, love, and act the way you do.* New York: Bantam Books.

O'Leary, A., & Brown, S. (1995). Self-efficacy and the physiological stress response. In J. E. Maddux (Ed.), *Self-efficacy, adaptation, and adjustment: Theory, research, and application* (pp. 227–248). New York: Plenum.

Ontario Consultants on Religious Tolerance (2004). *Taoism.* Retrieved May 3, 2005, from http://www.religioustolerance.org/taoism.htm

Ortony, A., Clore, G. L., & Collins, A. (1988). *The cognitive structure of emotions.* New York: Cambridge University Press.

Ortony, A., & Turner, T. J. (1990). What's basic about the basic emotions. *Psychological Review, 97,* 315–331.

Orwoll, L. (1989). *Wisdom in later adulthood: Personality and life history correlates.* Dissertation Abstracts International, *49,* 5054.

Orwoll, L., & Achenbaum, W. A. (1993). Gender and the development of wisdom. *Human Development, 36,* 274–296.

Ory, M. G., & Cox, M. (1994). Forging ahead: Linking health and behavior to improve quality of life in older people. *Social Indicator Research, 33,* 89–120.

Oyserman, D. (1993). The lens of personhood: Viewing the self, others, and conflict in a multicultural society. *Journal of Personality and Social Psychology, 65,* 993–1009.

Oyserman, D., Coon, H. M., & Kemmelmeier, M. (2002). Rethinking individualism and collectivism: Evaluation of theoretical assumptions and meta-analyses. *Psychological Bulletin, 128,* 3–72.

Paez, D., Velasco, C., & Gonzales, J. L. (1999). Expressive writing and the role of alexithymia as a dispositional deficit in self-disclosure and psychological health. *Journal of Personality and Social Psychology, 77,* 630–641.

Palmer, A. (November 2003). In brief: Positive emotion styles linked to the common cold. *The Monitor in Psychology, 34*(10), p. 16.

Palmer, S. (1970). *Deviance and conformity: Roles, situations, and reciprocity.* New Haven, CT: College and University Press.

Panter-Brick, C., Rowley-Conwy, P., & Layton, R. H. (Eds.). (2001). *Hunter-gatherers: An interdisciplinary perspective.* New York: Cambridge University Press.

Pargament, K. I. (1997). *The psychology of religion and coping: Theory, research, practice.* New York: Guilford Press.

Pargament, K. I., & Mahoney, A. (2002). Spirituality: Discovering and conserving the sacred. In C. R. Snyder & S. J. Lopez (Eds.), *The handbook of positive psychology* (pp. 646–659). New York: Oxford University Press.

Parham, T. A., White, J. L., & Ajamu, A. (1999). *The psychology of Blacks: An African centered perspective* (3rd ed.). Englewood Cliffs, NJ: Prentice Hall.

Parker, D. (1929, November). Interview with Ernest Hemingway. *The New Yorker, 30,* n.p.

Pascual-Leone, J. (1990). An essay on wisdom: Toward organismic processes that make it possible. In R. J. Sternberg (Ed.), *Wisdom: Its nature, origins, and development* (pp. 244–278). New York: Cambridge University Press.

Pasupathi, M., Staudinger, U., & Baltes, P. B. (1999). *The emergence of wisdom-related knowledge and judgment during adolescence.* Berlin, Germany: Max Planck Institute for Human Development.

Payne, B. P. (1977). The older volunteer: Social role continuity and development. *The Gerontologist, 29,* 710–711.

Pei, M. L. (2005). *Old horse knows the way.* Retrieved August 12, 2005, from http://www.chinapage.com/story/oldhorse.html

Pennebaker, J. W. (1989). Confession, inhibition, and disease. In L. Berkowitz (Ed.), *Advances in experimental social psychology* (Vol. 22, pp. 211–244). New York: Academic Press.

Pennebaker, J. W. (1990). *Opening up: The healing power of confiding in others.* New York: Morrow.

Pennebaker, J. W. (1997). *Opening up: The healing power of expressing emotions* (Rev. ed.). New York: Guilford Press.

Perry, S. K. (1999). *Writing in flow.* Cincinnati, OH: Writer's Digest Books.

Peterson, C. (2000). Optimistic explanatory style and health. In J. Gillham (Ed.), *The science of optimism and hope* (pp. 145–162). Philadelphia: Templeton Foundation Press.

Peterson, C., & Barrett, L. (1987). Explanatory style and academic performance among university freshmen. *Journal of Personality and Social Psychology, 53,* 603–607.

Peterson, C., Bettes, B. A., & Seligman, M. E. P. (1985). Depressive symptoms and unprompted causal attributions: Content analysis. *Behavior Research and Therapy, 23,* 379–382.

Peterson, C., Maier, S. F., & Seligman, M. E. P. (1993). *Learned helplessness: A theory for the age of personal control.* New York: Oxford University Press.

Peterson, C., & Park, N. (2003, March). *Assessment of character strengths among youth: Progress report on the Values in Action Inventory for Youth.* Paper presented at the Child Trends Conference on Indicators of Positive Youth Development, Washington, DC.

Peterson, C., Schulman, P., Castellon, C., & Seligman, M. (1992). CAVE: Content Analysis of Verbal Explanations. In C. Smith (Ed.), *Motivation and personality: Handbook of thematic content analysis* (pp. 383–392). New York: Cambridge University Press.

Peterson, C., & Seligman, M. E. P. (2004). *Character strengths and virtues: A handbook and classification.* Washington, DC: American Psychological Association.

Peterson, C., Seligman, M. E. P., Yurko, K. H., Martin, L. R., & Friedman, H. S. (1998). Catastrophizing and untimely death. *Psychological Science, 9,* 127–130.

Peterson, C., Semmel, A., von Baeyer, C., Abramson, L. Y., Metalsky, G. I., & Seligman, M. E. P. (1982). The Attributional Style Questionnaire. *Cognitive Therapy and Research, 6,* 287–299.

Peterson, C., & Steen, T. A. (2002). Optimistic explanatory style. In C. R. Snyder & S. J. Lopez (Eds.), *The handbook of positive psychology* (pp. 244–256). New York: Oxford University Press.

Peterson, C., & Villanova, P. (1988). An expanded attributional style questionnaire. *Journal of Abnormal Psychology, 97,* 87–89.

Peterson, P. E., & West, M. R. (Eds.). (2003). *No child left behind? The politics and practice of accountability.* Washington, DC: Brookings Institution.

Peterson, S. J., & Luthans, F. (2003). The positive impact and development of hopeful leaders. *Leadership and Organizational Development Journal, 24,* 26–31.

Phillips, V. (1998). *Empowering discipline: An approach that works with at-risk students.* Carmel Valley, CA: Personal Development Publishing.

Piaget, J. (1932). *The moral judgment of the child.* London: Routledge and Kegan Paul.

Piccard, B. (1999). Around at last! *National Geographic, 196*(3), 30–51.

Pickering, A., & Gray, J. (1999). The neuroscience of personality. In L. Pervin & O. John (Eds.), *Handbook of personality* (2nd edition, pp. 277–299). New York: Guilford Press.

Piedmont, R. (2004, November). *Spirituality predicts psychosocial outcomes: A cross-cultural analysis.* International Society for Quality of Life Studies Conference, Philadelphia.

Pieper, J. (1966). *The four cardinal virtues.* Notre Dame, IN: Notre Dame Press.

Pieper, J. (1969). *Hope and history.* (R. Winston & C. Winston, Trans.). England: Burns and Oates. (Original work published 1967)

Piliavin, J. A., & Charng, H.-W. (1990). Altruism: A review of recent theory and research. *American Sociological Review, 16,* 27–65.

Pines, A. M., Aronson, E., & Kafry, D. (1981). *Burnout: From tedium to personal growth.* New York: Free Press.

Pinker, S. (1997). *How the mind works.* New York: Norton.

Piper, W. (1989). *The little engine that could.* New York: Platt and Monk. (Original work published 1930)

Pipher, M. B. (1995). *Reviving Ophelia: Saving the selves of adolescent girls.* New York: Ballantine Books.

Pipher, M. B. (2003). *Letters to a young therapist.* New York: Basic Books.

Pittman, K. J., & Fleming, W. E. (1991). *A new vision: Promoting youth development.* Washington, DC: Center for Youth Development and Policy Research.

Plante, T. G. (2005). *Contemporary clinical psychology* (2nd ed.). New York: Wiley.

Plato. (1953). *The dialogues of Plato, Volume 1: Laches.* (B. Jowett, Trans.). New York: Modern Library.

Plomin, R., Scheier, M. F., Bergeman, C. S., Pederson, N. L., Nesselroade, J. R., & McClearn, G. E. (1992). Optimism, pessimism, and mental health: A twin/adoption analysis. *Personality and Individual Differences, 13,* 921–930.

Pretzer, J. L., & Walsh, C. A. (2001). Optimism, pessimism, and psychotherapy: Implications for clinical practice. In E. C. Chang (Ed.), *Optimism & pessimism: Implications for theory, research, and practice* (pp. 321–346). Washington, DC: American Psychological Association.

Prigatano, G. P. (1992). Disordered mind, wounded soul: The emerging role of psychotherapy in rehabilitation after brain injury. *Journal of Head Trauma and Rehabilitation, 6,* 1–10.

Pruyser, P. W. (1976). *The minister as diagnostician: Personal problems in pastoral perspective.* Philadelphia: Westminster Press.

Putman, D. (1997). Psychological courage. *Philosophy, Psychiatry and Psychology, 4*(1), 1–11.

Quinn, R. (2004). *Development and initial validation of the KU Strengths Cardsort for Adolescents.* Unpublished Master's thesis, University of Kansas, Lawrence.

Rachman, S. J. (1978). Human fears: A three-systems analysis. *Scandinavian Journal of Behaviour Therapy, 7,* 237–245.

Rachman, S. J. (1984). Fear and courage. *Behavior Therapy, 15,* 109–120.

Ramey, C. T., & Ramey, S. L. (1998). Early intervention and early experience. *American Psychologist, 53,* 109–120.

Rashid, T. (2006). *Promoting well-being through character strengths.* Unpublished manuscript, University of Pennsylvania.

Raskin, J. D., & Lewandowski, A. M. (2000). The construction of disorder as human enterprise. In R. A. Neimeyer & J. D. Raskin (Eds.), *Constructions of disorder: Meaning making frameworks for psychotherapy* (pp. 15–40). Washington, DC: American Psychological Association.

Rath, T. (2002). *Measuring the impact of Gallup's strengths-based development program for students.* Princeton, NJ: Gallup Organization.

Rath, T. (2006). *Vital friends: The people you can't afford to live without.* Washington, DC: Gallup Organization.

Rath, T., & Clifton, D. O. (2004). *How full is your bucket? Positive strategies for work and life.* New York: Gallup Organization.

Reis, H. T., & Gable, S. L. (2003). Toward a positive psychology of relationships. In C. L. M. Keyes & J. Haidt (Eds.), *Flourishing: Positive psychology and the life well lived* (pp. 129–159). Washington, DC: American Psychological Association.

Reykowski, J. (1994). Collectivism and individualism as dimensions of social change. In U. Kim, H. C. Triandis, C. Kagitcibasi, S.-C. Choi, & G. Yoon (Eds.), *Individualism and collectivism: Theory, method, and applications* (pp. 276–292). Newbury Park, CA: Sage.

Rice, E. F. (1958). *The Renaissance idea of wisdom.* Cambridge, MA: Harvard University Press.

Rice, J. K. (2003). *Teacher quality: Understanding the effectiveness of teacher attributes.* Washington, DC: Economic Policy Institute.

Riegel, K. F. (1973). Dialectical operations: The final period of cognitive development. *Human Development, 16,* 346–370.

Rigazio-DiGilio, S. A. (2000). Reconstructing psychological distress from a relational perspective: A systemic coconstructive-developmental framework. In R. A. Neimeyer & J. D. Raskin (Eds.), *Constructions of disorder: Meaning making frameworks for psychotherapy* (pp. 309–332). Washington, DC: American Psychological Association.

Rigsby, L. C. (1994). The Americanization of resilience: Deconstructing research practice. In M. Wang & E. Gordon (Eds.), *Educational resilience in inner-city America: Challenges and prospects* (pp. 85–94). Hillsdale, NJ: Lawrence Erlbaum.

Rime, B. (1995). Mental rumination, social sharing, and the recovery from emotional exposure. In J. W. Pennebaker (Ed.), *Emotion, disclosure, and health* (pp. 271–291). Washington, DC: American Psychological Association.

Ripley, J. S., & Worthington, E. L., Jr. (2002). Hope-focused and forgiveness-based group interventions to promote marital enrichment. *Journal of Counseling and Development, 80,* 452–472.

Riskind, J. H., Sarampote, C. S., & Mercier, M. A. (1996). For every malady a sovereign cure: Optimism training. *Journal of Cognitive Psychotherapy: An International Quarterly, 10,* 105–117.

Ritschel, L. (2005). Lessons in teaching hope: An interview with C. R. Snyder. *Teaching of Psychology, 32,* 74–78.

Roberts, M., Vernberg, E. & Jackson, Y. (2000). Psychotherapy with children and families. In C. R. Snyder & R. E. Ingram (Eds.), *Handbook of psychological change: Psychotherapy processes and practices for the 21st century* (pp. 500–519). New York: Wiley.

Robey, D., Khoo, H. M., & Powers, C. (2000). Situated learning in cross-functional virtual teams. *Professional Communication,* March, 51–61.

Robinson, D. N. (1990). Wisdom through the ages. In R. J. Sternberg (Ed.), *Wisdom: Its nature, origins, and development* (pp. 13–24). New York: Cambridge University Press.

Rodin, J., & Langer, E. J. (1977). Long-term effects of a control-relevant intervention among the institutionalized aged. *Journal of Personality and Social Psychology, 35,* 275–282.

Rodriguez-Hanley, A., & Snyder, C. R. (2000). The demise of hope: On losing positive thinking. In C. R. Snyder (Ed.), *Handbook of hope: Theory, measures, and applications* (pp. 39–54). San Diego, CA: Academic Press.

Rogers, R. W., & Prentice-Dunn, S. (1997). Protection motivation theory. In D. Gochman (Ed.), *Handbook of health behavior research 1: Personal and social determinants* (pp. 113–132). New York: Plenum.

Rokke, P. D., & Rehm, L. P. (2001). Management therapies. In K. S. Dobson (Ed.), *Handbook of cognitive-behavioral therapies* (pp. 173–210). New York: Guilford Press.

Rorty, A. O. (1988). *Mind in action: Essays in the philosophy of mind.* Boston: Beacon Press.

Ross, K. L. (2003). *Confucius.* Retrieved May 3, 2005, from http://friesian.com/confuci.htm

Roth, A., & Fonagy, P. (Eds.). (1996). *What works for whom? A critical review of psychotherapy research.* New York: Guilford Press.

Roth, A., Fonagy, P., & Parry, G. (1996). Psychotherapy research, funding, and evidence-based practice. In A. Roth & P. Fonagy (Eds.), *What works for whom? A critical review of psychotherapy research* (pp. 37–56). New York: Guilford Press.

Rotter, J. B. (1966). Generalized expectancies for internal versus external control of reinforcement. *Psychological Monographs, 80*(1, whole no. 609).

Rowan, C., Chiang, B. F., & Miller, R. J. (1997). Using research on employee's performance to study the effects of teachers on students' achievement. *Sociology of Education, 70,* 256–284.

Rowe, J. W., & Kahn, R. L. (1998). *Successful aging.* New York: Pantheon Books.

Royal, M. A., & Rossi, R. J. (1996). Individual-level correlates of sense of community: Findings from the workplace and school. *Journal of Community Psychology, 24,* 395–416.

Rue, L. (1994). *By the grace of guile: The role of deception in natural history and human affairs.* New York: Oxford University Press.

Ruehlman, L. S., & Wolchik, S. A. (1988). Personal goals and interpersonal support and hindrance as factors in psychological distress and well-being. *Journal of Personality and Social Psychology, 55,* 293–301.

Rushton, J. P., Chrisjohn, R. D., & Fekken, G. C. (1981). The altruistic personality and the Self-Report Altruism Scale. *Personality and Individual Differences, 2,* 293–302.

Rushton, J. P., Fulker, D. W., Neale, M. C., Nias, D. K., & Eysenck, H. J. (1986). Altruism and aggression: The heritability of individual differences. *Journal of Personality and Social Psychology, 50*, 1192–1198.

Rutter, M. (1985). Resilience in the face of adversity: Protective factors and resistance to psychiatric disorder. *British Journal of Psychiatry, 147*, 598–611.

Ryan, R. M., & Deci, E. L. (2001). On happiness and human potentials: A review of research on hedonic and eudaemonic well-being. *Annual Review of Psychology, 52*, 141–166.

Ryff, C. D. (1989). Happiness is everything, or is it? Explorations on the meaning of psychological well-being. *Journal of Personality and Social Psychology, 57*, 1069–1081.

Ryff, C. D., & Keyes, C. L. M. (1995). The structure of psychological well-being revisited. *Journal of Personality and Social Psychology, 57*, 1069–1081.

Saccuzzo, D. P., & Ingram, R. E. (1993). *Growth through choice: The psychology of personal adjustment.* New York: Harcourt Brace Jovanovich.

Sakade, F. (1958). Momotaro. In F. Sakade (Ed.), *Japanese children's favorite stories.* Rutland, VT: Tuttle.

Salovey, P., & Mayer, J. D. (1990). Emotional intelligence. *Imagination, Cognition, and Personality, 9*, 185–211.

Salovey, P., Mayer, J. D., & Caruso, D. (2002). The positive psychology of emotional intelligence. In C. R. Snyder & S. J. Lopez (Eds.), *The handbook of positive psychology* (pp. 159–171). New York: Oxford University Press.

Sameroff, A. J., Lewis, M., & Miller, S. M. (2000). *Handbook of developmental psychopathology.* New York: Plenum.

Sandage, S., Hill, P. C, & Vang, H. C. (2003). Toward a multicultural positive psychology: Indigenous forgiveness and Hmong culture. *The Counseling Psychologist, 31*, 564–592.

Sanders, M. R., Markie-Dadds, C., & Turner, K. M. T. (2003). Theoretical, scientific and clinical foundations of the Triple P-Positive Parenting Program: A population approach to the promotion of parenting competence. *Parenting Research and Practice, 1*, 1–21.

Sanders, M. R., Mazzucchelli, T. G., & Studman, L. (2004). Stepping Stones Triple P–An evidence-based positive parenting program for families with a child who has a disability: Its theoretical basis and development. *Journal of Intellectual and Developmental Disability, 29*, 1–19.

Sanders, M. R., & Turner, K.M.T. (in press). Dissemination of an evidence-based, population-level parenting and family support strategy: Our experience with the Triple P-Positive Parenting Program. *Journal of Family Violence.*

Sanders, W. L., & Rivers, J. C. (1996). *Cumulative and residual effects of teachers on future student academic achievement.* (Research progress report). University of Tennessee–Knoxville, Value-Added Research Assessment Center.

Sangharakshita (1991). *The three jewels: An introduction to Buddhism.* Glasgow, UK: Windhorse.

Sarafino, E. (2002). *Health psychology* (4th ed.). New York: Wiley.

Sarason, S. B. (1974). *The psychological sense of community: Prospects for a community psychology.* San Francisco: Jossey-Bass.

Satterfield, J. (2000). Optimism, culture, and history: The roles of explanatory style, integrative complexity, and pessimistic rumination. In J. Gillham (Ed.),

The science of optimism and hope (pp. 349–378). Philadelphia: Templeton Foundation Press.

Sayle, M. (1998). Japan's social crisis. *Atlantic Monthly, 281,* 84–94.

Schachter, S. (1951). Deviation, rejection, and communication. *Journal of Abnormal and Social Psychology, 46,* 190–207.

Schauber, A. C. (2001). Effecting extension organizational change toward cultural diversity: A conceptual framework. *Journal of Extension, 39,* 12–15.

Scheier, M. F., & Carver, C. S. (1985). Optimism, coping, and health: Assessment and implications of generalized outcome expectancies. *Health Psychology, 4,* 219–247.

Scheier, M. F., & Carver, C. S. (2001). Adapting to cancer: The importance of hope and purpose. In A. Baum & B. L. Anderson (Eds.), *Psychosocial interventions for cancer* (pp. 15–36). Washington, DC: American Psychological Association.

Scheier, M. F., Carver, C. S., & Bridges, M. W. (1994). Distinguishing optimism from neuroticism (and trait anxiety, self-mastery, and self-esteem): A reevaluation of the Life Orientation Test. *Journal of Personality and Social Psychology, 67,* 1063–1078.

Scheier, M. F., Carver, C. S., & Bridges, M. W. (2001). Optimism, pessimism, and psychological well-being. In E. C. Chang (Ed.), *Optimism & pessimism: Implications for theory, research, and practice* (pp. 189–216). Washington, DC: American Psychological Association.

Scheier, M. F., Weintraub, J. K., & Carver, C. S. (1986). Coping with stress: Divergent strategies of optimists and pessimists. *Journal of Personality and Social Psychology, 51,* 1257–1264.

Schimmel, S. (2000). Vices, virtues, and sources of human strength in historical perspective. *Journal of Social and Clinical Psychology, 19,* 137–150.

Schmidt, F. L., & Rader, M. (1999). Exploring the boundary conditions for interview validity: Meta-analytic findings for a new interview type. *Personnel Psychology, 52,* 445–464.

Schmidt, N. B., & Koselka, M. (2000). Gender differences in patients with panic disorder: Evaluating cognitive mediation of phobic avoidance. *Cognitive Therapy and Research, 24,* 531–548.

Schneider, S. L. (2001). In search of realistic optimism: Meaning, knowledge, and warm fuzziness. *American Psychologist, 56,* 250–263.

Schor, J. B. (1991). *The overworked American: The unexpected decline of leisure.* New York: Basic Books.

Schore, A. N. (1994). *Affect regulation and the origin of the self: The neurobiology of emotional development.* Hillsdale, NJ: Lawrence Erlbaum.

Schore, A. N. (2003). *Affect regulation and the repair of the self.* New York: Norton.

Schulman, P., Keith, D., & Seligman, M. E. P. (1993). Is optimism heritable? A study of twins. *Behaviour Research and Therapy, 31,* 569–574.

Schumacher, B. (2003). *A philosophy of hope: Joseph Pieper and the contemporary debate on hope.* (D. Schindler, Trans.). New York: Fordham University Press. (Original work published 2000)

Schumann, H. W. (1974). *Buddhism.* Wheaton, IL: Theosophical.

Schur, E. M. (1969). Reactions to deviance: A critical assessment. *American Journal of Sociology, 75,* 309–322.

Schutte, N. S., Malouff, J. M., Hall, L. E., Haggerty, D. J., Copper, J. T., Golden, C. J., et al. (1998). Development and validation of emotional intelligence. *Personality and Individual Differences, 25,* 167–177.

Schwartz, S. H. (1994). Beyond individualism and collectivism; New cultural dimensions of values. In U. Kim, H. C. Triandis, C. Kagitcibasi, S.-C. Choi, & G. Yoon (Eds.), *Individualism and collectivism: Theory, method, and applications* (pp. 85–122). Newbury Park, CA: Sage.

Schwarzer, R., & Renner, B. (2000). Social-cognitive predictors of health behavior: Action self-efficacy and coping self-efficacy. *Health Psychology, 19,* 487–495.

Seeman, T. E. (1996). Social ties and health: The benefits of social integration. *Annals of Epidemiology, 6,* 442–451.

Seligman, M. E. P. (1991). *Learned optimism.* New York: Knopf.

Seligman, M. E. P. (1994). *What you can change and what you can't.* New York: Knopf.

Seligman, M. E. P. (1995). The effectiveness of psychotherapy: The *Consumer Reports* study. *American Psychologist, 50,* 965–974.

Seligman, M. E. P. (1998a). Building human strength: Psychology's forgotten mission. *APA Monitor, 29*(1).

Seligman, M. E. P. (1998b). *Learned optimism: How to change your mind and your life* (2nd edition). New York: Pocket Books.

Seligman, M. E. P. (1998c). Positive social science. *APA Monitor, 29*(4), 2, 5.

Seligman, M. E. P. (1998d). The gifted and the extraordinary. *APA Monitor, 29* (11), 2–3.

Seligman, M. E. P. (1998e). Work, love, and play. *APA Monitor, 29.* Retrieved August 14, 2004, from www.apa.org/monitor/aug98/pc.html

Seligman, M. E. P. (2002). *Authentic happiness: Using the new positive psychology to realize your potential for lasting fulfillment.* New York: Free Press.

Seligman, M. E. P., Abramson, L. Y., Semmel, A., & von Baeyer, C. (1979). Depressive attributional style. *Journal of Abnormal Psychology, 88,* 242–247.

Seligman, M. E. P., & Csikszentmihalyi, M. (2000). Positive psychology: An introduction. *American Psychologist, 55,* 5–14.

Seligman, M. E. P., Kaslow, N. J., Alloy, L. B., Peterson, C., Tanenbaum, R., & Abramson, L. Y. (1984). Attributional style and depressive symptoms among children. *Journal of Abnormal Psychology, 93,* 235–238.

Seligman, M. E. P., Nolen-Hoeksema, S., Thornton, N., & Thornton, K. M. (1990). Explanatory style as a mechanism of disappointing athletic performance. *Psychological Science, 1,* 143–146.

Seligman, M. E. P., Reivich, K., Jaycox, L., & Gillham, J. (1995). *The optimistic child.* New York: Houghton Mifflin.

Seligman, M. E. P., & Schulman, P. (1986). Explanatory style as a predictor of performance as a life insurance agent. *Journal of Personality and Social Psychology, 50,* 832–838.

Seligman, M. E. P., Steen, T. A., Park, N., & Peterson, C. (2005). Positive psychology progress: Empirical validation of interventions. *American Psychologist, 60,* 410–421.

Selye, H. (1936). A syndrome produced by diverse nocuous agents. *Nature, 138,* 32.

Seuss, Dr. (1961). *Sneetches and other stories.* New York: Random House Books for Young Readers.

Shafranske, E. P., & Malony, H. N. (1990). Clinical psychologists' religious and spiritual orientations and their practices of psychotherapy. *Psychotherapy: Theory, Research, Practice, Training, 27,* 72–78.

Shapiro, D. A., & Shapiro, D. (1982). Meta-analysis of comparative therapy outcome studies. *Psychological Bulletin, 92,* 581–604.

Shapiro, D. H. (1980). *Meditation: Self-regulation strategy and altered state of consciousness.* New York: Aldine.

Shapiro, S. L., & Schwartz, G. E. (2000). The role of intention in self-regulation: Toward intentional systemic mindfulness. In M. Boekaerts, P. R. Pintrich, & M. Zeidner (Eds.), *Handbook of self-regulation* (pp. 253–273). New York: Academic Press.

Shapiro, S. L., Schwartz, G. E. R., & Bonner, G. (1998). The effects of mindfulness-based stress reduction on medical and pre-medical students. *Journal of Behavioral Medicine, 21,* 581–599.

Shapiro, S. L., Schwartz, G. E. R., & Santerre, C. (2002). Meditation and positive psychology. In C. R. Snyder & S. J. Lopez (Eds.), *The handbook of positive psychology* (pp. 632–645). New York: Oxford University Press.

Shaver, P., Hazan, C., & Bradshaw, D. (1988). Love as attachment. In R. J. Sternberg & M. L. Barnes (Eds.), *The psychology of love* (pp. 68–99). New Haven, CT: Yale University Press.

Shaw, W. S., Patterson, T. L., Semple, S. J., Grant, I., Yu, E. S. H., Zhang, M. Y., et al. (1997). A cross-cultural validation of coping strategies and their associations with caregiving distress. *The Gerontologist, 37, 490–504.*

Sheldon, K. M., & Lyubomirsky, S. (2004). Achieving sustainable new happiness: Prospects, practices, and prescriptions. In P. A. Linley and S. Joseph (Eds.), *Positive psychology in practice* (pp. 127–145). Hoboken, NJ: Wiley.

Shelp, E. E. (1984). Courage: A neglected virtue in the patient-physician relationship. *Social Science and Medicine, 18*(4), 351–360.

Sherer, M., Maddux, J. E., Mercandante, B., Prentice-Dunn, S., Jacobs, B., & Rogers, R. (1982). The self-efficacy scale: Construction and validation. *Psychological Reports, 51,* 663–671.

Sherwin, E. D., Elliott, T. R., Rybarczyk, B. D., Frank, R. G., Hanson, S., & Hoffman, J. (1992). Negotiating the reality of caregiving: Hope, burnout, and nursing. *Journal of Social and Clinical Psychology, 11,* 129–139.

Shi, D. (2004). *Dr. Brewer has passion for art of teaching.* Retrieved (n.d.) from david.shi@furman.edu

Shmotkin, D. (1998). Declarative and differential aspects of subjective well-being and implications for mental health in later life. In J. Lomranz (Ed.), *Handbook of aging and mental health: An integrative approach* (pp. 15–43). New York: Plenum.

Shmotkin, D. (2005). Happiness in the face of adversity: Reformulating the dynamic and modular bases of subjective well-being. *General Psychology Review, 9,* 291-325.

Shorey, H. S., Snyder, C. R., Yang, X., & Lewin, M. R. (2003). The role of hope as a mediator in recollecting parenting, adult attachment, and mental health. *Journal of Social and Clinical Psychology, 22,* 685–715.

Shure, M. B. (1974). Training children to solve interpersonal problems: A preventive mental health program. In R. F. Munoz, L. R. Snowden, & J. G. Kelly (Eds.), *Social and psychological research in community settings* (pp. 30–68). San Francisco: Jossey-Bass.

Shure, M. B., & Spivak, G. (1988). Interpersonal cognitive problem solving. In R. H. Price, E. L. Cowen, R. P. Lorion, & J. Ramos-McKay (Eds.), *Fourteen ounces of prevention: A casebook for practitioners* (pp. 69–82). Washington, DC: American Psychological Association.

Siegel, D. J. (1999). *The developing mind: Toward a neurobiology of interpersonal experience.* New York: Guilford Press.

Silberman, S. W. (1995). The relationship among love, marital satisfaction, and duration of marriage. *Dissertation Abstracts, 56,* 2341.

Simmel, G. (1950). *The sociology of Georg Simmel.* Glencoe, IL: Free Press.

Simonton, D. K., & Baumeister, R. F. (2005). Positive psychology at the summit. *Review of General Psychology, 9,* 99–102.

Singer, I. (1984a). *The nature of love: Vol. 1. Plato to Luther* (2nd ed.). Chicago: University of Chicago Press.

Singer, I. (1984b). *The nature of love: Vol. 2. Courtly and romantic.* Chicago: University of Chicago Press.

Singer, I. (1987). *The nature of love: Vol. 3. The modern world.* Chicago: University of Chicago Press.

Skinner, E. A. (1995). *Perceived control, motivation, and coping.* Thousand Oaks, CA: Sage.

Smith, A. (1976). *The theory of moral sentiments* (6th ed.). Oxford, England: Clarendon Press. (Original work published 1790)

Smith, B., & Rutigliano, T. (2003). *Discover your sales strengths: How the world's greatest salespeople develop winning careers.* New York: Warner Books.

Smith, C. A. (1991). The self, appraisal, and coping. In C. R. Snyder & D. R. Forsyth (Eds.), *Handbook of social and clinical psychology: The health perspective* (pp. 116–137). New York: Pergamon Press.

Smith, J., & Baltes, P. B. (1990). Wisdom-related knowledge: Age/cohort in response to life planning problems. *Developmental Psychology, 26,* 494–505.

Smith, J., Staudinger, U., & Baltes, P. B. (1994). Occupational settings facilitating wisdom-related knowledge: The sample case of clinical psychologists. *Journal of Consulting and Clinical Psychology, 66,* 989–999.

Smith, K. D., Türk-Smith, S., & Christopher, J. C. (1998, August). *Prototypes of the ideal person in seven cultures.* Paper presented at the International Congress of the International Association for Cross-Cultural Psychologists, Bellingham, WA.

Smith, M. L., Glass, G. V., & Miller, T. I. (1980). *The benefits of psychotherapy.* Baltimore: Johns Hopkins University Press.

Smith, R. (1987). *Unemployment and health: A disaster and a challenge.* Oxford, England: Oxford University Press.

Smith, T. W., Pope, M. K., Rhodewalt, F., & Poulton, J. L. (1989). Optimism, neuroticism, coping, and symptom reports: An alternative interpretation of the Life Orientation Test. *Journal of Personality and Social Psychology, 56,* 640–648.

Smyth, J. M., & Pennebaker, J. W. (1999). Sharing one's story: Translating emotional experiences into words as a coping tool. In C. R. Snyder (Ed.), *Coping: The psychology of what works* (pp. 70–89). New York: Oxford University Press.

Snyder, C. R. (1989). Reality negotiation: From excuses to hope and beyond. *Journal of Social and Clinical Psychology, 8,* 130–157.

Snyder, C. R. (1992). Product scarcity by need for uniqueness interaction: A consumer catch-22? *Basic and Applied Social Psychology, 13,* 9–24.

Snyder, C. R. (1994/2000). *The psychology of hope: You can get there from here.* New York: Free Press.

Snyder, C. R. (1997). Unique invulnerability: A classroom demonstration in estimating personal mortality. *Teaching of Psychology, 24,* 197–199.

Snyder, C. R. (Ed.). (1999a). *Coping: The psychology of what works.* New York: Oxford University Press.

Snyder, C. R. (1999b). Unique invulnerability as applied to personal mortality: The reports of its demise are exaggerated. *Teaching of Psychology, 26*(3), 217–219.

Snyder, C. R. (2000a). Genesis: The birth and growth of hope. In C. R. Snyder (Ed.), *Handbook of hope: Theory, measures, and applications* (pp. 25–38). San Diego, CA: Academic Press.

Snyder, C. R. (Ed.). (2000b). *Handbook of hope: Theory, measures, and applications.* San Diego, CA: Academic Press.

Snyder, C. R. (2000c). The past and the possible futures of hope. *Journal of Social and Clinical Psychology, 19,* 11–28.

Snyder, C. R. (2002a). Hope theory: Rainbows of the mind. *Psychological Inquiry, 13,* 249–275.

Snyder, C. R. (2002b). Part 2—The application, interview, and negotiation stages of obtaining a position in clinical psychology. *The Clinical Psychologist, 56,* 19–25.

Snyder, C. R. (2003, November). *Forgiveness and hope.* Paper presented at the International Campaign for Forgiveness Conference, Atlanta, GA.

Snyder, C. R. (2004a). The challenge: College students seem to be getting younger. *Reflections, 16,* 17–19.

Snyder, C. R. (2004b). *Measuring hope in American businesses.* Unpublished manuscript, University of Kansas, Lawrence.

Snyder, C. R. (2004c, November). *Hope and spirituality.* International Society for Quality of Life Studies Conference, Philadelphia.

Snyder, C. R. (2004d, December 17). Graceful attitude eases adversity. *Lawrence Journal-World,* p. D4.

Snyder, C. R. (2005a). Teaching: The lessons of hope. *Journal of Social and Clinical Psychology, 24,* 72–83.

Snyder, C. R. (Ed.). (2005b). The interface and teaching: A match made in the classroom. *Journal of Social and Clinical Psychology, 24,* 1–127.

Snyder, C. R., & Elliott, T. R. (2005). 21st-century graduate education in clinical psychology: A four-level matrix model. *Journal of Clinical Psychology, 61,* 1033–1054.

Snyder, C. R., & Feldman, D. (2000). Hope for the many: An empowering social agenda. In C. R. Snyder (Ed.), *Handbook of hope: Theory, measures, and applications* (pp. 389–412). San Diego, CA: Academic Press.

Snyder, C. R., Feldman, D. B., Taylor, J. D., Schroeder, L. L., & Adams III, V. (2000). The roles of hopeful thinking in preventing problems and promoting strengths. *Applied & Preventive Psychology: Current Scientific Perspectives, 15,* 262–295.

Snyder, C. R., & Fromkin, H. L. (1977). Abnormality as a positive characteristic: The development and validation of a scale measuring need for uniqueness. *Journal of Abnormal Psychology, 86*(5), 518–527.

Snyder, C. R., & Fromkin, H. L. (1980). *Uniqueness: The human pursuit of difference.* New York: Plenum.

Snyder, C. R., Harris, C., Anderson, J. R., Holleran, S. A., Irving, L. M., Sigmon, S. T., et al. (1991). The will and the ways: Development and validation of an individual-differences measure of hope. *Journal of Personality and Social Psychology, 60,* 570–585.

Snyder, C. R., & Higgins, R. L. (1997). Reality negotiation: Governing one's self and being governed by others. *General Psychology Review, 4,* 336–350.

Snyder, C. R., Higgins, R. L., & Stucky, R. J. (1983/2005). *Excuses: Masquerades in search of grace.* New York: Wiley Interscience. Republished 2005 by Percheron Press, Clinton Corners, NY.

Snyder, C. R., Hoza, B., Pelham, W. E., Rapoff, M., Ware, L., Danovsky, M., et al. (1997). The development and validation of the Children's Hope Scale. *Journal of Pediatric Psychology, 22,* 399–421.

Snyder, C. R., Ilardi, S. S., Cheavens, J., Michael, S. T., Yamhure, L., & Sympson, S. (2000). The role of hope in cognitive behavior therapies. *Cognitive Therapy and Research, 24,* 747–762.

Snyder, C. R., Ilardi, S., Michael, S., & Cheavens, J. (2000). Hope theory: Updating a common process for psychological change. In C. R. Snyder & R. E. Ingram (Eds.), *Handbook of psychological change: Psychotherapy processes and practices for the 21st century* (pp. 128–153). New York: Wiley.

Snyder, C. R., & Ingram, R. E. (1983). "Company motivates the miserable": The impact of consensus upon help-seeking for psychological problems. *Journal of Personality and Social Psychology, 45,* 1118–1126.

Snyder, C. R., & Ingram, R. E. (Eds.). (2000a). *Handbook of psychological change: Psychotherapy processes and practices for the 21st century.* New York: Wiley.

Snyder, C. R., & Ingram, R. E. (2000b). Psychotherapy: Questions for an evolving field. In C. R. Snyder & R. E. Ingram (Eds.), *Handbook of psychological change: Psychotherapy processes and practices for the 21st century* (pp. 707–726). New York: Wiley.

Snyder, C. R., LaPointe, A. B., Crowson Jr., J. J., & Early, S. (1998). Preferences of high- and low-hope people for self-referential input. *Cognition & Emotion, 12,* 807–823.

Snyder, C. R., & Lopez, S. J. (Eds). (2002). *The handbook of positive psychology.* New York: Oxford University Press.

Snyder, C. R., Lopez, S. J., Edwards, L. M., Pedrotti, J. T., Prosser, E. C., Larue-Walton, S., et al. (2003). Measuring and labeling the positive and the negative. *Positive psychological assessment: A handbook of models and measures* (pp. 21–40). Washington, DC: American Psychological Association.

Snyder, C. R., McDermott, D., Cook, W., & Rapoff, M. (2002). *Hope for the journey: Helping children through the good times and the bad* (Rev. ed.). Clinton Corners, NY: Percheron Press.

Snyder, C. R., McDermott, D. S., Leibowitz, R. Q., & Cheavens, J. (2000). The roles of female clinical psychologists in changing the field of psychotherapy. In C. R. Snyder & R. E. Ingram (Eds.), *Handbook of psychological change: Psychotherapy processes and practices for the 21st century* (pp. 640–659). New York: Wiley.

Snyder, C. R., Omens, A. E., & Bloom, L. J. (1977, April). *Signature size and personality: Some truth in graphology?* Paper presented at the Southwestern Psychological Association Convention, Dallas, TX.

Snyder, C. R., Parenteau, S., Shorey, H. S., Kahle, K. E., & Berg, C. (2002). Hope as the underlying process in Gestalt and other psychotherapy approaches. *International Gestalt Therapy Journal, 25,* 11–29.

Snyder, C. R., & Pulvers, K. (2001). Dr. Seuss, the coping machine, and "Oh, the places you will go." In Snyder, C. R. (Ed.), *Coping and copers: Adaptive processes and people* (pp. 3–19). New York: Oxford University Press.

Snyder, C. R., Rand, K., King, E., Feldman, D., & Taylor, J. (2002). "False" hope. *Journal of Clinical Psychology, 58,* 1003–1022.

Snyder, C. R., Ritschel, L. A., Rand, K. L., & Berg, C. J. (2006). Balancing psychological assessments: Including strengths and hope in client reports. *Journal of Clinical Psychology, 62,* 33–46.

Snyder, C. R., & Shorey, H. (2002). Hope in the classroom: The role of positive psychology in academic achievement and psychology curriculum. *Psychology Teacher Network, 12,* 1–9.

Snyder, C. R., & Shorey, H. (2004). Hope and leadership. In G. Goethals, G. J. Sorenson, & J. M. Burns (Eds.), *Encyclopedia of leadership* (pp. 673–675). Thousand Oaks, CA: Sage.

Snyder, C. R., Shorey, H., Cheavens, J., Pulvers, K. M., Adams III, V. H., & Wiklund, C. (2002). Hope and academic success in college. *Journal of Educational Psychology, 94,* 820–826.

Snyder, C. R., Sympson, S. C., Ybasco, F. C., Borders, T. F., Babyak, M. A., & Higgins, R. L. (1996). Development and validation of the State Hope Scale. *Journal of Personality and Social Psychology, 2,* 321–335.

Snyder, C. R., Tennen, H., Affleck, G., & Cheavens, J. (2000). Social, personality, clinical, and health psychology tributaries: The merging of a scholarly "river of dreams." *Personality and Social Psychology Review, 4,* 16–29.

Snyder, C. R., Thompson, L. Y., & Heinze, L. (2003). The hopeful ones. In G. Keinan (Eds.), *Between stress and hope* (pp. 57–80). Westport, CT: Greenwood.

Soldier, L. L. (1992). *Working with Native American children.* Unpublished ms., College of Education, Texas Tech University, Lubbock (National Association for the Education of Young Children at http://www.enc.org/features/focus/archive/multi/document.shtm?input=ACQ-111362–1362).

Soothill, W. E. (1968). *The analects of Confucius.* New York: Paragon.

Spera, S. P., Buhrfeind, E. D., & Pennebaker, J. W. (1994). Expressive writing and coping with job loss. *Academy of Management Journal, 37,* 722–733.

Spivak, G., & Shure, M. B. (1974). *Social adjustment of young children.* San Francisco: Jossey-Bass.

Staats, S. R. (1989). Hope: A comparison of two self-report measures for adults. *Journal of Personality Assessment, 53,* 366–375.

Stahl, J. M. (2005). Research is for everyone: Perspectives from teaching at historically Black colleges and universities. *Journal of Social and Clinical Psychology, 24,* 84–95.

Stajkovic, A. D., & Luthans, F. (1998). Self-efficacy and work-related performance: A meta-analysis. *Psychological Bulletin, 124,* 240–261.

Stanton, A. L., Danoff-Burg, S., Cameron, C. L., Bishop, M., Collins, C. A., Kirk, S. B., et al. (2000). Emotionally expressive coping predicts psychological and physical adjustment to breast cancer. *Journal of Consulting and Clinical Psychology, 68*(5), 875–882.

Stanton, A. L., Danoff-Burg, S., Cameron, C. L., & Ellis, A. P. (1994). Coping through emotional approach: Problems of conceptualizaton and confounding. *Journal of Personality and Social Psychology, 66*(2), 350–362.

Stanton, A. L., Danoff-Burg, S., & Huggins, M. E. (2002). The first year after breast cancer diagnosis: Hope and coping strategies as predictors of adjustment. *Psycho Oncology, 11*(2), 93–102.

Stanton, A. L., Kirk, S. B., Cameron, C. L., & Danoff-Burg, S. (2000). Coping through emotional approach: Scale construction and validation. *Journal of Personality and Social Psychology, 78*(6), 1150–1169.

Stanton, A. L., Parsa, A., & Austenfeld, J. L. (2002). The adaptive potential of coping through emotional approach. In C. R. Snyder & S. J. Lopez (Eds.), *The handbook of positive psychology* (pp. 148–158). New York: Oxford University Press.

Staudinger, U. (1999). Older and wiser? Integrating results from a psychological approach to study of wisdom. *International Journal of Behavioral Development, 23,* 641–664.

Staudinger, U., & Baltes, P. B. (1994). Psychology of wisdom. In R. J. Sternberg (Ed.), *Encyclopedia of human intelligence* (Vol. 2, pp. 143–152). New York: Macmillan.

Staudinger, U., & Baltes, P. B. (1996). Interactive minds: A facilitative setting for wisdom-related performance? *Journal of Personality and Social Psychology, 71,* 746–762.

Staudinger, U., & Leipold, B. (2003). The assessment of wisdom-related performance. In S. J. Lopez & C. R. Snyder (Eds.), *Positive psychological assessment: A handbook of models and measures* (pp. 171–184). Washington, DC: American Psychological Association.

Staudinger, U., Smith, J., & Baltes, P. B. (1992). Wisdom-related knowledge in a life-review task: Age differences and the role of professional specialization. *Psychology and Aging, 7,* 271–281.

Stein, M. (1989). Gratitude and attitude: A note on emotional welfare. *Social Psychology Quarterly, 52,* 242–248.

Sternberg, R. (1985). Implicit theories of intelligence, creativity, and wisdom. *Journal of Personality and Social Psychology, 49,* 607–627.

Sternberg, R. (1990). *Wisdom: Its nature, origins, and development.* New York: Cambridge University Press.

Sternberg, R. (1998). A balance theory of wisdom. *Review of General Psychology, 2,* 347–365.

Sternberg, R. J. (1986). A triangular theory of love. *Psychological Review, 93,* 119–135.

Sternberg, R. J. (1998). *Love is a story: A new theory of relationships.* New York: Oxford University Press.

Sternberg, R. J., & Hojjat, M. (1997). *Satisfaction in close relationships.* New York: Guilford Press.

Stevens, V., Hornbrook, M., Wingfield, D., Hollis, J., Greenlick, M., & Ory, M. (1992). Design and implementation of a falls prevention intervention for community-dwelling older persons. *Behavior, Health and Aging, 2,* 57–73.

Stevenson, L., & Haberman, D. L. (1998). *Ten theories of human nature.* New York: Oxford University Press.

Stewart, E. C. (1972). *American cultural patterns: A cross-cultural perspective.* Yarmouth, ME: Intercultural Press.

Stotland, E. (1969). *The psychology of hope.* San Francisco: Jossey-Bass.

Strecher, V. J., Champion, V. L., & Rosenstock, I. M. (1997). The health belief model and health behavior. In D. Gochman (Ed.), *Handbook of health behavior research 1: Personal and social determinants* (pp. 71–92). New York: Plenum.

Stuss, D. T., & Benson, D. S. (1984). Neuropsychological studies of frontal lobes. *Psychological Bulletin, 95,* 3-28.

Subkoviak, M. J., Enright, R. D., Wu, C. R., Gassin, E. A., Freedman, S., Olson, L. M., et al. (1995). Measuring interpersonal forgiveness in late adolescence and middle childhood. *Journal of Adolescence, 18,* 641–655.

Sue, D. W., & Constantine, M. G. (2003). Optimal human functioning in people of color in the United States. In W. B. Walsh (Ed.), *Counseling psychology and optimal human functioning* (pp. 151–169). Mahwah, NJ: Lawrence Erlbaum.

Sue, D. W., & Sue, D. (2003). *Counseling the culturally diverse: Theory and practice* (4th ed.). New York: Wiley.

Super, D. E., & Knasel, E. G. (1981). Career development in adulthood: Some theoretical problems and a possible solution. *British Journal of Guidance and Counselling, 9,* 194–201.

Swanson, J. L., & Gore, P. A., Jr. (2000). Advances in vocational psychology theory and research. In S. D. Brown & R. W. Lent (Eds.), *Handbook of counseling psychology* (3rd edition, pp. 233–269). New York: Wiley.

Szagun, G. (1992). Age-related changes in children's understanding of courage. *Journal of Genetic Psychology, 153,* 405–420.

Szagun, G., & Schauble, M. (1997). Children's and adults' understanding of the feeling experience of courage. *Cognition and Emotion, 11*(3), 291–306.

Szapocnik, J., Scopetta, M. A., & King, O. E. (1978). Theory and practice in matching treatment to the special characteristics and problems of Cuban immigrants. *Journal of Community Psychology, 6,* 112–122.

Szendre, E. N., & Jose, J. E. (1996). Telephone support by elderly volunteers to inner-city children. *Journal of Community Psychology, 24,* 87–96.

Tangney, J. P., Boone, A. L., & Dearing, R. (2005). Forgiving the self: Conceptual issues and empirical findings. In E. Worthington (Ed.), *Handbook of forgiveness* (pp. 143–158). New York: Routledge.

Tangney, J. P., Fee, R., Reinsmith, C., Boone, A. L., & Lee, N. (1999, August). *Assessing individual differences in the propensity to forgive.* Paper presented at the American Psychological Association Convention, Boston.

Taylor, S. E., Dickerson, S. S., & Klein, L. C. (2002). Toward a biology of social support. In C. R. Snyder & S. J. Lopez (Eds.), *The handbook of positive psychology* (pp. 556–572). New York: Oxford University Press.

Taylor, S. E., Kemeny, M. E., Aspinwall, L. G., Schneider, S. G., Rodriguez, R., & Herbert, M. (1992). Optimism, coping, psychological distress, and high-risk sexual behavior among men at risk for acquired immunodeficiency syndrome (AIDS). *Journal of Personality and Social Psychology, 63,* 460–473.

Tellegen, A., Lykken, D. T., Bouchard, T. J., Wilcox, K. J., Segal, N. L., & Rich, S. (1988). Personality similarity in twins reared apart and together. *Journal of Personality and Social Psychology, 54,* 1031–1039.

Teresa, J. S. (1991). *Increasing self-efficacy for careers in young adults from migrant farmworker backgrounds.* Unpublished doctoral dissertation, Washington State University, Pullman.

Terman, L. M., & Oden, M. H. (1947). *The gifted child grows up: Twenty five years' follow-up of a superior group.* Stanford, CA: Stanford University Press.

Thompson, L. W. (1996). Cognitive-behavioral therapy and treatment for late-life depression. *Journal of Clinical Psychiatry, 57*(Suppl. 5), 29–37.

Thompson, L. W., Gallagher, D., & Lovett, S. (1992). *Increasing life satisfaction: Class leaders' and participant manuals* (rev.). Palo Alto, CA: Dept. of Veterans Affairs Medical Center and Stanford University.

Thompson, L. Y., Snyder, C. R., Hoffman, L., Michael, S. T., Rasmussen, H. N., Billings, L. S., et al. (2005). Dispositional forgiveness of self, others, and situations: The Heartland Forgiveness Scale. *Journal of Personality, 73,* 313–359.

Thompson, M. G., & Heller, K. (1990). Facets of support related to well-being: Quantitative social isolation and perceived family support in a sample of elderly women. *Psychology and Aging, 5,* 535–544.

Thoresen, C. E., Harris, A. H. S., & Oman, D. (2001). Spirituality, religion, and health: Evidence, issues, and concerns. In T. G. Plante & A. C. Sherman (Eds.), *Faith and health: Psychological perspectives* (pp. 15–52). New York: Guilford Press.

Tian, K. T., Bearden, W. O., & Hunter, G. L. (2001). Consumers' need for uniqueness: Scale development and validation. *Journal of Consumer Research, 28,* 50–66.

Tian, K. T., & McKenzie, K. (2001). The long-term predictive validity of the Consumers' Need for Uniqueness Scale. *Journal of Consumer Psychology, 10,* 171–193.

Tierney, J. P., & Grossman, J. B. (2000). *Making a difference: An impact study of Big Brothers/Big Sisters.* Philadelphia: Public/Private Ventures.

Tiller, W. A., McCraty, R., & Atkinson, M. (1996). Cardiac coherence: A new, non-invasive measure of autonomic nervous system order. *Alternative Therapies in Health and Medicine, 2,* 52–65.

Tillich, P. (1980). *The courage to be.* New Haven & London: Yale University Press.

Ting-Toomey, S. (1994). Managing intercultural conflict in intercultural personal relationships. In D. D. Cahn (Ed.), *Intimate conflict in personal relationships.* Hillsdale, NJ: Lawrence Erlbaum.

Tipton, R. M., & Worthington, E. L. (1984). The measurement of generalized self-efficacy: A study of construct validity. *Journal of Personality Assessment, 48,* 545–548.

Triandis, H. C. (1988). Collectivism v. individualism: A reconceptualization of a basic concept in cross-cultural social psychology. In G. K. Verma & C. Bagley (Eds.), *Cross-cultural studies of personality, attitudes and cognition* (pp. 6–95). London: MacMillan.

Triandis, H. C. (1990). Cross-cultural studies of individualism and collectivism. In J. Berman (Ed.), *Nebraska Symposium on Motivation* (pp. 41–133). Lincoln: University of Nebraska Press.

Triandis, H. C. (1995). *Individualism and collectivism.* Boulder, CO: Westview Press.

Triandis, H. C., Brislin, R., & Hui, C. H. (1988). Cross-cultural training across the individualism-collectivism divide. *International Journal of Intercultural Relations, 12,* 269–289.

Trimble, J. E. (1976). Value differences among American Indians: Concerns for the concerned counselor. In P. Pederson, W. J. Lonner, & J. G. Graguns (Eds.), *Counseling across cultures* (pp. 65–81). Honolulu: University of Hawaii Press.

Trivers, R. L. (1971). The evolution of reciprocal altruism. *Quarterly Review of Biology, 46,* 35–57.

Trump, M. R. (1997). The impact of hopeful narratives on state hope, state self-esteem, and state positive and negative affect for adult female survivors of incest. *Dissertation Abstracts International, 58* (4A):1211.

Twenge, J., & King, L. A. (2003). *A good life is a good personal life: Relationship fulfillment and work fulfillment in judgments of life quality.* Unpublished manuscript, University of Missouri, Columbia.

Unger, J. B., McAvay, G., Bruce, M. L., Berkman, L., & Seeman, T. (1999). Variation in the impact of social network characteristics on physical functioning in elderly persons: MacArthur Studies of Successful Aging. *Journals of Gerontology, 54,* 245–251.

Urry, H. L., Nitschke, J. B., Dolski, I., Jackson, D. C., Dalton, K. M., Mueller, C. J., et al. (2004). Making a life worth living: Neural correlates of well-being. *Psychological Science, 15,* 367–372.

U.S. Department of Health and Human Services. (1998). *Suicide: A report of the surgeon general.* Rockville, MD: Author.

U.S. Department of Health and Human Services. (1999). *Mental Health: A report of the surgeon general.* Rockville, MD: Author.

U.S. Department of Health and Human Services. (2001). *Mental health: Culture, race, ethnicity,* supplement to *Mental health: Report of the surgeon general* (Inventory number SMA 01-3613). Rockville, MD: Author.

Vaillant, G. (1994). "Successful aging" and psychosocial well-being: Evidence from a 45-year study. In E. H. Thompson (Ed.), *Older men's lives: Research on men and masculinities series* (pp. 22–41). Thousand Oaks, CA: Sage.

Vaillant, G. E. (1977). *Adaptation to life.* New York: Little, Brown.

Vaillant, G. E. (2002). *Aging well: Surprising guideposts to a happier life from the landmark Harvard Study of Adult Development.* New York: Little, Brown.

Vandello, J. A., & Cohen, D. (1999). Patterns of individualism and collectivism across the United States. *Journal of Personality and Social Psychology, 77,* 279–292.

Veroff, J. B., Douvan, E., & Kulka, R. A. (1981). *The inner American: A self-portrait from 1957 to 1976.* New York: Basic Books.

Vessey, G. N. A. (1967). Volition. In P. Edwards (Ed.), *Encyclopedia of philosophy* (Vol. 8). New York: McMillan.

Vessey, J. T., & Howard, K. I. (1993). Who seeks psychotherapy? *Psychotherapy, 30,* 546–553.

Voss, M., Nylen, L., Floderus, B., Diderichsen, F., & Terry, P. (2004). Unemploy-ment and early causee-specific mortality: A study based on the Swedish twin registry. *American Journal of Public Health, 94,* 2155–2161.

Walker, L. J., & Hennig, K. H. (2004). Differing conceptions of moral exemplarity: Just, brave, and caring. *Journal of Personality and Social Psychology, 86,* 629–647.

Walker, L. J., & Pitts, R. C. (1998). Naturalistic conceptions of moral maturity. *Developmental Psychology, 34,* 403–419.

Wallach, M. A., & Wallach, L. (1983). *Psychology's sanction for selfishness: The error of egoism in theory and therapy.* San Francisco: Freeman.

Walsh, R. N. (1983). Meditation practice and research. *Journal of Humanistic Psychology, 23,* 18–50.

Walster, E., Walster, G. W., Piliavin, J., & Schmidt, L. (1973). "Playing hard to get": Understanding an elusive phenomenon. *Journal of Personality and Social Psychology, 26,* 113–121.

Wang, M., & Gordon, E. (Eds.). (1994). *Risk and resilience in inner-city America: Challenges and prospects.* Hillsdale, NJ: Lawrence Erlbaum.

Warr, P. (1987). *Work, unemployment and mental health.* Oxford, England: Clarendon Press.

Warr, P. (1999). Well-being and the workplace. In D. Kahneman, E. Diener, & N. Schwartz (Eds.), *Well-being: The foundations of hedonic psychology* (pp. 393–412). New York: Russell Sage.

Waterman, A. S. (1993). Two conceptions of happiness: Contrasts of personal expressiveness (eudaemonia) and hedonic enjoyment. *Journal of Personality and Social Psychology, 64,* 678–691.

Watkins, P. C., Grimm, D. L., & Hailu, L. (1998, June). *Counting your blessings: Grateful individuals recall more positive memories.* Paper presented at the American Psychological Society Convention, Denver, CO.

Watson, D. (1988). The vicissitudes of mood measurement: Effects of varying descriptors, time frames, and response formats on measures of positive and negative affect. *Journal of Personality and Social Psychology, 55,* 128–141.

Watson, D. (2000). *Mood and temperament.* New York: Guilford Press.

Watson, D. (2002). Positive affectivity: The disposition to experience pleasurable emotional states. In C. R. Snyder & S. J. Lopez (Eds.), *The handbook of positive psychology* (pp. 106–119). New York: Oxford University Press.

Watson, D., & Clark, L. A. (1994). *The PANAS-X: Manual for the Positive and Negative Affect Schedule–Expanded Form.* Unpublished manuscript, University of Iowa, Iowa City.

Watson, D., Clark, L., & Tellegen, A. (1988). Development and validation of brief measures of positive and negative affect: The PANAS scales. *Journal of Personality and Social Psychology, 54,* 1063–1070.

Watson, M., & Ecken, L. (2003). *Learning to trust: Transforming difficult elementary classrooms through developmental discipline.* San Francisco: Jossey-Bass.

Weinberger, J., McLeod, C., McClelland, D., Santorelli, S. F., & Kabat-Zinn, J. (1990). *Motivational change following a meditation-based stress reduction pro-gram for medical outpatients.* Poster presented at the 1st International Congress of Behavioral Medicine, Uppsala, Sweden.

Weir, H. B. (1971). *Deprivation of the need for uniqueness and some variables moderating its effects.* Unpublished doctoral dissertation, University of Georgia, Athens.

Weir, K., & Duveen, G. (1981). Further development and validation of the Prosocial Behavior Questionnaire for use by teachers. *Journal of Child Psychology and Psychiatry, 22,* 357–374.

Weissberg, R. P., Barton, H. A., & Shriver, T. P. (1997). The social-competence promotion program for young adolescents. In G. W. Albee & T. P. Gullotta (Eds.), *Primary prevention works* (pp. 268–290). Thousand Oaks, CA: Sage.

Weisz, J. R., Rothbaum, R. M., & Blackburn, T. C. (1984). Standing out and standing in: The psychology of control in America and Japan. *American Psychologist, 39,* 955–969.

Weisz, J. R., Weiss, B., Alicke, M. D., & Klotz, M. L. (1987). Effectiveness of psychotherapy with children and adolescents: Meta-analytic findings for clinicians. *Journal of Consulting and Clinical Psychology, 55,* 542–549.

Wenar, C., & Kerig, P. (1999). *Developmental psychopathology.* New York: McGraw-Hill.

Werner, E. E. (1984). Resilient children. *Young Children, 40,* 68–72.

Werner, E. E., & Smith, R. S. (1982). *Vulnerable but invincible: A study of resilient children.* New York: McGraw-Hill.

Werner, E. E., & Smith, R. S. (1992). *Overcoming the odds: High-risk children from birth to adulthood.* Ithaca, NY: Cornell University Press.

Westburg, N. G. (2001). Hope in older women: The importance of past and current relationships. *Journal of Social and Clinical Psychology, 20,* 354–365.

Western Reform Taoism. (2003). *Our beliefs.* Retrieved May 3, 2005, from http://wrt.org

Whalen, S. (1999). Challenging play and the cultivation of talent: Lessons from the Key School's flow activities room. In N. Colangelo & S. Assouline (Eds.), *Talent development III* (pp. 409–411). Scottsdale, AZ: Gifted Psychology Press.

White, R. W. (1959). Motivation reconsidered: The concept of competence. *Psychological Review, 66,* 297–333.

Williams, S. L. (1995). Self-efficacy, anxiety, and phobic disorders. In J. E. Maddux (Ed.), *Self-efficacy, adaptation, and adjustment: Theory, research, and application* (pp. 69–107). New York: Plenum.

Williamson, G. M. (2002). Aging well: Outlook for the 21st century. In C. R. Snyder & S. J. Lopez (Eds.), *The handbook of positive psychology* (pp. 676–686). New York: Oxford University Press.

Williamson, G. M., Shaffer, D. R., & Parmalee, P. A. (Eds.). (2000). *Physical illness and depression in older adults: A handbook of theory, research, and practice.* New York: Plenum.

Wills, T. A., & DePaulo, B. M. (1991). Interpersonal analyses of the help-seeking process. In C. R. Snyder & D. R. Forsyth (Eds.), *Handbook of social and clinical psychology: The health perspective* (pp. 350–375). Elmsford, NY: Pergamon.

Winerman, L. (2005). Mirror neurons: The mind's mirror. *Monitor, 36,* 49–50.

Winseman, A. L. (2003). Doing what they do best. *Gallup Management Journal, 2,* 1–4.

Winseman, A. L., Clifton, D. O., & Liesveld, C. (2003). *Living your strengths: Discover your God-given talents, and inspire your congregation and community.* Washington, DC: Gallup Organization.

Woodard, C. (2004). *Hardiness and the concept of courage.* Unpublished manuscript, The Groden Center, Providence, RI.

Woods, R., & Roth, A. (1996). Effectiveness of psychological interventions with older people. In A. Roth & P. Fonagy (Eds.), *What works for whom? A critical review of psychotherapy research* (pp. 321–340). New York: Guilford Press.

Woolfolk, R. L. (2002). The power of negative thinking: Truth, melancholia, and the tragic sense of life. *Journal of Theoretical & Philosophical Psychology, 22,* 19–27.

World Health Organization. (1992). *ICD 10: International statistical classification of diseases and related health problems.* Washington, DC: American Psychiatric Association.

Worley, D. W. (2001). Central states outstanding teaching award winners: A philosophy for teaching. *Communication Studies, 52,* 278–283.

Worthington, E. L., Jr. (1998). An empathy-humility-commitment model of forgiveness applied within family dyads. *Journal of Family Therapy, 20,* 59–71.

Worthington, E. L., Jr. (Ed.). (2005). *Handbook of forgiveness.* New York: Routledge.

Worthington, E. L., Jr., & Drinkard, D. T. (2000). Promoting reconciliation through psycho-educational and therapeutic interventions. *Journal of Marital and Family Therapy, 26,* 93–101.

Worthington, E. L., Jr., Hight, T. L., Ripley, J. S., Perrone, K. M., Kurusu, T. A., & Jones, D. R. (1997). Strategic hope-focused relationship-enrichment counseling with individuals. *Journal of Counseling Psychology, 44,* 381–389.

Wright, B. A. (1988). Attitudes and fundamental negative bias. In H. E. Yuker (Ed.), *Attitudes toward persons with disabilities* (pp. 3–21). New York: Springer.

Wright, B. A. (1991). Labeling: The need for greater person-environment individuation. In C. R. Snyder & D. R. Forsyth (Eds.), *The handbook of social and clinical psychology: A health perspective* (pp. 469–487). New York: Pergamon.

Wright, B. A., & Lopez, S. J. (2002). Widening the diagnostic focus: A case for including human strengths and environmental resources. In C. R. Snyder & S. J. Lopez (Eds.), *The handbook of positive psychology* (pp. 26–44). New York: Oxford University Press.

Wright, R. (1994). *The moral animal: The new sciences of evolutionary psychology.* New York: Pantheon.

Wrzesniewski, A., McCauley, C. R., Rozin, P., & Schwartz, B. (1997). Jobs, careers, and callings: People's relations to their work. *Journal of Research in Personality, 31,* 21–33.

Wrzesniewski, A., Rozin, P., & Bennett, G. (2001). Working, playing, and eating: Making the most of most moments. In C. Keyes & J. Haidt (Eds.), *Flourishing: The positive person and the good life* (pp. 185–204). Washington, DC: American Psychological Association.

Yamaguchi, S., Kuhlman, D. M., & Sugimori, S. (1995). Personality correlates of allocentric tendencies in individualist and collectivist cultures. *Journal of Cross-Cultural Psychology, 26,* 658–672.

Yang, S. (2001). Conceptions of wisdom among Taiwanese Chinese. *Journal of Cross-Cultural Psychology, 32,* 662–680.

Yoshikawa, H. (1994). Prevention as cumulative protection: Effects of early family support and education on chronic delinquency and its risks. *Psychological Bulletin, 115,* 28–54.

Zahn-Wexler, C., Robinson, J., & Emde, R. N. (1992). The development of empathy in twins. *Developmental Psychology, 28,* 1038–1047.

Zautra, A. J., Potter, P. T., & Reich, J. W. (1997). The independence of affect is context dependent: An integrative model of the relationship between positive and negative affect. In K. W. Schaie & M. P. Lawton (Eds.), *Annual review of gerontology and geriatrics* (Vol. 17, pp. 75–103). New York: Springer.

Zeidner, M., & Hammer, A. L. (1992). Coping with missile attack: Resources, strategies, and outcomes. *Journal of Personality, 60,* 184–199.

Zillman, D. (1979). *Hostility and aggression.* Hillsdale, NJ: Lawrence Erlbaum.

Zimbardo, P. G. (1999). A generalist looks at his career in teaching: An interview with Dr. Phil Zimbardo. *North American Journal of Psychology, 1,* 1–16.

Zimbardo, P. G. (2005). Optimizing the power and magic of teaching. *Journal of Social and Clinical Psychology, 24,* 11–21.

Zimbardo, P. G., & Boyd, J. N. (1999). Putting time in perspective: A valid, reliable individual-differences metric. *Journal of Personality and Social Psychology, 77,* 1271–1288.

Zimmerman, F. J., Glew, G. M., Christakis, D. A., & Katon, W. (2005). Early cognitive stimulation, emotional support, and television watching as predictors of subsequent bullying among grade-school children. *Archives of Pediatric Adolescent Medicine, 159,* 384–388.

Zinnbauer, G. J., Pargament, K. I., Cole, B. C., Rye, M. S., Butter, E. M., Belavich, T. G., et al. (1997). Religion and spirituality: Unfuzzying the fuzzy. *Journal for the Scientific Study of Religion, 36,* 549–564.

Author Index

Subject Index

About the Authors

C. R. (Rick) Snyder (1944–2006) was the Wright Distinguished Professor of Clinical Psychology at the University of Kansas, Lawrence. Internationally known for his work at the interface of clinical, social, personality, and health psychology, his theories pertained to how people react to personal feedback, the human need for uniqueness, the ubiquitous drive to excuse transgressions and, most recently, the hope motive. He received 31 research awards and 27 teaching awards at the university, state, and national levels. In 2005, he received an honorary doctorate from Indiana Wesleyan University.

Snyder appeared many times on nationally broadcast American television shows, and he was a regular contributor to National Public Radio. His scholarly work on the human need for uniqueness received the rare distinction of being the subject matter of an entire Sunday cartoon sequence by Garry Trudeau. All these accomplishments were packaged as a graying, self-effacing, absent-minded professor who said of himself, "If you don't laugh at yourself, you have missed the biggest joke of all!"

Rick lived with his wife, Rebecca, within walking distance of the Psychology Department at the University of Kansas, Lawrence. In Lawrence, the Snyders raised three children (Staci, James, and Zach) and two grandchildren (Drew and Trenton).

Shane J. Lopez is Associate Professor of Counseling Psychology at the University of Kansas, Lawrence, where he teaches courses in positive psychology, psychological assessment, and educational leadership. He also is a Gallup senior scientist, a role in which he consults primarily with the Gallup Education Division and Gallup University. He serves on the editorial board of the *Journal of Positive Psychology* and on the advisory board of *Ready, Set, Learn,* the Discovery Channel's preschool educational television program.

Through his current research programs, Lopez is examining the effectiveness of hope training programs in the schools (under the auspices of the Making Hope Happen Program), refining a model of psychological courage, and exploring the link between soft life skills and hard outcomes in education, work, health, and family functioning. His books include *The Handbook of Positive Psychology* (Oxford University Press) and *Positive Psychological Assessment: A Handbook of Models and Measures* (American Psychological Association), both with C. R. Snyder.

Lopez and his wife, Allison, live with their son, Parrish, in Lawrence, Kansas, where they attempt to live the good life every day and long for the temperate Louisiana winters of their childhoods every February.